NEW YORK STORIES

RANDOM HOUSE

TRADE PAPERBACKS

New York

NEW YORK STORIES

Landmark
Writing from
Four Decades
of

**NEW YORK
MAGAZINE**

★

Edited by

STEVE FISHMAN, JOHN HOMANS, AND ADAM MOSS

A Random House Trade Paperback Original

Copyright © 2008 by *New York* Magazine Holdings LLC

All rights reserved.

Published in the United States by Random House Trade Paperbacks,
an imprint of The Random House Publishing Group,
a division of Random House, Inc., New York.

RANDOM HOUSE TRADE PAPERBACKS and colophon
are trademarks of Random House, Inc.

All of the articles that appear in this volume were originally published in *New York*.

Library of Congress Cataloging-in-Publication Data

New York stories : landmark writing from four decades of New York magazine / The editors of
New York magazine.

p.   cm.

ISBN 978-0-8129-7992-3

1. New York (N.Y.)—Literary collections.   2. American literature—New York (State)—New York.
I. New York magazine.

PS549.N5N48 2008

810.8'0327471—dc22   2008028844

Printed in the United States of America

www.atrandom.com

2 4 6 8 9 7 5 3 1

Book design by Barbara M. Bachman

to

CLAY FELKER

1925–2008

CONTENTS

....

PART FOUR: THE PERMANENT REVOLUTION

PART FIVE: CRIMINAL ACTS

PART SIX: THE NATIONAL INTEREST

TOM WOLFE

*

*I*TOOK A SECOND LOOK—I was right the first time. The man's shirt had a button-down collar . . . *and* . . . French cuffs with engraved gold cuff links . . . *a boy's lolly boarding-school collar* . . . and . . . *a set of cuffs from a partners meeting at Debevoise & Plimpton* . . . This shirt had to be custom-made . . . *had* to be. Likewise, the man's jacket . . . Catch the high armholes and the narrow cut of the sleeves. They clear the French cuffs by a precise eighth of an inch. They're just short enough—*just so!*—to reveal the gold cuff links and not a sixteenth of an inch shorter. *Check out the shoes!*—brown leather cap-toed English oxfords custom-fitted so closely to his high-arched feet, they look absolutely petite, his feet do, as if he were some unaccountably great strapping Chinese maiden whose feet had been bound in infancy to make sure they would be forever tiny at teatime . . . I could not imagine how a man his size, six feet tall and two hundred pounds at the very least, with a big neck, a burly build, a square-jawed face, could possibly rise up from his chair here in a little bullpen slapped together out of four-foot-high partitions in the sludge-caked exposed-pipe-joint offices of a newspaper not long for this world, the *New York Herald Tribune,* and support himself, no hands, teetering atop that implausibly little pair of high-arched bench-made British cap-toed cinderella shoes.

Yet rise and stand he did. He introduced himself. His name was Clay Felker. He had a booming voice, but it wasn't so much the boom that struck me. It was his honk. The New York Honk, as it was called, was the most fashionable accent an American male could have at that time, namely, the spring of 1963. One achieved it by forcing all words out through the nostrils rather than the mouth. It was at once virile . . . and utterly affected. Nelson Rockefeller had a New York Honk. Huntington Hartford had one. The editor of *Newsweek*, Osborn Elliot, had one. The financier Robert Dowling, publishers Roger Straus and Tom Guinzburg had the Honk, and so did Robert Morgenthau, who still does, as far as that goes.

Unfortunately, Clay Felker didn't even rate being in the same paragraph with toffs like them. Custom-made toffery he was clad in, BUT he was also pushing forty and jobless, on the beach, as the phrase went, panting, gasping for air, a beached whale, after coming out the loser in a battle for the editorship of *Esquire* magazine . . . not to mention the corner suite with north and east views of 1963's street of dreams, Madison Avenue in the Fifties, that came with it.

Yet in less than six months from that same day, in that same jerry-built eight-by-ten-foot bullpen at a doomed newspaper, he created the hottest magazine in America in the second half of the twentieth century: *New York*.

IN OUR STORY, the shirt (Turnbull & Asser of Jermyn Street, London), the suit (Huntsman of Savile Row, London), the shoes (John Lobb, also of Jermyn Street, London), as well as the accent, are not thrust into the reader's face idly. All provide microscopic glimpses into our story's very heart. And the duplex apartment Clay Felker lived in at 322 East 57th Street—well, from up here the view becomes what has to be termed macroscopic. The living room was a twenty-five-by-twenty-five-foot grand salon with a two-story, twenty-five-foot-high ceiling and two huge House of Parliament–scale windows, overlooking 57th Street, each twenty-two feet high and eight feet wide, divided into colossal panes of glass by muntins as thick as your wrist. There was a vast fireplace of the sort writers searching for adjectives always call baronial. Fourteen status seekers could sit at the same time on the needlepoint-upholstered fender that went around it, supported by gleaming brass columns. When you arrived *chez* Felker and walked out of the elevator, you found yourself on a balcony big as a lobby overlooking the meticulously conspicuous consumption below. Guests descended to the salon down a staircase that made the Paris Opera's look like my old front stoop. Standing on the gigantic Aubusson rug at the foot of the stairs to welcome you, on a good night, would be Felker's wife, a twenty-year-old movie actress named Pamela Tiffin, who had starred in the screen version of *Summer and Smoke*. She had a fair white face smooth as a Ming figurine's. She was gorgeous. She had something else, too, a career that was taking off so fast she had not one but two personal managers, Irwin Winkler and Robert Chartoff. She could afford them and two more like them, but there were no two more like them. Fifteen years later Chartoff and Winkler would win an Academy Award for a movie they produced called *Rocky*. For a man on the beach, Pamela Tiffin was a lovely helpmate to have. Clay Felker was broke.

So what inna nameagod *was* all this? He who had staged this style of life, Clay Felker, was a Midwestern boy, from Webster Groves, Missouri, which always made me think of Grover's Corners in *Our Town*. Like the two great American magazine founders of the first half of the twentieth century, Harold Ross of *The New Yorker*, a real Colorado boy, and Henry Luce of *Time* and *Life*, born to missionaries in China, Felker grew up far from the magnetic pull of New York's much-vaunted glamour and excitement. His obsession with New York seems to have begun so early in his life that no one, not even the man himself, can remember what set it off. Introducing him many, many years later at a fund-raiser for the Felker Magazine Center of the University of California, Berkeley, I claimed his sister had told me Baby Clay's first complete sentence was "Whaddaya mean, I '*don't have a reservation*'?" At the time I thought I was only making a little joke.

The standard line about boys from Missouri is, "I'm from Missouri. You've got to show me," meaning, "Don't you glib city slickers try to slicktalk me. You've got to prove it." But to Clay Felker it was the Dionysian cry of a Midwesterner who had come to New York to swallow America's great City of Ambition whole, slick talk and all. "You've got to *show* me!"—all of it, the very process of status competition, the status details, the status symbols, the styles of life, everything that indicated how one ranked. The posh details of his private life were the reverse, like the reverse surface of a silk *le smoking,* an inside look at his obsession with status as the drive that runs the world—certainly the New York part of it.

At *Esquire* our man had produced an article comprised mainly of elaborate illustrations of the interiors of Manhattan's most fashionable nightspots—"21," El Morocco, Sardi's—carefully designating where the social ringmasters, the maître d's, seated VIPs . . . and where they stowed very unimportant people, the nobodies, usually out of sight in the rear of the room. At "21" they took no chances. They put the poor devils up on an entirely separate floor. Either way, these dead zones were known in the business as "Siberia." As soon as Felker published it, the term spread like a smell to swell restaurants all over the country. To this day unsteady souls enter such joints in a state of dread, resentment on the hair trigger, fearful lest the wardens, i.e., the maître d's, icy smiles of welcome frozen on their faces, lead them straight to the gulag. Such are the status details that intrigue the human mind and, once inside it, never leave. They get under your skin—so much so that there would come a day when one author would write in *New York* magazine's pages that Clay Felker had "Felkerized" New York.

AT *THAT MOMENT,* the moment I first saw the big man accomplish the improbable stunt of standing up and balancing himself on two elfin feet, the *Herald Tribune* was trying to pull itself together after a four-month-long American Newspaper Guild strike. The sheet had brought our Whale in from the beach as a consultant in a total revamping of its Sunday edition and especially the Sunday supplement, whose name had been changed from *Today's Living* to *New York.* A . . . *Sunday supplement!* The Sunday supplement was the lowest form of newspaper journalism in America at that time. With the single exception of *The New York Times Magazine,* Sunday supplements were cotton candy for the two areas of the brain (Broca's and Wernicke's) that process language.

New York's first editor, Sheldon Zalaznick, had a mandate to turn it into a serious enough sheet to compete with *The New York Times Magazine.* He arranged to have Jimmy Breslin and me do an article for *New York,* both of us, every week, in addition to our daily chores for the City Desk. Zalaznick proved to be serious enough, all right. The *Trib* had recruited its most famous literary alumnus, John O'Hara, who certainly didn't need the work, to do a column for *New York* once a month. His first contribution was so sloppy, not to mention surly, it was obvious he had dashed the thing off during some quick fit of pique or other. Zalaznick rejected it, and O'Hara piqued into just as quick a fit and quit—to the profound consternation of the *Trib's* advertising department. They were using O'Hara's name as their lead lure for the renovated Sunday edition. Right away I could see this was a very different sort of Sunday supplement. I was good enough to write for it, but John O'Hara wasn't.

After no more than six weeks, Zalaznick was promoted to editor of the entire Sunday edition. At that point the newspaper's maximum editor, Jim Bellows, brought Clay Felker on staff to edit *New York*.

Not long thereafter Clay was sitting in the bullpen with his staff. *Staff* . . . The staff, the entire staff, consisted of one full-time editorial assistant, Walter Stovall, and two part-time writers, Jimmy Breslin and myself. What with two metal desks taking up more than half the space, you couldn't have fitted more than four people in there, anyway.

I remember Clay saying, "Look . . . we're coming out once a week, right? And *The New Yorker* comes out once a week. And we start out the week the same way they do, with blank paper and ink. Is there any reason why we can't be as good as *The New Yorker*? . . . Or better. They're so damned dull."

At first I wrote that off as brave bluster. *The New Yorker* was also so damned solid. They had long ago established themselves as the very embodiment of New York sophistication. You could make the argument that it was the most prestigious magazine in America. College-educated souls all over the country subscribed to *The New Yorker* to be . . . *with it*. High-end retail companies loved all these people above the B.A. line. They were positively *stoking* the magazine with ads.

At *The New Yorker* they had not an inkling of what was about to hit them, namely, Clay Felker's new kind of news.

As I recall, the first assignment Clay gave me was a story on the promenade *les chic* and *les chic*-lets took every Saturday morning through the art galleries along Madison Avenue from 57th Street to 79th. I was totally unaware of any such custom. Fortunately for me, Clay assigned a photographer, Freddie Eberstadt, to the story, too. Freddie knew his way around in that world already. The next Saturday morning we set out on the promenade and ran across half the *what's happ'nin'* population of Manhattan, everyone from Greta Garbo, looking as inconspicuous as possible in the Wildenstein gallery—but Freddie recognized her immediately—to Tiger Morse, a flamboyant fashionista of the time, walking along the Avenue and gaily waving . . . to Freddie. When the piece, entitled "The Saturday Route," came out, people thought of me (not Freddie) as an ingenious reporter capable of sniffing out all these icons and novoscenti on a single Saturday-morning stroll. They were also astonished . . . and thrilled . . . that any such promenade took place . . . and now *les* proto-*chic*-lettes came skipping and screaming onto the Madison Avenue Saturday morning gallery scene, pretty young things in short skirts and jeans molded to their pelvic saddles. They became known as the "art birds." As late as 1989 Japanese art collectors liked to have these pretty little American girls by their sides in the front rows for the "important" auctions at Sotheby's and Christie's. They loved the pretty things' lithe young legs with their epidermi of sheerest ravage-me nylon shimmering up to the most tumescent swells of their thighs as they crossed and then re-crossed and then re-re-crossed and then re-re-re-crossed them *shimmer shimmer shimmer shimmer* beneath the downlighters.

As I say, I had never heard of this Saturday-morning art promenade before, but Clay had. He made it a point to hear about such things. I had never worked with an editor who generated so many story ideas himself. He was his own best reporter. He always kept a small pad of paper in the left-hand inside pocket of his jacket. At dinner, even a formal dinner in some swell private home, as soon as he heard a wisp of conversation that gave him a story idea, Clay would draw the pad from his pocket and draw it fast, as if he kept it in a shoulder holster, slap it flat on the table, and write his inspiration down with a fourteen-karat-gold ballpoint pen. The pen inevitably created a flash in electric light. I saw him do it many times.

One afternoon I came by to see Clay at his Xanadu on 57th Street and found him sitting at a desk going through a date book to put together some income-tax data.

"Look at this," he told me, riffling through the date book, "I only ate dinner at home eight times last year!"

I don't think I can adequately convey the pride he took in this discovery. He had developed night vision for detecting new styles of life. "Style of life"—*Lebensstil* in German—was a term invented a hundred years ago by the German sociologist Max Weber, the father of status theory itself. All new styles of life, he said, were created by "status groups," like-minded souls who try to create spheres of their own, insulated from the opinions of people outside. The socialites of the Saturday route had their style of life in the 1960s . . . and hippies had theirs. It was not until the late 1950s that the terms themselves, "status," referring to social position, and "style of life," referring to the manners and mores of status groups, emerged from academic sociology and became part of everyday language.

I don't think Clay even knew who Max Weber was or what "status," let alone "styles of life," meant in sociology. But his *Show me!* instincts led him directly to the same line of thought and toward styles of life that made big news. When Clay edited *New York* as a Sunday supplement and when he turned it into the magazine you can buy on newsstands today, the range of exclusives, of scoops, as it were, was extraordinary, looking back on it.

He published an astonishing report by Gail Sheehy—represented in this anthology by her lovely piece on the mysteries of Grey Gardens—on prostitution in New York. She had taken to the streets herself in hot pants that came up to *here,* white vinyl Courrèges boots, and an aureolae-oriented top in order to mingle with the "working girls." What she brought back to Clay at *New York* was not only an eyewitness account of the trade, which was remarkable enough, but also an analysis of prostitutes as a status group with six distinct social gradations. He published the first account of how the megawattage of newspaper, magazine, and television coverage, abetted by PR resources of the fashion industry, had created an entirely new kind of socialite, who so outdazzled the old capital-S Society based on Protestant family lineage that it was reduced to obscurity. He even published the first report from inside a hippie commune at a time when hippies were still called acid-heads. The material was hot—but how could you expect readers to *thrill* to the lives of people called acid-heads?

For that matter, he published the first account of life within a California surfer commune, "The Pump House Gang," and the first account of life among the student radicals who stormed Columbia University and took it over for a week in 1968. These three styles of life, the hippie, the surfer, and the radical, would change the lives of American youth and with them American life in general in ways beyond imagining at the time.

Clay's magazine brought to life the inner emotional lives, not just the financial adventures, of the boom-time financiers in the voice of Adam Smith, the pseudonym for George J. W. Goodman. Goodman was an investor who had made a modest fortune, set up an investment fund, lost several modest fortunes, his own and the investors', before making what was to be his real fortune by creating an irresistible new approach to business news. His stories for *New York*, reworked only slightly, became the best-selling book *The Money Game*. Jimmy Breslin wrote a priceless piece for Clay, "Namath All Night Long," about life as lived by the first Bad Boy professional athlete who became the prototype for all the Bad Boys, the John McEnroes, the Jimmy Connorses, who were to follow. Clay published Mark Jacobson's bizarre account of "the hip fleet," the world of the Dover Taxi Garage's nighttime cabbies, a superiority complex of professors, former priests, artists, musicians, MAs, DJs, and others who classified themselves as intellectuals, padding out their miserable livings by driving at night—and whose greatest fear was working the day shift, which would mean the worst had now happened: they had become *real* cabdrivers. He published Nik Cohn's "The Tribal Rites of the New Saturday Night," depicting a world of lower-middle-class, lower-IQ youths in Queens, Brooklyn, and the Bronx in the mid-1970s who *lived* for Saturday nights in disco joints. Cohn's piece was the basis of the movie *Saturday Night Fever*, starring John Travolta. The white suits Travolta wore throughout created a sudden effulgence of white suits in the men's clothing stores that made my own look trite ... until the travolting faddists found out how much trouble and expense they require to maintain, and the *Saturday Night Fever* whites vanished as fast as they had appeared. He published a remarkable account of 1970s hangover of all of New York's young hipsters and yipsters and granolas who had based their status dreams completely on one "Counter Culture" style of life or another. And he published Gael Greene's reprise in 1970—"How Not to Be Humiliated in Snob Restaurants"—of Clay's own "Siberia" piece in *Esquire* a decade before.

Up against work of this sort, based on reporting this solid, *The New Yorker* never had a chance. In its "Talk of the Town" column, the magazine began to fling zingers obviously aimed at us, always omitting the name of the magazine, *New York*, that was already making them look second-rate. We were working for an old newspaper, the *Herald Tribune*, that was all. This culminated in a full-blown parody in the body of *The New Yorker* of Breslin's work for *New York* and mine . . . without mentioning *New York*. (To tell the truth, it was pretty clever stuff, that parody.) So they wanted to play. That much they made clear, as Clay and I saw it, and we certainly didn't mind obliging them. Why should we?

We were sitting in Clay's office one afternoon grousing about and begrudging all the outrageously worshipful rose petals and laurel wreaths other publications were heaping upon *The New Yorker*. The damned thing was easier to praise than to read . . . right? Right . . . They're really heaping all this praise on the dead body of Harold Ross and the way the magazine used to be when he ran it in the old days . . . right? Right . . . That was when we had an inspiration. What about the man who runs it now, the Sandman who puts everybody to sleep these days? William Shawn was his name. Ross had handpicked Shawn to succeed him, which he did, in 1952. That was it! We'd do a profile of William Shawn. That would be rich, wouldn't it? The "profile" was a genre *The New Yorker* itself had dreamed up and named. Nobody had ever written much of anything about William Shawn. From what we soon learned about him, it wasn't hard to guess why. Shawn was a very apprehensive little man, a regular homunculus, and a claustrophobe. The thought of getting on an elevator petrified him. So did the idea of appearing in public, let alone speaking in public. So did the idea of being photographed, never mind submitting to an interview. There was only one known photograph of William Shawn as an adult. He had commissioned and paid for it himself and executed total . . . and very wary . . . control over who could use it.

The more Clay and I talked about it the funnier the idea became. This presumed-to-be Dr. Johnson of Urbanity, Wit, Sophistication, Glamour, and Excitement in New York was a gnome who apparently had no life outside his office on West 43rd Street and a building on Fifth Avenue, where he lived *quietly quietly quietly quietly* with his wife and child in an apartment on the second floor . . . and therefore easily accessible without enclosing anybody's body in the windowless metal coffin called "elevator." He was as close to a hermit as a man could be and still hold a day job.

There, in sum, you have the Editor Shawn I presented in a two-part profile headed "Tiny Mummies! The True Story of the Rulers of 43rd Street's Land of the Walking Dead." I didn't accuse him of doing anything other than being himself. But you've heard of "bloody murder"? That was what greeted my playful profile—screams and howls of bloody murder such as you've never heard in your life! Shawn himself wrote a letter to the owner of the *Trib*, Jock Whitney, and had it hand-delivered. He called my "Tiny Mummies" more than libelous, at the same time making it clear it was that, too. No, it was worse. It was "murderous." And *they* were the ones who had wanted to *play* . . .

Bloody murder! Somebody at *The New Yorker*—the asphalt jungle drums said it was one of the magazine's oldest and best writers, Lillian Ross—marshaled the troops, drafting every writer who had written, was writing, or sure would like to write for *The New Yorker*. Godalmighty there were a lot of them! Famous, too! J. D. Salinger, who was even more of a recluse than Shawn and hadn't uttered or written a public word in seven years, popped up out of his hole in rural New Hampshire like The Groundhog and sent Whitney a telegram accusing him, our former Ambassador to the Court of St. James, of having destroyed his own and the *Trib*'s reputation, *forever*, with a single "poisonous" article. Among the angriest sure-would-like-to-bes (a yearning we would learn of later) was one of the two most prestigious political columnists in the country, Joseph Alsop. Alsop said I was part of the Ho Chi Minh–loving America-hating madness now sweeping a generation of young Americans into the arms of the totalitarian Left. Guess what newspaper was Alsop's home office . . . the *Trib*! The British writer Muriel Spark at least added some balance by calling me a Joe McCarthy–style bully. So what about the other of the two most prestigious political columnists in America, namely, Walter Lippmann? You won't believe this—*but he checked in too!* Lest he be seen as shading his meaning in any fashion, Walter Lippmann wrote, "Tom Wolfe is an incompetent ass." You won't believe this either but his home office was . . . the *Trib* too! That was how bad it got.

Our little magazine was suddenly lit up lurid with publicity. *Time, Newsweek,* the press all over America—they couldn't get enough of this "murderous" Manhattan magazine feud. A lot of the coverage was negative, but *le tout America* now knew that here was a magazine called *New York* that had become a major player.

IN 1966 THE *Trib* had folded after yet another suicidal strike. Two other stricken newspapers, the *Journal-American* and the *World-Telegram & Sun,* anted up along with the *Trib* to stay alive with life-support in the form of a now mercifully forgotten, stillborn sheet called the *World Journal Tribune.* It lasted eight months, and the three comrades-of-convenience said goodbye to the business forever in 1967. I bade a sentimental goodbye to the *Trib,* which I had loved working for. Such wild and crazy, lovely times . . . like the time a mob of Cuban refugees burst into the City Room wanting my head—my *head!*—and I—

—but Clay didn't have time to listen to my old war stories. I doubt that he wasted five seconds reminiscing. He knew immediately what was to be done: breathe life back into the corpse of the dear departed Sunday supplement and resurrect it as an independent national weekly magazine called *New York.*

Getting a weekly publication rolling from a dead start has been compared to slicing a wrist to find out how fast you can bleed. It had taken Time Inc. half a dozen years and massive transfusions of money to bring *Sports Illustrated* to the point where it began to turn a profit, and Clay Felker and Time Inc. didn't belong on the same page, much less in the same paragraph. Jock Whitney had agreed to sell the name *New York* for $6,500, but Clay couldn't even come up with that. He finally borrowed it from a writer, Barbara Goldsmith.

Ironically, it was probably the intense coverage of the set-to with *The New Yorker,* bad as much of it was, that enabled Clay to raise the small fortune required to start up a slick-paper weekly magazine like this in less than a year. *The New Yorker* Affair, as people called it, had sunk Clay's name and *New York*'s into everybody's bean. I remember the day in April

1968 that *New York,* the freestanding magazine, made its debut. The scene was a breakfast at the Four Seasons for a thousand advertisers, potential advertisers, media folk, PR people . . . in short, the cast of characters needed most by a magazine as a bottom-line business. The first one thousand *New York*s to come off the press were to be presented to the guests as they arrived. Start-ups have their problems. The most interesting was the sight of one of the country's best-known illustrators and designers, Milton Glaser, now art director for Clay, desperately trying to add a decorative black bar above the logo, *New York,* with a straight-edge and a drafting pen—*upon each of the thousand copies*—at a rate faster than the guests could come in. Somehow the bar had disappeared in the printing process. There in the grand luxe Four Seasons a desperate man was trying to show Fate what for.

New York's first offices were on the top floor, the fourth, of Glaser's Push Pin Studio's loft building on East 32nd Street. The building was a walk-up all the way, but who cared? Oh, to be young and in New York! Still in a blessed state of rude animal health! With virgin optimism and brand-new shrink-wrapped ambition! So it was up on the fourth floor at 207 East 32nd Street . . . as *New York* published right on time its second issue . . . and then the third . . . and then—

I was up there in *New York's* new office when Clay came over to me and said, "Take a look at this. The advertising department says if we run it, we'll lose every advertiser we have on Madison Avenue."

This was no small thing. The new *New York* had been ably sold to high-end retailers on Madison Avenue and elsewhere with assurances of what a high-end magazine it would be and how much people flush with high-end boom money would love it.

Clay handed me an article entitled "La Dolce Viva," by Barbara Goldsmith, the very one who had lent him $6,500 to buy the name *New York* from Jock Whitney in the first place. With it was a photograph.

I was standing up when I started reading—and found I was unwilling to interrupt myself long enough to sit down. What I had in my hands was dynamite. *Tout le monde* knew about the famous Andy Warhol and his famous Factory full of helpers and hangers-on. But Barbara Goldsmith's was the first story to capture the campy creepy K-Y/vaseline-y queasiness of it . . . the Warhol style of life—a classic example, incidentally, of what Weber meant by a status group generating a style of life . . . (Not only that, for an even forty years now St. Andy's has remained the dominant style of the lives of the artists in New York.) I looked at the photograph. I had never seen anything like it. It was a portrait of one of Warhol's "superstars," as he called the unknown actresses in his high-camp movies. She went by one name, Viva, the same way real celebrities such as a Liz (Taylor), Jackie (O.), and Andy did. In the photograph, Viva was reclining nude upon a ratty version of a Récamier sofa. This vision was not what one would call arousing. She looked like a hairless rabbit. You could see her entire rib cage beneath her skin except where a pair of tiny shrunken breasts were in the way. Seems she was a sometime model. She had rolled her eyes up under her skull, as if she were stoned, as being high on drugs was called at that time. Somehow the defining touch was an empty milk carton on the coffee table in the foreground. Not a syringe, not a stubbed-out reefer, not even an empty liquor bottle—but an empty milk carton. Somehow that milk carton was the perfect objective correlative, as the literary critics of the 1950s and 1960s used to say, of the mental rubbish the picture captured. The photographer's name was Diane Arbus.

I looked up at Clay and said, "I don't see how you can *not* run it."

"That's the way I feel," said Clay. And he ran it, story and photograph, in *New York*'s fourth issue.

Dynamite! Dynamite this story and this photograph were! So where did that leave the advertising department? Had they been a bunch of panicky philistines and Mrs. Grundys? As it turned out . . . no. *New York* lost every high-end retailer on Madison Avenue and beyond. This precipitated a crisis. The board, made up of the big investors, summoned Clay to a meeting at the Park Avenue apartment of one of them, a much respected elder statesman of Wall Street named Armand Erpf. I came along, too, since technically (and technically only) I was a vice-president of the magazine. Erpf's apartment was nowhere near as grand as Clay's, but the living room was lined—*lined*—with paintings such as I had seen before only in museums or Skira art books, Impressionists and the like. In terms of current prices, there must have been a billion dollars worth of pictures hanging on those walls. The directors weren't looking at the pictures.

They were hopping mad over this "Viva" business. They could see their investment sinking without a bubble after only four issues. They were ready to can Clay then and there and probably would have, had not the elder statesman and maximum art collector, Erpf, exercised moral suasion.

Incidentally, Diane Arbus is today the St. Diane of photography as an art. An original print of *Viva* would fetch $500,000 and possibly much more, judging by the latest auction prices of her work. Clay's writers could only admire him for the risk he had taken, for brushing aside all the business types and seeing to it that a great story and a great photograph got published. *His* writers . . . for by now, quite without intending to, he had cast his own spell over *New York*'s writers and editors and illustrators, graphic artists, photographers—in short, the entire creative side of the operation. Soon we were all breathing Clay's own mental atmosphere of boundless ambition, his conviction that we were involved in the greatest experiment in the history of journalism. Even back when his platform was nothing more than that miserable little bullpen at the *Trib,* he had a way of convincing you that his dream was as good as an *action accompli.* What we're doing with this magazine is . . . Big League stuff! . . . If you put everything you've got into what I'm asking you to do . . . "I'll make you a star." According to the fast-accumulating Felker lore, that was the way he always put it, "I'll make you a star." I never heard him utter those very words, but one way or another he imparted that heady prospect to me and everyone else who worked for *New York* . . . *He'll make me a star.* He wasn't just blowing smoke, either. He did exactly that many times. And now that *New York* was a magazine on its own, more and more writers . . . *believed.* This . . . is . . . Big League stuff. And most of them—once they got a look at Clay's Xanadu on 57th Street, they surrendered all doubts. Either this is the Big League . . . or there *is* no Big League. The only grandeur missing from Xanadu was Pamela. She was spending more and more time acting in movies in Italy, and by and by she and Clay went their separate ways. Years later he married Gail Sheehy.

If Clay was crazy about some story a writer had done for him, then he couldn't do enough for the writer. The ultimate case was Gloria Steinem. Glo-Glo, as Clay called her, had done some great pieces for *New York* on the subject of feminism. So when she founded *Ms.* magazine, Clay gave her a hoist and a half. He printed the entire first issue of *Ms.*, featuring a piece by Glo-Glo herself entitled "Sisterhood," as a pull-out within an issue of *New York*. That was her start-up: a debut under the aegis of the most talked-about magazine in the country. It reminded me at the time of the way NASA used to carry rocket airplanes such as the X-1, the first ship to break the sound barrier, up to an altitude of ten thousand feet in the belly of a cargo plane. Then they would cut the little beast loose on its own so some pilot like Chuck Yeager (and there *were* two or three other pilots like Chuck Yeager) could take it "booming and zooming" up into the thin atmosphere on the edge of space. That way they didn't have to use up most of the rocket fuel overcoming gravity. Likewise, Glo-Glo didn't have to burn up a fortune in start-up money getting the perfect audience to look at *Ms.*—and the novelty of the stunt generated publicity money couldn't buy.

Clay made sure I got a great ride, too. Late in 1969 I came up with the idea of writing a non-fiction version of Thackeray's *Vanity Fair* about New York, a "non-fiction novel," to use the label Truman Capote had stuck onto *In Cold Blood*, as if to say, "Let's get one thing clear: this isn't journalism, this is literature." (Even Solzhenitsyn . . . even he . . . stuck a label on *The Gulag Archipelago* reading "an experiment in literary investigation," that being its subtitle.) So one day I was hanging around a hallway at *Harper's* magazine. *Harper's* had a knockout of an art director named Sheila, and I got the bright idea of maybe asking her out for lunch, which was marginally more serious than *wanna go get a cup of coffee*. While I was waiting for her to finish up whatever she was doing in the art department, I wandered next door into the office of David Halberstam, who wasn't there. Nosily I noticed a rather fancy card on his desktop . . . I couldn't believe it. It was an invitation from Leonard Bernstein and his wife, Felicia, for a reception at their apartment at 895 Park Avenue, corner of Park and 79th Street, in support of the Black Panthers. Now, there was a match made on Donkey Island for you . . . Leonard Bernstein gives a party for the Black Panthers on Park Avenue, in the Seventies, no less. If this wouldn't make a chapter in a non-fiction *Vanity Fair* about New York, what *would*? You were supposed to RSVP to a certain telephone number. So I called it, using David Halberstam's telephone, and said,

"This is Tom Wolfe, and I accept." On the other end there must have been a functionary working for some sort of Panther defense committee, writing down acceptances on a yellow legal pad or whatever, because that was that.

When I reached Leonard Bernstein's apartment on the appointed evening, there was a security check at a desk outside the door. I said, "Tom Wolfe," and sure enough, there he was, Tom Wolfe, listed on a yellow legal pad. Inside, I could see immediately that the entryway hadn't begun to reveal the scale of the place. It was a thirteen-room penthouse duplex, not nearly so swell and overwhelming as Clay's duplex, but it had its own swell touches. In the living room, near the windows, there was a pair of grand pianos, the indisputably *grand* sort of grand pianos. One look, and you couldn't help but imagine sublime evenings *chez* Bernstein . . . playful yet magical piano duets with Bernstein himself at one piano and some other not merely sophisticated but *knowing* artist at the other piano trying to out-descant one another with great garlands of notes in elliptical orbits only barely and yet always subject to the gravitational pull of the cantus firmus . . . Like any boy who has been instructed at cotillion to pay his respects to the host and hostess first and then be gracious and circulate, I sought out Leonard and Felicia Bernstein and introduced myself. I kept my National Brand shorthand pad and ballpoint pen in plain view. I mention that because afterward I can't tell you how many people accused me of perfidiously turning on my hosts. Bernstein's sister wrote a letter enumerating my sins in an ascending order of perfidy. Serving the forces of oppression wasn't the worst and ultimate. The worst and ultimate was sneaking a hidden tape recorder into her brother's home. I took that as a great compliment, since in this life one should take his satisfactions where he can. It meant that my shorthand recording of the evening's dialogue, which I did quite openly, must have struck Leonard Bernstein as a bull's-eye. The evening's cast of characters . . . leonine Leonard Bernstein and his beautiful blond former actress wife, Felicia, three fiercely-turned-out Black Panther dudes and "the Panther women," as they were referred to, a couple of organizers in gray suits who had Engineers on the Freight Train of History written all over them, the two dozen or so celebrities (e.g., Barbara Walters, Otto Preminger), socialites (e.g., Jean vanden Heuvel, Cynthia Phipps), and "intellectuals" (e.g., Robert Silvers, Harold Taylor) . . . this cast would have been pure gold for any writer. The sight of the rich, the famous, and the brainy kowtowing to a band of black radicals from Oakland, California, in Leonard Bernstein's living room, baring their soft white backs the more poignantly to feel the Panthers' vengeful lash, then imploring them not to kill their children—no writer would have ever dreamed of a bonanza quite this rich. In any case, my description appears within the tome before you (pages 3 to 46). It was all too much for me to try to keep penned up in a shorthand pad until I was ready to fit it in as a chapter of a "non-fiction novel." That scene cried out for *New York* magazine—*now*. Just about any magazine other than *The Nation* and *Mother Jones,* which would have raised their forearms to shield their eyes from the light like werewolves shrinking from the dawn—just about any magazine would have published material like that. But only Clay would understand how potent it was. Only Clay would give the writer his head and publish it down to the last detail, no matter how many pages it took. It took thirty pages, it so happened. He devoted almost the entire June 8, 1970, issue of *New York* to "That Party at Lenny's," as the cover line read.

"Down to every last detail" . . . Again, this was mainly instinctive, I think, but Clay realized the importance of detail as metonymy to bring alive the scenes that illustrated new styles of life. The new styles of life in turn revealed new status groups, some of which have proven influential enough to change life not merely in New York but all over the United States. "Radical Chic: That Party at Lenny's" was a herald—or an early warning, depending on one's take on the matter—of what is well known today as "political correctness." Political correctness today transcends or is blithely oblivious of ideology. It has become an intellectual fashion, just as membership in the Baptist Church once was, believe it or not, essential to establishing one's spiritual enlightenment. Dignified, prominent, fashionable people dread being asked their opinion of, say, soft-porn photographs of the bare haunches and school-of-bare breasts of vulvacious young things with *I gotta have it* leers on their lips . . . in fashion ads in the most elegant magazines. They shudder. Honest answers might strip them of their socially compulsory spiritual enlightenment.

Clay's eye for styles of life and the status groups that created them, his journalist's awareness of such things as hot news, profoundly changed magazine and newspaper publishing in the United States and, for that matter, England. So-called "city" magazines doing their best to imitate *New York* cropped up all over the country. Newspapers created sections called "Style," "Lifestyle," or, using the new corporate jam-bam style of logo, "LifeStyle," all to try to capture some of the *New York* mojo. *The New York Times* would seek to duplicate *New York* by slipping a multitude of new sections into the newspaper daily and on Sunday—the jumbo Sunday *Times* might contain three or more of them—with titles such as "Styles," "City" (more styles), "Escapes," "Arts" (consisting of two subsections, one for the Fine and one for the Fun), "Dining Out," "Dining In," "Circuits." But the city magazines, the newspaper jam-bammers, and the *Times*'s one-a-day magazine (if not two- or three-a-day) quickly degenerated into coverage not of styles of life in the Max Weber sense but styles of living in the Martha Stewart sense, the right kitchenware, the right party planning, the right trips abroad, the right décors, neighborhoods, nanny services, iCommunicators, fitness programs, and "parenting."

Throughout the fourteen years he ran *New York* magazine, Clay Felker oversaw sociological studies of urban life that academic sociology had never even attempted: the culture of Wall Street, the culture of political graft in New York, cop culture, Mob culture, youth cultures in California as well as New York, New York's self-aborting, dysfunctional, deconstructed power structure, capital-S Society and its discontents. And yet no one ever thought of it as sociology. That was thanks to one of Clay's finest instincts. He demanded—or, better said, inspired as well as required—such depth of reporting that his writers came up with the same sort of scenes, status details, and detailed dialogue that in the past had rarely been found except in novels, short stories, and the most outrageous form of fiction, as Orwell put it, which is autobiography. (Autobiography is like Wikipedia: Some of it may be true.) And although it remains controversial, Clay's writers often used the other favorite device of fiction writers: namely, putting the reader inside the skin, inside the head, behind the eyes of characters in the story. The New Journalism, *c'est moi*, Clay could have easily claimed.

One could argue—and I don't hesitate to do it—that in those fourteen years, 1963–1977, Clay produced a huge sprawling *Vanity Fair* himself . . . only having it written, chapter by chapter, by his writers . . . all of them absorbed in, exhilarated by, a Missouri boy's wide-eyed obsession with New York as the Rome, the Paris, the London of the twentieth century, the capital of the world . . . the radiant City of Ambition.

In 1977 Clay, in his early fifties, at the very zenith of his creative powers, proved to be still an innocent Missouri boy beneath his heavy baggage of sophisticated knowledge. He looked on helplessly, utterly baffled, as a handful of what today are called "activist investors" euchred *New York* magazine right out from under him. If you know the type, you can imagine their peculiar *hee hee hee* viperous glee.

The look on his face! It was so easy, the gang had to chuckle. Such Big Talk . . . the poor chump. The gang stared at the magazine for a while, and then they looked at each other. Why the hell wouldn't the damned thing lay those golden eggs it was supposed to be so hot at doing? Presently they sold it, at a loss. But hey, that's business. You take the bitter with the better. Looking back on the whole thing, though, you couldn't help *hee hee hee* laughing again. The big talker with the big apartment and the big ideas— they sure had cooked his goose!

INTRODUCTION

....

IT'S AN IRONY, but not an entirely surprising one, that *New York* magazine was founded by an out-of-towner. Clay Felker, who built the magazine on the ashes of the old *New York Herald Tribune,* was born in Missouri, went to college at Duke, in North Carolina, and never lost the hint of a twang in his foghorn voice. At the core of the magazine's journalistic mission has always been an outsider's excitement at New York's particular brand of urban life. Felker, who began his journalistic career as a sportswriter at *Life* magazine, spent most of the early sixties as a top editor at *Esquire,* where he helped invent what came to be known as the New Journalism, with its vivid, highly subjective storytelling techniques.

While *New York* magazine came out of that tradition, and published some excellent examples (including Tom Wolfe's manifesto on the subject), that was never primarily its focus. Rather, Felker conceived of New York as a place of constant revolutionary tumult, with its own particular mind-set and a distinctive set of interests. Under Felker and subsequent editors, *New York* expanded the palette of what a magazine could be and made it more responsive to what was actually going through the heads of actual people in an actual city. This collection, on the occasion of the magazine's fortieth anniversary, reflects this new sensibility as it has evolved over the past decades.

NEW YORK PUBLISHED ITS FIRST issue in April 1968. Felker had been editing a Sunday supplement, also called *New York,* that came tucked inside the *Herald Tribune*—the magazine had been his consolation prize after he'd lost out on becoming editor of *Esquire*. When the *Herald Tribune* was shuttered, Felker organized a group of investors to buy the name and publish the magazine on its own.

He'd been lucky to lose *Esquire; New York* was his perfect vehicle. He set about immediately trying to codify the new urban mood. Felker had an instinctive opposition to categorizing experience in a hierarchical way; he was never a highbrow, and he tended not to make brow distinctions of any kind. He was fascinated by power and had plenty of ego, but very little pretense. He was the most curious person anyone had ever met, and every bit as good a reporter as any of the famous names who worked for him.

His social life and his professional life were fused. He was out every night listening to people, jotting down their insights on a special pad he carried around, and turning what he heard into stories. To a large degree, the magazine operated according to this guideline: to cover not only the great questions of the day but who discussed them, and where they were eating, and what they were eating, and what they did when they went home.

It's a truism that the late sixties was a period of great cultural ferment, and the changes that washed over the nation swept the city too. But New York City's own evolution took on an idiosyncratic form. A new kind of metropolis was being born, and *New York* magazine's editors and writers were among the first to attempt to map it. The sixties and seventies ethics of personal discovery were transformed in *New York* into something brasher and glossier. In the new city, personal choice became a kind of fetish, an indicator of deeper identity: downtown or uptown, French or Chinese, bohemian or yuppie (in fact, in a not entirely flattering formulation, Felker can be said to have invented the yuppie). The immigrant city, of factory workers and longshoremen and *dese* and *dem* and *dose*, was losing its sway. Increasingly, the city's energy would be defined by a different kind of immigrant, one like Felker: out-of-towners who came to New York because it was the biggest American stage.

At the center of the magazine, then and now, has always been an aspirational fervor that was a personal characteristic of Felker himself and of many of the magazine's writers. This characteristic was mirrored in the mental landscape of many of the new city dwellers, people who came to escape not war and famine in faraway places but the boredom of the suburbs or their families anywhere else.

In a sense, the magazine's writers were the original "Me" that went on to become the "Me Decade." They were prodigious consumers of the urban experience, and they expected readers to live vicariously through their stories. They didn't hesitate to use the first person, to speak with authority, to get on the soapbox and pontificate. They were often, like Felker, outsize, ambitious characters, some civically involved, some hedonistic, mostly both, and divahood was an expected part of the job, for editors an occupational hazard. "Talent," Felker liked to say, "comes in inconvenient packages."

Some of the writers in the early days of *New York* were children of the old immigrants, writers like Jimmy Breslin and Pete Hamill, men who'd graduated from egg creams and spaldeens, who had a deep—sometimes too deep—understanding of what went on in the city's saloons, and who had an understanding of what was being lost as the new city was being born. Breslin came by his first-person voice not by his commitment to expanding journalistic horizons but because he is a master storyteller—he wrote like he talked, pulling no punches but managing to charm even when he was. In 1969, he ran for president of the city council. His article "I Run to Win," published in May 1969, manages to distill the state of the world, his mood, his friend and running mate Norman Mailer, the mayoral race, and his wife's thoughts about the same into an effortlessly offhand piece that encapsulated the fusion of the writer's life and the public life. Many of *New York*'s early writers were prominent cultural figures in their own right. (Some had distinctly odd roles at the magazine: Stephen Sondheim edited the crossword puzzle for a year.)

Change, then and always, was the magazine's central subject (which is true of all journalism, certainly, but always maniacally true at *New York*). Pete Hamill, in "The Revolt of the White Lower Middle Class," confronted head-on the tumult the city was experiencing and diagnosed with clear eyes and great sympathy the psychic conditions of his neighbors in the old neighborhood. And Gloria Steinem, not yet the activist that she would become, presaged the birth of feminism in a column titled simply "After

Black Power, Women's Liberation." Later, she would publish the first issue of *Ms.* as an insert in *New York's* pages.

IT WAS NO accident that the early feminist movement was covered with such passion in *New York*. Once, magazines tended to be segregated by gender. There were women's magazines and men's magazines. And then there was *New York*. Felker and his colleagues broke down the wall between male and female subject matter and opened the door to female voices of many different kinds. Beyond publishing an unusual number of women writers for the time, the magazine legitimized and even reveled in certain sorts of psychic and cultural exploration that had been stereotypically female. There was no set doctrine about women's subjects, or any other. Steinem wrote (powerfully) about national politics. Gail Sheehy, one of the magazine's early stars, is here represented by "The Secret of Grey Gardens," about Edie and Edith Beale. Long after Felker was gone, the editors of *New York* would take traditional women's-magazine material and proudly publish the work to its dual-gender audience. Joyce Wadler's "My Breast," a masterpiece of confessional journalism published in 1992, is a good example, yet this is also true of essays that dealt directly with the politics of women, such as Ariel Levy's "Female Chauvinist Pigs," written in 2001, after Levy noticed that women, increasingly, were cheerfully, bawdily participating in their own exploitation, and coined the term of its title to describe this complicated new consciousness.

And the stuff of the "women's" pages in newspapers was given an entirely different spin in *New York*. Food, especially, has always been an obsession of the magazine, an obsession that extends well beyond what is on the plate. Nora Ephron's prescient article about the food establishment, "Critics in the World of the Rising Soufflé," published in September 1968, saw the ingredients—ego, obsession, fierce competition—that would eventually be whipped up into the overheated confection that is the culinary world today. Where Ephron wrote as an observer, Gael Greene, the only writer to have been with the magazine from its founding to the present day, had no direct experience as a food critic. But she was a sensualist (famously, she'd slept with Elvis Presley) with enormous enthusiasm and a gift for getting past the velvet rope. As the magazine's first restaurant critic, she quickly developed wide connoisseurship, and so too did her audience. The magazine's idea about restaurants was that the food was often only the appetizer. Restaurants were a stage for the power and status dramas of the city—not to mention the romance. Greene's story in this volume, "How Not to Be Humiliated in Snob Restaurants," showed how regular people could take their place on the stage, providing extensive cues and directions and a script.

AT THE BEGINNING, *New York* magazine was the bomb-throwing upstart, eager to make a loud noise to get people's attention. At the *Herald Tribune*'s Sunday magazine, Felker and his marquee writer, Tom Wolfe, loved to push buttons, to assess the state of the emperor's wardrobe. "Tiny Mummies," a deliciously savage piece Wolfe wrote for the *Trib* about William Shawn and *The New Yorker*, began because Felker had the insight one afternoon that *The New Yorker* is "so . . . BORING!" *New York* has never fully evolved away from a sometimes frantic desire to get noticed, but its diffidence about conventions has resulted in some spectacular journalism. Perhaps the most famous story in the magazine's history is "Radical Chic," also written by Wolfe.

Felker and Wolfe were obsessed with the workings of class in the city. Wolfe's 1970 story, about a dinner party Leonard Bernstein and his wife threw for the Black Panthers, isn't simply an attack on limousine liberals, though it certainly functions as that. It goes past politics into a novelistic exploration of a specific kind of contradiction-laden Manhattan consciousness.

"Radical Chic" was a kind of obituary for the left coalition that had driven the sixties, for good and ill, the coalition that decisively collapsed with the defeat of George McGovern. After its publication, it was impossible to look at the political world in quite the same way.

Felker was a Democrat and was fascinated by politics at all levels. But he was never a wringer of hands about the fate of the world. And the magazine never had a strong superego. The kinds of stories that magazine editors sometimes call "worthy," with faint condescension, have never had much purchase.

Felker was an adherent of the Great Man theory of history. Personality was central to his understanding of the world—personality and conflict were, for him, the two essential ingredients of great journalism. He was captivated by the doings of powerful people, even when their doings were done to him. Years after Rupert Murdoch had bought the magazine out from under him, he was still awed by the mogul's hunger. "He's . . . insatiable!" he sometimes said, wide-eyed.

Personalities have been, for Felker and all his successors, an avenue into a domain. The pieces in this book profiling figures from Joe Namath in 1969 (by Breslin) to Augusten Burroughs in 2008 (by Sam Anderson) stand for a whole class of journalistic endeavor in *New York* magazine. Often satirical in spirit, they explore the idiosyncrasies of prominent figures, especially at moments when they are teetering between triumph and defeat. In many of these stories, such as an odd and interesting sketch of Bess Myerson by the late Susan Berman, writerly flourishes were secondary to the main event, which was to let the subject speak. In Nick Pileggi's 1986 portrait of Henry Hill, the mafioso and another wonderful New York character, Hill does the talking—and what a talker he is. Julie Baumgold's 1984 portrait of Truman Capote is a particularly artful example of a story the magazine came to specialize in—a literary obituary written soon after a subject's death that has all the qualities of a biography that might take a writer years to complete. Many of the magazine's profiles are vividly unconventional—in 1993, Nancy Jo Sales wrote an account of an epistolary relationship she'd had with Woody Allen when she was younger that offered an unusual lens on what was the big tabloid story of that moment—the relationship of Allen and his girlfriend Mia Farrow's adopted daughter, Soon-Yi Previn.

NEW YORK HAS long been a tabloid city; the tabloids are where emotions boil. It's the stories these papers specialize in that have occupied the city's popular imagination, and so, like it or not, the tabloids have long set much of the city's agenda, even that of the august *Times. New York* magazine has always seen itself as something of the tabloid-of-record, the publication where unfiltered emotions are transformed, often on short deadlines, into dramas with characters and motives.

By the early eighties, the city of the magazine's founding had given way to something else entirely. New York might have been, as the magazine once saw it, a promised land, at once magical and distant from the rest of the country, but in the eighties it inhabited Reagan's America. Suddenly, New York seemed to be Wall Street's city.

One of the magazine's obsessions (also an obsession of the tabloids, of course) became the psychopathologies and distortions of wealth, especially where the wealthy were exhibiting some really bad behavior. Anthony Haden-Guest's "The Headmistress and the Diet Doctor," about Jean Harris's murder of Herman Tarnower, is exemplary of the kind of story that came to be seen as particularly *New York*-ian.

But really, the rich didn't have to kill anybody to get noticed in *New York* at that time. It was hard to miss, a newly imposed class structure dominating headlines. The fascination with the wealthy was significantly amped up, and not just the wealthy but the superwealthy who lorded their money over them (and us). Business, scorned in the sixties, became a path to fulfilling one's dreams. New York was now a place where the unwashed wealthy—those who earned their fortune through enterprise, not bloodlines—drove the city's story. To those left behind, it seemed a fiction, and a source of resentment. But few could deny that the nouveau riche set the tone.

The new titans had broken from the Waspy social register and were engaged in their own breathtakingly public status pursuits. Like the barons of capitalism who first populated Fifth Avenue, when Central Park was mostly pastureland, the new wealthy took over the block, the zip code, and all the city's prestigious institutions. John Taylor's 1988 article on the extravagant self-inventions of John Gutfreund, then the head of Salomon Brothers, Wall Street's wealthiest investment house, and his up-from-very-little wife, Susan Gutfreund, is a nicely turned satiric morality tale on the perils of great wealth and typical of many of the stories *New York* published during that time.

BESIDES MONEY, the tabloids' other great subject is crime, and there was plenty of that over the magazine's four decades for *New York* to cover. As we looked over back issues of the magazine, we were struck by how crime—flashy criminals and street thugs, heroic and corrupt police—

dominated *New York*'s pages. Until Giuliani's ascent in 1993, the city seemed hopelessly mired in the late-night comic's view of New York: perils at every crosswalk and in every cab. Michael Daly's 1986 piece on the dirty 77th Precinct in Brooklyn is a kind of parable of the ungovernable city. Much of the panic about crime also came to infect the dialogue about race, as one racially charged crime after another hit the headlines. In his 1989 cover story "Race," Joe Klein's point of departure is the rape of a Central Park jogger, a white woman said to have been brutalized by a group of young black and Latino men (ultimately, the men were exonerated). We have included it here, but it is only one of many the magazine published that struggled to understand a city increasingly polarized by skin color.

The crime sweep in the nineties, for which Giuliani inevitably grabbed credit, eventually helped to change all that (even while it further inflamed racial tensions). The city was detoxified, and simultaneously suburbanized. No difference in the magazine's history is as conspicuous as its coverage of pre- and post-Giuliani New York. Even as New Yorkers seemed to welcome the quieter city, others seemed to mourn the one left in its wake. No doubt Felker, if he'd still been making his nightly rounds, would have heard nostalgic talk about the swaths of disappearing "authentic" New York, and sensed a longing for the offbeat energy that thrived before everyone at the café had their heads buried in a BlackBerry. (See Gary Indiana's hilarious "One Brief, Scuzzy Moment" for its knowing, nostalgic look at the disappeared East Village of the late seventies.) But the members of a new upper-middle class were ecstatic at the Giuliani version of the city even as they experienced a heightened feeling of class anxiety, one captured perfectly by Michael Wolff in his 2002 story "The Price of Perfection," about the lengths to which one would go to get one's child into the right preschool.

THE TWIN ENGINES of urban change, a decline in crime and a jump in tax brackets, cleared the way for rampant gentrification, perhaps the greatest social revolution in New York since the sixties. In the new century, the magazine ran (and is still running) story after story about the gentrifying of struggling neighborhoods and the broadening of the city's center of social gravity from Manhattan to the other boroughs. Adam

Sternbergh's 2006 "Up With Grups" introduced readers to a new kind of archetype that was a product of this change. And in that same year, Jay McInerney's "The Death of (the Idea of) the Upper East Side" documented a shift among the moneyed class from the 10021 zip code to the southern edge of the island that a '68 reader would have found unthinkable.

In some respects, New York is now a very different place than the city of the magazine's founding. Technology has had a good deal to do with that. In "Say Everything," Emily Nussbaum observes the widening of a new generation gap between Web-addicted young people and their elders; her article is not only an analysis but an argument, a defense of the new openness of the younger generation. And in "Everybody Sucks," Vanessa Grigoriadis explicates a new sensibility among a segment of young Manhattanites Grigoriadis calls the "creative underclass" within whom seems to flow a river of bile; Gawker, a website founded in 2002, became a highly public forum for their angry feelings.

But the single biggest event in New York in the twenty-first century wasn't a product of technology or money—or perhaps it was. That was the attacks of September 11, 2001. Just as the magazine had covered the fiscal collapse in the seventies, the city's racial strife and the AIDS epidemic in the eighties and nineties, the magazine turned its attention to the effects of this singular American tragedy on its home turf. In just one example, Steve Fishman reduced this cataclysmic event to an intimate drama. "The Dead Wives Club" explored the conflicts among a group of 9/11 widows who grew uncomfortable with their assigned station as national symbols of grief.

IN PART AS A consequence of being the epicenter of the nation's crisis, and in part because of other factors—a politics that became more purple than blue, a consumer culture that more closely mirrors everyone else's— New York is less an island off the coast of America and more the national capital it should have been in the first place. The magazine has always treated Washington as a kind of suburb—or as the home of a strange, sometimes hostile tribe. Kurt Andersen, a columnist who used to be editor of the magazine, writes about the distortions of life under George W.

Bush in a section devoted to the magazine's writings on national politics that, true to the rest of the magazine's method, is especially interested in the engine of personality. Andersen is in excellent company here. Gloria Steinem's story on Richard Nixon ("In Your Heart, You Know He's Nixon") leads off the chapter, and is joined by David Halberstam on Spiro Agnew, Richard Reeves on Gerald Ford, Garry Wills on George Wallace, and Joe Klein on Bill Clinton. This book is being published in the midst of a presidential race that is—almost—as momentous and dramatic as the one that was under way the year the magazine was founded. So because we are magazine editors and therefore especially caught up in the moment, we have included some writings from the 2008 campaign. John Heilemann is represented by stories about Hillary Clinton and John McCain. And in "Dreaming of Obama," Jennifer Senior captures the candidate just as he was turning from a fantasy into a flesh-and-blood contender.

We call that section "The National Interest," after a long-standing column in the magazine. We've organized the rest of the book in parts that correspond to some of the themes we've touched upon here (though which stories fit into which parts is in some cases fairly arbitrary). You'll notice that several stories in this anthology had other, later lives in the popular culture. "Night-Shifting for the Hip Fleet," written by Mark Jacobson (who has written memorable stories for the magazine in almost all of its decades), was purchased for television for what, in Hollywood terms, was a pittance, unfortunately for Jacobson, and made into the long-running television series *Taxi*. Henry Hill's saga became the movie *GoodFellas*. And, perhaps most famously, "Tribal Rites of the New Saturday Night," by Nik Cohn, became *Saturday Night Fever*, launched John Travolta as a megastar with his own private plane, and was a shining light of what could happen to a journalist if he kept his nose to the ground for new and interesting scenes. As it happened, some twenty years later, he revealed in the pages of *New York* that he'd made up most of it. (At all magazines, truth standards and rules involving composite characters and quotations were much less rigorous in the past, but Cohn shredded even these loose rules.)

This anthology is not meant to be a history of the city, or even of the magazine. Inevitably, certain kinds of pieces (essays, mostly) work better in a book context than others (mainly reporting of particularly topical stories). Many excellent writers who were crucial to the history of the magazine are not included, for which we feel considerable regret. Even more galling to us are the exclusions, partial or complete, of epochal news stories and figures of the period. September 11 itself is given short shrift. Giuliani is barely mentioned, nor are Ed Koch or John Lindsay or Michael Bloomberg. But this book was not edited with an eye toward completeness. Rather, we've looked for stories that had dimensions beyond just journalism or history. We've looked for stories that seemed like particularly good examples of *New York* magazine's contributions to the life of the city over its four decades. We've also tried to illustrate the continuities between the original magazine and the one you can pick up on the newsstand today. Aside from some judicious editing, mostly for length, we've left the articles much as we found them in the original magazine. This means that some of the names that were on everyone's lips decades ago and thus needed no explanation will now produce blank stares. In most places, a prudent use of Wikipedia will serve in place of the footnotes that we decided would be too cumbersome.

This anthology is, thus, not comprehensive and isn't intended to be. Rather, it celebrates what Tom Wolfe once called the billion-footed beast—life as it's lived, in all its complexities, in the city in which the magazine's writers have stalked it over the past four decades.

NEW YORK STORIES

PART ONE

. . . .

MATTERS
OF CLASS

★

RADICAL CHIC
That Party at Lenny's

TOM WOLFE

JUNE 8, 1970

In 1970, Leonard Bernstein, the composer and conductor, hosted a fund-raiser for the Black Panther Party at his Park Avenue duplex. Tom Wolfe's twenty-five-thousand-word piece on the party, which took up almost an entire issue of New York, *was set in motion by an invitation—though not to him. He spotted it on the desk of David Halberstam, then a writer at* Harper's *magazine, whose offices Wolfe was visiting. Wolfe called to say he'd be delighted to attend. Guests assumed anyone there shared their views. "I just thought it was a scream," said Wolfe. "To think that somebody living in an absolutely stunning duplex could be having in all these guys who were saying, 'We will take everything away from you if we get the chance,' which is what their program spelled out, was the funniest thing I had ever witnessed."*

A T 2 OR 3 OR 4 A.M., somewhere along in there, on August 25, 1966, his forty-eighth birthday, in fact, Leonard Bernstein woke up in the dark in a state of wild alarm. That had happened before. It was one of the forms his insomnia took. So he did the usual. He got up and walked around a bit. He felt groggy. Suddenly he had a vision, an inspiration. He could see himself, Leonard Bernstein, the *egregio maestro*, walking out on stage in white tie and tails in front of a full orchestra. On one side of the conductor's podium is a piano. On the other is a chair with a guitar leaning against it. He sits in the chair and picks up the guitar. A guitar! One of those half-witted instruments, like the accordion, that are made for the Learn-to-Play-in-Eight-Days E-Z-Diagram 110-IQ fourteen-year-olds of Levittown! But there's a reason. He has an anti-war message to deliver to this great starched white-throated audience in the symphony hall. He announces to them: "I love." Just that. The effect is mortifying. All at once a Negro rises up from out of the curve of the grand piano and starts saying things like, "The audience is curiously embarrassed." Lenny tries to start again, plays some quick numbers on the piano, says, "I love. *Amo, ergo sum.*" The Negro rises again and says, "The audience thinks he ought to get up and walk out. The audience thinks, 'I am ashamed even to nudge my neighbor.' " Finally, Lenny gets off a heartfelt anti-war speech and exits.

For a moment, sitting there alone in his home in the small hours of the morning, Lenny thought it might just work and he jotted the idea down. Think of the headlines: BERNSTEIN ELECTRIFIES CONCERT AUDIENCE WITH ANTI-WAR APPEAL. But then his enthusiasm collapsed. He lost heart. Who the hell was this Negro rising up from the piano and informing the world what an ass Leonard Bernstein was making of himself? It didn't make sense, this superego Negro by the concert grand.

MMMMMMMMMMMMMMMM. These are nice. Little Roquefort cheese morsels rolled in crushed nuts. Very tasty. Very subtle. It's the way the dry sackiness of the nuts tiptoes up against the dour savor of the cheese that is so nice, so subtle. Wonder what the Black Panthers eat here on the hors d'oeuvre trail? Do the Panthers like little Roquefort cheese morsels wrapped in crushed nuts this way, and asparagus tips in mayonnaise dabs, and *meatballs petites au Coq Hardi,* all of which are at this very moment being offered to them on gadrooned silver platters by maids in black uniforms with hand-ironed white aprons . . . The butler will bring them their drinks . . . Deny it if you wish to, but such are the *pensées métaphysiques* that rush through one's head on these Radical Chic evenings just now in New York. For example, does that huge Black Panther there in the hallway, the one shaking hands with Felicia Bernstein herself, the one with the black leather coat and the dark glasses and the absolutely unbelievable

Afro, Fuzzy Wuzzy–scale in fact—is he, a Black Panther, going on to pick up a Roquefort cheese morsel rolled in crushed nuts from off the tray, from a maid in uniform, and just pop it down the gullet without so much as missing a beat of Felicia's perfect Mary Astor voice . . .

Felicia is remarkable. She is beautiful, with that rare burnished beauty that lasts through the years. Her hair is pale blond and set just so. She has a voice that is "theatrical," to use a term from her youth. She greets the Black Panthers with the same bend of the wrist, the same tilt of the head, the same perfect Mary Astor voice with which she greets people like Jason, D. D., Adolph, Betty, Gian Carlo, Schuyler, and Goddard, during those *après*-concert suppers she and Lenny are so famous for. What evenings! She lights the candles over the dining room table, and in the Gotham gloaming the little tremulous tips of flame are reflected in the mirrored surface of the table, a bottomless blackness with a thousand stars, and it is that moment that Lenny loves. There seem to be a thousand stars above and a thousand stars below, a room full of stars, a penthouse duplex full of stars, a Manhattan tower full of stars, with marvelous people drifting through the heavens, Jason Robards, John and D. D. Ryan, Gian Carlo Menotti, Schuyler Chapin, Goddard Lieberson, Mike Nichols, Lillian Hellman, Larry Rivers, Aaron Copland, Richard Avedon, Milton and Amy Greene, Lukas Foss, Jennie Tourel, Samuel Barber, Jerome Robbins, Steve Sondheim, Adolph and Phyllis Green, Betty Comden, and the Patrick O'Neals . . .

. . . and now, in the season of Radical Chic, the Black Panthers. That huge Panther there, the one Felicia is smiling her tango smile at, is Robert Bay, who just forty-one hours ago was arrested in an altercation with the police, supposedly over a .38-caliber revolver that someone had, in a parked car in Queens at Northern Boulevard and 104th Street or some such unbelievable place, and taken to jail on a most unusual charge called "criminal facilitation." And now he is out on bail and walking into Leonard and Felicia Bernstein's thirteen-room penthouse duplex on Park Avenue. Harassment & Hassles, Guns & Pigs, Jail & Bail—they're *real*, these Black Panthers. The very idea of them, these real revolutionaries, who actually put their lives on the line, runs through Lenny's duplex like a rogue hormone. Everyone casts a glance, or stares, or tries a smile, and then sizes up the house for the somehow delicious counterpoint . . . Deny it if you want to! but one *does* end up making such sweet furtive comparisons in this season of Radical Chic . . . There's Otto Preminger in the library and Jean vanden Heuvel in the hall, and Peter and Cheray Duchin in the living room, and Frank and Domna Stanton, Gail Lumet, Sheldon Harnick, Cynthia Phipps, Burton Lane, Mrs. August Heckscher, Roger Wilkins, Barbara Walters, Bob Silvers, Mrs. Richard Avedon, Mrs. Arthur Penn, Julie Belafonte, Harold Taylor, and scores more, including Charlotte Curtis, women's news editor of *The New York Times,* America's foremost chronicler of Society, a lean woman in black, with her notebook out, standing near Felicia and big Robert Bay, and talking to Cheray Duchin.

Cheray tells her: "I've never met a Panther—this is a first for me!" . . . never dreaming that within forty-eight hours her words will be on the desk of the President of the United States . . .

THIS IS A FIRST FOR ME. But she is not alone in her thrill as the Black Panthers come trucking on in, into Lenny's house, Robert Bay, Don Cox the Panthers' Field Marshal from Oakland, Henry Miller the Harlem Panther defense captain, the Panther women—Christ, if the Panthers don't know how to get it all together, as they say, the tight pants, the tight black turtlenecks, the leather coats, Cuban shades, Afros. But real Afros, not the ones that have been shaped and trimmed like a topiary hedge and sprayed until they have a sheen like acrylic wall-to-wall—but like funky, natural, scraggly . . . wild . . .

These are no civil-rights Negroes *wearing gray suits three sizes too big—*

—no more interminable Urban League banquets in hotel ballrooms where they try to alternate the blacks and whites around the tables as if they were stringing Arapaho beads—

—*these are* real men!

Shootouts, revolutions, pictures in *Life* magazine of policemen grabbing Black Panthers like they were Viet Cong—somehow it all runs together in the head with the whole thing of how *beautiful* they are. *Sharp as a blade.* The Panther women—there are three or four of them on hand, wives of the Panther 21 defendants, and they are so lean, so *lithe,* as they say, with tight pants and Yoruba-style headdresses, almost like turbans, as if they'd stepped out of the pages of *Vogue*, although no doubt *Vogue* got it from them. All at once every woman in the room knows exactly what Amanda Burden meant when she said she was now anti-fashion because "the sophistication of the baby blacks made me rethink my attitudes." God knows the Panther women don't spend thirty minutes in front of the mirror in the morning shoring up their eye holes with contact lenses, eyeliner, eye shadow, eyebrow pencil, occipital rim brush, false eyelashes, mascara, Shadow-Ban for undereye and Eterna Creme for the corners . . . And here they are, right in front of you, trucking on into the Bernsteins' Chinese yellow duplex, amid the sconces, silver bowls full of white and lavender anemones, and uniformed servants serving drinks and Roquefort cheese morsels rolled in crushed nuts—

But it's all right. They're *white* servants, not Claude and Maude, but white South Americans. Lenny and Felicia are geniuses. After a while, it all comes down to servants. They are the cutting edge in Radical Chic. Obviously, if you are giving a party for the Black Panthers, as Lenny and Felicia are this evening, or as Sidney and Gail Lumet did last week, or as John Simon of Random House and Richard Baron, the publisher, did before that; or for the Chicago Eight, such as the party Jean vanden Heuvel gave; or for the grape workers or Bernadette Devlin, such as the parties Andrew Stein gave; or for the Young Lords, such as the party Ellie Guggenheimer is giving next week in her Park Avenue duplex; or for the Indians or the SDS or the G.I. Coffee Shops or even for the Friends of the Earth—well, then, obviously you can't have a Negro butler and maid, Claude and Maude, in uniform, circulating through the living room, the library and the main hall serving drinks and canapés. Plenty of people have tried to think it out. They try to picture the Panthers or whoever walking in bristling with electric hair and Cuban shades and leather pieces and the rest of it, and they try to picture Claude and Maude with the black uniforms coming up and saying, "Would you care for a drink, sir?" They close their eyes and try to picture it *some way*, but there *is* no way. One simply cannot see that moment. So the current wave of Radical Chic has touched off the most desperate search for white servants.

Just at this point some well-meaning soul is going to say, Why not do without servants altogether if the matter creates such unbearable tension and one truly believes in equality? Well, even to raise the question is to reveal the most fundamental ignorance of life in the great co-ops and townhouses of the East Side in the age of Radical Chic. Why, my God! servants are not a mere convenience, they're an absolute psychological necessity. Once one is into that life, truly into it, with the morning workout on the velvet swings at Kounovsky's and the late mornings on the telephone, and lunch at the Running Footman, which is now regarded as really better than La Grenouille, Lutèce, Lafayette, La Caravelle and the rest of the general Frog Pond, less ostentatious, more of the David Hicks feeling, less of the Parish-Hadley look, and then—well, then, the idea of not having servants is unthinkable. But even that does not say it all. It makes it sound like a matter of convenience, when actually it is a sheer and fundamental matter of—having *servants*. Does one comprehend?

God, what a flood of taboo thoughts runs through one's head at these Radical Chic events . . . But it's delicious. It is as if one's nerve-endings were on red alert to the most intimate nuances of status. Deny it if you want to! Nevertheless, it runs through every soul here. It is the matter of the marvelous contradictions on all sides. It is like the delicious shudder you get when you try to force the prongs of two horseshoe magnets together . . . them and *us* . . .

Or—what does one wear to these parties for the Panthers or the Young Lords or the grape workers? What does a woman wear? Obviously one does not want to wear something frivolously and pompously expensive, such as a Gerard Pipart party dress. On the other hand one does not want to arrive "poor-mouthing it" in some outrageous turtleneck and West Eighth Street bell-jean combination, as if one is "funky" and of "the people." Frankly, Jean vanden Heuvel—that's Jean there in the hallway giving everyone her famous smile, in which her eyes narrow down to f/16— frankly, Jean tends too much toward the funky fallacy. Felicia Bernstein seems to understand the whole thing better. Look at Felicia. She is wearing the simplest little black frock imaginable, with absolutely no ornamentation save for a plain gold necklace. It is perfect. It has dignity without any overt class symbolism.

Lenny? Lenny himself has been in the living room all this time, talking to old friends like the Duchins and the Stantons and the Lanes. Lenny is wearing a black turtleneck, navy blazer, Black Watch plaid trousers and a necklace with a pendant hanging down to his sternum. His tailor comes here to the apartment to take the measurements and do the fittings. Lenny is a short, trim man, and yet he always seems tall. It is his head. He has a noble head, with a face that is at once sensitive and rugged, and a full stand of iron-gray hair, with sideburns, all set off nicely by the Chinese yellow of the room. His success radiates from his eyes and his smile with a charm that illustrates Lord Jersey's adage that "contrary to what the Methodists tell us, money and success are good for the soul." Lenny may be fifty-one, but he is still the *Wunderkind* of American music. Everyone says so. He is not only one of the world's outstanding conductors, but a more than competent composer and pianist as well. He is the man who more than any other has broken down the wall between elite music and popular tastes, with *West Side Story* and his children's concerts on television. How natural that he should stand here in his own home radiating the charm and grace that make him an easy host for leaders of the oppressed. How ironic that the next hour should prove so shattering for this *egregio maestro*! How curious that the Negro by the piano should emerge tonight!

A bell rang, a dinner table bell, by the sound of it, the sort one summons the maid out of the kitchen with, and the party shifted from out of the hall and into the living room. Felicia led the way, Felicia and a small gray man, with gray hair, a gray face, a gray suit, and a pair of Groovy but gray sideburns. A little gray man, in short, who would be popping up at key moments . . . to keep the freight train of history on the track, as it were . . .

Felicia was down at the far end of the living room trying to coax everybody in.

"Lenny!" she said. "Tell the fringes to come on in!" Lenny was still in the back of the living room, near the hall. "Fringes!" said Lenny. "Come on in!"

Once Lenny got "the fringes" moving in, the room filled up rapidly. It was jammed, in fact. People were sitting on sofas and easy chairs along the sides, as well as on the folding chairs, and were standing in the back, where Lenny was. Otto Preminger was sitting on a sofa down by the pianos, where the speakers were going to stand. The Panther wives were sitting in the first two rows with their Yoruba headdresses on, along with Henry Mitchell and Julie Belafonte, Harry Belafonte's wife. Julie is white, but they all greeted her warmly as "Sister." Behind her was sitting Barbara Walters, hostess of the *Today* show on television, wearing a checked pants suit with a great fluffy fur collar on the coat. Harold Taylor, the former "Boy President" of Sarah Lawrence, now fifty-five and silver-haired, but still youthful looking, came walking down toward the front and gave a hug and a big social kiss to Gail Lumet. Robert Bay settled down in the middle of the folding chairs. Jean vanden Heuvel stood in the back and sought to focus . . . f/16 . . . on the pianos . . . Charlotte Curtis stood beside the door, taking notes. And then Felicia stood up beside the pianos and said:

"I want to thank you all very, very much for coming. I'm very, very glad to see so many of you here." Everything was fine. Her voice was rich as a woodwind. She introduced a man named Leon Quat, one of the lawyers for the "Panther 21," twenty-one Black Panthers who had been arrested on a charge of conspiring to blow up five New York department stores, New Haven Railroad facilities, a police station and the Bronx Botanical Gardens.

Leon Quat, oddly enough, had the general look of those fifty-two-year-old men who run a combination law office, real estate and insurance operation on the second floor of a two-story taxpayer out on Queens Boulevard. And yet that wasn't the kind of man Leon Quat really was. He had the sideburns. Quite a pair. They didn't come down just to the incisura intertragica, which is that little notch in the lower rim of the ear, and which so many tentative Swingers aim their sideburns toward. No, on top of this complete Queens Boulevard insurance agent look, he had real sideburns, to the bottom of the lobe, virtual muttonchops, which somehow have become the mark of the Movement. Leon Quat rose up smiling:

"We are very grateful to Mrs. Bernstein"—only he pronounced it "steen."

"STEIN!"—a great smoke-cured voice booming out from the rear of the room! It's Lenny! Leon Quat and the Black Panthers will have a chance to hear from Lenny. That much is sure. He is on the case. Leon

Quat must be the only man in the room who does not know about Lenny and the Mental Jotto at 3 A.M. . . . For years, twenty at the least, Lenny has insisted on *-stein* not *-steen,* as if to say, I am not one of those 1921 Jews who try to tone down their Jewishness by watering their names down with a bad soft English pronunciation. Lenny has made such a point of *-stein* not *-steen,* in fact, that some people in this room think at once of the story of how someone approached Larry Rivers, the artist, and said, "What's this I hear about you and Leonard Bernstein"—*steen,* he pronounced it— "not speaking to each other anymore?"—to which Rivers said, "*STEIN!*"

"We are very grateful . . . for her marvelous hospitality," says Quat, apparently not wanting to try the name again right away. Then he beams toward the crowd:

"I assume we are all just an effete clique of snobs and intellectuals in this room . . . I am referring to the words of Vice-President Agnew, of course, who can't be with us today because he is in the South Pacific explaining the Nixon doctrine to the Australians. All vice-presidents suffer from the Avis complex—they're second best, so they try harder, like General Ky or Hubert Humphrey . . ." He keeps waiting for the grins and chuckles after each of these mots, but all the celebrities and culturati are nonplussed. They give him a kind of dumb attention. They came here for the Panthers and Radical Chic, and here is Old Queens Boulevard Real Estate Man with sideburns on telling them Agnew jokes. But Quat is too deep into his weird hole to get out. "Whatever respect I have had for Lester Maddox, I lost it when I saw Humphrey put his arm around his shoulder . . ." and somehow Quat begins disappearing down a hole bunging Hubert Humphrey with lumps of old Shelley Berman material. Slowly he climbs back out. He starts telling about the oppression of the Panther 21. They have been in jail since February 2, 1969, awaiting trial on ludicrous charges such as conspiring to blow up the Bronx Botanical Gardens. Their bail has been a preposterous $100,000 per person, which has in effect denied them the right to bail. They have been kept split up and moved from jail to jail. For all intents and purposes they have been denied the right to confer with their lawyers to prepare a defense. They have been subjected to inhuman treatment in jail—such as the case of Lee Berry, an epileptic, who was snatched out of a hospital bed and thrown in jail and kept in solitary confinement with a light bulb burning over his head night and day. The Panthers who have not been thrown in jail or killed, like Fred Hampton, are being stalked and harassed everywhere they go. "One of the few higher officials who is still . . . in the clear"—Quat smiles—"is here today. Don Cox, Field Marshal of the Black Panther Party."

"Right on," a voice says to Leon Quat, rather softly. And a tall black man rises from behind one of Lenny's grand pianos . . . The Negro by the piano . . .

The Field Marshal of the Black Panther Party has been sitting in a chair between the piano and the wall. He rises up; he has the hardrock look, all right; he is a big tall man with brown skin and an Afro and a goatee and a black turtleneck much like Lenny's, and he stands up beside the piano, next to Lenny's million-dollar *chatchka* flotilla of family photographs. In fact, there is a certain perfection as the first Black Panther rises within a Park Avenue living room to lay the Panthers' ten-point program on New York Society in the age of Radical Chic. Cox is silhouetted—well, about nineteen feet behind him is a white silk shade with an Empire scallop over one of the windows overlooking Park Avenue. Or maybe it isn't silk, but a Jack Lenor Larsen mercerized cotton, something like that, lustrous but more subtle than silk. The whole image, the white shade and the Negro by the piano silhouetted against it, is framed by a pair of bottle-green velvet curtains, pulled back.

And does it begin now?—but this Cox is a cool number. He doesn't come on with the street epithets and interjections and the rest of the rhetoric and red eyes used for mau-mauing the white liberals, as it is called.

"The Black Panther Party," he starts off, "stands for a ten-point program that was handed down in October, 1966, by our Minister of Defense, Huey P. Newton . . ." and he starts going through the ten points . . . "We want an educational system that expresses the true nature of this decadent society" . . . "We want all black men exempt from military service" . . . "We want all black men who are in jail to be set free. We want them to be set free because they have not had fair trials. We've been tried by predominantly middle-class, all-white juries" . . . "And most important of all, we want peace . . . see . . . We want peace, but there can be no peace as long as a society is racist and one part of society engages in systematic oppression of another" . . . "We want a plebiscite by the United Nations to be held in black communities, so that we can control our own destiny" . . .

Everyone in the room, of course, is drinking in his performance like tiger's milk, for the . . . Soul, as it were. All love the tone of his voice, which is Confidential Hip. And yet his delivery falls into strangely formal patterns. What are these block phrases, such as "our Minister of Defense, Huey P. Newton"—

"Some people think that we are racist, because the news media find it useful to create that impression in order to support the power structure, which we have nothing to do with . . . see . . . They like for the Black Panther Party to be made to look like a racist organization, because that camouflages the true class nature of the struggle. But they find it harder and harder to keep up that camouflage and are driven to campaigns of harassment and violence to try to eliminate the Black Panther Party. Here in New York twenty-one members of the Black Panther Party were indicted last April on ridiculous charges of conspiring to blow up department stores and flower gardens. They've had twenty-seven bail hearings since last April . . . see . . ."

—But everyone in here loves the *sees* and the *you knows*. They are so, somehow . . . *black* . . . so *funky* . . . so metrical . . . Without ever bringing it fully into consciousness everyone responds—communes over—the fact that he uses them not for emphasis, but for punctuation, metrically, much like the *uhs* favored by High Church Episcopal ministers, as in, "And bless, uh, these gifts, uh, to Thy use and us to, uh, Thy service"—

"The situation here in New York is very explosive, as you can see, with people stacked up on top of each other. They can hardly deal with them when they're *un*organized, so that when a group comes along like the Black Panthers, they want to eliminate that group by any means . . . see . . . and so that stand has been embraced by J. Edgar Hoover, who feels that we are the greatest threat to the power structure. They try to create the impression that we are engaged in criminal activities. What are these 'criminal activities'? We have instituted a breakfast program, to address ourselves to the needs of the community. We feed hungry children every morning before they go to school. So far this program is on a small scale. We're only feeding fifty thousand children nationwide, but the only money we have for this program is donations from the merchants in the neighborhoods. We have a program to establish clinics in the black communities and in other ways also we are addressing ourselves to the needs of the community . . . see . . . So the people know the power structure is lying when they say we are engaged in criminal activities. So the pigs are driven to desperate acts, like the murder of our deputy chairman, Fred Hampton, in his bed . . . see . . . in his sleep . . . But when they got desperate and took off their camouflage and murdered Fred Hampton, in his bed, in his sleep, see, that kind of shook people up, because they saw the tactics of the power structure for what they were . . .

"We relate to a phrase coined by Malcolm X: 'By any means necessary' . . . you see . . . 'By any means necessary' . . . and by that we mean that we recognize that if you're attacked, you have the right to defend yourself. The pigs, they say the Black Panthers are armed, the Black Panthers have weapons . . . see . . . and therefore they have the right to break in and murder us in our beds. I don't think there's anybody in here who wouldn't defend themselves if somebody came in and attacked them or their families . . . see . . . I don't think there's anybody in here who wouldn't defend themselves . . ."

—and every woman in the room thinks of her husband . . . with his cocoa-butter jowls and Dior Men's Boutique pajamas . . . ducking into the bathroom and locking the door and turning the shower on, so he can say later that he didn't hear a thing—

"We call them pigs, and rightly so," says Don Cox, "because they have the way of making the victim look like the criminal, and the criminal look like the victim. So every Panther must be ready to defend himself. That was handed down by our Minister of Defense, Huey P. Newton: Everybody who does not have the means to defend himself in his home, or if he does have the means and he does not defend himself—we expel *that man* . . . see . . . As our Minister of Defense, Huey P. Newton, says, 'Any unarmed people are slaves, or are slaves in the real meaning of the word' . . . We recognize that this country is the most oppressive country in the world, maybe in the history of the world. The pigs have the weapons and they are ready to use them on the people, and we recognize this as being very bad. They are ready to commit genocide against those who stand up against them, and we recognize this as being very bad.

"All we want is the good life, the same as you. To live in peace and lead the good life, that's all we want . . . see . . . But right now there's no way we can do that. I want to read something to you:

" 'When in the course of human events, it becomes necessary for one people to dissolve the political bands which have connected them with another, and . . .' " He reads straight through it, every word. " '. . . And, accordingly, all experience hath shown, that mankind are more disposed to suffer, while evils are sufferable, than to right themselves by abolishing the forms to which they are accustomed. But when a long train of abuses and usurpations, pursuing invariably the same object, evinces a design to reduce them under absolute despotism, it is their right, it is their duty, to throw off such government, and to provide new guards for their future security.'

"You know what that's from?"—and he looks out at everyone and hesitates before laying this gasper on them—"That's from the Declaration of Independence, the American Declaration of Independence. And we will defend ourselves and do like it says . . . you know . . . and that's about it."

The "that's about it" part seems so casual, so funky, so right, after the rhetoric of what he has been saying. And then he sits down and sinks out of sight behind one of the grand pianos.

The thing is beginning to move. And—hell, yes, the *Reichstag fire*! Another man gets up, a white named Gerald Lefcourt, who is chief counsel for the Panther 21, a young man with thick black hair and the muttonchops of the Movement and that great motor inside of him that young courtroom lawyers ought to have. He lays the Reichstag fire on them. He reviews the Panther case and then he says:

"I believe that this odious situation could be compared to the Reichstag fire attempt"—he's talking about the way the Nazis used the burning of the Reichstag as the pretext for first turning loose the Gestapo and exterminating all political opposition in Germany—"and I believe that this trial could also be compared to the Reichstag trial . . . in many ways . . . and that opened an era that this country could be heading for.

That could be the outcome of this case, an era of the Right, and the only thing that can stop it is for people like ourselves to make a noise and make a noise now."

Leon Quat says: "Fascism always begins by persecuting the least powerful and least popular movement. It will be the Panthers today, the students tomorrow—and then . . . the Jews and other troublesome minorities! . . . What price civil liberties! . . . Now let's start this off with the gifts in four figures. Who is ready to make a contribution of a thousand dollars or more?"

All at once—nothing. But the little gray man sitting next to Felicia, the gray man with the sideburns, pops up and hands a piece of paper to Quat and says: "Mr. Clarence Jones asked me to say—he couldn't be here, but he's contributing $7,500 to the defense fund!"

"Oh! That's marvelous!" says Felicia.

Then the voice of Lenny from the back of the room: "As a guest of my wife"—he smiles—"I'll give my fee for the next performance of *Cavalleria Rusticana*." Comradely laughter. Applause. "I *hope* that will be four figures!"

Things are moving again. Otto Preminger speaks up from the sofa down front:

"I geeve a t'ousand dollars!"

Right on. Quat says: "I can't assure you that it's tax deductible." He smiles. "I wish I could, but I can't." Well, the man looks brighter and brighter every minute. He knows a Radical Chic audience when he sees one. Those words are magic in the age of Radical Chic: it's *not* tax deductible.

The contributions start coming faster, only $250 or $300 at a clip, but faster . . . Sheldon Harnick . . . Bernie and Hilda Fishman . . . Judith Bernstein . . . Mr. and Mrs. Burton Lane . . .

"We'll take *any*thing!" says Quat. "We'll take it all!" . . . he's high on the momentum of his fund-raiser voice . . . "You'll leave here with nothing!"

But finally he wraps it up. Suddenly there is a much more urgent question from the rear:

"Who do you call to give a party? Who do you call to give a party?"

Every head spins around . . . Quite a sight . . . It's a slender blond man who has pushed his way up to the front ranks of the standees. He's wearing a tuxedo. He's wearing black-frame glasses and his blond hair is combed back straight in the Eaton Square manner. He looks like the intense Yale man from out of one of those 1927 Frigidaire ads in *The Saturday Evening Post,* when the way to sell anything was to show Harry Yale in the background, in a tuxedo, with his pageboy-bobbed young lovely, heading off to dinner at the New Haven Lawn Club. The man still has his hand up in the air like the star student of the junior class.

"I won't be able to stay for everything you have to say," he says, "but who do you call to give a party?"

In fact, it is Richard Feigen, owner of the Feigen Gallery, 79th and Madison. He arrived on the art scene and the social scene from Chicago three years ago . . . He's been moving up hand over hand ever since . . . like a champion . . . Tonight—the tuxedo—tonight there is a reception at the Museum of Modern Art . . . right on . . . a "contributing members' " reception, a private viewing not open to mere "members" . . . But before the museum reception itself, which is at 8:30, there are private dinners . . . right? . . . which are the *real* openings . . . in the homes of great collectors or great climbers or the old Protestant elite, marvelous dinner parties, the real thing, black tie, and these dinners are the only true certification of where one stands in this whole realm of Art & Society . . . The whole game depends on whose home one is invited to before the opening . . . And the game ends as the host gathers everyone up about 8:45 for the trek to the museum itself, and the guests say, almost ritually, "God! I wish we could see the show from here! It's too delightful! I simply don't want to *move*!!' . . . And, of course, they mean it! Absolutely! For them, the opening is already over, the hand is played . . . And Richard Feigen, man of the hour, replica 1927 Yale man, black tie and Eaton Square hair, has dropped in, on the way, *en passant,* to the Bernsteins', to take in the other end of the Culture tandem, Radical Chic . . . and the rightness of it, the exhilaration, seems to sweep through him, and he thrusts his hand into the air, and somehow Radical Chic reaches its highest, purest state in that moment . . . as Richard Feigen, in his tuxedo, breaks in to ask, from the bottom of his heart, "Who do you call to give a party?" There you had a trend, a fashion, in its moment of naked triumph. How extraordinary that just thirty minutes later Radical Chic would be—

BUT AT THAT MOMENT Radical Chic was the new wave supreme in New York Society. It had been building for more than six months. It had already reached the fashion pages of *Vogue* and was moving into the food column. *Vogue* was already preparing a column entitled "Soul Food."

"The cult of Soul Food," it began, "is a form of Black self-awareness and, to a lesser degree, of white sympathy for the Black drive to self-reliance. It is as if those who ate the beans and greens of necessity in the cabin doorways were brought into communion with those who, not having to, eat those foods voluntarily as a sacrament."

Very nice! In fact, this sort of *nostalgie de la boue*, or romanticizing of primitive souls, was one of the things that brought Radical Chic to the fore in New York Society. *Nostalgie de la boue* is a nineteenth-century French term that means, literally, "nostalgia for the mud." Within New York Society *nostalgie de la boue* was a great motif throughout the 1960s, from the moment two socialites, Susan Stein and Christina Paolozzi, discovered the Peppermint Lounge and the twist and two of the era's first pet primitives, Joey Dee and Killer Joe Piro. *Nostalgie de la boue* tends to be a favorite motif whenever a great many new faces and a lot of new money enter Society. New arrivals have always had two ways of certifying their superiority over the hated "middle class." They can take on the trappings of aristocracy, such as grand architecture, servants, parterre boxes and high protocol; and they can indulge in the gauche thrill of taking on certain styles of the lower orders. The two are by no means mutually exclusive; in fact, they are always used in combination.

By the 1960s yet another new industry had begun to dominate New York life, namely, communications—the media. At the same time the erstwhile "minorities" of the first quarter of the century had begun to come into their own. Jews, especially, but also many Catholics, were eminent in the media and in Culture. So, by 1965—as in 1935, as in 1926, as in 1883, as in 1866, as in 1820—New York had two Societies, "Old New York" and "New Society." In every era, "Old New York" has taken a horrified look at

"New Society" and expressed the devout conviction that a genuine aristoc-racy, good blood, good bone—themselves—was being defiled by a horde of rank climbers. This has been an all-time favorite number. In the 1960s this quaint belief was magnified by the fact that many members of "New Society," for the first time, were not Protestant. The names and addresses of "Old New York" were to be found in the Social Register, which even ten years ago was still confidently spoken of as the Stud Book and the Good Book. It was, and still is, almost exclusively a roster of Protestant families. Today, however, the Social Register's annual shuffle, in which errant so-cialites, e.g., John Jacob Astor, are dropped from the Good Book, hardly even rates a yawn. The fact is that "Old New York"—except for those mem-bers who also figure in "New Society," e.g., Nelson Rockefeller, John Hay Whitney, Mrs. Wyatt Cooper—is no longer good copy, and without public-ity it has *never* been easy to rank as a fashionable person in New York City.

Among the new socialites of the 1960s, especially those from the one-time "minorities," this old social urge to do well by doing good, as it says in the song, has taken a more specific political direction. This has often been true of Jewish socialites and culturati, although it has by no means been confined to them. Politically, Jews have been unique among the groups that came to New York in the great migrations of the late nineteenth and early twentieth centuries. Many such groups, of course, were Left or lib-eral during the first generation, but as families began to achieve wealth, success, or, simply, security, they tended to grow more and more conserva-tive in philosophy. The Irish are a case in point. But forced by twentieth as well as nineteenth century history to remain on guard against right-wing movements, even wealthy and successful Jewish families have tended to remain faithful to their original liberal-left worldview. In fact, according to Seymour Martin Lipset, Nathan Glazer, and Kenneth Keniston, an un-usually high proportion of campus militants come from well-to-do Jewish families. They have developed the so-called "red diaper baby" theory to ex-plain it. According to Lipset, many Jewish children have grown up in fam-ilies which "around the breakfast table, day after day, in Scarsdale, Newton, Great Neck and Beverly Hills," have discussed racist and reac-tionary tendencies in American society. Lipset speaks of the wealthy Jew-ish family with the "right-wing life style" (e.g. a majority of Americans outside of the South who have full-time servants are Jewish, according to a study by Lipset, Glazer and Herbert Hyman) and the "left-wing outlook."

For years many Jewish members of New Society have supported black organizations such as the NAACP, the Urban League and CORE. And no doubt they have been sincere about it, because these organizations have never had much social cachet, i.e., they have had "middle class" written all over them. All one had to do was look at the "Negro leaders" involved. There they were, up on the dais at the big hotel banquet, wearing their white shirts, their Hart Schaffner & Marx suits three sizes too big, and their academic solemnity. By last year, however, the picture had changed. In 1965 two new political movements, the anti-war movement and black power, began to gain great backing among culturati in New York.

The black movement itself, of course, had taken on a much more electric and romantic cast. What a relief it was—socially—in New York—when the leadership seemed to shift from middle class to . . . *funky*! From A. Philip Randolph, Dr. Martin Luther King and James Farmer . . . to Stokely, Rap, LeRoi and Eldridge! This meant that the tricky business of the fashionable new politics could now be integrated with a tried and true social motif: *Nostalgie de la boue*. The upshot was Radical Chic.

From the beginning it was pointless to argue about the sincerity of Radical Chic. Unquestionably the basic impulse, "red diaper" or otherwise, was sincere. But, as in most human endeavors focused upon an ideal, there seemed to be some double-track thinking going on. On the first track—well, one *does* have a sincere concern for the poor and the underprivileged and an honest outrage against discrimination. One's heart does cry out—quite spontaneously!—upon hearing how the police have dealt with the Panthers, dragging an epileptic like Lee Berry out of his hospital bed and throwing him into the Tombs. When one thinks of Mitchell and Agnew and Nixon and all of their Captain Beefheart Maggie & Jiggs New York Athletic Club troglodyte crypto-Horst Wessel Irish Oyster Bar Construction Worker followers, then one understands why poor blacks like the Panthers might feel driven to drastic solutions, and—well, anyway, one truly feels for them. One really does. On the other hand—on the second track in one's mind, that is—one also has a sincere concern for maintaining a proper East Side lifestyle in New York Society. And this concern is just as sincere as the first, and just as deep. It really is. It really *does* become part of one's psyche. For example, one must have a weekend place, in the country or by the shore, all year round preferably, but certainly from the middle of May to the middle of September. It is hard to get across to outsiders an understanding of how *absolute* such apparently trivial needs are. One *feels* them in his solar plexus. When one thinks of being trapped in New York Saturday after Saturday in July or August, doomed to be a part of those fantastically dowdy herds roaming past Bonwit's and Tiffany's at dead noon in the sandstone sun-broil, 92 degrees, daddies from Long Island in balloon-seat Bermuda shorts bought at the Times Square Store in Oceanside and fat mommies with white belled pants stretching over their lower bellies and crinkling up in the crotch like some kind of Dacron polyester labia—well, anyway, then one truly *feels* the need to obey at least the minimal rules of New York Society. One really does.

One rule is that *nostalgie de la boue*—i.e., the styles of romantic, raw-vital, Low Rent primitives—are good; and *middle class*, whether black or white, is bad. Therefore, Radical Chic invariably favors radicals who seem primitive, exotic and romantic, such as the grape workers, who are not merely radical and "of the soil," but also Latin; the Panthers, with their leather pieces, Afros, shades, and shoot-outs; and the Red Indians, who, of course, had always seemed primitive, exotic, and romantic. At the outset, at least, all three groups had something else to recommend them, as well: they were headquartered three thousand miles away from the East Side of Manhattan, in places like Delano (the grape workers), Oakland (the Panthers) and Arizona and New Mexico (the Indians). They weren't likely to become too much . . . *underfoot,* as it were. Exotic, Romantic, Far Off . . . as we shall soon see, other favorite creatures of Radical Chic had the same attractive qualities; namely, the ocelots, jaguars, cheetahs and Somali leopards.

Rule No. 2 was that no matter what, one should always maintain a proper address, a proper scale of interior decoration, and servants. Servants, especially, were one of the last absolute dividing lines between those truly "in Society," New or Old, and the great scuffling mass of middle-class strivers paying up to $1,250-a-month rent or buying expensive co-ops all over the East Side. There are no two ways about it. One *must* have servants. Having servants becomes such a psychological necessity that there are many women in Society today who may be heard to complain in all honesty about how hard it is to find a nurse for the children to fill in on the regular nurse's day off. There is the famous Mrs. C——, one of New York's richest widows, who has a ten-room duplex on Sutton Place, the good part of Sutton Place as opposed to the Miami Beach–looking part, one understands, but who is somehow absolute poison with servants and can't keep anything but day help and is constantly heard to lament: "What good is all the money in the world if you can't come home at night and know there will be someone there to take your coat and fix you a drink?" There is true anguish behind that remark!

In the era of Radical Chic, then, what a collision course was set between the absolute need for servants—and the fact that the servant was the absolute symbol of what the new movements, black or brown, were struggling against! How absolutely urgent, then, became the search for the only way out: white servants!

The first big Radical Chic party, the epochal event, so to speak, was the party that Assemblyman Andrew Stein gave for the grape workers on his father's estate in Southampton on June 29, 1969. The grape workers had already been brought into New York social life. Carter and Amanda Burden, the "Moonflower Couple" of the 1960s, had given a party for them in their duplex in River House, on East 52nd Street overlooking the East River. Some of New York's best graphic artists, such as Paul Davis, had done exquisite posters for "La Causa" and "La Huelga."

The grape workers had begun a national campaign urging consumers to boycott California table grapes, and nowhere was the ban more strictly observed than in Radically Chic circles. Chavez became one of the few union leaders with a romantic image.

Andrew Stein's party, then, was the epochal event, not so much because he was fashionable as because the grape workers were. Stein himself was the twenty-four-year-old son of Jerry Finkelstein, who had made a small fortune in public relations and built it up into a firm called Struthers Wells. Finkelstein was also a power in the New York State Democratic party and, in fact, recently became the party's New York City chairman. His son Andrew had shortened his name from Finkelstein to Stein and was noted not only for the impressive parties he gave but for his election to the State Assembly from Manhattan's Upper West Side. The rumor was that his father had spent $500,000 on his campaign. No one who knew state politics believed that, however, since for half that sum he could have bought enough of Albany to have the boy declared king.

The party was held on the lawn outside Finkelstein's huge *cottage orné* by the sea in Southampton. There were two signs by the main entrance to the estate. One said Finkelstein and the other said Stein. The guests came in saying the usual, which was, "You can't take the Fink out of Finkelstein." No one turned back, however. From the beginning the afternoon was full of the delicious status contradictions and incongruities that provide much of the electricity for Radical Chic. Chavez himself was not there, but a contingent of grape workers was on hand, including Chavez's first lieutenant, Andrew Imutan, and Imutan's wife and three sons. The grape workers were all in work clothes, Levis, chinos, Sears balloon-seat twills, K-Mart sports shirts, and so forth. The socialites, meanwhile, arrived at the height of the 1969 summer season of bell-bottom silk pants suits, Pucci clings, Dunhill blazers, and Turnbull & Asser neckerchiefs. A mariachi band played for the guests as they arrived. Marvelous! Everyone's status radar was now so sensitive that the mariachi band seemed like a *faux pas*.

When the fund-raising began, Andrew Imutan took a microphone up on the terrace above the lawn and asked everybody to shut their eyes and pretend they were a farm worker's wife in the dusty plains of Delano, California, eating baloney sandwiches for breakfast at 3 A.M. before heading out into the fields . . . So they all stood there in their Pucci dresses, Gucci shoes, Capucci scarves, either imagining they were grape workers' wives or wondering if the goddamned wind would ever stop. The wind had come up off the ocean and it was wrecking everybody's hair. People were standing there with their hands pressed against their heads as if the place had been struck by a brain-piercing ray from the Purple Dimension. Andrew Stein's hair was long, full, and at the outset had been especially well coifed in the Roger's 58th Street French manner, and now it was . . . a wreck. . . .

Then Frank Mankiewicz, who had been Robert Kennedy's press secretary, got up and said, "Well, all I know, if we can only raise 20 percent of the money that has gone into all the Puccis I see here today, we'll be doing all right!" He waited for the laughter, and all he got was the ocean breeze in his face. By then everyone present was thinking approximately the same thing . . . and it was *delicious* in that weird way . . . but to just blurt it out was a strange sort of counter-gaffe.

Nevertheless, Radical Chic had arrived. The fall social season of 1969 was a big time for it. People like Jean vanden Heuvel gave parties for *Ramparts* magazine, which had by now become completely a magazine of the barricades, and for the Chicago Eight. Jules Feiffer gave a party for the G.I. Coffee Houses, at which Richard Avedon, America's most famous fashion photographer, took portraits of everybody who made a $25 contribution to the cause. He had his camera and lights set up in the dining room. As a matter of fact, Avedon had become a kind of court photographer to the Movement. He was making his pentennial emergence to see where it was now at. Five years before he had emerged from his studio to take a look around and had photographed and edited an entire issue of *Harper's Bazaar* to record his findings, which were of the Pop, Op, Rock, Andy, Rudi and Go-Go variety. Now Avedon was putting together a book about the Movement. He went to Chicago for the trial of The Eight and set up a studio in a hotel near the courthouse to do portraits of the celebrities and activists who testified at the trial or watched it or circled around it in one way or another.

Meanwhile, some of the most prestigious young matrons in San Francisco and New York were into an organization called Friends of the Earth. Friends of the Earth was devoted to the proposition that women should not buy coats or other apparel made from the hides of such dying species as leopards, cheetahs, jaguars, ocelots, tigers, Spanish lynx, Asiatic lions, red wolves, sea otter, giant otter, polar bear, mountain zebra, alligators, crocodiles, sea turtles, vicuñas, timber wolves, wolverines, margays, kolinskies, martens, fishers, fitch, sables, servals, and mountain lions. On the face of it, there was nothing very radical about this small gesture in the direction of conservation, or ecology, as it is now known. Yet Friends of the

Earth was Radical Chic, all right. The radical part began with the simple fact that the movement was not tax deductible. Friends of the Earth is a subsidiary of the Sierra Club. The Sierra Club's pre-eminence in the conservation movement began at precisely the moment when the federal government declared it a political organization, chiefly due to its fight against proposed dam projects in the Grand Canyon. That meant that contributions to it were no longer tax deductible. One of the Sierra Club's backstage masterminds, the late Howard Gossage, used to tell David Brower, the Sierra Club's president: "That's the grea-a-a-atest thing that ever happened to you. It removed all the guilt! Now the money's just rolllllllling in." Then he would go into his cosmic laugh. He had an incredible cosmic laugh, Gossage did. It started way back in his throat and came rolllling out, as if from Lane 27 of the Heavenly bowling alley.

No tax deduction! That became part of the canon of Radical Chic. Lay it on the line! Matrons soliciting funds for Friends of the Earth and other organizations took to making telephone calls that ended with: "All right, now, I'll expect to see your check in the mail—and it's *not* tax deductible." That was a challenge, the unspoken part of which was: You can be a tax deductible Heart Funder, April in Paris Baller, Day Care Center-of-the-Roader, if that's all you want out of your jiveass life . . . As for themselves, the Friends of the Earth actually took to the streets, picketing stores and ragging women who walked down the street with their new Somali leopard coats on. A woman's only acceptable defense was to say she had shot the animal and eaten it. The Friends of the Earth movement was not only a fight in behalf of the poor beasts but a fight against greed, against the spirit of capitalistic marauding, to call it by its right name . . . although the fight took some weird skews here and there, as Radical Chic is apt to do.

So . . . Radical Chic was already in full swing by the time the Black Panther Party began a national fund-raising campaign late in 1969. The Panthers' organizers, like the grape workers', counted on the "cause party"—to use a term for it that was current thirty-five years ago—not merely in order to raise money. The Panthers' status was quite confused in the minds of many liberals, and to have the Panthers feted in the homes of a series of social and cultural leaders could make an important difference.

Ideally, it would work out well for the socialites and culturati, too, for if there was ever a group that embodied the romance and excitement of which Radical Chic is made, it was the Panthers.

Even before the Bernsteins' party for the Panthers, there had been at least three others, at the homes of John Simon of Random House, on Hudson Street, Richard Baron, the publisher, in Chappaqua, and Sidney and Gail Lumet, in their townhouse at Lexington Avenue and 91st Street. It was the Lumets' party that led directly to the Bernsteins'. A veteran cause organizer named Hannah Weinstein had called up Gail Lumet. She said that Murray Kempton had asked her to try to organize a party for the Black Panthers to raise money for the defense of the Panther 21.

The party was a curious one, even by the standards of Radical Chic. Many of the guests appeared not to be particularly "social" . . . more like Mr. and Mrs. Wealthy Dentist from New Rochelle. Yet there was a certain social wattage in the presence of people like Murray Kempton, Peter Stone, writer of *1776*, the Lumets themselves, and several Park Avenue matrons, the most notable being Leonard Bernstein's wife, Felicia.

The first half of the session generated the Radical Chic emotion in its purest and most penetrating form. Not only was there the electrifying spectacle of the massed Panthers, but Mrs. Lee Berry rose and delivered a moving account of how her husband had been seized by police in his hospital room and removed summarily to jail. To tell the truth, some of the matrons were disappointed when she first opened her mouth. She had such a small, quiet voice. "I am a Panther wife," she said. *I am a Panther wife?* But her story *was* moving. Felicia Bernstein had been present up to this point and, as a longtime supporter of civil liberties, had been quite upset by what she had heard. But she had had to leave before the session was over. Each guest, as he left, was presented with a sheet of paper and asked to do one of three things: pledge a contribution to the defense fund, lend his name to an advertisement that was to appear in *The New York Times,* or to make his home available for another party and fund-raising event. By the time she left, Felicia was quite ready to open her doors.

The emotional momentum was building rapidly when Ray "Masai" Hewitt, the Panthers' Minister of Education and member of the Central Committee, rose to speak. Hewitt was an intense, powerful young man and in no mood to play the diplomacy game. Some of you here, he said, may have some feelings left for the establishment, but we don't. We want to see it die. We're Maoist revolutionaries, and we have no choice but to fight to the finish. For about thirty minutes Masai Hewitt laid it on the line. He referred now and again to "that M—— F—— Nixon" and to how the struggle would not be easy, and that if buildings were burned and other violence ensued, that was only part of the struggle that the power structure had forced the oppressed minorities into. Hewitt's words tended to provoke an all-or-nothing reaction. A few who remembered the struggles of the Depression were profoundly moved, fired up with a kind of *nostalgie de that old-time religion*. But more than one Park Avenue matron was thrown into a Radical Chic confusion. The most memorable quote was: "He's a magnificent man, but suppose some simple-minded schmucks take all that business about burning down buildings *seriously*?"

Murray Kempton cooled things down a bit. He stood up and, in his professorial way, in the tweedy tones of the lecturer who clicks his pipe against his teeth like a mental metronome, he summed up the matter. Dependable old Murray put it all in the more comfortable terms of Reason Devout, after the manner of a lead piece in the periodicals he worshipped, *The New Statesman* and *The Spectator*. Murray, it turned out, was writing a book on the Panthers and otherwise doing his best for the cause. Yes, Masai Hewitt may have set the message down too hard, but that was of little consequence. In no time at all another party for the Panthers had been arranged. And this time in the home of one of the most famous men in the United States, Leonard Bernstein.

"Who do you call to give a party!" says Richard Feigen. "Who do you call to give a party!"

And all at once the candid voice of Radical Chic, just ringing out like that, seems about to drop Don Cox, Field Marshal of the Black Panthers, in his tracks, by Lenny's grand piano. He just stares at Feigen . . . this Yale-style blond in a tuxedo . . . And from that moment on, the evening begins to take on a weird reversal. Rather than Cox being in the role of the black militant mau-mauing the rich white liberals, he is slowly backed into a weird corner. Afro, goatee, turtleneck and all, *he* has to be the diplomat . . . *He* has to play that all-time-loser role of the house guest trying to deal with a bunch of leaping, prancing, palsied happy-slobber Saint Bernards . . . It's a ball-breaker . . . And no wonder! For what man in all history has ever before come face to face with naked white Radical Chic running ecstatically through a Park Avenue duplex and letting it all hang out.

One of the members of the Panther defense committee, a white, manages to come up with a phone number, "691–8787," but Feigen is already pressing on:

"There is one candidate for governor," he says—quite an impressive voice—"who feels very deeply about what is going on here. He had hoped to be here tonight, but unfortunately he was detained upstate. And that's Howard Samuels. Now, what I want to know is, if he were willing to come before you and present his program, would you be willing to consider supporting it? In other words, are the Black Panthers interested in getting any political leverage within the System?"

Cox stares at him again. "Well," he says—and it is the first time he falls into that old hesitant thing of beginning a sentence with *well*—"any politician who is willing to relate to our ten-point program, we will support him actively, but we have no use for the traditional political—"

"But would you be willing to listen to such a candidate?" says Feigen.

"—the traditional political arena, because if you try to oppose the system from within the traditional political arena, you're wasting your time. Look at Powell. As soon as he began to speak for the people, they threw him out. We have no power within the system, and we will never have any power within the system. The only power we have is the power to destroy, the power to disrupt. If black people are armed with knowledge—"

"But would you be willing to listen to such a candidate?" says Feigen.

"Well," says Cox, a bit wearily, "we would refer him to our Central Committee, and if he was willing to support our ten-point program, then we would support that man."

Feigen muses sagely inside of his tuxedo. *Dapper.* A dapper dude in pinstripe suit and pencil moustache in the rear of the room, a black named Rick Haynes, president of Management Formation Inc., an organization promoting black capitalism, asks about the arrest the other night of Robert Bay and another Panther named Jolly.

"Right on," says Cox, softly, raising his left fist a bit, but only as a fraternal gesture—and through every white cortex rushes the flash about how the world here is divided between those who rate that acknowledgement—*right on*—and those who don't . . . Right on . . . Cox asks Robert Bay to stand, and his powerful form and his ferocious Afro rise from out of the midst of the people in the rows of chairs in the center of the room, he nods briefly towards Haynes and smiles and says "Right on"—there it is—and then he sits down. And Cox tells how the three detectives rousted and hassled Bay and Jolly and another man, and then the detectives went on radio station WINS and "lied about it all day." And Lefcourt gets up and tells how this has become a pattern, the cops incessantly harassing the Panthers, wherever they may be, everything from stopping them for doing 52 in a 50-mile-an-hour zone to killing Fred Hampton in his bed.

The beautiful ash-blond girl speaks up: "People like myself who feel that up to now the Panthers have been very badly treated—we don't know what to do. I mean, if you don't have money and you don't have influence, what can you do? What other community programs are there? We want to do something, but what can we do? Is there some kind of committee, or some kind of . . . I don't know . . ."

Well baby, if you really—but Cox tells her that one of the big problems is finding churches in the black community that will help the Panthers in their breakfast program for ghetto children, and maybe people like her could help the Panthers approach the churches. "It's basically the churches who have the large kitchens that we need," he says, "but when we come to them to use their kitchens, to feed hot breakfasts to hungry children, they close the door in our faces. That's where the churches in the black community are at."

"Tell why!" says Leonard Bernstein. Hardly anybody has noticed it up to now, but Leonard Bernstein has moved from the back of the room to an easy chair up front. He's only a couple of feet from Cox. But Cox is standing up, by the piano, and Lenny is sunk down to his hip sockets in the easy chair . . . They really don't know what they're in for. Lenny is on the move. As more than one person in this room knows, Lenny treasures "the art of conversation." He treasures it, monopolizes it, conglomerates it, like a Jay Gould, an Onassis, a Cornfeld of Conversation. Anyone who has spent a three-day weekend with Lenny in the country, by the shore, or captive on some lonesome cay in the Windward Islands, knows that feeling—the alternating spells of adrenal stimulation and insulin coma as the Great Interrupter, the Village Explainer, the champion of Mental Jotto, the Free Analyst, Mr. Let's Find Out, leads the troops on a seventy-two-hour forced march through the lateral geniculate and the pyramids of Betz, no breathers allowed, until every human brain is reduced finally to a clump of dried seaweed inside a burnt-out husk and collapses, implodes, in one last crunch of terminal boredom. Mr. Pull! Mr. Push! Mr. Auricularis! . . . But how could the Black Panther Party of America know that? Just now Lenny looks so sunk-down-low in the easy chair. Almost at Don Cox's feet he is, way down in an easy chair with his turtleneck and blazer on, and his neckpiece. Also right down front, on the couch next to the wall, is Otto Preminger, no piece of wallpaper himself, with his great head and neck rising up like a howitzer shell from out of his six-button double-breasted, after the manner of the eternal Occupation Zone commandant.

"Tell why," says Lenny.

"Well," says Cox, "that gets into the whole history of the church in the black community. It's a long story."

"Go ahead and tell it," says Lenny.

"Well," says Cox, "when the slaves were brought to America, they were always met at the boat by the cat with the whip and the gun . . . see . . . and along with him was the black preacher, who said, Everything's gonna be all right, as long as you're right with Jesus. It's like, the normal thing in the black community. The preacher was always the go-between the slavemasters and the slave, and the preacher would get a little extra crumb off the table for performing this service . . . you know . . . It's the same situation in the black community today. The preacher is riding around in a gold Cadillac, but it's the same thing. If you ask a lot of these churches to start working for the people instead of for The Man, they start worrying about that crumb . . . see . . . Because if the preacher starts working for the people, then the power structure starts harassing him. Like we found this one minister who was willing for us to use his church for the breakfast program. So okay, and then one day he comes in, and he's terrified . . . see . . . and he says we have to leave, that's all there is to it. The cat's terrified . . . So we say, okay, we'll leave, but just tell us what they said to you. Tell us what they did to intimidate you. But he won't even talk about it, he just says, Leave. He's too terrified to even talk about it."

Bernstein says, "Don, what's really worrying a lot of us here is the friction between groups like the Black Panthers and the established black community."

No problem. Cox says, "We recognize that there is not only a racial struggle going on in this country, but a class struggle. The class structure doesn't exist in the same way in the black community, but what we have are very bourgeois-minded people"—he uses the standard New Left pronunciation, which is "boooooooozh-wah"—"petty bourgeois-minded people . . . you see . . . and they have the same mentality as bourgeois-minded people in the white power structure."

"Yes," says Bernstein, "but a lot of us here are worried about things like threats against the lives of leaders of the established black community—"

Suddenly Rick Haynes speaks out from the back of the room: "This thing about 'the black community' galls me!" He's really put out, but it's hard to tell what over, because what he does is look down at the Ash-Blond Beauty, who is only about ten feet away: "*This lovely young lady* here was asking about *what she could do . . .*" What a look . . . if sarcasm could reach 550 degrees, she would shrivel up like a slice of Oscar Mayer bacon. "Well, I suggest that she forget about going into *the black community*. I suggest that she think about the white community. Like *The Wall Street Journal—The Wall Street Journal* just printed an article about the Black Panthers, and they came to the shocking conclusion—for them— that a majority of the black community supports the Black Panthers. Well, I suggest that this lovely young lady get somebody like her *daddy*, who just might have a little more *pull* than she does, to call up *The Wall Street Journal* and congratulate them when they write it straight like that. Just call up and say, We like that. The name of the game is to use the media, because the media have been using us."

"Right on," says Don Cox.

Curiously, Ash Blonde doesn't seem particularly taken aback by all this. If this dude in a pin-stripe suit thinks he's going to keep her off The All-Weather Panther Committee, he's bananas . . .

And if they think this is going to deflect Leonard Bernstein, they're *all* out to lunch. About five people are talking at once—Quat—Lefcourt—Lenny—Cox—Barbara Walters is on the edge of her chair, bursting to ask a question—but it is the Pastmaster who cuts through:

"I want to know what the Panthers' attitude is toward the threats against these black leaders!" says Lenny.

Lefcourt the lawyer jumps up: "Mr. Bernsteen—"

"*STEIN!*" roars Lenny. He's become a veritable tiger, except that he is sunk down so low into the Margaret Owen billows of the easy chair, with his eyes peering up from way down in the downy hollow, that everything he says seems to be delivered into the left knee of Don Cox.

"Mr. Bernstein," says Lefcourt, "every time there are threats, every time there is violence, it's used as an indictment of the Black Panthers, even if they had nothing whatsoever to do with it."

"I'm hip," says Lenny.

"I think everybody in this room buys that, and everybody buys the distinction between what the media, what the newspapers and television say about the Panthers and what they really are. But this thing of the threats is in our collective memory. Bayard Rustin was supposed to be here tonight, but he isn't here, and for an important reason. The reason he isn't here tonight is that he was warned that his life would be in danger, and that's what I want to know about."

It's a gasper, this remark. Lefcourt and Quat start talking, but then, suddenly, before Don Cox can open his mouth, Lenny reaches up from out of the depths of the easy chair and hands him a mint. There it is, rising up on the tips of his fingers, a mint. It is what is known as a puffed mint, an after-dinner mint, of the sort that suddenly appears on the table in little silver Marthinsen bowls, as if deposited by the mint fairy, along with the coffee, but before the ladies leave the room, a mint so small, fragile, angel-white and melt-crazed that you have to pick it up with the papillae of your forefinger and thumb lest it get its thing on a straightaway, namely, one tiny sweet salivary peppermint melt . . . in mid-air, so to speak . . . just so . . . Cox takes the mint and stares at Bernstein with a strange Plexiglas gaze . . . This little man sitting down around his kneecaps with his Groovy gear and love beads on . . .

Finally Cox comes around. "We don't know anything about that," he says. "We don't threaten anybody. Like, we only advocate violence in self-defense, because we are a colonial people in a capitalist country . . . you know? . . . and the only thing we can do is defend ourselves against oppression."

Quat is trying to steer the whole thing away—but suddenly Otto Preminger speaks up from the sofa where he's sitting, also just a couple of feet from Cox:

"He used von important vord"—then he looks at Cox—"you said zis is de most repressive country in de vorld. I dun't be*leef* zat."

Cox says, "Let me answer the question—"

Lenny breaks in: "When you say 'capitalist' in that pejorative tone, it reminds me of Stokely. When you read Stokely's statement in *The New York Review of Books,* there's only one place where he says what he really means, and that's way down in paragraph 28 or something, and you realize he is talking about setting up a socialist government—"

Preminger is still talking to Cox: "Do you mean dat zis government is more repressive zan de government of Nigeria?"

"I don't know anything about the government of Nigeria," says Cox. "Let me answer the question—"

"You dun't eefen *lis*ten to de kvestion," says Preminger. "How can you *answer* de kvestion?"

"Let me answer the question," Cox says, and he says to Lenny: "We believe that the government is obligated to give every man employment or a guaranteed income . . . see . . . but if the white businessman will not give full employment, then the means of production should be taken from the businessman and placed in the community, with the people."

Lenny says: "How? I dig it! But how?"

"Right on!" Someone in the back digs it, too.

"Right on!"

Julie Belafonte pipes up: "That's a very difficult question!"

"You can't blueprint the future," says Cox.

"You mean you're just going to *wing* it?" says Lenny.

"Like . . . this is what we want, man," says Cox, "we want the same thing as you, we want peace. We want to come home at night and be with the family . . . and turn on the TV . . . and smoke a little *weed* . . . you know . . . and get a little *high* . . . you dig? . . . and we'd like to get into that bag, like anybody else. But we can't do that . . . see . . . because if they send in the pigs to rip us off and brutalize our families, then we have to fight."

"I couldn't agree with you more!" says Lenny. "But what do you do—"

Cox says: "We think that this country is going more and more toward fascism to oppress those people who have the will to fight back—"

"I agree with you one hundred percent!" says Lenny. "But you're putting it in defensive terms, and don't you really mean it in offensive terms—"

"That's the language of the oppressor," says Cox. "As soon as—"

"Dat's not—" says Preminger.

"Let me finish!" says Cox. "As a Black Panther, you get used to—"

"Dat's not—"

"Let me finish! As a Black Panther, you learn that language is used as an instrument of control, and—"

"He doesn't *mean* dat!"

"Let me finish!"

Cox to Preminger to Bernstein to . . . they're wrestling for the Big Ear . . . quite a struggle . . . Cox standing up by the piano covered in the million-dollar *chatchkas* . . . Lenny sunk down into the Margaret Owen easy chair . . . Preminger, the irresistible commandant of the sofa . . . they're pulling and tugging—

Then Cox seizes the moment: "Our Minister of Defense, Huey P. Newton, has said if we can't find a meaningful life . . . you know . . . maybe we can have a meaningful death . . . and one reason the power structure fears the Black Panthers is that they know the Black Panthers are ready to die for what they believe in, and a lot of us have already died."

Lenny seems like a changed man. He looks up at Cox and says, "When you walk into this house, into this building"—and he gestures vaguely as if to take it all in, the moldings, the sconces, the Roquefort morsels rolled in crushed nuts, the servants, the elevator attendant and the doorman downstairs in their white dickeys, the marble lobby, the brass struts on the marquee out front—"when you walk into this house, you must feel infuriated!"

Cox looks embarrassed. "No, man . . . I manage to overcome

that . . . That's a personal thing . . . I used to get very uptight about things like that, but—"

"Don't you get bitter? Doesn't that make you mad?"

"Noooo, man . . . That's a personal thing . . . see . . . and I don't get mad about that personally. I'm over that."

"Well," says Lenny, "it makes *me* mad!"

And Cox stares at him, and the Plexiglas lowers over his eyes once more . . . These cats—if I wasn't here to see it—

"This is a very paradoxical situation," says Lenny. "Having this apartment makes this meeting possible, and if this apartment didn't exist, you wouldn't have it. And yet—well, it's a very paradoxical situation."

"I don't get uptight about all that," says Cox. "I've been through all that. I grew up in the country, in a farming community, and I finally became a 'respectable Negro' . . . you know . . . I did all the right things. I got a job and a car, and I was wearing a suit and getting good pay, and as long as I didn't break any rules I could go to work and wear my suit and get paid. But then one day it dawned on me that I was only kidding myself, because that wasn't where it was at. In a society like ours I might as well have had my hair-guard on and my purple pants, because when I walked down the street I was just another *nigger* . . . see . . . just another *nigger* . . . But I don't have that hate thing going. Like, I mean, I can *feel* it, I can *get* uptight. Like the other day I was coming out of the courthouse in Queens and there was this off-duty pig going by . . . see . . . and he gives me the finger. That's the pig's way of letting you know he's got his eye on you. He gives me the finger . . . and for some reason or other, this kind of got the old *anger* boiling . . . you know?"

"God," says Lenny, and he swings his head around toward the rest of the room, "most of the people in this room have had a problem about being unwanted!"

Most of the people in this room have had a problem about being unwanted. There it is. It's an odd feeling. Most-of-the-people-in-this-room's . . . heads have just spun out over this one. Lenny is unbeatable. Mental Jotto at 3 A.M. He has done it. He has just steered the Black Panther movement into a 1955 Jules Feiffer cartoon. Rejection, Security, Anxiety, Oedipus, Electra, Neurosis, Transference, Id, Superego, Archetype and Field of Perception, that wonderful 1950s game, beloved by all educated young men and women in the East who grew up in the era of the great cresting tide of Freud, Jung, Adler, Reik & Reich, when everyone either had an analyst or quoted Ernest Dichter telling Maytag that dishwashing machines were bought by women with anal compulsions. And in the gathering insulin coma Lenny has the Panthers and seventy-five assorted celebrities and culturati heading off on the long march into the neural jungle, 1955 Forever. One way or another we all feel insecure— right? And so long as we repress our—it's marvelous! Mr. Auricularis! The Village Explainer! *Most of the people in this room have had a problem about being unwanted—*

Everybody is talking at once, but then Barbara Walters, who has had this certain thing building up inside of her, springs it loose. Everybody knows that voice, Barbara Walters of the *Today* show, televised coast to coast every morning, a mid-Atlantic voice, several miles east of Newfoundland and heading for Blackpool, and she leans forward, sitting in the third row in her checked pantsuit with the great fur collar:

"I'm a member of the news media, but I'm here as an individual, because I'm concerned about the questions raised here, and there has been a lot of talk about the media. Last year we interviewed Mrs. Eldridge Cleaver, Kathleen Cleaver, and it was not an edited report or anything of that sort. She had a chance to say whatever she wanted, and this is a very knowledgeable, very brilliant, very articulate woman . . . And I asked her, I said, 'I have a child, and you have a child,' and I said, 'Do you see any possibility that our children will be able to grow up and live side by side in peace and harmony?' and she said, 'Not with the conditions that prevail in this society today, not without the overthrow of the system.' So I asked her, 'How do you feel, as a mother, about the prospect of your child being in that kind of confrontation, a nation in flames?' and she said, 'Let it burn!' And I said, 'What about your own child?' and she said, 'May he light the first match!' And that's what I want to ask you about. I'm still here as a concerned person, not as a reporter, but what I'm talking about, and what Mr. Bernstein and Mr. Preminger are talking about, when they ask you about the way you refer to capitalism, is whether you see any chance at all for a peaceful solution to these problems, some way out without violence."

Cox says, "Not with the present system. I can't see that. Like, what can change? There's 750 families that own all the wealth of this country—"

"Dat's not *tdrue*!" says Preminger. "Dere are many people vid vealth all over—"

"Let me finish!—and these families are the most reactionary elements in the country. A man like H. L. Hunt wouldn't let me in his house."

Barbara Walters says: "I'm not talking about—"

"I wouldn't *go* to his house eef he *asked me*," says Preminger.

"Well I almost—"

"Vot about Ross Perot? He's a Texan, too, and is spending millions of dollars trying to get de vives of prisoners of war in touch with the government of North Vietnam—"

Cox says: "I would respect him more if he was giving his money to hungry children."

"He is!" says Preminger. "He is! You dun't *read* anyt'ing! Dat's your tdrouble!"

"I'm not talking about that," Barbara Walters says to Cox. "I'm talking about what's supposed to happen to other people if you achieve your goals."

"You can't just put it like that!" says Julie Belafonte. "That needs clarification."

Barbara Walters says: "I'm talking as a white woman who has a white husband, who is a capitalist, or an agent of capitalists, and I am, too, and I want to know if you are to have your freedom, does that mean we have to go!"

Barbara Walters and her husband, Lee Guber, a producer, up against the wall in the cellar in Ekaterinburg.

Cox says, "For one person to be free, everybody must be free. As long as one whole class is oppressed, there is no freedom in a society. A lot of young white people are beginning to—"

"Dat eesn't vat she's asking—"

"Let me finish—let me answer the question—"

"You dun't even *lis*ten to de kvestion—"

"Let me finish—A lot of young white people are beginning to understand about oppression. They're part of the petty bourgeoisie. It's a different class from the black community, but there's a common oppressor. They're protesting about individual freedoms, to have their music and smoke weed and have sex. These are individual freedoms but they are beginning to understand—"

"If you're for freedom," says Preminger, "tell me dis: Is it all right for a Jew to leave Russia and settle in Israel?"

"Let me finish—"

"Is it all right for a Jew to leave Russia and settle in Israel?"

Most people in the room don't know what the hell Preminger is driving at, but Leon Quat and the little gray man know right away. They're trying to wedge into the argument. The hell with that little number, that Israel and Al Fatah and U.A.R. and MIGS and USSR and Zionist imperialist number—not in this room you don't—

Quat stands up with a terrific one-big-happy-family smile on and says: "I think we're all ready to agree that the crisis in this country today comes not from the Black Panthers but from the war in Vietnam, and—"

But there is a commotion right down front. Barbara Walters is saying something to one of the Panther wives, Mrs. Lee Berry, in the front row.

"What did she say to you?" says Lenny.

"I was talking to this very nice lady," says Barbara Walters, "and she said, 'You sound like you're afraid.'"

Mrs. Berry laughs softly and shakes her head.

"I'm not afraid of you," Barbara Walters says to her, "but maybe I am about the idea of the death of my children!"

"Please!" says Quat.

"All I'm asking is if we can work together to create justice without violence and destruction!"

"Please!" says Quat.

"He never answered her kvestion!" says Preminger.

"Please!"

"I can answer the question—"

"You dun't eefen *lis*ten—"

"So—"

"Let me answer the question! I can deal with that. We don't believe that it will happen within the present system, but—"

Lenny says: "So you're going to start a revolution from a Park Avenue apartment!"

Right on!

Quat sings out desperately: "Livingston Wingate is here! Can we please have a word from Mr. Livingston Wingate of the Urban League?" Christ, yes, bring in Livingston Wingate.

So Livingston Wingate, executive director of the New York Urban League, starts threading his way down to the front. He hasn't got the vaguest notion of what has been going on, except that this is Panther night at the Bernsteins'. He apparently thinks he is called upon to wax forensic, because he starts into a long disquisition on the changing mood of black youth.

"I was on television this morning with a leader of the Panther movement," he says, "and—"

"That was me—" Cox from his chair beside the piano.

Wingate wheels around. "Oh, yes . . ." He does a double take. "I didn't see you here . . . That was *you* . . . Hah . . ." And then he continues, excoriating himself and his generation of black leaders for their failures, because non-violence didn't work, and he can no longer tell the black youth not to throw that rock—

In the corner, meanwhile, by the piano, Preminger has reached out and grabbed Cox by the forearm in some kind of grip of goodwill and brotherhood and is beaming as if to say, I didn't mean anything by it, and Cox is trying to grab his hand and shake hands and say that's OK, and Preminger keeps going for the forearm, and Cox keeps going for the hand, and they're lost there in a weird eccentric tangle of fingers and wrist bones between the sofa and the grand piano, groping and tugging—

—because, says Livingston Wingate, he cannot prove to the ghetto youth that anything else will work, and so forth and so on, "and they are firmly convinced that there can be no change unless the system is changed."

"Less than 5 percent of the people of this country have 90 percent of the wealth," says Lefcourt the lawyer, "and 10 percent of them have most of the 90 percent. The mass of the people by following the system can never make changes, and there is no use continuing to tell people about constitutional guarantees, either. Leon and I could draw up a constitution that would give us all the power, and we could make it so deep and legitimate that you would have to kill us to change it!"

Julie Belafonte rises up in front and says: "Then we'll kill you!"

"Power to the people!" says Leon Quat . . . and all rise to their feet . . . and Charlotte Curtis puts the finishing touches in her notebook . . . and the white servants wait patiently in the wings to wipe the drink rings off the Amboina tables . . .

STILL WOUND UP with the excitement of the mental Jotto they had all just been through, Lenny, Felicia and Don Cox kept on talking there in the duplex, long after most guests had gone, up to about 10 P.M., in fact. Lenny and Felicia knew they had been through a unique experience, but they had no idea of the furor that was going to break the next day when Charlotte Curtis's account of the party would appear in *The New York Times*.

The story appeared in two forms—a preliminary report rushed through for the first edition, which reaches the streets about 10:30 P.M., and a much fuller one for the late city edition, the one most New Yorkers see in the morning. Neither account was in any way critical of what had gone on. Even after reading them, Lenny and Felicia probably had little inkling of what was going to happen next. The early version began:

"Mrs. Leonard Bernstein, who has raised money for such diverse causes as indigent Chileans, the New York Philharmonic, Church World Service, Israeli student scholarships, emotionally disturbed children, the New York Civil Liberties Union, a Greek boys' school and Another Mother for Peace, was into what she herself admitted yesterday was a whole new thing. She gave a cocktail party for the Black Panthers. 'Not a frivolous party,' she explained before perhaps thirty guests arrived, 'but a chance for all of us to hear what's happening to them. They've really been treated very inhumanely.' "

Felicia herself couldn't have asked for it to be put any better. In the later edition it began: "Leonard Bernstein and a Black Panther leader ar-

gued the merits of the Black Panther party's philosophy before nearly
ninety guests last night in the Bernsteins' elegant Park Avenue duplex"—
and went on to give some of the dialogue of Lenny's, Cox's and Preminger's
argument over Panther tactics and Lenny's refrain of "I dig it." There was
also a picture of Cox standing beside the piano and talking to the group,
with Felicia in the background. No one in the season of Radical Chic could
have asked for better coverage. It took up a whole page in the fashion section, along with ads for B. Altman's, Edith Imre wigs, fur coats, the
Sherry-Netherland Hotel, and The Sun and Surf (Palm Beach).

What the Bernsteins probably did not realize at first was that the story
was going out on *The New York Times* News Service wires. In other cities
throughout the United States and Europe it was played on page one, typically, to an international chorus of horse laughs or nausea, depending on
one's *Weltanschauung*. The English, particularly, milked the story for all
it was worth and seemed to derive one of the great cackles of the year
from it.

BY THE SECOND DAY, however—Friday—the Bernsteins certainly knew
they were in for it. The *Times* ran an editorial! on the party. It was headed
"False Note on Black Panthers":

"Emergence of the Black Panthers as the romanticized darlings of the
politico-cultural jet set is an affront to the majority of black Americans.
This so-called party, with its confusion of Mao-Marxist ideology and Fascist paramilitarism, is fully entitled to protection of its members' constitutional rights. It was to make sure that those rights are not abridged by
persecution masquerading as law-enforcement that a committee of distinguished citizens has recently been formed [a group headed by Arthur
Goldberg that sought to investigate the killing of Fred Hampton by
Chicago police].

" . . . The so-called 'party' for the Panthers had not been a party at all.
It had been a meeting. Nothing social about it . . .

"In contrast, the group therapy plus fund-raising soiree at the home of
Leonard Bernstein, as reported in this newspaper yesterday, represents
the sort of elegant slumming that degrades patrons and patronized alike.
It might be dismissed as guilt-relieving fun spiked with social conscious-

ness, except for its impact on those blacks and whites seriously working for complete equality and social justice. It mocked the memory of Martin Luther King Jr., whose birthday was solemnly observed throughout the nation yesterday.

"Black Panthers on a Park Avenue pedestal create one more distortion of the Negro image. Responsible black leadership is not likely to cheer as the Beautiful People create a new myth that Black Panther is beautiful."

Elegant slumming . . . mocked the memory of Martin Luther King . . . Black Panthers on a Park Avenue pedestal . . . the Beautiful People . . . It was a stunner. And this was not the voice of some right-wing columnist like William Buckley (although he would be heard from)—this was an editorial, on the editorial page, underneath the eagle medallion with "All the News That's Fit to Print" and "Established 1851" on it . . . in the very *New York Times* itself.

A controversy they were apparently oblivious of suddenly erupted around them. Namely, the bitterness between Jews and blacks over an issue that had been building for three years, ever since Black Power became important. The first inkling the Bernsteins had was when they started getting hate mail, some of it apparently from Jews of the Queens-Brooklyn Jewish Defense League variety. Then the League's national chairman, Rabbi Meir Kahane, blasted Lenny publicly for joining a "trend in liberal and intellectual circles to lionize the Black Panthers . . . We defend the right of blacks to form defense groups, but they've gone beyond this to a group which hates other people. That's not nationalism, that's Naziism. And if Bernstein and other such intellectuals do not know this, they know nothing."

Black Power groups such as SNCC and the Black Panthers were voicing support for the Arabs against Israel. This sometimes looked like a mere matter of black nationalism; after all, Egypt was a part of Africa, and black nationalist literature sometimes seemed to identify the Arabs as blacks fighting the white Israelis. Or else it looked like merely a commitment to world socialism; the Soviet Union and China supported the Arabs against the imperialist tools, the Israelis. But many Jewish leaders regarded the anti-Zionist stances of groups like the Panthers as a veiled American-brand anti-Semitism, tied up with such less theoretical matters as extortion, robbery and mayhem by blacks against Jews in ghetto areas. They cited things like the August 30, 1969, issue of *Black Panther*, which carried an article entitled "Zionism (Kosher Nationalism) + Imperialism = Fascism" and spoke of "the fascist pigs." The June, 1967, issue of another Panther publication, *Black Power*, had carried a poem entitled "Jew-Land," which said:

> *Jew-Land, On a summer afternoon, Really, Couldn't kill the Jews*
> > *too soon,*
> *Now dig. The Jews have stolen our bread*
> *Their filthy women tricked our men into bed*
> *So I won't rest until the Jews are dead . . .*
> *In Jew-Land, Don't be a Tom on Israel's side*
> *Really, Cause that's where Christ was crucified.*

But in the most literate circles of the New Left—well, the Panthers' pronouncements on foreign affairs couldn't be taken too seriously. Ideologically, they were still feeling their way around. To be a UJA Zionist about the whole thing was to be old-fashioned, middle-class middle-aged, suburban, Oceanside-Cedarhurstian, in an age when the youth of the New Left had re-programmed the whole circuitry of Left opposition to oppression. The main thing was that the Panthers were the legitimate vanguard of the black struggle for liberation—among the culturati whom Leonard Bernstein could be expected to know and respect, this was not a point of debate, it was an axiom. The chief theoretical organ of Radical Chic, *The New York Review of Books*, regularly cast Huey Newton and Eldridge Cleaver as the Simón Bolívar and José Martí of the black ghettos. On August 24, 1967, *The New York Review of Books* paid homage to the summer urban riot season by printing a diagram for the making of a Molotov cocktail on its front page. In fact, the journal was sometimes referred to good-naturedly as *The Parlour Panther*, with the *-our* spelling of *Parlour* being an allusion to its concurrent motif of anglophilia. The *Review's* embracing of such apparently contradictory attitudes—the nitty-gritty of the ghetto warriors and the preciosity of traditional English Leavis & Loomis intellectualism—was really no contradiction at all, of course. It was merely the essential double-track mentality of Radical Chic—*nostagie de la boue* and high protocol—in its literary form. In any case, given all this, people like Lenny and Felicia could hardly have been expected to comprehend a complex matter like the latter-day friction between blacks and Jews.

To other people involved in Radical Chic, however, the picture was now becoming clear as day. This was no time for Custer's last stand. This was time . . . to panic. Two more couples had already agreed to give parties for the Panthers: Peter and Cheray Duchin and Frank and Domna Stanton. The Duchins had already gotten some of the static themselves. Peter had gone to Columbus, Ohio, with his orchestra . . . and the way some of the locals let him have it! All because Charlotte Curtis's article had quoted Cheray saying how thrilled she was at the prospect of meeting her first Black Panther at Felicia's. Columbus freaking *Ohio*, yet. Nor did it take the Stantons long to put two and two together. Frank Stanton, the entrepreneur, not the broadcaster, had a duplex co-op that made Lenny's look like a fourth-floor walkup. It had marble floors, apricot velvet walls, trompe l'oeil murals in the dining room, the works. A few photos of the Panthers against this little backdrop—well, you could write the story yourself.

On Saturday evening, the twenty-fourth, the Duchins, the Stantons, Sidney and Gail Lumet, and Lenny and Felicia met at the Bernsteins' to try to think out the whole situation. Sidney Lumet was convinced that a new era of "McCarthyism" had begun.

LENNY COULDN'T GET OVER the whole affair. Earlier in the evening he had talked to a reporter and told him it was "nauseating." The so-called "party" for the Panthers had not been a party at all. It had been a meeting. There was nothing social about it. As to whether he thought parties were held in the homes of socially prominent people simply because the living rooms were large and the acoustics were good, he didn't say. In any case, he and Felicia didn't give parties, and they didn't go to parties, and they were certainly not in anybody's "jet set." And they were not "masochists," either.

So four nights later Lenny, in a tuxedo, and Felicia, in a black dress, walked into a party in the triplex of one of New York's great hostesses, overlooking the East River, on the street of social dreams, East 52nd, and right off the bat some woman walks right up to him and says, "Lenny, I just think you're a masochist." It was unbelievable.

In general, the Radically Chic made a strategic withdrawal, denouncing the "witchhunt" of the press as they went. There was brief talk of a whole series of parties for the Panthers in and around New York, by way of showing the world that socialites and culturati were ready to stand up and be counted in defense of what the Panthers, and, for that matter, the Bernsteins, stood for. But it never happened. In fact, if the socialites already in line for Panther parties had gone ahead and given them in clear defiance of the opening round of attacks on the Panthers and the Bernsteins, they might well have struck an extraordinary counterblow in behalf of the Movement. This is, after all, a period of great confusion among culturati and liberal intellectuals generally, and one in which a decisive display of conviction and self-confidence can be overwhelming. But for the Radically Chic to have fought back in this way would have been a violation of their own innermost convictions. Radical Chic, after all, is only radical in style; in its heart it is part of Society and its traditions. Politics, like Rock, Pop and Camp, has its uses; but to put one's whole status on the line for *nostalgie de la boue* in any of its forms would be unprincipled.

And still this damned nauseating furor would not lie down and die. Wouldn't you know it—two days after the, well, meeting, on the very day he and Felicia were reeling from the *Times* editorial, Daniel Patrick Moynihan, that renegade, had been down in Washington writing his famous "benign neglect" memo to Nixon. In it Moynihan had presented him and Felicia and their "party" as Exhibit A of the way black revolutionaries like the Panthers had become the "culture heroes" of the Beautiful People. Couldn't you just see Nixon sitting in the Oval Room and clucking and fuming and muttering things like "rich snob bums" as he read: "You perhaps did not note on the society page of yesterday's *Times* that Mrs. Leonard Bernstein gave a cocktail party on Wednesday to raise money for the Panthers. Mrs. W. Vincent Astor was among the guests. Mrs. Peter Duchin, 'the rich blonde wife of the orchestra leader,' was thrilled. 'I've never met a Panther,' she said. 'This is a first for me.' "

On February 29 someone leaked the damned memo to the damned

New York Times, and that did it. Now he was invested, installed, inaugurated, instituted, transmogrified as Mr. Parlour Panther for all time. The part about their "cocktail party" was right in the same paragraph with the phrase "benign neglect." And it didn't particularly help the situation that Mrs. Astor got off a rapid letter to the *Times* informing them that she was not at the "party." She received an invitation, like all sorts of other people, she supposed, but, in fact, she had *not* gone. Thanks a lot, Brooke Astor.

Fools, boors, philistines, Birchers, B'nai B'rithees, Defense Leaguers, Hadassah theatre party pirhanas, UJAviators, concert hall Irishmen, WASP ignorati, toads, newspaper readers—they were booing him, Leonard Bernstein, the *egregio maestro* . . . *Boooooo.* No two ways about it. They weren't clearing their throats. They were squeezed into their $14.50 bequested seats, bringing up from out of the false bottoms of their bellies the old Low Rent raspberry boos of days gone by. *Boooooo.* Newspaper readers! That harebrained story in the *Times* had told how he and Felicia had given a party for the Black Panthers and how he had pledged a conducting fee to their defense fund, and now, stretching out before him in New York, was a great starched white-throated audience of secret candystore bigots, greengrocer Moshe Dayans with patches over both eyes . . .

—*Boooooooooo! Booooooooooo!* it was unbelievable. But it was real. These greengrocers—he was their whipping boy, and a bunch of $14.50 white-throated cretins were booing him, and it was no insomniac hallucination in the loneliness of 3 A.M.

Would that black apparition, that damnable Negro by the piano, be rising up from the belly of a concert grand for the rest of his natural life?

THE REVOLT OF THE
WHITE LOWER MIDDLE CLASS

PETE HAMILL

APRIL 14, 1969

Pete Hamill was born into a Brooklyn world that has long since ceased to exist. Hamill's father supported seven children on a factory job, until the factory departed in search of cheaper labor. "I was part of the last generation of working-class white people who could survive in New York," says Hamill. But Hamill was also among the first to understand the implications of that loss. His research for this article began in the working bars of his old neighborhood, which were populated with embittered workers whose standard of living had been slipping in the face of immigration and jobs moving overseas. In years to come, white working-class anger would radically alter America's political landscape, pushing the blue-collar Democrats of Hamill's childhood—Hamill grew up with a photo of FDR on one wall—into the Reagan coalition. Hamill, former editor of the New York Post *and the New York* Daily News, *is author of nine novels, two collections of short stories, and ten works of nonfiction, including* A Drinking Life, *which began as a* New York *story.*

THEY CALL MY PEOPLE the White Lower Middle Class these days. It is an ugly, ice-cold phrase, the result, I suppose, of the missionary zeal of those sociologists who still think you can place human beings on charts. It most certainly does not sound like a description of people on the edge of open, sustained and possibly violent revolt. And yet, that is the case. All over New York City tonight, in places like Inwood, South Brooklyn, Corona, East Flatbush and Bay Ridge, men are standing around saloons talking darkly about their grievances, and even more darkly about possible remedies. Their grievances are real and deep; their remedies could blow this city apart.

The White Lower Middle Class? Say that magic phrase at a cocktail party on the Upper East Side of Manhattan and monstrous images arise from the American demonology. Here comes the murderous rabble: fat, well-fed, bigoted, ignorant, an army of beer-soaked Irishmen, violence-loving Italians, hate-filled Poles. Lithuanians and Hungarians (they are never referred to as Americans). They are the people who assault peace marchers, who start groups like the Society for the Prevention of Negroes Getting Everything (S.P.O.N.G.E.), the people who hate John Lindsay and vote for George Wallace, presumably because they believe that Wallace will eventually march every black man in America to the gas chambers, sending Lindsay and the rest of the Liberal Establishment along with them. Sometimes these brutes are referred to as "the ethnics" or "the blue-collar types." But the bureaucratic, sociological phrase is White Lower Middle Class. Nobody calls it the Working Class anymore.

But basically, the people I'm speaking about *are* the working class. That is, they stand somewhere in the economy between the poor—most of whom are the aged, the sick and those unemployable women and children who live on welfare—and the semi-professionals and professionals who earn their way with talents or skills acquired through education. The working class earns its living with its hands or its backs; its members do not exist on welfare payments; they do not live in abject, swinish poverty, nor in safe, remote suburban comfort. They earn between $5,000 and $10,000 a year. And they can no longer make it in New York.

"I'm going out of my mind," an ironworker friend named Eddie Cush told me a few weeks ago. "I average about $8,500 a year, pretty good money. I work my ass off. But I can't make it. I come home at the end of the week, I start paying the bills, I give my wife some money for food. And there's nothing left. Maybe, if I work overtime, I get $15 or $20 to spend on myself. But most of the time, there's nothin'. They take $65 a week out of my pay. I have to come up with $90 a month rent. But every time I turn around, one of the kids needs shoes or a dress or something for school. And then I pick up a paper and read about a million people on welfare in New York or spades rioting in some college or some fat welfare bitch *demanding*—you know, not askin', demanding—a credit card at Korvette's . . . I work for a living and *I* can't get a credit card at Korvette's . . . You know, you see that, and you want to go out and strangle someone."

Cush was not drunk, and he was not talking loudly, or viciously, or with any bombast; but the tone was similar to the tone you can hear in conversations in bars like Farrell's all over this town; the tone was quiet bitterness.

"Look around," another guy told me, in a place called Mister Kelly's on Eighth Avenue and 13th Street in Brooklyn. "Look in the papers. Look on TV. What the hell does Lindsay care about me? He don't care whether my kid has shoes, whether my boy gets a new suit at Easter, whether I got any money in the bank. None of them politicians gives a good goddam. All they worry about is the niggers. And everything is for the niggers. The niggers get the schools. The niggers go to summer camp. The niggers get the new playgrounds. The niggers get nursery schools. And they get it all without workin'. I'm an ironworker, a connector; when I go to work in the mornin', I don't even know if I'm gonna make it back. My wife is scared to death, every mornin', all day. Up on the iron, if the wind blows hard or the steel gets icy or I make a wrong step, bango, forget it, I'm dead. Who feeds my wife and kid if I'm dead? Lindsay? The poverty program? You know the answer: nobody. But the niggers, they don't worry about it. They take the welfare and sit out on the stoop drinkin' cheap wine and throwin' the bottles on the street. They never gotta walk outta the house. They take the money outta my paycheck and they just turn it over to some lazy son of a bitch who won't work. I gotta carry him on my back. You know what I am? I'm a sucker. I really am. You shouldn't have to put up with this. And I'll tell ya somethin'. There's a lotta people who just ain't gonna put up with it much longer."

"The black man has hope; his life is slowly getting better. The white man of forty who makes $7,000 sees things getting worse."

It is very difficult to explain to these people that more than 600,000 of those on welfare are women and children; that one reason the black family is in trouble is because outfits like the Iron Workers Union have practically excluded blacks through most of their history; that a hell of a lot more of their tax dollars go to Vietnam or the planning for future wars than to Harlem or Bed-Stuy; that the effort of the past four or five years was an effort forced by bloody events, and that they are paying taxes to relieve some forms of poverty because of more than 100 years of neglect on top of 300 years of slavery. The working-class white man has no more patience for explanations.

"If I hear that 400-years-of-slavery bit one more time," a man said to me in Farrell's one night, "I'll go outta my mind!"

One night in Farrell's, I showed the following passage by Eldridge Cleaver to some people. It is from the recently-published collection of Cleaver's journalism:

> The very least of your responsibility now is to compensate me, however inadequately, for centuries of degradation and disenfranchisement by granting peacefully—before I take them forcefully—the same rights and opportunities for a decent life that you've taken for granted as an American birth-right. This isn't a request but a *demand* . . .

The response was peculiarly mixed. Some people said that the black man had already been given too much, and if he still couldn't make it, to hell with him. Some said they agreed with Cleaver, that the black man "got the shaft" for a long time, and whether we like it or not, we have to do something. But most of them reacted ferociously.

"Compensate him?" one man said. "Compensate him? Look, the English ruled Ireland for 700 years, that's hundreds of years longer than Negroes have been slaves. Why don't the British government compensate me? In Boston, they had signs like 'No Irish Need Apply' on the jobs, so why don't the American government compensate *me*?"

IN ANY CONVERSATION with working-class whites, you are struck by how the information explosion has hit them. Television has made an enormous impact on them, and because of the nature of that medium—its preference for the politics of theatre, its seeming inability to ever explain what is happening behind the photographed image—much of their understanding of what happens is superficial. Most of them have only a passing acquaintance with blacks, and very few have any black friends. So they see blacks in terms of militants with Afros and shades, or crushed people on welfare. Television never bothers reporting about the black man who gets up in the morning, eats a fast breakfast, says goodbye to his wife and children, and rushes out to work. That is not news. So the people who live in working-class white ghettos seldom meet blacks who are not threatening to burn down America or asking for help or receiving welfare or committing crime. And in the past five or six years, with urban rioting on everyone's minds, they have provided themselves (or been provided with) a confused, threatening stereotype of blacks that has made it almost impossible to suggest any sort of black-white working-class coalition.

"Why the hell should I work with spades," he says, "when they are threatening to burn down my house?"

The Puerto Ricans, by the way, seem well on the way to assimilation with the larger community. It has been a long time since anyone has written about "the Puerto Rican problem" (though Puerto Rican poverty remains worse than black poverty), and in white working-class areas you don't hear many people muttering about "spics" anymore.

"At least the Puerto Ricans are working," a carpenter named Jimmy Dolan told me one night, in a place called the Green Oak in Bay Ridge. "They open a grocery store, they work from six in the mornin' till midnight. The P.R.'s are willin' to work for their money. The colored guys just don't wanna work. They want the big Buicks and the fancy suits, but they jus' don't wanna do the work they have ta do ta pay for them."

The working-class white man sees injustice and politicking everywhere in this town now, with himself in the role of victim. He does not like John Lindsay, because he feels Lindsay is only concerned about the needs of blacks; he sees Lindsay walking the streets of the ghettos or opening a privately-financed housing project in East Harlem or delivering lectures about tolerance and brotherhood, and he wonders what it all means to *him.* Usually, the working-class white man is a veteran; he remembers coming back from the Korean War to discover that the GI Bill only gave him $110 a month out of which he had to pay his own tuition; so he did not go to college because he could not afford it. Then he reads about protesting blacks in the SEEK program at Queens College, learns that they are being paid up to $200 a month to go to school, with tuition free, and he starts going a little wild.

The working-class white man spends much of his time complaining almost desperately about the way he has become a victim. Taxes and the rising cost of living keep him broke, and he sees nothing in return for the taxes he pays. The Department of Sanitation comes to his street at three in the morning, and a day late, and slams garbage cans around like an invading regiment. His streets were the last to be cleaned in the big snowstorm, and they are now sliced up with trenches that could only be called potholes by the myopic. His neighborhood is a dumping ground for abandoned automobiles, which rust and rot for as long as six weeks before someone from the city finally takes them away. He works very hard, frequently on a dangerous job, and then discovers that he still can't pay his way; his wife takes a Thursday night job in a department store and he gets a weekend job, pumping gas or pushing a hack. For him, life in New York is not much of a life.

"The revolt involves guns. In places like East Flatbush and Corona, people are forming gun clubs and self-defense leagues."

"THE AVERAGE WORKING stiff is not asking for very much," says Congressman Hugh Carey, the Brooklyn Democrat whose district includes large numbers of working-class whites. "He wants a decent apartment, he wants a few beers on the weekend, he wants his kids to have decent clothes, he wants to go to a ballgame once in a while, and he would like to put a little money away so that his kids can have the education that he never could afford. That's not asking a hell of a lot. But he's not getting that. He thinks society has failed him and, in a way, if he is white, he is often more alienated than the black man. At least the black man has his own organizations, and can submerge himself in the struggle for justice and equality, or elevate himself, whatever the case might be. The black man has hope, because no matter what some of the militants say, his life is slowly getting better in a number of ways. The white man who makes $7,000 a year, who is forty, knows that he is never going to earn much more than that for the rest of his life, and he sees things getting worse, more hopeless. John Lindsay has made a number of bad moves as mayor of this town, but the alienation of the white lower middle class might have been the worst."

Carey is probably right. The middle class, that cadre of professionals, semi-professionals and businessmen who are the backbone of any living city, are the children of the white working class. If they are brought up believing that the city government does not care whether they live or die (or how they live or die), they will not stay here very long as adults. They will go to college, graduate, marry, get jobs and depart. Right now, thousands of them are leaving New York, because New York doesn't *work* for them. The public schools, when they are open, are desperate; the private schools cost too much (and if they can afford private school, they realize that their taxes are paying for the public schools whose poor quality prevent them from using them). The streets are filthy, the air is polluted, the parks are dangerous, prices are too high. They end up in California, or Rahway, or Islip.

Patriotism is very important to the working-class white man. Most of the time he is the son of an immigrant, and most immigrants sincerely believe that the Pledge of Allegiance, "The Star-Spangled Banner," the American Flag are symbols of what it means to be Americans. They might not have become rich in America, but most of the time they were much better off than they were in the old country. On "I Am an American" Day they march in parades with a kind of religious fervor that can look absurd to the outsider (imagine marching through Copenhagen on "I Am a Dane" Day), but that can also be oddly touching. Walk through any working-class white neighborhood and you will see dozens of veterans' clubs, named after neighborhood men who were killed in World War Two or Korea. There are not really orgies of jingoism going on inside; most of the time the veterans' clubs serve as places in which to drink on Sunday morning before the bars open at 1 P.M., or as places in which to hold baptisms and wedding receptions. But they are places where an odd sort of know-nothingism is fostered. The war in Vietnam was almost never questioned until last year. It was an American war, with Americans dying in action, and it could not be questioned.

The reasons for this simplistic view of the world are complicated. But one reason is that the working-class white man fights in every American war. Because of poor educations, large numbers of blacks are rejected by the draft because they can't pass the mental examinations; the high numbers of black casualties are due to the disproportionate number of black career NCOs and the large number of blacks who go into airborne units because of higher pay. The working-class white man (and his brothers, sons and cousins) only get deferments if they are crippled; their educations, usually in parochial schools, are good enough to pass Army requirements, but not good enough to get them into the city college system (which, being free, is the only kind of college they could afford). It is the children of the rich and the middle class who get all those college deferments.

While he is in the service, the working-class white hates it; he bitches about the food, the brass, the living conditions; he tries to come back to New York at every opportunity, even if it means two fourteen-hour car rides on a weekend. But after he is out, and especially if he has seen combat, a romantic glaze covers the experience. He is a veteran, he is a man, he can drink with the men at the corner saloon. And as he goes into his thirties and forties, he resents those who don't serve, or bitch about the service the way he used to bitch. He becomes quarrelsome. When he gets drunk, he tells you about Saipan. And he sees any form of antiwar protest as a denial of his own young manhood, and a form of spitting on the graves of the people he served with who died in his war.

The past lives on. When I visit my old neighborhood, we still talk about things we did when we were eighteen, fights we had, and who was "good with his hands" in the main events at the Caton Inn, and how great it was eating sandwiches from Mary's down near Oceantide in Coney Island. Or we talk about the Zale-Graziano fights, or what a great team the Dodgers were when Duke Snyder played center field and Roy Campanella was the catcher, and what a shame it was that Rex Barney never learned how to control the fast ball. Nostalgia was always a curse: I remember one night when I was seventeen, drinking beer from cardboard containers on a bench at the side of Prospect Park, and one of my friends said that it was a shame we were getting old, that there would never be another summer like the one we had the year before, when we were sixteen. It was absurd, of course, and yet it was true; the summer we were seventeen, guys we knew were already dying on the frozen ridges of Korea.

A LARGE REASON for the growing alienation of the white working class is their belief that they are not respected. It is an important thing for the son of an immigrant to be respected. When he is young, physical prowess is usually the most important thing; the guy who can fight or hit a ball or run with a football has more initial respect than the guy who gets good marks in school. But later, the man wants to be respected as a good provider, a reasonably good husband, a good drinker, a good credit risk (the worse thing you can do in a working-class saloon is borrow $20 and forget about it, or stiff the guy you borrowed it from).

It is no accident that the two New York City politicians who most represent the discontent of the white working class are Brooklyn Assemblyman Vito Battista and Councilman Matty Troy of Queens. Both are usually covered in the press as if they were refugees from a freak show (I've been guilty of this sneering, patronizing attitude towards Battista and Troy myself at times). Battista claims to be the spokesman for the small home owner and many small home owners believe in him; but a lot of the people who are listening to him now see him as the spokesman for the small home owner they would like to be. "I like that Battista," a guy told me a couple of weeks ago. "He talks our language. That Lindsay sounds like a college professor." Troy speaks for the man who can't get his streets cleaned, who has to take a train and a bus to get to his home, who is being taxed into suburban exile; he is also very big on patriotism, but he shocked his old auditors at the Democratic convention in Chicago last year when he supported the minority peace plank on Vietnam.

There is one further problem involved here. That is the failure of the literary/intellectual world to fully recognize the existence of the white working class, except to abhor them. With the exception of James T. Farrell, no major American novelist has dealt with the working-class white man, except in war novels. Our novelists write about bullfighters, migrant workers, screenwriters, psychiatrists, failing novelists, homosexuals, advertising men, gangsters, actors, politicians, drifters, hippies, spies and millionaires; I have yet to see a work of the imagination deal with the life of a wirelather, a carpenter, a subway conductor, an ironworker or a derrick operator. There hasn't even been much inquiry by the sociologists; *Beyond the Melting Pot,* by Nathan Glazer and Pat Moynihan, is the most useful book, but we have yet to see an Oscar Lewis–style book called, say, *The Children of Flaherty.* I suppose there are reasons for this neglect, caused by a century of intellectual sneering at bourgeois values, etc. But the result has been the inability of many intellectuals to imagine themselves in the plight of the American white working man. They don't understand his virtues (loyalty, endurance, courage, among others) and see him only through his faults (narrowness, bigotry, the worship of machismo, among others). The result is the stereotype. Black writers have finally begun to reveal what it means to be black in this country; I suppose it will take a working-class novelist to do the same for his people. It is certainly a rich, complex and unworked mine.

But for the moment, it is imperative for New York politicians to begin to deal with the growing alienation and paranoia of the working-class white man. I really don't think they can wait much longer, because the present situation is working its way to the point of no return. The working-class white man feels trapped and, even worse, in a society that purports to be democratic, ignored. The tax burden is crushing him, and the quality of his life does not seem to justify his exertions. He cannot leave New York City because he can't afford it, and he is beginning to look for someone to blame. That someone is almost certainly going to be the black man.

This does not have to be the situation, of course. If the government were more responsive to the working-class white man, if the distribution of benefits were spread more widely, if the government's presence were felt more strongly in ways that benefit white communities, there would be a chance to turn this situation around. The working-class white man does not care if a black man gets a job in his union, as long as it does not mean the loss of his own job, or the small privileges and sense of self-respect that go with it. I mean it; I know these people, and know that they largely would not care what happens in the city, if what happens at least has the virtue of fairness. For now, they see a terrible unfairness in their lives, and an increasing lack of personal control over what happens to them. And the result is growing talk of revolt.

The revolt involves the use of guns. In East Flatbush, and Corona, and all those other places where the white working class lives, people are forming gun clubs and self-defense leagues and talking about what they will do if real race rioting breaks out. It is a tragic situation, because the poor blacks and the working-class whites should be natural allies. Instead, the black man has become the symbol of all the working-class white man's resentments.

"I never had a gun in my life before," a thirty-four-year-old Queens bartender named James Giuliano told me a couple of weeks ago. "But I got me a shotgun, license and all. I hate to have the thing in the house, be-cause of the kids. But the way things are goin' I might have to use it on someone. I really might. It's comin' to that. Believe me, it's comin' to that."

The working-class white man is actually in revolt against taxes, joyless work, the double standards and short memories of professional politi-cians, hypocrisy, and what he considers the debasement of the American dream. But George Wallace received ten million votes last year, not all of them from rednecked racists. That should have been a warning, strong and clear. If the stereotyped black man is becoming the working-class white man's enemy, the eventual enemy might be the democratic process itself. Any politician who leaves that white man out of the political equa-tion, does so at very large risk. The next round of race riots might not be between people and property, but between people and people. And that could be the end of us.

UP WITH GRUPS

ADAM STERNBERGH

APRIL 3, 2006

Stereotypically, adulthood was something people entered after college, or maybe the military, with new suits and shined shoes and a big list of responsibilities that necessitated leaving juvenile pop-cultural enthusiasms behind. But, culturally, the line between youth and adulthood has grown increasingly blurry. It's not only that every ten-year-old has an encyclopedic knowledge of the Beatles. Especially in New York, a large cohort of people in their thirties and forties are indistinguishable, save for a wrinkle here and there, from people a decade or two younger. Adam Sternbergh borrowed the name for this new tribe, with their shoulder bags and iPods, from a famous Star Trek *episode. "The story kind of metastasized from a limited observation to become a story about the reinvention of adulthood," he says. Sternbergh is an editor-at-large at* New York.

*L*ET'S START WITH A QUESTION. A few questions, actually: When did it become normal for your average thirty-five-year-old New Yorker to (a) walk around with an iPod plugged into his ears at all times, listening to the latest from Bloc Party; (b) regularly buy his clothes at Urban Outfitters; (c) take her toddler to a Mommy's Happy Hour at a Brooklyn bar; (d) stay out till 4 A.M. because he just can't miss the latest New Pornographers show, because who knows when Neko Case will decide to stop touring with them, and *everyone knows she's the heart of the band;* (e) spend $250 on a pair of jeans that are artfully shredded to look like they just fell through a wheat thresher and are designed, eventually, to artfully fall totally apart; (f) decide that Sufjan Stevens is the perfect music to play for her two-year-old, because, let's face it, two-year-olds have lousy taste in music, and *we will not listen to the Wiggles in this house;* (g) wear sneakers as a fashion statement; (h) wear the same vintage New Balance sneakers that he wore on his first day of school in the seventh grade as a fashion statement; (i) wear said sneakers to the office; (j) quit the office job because—you know what?—screw the office and screw jockeying for that *promotion* to VP, because isn't promotion just another word for "slavery"?; (k) and besides, now that she's a freelancer, working on her own projects, on her own terms, it's that much easier to kick off in the middle of the week for a quick snowboarding trip to Sugarbush, because she's got to have some balance, right? And she can write it off, too, because who knows? She might bump into Spike Jonze on the slopes; (l) wear a Misfits T-shirt; (m) make his two-year-old wear a Misfits T-shirt; (n) never shave; (o) take pride in never shaving; (p) take pride in never shaving while spending $200 on a bedhead haircut and $600 on a messenger bag, because, seriously, only his grandfather or some frat-boy Wall Street flunky still carries a briefcase; or (q) all of the above?

This is an obituary for the generation gap. It is a story about forty-year-old men and women who look, talk, act, and dress like people who are twenty-two years old. It's about the hedge-fund guy in Park Slope with the chunky square glasses, brown rock T-shirt, slight paunch, expensive jeans, Puma sneakers, and shoulder-slung messenger bag, with two kids squirming over his lap like itchy chimps at the Tea Lounge on Sunday morning. It's about the mom in the low-slung Sevens and ankle boots and vaguely Berlin-art-scene blouse with the $800 stroller and the TV-screen-size Olsen-twins sunglasses perched on her head walking through Bryant Park listening to Death Cab for Cutie on her Nano.

And because this phenomenon wears itself so clearly as the convergence of downtown cool and easy, abundant money, it is also, of course, about *stuff*—though that's not all it's about. It's more interesting as evidence of the slow erosion of the long-held idea that in some fundamental way, you cross through a portal when you become an adult, a portal inscribed with the biblical imperative "When I was a child, I spake as a child, I understood as a child, I thought as a child: But when I became a man, I put away childish things." This cohort is not interested in putting away childish things. They are a generation or two of affluent, urban adults who are now happily sailing through their thirties and forties, and even *fifties*, clad in beat-up sneakers and cashmere hoodies, content that they can enjoy all the good parts of being a grown-up (a real paycheck, a family, the warm touch of cashmere) with none of the bad parts (Dockers, management seminars, indentured servitude at the local Gymboree). It's about a brave new world whose citizens are radically rethinking what it means to be a grown-up and whether being a grown-up still requires, you know, actually growing up.

And it's been a long time coming. It showed up in the early eighties as "the Peter Pan Syndrome," then mutated to the *yuppie*, which, let's face it, has had a pretty good run. Later, it took the form that David Brooks called "bourgeois bohemians," or bobos (as in *Bobos in Paradise*). Over in England, they're now calling them *yindies* (that's yuppie plus indie), and here, the term *yupster* (you can figure that out) has been gaining some traction of late. And as this movement evolves, something pivotal is happening. This cascade of pioneering immaturity is no longer a case of a generation's being stuck in its own youth. This generation is now, if you happen to be under twenty-five, more interested in being stuck in *your* youth.

This article being what it is, I wanted to come up with my own term to describe them. But what? Dadsters? Sceniors? Dorian Graybeards? Over the course of my investigation, I started calling them *Grups*. It's not the most elegant term, but it passes the field test of real-world utility. *(Here a Grup, there a Grup, everywhere a Grup-Grup.)* "Grups" is a nerdy reference to an old *Star Trek* episode in which Kirk and crew land on a planet run entirely by kids, who call grown-ups "grups." All the adults have been killed off by a terrible virus, which also slows the natural aging process, so the kids are trapped in a state of extended prepubescence. They will never grow up. And they are running the show.

Oh, and there's one more thing I learned, in answer to my opening questions: If being a Grup means being thirty-five, and having a job, and using a messenger bag instead of a briefcase, and staying out too late too often, and owning more pairs of sneakers (eleven) than suits (one), and downloading a Hot Hot Heat song from iTunes because it was on a playlist titled "Saturday Errands," and generally being uneasy and slightly confused about just what it means to be an adult in these modern times—in short, if it means living your life in fundamentally the same way that you did when you were, say, twenty-two—then, let's face it, I'm a Grup. In fact, take a minute and look up from these pages—if you're in public, you'll see them everywhere. If you're in front of a mirror, you might see one there too.

1. The Grup Music, or the Brand-new Sound of Twenty Years Ago

Once upon a time, pop culture, and in particular pop music, followed a certain reliable pattern: People listened to bands, like the Doobie Brothers or Cream or Steely Dan, that their Frank Sinatra–loving parents absolutely despised. Then these people had kids, and their kids became teens, and they started listening to bands, like the Clash or Elvis Costello or Joy Division, that their Cream-loving parents absolutely despised. And, lo, the Lord looked down and saw that it was good, and on the eighth day, He created the generation gap.

And then these Clash-listening kids grew up and had kids of their own, and the next generation of kids started listening to music, like Franz Ferdinand and Interpol and Bloc Party, that you might assume their parents would absolutely despise. Except it doesn't really work that way anymore. In part, because how can their parents hate Interpol when they sound *exactly like Joy Division*? And in part, because how can their parents hate Bloc Party when their parents just downloaded Bloc Party and think *it's awesome and totally better than the Bravery*!

This, of course, is a seismic shift in intergenerational relationships. It means there is no fundamental generation gap anymore. This is unprecedented in human history. And it's kind of weird.

Take the case of Andy Chase and Dominique Durand, a married couple, both well into their thirties and now with kids of their own, who play in a successful rock band called Ivy. "Most of our fans are in their twenties or even teenagers," says Chase. "And that keeps you young. Because you're friends with people who are much younger than you. Our keyboard player is twenty-one years old. And we dress the same—"

"Our interests are the same," adds Durand. "The passion is the same. There's a real connection."

Andy interjects, "Well, let's talk to the keyboard player and see if he says the same thing."

Or take Michael Rauch, the creator of the recently canceled CBS show *Love Monkey*, which chronicled the life of a late-thirties single A&R guy in New York who frets openly about being a "suit" while working at the plucky indie label he joined after leaving his evil corporate record company, because for him, it was *all about the music*. Isn't a guy like that—late thirties, still single, still bar-hopping, still chasing the latest hot rock band, his whole life, in fact, still defined by the word *still*—kind of, I don't know, pathetic? "If this show existed ten years ago, the answer would be yes," says Rauch. "But now, absolutely not. Now it's less the exception than the rule. Especially in New York." Rauch himself is thirty-eight. "I spoke to an undergrad class at NYU recently. And it was terrifying how much we had in common. I'm looking at these kids who look about twelve, and we're all going to the same movies and watching the same TV shows and listening to the same music. I don't know if it's scarier for them or scarier for me."

Think of it this way: For Gen X, just fifteen years ago, the big complaint was that boomers, with their lingering sixties-era musical attachments and smug sense of cultural centrality, refused to pass the torch and get the hell out of the way. In a 1997 sociology essay titled "Generation X: Who Are They? What Do They Want?" one twentysomething student lamented, "We still are bombarded with 'Classic Rock' and moldy oldies. Bands like the Eagles, Rolling Stones, and Aerosmith need to back off so we can define our own music, lifestyle." It's ironic, then, that those self-same slackers—the twentysomethings of the early nineties (and, hey, I was right there, too: Rock on, Screaming Trees)—aren't standing in the way of the next generation. Rather, they're joining right in at the front of the crowd at the sold-out Decemberists show. *Hey, kids, you can define your own music, lifestyle—that's our music and lifestyle, too!*

"All of the really good music right now has absolutely precise parallels to the best music of the eighties, from Franz Ferdinand to Interpol to Death Cab—anything you can name," says Michael Hirschorn, the forty-two-year-old executive vice-president of original programming and production at VH1. "Plus, the twenty-year-olds are all listening to the Cure and New Order anyway. It's created a kind of mass confusion. I was at the Coachella festival last year, and the groups people were most stoked about were Gang of Four and New Order." No wonder Grups like today's indie music: It sounds exactly like the indie music of their youth. Which, as it happens, is what kids today like, too, which is why today's new music all sounds like it's twenty years old. And thus the culture grinds to a halt, in a screech of guitar feedback.

As a result, says Hirschorn, "some of the older parents I know who have teenagers claim that there's no generation gap anymore. They say they get along perfectly with their kids. They listen to the same music. To me, that seems somewhat laughable. But I do remember when I was young, trying to explain the Beatles to my dad, and he didn't even know who they were. I don't think that's possible today."

And it's not just music that's collapsed on itself in this way. During Hirschorn's tenure at VH1, the channel was cunningly transformed from the frumpy, easy-listening older sibling of MTV to a retro-culture-celebrating mother ship for Grups. Trademark shows such as *I Love the 80s* feature a parade of thirtysomething comedians making funny comments about music and fashions and TV shows that were popular back when they were teens. The canny success of this concept rests on the fact that it appeals both to the thirtysomethings who lived through Mr. T and Kajagoogoo the first time around and twentysomethings who are fascinated with semi-ironically recycling cultural trends. In a prescient essay in 1994 titled "The Nostalgia Gap," Tom Vanderbilt jokingly predicted that thanks to an ever-quickening cultural churn, we'd soon see manufactured nostalgia for trends of two weeks ago. He was off by a week. VH1's *Best Week Ever* consists of comedians looking back with fond, ironic eyes on the events of the last seven days.

"The embarrassing thing for me," says Hirschorn, "is seeing the actual culture of my youth recycled as a kind of ironic hipster kitsch. What's my access point into that? If I still have the clothes from the first time around, does that mean I get to wear them again?" In other words, if you're thirty-five and wearing the same Converse All-Stars to work that you wore to junior high, are you an old guy sadly aping the Strokes? Or are the young guys simply copying you? Wait, how old are the Strokes, anyway?

2. *The Grup Look, or I Swear These Jeans Were Here a Minute Ago*

My father did not wear T-shirts. He did not own sneakers. He may have had one pair of jeans, crisp and stiff and store-bought blue, to wear on the weekends when we'd do things like go apple-picking. At all other times, he wore suits.

So I wonder what he would make of the offices of Rogan, a very hot, very hip fashion label that operates out of the third floor of a building just off Broadway, north of Canal. The office is cluttered with large cardboard boxes and long tables, where twentysomething staffers fulfill orders by hand, among rolling racks of carefully crafted vintage-style shirts and down ski vests. Paper patterns for future clothes hang from a bar overhead like thought bubbles suspended in midair.

Rogan is run by Rogan Gregory, a thirty-three-year-old designer who, when I meet him, is wearing a faded pink vintage surf-shop T-shirt, dirty white Vans slip-ons with seagull silhouettes, and a pair of his famous jeans. Famous, at least, within certain circles: namely, denim hounds who will pay $450 for a pair of jeans that are so distressed—so tattered, so frayed, so worked over and beaten down—that they will likely fall apart within two years.

Rogan is tall and slim, with a trim beard and jaw-length hair that's tucked back behind one ear. He specializes in clothes that are handcrafted to look like you exhumed them from a rack at the back of a dusty vintage store when, in fact, you bought them at Barneys for several hundred dollars each. He understands that this market did not always exist. "I've been wearing the same thing my entire life," he says. "But ten years ago, people gave me a hard time. If I was checking into a hotel, they wouldn't believe that I was actually staying there. Now it's accepted that just because that dude doesn't look like some fancy-pants—well, you never know."

Rogan sees this as a good thing, and not just for the obvious business reasons. It used to be, he explains, that each stage of life had its uniform, from kid to teenager to fancy-pants. Now, though, that fashion progression has flattened out, and everyone just wears the uniform of his choice. "It's absolutely not a hierarchical thing," he says. "It's a look thing. They're all spending about the same amount of money on their wardrobes. It's just about how you like to be perceived."

A number of trends have nudged us in this direction, from the increasingly casual dress codes at work to the persistent marketing of counterculture "rebellion" as an easily attainable, catchall symbol for cool. During the dot-com boom, businesses not only allowed people to come to work in clothes they might usually wear to clean out the attic but encouraged this as a celebration of youthful vivacity and an upheaval of the fusty corporate order. Suits were thought to be the provenance of, well, suits. The dot-com bubble burst, but the aesthetic remained, as part of the ongoing rock star–ification of America. Three-day stubble and shredded jeans are the now-familiar symbols of the most desirable kind of affluence and freedom. So why would anyone dress up anymore? A suit says, *My mother made me wear this to go to a bar mitzvah.* The Grup outfit says, *I'm so cool, and so damned good at what I do, I can wear whatever the hell I want. At least when I go out to brunch.*

So now, for many people—many grown-up people—the uniform of choice is rock tees and sneakers and artfully destroyed denim. Of course, when you're forty, with a regular paycheck, yet still want to resemble a rock star who resembles a garage mechanic, well, what's a guy to do? Status symbols still have their uses, especially in the world of clothes. And this is where the $200 ripped jeans come in. Or $450. Or $600. You want the tattered jeans, but you also want the world to know, *I can afford the very best in tattered jeans.*

"One thing happened that I thought was funny," says Rogan. "I made a run of a hundred jeans, and I made them as perfectly as I could. Which for me means essentially destroying the fabric, to the point where if you wear them for a month, they'll disintegrate. And I literally sold them out in a week. And they'll completely disintegrate. You wear them for a couple of weeks and go out one night and there'll be a giant tear. I mean, it's embarrassing. I was surprised that people would pay that amount of money for something that literally falls apart."

At one point, I spoke to a thirty-nine-year-old musician who had lived briefly in Park Slope and then fled, largely because of the prevalence of exactly the kind of person who would buy jeans designed to fall apart in a month. This musician is old school in his fashion tastes—which is to say, one day he came to a point where he pulled that old concert T-shirt from his dresser and thought, *Yeah, I just can't pull this off anymore.* (For me, this moment came with a thrift-store T-shirt with QUALITY PLASTIC SUPPLIES decaled across the chest.) These days, though, especially in New York, there just aren't many people saying *I just can't pull this off anymore.*

"If really hard-pressed, I would admit that I actually own a Clash T-shirt that I got from that last Clash tour," the musician told me. "But I don't wear it! And I'm certainly not going to wear it under an Armani black blazer. I even remember meeting this guy who was around my age, who was wearing an expensive blazer, and on the lapel was a *London Calling* button. Who the fuck wears that? That's what I wore when I was eighteen in art school! And you're the same age as me? And you're wearing it again?" He pauses, then adds, "And you know what? Giving your kid a mohawk is fucked up, too."

3. The Grup Children, or Daddy, Please Turn That Music Down

Here's the bad news about kids: They're not cool. Especially little kids. Like, two-year-olds? Forget it. Left to their own devices, they don't dress well, they have no sense of style, and frankly, their musical taste sucks.

Here's the good news about kids: They're defenseless. So if you want to put a Ramones T-shirt on your two-year-old, you don't need his permission. All you need is for someone to have the great idea to make a two-year-old-size Ramones T-shirt. (And trust me—someone's had that idea.) And if you want to play the Strokes for your four-year-old son, what's he going to do? I'll tell you what—*he's going to learn to love the Strokes.*

"My son seems to like the Hives a lot," says Neal Pollack, the author of the forthcoming memoir *Alternadad: The True Story of One Family's*

Struggle to Raise a Cool Kid in America, of his three-year-old son, Elijah, and the raucous Swedish fivesome the Hives. "I mean, he doesn't know who they are. He calls it 'thunder music' when I put it on. He gets very excited by that. That makes me sort of proud."

See, Grups aren't afraid of parenting. Grups don't avoid having kids. Grups love kids. In part, though, this is because Grups find kids to be perfect little Mr. Potato Head versions of themselves. Of course, there's more to Grup parenting than simply molding your kid's tastes. You must be vigilant that you don't grow up and become uncool yourself. "I recognize that changes and sacrifices are necessary. I do occasionally wake up before nine these days," says Pollack of parenthood. "But I didn't want to lose touch with the world's cultural progress. I didn't want to freeze myself in time." So instead of playdates, Pollack invites other cool dads and their kids over for playing (kids), beers (dads), and sampling new CDs (everyone). Or he packs up his toddler for the Austin City Limits Music Festival. Though that plan didn't work so well. "It was really hot and crowded," he says. "And the music sucked." His son apparently concurred.

Pollack's philosophy, when you hear him talk about it, makes a lot of sense, at least at first. "Mainstream American adulthood is so narrowly defined, it's only natural that people who have time and leisure to think about it are going to rebel against it." *Yes, of course, why not?* "We want to be good parents. We want to love our kid and raise our kid up properly, with decent values." *Right on!* "But we don't want our lives to become nothing but Mommy & Me classes." *Who would? Fuck Mommy & Me!*

"You have to have a little bit of Dora the Explorer in your life," he says. "But you can do what you can to mute its influence." *Okay.* "And there's no shame, when your kid's watching a show, and you don't like it, in telling him it sucks." *Yeah! There's no—wait. What?* "If you start telling him it sucks, maybe he might develop an aesthetic." *Sorry, son. No more* Thomas the Tank Engine *for you.* Thomas *sucks. Stop crying. Daddy's helping you develop an aesthetic. Now Daddy's going to go put on some thunder music.*

But isn't there something unsavory in the idea of your kid as a kind of *tabula rasa* for you to overwrite with your tastes? Less a child than a malleable Mini-Me?

"It's hard to say right now, because most of these kids are between the age of zero and five," says Pollack. "So they're still . . . I don't want to say accessories, but they're still moldable. You can still sort of play with them." Although, if you're planning to take this parental approach, you'd better make damn sure you've got good taste. "I find myself arguing with dads about the music their kids like," he says. "One guy was telling me his son was really into Wilco. And I was telling him that's lame. Because Wilco is so over."

I don't mean to be so hard on Pollack, who does seem genuinely interested in exploring a new kind of parenting—a kind that doesn't involve totally losing any sense of who you were ten minutes before your baby was born. In fact, I got a much saner version of more or less the same philosophy from Adam Levite and Francine Hermelin, a couple in their thirties (he's 38, she's 36) with three (yes, three) kids: Asa, 6; Dora, 3; and Ester, 0.5. Levite directs music videos for artists like Beck and Interpol, and Hermelin spends most of her time with the kids while also organizing events like Downtown for Democracy's mock election, in which eight-year-olds ran for president. Levite wears cool little geometric glasses and Hermelin wears slightly thinner cool little geometric glasses. The family lives in a large white envy-inducing loft apartment in Tribeca that looks like a design-magazine photo shoot. As you enter, you'll find Levite's guitar collection propped against the wall, right next to which you'll find similar, miniature versions of the same guitars for his son, Asa. "From a very young age, we've always decided to try not to, you know, vanilla the kids in the things that we present to them," says Levite. A-ha! Here we go— *thunder music.* "We've been listening to the Beatles since the moment they were born. They're classic pop songs, but not full of anger and angst. And we still listen to some kids' music. Music for Aardvarks is really great."

"It's really important for us to be whole people, and not feel like our kids have . . . look, we love our kids," says Hermelin. "The point isn't to raise cool kids. We want passionate kids. And I think that by us doing the things that we love to do, that models that passion for our kids."

Later, when I talk to Andy Chase, the dad–slash–rock star, he says almost the exact same thing. "How great for a child to see their parents loving what they're doing? It's a delicate balance to strike, but when you maintain that balance, its a great thing to teach your children—that they can look forward to doing something they love doing."

"Of course, there have to be some priorities," says Levite. "Even if you come home and you just bought a great new CD, and you really want to listen to it with your kids, sometimes it's their bedtime. You just learn. You can't always play guitar with them." I wonder, though, what will happen when Asa becomes a teenager. Will he still want to jam with Dad on matching guitars? Or will he find his own way to grow up? The last time teenagers weren't expected to rebel, it was because they were heading off to work in the coal mines at age thirteen. Can we really expect to be cool parents and also raise cool kids? Is this youth big enough for the both of us?

Or perhaps we can look forward—at least if *Family Ties* can be trusted—to a new generation of buttoned-down, high-strung Alex P. Keaton–type conservative teenagers. This is something the Grups have considered. When I asked Hermelin her worst fear, she laughed and said, "Our kids are going to become Republicans."

In college, I remember a friend of mine playing Public Enemy at high volume at his mother's house, at which point she sputtered into paroxysms of clichéd parental dismay, saying, quite unironically, "Turn that off! It's nothing but noise!" Later, we tried to imagine what kind of high-decibel air-raid-siren music our teens might one day listen to, causing us to react the same way. It's a concept that Pollack, for one, seems literally incapable of processing. "I don't know if that's going to happen with this generation," he says. Besides, he explains, the alternadad's worst nightmare isn't that his kid will grow up to be something he doesn't want him to be. "The worst nightmare for a quote-unquote alternadad," he says, "is that he'll grow up to be something he doesn't want to be."

We might consider, then, the case of Chad Ruble. At age thirty-two, with a wife who was four months pregnant with their first child, Ruble had a bright idea—he decided to take up skateboarding. "I had never noticed that there's a half-pipe at Chelsea Piers," he said. "I thought, *Too bad I'm too old to do that.* Then I thought, *I'm not too old!*" So he went to Paragon Sports in Union Square to buy some skateboarding gear (avoiding the hard-core East Village skate shops, because he found them too intimidating). "I was heartened because there was another older guy there getting a whole setup, too. I was like, *Oh, cool. I'm not the only one*," he said. "Turns out he was getting it for his kid."

Ruble need not have worried, though—once he hit the Chelsea Piers half-pipe, there were lots of thirtysomething guys skateboarding there, along with the usual kids. So he mounted his board and set out on the pipe. He hadn't skateboarded since he was twelve, but it turns out he still remembered most of the moves. Until his fourth try that is, when he wiped out and dislocated his shoulder. "But I was having the time of my life," he said. "Those four times were really fun."

His tale conjures an uneasy vision of an all-too-possible future: of a young boy, maybe twelve, in a tiny suit, standing in a hospital room where his dad lies in traction after a gnarly kickflip-and-nosegrind combination gone horribly wrong. The boy comforts his father, perhaps fluffs his pillow, perhaps delivers to him a freshly laundered Cramps T-shirt brought from home. Then he replaces the earbuds of an iPod that's playing Burl Ives, straightens his bow tie, and heads out to grab the bus home.

4. The Grup Career, or Take This Job and Allow Me to Do It From Home, With Occasional Snowboarding Trips

Matt Peccini is a tall, slim, thirty-four-year-old guy with a shaved head and a dry sense of humor. He becomes immediately more interesting to me when he reveals that he once played Boo-Boo, Yogi Bear's sidekick, in an episode of *Harvey Birdman, Attorney at Law*. He earned that cameo in the Cartoon Network's cult hit during his successful career in television, first at TNT—"working my way through titles and responsibility levels"—and then as a creative director at the AMC channel in New York. "It was a big bump in pay and a big bump in responsibility and in title. I had a staff. On paper, it was a great job," he says. So after two and a half years, he did what any self-respecting Grup would do—he quit.

This is where the Grup diverges from the bobo, the yuppie, even the yupster. The Grup does not want a corner office. The Grup does not yearn for a fancy title. The Grup does not want—oh, please, do not ask the Grup to manage—a *staff.* "I just wanted to make fun stuff that went on TV," says

Peccini. "Then all of a sudden I'm doing performance appraisals and going to management seminars."

A human-resources executive told me recently that there's a golden rule of HR: To motivate a baby boomer, offer him a bonus. To motivate a Generation-Xer, offer him a day off. The Grup, I think, would go for the day off, too. If the boomer's icon of success was an empire-building maverick magnate like Ted Turner, the Grup's model would be Spike Jonze, the thirty-six-year-old *Jackass*-producing, skateboarding, awesome-indie-movie-directing free agent. Remember, the Grup of today is the slacker from 1990 who, fresh out of college, ran smack into the recession and maybe fiddled around with a riot-grrl band, then got a job at twenty-five for a Web-development company where she wore jeans to work and played Ping-Pong and stayed late and covered her desk in rare Japanese action figures. Now that woman is thirty-five, a VP at a viral-marketing firm, still dressing down because *everyone knows that the youth market is where it's at,* yet is scared to death she's going to ossify into the same kind of corporate stooge she swore she'd never become. For a Grup, success isn't about how many employees you have but how much freedom you have to walk, or boogie-board, away.

So now Peccini works as a freelancer, making TV promos and animated shorts that he sells back to the Cartoon Network. It's been tough getting set up—"I'd gotten used to a certain lifestyle," he says—and it hasn't been all unfettered freedom. He's currently alternating between animation projects and industrial films, like one about sustainability to be played for Wal-Mart employees. But for him, quitting was the best career move. As it was, too, for Nicholas Nathanson, who left his job as an Internet equity research associate at a New York investment bank in 1999—just when that field promised unlimited advancement and riches—at age twenty-nine to start an online surfwear store called Swell. You see, it's not that Grups don't want to work; they just don't want to work for you. In a recent *Money* magazine poll about bosses, 54 percent of the respondents said they wouldn't want their boss's job no matter how much money you paid them. *Fifty-four percent.*

"If I had spent the last six years working at that job and progressed, I would have made a lot of money," Nathanson told me from San Juan

Capistrano, California, where his surfwear company is based. "But honestly, there have been very few days in the past six years where I've gotten in my car to go to work and thought, *Fuck, I'm going to work.* When I was at the investment bank, that was happening 50 percent of the days. And now I can go snowboarding at Mammoth in the middle of the week if there's a good storm, rather than worrying about being at work at six in the morning. And there's another upside as well: I have a total and complete *passion* for this business."

There's that tricky word again: passion. What's with the Grups and passion? It's all anyone wants to talk about. Passionate parents, passionate workers, passionate listeners to the new album by Wolf Parade. Even Rogan lights up when he talks about touring Japanese textile factories to find the perfect denim for his jeans. And I start to realize: Under the skin of the iPods and the $400 ripped jeans, this is the spine of the Grup ethos: passion, and the fear of losing it.

Which brings me back to my father: the one who wore suits, not jeans; the one who, when he was my age, already had four kids; the one who logged a lifetime at exactly the kind of middle-management jobs that no one wakes up excited about going to in the morning, and who then found himself sandbagged by the late-eighties recession, laid off in what must have felt like the worst kind of double whammy. All the adult trade-offs he'd made turned out to be a brutal bait-and-switch. Is it any wonder that the Grups have looked at that brand of adulthood and said, "No thanks, you can keep your carrot and your stick." Especially once we saw just how easily that stick can be turned around to whap your ass as you're ushered out the door, suit and all. Just how easily a bona fide, by-the-book adult can be made to wonder where it all went wrong, and why you ever bothered to grow up in the first place.

5. *The Happy Ending*

And this, improbably, is the happy ending to our story. (And, I admit, I'd hoped for a happy ending; for all the bedhead haircuts and Hives-peddling parents, I wanted this to end well.) Being a Grup isn't, as it turns out, all about holding on to some misguided, well-marketed idea of youth—or, at least, isn't just about that. It's also about rejecting a hand-me-down model of adulthood that asks, or even necessitates, that you let go of everything you ever felt passionate about. It's about reimagining adulthood as a period defined by promise, rather than compromise. And who can't relate to that?

Of course, that's not a real ending—even the Grups don't know how this will end. They know they're making up adulthood as they go. "My dad's worked at the same place he's worked for thirty years," says Peccini. "But when I left my job, he said to me, 'If I was your age—and if I hadn't had three kids and a mortgage—I would have done the same thing.' " When I ask Peccini what he sees himself doing in ten years, or at his dad's age, he gives the typical Grup answer. "That's a great question," he says. "I don't know. But I like my life."

Even Andy and Dominique, the startlingly cool rock-star parents, aren't quite sure where this is headed. "All I know is that the end point you give yourself keeps shifting by five years," says Andy. "When we were in our twenties, we were like, 'When we get in our mid-thirties, we'll have to call it quits, because it's too pathetic after that.' Then we got to our mid-thirties, and the timetable became the early forties. I suppose when we get there, we'll say, 'Once we hit fifty . . . ' " Then he says, with more resolve, "On our fiftieth birthday, it will be official. No more touring."

HOW NOT TO BE HUMILIATED
IN SNOB RESTAURANTS

GAEL GREENE

APRIL 13, 1970

In 1968, when New York *began reviewing restaurants, almost all of the city's best menus were in French. "There were no American chefs," says* New York*'s first food critic, Gael Greene. And restaurants were forbidding places, with their fearsome, crisply attired maître d's looking down their noses at anyone they perceived as not up to snuff. Greene's mission was, in bourgeois terms, a revolutionary one—she wanted to help New York's ordinary people storm the gates of the city's most exclusive bastions. In this piece, Greene mapped out the lay of the land of a few of New York's exclusive restaurants, along with strategies by which their defenses could be breached. The food world had rarely encountered such impudence. Greene is still a contributing editor of the magazine, the only writer who has appeared regularly for all of its forty years. Her memoir,* Insatiable: Tales From a Life of Delicious Excess, *was published in 2006.*

I WISH TO INTRODUCE M. Martin Decré. His face is pink. His hair is gray. His feet are flat. His cufflinks, by Cartier. He is the sentinel of La Seine Restaurant . . . a *beau monde* cloister of drop-dead chic. Martin Decré stands between you and a good dinner in a great restaurant.

Martin is a warm, sympathetic, earthy good fellow. But that is the seven-eighths of the Decré iceberg *you* may never see. It is not that Martin is a born fascist. He does not eat ground glass for breakfast. He is simply a highly trained despot. A maître among the town's haughtiest maîtres d'. Let us not hack the tiniest chink in his armor of unshakable arrogance, thus tarnishing La Seine's snob cachet. If it were a snap to seduce Martin, would it be worth the effort? The canons of *haut snobisme* are perfectly clear: there are clients who adorn La Seine and clients who pollute its elegance. It is for Martin to court the former and discourage the latter.

It hurts so nice! The card-carrying Manhattan masochist thrives on a diet of flageolets and flagellation, so often the *spécialité du jour* in the posh Pleiades of restaurants where the snub is often more creative than the cuisine. Nor must one be French to subscribe to the tyranny de gall. The Colony, "21" and Orsini's serve memorable cold shoulder. And for the discriminating masochist, the chill of Miss Pearl on West 48th Street is a snub with its own scrutable ouch.

Perhaps your ego is as neat as a nicely poached egg. Deep down inside you know you're more fun on a hayride than Babe Paley. In a pinch you're more pinchable than the Duchess. You bring money, lots of money, in your Hermès *sac* or your Vuitton duffle. But mere money will not spring you from the bitter frostbite of Siberia, from neglect, glazed ennui, under-age wines, snarled lectures on gastronomic propriety, and other lessons in humility.

If you are a Machiavellian radical like Saul Alinsky, you slam your glass to the floor and bellow insults right back. If you are Uriah Heep, Pariah Emeritus, you practice absolute submission, take a table at 5:30 if there's nothing at 8, make like a meek little kipper in your crowded corner, dutifully order the *plat du jour*, and carry your Gelusil in a discreet flask.

When simple everyday *snobisme* escalates into assault, with intimations of sadism verging on assassination, you may decide to kick the humble-pie habit and abandon the scene. It will be an autocrat's nightmare if tight money, the ides of April and a growing sea of white tablecloths turn the usual chill positively toasty. Meanwhile, if you have only one masochistic bone in your body, stick it out. Decré can learn to love you. Dedicate yourself to "making it" on the *haute* eating scene.

Stardom

    a) You write a best seller . . . get lionized by your publisher . . . get sued by the Kennedys.

   b) You are named co-respondent in a fancy divorce, preferably
      royal.
   c) You are being rushed by Frank Sinatra.
   d) Or Truman Capote.
   e) Your husband's renegade conglomerate swallows a major com-
      munications empire.
   f) Daddy gets elected President.

If instant stardom eludes you, hire a press agent. Call her "my dear
friend." Her name is Marianne (Mimi) Van Rensselaer Strong. She will tell
you, "Really chic people don't go out on Saturday night . . . only the
crumbs go out on Saturday. The chic people go to the country . . . or a
movie. Sunday night has become very chic, very 'in.' " She will help you
plan "drop-dead little dinner parties" at La Seine. "There are only two
restaurants for dinner, my dear," says Mimi, "La Seine and '21.' " She will
keep *Women's Wear* and Suzy panting for news of your labels and your
Longuettes and your lunches with your decorator.

   Does that sound too calculated? Too costly? Then go it alone. Try this
cram course in humility-and-chutzpah. Essentially the snob maître d' is
somewhat human. He respects fidelity, celebrity and wanton extravagance. Be loyal to your chosen restaurant. Open a house account. Spend
lots.

On the Phone

   Your secretary calls for a reservation. Your English secretary, prefer-
ably. Or your wife, cleverly passing herself off as your English secretary.
"This is Mr. Ford's office. Mr. Ford would like a table for two at lunch."
When the cagey maître d' asks for Mr. Ford's initial, cagey wife answers
"E." Roosevelt and Vanderbilt are also good names. As Mimi Strong ob-
serves, "Not every Vanderbilt is a Vanderbilt, you know."

   If you are Miss Nobody lunching with Ava Gardner or Dorothy Schiff
or Happy Rockefeller, say so boldly, or slyly: "By the way Martin, I am
meeting Mrs. Rockefeller. Please watch for her in case I'm a few minutes
late." And you *are* late, to insure getting a Rockefeller table instead of a nobody table. If your family name is Orlovsky, change your first name to

Prince. I have a friend who has vowed to name her next son Count. "Count Kaufman's table, please." If he is stabbed by the *petit pain* boy, he needn't bleed blue—merely profusely, muttering darkly about hemophilia.

For really advanced knavery, it takes a rogue—"preferably Hungarian," says writer-rogue Bela von Block, John Paul Getty's ghost. "This is von Block," Bela announces, demanding a table. Then he asks for a rundown on the house's clarets, or orders champagne to be waiting in a bucket. "I ask for Pol Roger and I accept nothing older than the forties." What if the restaurant has an acceptable Pol Roger? "I doubt if five restaurants in New York have," says von Block. "If they do, you'll be stuck for about $60, but when you play Russian Roulette, you've got to be ready to take an occasional shot in the wallet." Next von Block deploys a messenger with an envelope addressed to himself care of the maître d'. "I steal impressive letterheads and use a wax seal." When he arrives at the restaurant, the headwaiter takes him aside. "We have an instant intimacy."

The Arrival

For sheer class, you may never beat the wispy plaster-cast dowager whose chauffeur carried her into La Caravelle. But sables never hurt. Jonathan Dolger, author of *The Expense Account Diet*, advocates a confident smile. "Definitely have your teeth capped."

Don't rush . . . glide. Greet the maître d' by name. As he teeters off-balance (Who are you? Should he know you?), quickly give your name. "Ford. Table for two." "Of course, Mr. Ford." (He juggles tables mentally. Perhaps you don't belong quite so deep in Siberia.)

"Good" table and "bad" table can be crucial. Ludwig Bemelmans told of a woman who was always given an undesirable table in a certain posh restaurant whenever she dined with her husband. One day she came in with another man and was immediately led to the best table in the house. Divorce inevitably followed.

Just as water seeks its own level, tables find their own status. The most desirable tables are in the heart of tumult and traffic. Not even the iron-willed Henri Soulé could de-status a table once Le Pavillon pets had charted their own perverse social topography. "They would rather dine in the telephone booth than in the dining room," he would complain. True, it's the same *mousse de sole* no matter where you sit, but the service can vary erratically. Of course, the snobbery of status-seekers breeds reverse snobbery. At "21," says Mimi Strong, "the nouveau status-seekers will stay at the bar till they get a seat in the front room . . . they're afraid to sit down anywhere else. The most important people insist on a table upstairs with the nobodies."

Money liquefies some glaciers, but not those of the *Académie* Pavillon.

Money will not melt Robert Meyzen of La Caravelle: "You cannot buy a table—not for $200," Meyzen has said. "If you belong here, you get a table."

The Belonging

Martin Decré likes simplicity. Simple black dresses and simple diamonds. Mme. Henriette of Côte Basque and the cantankerous Fayets of Lafayette have never warmed to ladies in pants. Soulé's disciples are stodgily conservative. La Grenouille is more permissive. There, in the castle of the Seventh Avenue kings, anything goes: see-through jumpsuits, unfettered bosoms, Sioux rain-dance togs. Le Pavillon under Stuart Levin has softened its formidable mien. But after five, dark suits and white shirt are still *de rigueur.* And no turtlenecks at lunch. "Not even for Sammy Davis Jr.," Levin warned. "Of course, if he comes in dashiki I'll have to let him in . . . dashiki is national dress."

The wrong purse and a voluminous suburban bag (unless it's alligator) are dead giveaways, Mimi Strong cautions.

The lady checks her coat. Yes, even her sable. "We like to think our customers are secure," Levin observes. So, check the security blanket. Martin demoted a very impressively dressed couple from the plains to the frozen tundra. "When he passed by I saw his rundown heels and white socks."

Even the consummate arbiters of "in" have their astigmatisms. Henri Soulé himself once seated two matrons in the farthest reaches of Outer Mongolia. They ate lunch without protest. "You have a nice restaurant— it's a pity you don't know your New York," the former Mrs. Nelson Rockefeller admonished Soulé as she exited. La Grenouille's headwaiter failed to recognize Alice Longworth. "Howard Hughes in his dusty sneakers would probably get the same rebuff," predicts Jonathan Dolger. "I assume he'd walk around the corner, step into a phone booth and buy the block."

No reservation? The snob maître d' keeps a few empty tables for the eleven-hour whims of his favorites. Present yourself, discreetly costumed, to the benevolent ogre. You may get the table you couldn't reserve on the phone that same morning.

A Little Knowledge

You can never know too much about food. If you care what crosses your palate, you may fire a bored captain's imagination. I favor an academic approach. Cooking lessons . . . a year at the Cordon Bleu. A tutor in French . . . frequent research trips to France. Waverly Root is my muse, and *Larousse Gastronomique* the companion of my insomnia. At the very minimum, memorize a few common terms: *Florentine* (spinach); *Veronique* (with white grapes); *en gelée* (jellied); *fumé* (smoked). If something is cold or singed or spoiled or rotten, send it back. If you order ris de veau expecting rice and veal, you lose points complaining that you didn't order sweetbreads. Try not to weep when you discover *pamplemousse* is not exotic mousse of pamples but merely everyday grapefruit.

Caviar is always impressive. May and June, October and November are the best months for caviar. *Malossol* means "lightly salted." Daddy O prefers the slightly less expensive caviar. Restaurants Ari favors keep a supply on hand. Ask if the house can spare some. Champagne goes well, Polish vodka even better.

Bela von Block always demands fresh horseradish. "That throws them. Not too many places have it." If they do, he commands it cut in paper-thin curls. "Delicious with Bloody Marys. Put a strip between your teeth and drink the Bloody Mary through it."

Devastate the chocolate mousse-swilling proles with your dessert order: "A nice crisp apple would be pleasant."

For the best possible meal, restaurateurs wish you would order ahead. "Especially if you are more than four at dinner," Stu Levin urges. "But even for a party of two." Paul Kovi at the Four Seasons outdoes himself when you say, "We put ourselves entirely into your hands." Martin at La Seine says, "We knock ourselves out for out-of-towners who confide they've come because of the *Gourmet* magazine rave, have saved for a year and hope they won't be disappointed." Alfred Knopf Jr. asks to meet the chef.

The Grape

Any fool knows that Lafite Rothschild is a hotshot label. And the average child of eleven knows that 1959 was a great year. A great wine demands a great dinner. Nothing is less cool than ordering a Lafite with calf's liver. If you can't pronounce French, Anglicize it with a pronounced Cambridge accent. Imagine that you are David Frost. The wine thermometer as a weapon demands élan and knowledge. You can impress even a journeyman oenophile if you know what vineyards got rained on just before the '64 harvest. Study Schoonmaker's *Encyclopedia of Wine*. For classic one-upsmanship, grape division, memorize the Morrell liquor shop catalogue. Eye the cork stonily as the captain presents it to you. Sniff. You needn't close off one nostril—it isn't a Benzedrex inhaler. If the wine smells dirty, it is safe to say: "It has a lovely nose." If it costs over $20, you may comment: "It isn't quite what it could be. Let's allow it to breathe awhile."

The Payoff

Overtipping the waiter is wanton. It is impossible to overtip the maître d'. Some innocents still tip 15 percent and some tip 25 percent. But 20 percent (before tax) is the going rate—15 percent for the waiter, 5 percent to the captain. If you sign the check, you *must* specify so much for each. Otherwise, the waiter claims it all and the captain is miffed. If there is a wine steward, he gets 15 percent on the wine (subtracted from the waiter's total at the risk of his wrath) or a dollar (on half a bottle). There is infinite cachet in the invisible payoff: Ask the maître d' in advance to sign your check and add the usual tips—he will be impeccably discreet. Regulars tip the maître d' $2 to $5 every three or four visits or generously at Christmas and before his vacation. A painting magnate hates to see his tips pocketed discreetly, with minimum impact. He likes to thank the maître d' for a fine evening by sending $20 to his house with a note—"Makes the guy feel big at breakfast in front of his wife, and he remembers where it came from."

He did it after an impressively flambéed evening at the Forum of the Twelve Caesars. "Now whenever I walk in, I'm the thirteenth Caesar."

If the evening was great, put it in writing—on Tiffany note paper, of course. If dinner was an outrage, definitely write. You may be invited back as guests of the house.

You can do better than gross currency. Martin's Cartier cufflinks came from Mrs. Charles Engelhard. Frederick Brisson gives him tickets to *Coco*. When Martin and his wife arrived in St. Thomas on vacation, they were met at the airport by Charles Revson's chauffeured limousine and invited to lunch on the yacht that "Fire and Ice" built. When Martin visits Rome or Milan or Washington, he sees the town in a car dispatched by J. Edgar Hoover, complete with FBI men.

What have you done for your favorite maître d' lately?

Perhaps you can get his son into St. Bernard's.

In fleeting moments of sanity, the lust to be be loved in *haute* eating circles may wane. If so, take a few deep breaths. Attacks of sanity usually pass quickly.

DAVID AND HIS
TWENTY-SIX ROOMMATES

DEBBIE NATHAN

MAY 16, 2005

New York, along with much of the country, runs on undocumented immigrants. They're in every restaurant and deli, in many homes working as nannies, on construction jobs. They're also largely invisible, a kind of submerged culture. When Debbie Nathan set out to learn how immigrants live in New York, she called David, who had moved to the city in search of a better life. "I live with twenty-six roommates," he said. Nathan, who speaks Spanish and had worked as a civil-rights organizer in Texas, says she was surprised by the New York illegals. Put simply, they love New York. "It's so much less repressive here in terms of immigration enforcement than in places like Texas," she says, "Despite all the horrible misery, it's a generous experience for them." After her article appeared, Nathan offered her subjects ESL classes, which they took. Nathan is the author of Women and Other Aliens: Essays From the U.S.–Mexico Border *and* Satan's Silence: Ritual Abuse and the Making of a Modern American Witch Hunt.

D AVID HAS A RECURRING DREAM. "Mi sueño nuyorquino," he calls it. His New York dream. He's flying high above Manhattan—his arms outstretched, a cool wind in his face. Far below on the streets, people point up at him, their eyes wide. It's his favorite dream. "I have it often when I'm sleeping," he says. "Being up so high, a loneliness that actually feels good. And the *americanos* noticing me."

David doesn't attract much notice in his waking life. He's short and soft-spoken, with a face the color and shape of a homemade cookie. He dresses in bargain jeans and a sensible sweatshirt and keeps his head down. He decorates dishes with artful streaks of sauce and careful radish rosettes at an upscale West Village restaurant. When, after a few margaritas and some pato en mole verde, diners ask to tour the kitchen and compliment the staff, he greets them with a courteous nod and labored English: "How are you? Have a nice day."

His housemates work at similarly bright and airy places such as Fairway and Citarella, bustling about the frisée bins and sautéing the portobellos and packing up comfort foods for harried professionals. As a household, they do pretty well even by New York standards, pulling in six figures a year. But this household is different from most in Manhattan. For one thing, there are twenty-seven people in it—all Mexicans, most of them undocumented.

To get to his home, David walks past a phalanx of grand old Washington Heights high-rises full of classic sixes with Hudson River views and turns down a stairway that's practically hidden from the street. He crosses a reeking courtyard strewn with waterlogged cardboard boxes, rotting chicken bones, and junked toilets and comes to a greasy window guarded by a Yosemite Sam doll holding a sign that reads BACK OFF, VARMINT. Next to the warning is a locked door, and past that, the dank, dark basement bowels of a pre–World War I apartment building. He passes the ancient and rumbling boiler and proceeds down a moldy hall not much wider than the corridor of a Pullman sleeper. To the right is the bathroom, whose ceiling opens to a maw of boards, with water and roaches seeping in. Farther on are several tiny rooms whose rickety doors are bolted with padlocks. One is David's.

"Welcome to *mi casa*," he says, opening the door to an eight-by-ten-foot space jammed with a children's bunk bed, a refrigerator salvaged from the trash, and an outsize, cast-off TV. He shares the tiny room with a construction worker named José, who rehabs bathrooms and baby nurseries on the Upper West Side. For $100 each, they get forty square feet apiece—half the eighty square feet required by law for each person in a household. It's hard to turn around and impossible to walk anywhere but to the leaking bathroom down the claustrophobic hall, or to the small living room with the scavenged sofa and the saint-and-candle-clotted shrine to the Virgin of Guadalupe.

Twelve of the twenty-seven people in the basement live in this 750-square-foot section. In addition to David and José, there's Leo, Giovanny, and Paco, who work at Citarella. Mateo, Jacobo, and their roommate work at Fairway. Another guy works in a bar on 24th Street; his roommate does odd jobs in Washington Heights. Arianna boxes crayons at a factory in New Jersey. And Francisca trucks through the neighborhood with an old shopping cart, collecting soda cans for recycling. Individually, they're poor. Collectively, they earn over $150,000 a year and pay $1,200 a month in rent.

Their decrepit basement apartment is illegal, of course. It was converted by a rotund Mexican affectionately known to the housemates as El Gato (the Cat). First he cleared out a half-dozen tiny toolrooms and wired them for electricity. Then he jerry-rigged a toilet and shower near the coin-operated washer-dryers used by residents of the forty-plus legal units upstairs. The building's landlord collects almost $3,000 in monthly rent from the two sides of the basement. Half he kicks back to the super, a Cuban. The super lets Gato live in the basement for free and funnels him some of the kickback in exchange for keeping up the apartments and recruiting a continuing supply of Mexicans. Gato has been here twelve years and has a rep for helping newcomer compatriots. He rounds up used clothing for them and organizes Sunday pickup basketball games so they won't feel homesick.

But Gato's efforts don't help much. David and the others are "lonely boys," men who come by themselves from Mexico to support the families they've left behind. Inside their crowded dwellings, they lead strangely isolated lives. "You feel like a ghost," says David. "A ghost in a basement."

DAVID COMES FROM a slum just south of Mexico City. His father used to work in construction, but he had an accident a few years ago that left him paralyzed. Now his mother sells fruit and vegetables on the street and makes the peso equivalent of $10 a day—which sounds impossible but is still twice the Mexican minimum daily wage. There are eight children in the family. Though all are now adults, the younger ones attend junior and business colleges and still have to be supported on that $10. David, thirty-five, is the oldest and has always felt responsible for his sisters and brothers. At the same time, he harbors a certain irresponsibility, a yen for what he calls *aventura*.

New York City, he started thinking in 1999, would be the perfect compromise: a fine *aventura,* but also a place to make money for the family. One of his brothers had immigrated to Manhattan a year earlier, and the dispatches he sent back were of the streets-lined-with-gold variety. In Mexico, David had been working in the basement of a fabrics store, earning the minimum wage of $25 a week. He imagined himself with a cool job in New York and his own apartment—or even a house! Not to mention a new car.

He sold his Mexico junker for $1,500, the price the coyote charged to smuggle him north. That fee covered a flight—the first in his life—to the Arizona border, a nine-hour trek through the desert, a van ride to Phoenix lying atop twenty other smuggled passengers, a safe house, a secret drive to California, and finally a flight from LAX to JFK. To David, it was all a lark, a prelude to excitement and riches.

Reality hit on the first day in New York. "From the airport, I went to my brother's place in Washington Heights," David says. "He was living with his child and pregnant wife, along with another couple and their kid. Six people. I was the seventh. In one room."

Over the next few days, David discovered that virtually every Mexican he met was in the same insanely cramped boat. He walked around in a state of low-grade shock, compounded by his inability to understand "the language, the street signs, the money, anything." He planned to flee as soon as he'd saved enough for a flight or a Greyhound back to Mexico, plus $1,500 to buy another car back home. Within days, he'd found a minimum-wage job as a restaurant delivery boy. He figured it would take almost a year to save what he needed to get out of this mess.

To his surprise, it took him only three months. "It was so fast that I thought, *Well, why not stay a little longer and save even more?*" he says. Three months stretched into six months, then a year. Then another.

"I kept postponing my departure because, to tell the truth, I was starting to like it here," he says. He liked riding the ferry to Staten Island. He especially liked Times Square, with its amazing variety of people "that you never see in Mexico City, though it's much bigger than New York." He was delighted one day on 42nd Street when a tourist about his age named Julie, from Albany, spoke to him in English, asking where he was from and noting that she loved Latino music—and he was able to carry on a rudimentary flirtation in the same language. He found himself invigorated by the sheer pace of things: New York's *ritmo*, he calls it.

The city was exciting, but David's place in it was fragile. After his brother's marriage foundered—perhaps owing to the strain of living in one room with another family—he and David moved with the children into an $800 Washington Heights studio. The two men babysat in shifts so David's brother could keep his job as a mechanic. They were barely holding on to the pricey apartment when David lost his job because the restaurant closed.

He had just found a new minimum-wage job—at an upscale seafood market on Broadway in the Eighties—when David's sister-in-law returned to her family, tried to reconcile with her husband, and ended up kicking him out, along with David. After knocking from bunk to bunk for three weeks, David decided it would be easier to live on the subways.

"I slept on the No. 1 sometimes but mostly on the A, because the trip is very long," he remembers. "I made sure to wear clean clothes, and I never lay down—never took up two seats. I always slept sitting up so the police wouldn't bother me. Mornings I would wash my face at work, and every few days I'd buy a bar of soap and go to a public swimming pool. I would take a shower, then a swim, then another shower."

Meanwhile, he reported to the fish market every day to cut fancy fillets and smile at his Upper West Side customers, who, as he puts it in literally translated Spanish, were "people of category." No one noticed anything amiss.

Eventually a friend told him about Gato's place. He moved into the illegal basement with the Yosemite Sam doll and the twenty-six other tenants.

ONE SUNDAY AFTERNOON, David stumbles from his bunk and heads to the bathroom to prepare for his four-to-midnight shift at the restaurant. Most of the other housemates are savoring their day off. A new month is nearing, and people are getting their rents together for when El Gato comes by to collect.

Gato's live-in girlfriend—a large woman who works as a cleaning lady in several midtown high-rises—drops by from across the courtyard to chat. The ultimate recipient of the basement rent, she says, is "the little old *judío*"—the Jew—who owns the building. She knows his religion because "he's got the hat and big beard and the long black coat." The *judío*'s son usually comes to pick up the money. His name is something like Barry, but when Mexicans pronounce it with their trilling *r*, it comes out like Body.

Everyone loves Body because he lets them keep animals. "I thought he'd kick us out when he saw my dog and her two puppies," says Gato's girlfriend. "Instead, he said, 'Oh, they're so cute!' " Nor does he seem perturbed by Francisca's caged doves, which live by the boiler. Or her rabbit.

Once when Body, who lives in New Jersey, drove over for the rent, he brought along his family's cocker spaniel. The dog ran out into traffic and died instantly. Body went to pieces. "He cried and cried," remembers Gato's girlfriend. "Just like a child. A baby!" The Mexicans chipped in and bought him a new purebred spaniel. Sure, it was expensive. Sure, they couldn't afford it. But what can you do when your landlord "has such a big heart?"

David's roommates have excellent neighbors. They listen to their music with headphones, wait patiently to use the bathroom, and no one fights. The apartment is peaceful, even conducive to study. David and his roommate José use their bilingual dictionaries to pore over old copies of *Vogue* retrieved from the trash. José doesn't need too many words; he has a wife and five children back home and plans to leave in a couple of years. But David wants a larger vocabulary. "I've got to learn what my legal rights are, how to open a bank account, how to put away some savings," he says. He's thinking he might stick around for a while.

When they're not studying, they lie in bed and listen to music. (David's favorite songs: "Great Balls of Fire," by Jerry Lee Lewis, and "Who'll Stop the Rain" by Creedence Clearwater Revival.) "Or watch *telenovelas*," he adds sheepishly, to José's guffaws. These are the Spanish-language soap operas so popular among women in Latin America and so don't-watch-or-you'll-be-a-*maricón* for men.

"Okay, there's this one I really like," confesses Mateo, popping over from across the hall. "*Rubí*. It's about a ruthless girl who's poor but wants to have everything that her rich friend, Maribel, does. Rubí dumps her poor boyfriend and steals Maribel's rich boyfriend, the architect. She marries him strictly for his money, so of course she's not happy. Meanwhile, the poor ex has all the luck and gets rich."

There's not much to do in New York when you're pinching pennies. After sending half their wages to Mexico and paying rent, they're each left with about $80 a week in pocket money. Much of it goes for takeout and restaurant food.

Part of the reason David and José and the other men eat out rather than cook at home is that they feel awkward using the apartment's kitchen. Even in this workable living arrangement, there's tension. Thirty-three-year-old Leo, the Citarella employee, is carrying on a May-December romance with fifty-year-old Francisca, the can collector. Leo helped Francisca bring her grown kids—Arianna, twenty, Giovanny, twenty-one, and Paco, twenty-six—to New York last fall from Oaxaca. Suddenly, the apartment had a whole family living in it.

If things were more relaxed, David and the others would probably flirt with Arianna, who's cute, gracious, and good with her eyeliner. But instead of wooing her, "they rush by and say 'Excuse me' or 'Have a nice day,' " she says. The men's standoffishness reassures Arianna; it's hard enough sharing a bedroom with her two brothers—at least she's not imposed upon by men who are no relation. But the formality "makes us uncomfortable," says Leo, "and we don't know what to do about it." A house meeting hardly seems possible, since the men and the family barely know each other after months of living together. "Last names?" says Arianna. "We don't even know their first names."

HE GOES TO bars like Los Compadres, near the last stop on the north-bound A train. Years ago, it would have been called a dime-a-dance hall. Today, the going rate is $2; for that, lonely Mexican guys can spend three minutes twirling Latina women who call themselves *bailarinas.* But this isn't ballet. It's herky-jerk Mexican polka, rolling cumbia, and slithering bachata, with women in low-cut jeans and even lower shirts. Every few weekends, David says to hell with thrift and visits places like this.

On a recent Saturday night at Los Compadres, the year-round Christmas lights were glaring and a cheesy band was belting out Mexican favorites. No matter that their voices sometimes cracked, and that stage smoke puffed wholly out of sync with the music. The important thing was the *bailarinas,* and there were plenty to go around—demure Mexicans wearing little makeup, and slinky Caribbeans with lots of lipstick. David grabbed a Dominican for his first dance. She was a big girl, with light, frizzy hair and studious eyeglasses. He would go on to pay for dozens more dances. He often drops $150 in an evening.

But "I can't meet any good women," he complains, and by good he means practically anyone but *bailarinas.* Back home, women who earn a living with their bodies are considered the scum of the earth. But that's Mexico. In New York, David is having a change of heart. "I talk to the *bailarinas.* They've left their families behind and risked their lives with coyotes. I used to despise them, but now I see they're human beings just trying to get through hard times like I am. I could see marrying one." In fact, he'd like to marry one in particular.

DIANA IS BEAUTIFUL, with fair skin, long honey-colored hair, and big dark eyes. A Colombian, she came to New York five years ago on a tourist visa but stayed on after it expired, hoping to earn a living as a hairdresser in Queens. She turned to taxi-dancing after finding it impossible to support herself with salon work. David says he knew she was special from the moment he saw her. "Not once did I ever touch her improperly or try to kiss her," he says. "At first I paid her for dances, especially after I noticed she would ignore other men to seek me out. Then I paid her just to sit at the table and talk. After a while, I asked her out."

For their first date, David took Diana to a family birthday party. He keeps a framed picture that was taken there. In it, he looks radiant and she looks grave. It's a complicated relationship. "She told me from the beginning that the priority in her life was the baby," he says. She'd gotten involved with a Mexican who'd abandoned her after getting her pregnant. She sent the baby to live with her parents in Colombia, and she was torn by the fact that when she called long distance, her son no longer knew who she was.

The two became a couple, and though David had always been skittish about getting serious with a woman, he sometimes told Diana he loved her. "Once when I said that, she just said 'Yo también' "—me too. Other times, she laughed, and he laughed back to stay close to her. "Still, I believe she has real feelings for me," David says. "And even though people warn not to get involved with a *bailarina,* I think that for me, it's love."

David and Diana went out for a year before she returned to Colombia to be with her child. Feeling like there was nothing left for him here, David also decided to go home. After five years, the great *aventura* was over. He left in early 2004.

David's return to Mexico was more shocking than his first days in Manhattan. "My family was hardly eating. We couldn't afford meat. She was using spoiled fruit and vegetables."

While David watched in horror as his mother cooked rotten onions, Diana called from Colombia. She too was chilled by life back home, not just the poverty but also the monotony. They came up with a plan: They would meet in Mexico, hire the same coyote, and sneak north together. This time, there was no used-car capital to finance the return, so David would have to borrow from a friend. The coyote's fee had gone up from five years earlier: Now it was $2,000.

Last fall, they set their plan in motion—and immediately ran into trouble. Diana flew to Mexico City, but Immigration authorities turned her back at the airport. Thinking she'd never return to America, she had flown from New York to Colombia on her long-expired visa, which immediately alerted authorities that she'd been in the States illegally. She was forced to return to Colombia and apply for another U.S. visa.

Heartbroken, David returned to New York alone. The fish market had gone out of business in his absence, but the West Village restaurant had finished its remodeling and took him back, promoting him from delivery boy to cook's assistant (at a wage still only slightly more than minimum). His cheap basement space was still available, too. His life is pretty much the same as when he left it—except Diana's not here.

Since he's been back, David has become a habitué of those little Washington Heights storefronts with lines of wooden phone booths. From there, he places calls to Diana in Colombia—at a cost of $10 to $20 each. They've been waiting to hear from the U.S. Consulate about a new tourist visa for Diana, but since she abused her last visa, it's hard to imagine the consulate's accommodating her. In a pinch, Diana thinks she could get a visa from Spain. But David is desperate to stay in New York. At work, on the subway, lying on his bunk bed, he's been hatching complicated schemes involving flying to Colombia, marrying Diana, bringing her to Mexico, and paying the coyote $4,000 for the two of them. He figures it would cost $10,000 to cover all the flights and the smuggling fees.

A few weeks ago, Diana was due to hear about the consular decision, and David called to learn their fate.

"Diana? What's wrong?" he said into the receiver. "Oh, no, that's bad! *¡Ay, mujer!* I've been thinking that this is my fault—if I'd gone straight after you in Colombia when I was in Mexico, you'd be here now. Dianita, I'd like to come for you, to do everything for you."

Suddenly David looked up, puzzled. The connection had gone dead— Diana's little boy had hung up the phone. David kept trying to call back, but a recording said there were too many calls to Colombia just then.

He had two hours to kill before starting his shift at the restaurant and nowhere else to go. So David went back home to the basement—with the roommates watching *telenovelas* and the doves cooing and the family in the kitchen and someone in the bathroom and Gato trying to drum up a basketball game. It was crowded, but David felt very lonely.

THE SECRET OF GREY GARDENS

GAIL SHEEHY

JANUARY 10, 1972

It's hard to remember, in the ever-expanding cult of Grey Gardens, that the Edith Beales, mère et fille, were real-life people, and you could actually go up and knock on the door of their dilapidated East Hampton mansion and Edie Beale would answer in her headband and talk to you in the loopily charming way that's now become world famous. That's what Gail Sheehy did in 1971, just as the town of East Hampton was moving toward condemning their glorious wreck. Big and Little Edie, as they were called, were the aunt and first cousin of former First Lady Jacqueline Bouvier Kennedy Onassis, and as their fame grew, Onassis tried to help her relatives and tamp down the scandal, but Sheehy's portrait had already helped make the two into a legend, which the Maysles brothers' documentary, which came out in 1975, cemented (Grey Gardens also later became a Broadway musical). Eventually, the Beales' house was purchased by Sally Quinn and Ben Bradlee. As for Sheehy, a penalty for revealing East Hampton's secrets was the loss of her East Hampton rental. Sheehy, who is now a contributing editor at Vanity Fair, *is author of the best-selling* Passages, *and many other books.*

THIS IS A TALE of wealth and rebellion in one American Gothic family. It begins and ends at the juncture of Lily Pond Lane—the new Gold Coast—and West End Road, which is a dead end. There, in total seclusion, live two women, twelve cats, and occasional raccoons who drop through the roof of a house like no other in East Hampton. Ropes of bittersweet hang from its frail shoulders. A pair of twisted catalpa trees guard its occupants, but nothing is safe for long from invasion by the bureaucrats and Babbitts. Least of all a mother and daughter of unconventional tastes who long ago turned their backs on public opinion.

The seeds of their tale go back to 1915 when the family first discovered, beyond "dressy" Southampton, a "simple" summer resort composed of saltbox houses and village greens. The sea was still tucked then behind great cushions of sand dunes. Behind them potato fields stretched in white-tufted rows clear to the horizon like a natural Nettle Creek bedspread. Right from the start, East Hampton provided a refuge for the family's scandals and divorces and all manner of idiosyncrasies common to those of high breeding.

The family brought the wealth of Wall Street to this simple resort. It casually purchased a cabana at the Maidstone Club for $8,000 in 1926. The men set down roots in four houses and sired beautiful women. In due time the little girls' names entered the Social Register. Later they would appear in the creamy pages of *The Social Spectator* . . ." Seen at the recent East Hampton Village Fair, 'Little Edie' Beale," under the picture of a full-lipped blonde shamelessly vamping through the brim of her beach hat, or, "Picking up another blue ribbon at the East Hampton horse show, Miss Jacqueline Bouvier with her father, John Vernou Bouvier III" captions which reflected the infinite self-confidence of the indomitably rich.

The Social Spectator described an era which will never be again. The family's homes are gone now, all but one. And the family itself, after three hundred years, has slipped back into the abominable middle class. All except a few. One became the most celebrated woman in the world, Jacqueline Bouvier Kennedy Onassis. Two others never gave a damn about all that. They rebelled against the Maidstone, shunned garden parties to pursue the artistic life. Now, passed over by history, they are left to the wreck of their house.

Contemporary East Hampton is caught up in a war of land values. It is no longer a refuge for artists and eccentrics. The dropouts at the foot of the lane do not conform to the new values exhibited by "beach houses" with elevators. Their lives are remote from the Friday afternoon helicopters which ferry high-powered businessmen out from the city and drop them into pastel sports cars on D. Blinken's lawn. Around the corner from them, on West End, a parade of tycoons' castles, one owned by Revlon's Charles Revson (who copied the house next door), ends in a nest of five mansionettes owned by Pan Am's Juan Trippe and family. But the grounds belonging to the dropouts bear no resemblance to putting-green lawns, nor to the wedding-cake trees created by topiary gardening on estates which retreat from them behind trimmed privet hedges. These two have lived beyond their time at the juncture of Lily Pond Lane and West End, where the privet runs wild over a house called Grey Gardens.

LAST SUMMER our lives crossed by chance. My daughter and I often walked past Grey Gardens on the way back from Georgica Beach. We could see little of the house because on that side it was obscured by a tall hedge with an overpowering fragrance of honeysuckle. But my daughter had seen fat cats in the high grass. She also reported a light in the second-floor window at night. On this scanty evidence she had dubbed it the Witch House.

One Sunday morning's discovery changed all that. My daughter came running, tearful, holding three baby rabbits in a Tide box. She had found them motherless by the side of the road. "Can't we take them home?" she asked. I explained they would never survive the train ride. She had another idea: if the Witch House had all those cats, whoever lived there must like animals. Before I could protest, we had ducked under the hedge, skittered past a 1937 Cadillac brooding in the tangled grasses, and we were deep into the preserve of twelve devil-eyed cats. There was no turning back.

"Mother?"

We whirled at the sound of an alien voice. She was coming through the catalpa trees as a taxi pulled away, and she was covered everywhere except for her face, which was beautiful. "Are you looking for Mother, too?" she asked, more unnerved than we.

My little girl held out the Tide box to show her the trembling bunnies.

"Did you think we care for animals here?" The woman smiled and bent down close to the face of the child, who silently considered her. This was not at all a proper witch. She looked sweet sixteen going on thirty-odd and had carefully applied lipstick, eyeliner and powder to her faintly freckled face. The child nodded solemnly: "This *is* an animal house."

"You see! Children sense it." The woman clapped her hands in delight. "The old people don't like us. They think I'm crazy. The Bouviers don't like me at all, Mother says. But the children understand."

My little girl said it must be fun to live in a house where you never have to clean up.

"Oh, Mother thinks it's artistic this way, like a Frank Lloyd Wright house. Don't you love the overgrown Louisiana Bayou look?"

My daughter nodded vigorously. At this point the woman looked shyly up to include me in the conversation. "Where do you come from?"

"Across the way."

"My goodness, it's about time we got together! How many years have you been here?" She rushed on before I could answer, as though reviving a numb habit of social conversation and desperate not to lose the knack. "You phone me. Beale. That's the name, Edith Beale."

As she swept past us in a long trench coat and sandals, her head wrapped in a silk scarf knotted at the back of the neck, I could have sworn she was—who? I'd seen her picture hundreds of times.

Edie Beale, safe on her porch, pointed out the formally lettered sign she had made for the front door: DO NOT TRESPASS, POLICE ON THE PLACE.

"Are there really?" my daughter breathed.

"Not really, but Mother is frightened of anyone who comes by." She then described a neighbor who tries to club the cats to death at night, and the boys from across the street whose surfer friends try to break in. I suggested the boys might just be prankish.

"Oh no, they're dangerous. I can tell what's inside a person right away. Mother and I can see behind the masks; we're artists, it's the artist's eye. I wish I didn't have it. Jackie has it too. She's a fine artist."

"Jackie?"

"I'm Jacqueline Bouvier's first cousin. Mother is her aunt. Did you know that?"

"No, we didn't."

"Oh yes, we're all descended from fourteenth-century French kings. Now a relative has written a book saying it's all a lie, that we don't really have royal blood. He's a professor, John H. Davis, and *he's* breaking with history. Everyone is. That's how I know the millennium is coming. *The Bouviers: Portrait of an American Family.* Not a bad book really."

(Subsequently, I read the Davis book and was struck by the parallel courses of their two lives—Little Edie, better known as Body Beautiful Beale, but so breakable; her young cousin Jackie, whose heart developed a steel safety catch—until an accident of fate drove one to the top and condemned the other to obscurity. It came out in the inauguration scene:

> "The Reception for Members of President and Mrs. Kennedy's Families" was the first Kennedy party held in the White House. Peter Lawford and Ted Kennedy showed up. Little Edie Beale approached J. P. Kennedy, who was looking his usual unassuming self, and reminded him jokingly that she had once almost been engaged to his first-born son, Joe, Jr. And if he had lived, she probably would have married him and he would have become President instead of Jack and she would have become First Lady instead of Jackie! J. P. Kennedy smiled and took another drink.)

"I've just come from church, which put the millennium in my mind," the lady of Grey Gardens was saying. The woman before me, a version of Jackie coming from church on a Greek island, was Little Edie in the summer of her 54th year!

"You . . . resemble your cousin," I faltered.

"Mmmm, Jackie had a very hard time. Did you like the Kennedys?" She didn't skip a beat. "They brought such art to the country! Besides the clothes and makeup, politics is the most exciting thing about America. Didn't you think the Kennedys would be around forever—at least three terms?" Her eyes danced.

My daughter wanted to know if she knew President Kennedy well.

"Jack never liked society girls, he only dated showgirls," she began, synchronizing only with her memories. "I tried to show him I'd broken with society, I was a *dancer*. But Jack never gave me a tumble. Then I met Joe

Jr. at a Princeton dance, and oh my!" She swooned. "Joe was the most
wonderful person in the world. There will never be another man like him."

"But you were a ballerina?" My daughter wanted to stick to the facts.

"What, sweetheart?" Edie Beale was off in her private world again; this
brought her back. "Oh yes, I started in ballet. Ran away from home three
times. First to Palm Beach; everyone thought I'd eloped with Bruce Cabot,
the movie actor—I didn't even know him! I never did anything but flirt—
you know, the Southern belle. My father brought me back. He'd always
thought my mother was crazy because she was an artist. Then I went into
interpretive dancing and ran away to New York. Mother caught me moving out of the Barbizon, she thought it was the correct spot. But I moved
into New York's oldest theatrical hotel. On the sly a friend sent me to Max
Gordon. The minute he saw me he said: 'You're a musical comedienne.' I
said, 'That's funny, I did Shakespearean tragedy at Spence.' Max Gordon
said the two were very close. I was all set to audition for the Theatre Guild
that summer. Shaking with fear, you can imagine with my father still
alive—he'd left Mother for the very same thing! I modeled for Bachrach
while I was waiting for the summer to audition. Someone squealed to my
father. Do you know, he marched up Madison Avenue and saw my picture
and put his fist right through Mr. Bachrach's window?"

At that, Little Edie threw back her head and giggled so contagiously
we caught it ourselves. "But"—we were gasping for the end of the story—
"did you ever go for the audition?"

"Oh no. Mother got the cats. That's when she brought me down from
New York to take care of them."

It was a stunning *non sequitur*, but the empty finality of her voice
made the meaning clear. We had come to the dead end of a human life.

Cats crouched all around in the grass, rattling in their throats, mean
and stricken.

"Are they wild?" I asked.

She called for Tedsy Kennedy, a Persian. "Mother bred them all. We've
had three hundred cats altogether. Now we have twelve, but they're not
wild. They're fur people." Tedsy Kennedy leaped out of her arms. She tried
for Hipperino, Little Jimmy, Zeppo, Champion—"He's a mother's boy"—
and finally she succeeded in scooping up Bigelow. "It's true about old

maids, they don't need men if they have cats." She put her lips to the ear of the fur person named Bigelow: "We're going away together, all right, Bigs? Just you and me?"

Bigs writhed out of the embrace too, giving her nothing but a blood bubble on one finger.

Then an operatic voice sang its lament through the upstairs window.

EeeDIE? I'm about to die.

"Oh dear, Mother's furious because she's not getting attention. *I'll be right up, Mother.*"

"The bunnies—" My daughter offered the Tide box.

"They are sweet, but you see, Mother runs everything around here. I work for her and she might throw me out. . . ." Little Edie accepted the bunnies anyway. She walked us up to the catalpa trees. Suddenly she gasped, shrank back:

"Oh dear, it's fall."

We followed her eyes to the ground where a dead mouse lay in our path. "That's the sign of an early fall. There's evil ahead," she said.

IT WAS NOT AN early fall. But Edith Beale was right about evil in the wings. Late August Saturdays still found the new rich along the Gold Coast entertaining the "fun people" in lime pants from Southampton. At high noon they sat beside gelid pools exercising little but their mouths; talking business, nibbling quiche, complaining about neighbors who drive down the land values.

These are the city people who send out their architects to order the shoulders of the sea broken, crushed, swept back into the potato fields. On the leveled stage they set down their implausible houses and bathwater pools. New dune grass eventually appears in patches, row on row, like hair transplants. But dunes never grow back. The new people use the sea only as a backdrop ("You don't swim in it, do you?"), insulting it, hating it really. The wind wrecks their hairdos. Sand nicks their glass window walls. They use the sand only as a mine field to hide the wires leading to their Baroque burglar alarm systems.

So long as real-estate moguls and barons of Wall Street and their shrill, competitive wives keep coming out from the city to erect display cases on the dunes, the Village Fathers will appease them. The new people create jobs and pay obscene beachfront taxes. Nothing is likely to be said aloud about what *they* violate of East Hampton. But when a few of them complain about *those two* living in an "eyesore" near their precious land values, the Village Fathers can be very quickly turned into a posse. Even as Labor Day approached, such a posse was being assembled against the Beales.

The sea comes into its wild season with September riptides. Gathering far out, it hurls its weight against the land, smearing the beach with tidal pools, while opposing waves tear at virgin sand and drag it back. Most people in East End stay away from the beach then.

Who was that lone figure in black?

Both Sundays after Labor Day she ran off the dunes like an escapee and plunged into the surf. Alarmed at first, I watched her draw the water hungrily around her. But she was a strong swimmer, a child-woman of such unspent exuberance. Her body was still beautiful, I thought, as Edith Beale came up the beach in a black net bathing suit.

"I haven't seen you in so long!" she called. "Mother never allows me to show myself on the beach after summer, but this fall I had to come out."

I said she still looked like a model.

"Shall I tell you what I've done for twenty years? Fed cats. Mother wouldn't let me go around with American men, they were too rich and fast. She was afraid I'd get married. *Nothing has happened* in twenty years, so I haven't changed in any way."

She remembered every detail from our last encounter. How was my trip to Russia? she asked. How are dancers treated there?

"The simple life is not understood in America," she broke in with a deep whisper. "They're all so rich and spoiled. I would have loved this life, except—I never got to say goodbye to any of my friends." She blushed to the edges of her flowered cap, admitting she had always preferred older men. "They're all dead now and I'm alone. . . ."

We walked toward the sea, which seemed to revive her spirits. "So I had to make friends with the younger generation," the voice lilting now,

"the boys who come by and like the overgrown look. We sketch together."
She turned quickly and scanned the beach. "Maybe they thought I was
getting too friendly with the young boys."

They?

Her eyes focused on a dark blur, maybe a mile away. She recounted a
strange phone call from one of her brother's sons last February: *You're in
the soup,* he kept saying, *the County's going to take your house.* "I'm psychic and I feel it coming."

That was her brother coming now, in the jeep down the beach; she
grew stiff and asked me to stay and meet him. I wondered which brother
it would be, having read of the contrast between them. While Little Edie
confounded her Bouvier relatives by imitating her mother's rebellion
against bourgeois conformity, her younger brother, Bouvier Beale, was
following in the footsteps of his lawyer father and grandfather. He married a society girl and established his own law firm in New York—Walker,
Beale, Wainwright and Wolf. Today he lives in Glen Cove, belongs to Pip-
ing Rock, as did his grandfather, and only last summer built his own summer home in Bridgehampton. The other brother, Phelan Jr., escaped to
Oklahoma and never came back.

But why hadn't they come to the rescue of their seventy-six-year-old
recluse mother and pathetic sister buried alive in Grey Gardens? Edith
Beale must have read my thoughts.

"Now my brothers, they're great successes. But the way they've been
acting has put Mother more on my neck than ever. They refuse to give one
penny to the house. The trust from my grandfather is about gone. Mother
suffered reverses in the stock market last year, so my brothers sold her
blue chip stock."

I asked a sensitive question about her present financial situation.

"Oh we're not destitute, Mother has *collateral.* It's been my life's work
to protect her collections, *we don't trust anybody.*" The rest was hurriedly
whispered: "My brother, Bouvier Beale, has been after Mother for a year
now to sign over power of attorney. I think he wants to take over the house
and put poor Mother into an institution. He treats her just as her father
did, you know, because she's an artist. It all goes back to Mother deciding
she wanted to sing . . . she was so advanced. Grandfather threatened to

disown her but she made plenty of appearances in clubs around New York. She is still totally modern and correct in everything, with one exception. My career."

But how could Mother deny her the very freedom of expression for which she had defied an entire family? I pressed.

"Two women can't live together for twenty years without some jealousy," Little Edie Beale said reluctantly. "Not that my voice is better than Mother's, but *she* can't dance."

The jeep was upon us. Its driver, a stiffly formal man, was introduced as Bouvier Beale. Seemingly embarrassed, he walked off with his sister for a private conference. As I climbed the dunes, their bodies were turning rigid in dispute, necks stiff. A shout came back in a man's voice: "You must go to a room in the Village!"

Little Edie broke away and ran for the sea.

OCTOBER BEGINS the bad months. When summer finishes with East Hampton and black ice begins to form, the stupid puddle ducks freeze in the Village pond and the caretakers stay drunk, and besides family fights and inbreeding there is very little to do. The Village Fathers had cut out their work in advance. The new Village building inspector, A. Victor Amann, had sent a letter to the Beales back last February, demanding the overgrowth be cut back: the Village would do it for $5,000. He sent a copy to the trust fund, which replied there was no money left. Another letter from P. C. Schenck's fuel company of East Hampton warned the Beales their furnace was unsafe. A copy of *that* was mailed to Bouvier Beale, along with his mother's unpaid bill of $800.

Ignored, the Village Fathers moved in on October 20. Little Edie was on the porch of Grey Gardens when five people materialized. She thought they were wearing costumes, she told me. One said: "You have no heat." Another said: "You have no food." A public nurse said: "You're sick."

"Mother, did you hear that? This horrible public health nurse says we're sick!" Little Edie stamped her feet furiously, informing her invaders: "We're Christian Scientists. The only medicine is work." Mother's voice boomed from the window: *SEND that nurse AWAY—SHE'S been in contact with ALL the GERMS of SUFFOLK COUNTY!*

The invaders retreated, but only to assemble a proper posse (which took all of two days). East Hampton's Mayor Rioux was away on vacation and his deputy, Dr. William Abel, was determined to have done with the misfits.

"People are basically no damned good," the Acting Mayor later expressed himself to me. I thought this odd coming from a chief surgeon at Southhampton Hospital, but Dr. Abel added, "I prefer animals." The very mention of the Beale house caused him to grip his knees and go white: "The house is unfit for human habitation—*animals* don't live like this. The two sweet old things won't move unless they are forcibly moved because, unfortunately, they're not mentally competent." He declined to go into the reasons for his diagnosis because "I get so wrapped up in it." But as a public official he felt it his duty to leave me with a warning. "Are you aware that many of the most horrible murders in our country are committed by schizophrenics who appeared perfectly stable, maybe even saner than I?"

In an unusual move, the Village sought help from the County. On the 22nd of October a raiding party of twelve made its move. County sanitarians, detectives, and ASPCA representatives from New York forced their way past the ladies of Grey Gardens armed with a search warrant issued by a Town Justice on the ground that the Beales were harboring diseased cats. Cameras recorded the sorry scene: cat manure covering the floors; a five-foot-high mound of empty cans in the dining room; the Sterno stove on Mother's bed; cobwebs, cats, and all sorts of juicy building-code violations. Mother thought it was a stickup. The sanitarians had the dry heaves. It remained for the ASPCA man, alone, to report he'd seen human fecal matter in the upstairs bedroom.

"They never said why it was they'd come," Little Edie told *The East Hampton Star.*

Sidney Beckwith, of the County Health Department, got on the phone with Bouvier Beale and quoted the hot report of his inspection.

"Mr. Beckwith, you've described it very well, but it's nothing new— Mother is the original hippie," said Bouvier Beale. Astonished that such a prominent family would sit back and let their relations be condemned, Mr. Beckwith warned that the next inspection would create a national scandal.

"If that's what it takes to get Mother out of the house, sobeit," said Beale.

It was never clear after the whole mess hit the newspapers, a month later, who had put whom up to what. But three forces conspired to finish off the ladies of Grey Gardens: Village Fathers, a few nameless neighbors, and their closest kin. My first clue to their plight was a *New York Post* headline of November 20: JACKIE'S AUNT TOLD: CLEAN UP MANSION.

I called immediately but the Beales' phone was "out of order." There was nothing to do but drive out to Grey Gardens. Stripped of summer foliage, it stood naked to prying eyes.

Shades of Chappaquiddick. Five girls from Huntington sat in a car across the street, trading binoculars: "We've been here all day." An old local jumped out of his station wagon, armed with an Instamatic, and posed his niece before the pariahs' house. "Sure, I knew old Black Jack Bouvier, used to caddy for him up the Maidstone," the old man said. "Knew the Beales too, delivered a lot of packages up here."

But wasn't he horrified at this invasion of their privacy? "We swim in different schools. I don't have much in common with the Beales," he said. "I'm a local working person."

At dawn the following day I reached young Edie Beale by phone. She was terrified, but adamant: "Mother would never be put out of this house. She's going to roof it, plaster it, paint it, and sell it. We're artists against the bureaucrats. Mother's French operetta. I dance, I write poetry, I sketch. But that doesn't mean we're crazy or taking heroin or anything! Please—" her voice pleaded for all she was worth—"please *tell them what we are.*"

IN THE EARLY twenties "Big Edie"—sister of Black Jack Bouvier (Jackie's father), wife of lawyer Phelan Beale, and mother of Little Edie—became the first lady of Grey Gardens. It was a proper twenty-eight-room mansion when they bought it. The box hedges surrounding it were trimmed. But even then a mantle of ivy draped its gables and the lush walled-in garden to one side suited Big Edie's unconventional personality.

By 1925 her husband was prospering. Her children, Little Edie, Phelan Jr. and Bouvier, were small. But Edie had a retinue of servants that freed her to cultivate interests and opinions which the Bouviers considered downright subversive. She played the grand piano in her living room by the hour and sang, in her rich mezzo soprano, "Indian Love Call" and "Begin the Beguine" to a husband who was generally upstairs hollering for his tuxedo to be pressed. He'd go off to stuffy cocktail parties and Maidstone dances which bored her to tears. Since she was likely to wear a sweater over her evening gown and discuss Christian Science, the family became less and less insistent that Big Edie come along.

Big Edie's two brothers were then in fierce competition to become rich men. Before they reached thirty-five, Black Jack Bouvier had reaped a fortune of $750,000 on Wall Street, while Bud Bouvier made his money in the Texas oil fields. Jack was always one up on his brother, which drove Bud to destroy his marriage and caused the first Bouvier divorce in a hundred years. In 1929, the same year that the beautiful Jacqueline was born to Black Jack, his brother drank himself to death.

Material success had become the real Bouvier god, as it was for so many others of that wildly prosperous era. Only Big Edie, among the Bouviers, dropped away from bourgeois conventions. Her brother's demise foreshadowed the family's deterioration. Within two weeks of Bud's death, and with the entire clan at the peak of its fortunes, the stock market crashed.

Black Friday found the old family broker, M. C. Bouvier, at his office at 20 Broad, congratulating himself on his cash reserves and the quality of his bonds.

Black Jack was much less serene. He was forced to ask for help from his father-in-law. James T. Lee agreed on the condition Black Jack curb his flamboyant lifestyle—Jackie's father was fatally susceptible to beautiful women and big money, which he spent faster than he earned. It was a great humiliation to move his wife and Jacqueline to a rent-free apartment, provided by his father-in-law, at 740 Park Avenue. By 1935 his net worth had plummeted to $106,444.

The family's lot began to improve only when M. C. Bouvier died in 1935, leaving his brokerage firm to Black Jack, and his fortune to Major Bouvier, who became the family patriarch. But as for Big Edie, her husband had left her in Grey Gardens and disappeared into the Northwest woods, where he built his own hunting lodge, Grey Goose Gun Club. He sent only child support. Big Edie became dependent on her father, Major

Bouvier, for a subsistence of $3,500 a year, and began to withdraw into seclusion.

The Bouviers lived their golden East Hampton summers through the thirties and forties, seemingly exempt from the country's economic despair. Ignoring Depression and war, they divided their time between the Maidstone Club and Lasata, Major Bouvier's great house on Further Lane. But the Major's flamboyant reign was accomplished at a gruesome price, to be paid much later by his heirs. By living off principal, he assured the family comfort and style only for as long as he lived.

But for the moment, his grandchildren were dazzling the cabana owners of the Maidstone. The Bouvier who attracted all the stares as she sauntered down the midway was Little Edie. The Body Beautiful at twenty-four. Her cousin Jackie was a solemn twelve and generally in jodhpurs. About the contrast Black Jack was fiercely defensive. During luncheons at Lasata he would announce to the family: "Jackie's got every boy at the club after her, and the kid's only twelve!" Everyone knew Little Edie was It, but her mother never rose to the bait. Big Edie was always busy directing the attention to herself. The excuse might be Albert Herter's portrait of her in a blue dress, done twenty years before. "Did you know the blue dress in that painting is the same one I'm wearing now?" She would pause for effect. "*That's* how poor I am."

Black Jack would remind her that a clever woman would have gotten some alimony out of her husband. Big Edie would remind her family that she was not a golddigger. Whereupon she would head for the piano with ten adoring children traipsing at her heels.

The last of the fashionable family affairs was the 1942 wedding of Big Edie's son, Bouvier Beale. A ceremony at St. James's was scheduled for four, and almost the entire Bouvier family was in place. Big Edith was the missing guest. The wedding was half over when she arrived, dressed like an opera star. The bride and groom took the incident in stride, but Major Bouvier had had his fill of Edith's outlandish behavior. Two days later he cut her out of his will. From then until his death in 1948, the moralizing Major used his changing will as a club, but Edie had already become the recluse of Grey Gardens when the news came that her share of the dead Major's dwindled fortune was a $65,000 trust fund, her sons in control.

On that sum, Big and Little Edie have lived for the past twenty-three years. Little Edie always talked about getting away . . . "I've got to get out of East Hampton, fast," she told her neighbor, Barbara Mahoney. That was sixteen years ago, when she crossed the street to take her a friendship card with a red sachet: *Thank you, Barbara, for being my friend,* it read. "You know," she whimpered, "I'm thirty-eight and I'm an old maid. I don't have any friends. Ought to get away. I don't know where to go!"

About that time the ladies of Grey Gardens met Tex Logan in Montauk. He was playing steel guitar and looking for jobs. "He was mad about my mother," Little Edie recalls, "so you know, he came in as a carpenter–maintenance man–cook. Tex did just about everything for nine years, on and off." But Tex was a wanderer. When he grew bored, he'd hitchhike out of town and when he came back he was inevitably drunk. Then there was the night Tex was arrested for possession of a pistol at Mrs. Morgan Belmont's bridge party. *The East Hampton Star* gave the Beale house as his address. How the ladies of Grey Gardens did fuss! Tex didn't come back again until the winter he contracted pneumonia. He was found a week later, dead, in the kitchen of Grey Gardens. This time *The East Hampton Star* noted, discreetly, the man was the Beales' "caretaker."

"We never let anybody in here after that," Little Edie recalled, "because the house is loaded with valuables. Except once, in the early spring of '68, when the Wainwrights invited Mother and me to a big dance. Mother said we should make one last appearance before the Old Guard of East Hampton. I was so excited—but Mother said, 'You are absolutely not going to that dance unless you get somebody to help clean up this mess.'"

Little Edie hired two boys, sons of old natives, who were home from the Navy. She noticed they were acting funny on the second floor, but in her excitement she ignored it. The party was being given by young Edie's childhood friend, Carolyn Wainwright, for her daughter's debut. The reclusive Beales made a breathtaking entrance.

Mother wore a wrapper open to the waist and clasped with a dazzling brooch. In her hair, which looked as though it hadn't seen a comb in years, she had wound faded silk violets. Little Edie arrived desperate to dance, trailing a black net stole over her black bathing suit and fishnet tights.

Edie danced by herself with one red rose. Somebody's sympathetic husband got up to dance with her, but she was inexhaustible. The rock music grew wild and Little Edie even wilder—"I flew into a jungle rock and nobody could control me, not even Mother!" Late in the evening, Big Edie dragged her wayward daughter home, scolding all the way: her disgraceful behavior would release evil spirits, just wait. They entered Grey Gardens to find $15,000 worth of heirlooms stolen.

LAST AUGUST the Beales paid $1,790 in taxes to the Village of East Hampton for one more year in the life of Grey Gardens. "Why are my brothers so anxious to get Mother out?" Little Edie kept asking. "She was going to sell the house anyway, before the taxes are due next August. She's just a little superstitious. Mother thinks if she makes a will, she'll die."

Meanwhile a Village official was calculating out loud: "It would take about $10,000 to demolish the house. With the land cleared you could easily get $80,000, a sum that would be of considerable interest to members of the family . . ." Other estimates run as high as $300,000.

"The final degradation for Grey Gardens," moaned Edith Beale.

When the raids began, the Beales decided the Village was out to break them. "I don't think we can live in America any more," sighed Little Edie. "The only freedom we have left is the press. Thank God I could tell my side of the story to *The East Hampton Star.* Isn't it a terrific paper; it's our *Daily News!*"

Meanwhile the international press was having a field day with the sordid tale—"They keep saying we're old and ill and have to be institutionalized," Little Edie wept to her lawyer, Mr. LaGattuta from The Springs. "I don't look old, do I?" But Mother felt she was smarter than any lawyer and refused to pay LaGattuta a fee.

After a third inspection on December 7, Mr. Beckwith informed the Beales by letter: "Should you continue living in this dwelling under the existing conditions, this department will have no recourse but to take action to remove you." That action would be an eviction hearing immediately after Christmas. Mr. Beckwith took the liberty of sending a copy to Mrs. Onassis with a personal note, mentioning that her aunt and cousin had spoken fondly of Jackie and if she could do anything to help, the Beales certainly needed it. Although Mrs. Onassis was in New York partying all month, she made no effort to contact her brutalized relatives. Her social secretary, Nancy Tuckerman, insisted that Mrs. Onassis was always very fond of *them,* too. In her opinion, however, it was not a matter of money but of how they chose to live.

THE LAST TIME I saw Little Edie was the week before Christmas, when she invited us out to take pictures. Prepared as though for her stage debut, garbed in black net and flashy reds and heavily perfumed, she swept out the door in grand theatrical tradition.

EeeDIE! WEAR YOUR MINK! a voice called to her.

"Mother always tells me how to dress," she exclaimed, returning with a bottle of frosted fuchsia nail polish and a mangy fur jacket. When we had finished, she invited us in. "What can they possibly have against this house? They haven't seen the *inside.*"

She led us into the narrow damp hall and up the lightless staircase, pointing out the carved banister and paneled doors . . ." These are very much in demand these days." Animals hid still as stone in the gloomy deeps until we passed; suddenly dust would scatter and . . . something leapt past our heads—a bat, no, a *cat*—flying to some ceiling perch. The windows at the top of the stairs were blinded with cobwebs and pawing vines, the bittersweet vines of Grey Gardens grown thick as boa constrictors. Mother had set out some crackers and Taylor's port for our refreshment. Little Edie poured. "Only students of architecture can fully appreciate this place," she said. Her performance was exquisite. We scarcely noticed a cat eating his own droppings in one corner. We were completely entranced by this bizarre version of a White House tour led by Jackie Kennedy.

Mother kept wheezing inside and banging on the floor. "She's furious because I'm getting all the attention," confided Little Edie. Would Mother like her picture taken? we ventured. "You don't want your picture, do you, Mother?" she called out. And then to us, in a theatrical aside, "Mother looks like she's about to die."

I AM. I'M GOING TO DIE TODAY!

"You see?"

EeeDIE? My MAKEUP is under the BED.

"Never mind, Mother."

We reminded Edie of a beautiful girl whose picture ran thirty years ago in *The Social Spectator*, Little Edie Beale at the East Hampton Fair.

"I hate it when people say I was beautiful in the old days," she grimaced. "I want to *detach* myself from the past! Do you understand? I like to think I'm good now. I'm *terrific* now!"

But what does she do here for twelve hours of every day? we asked the second lady of Grey Gardens.

"I wake up and write poetry, like other people have coffee. I love the late movies on TV."

And in between?

Something snapped in Little Edie at that moment. Her mask dropped and she whispered with urgency of a child:

"I've been a subterranean prisoner here for twenty years. If you only knew how I've loathed East Hampton, but I love Mother. . . . They must have found out how I hated this house. They must have heard my scream—"

What scream?

"Last summer, out that broken window, when I screamed at Mother for the first time—'It's boring, boring, boring here! I'll go anywhere to be free!' "

THIS WAS THE Secret of Grey Gardens—the unfinished woman who stood before us, consumed by cats, fed upon for decades by her broken mother, was far from buried in Grey Gardens. She was only now ready to live! Her family has disintegrated, the survivors have turned away, preferring scandal to parting with a sou from their fortunes to ameliorate this shame. There is nothing left now, nothing, but the hope in Little Edie's wound-shattering scream.

As we backed toward the car her lower lip trembled. She came running to the edge of the catalpa trees and cried out: "Call me anything, but don't call me old!"

THE PRICE OF PERFECTION

MICHAEL WOLFF

DECEMBER 2, 2002

It was never surprising when Eliot Spitzer, as New York's attorney general, put a high-level financial player in his crosshairs. But when he subpoenaed the e-mails of Citigroup's Jack Grubman, who'd been the most powerful telecommunications analyst on Wall Street, what was surprising was the bargain Grubman appeared to have struck. The e-mails suggested that Grubman had upgraded his rating of AT&T in a deal to help get his twins into preschool at the 92nd Street Y. For Michael Wolff, then a New York *magazine columnist, this was a powerful statement: that there are things in New York that are more important than money. "New York is one of the most socially and psychologically competitive places in the world," says Wolff. "One of the most unnerving measures of one's success is getting your kids into the right school." Wolff, now a columnist at* Vanity Fair, *is working on a biography of Rupert Murdoch.*

I'D BEEN SAVING UP to write about New York private schools—possibly the subject I have dwelled on most obsessively for the past fifteen years—until my children got out of them.

But it's likely that Jack Grubman and Sandy Weill and an injudicious use of e-mail will have an effect on independent schools—a rarefied circle of these schools, at least—similar to the effect pedophilic priests in Boston have had on the Catholic Church. There's no hiding anymore. It's all going to come out.

This is what money buys.

Let me first come clean as to what bank or institution or sugar daddy or influence peddler has secured my children's ascension, as Citigroup underwrote Jack Grubman's kids' entrance to the 92nd Street Y preschool. That would be my wife, Alison: Brearley class of 1970. Her legacy is a kind of pass, or lifetime membership, or punched ticket, evidently as valuable as a "strong buy" recommendation for AT&T and a million-dollar gift from Citigroup.

She provides our children entrée not just to schools that are, in Mr. Grubman's description, "harder than Harvard" to get into, but to the entire Upper East Side culture—which is surely what this is about. The faded world of Holden Caulfield and Henry Orient and Butterfield 8 and the Knickerbocker Grays (if you have to ask, you're going to have to donate more) as well as the shinier new world of the investment-banking community.

I was, when I first met my wife, an ambitious know-nothing from New Jersey (I went to an upwardly mobile private day school, but its celebrity children were the children of mobsters and golf-course developers), alternately mystified and amused by the folk customs and secret rituals she had to impart about this weird archipelago of privilege and status. Among the islands in her tales were Dalton, Trinity, Spence, Chapin (the day before our wedding, my wife's distraught mother told my wife that she would have had much better marital prospects if only she'd gone to Chapin), Collegiate, Nightingale, Horace Mann, Brearley. (Here's a secret-ritual detail: the nude posture pictures taken of generations of Brearley girls well into the modern age. What are the chances they still exist somewhere in some school closet or fetishist's file?) Then there's the uniformed-nanny world of feeder preschools, and, for really doctrinaire East Siders, the boys K-to-9's (Buckley, St. Bernard's, Allen-Stevenson), which lead to boarding schools.

Still, in my twenties, I thought this world, this Wasp culture, was not just ridiculous and long-in-the-tooth but dying too. *I* thought I was rescuing *Alison*.

Well, as it happened, neither of us paid any real attention when our daughter, Elizabeth, applied to preschool (there is something odd about adults even saying the word *preschool*—saying it as though preschool were a monumental life passage, a historic institution). We weren't ready for this—we'd deal with such stuff later. Any nursery school would do . . . whatever. But then Elizabeth, age three, didn't get in—anywhere.

Now, I would not have thought that Jack Grubman and I have much in common. And yet I understand what he was willing to trade his honor for.

There were, suddenly, when Elizabeth was turned down, two stark paths: a hopeful one and a lesser one. And there were two kinds of parents: ones who made the effort and ones who did not. And two kinds of New Yorkers: the in and the out. Wounded in some deep place, I screamed at Alison to fix it. I became, I believe, seriously unhinged.

Alison, finally accepting or acquiescing to her place in the social order, got on the phone. I do not even think it took her that many calls. No bribes. No money. Just a little chatting. Just being an insider, and knowing what an insider knows. The next day, Elizabeth was accepted at the much-vaunted All Souls School on 80th and Lexington.

I wonder how that would make Jack Grubman feel (as "someone," he confided to Sandy Weill, "who grew up in a household with a father making $8,000 a year"). I wonder if influence like my wife's (Alison, in the face of my great trepidation, applied for our daughters after preschool only to Brearley; and for our son, only to Collegiate—where the director of admissions is a Brearley girl) is exactly the reason he felt justified leveling the playing field with his own kind of influence. And why not? Isn't it good that anyone can acquire influence to balance the influence of people who were born with it?

Why they would want to is another question.

IT'S CONFOUNDING, but true, that most people in New York are not dying of regret that their children are not in these schools. Even among the seriously upwardly mobile, most do not have these deep pangs. I know people downtown who—hard to believe—could not readily tell you the difference between Episcopal and Brick, between Spence and Nightingale. This could mean they're not smart enough to appreciate value as

Jack Grubman does (on the other hand, he thought WorldCom had value), or they're wise enough to suspect it's all a crock, or so selfish as to think they might have better uses for their dough—of course, they could just be too poor to compete in this world.

Or it could be that Jack Grubman and I and a few thousand highly parochial others are part of a separate world, with specialized, even slightly perverse values and needs.

We, it seems, have a greater craving for validation, for competitive success, for status, for institutional acceptance, for class standing (we are the real soldiers of American ambition and everyone else is a civilian, I think we feel)—for having something tangible, some identifiable brand, to show for our troubles. And possibly—and this should not be underestimated—for taking something that used to belong to somebody else. (*I'll take that social milieu. Throw in some extra uptightness.*) We're drawn to the exclusive thing, the formal thing, the Establishment thing—like Ralph Lauren to the Rhinelander Mansion. Jack Grubman's nursery-school payoff, in other words, is just a logical extension of what makes Jack Grubman Jack Grubman.

We are not so exceptional or perverse, of course. As class barriers have fallen and private education has become a more meritocratic enterprise (well, meritocratic in the sense of your parents having succeeded in the meritocracy), vastly more people everywhere in the country are applying and donating and tapping connections and getting their children tutored and arranging internships and hiring essay writers, all in an effort to get into some formerly off-limits heaven-on-earth school.

Still—I don't think I have to argue this—the connections are grander, the dollars greater, the life-and-death struggle more dramatic, here in Manhattan and most of all on the Upper East Side (there are important West Side schools, too, which does not so much change the demographic point as introduce the parallel and ever-converging competition of Wasps and Jews into the equation—indeed, the Grubman brouhaha involves a Jewish school on the East Side).

So what *are* we getting? Or, what do we *think* we're getting?

True, as Jack says, "there are no bounds for what you do for your children." But I've never known a rich guy who at some point didn't want a return on his investment (the big donations together with the $300,000 in ordinary costs to get your kid from preschool through the twelfth grade). What's more, there are lots of normal upper-middle-class Manhattanites sucking up like crazy to get into these schools, and then straining mightily to pay these bills.

Certainly, we think we'll be absolved of future guilt—going all-out now means we won't have to blame ourselves later. But surely it's something more (who hasn't rationalized guilt in cheaper ways?). Something much grander draws us.

It's a notion of perfection. And of order. A Platonic ideal.

When you show up at these schools, you can't *not* be bowled over by the scene. These kids *look* perfect! Straight from a high-end catalogue. The catalogues imitate these kids—they are the archetype! This is no overnight tradition. They've been working on carriage and posture here for generations—and truly, they don't slouch very much; there really isn't much visible attitude. From the groomed and tended preschool youngsters to the gamine girls and Harry Potter boys lounging in common rooms and on window seats—there are no sore thumbs. This is incredible packaging. *This is what the rich are supposed to look like.* And the better the school, the better the packaging. The better the school, the stricter the homogeneity of style and tone and manners. (This is actually the result of a harsh Darwinian process: You have to look or fit the part to get in, and then, if you don't continue to stay in character, you're weeded out—indeed, almost no amount of money can keep a misfit or underperformer in.)

Who isn't, even unreasonably, attracted to the idea that the right circumstance, milieu, window seats, might help make a perfect kid?

There is, of course, a stricter economic interpretation. Value is created by supply and demand. The greater the chance that you can't get it, the greater the desire to get in, the greater the willingness to pay the price—and to believe it's really worth it. In other words, the admissions *Sturm und Drang* is self-perpetuating. The more they extort you, the more you want to be extorted.

There's more:

There's the pure joy of *not* being rejected (happiness being nothing but the remission of pain).

There's the perceived higher value of your children—you no longer have just a kid, you have a 92nd Street Y kid, or a Spence daughter, or a Horace Mann son. It's something you can take to the bank. It's a social currency—even a business currency. You'll drop the name of your kid's school—you will.

There's your recalibrated social station—you enter a truly exclusive club, and a wildly charming novel of manners. (There is, too, for many, a more subtle sense of *diminished* social station, which grows over time when you realize that everyone is richer than you—you're the person lingering uncomfortably at the fringe of parent cocktail parties.) Very public people become part of your private life. It's surreal. There was the time Itzhak Perlman called me up to ask if it was okay if he took his daughter and mine to see *Wayne's World*. While it is important to be cool, everybody is also giddy with in-ness and proximity (to be fair, the giddiness is much greater in Los Angeles private schools; the LA people, interestingly, seem less cool about this than New Yorkers).

There's peace in your household—rejection can be a marital disaster, a grievance carried for years. Who did not make the calls? Who failed to write the letters—or write good enough letters? Who did not know when and how to offer the money?

There's a (temporary) quieting of your own unquiet ambitions—it is, of course, about you. There is the earning of position as a certain kind of New Yorker—an official New Yorker, a sophisticated New Yorker. It's a tribal thing.

Nursery school is where it begins—it's a portal, or, perhaps more accurately, a test. The first test. (The fact is, many of these schools get easier to get into rather than harder; but there is something about being at the starting line, about being the first out of the box, about being the early bird.) Are you up to it?

OF COURSE, there is the issue of whether Jack Grubman really, in the end, wants to be a member of a club that would have him.

My wife's Brearley class differs substantially from my daughters' classes. My wife's classmates were children of writers (predominantly, it seems, *New Yorker* writers), Columbia academics, publishers, doctors, and lawyers as well as socialites and product brand names—most of whom have largely been replaced in my daughters' classes by the children of people in the financial industry. This clearly mirrors what has happened in the city itself—banking, providing never-before-imagined levels of cash flow and vastly scaled-up net worths, has changed these schools as it has changed (sleeked up, amped up, intensified, competitied) Manhattan life.

Money, in other words, really, really big money, is everywhere. Money is the mother's milk of private education—as distorting and corrupting as it is to politics and to executives and accountants whose compensation depends on a market uptick.

Money, of course, understands and accepts the ways of money.

It's widely assumed, for instance, that the 92nd Street Y is pretty much off limits for anyone without a major donation or major connection. All Souls, where Alison so easily opened the door, is, after a preference for church members (joining a church is a back door to various preschools), siblings, and people who know people, mostly a closed world.

Spence seems like a kind of banana republic for people with boatloads of dough; its billionaires are would-be Noriegas.

Dalton, with large aspirations but a shallow endowment, will do anything to attract more billionaires.

Collegiate, with some West Side consciousness, often seems in a moral dilemma about its billionaires (although it certainly has as many as any other school—and has a special penchant for media moguls); its former headmaster was strongly criticized for being too cozy with investment bankers.

Brearley, playing it ever-so-close to the vest, acts as though it were unaware of its billionaires: *Aren't we all just folks? Can't we all just get along?*

Now, the issue, in a further complication, is not just that money is a weighted factor in every admissions decision. It is not just that every year the number of truly open positions is winnowed down by the pressure of money (every new centa-millionaire who comes into the system comes with a set of people he's going to be pushing strongly for each year), and that nice kids are left outside and awful kids with punch let in. Nor that money infuses *every* aspect of the life of each of these schools. But that this is all deeply denied.

The system of denial is exactly why Jack Grubman couldn't just whip out his checkbook and instead had to do it under the cover of a donation from Citigroup (schools, of course, understand that there is a big value distinction between someone who can write a check and someone who can cause Citigroup to write one).

Denial and artifice are everywhere. It's a laundering enterprise of the greatest ritual and propriety. (Never ask, "How much?" Or ever demand clear value for what you have given. There is no greater vulgarism than quid pro quo.) Even in Spence's Panama, you must know *how* to do the deal.

In part, this denial and artifice reflect the need to prop up the whole range of conceits about these schools (after all, no self-respecting rich person would want to send his children to a school that you could just *buy* your way into), but, perhaps more profoundly, they also reflect the deep ambivalence (and often real distaste) that these schools—or the people who actually work in these schools—have for the people who are buying their children in.

Consider the disparity between the nursery-school teacher making what a nanny makes and the billion-dollar three-year-old (with a bodyguard or two) to whom she is teaching "community values"; or the dynamic in the meeting between the $65,000 upper-school administrator and the titan of industry.

The effect, though, is not so much that the schools and teachers bow and scrape (they have a finely honed understanding of when and to whom they must bow and scrape and whom they can high-hand) but rather that they come to understand the full extent of their power (as well as being convinced of their own superiority), and, accordingly, the battle lines are drawn.

These people really know how to manage powerful parents. (It may well be that the rich and powerful like to be slapped around.)

This is a class issue—ALERT: VULGARIAN ON THE PREMISES— but it is also, much more, a power issue. Who is in charge?

The job of the school administrator is to outwit the rich and powerful (while all rich people are valued and despised, the rich and malleable are especially valued and despised). It is to get as much as he can from the rich while giving in return as little control as possible. (Interestingly, a school that gets a reputation for being controlled by its wealthy parents is thought to be a lesser school.)

Almost all administrators have perfected a language of diffuseness and avoidance and euphemism (in the girls' schools, every issue is reduced to eating disorders). A good private-school administrator is a Clausewitz of passive aggression. The schools have the ultimate weapon, too, of possession of the children; everybody is fearful of how it will "affect my kid." Special tutoring? Ritalin? Lukewarm college recommendations? The boot? And so, in almost every negotiation—and every discussion is a negotiation—parents lose.

On some level, the issue is an irresolvable conflict and long-simmering war between Alison's school and Jack Grubman's school—Jack is paying for the former while, of course, creating the latter.

So the artifice is breathtaking.

Against the background of vast corruption in any private school of any standing, there is an intense, near-religious focus on tradition, standards, values, and preparation, together with vast, almost theatrical, amounts of homework and a Stepford degree of conformity (helped by that constant weeding-out of the people who just don't fit in) and an ever-more-idealized notion of *our* community (this includes the diversity thing— a weird, horrifying elephant in the middle of the table—wherein perfectly innocent kids from more normal worlds are forced into this drama of artifice and denial). The more corrupt, the better the school—or the better the pretense of a better school.

The interesting and ironic result is that at the end, after all the struggle to be a part of this, nobody is too happy with the outcome (it starts happy, with great cosseting and niceness, and then, slowly, the tensions build). The price is too high, the pretense too demanding, the negotiating too exhausting, the pressure too great. It is not too much of an overstatement to say that every parent, no matter how little or how much he or she has paid, graduates from the rich-school experience with a chip on his or her shoulder. *Was it worth it?* is the silent and traumatic question.

And yet, possibly because the alternative would be to admit that we have not only wasted millions of dollars and vast reserves of psychic energy but maybe even screwed up our kids, we do believe we have paid the going price for more-perfect children.

I'm not sure Jack Grubman, who has clearly messed up his chances for such perfect offspring, should be so unhappy to be out of this game.

EVERYBODY SUCKS

VANESSA GRIGORIADIS

OCTOBER 15, 2007

For almost all of the world, what appears on a website known as Gawker is of minuscule consequence. But for a few years in the mid-2000s, for a small, catty, parochial, privileged segment of New York—which happens to be a part of the city that New York *magazine and much of the rest of the media world occupy—Gawker seemed to be at the center of the universe. Vanessa Grigoriadis's piece explored the rise of Gawker and other blogs as a kind of class struggle between media world haves and have-nots—the rise of "the creative underclass," as she called it. In fact, one of their targets had been Grigoriadis, but that didn't stop her from infiltrating their world. "I hadn't ever hung out with bloggers," she says. "It was a scene with a hierarchy and interesting characters. They're people who believe in what they're doing even if they're misguided." Grigoriadis is a contributing editor at* New York.

—

AT THE RISK OF SOUNDING like a wounded old-media journalist, let me share a story about my experience with the media-gossip blog Gawker.com, which I, like most journalists who cover stylish topics in New York, have read almost every day for five years. In addition to recently finding attacks on some of my female journalist friends—one of whom was described as slutty and "increasingly sundamaged"; another variously called a "tardblogger," "specialblogger," and "developmentallydisabledblogger"—as well as a friend's peppy little sister, who was put down for wanting to write a "self-actualizing screenplay or book proposal or whatever," I woke up the day after my wedding to find that Gawker had written about me. "The prize," said the website, "for the most annoying romance in this week's [*New York Times*] 'Vows' [column] goes to the following couple," and I'll bet you can guess which newly merged partnership that was. It seems that our last names, composed of too many syllables, as well as my alma mater, Wesleyan; the place we fell in love, Burning Man; our mothers' occupations as artists; and my husband's employer, David LaChapelle—in short, the quirky graphed points of my life—added up to an irredeemably idiotic persona (the lesson here, at the least, is that talking to the *Times*' "Vows" column is a dangerous act of amour propre). Gawker's commenters, the unpaid vigilantes who are taking an increasingly prominent role in the site, heaved insults my way:

"Grigoriadis writes for *New York* magazine. Her last article was entitled, 'You Too Can Be a Celebrity Journalist!' With that kind of work and the newfound fame that comes with a *Times* wedding announcement, she's on the fast track to teaching a class at The Learning Annex."

"Sorry, but I'm obsessed with these two. The last names alone? They have nine vowels between them. And can't you see it when they have their painful hyphenated named children? Does anyone out there know them? Please offer up some stories. Perhaps their trip to Nepal, or her internship with Cindy Sherman. I need more . . ."

"Those two are such easy targets they have to be made up. C'mon, Wesleyan? LaChapelle? The immigrant artist parents? No two people could be that painful."

"Immigrant artist parents = house painters."

Are we ridiculous? Perhaps a little, and I was contemplating this, nervously, when I got a call from my new mother-in-law, who had received the news by way of a Google alert on her son's name. She was mortified, and I = pissed: High-minded citizen journalism, it seems, can also involve insulting people's ethnic backgrounds. I felt terrible about dragging my family into the foul, bloggy sewer of Gawker, one I have increasingly accepted as a normal part of participating in city media. A blog that is read by the vast majority of your colleagues, particularly younger ones, is as powerful a weapon as exists in the working world; that most of the blog is unintelligible except to a certain media class and other types of New York bitches does not diminish its impact on that group.

Like most journalists, I tend to have a defeatist attitude about Gawker, dismissing it as the *Mystery Science Theater 3000* of journalism, or accepting its vague put-downs under the principle that any press is good press. After all, there aren't lots of other news outlets that cover the minutiae of our lives, and we're all happy for any smidge of attention and desperate for its pickups of our stories, which are increasingly essential to getting our work read. The prospect and high probability of revenge makes one think twice about retaliation. Plus, only pansies get upset about Gawker, and no real journalist considers himself a pansy. But there is a cost to this way of thinking, a cost that can be as high as getting mocked on your wedding day.

Nearly five years ago, in December 2002, Gawker made its debut under the leadership of Nick Denton, the complicated owner of the blog network Gawker Media, and Elizabeth Spiers, a twenty-five-year-old banker turned blogger who was fragile in person but displayed a streak of dark cunning on the page. They didn't exactly invent the blog, but the tone they used for Gawker became the most important stylistic influence on the emerging field of blogging and has turned into the de facto voice of blogs today. Under Spiers's aegis, Gawker was a fun inside look at the media fishbowl by a woman who was, indeed, "snarky" but also seemed to genuinely enjoy both journalism and journalists—Spiers was a gawker at them—and took delight in putting out a sort of industry fanzine or yearbook, for which she was rewarded with fawning newspaper articles casting her as the new Dorothy Parker. Ironically enough, Spiers craved a job at a magazine. She soon left for a position here, at *New York* magazine; two subsequent Gawker editors, Jesse Oxfeld and Jessica Coen, have followed in the past year.

To be enticed, as these writers were, by the credentials extended by an old-media publication is a source of hilarity at the Gawker offices, where, beneath a veneer of self-deprecation, the core belief is that bloggers are cutting-edge journalists—the new "anti-media." No other form has lent itself so perfectly to capturing the current ethos of young New York, which is overwhelmingly tipped toward anger, envy, and resentment at those who control the culture and apartments. "New York is a city for the rich by the rich, and all of us work at the mercy of rich people and their projects," says Choire Sicha, Gawker's top editor (he currently employs a staff of five full-time writers). "If you work at any publication in this town, you work for a millionaire or billionaire. In some ways, that's functional, and it works as a feudal society. But what's happened now, related to that, is that culture has dried up and blown away: The Weimar-resurgence baloney is hideous; the rock-band scene is completely unexciting; the young artists have a little more juice, but they're just bleak intellectual kids; and I am really dissatisfied with young fiction writers." Sicha, a handsome ex-gallerist who spends his downtime gardening on Fire Island, is generally warm and even-tempered, but on this last point, he looks truly disgusted. "Not a week goes by I don't want to quit this job," he says, "because staring at New York this way makes me sick."

IT'S LONG BEEN known to magazine journalists that there's an audience out there that's hungry to see the grasping and vainglorious and undeservedly successful ("douchebags" or "asshats," in Gawker parlance) put in the tumbrel and taken to their doom. It's not necessarily a pleasant job, but someone's got to do it. Young writers have always had the option of making their name by meting out character assassinations—I have been guilty of taking this path myself—but Gawker's ad hominem attacks and piss-on-a-baby humor far outstrip even *Spy* magazine's. It's an inevitable consequence of living in today's New York: Youthful anxiety and generational angst about having been completely cheated out of ownership of Manhattan, and only sporadically gaining it in Brooklyn and Queens, has fostered a bloodlust for the heads of the douchebags who stole the city. It's that old story of haves and have-nots, rewritten once again.

Gawker is the finest mechanism to date for satisfying this craving. Two weeks ago, Gawker writer Josh Stein jumped on the four-year-old son of satirist Neal Pollack, calling him a "horror" and "the worst" for providing his father with some cute quips about expensive cheese at a gourmet store. Pollack responded by sending an e-mail blast about his feelings to his friends, but Gawker got hold of the e-mail and relentlessly dug into him again and again. When Pollock first saw the post, "my heart sank to my knees," he says. "Instinctively, and stupidly, I sent out that e-mail, which I should never have done, because it just gave them the satisfaction of knowing that they'd gotten to me. That's all bullies want, really."

A friend of Pollack later sent him a link to a blog written by a woman who'd dated Stein, which he passed along to me: "It's nice to know that my antagonist is an emotionally manipulative premature ejaculator with a Serge Gainsbourg tattoo on his back," explains Pollack, who'd realized a truth of the bile culture—shame is a weapon.

"Only two of those things are true," jokes Stein. "Look, if I was Neal Pollack, I would be mad too. But when you create a character out of your son, and you develop that character in your prose, that character is open to criticism. I'm actually looking forward to the moment when Neal Pollack is an old person and Elijah Pollack is writing stories about him in a nursing home."

Journalists are both haves and have-nots. They're at the feast, but know they don't really belong—they're fighting for table scraps, essentially—and it could all fall apart at any moment. Success is not solid. That's part of the weird fascination with Gawker, part of why it still works, five years on—it's about the anxiety and class rage of New York's creative underclass. Gawker's social policing and snipe-trading sideshow has been impossible to resist as a kind of moral drama about who deserves success and who doesn't. It supplies a Manhattan version of social justice. In the past couple of years, Gawker has expanded its mission to include celebrity gossip, sacrificing some of its insider voice in the process, but on a most basic level, it remains a blog about being a writer in New York, with all the competition, envy, and self-hate that goes along with the insecurity of that position.

It's not a secret that these are hard times for journalists. In fact, the rise of Gawker over the past half-decade has dovetailed with the general decline of newspaper and magazine publishing, which, like the rest of the publishing industry, has seen revenues stagnate as advertisers are increasingly drawn to the Web. This has made for wholesale changes within magazines, including our own, with Web departments, a few years ago considered a convenient place to dump unimpressive employees, now led by the favored (our own website now counts over forty workers). At the same time, the $200,000-a-year print-publishing job, once an attainable goal for those who had climbed near the top of the ladder in editorial departments, has all but disappeared.

CONSIDER THE GAWKER mind-fuck at a time of rapid deterioration of our industry: Young print journalists are depressed over the state of the industry and their inability to locate challenging work or a job with health insurance. Although the situation may not be as dire as they might imagine—a healthy magazine is constantly on the hunt for young writers, because it wants the fresh take on the world found only in the young, and because young writers tend to be cheap—they need a release, the daily dose of Schadenfreude offered by Gawker's gallows humor, its ritualistic flogging of working journalists and relentless cataloguing of the industry's fall (e.g., items like "*New Republic* Page Count Watch"). Though reading Gawker subtly reinforces their misery, they generate an emotional bond and soon begin to tip it with their own inside information (and misinformation, as reserved for their enemies). The system keeps getting stronger, a KGB of media gossip, a complex network of journalist spies and enforcers communicating via e-mail and IM, until Gawker knocks print out of the box. With Gawker, there is now little need for the usual gossip players like *The New York Observer*, vastly diminished in its news-breaking capacity and influence, or even the *New York Post*'s "Page Six," emasculated by the Murdoch hierarchy after the Jared Paul Stern scandal. The panopticon is complete. "Peering into my in-box in the morning is like looking at the id of every journalist in the city," says Gawker writer Emily Gould.

It's almost part of Gawker's business plan to ensure that its young writers, by attracting the attention of those they are sniping at, are able to leap into the waiting arms of the mainstream media before they become too expensive to employ. One afternoon, I meet Gould for tea before her early-evening meeting with an agent for appetizers at Serafina. She has the look of a studious but sexy punk rocker: twenty-six, dirty-blond hair caught in a high ponytail that shakes back and forth like a wagging tail as she speaks, tattoos crawling over a shoulder and back exposed today by a purple-plaid jumper. "I don't even really want to be a writer, but I feel like I don't have a choice," she says quietly. "It's all I've ever known how to do."

Ten or twenty years ago, Gould would have likely emulated Joan Didion, but she is trying to play the blog game now. She means to win, and to grab some attention for herself in the process. This summer, she took some time off in Maine, and before she went posted a picture of herself on Gawker in a bathing suit flipping the bird—"At least I didn't put up the ones of myself in a silver-lamé bikini. That would have been a little much," she says, laughing. She even used to do a lot of TV spots for Gawker, but then got badly beat up by Jimmy Kimmel, who told her on-air (he was subbing for Larry King), "I just want you to think about your life . . . because I would hate to see you arriving in hell and somebody sending a text message saying, 'Guess who's here?' " She was panicked about this at the time, but she's moved past it now. "It's funny," she drawls. "People in publishing treat you like a celebrity when you do this job, but you live in Brooklyn, make $55,000 a year, and don't feel like a celebrity until someone comes up to you on the street and says, 'Buck up, kid. Jimmy Kimmel's an asshole.' "

Though Gould is ruthless in pointing out other writers' shortcomings on Gawker, she is sensitive about her line of work. "In Maine, I was telling the guys I met that I was a yoga teacher," she says. "What am I supposed to say, 'I work for a media-gossip website in New York?' " She shakes her head, and the ponytail bops around. "Who knows how this will all play out for me?" she says. "I could be ruining my life."

If there's one person who is most certainly a "have," it's Nick Denton, forty-one, the attractive, upper-class gay Jewish Briton who owns almost all of Gawker Media. He seems to control an entire Soho street, presiding over his empire from his apartment, which is around the corner from the Gawker offices and across the street from his unofficial office, Balthazar (hence his *faux* IM name on Gawker.com, DarkLordBalthazar). Occasional unpleasantness with employees, who describe him as "less passive-aggressive and more aggressive-aggressive," and rampant speculation as to his skyrocketing net worth fuel his image, and in fact he has a Machiavellian bent. Denton likes to say that his celebrity look-alike is Morrissey, and he does have the same enormous head, but his hair is worn short, at almost the same length as his graying stubble. The pumpkin head bobs over his uniform of hip business casual—collarless navy T-shirt, iPhone in palm, clean dark jeans tapering off to thin-soled shiny black sneakers. He's polite, quiet, and relentlessly confident, an effective, poised leader whose true nature is amoral recklessness, an unrufflable libertarian and libertine. Like Tina Brown, with whom he was intrigued in the past, he's always loved using his position to play-cast a social network with himself at the center.

DENTON IS FOND of denying interview requests while secretly helping writers formulate stories about him via off-the-record conversations, then slagging their work later on his blog, calling one journalist who profiled him "about as reliable as a journalist who turns to an Iraqi exile for intelligence on Saddam's hidden nukes." The moment that he told me that he would not conduct an official interview with me, and I said I'd continue reporting without him, was perhaps the only one where I've seen him express emotion. For a split second, he was furious. His eyes flicked back and forth over mine like a metronome, searching for some clue to what I was planning, what angle I might be playing, and he spat out his denial with the intensity of a losing tennis player. "Nick loves press, but only press he can control," says a colleague.

A successful former journalist for the *Financial Times* who never quite became an opinion leader, and the co-founder of two Web 1.0 Internet companies that didn't exactly set Silicon Valley on fire, though one of them was nevertheless reported to have been sold for $50 million to Israeli venture capitalists, Denton has been jubilant over the success of Gawker, taking on the self-image of a maverick who has thumbed his nose at both of his former industries. Like most journalists trained in the British system, Denton does not believe in privacy for public figures, nor really for anyone else (except himself, apparently). "Everyone suspects Nick's motives, and he has defiantly lower print standards than any of us," says Sicha. "I'll tell him, 'That guy's gay,' or 'That guy's having an affair,' and he'll say, 'Then write that.' Well, I haven't slept with the guy, so I don't want to go to court over that. Nick communicates such things intentionally to us, to continually erode our standards." According to a post by another Gawker writer, one day Denton harangued Gawker's editors about being too mean on the site; a few minutes later, he began suggesting ideas for posts, like "Who's shorter in real life than you'd think they'd be? Who has dandruff?" "Does Nick believe in quality, or does Nick believe in respecting other people's idea of quality he doesn't believe in?" Sicha muses. "He has to believe not just in page views. But I don't know how exactly."

Of all the ways in which Gawker is antithetical to journalistic ethics—it's self-referential, judgmental, ad hominem, and resolutely against effecting change in the world—it pushes its writers to be honest in a way that's not always found in print publications. Little is repressed; the id, and everything else, is part of the discourse (including exhibition and narcissism). Even the Gawker office, a kind of journalistic boiler room, can serve as a metaphor for transparency, open for anyone to see, operating behind a plate-glass window in a Crosby Street storefront. Some of Denton's bloggers are onboard with this mission: "Quite frankly, fuck discretion," writes Moe Tkacik, a former newspaper reporter, on Denton's newest site, Jezebel. "Discretion is how I didn't figure out how to come until I was twenty-four years old; discretion is why women's magazine editors persist in treating their fellow humans like total shit; and when you've spent a career trying to catch others in their own indiscretions, discretion just feels a little dishonest and superior."

It's a good trick, taking the one thing that journalists have in the world—honesty—from them, and setting up Gawker.com to instill fear of being caught in their foibles. It's what someone would do if they were trying to usurp an industry, which is exactly what Denton has always wanted. These days, Gawker is merely the flagship property of a Gawker Media empire, one Denton likes to compare to Condé Nast. Employees have started talking about his blogs as "magazines," and the company as a "stable of magazines." All fourteen Gawker blogs maintain standards of stratospherically higher writing quality than other websites in this LOL-cat era, displaying their wares on sites with hilarious, deadpan names: Fleshbot (porn), Jalopnik (cars), Gizmodo (gadgets), and Kotaku (games); an early name for Gawker was "YouNork." Half of Denton's sites are modeled on Gawker's model of pairing a mannered gossip column with the industry of a given city, including Wonkette (DC politics), Defamer (Hollywood), Valleywag (Silicon Valley), and the new, excellent Jezebel (women's magazines and fashion). Denton is only intermittently involved in content and gives free rein to his editors to attack anyone they'd like (only ex-employees get a pass).

Denton's most successful blogs are, unsurprisingly, Gizmodo and Kotaku, at about 11 and 4 million visits per week. Or, to use the preferred metric, which has the benefit of being a higher number, the two blogs receive about 12 and 5 million "page views" per week, which is the number of times each visitor clicks on any blog page. Page views are very important: Advertisers usually pay for online ads in a unit of 1,000 ad impressions, and the number of page views a website receives have become like points for content-driven Internet properties, a way to keep score on competitors. Gawker nearly doubled in size last year, but the rate slowed to perhaps 30 percent last year, and the site now does about 2.5 million page views per week. For years, Denton told colleagues that there was no money to be made in blogs, even providing such a quotation to *The New York Times*. He didn't see the advantage in talking it up. Today, Gawker Media has approximately 100 employees and contractors. "Nick made us all join Facebook," says Sicha. "I think he came to the office one day and couldn't recognize anybody—'Which one are you?' " Very few websites provide their traffic information, but Denton has chosen to do so with a link on his home page: No one can accuse him of not keeping his business transparent, at least superficially. Brightly colored traffic graphs provide the curious illusion of being able to figure out his earnings, but without knowing the percentage of ad inventory sold across all blogs, it's impossible to generate more than a back-of-the-envelope guess of $10 to $12 million in revenue annually if most of his blogs sell ads at the industry standard.

"How many page views are you getting?" That's Denton's favorite question to ask fellow Internet entrepreneurs at a party.

DENTON'S PLACE is one of the great Manhattan apartments for a party, a cavernous loft that seems to be decorated only in titanium and suede in a Soho building whose other tenants include Kelly Ripa and Harvey

Weinstein. Sometimes he throws open his doors to everyone in town, on Halloween and during the holiday season, but more often he plays host to a select group of entrepreneurs and writers.

Over the summer, at the tail end of a cocktail hour, he's cleaning up the wrappers of White Castle hamburgers he provided as hors d'oeuvre. "I had a book party for Rebecca Mead at the New York Public Library last week, and they gouged me on the catering," he says, pursing his lips slightly. "These were so cheap!" Denton's boyfriend, a lovely African-American artist, begins to get ready for their next stop of the evening, a going-away party for Gawker Media managing editor Lockhart Steele, leaving to build his own blog network with Denton joining an angel investment round. "Are there going to be a lot of bloggers there?" his boyfriend asks, and Denton nods. He sighs.

At Steele's party, at a dirty bar on Clinton Street, a white limousine with the license plate FILTHYNY rolls by as dozens of bloggers spill onto the sidewalk, surreptitiously drinking beers until a couple of cops begin handing out tickets. Everyone has a slightly hunted look, born of spending all day at a computer with a gun to their heads: Most bloggers in Denton's network work under the most severe deadlines imaginable, with many contracted to write twelve posts per day. At the same time, they are unbelievably fulfilled: Bloggers get to experience the fantastic feeling of looking at everything in the world and then having everyone look at them through their blog, of being both subject and object, voyeur and voyeurant. To get more of that feeling, some bloggers—if we were a blog, we'd tell you who—are in the bathroom snorting cocaine, or Adderall, the ADHD drug popular among college kids on finals week, the constant use of which is one of the only ways a blogger can write that much ("We're a drug ring, not a bunch of bloggers," one Gawker Media employee tells me cheerily). Pinched nerves, carpal tunnel, swollen feet—it's all part of the dastardly job, which at the top level can involve editing one post every fifteen minutes for nine hours a day, scanning 500 websites via RSS for news every half-hour, and on "off-hours" keeping up with the news to prepare for tomorrow.

The Gawker.com editors stand mostly to the side, in a cool-kid clique. Although they may in some sense be outsiders with their noses pressed to the glass, horrified by a world of New York that doesn't quite want to have

them as members, in the bubble of blogs, they're the elite, especially because lots of smaller bloggers' traffic relies on "link-whoring" (i.e., Gawker
editors being solicited for links by smaller sites). Sicha leans against the
back of a parked car, tanned and lean, his jeans slung low enough to reveal
the waistband of his underwear, talking to Alex Balk, a former copywriter
who tweaks Denton's desire for lowbrow posts that generate page views by
dialoguing with a character known as "My Cock" (his bitterness conceals
an emo side: Balk's previous blog was named after a line from a Leonard
Cohen song). One Gawker Media videographer, widely known in the office
as the guy who had sex after-hours on the office couch, lurches around in
tight white jeans. "I was talking to this writer from *Elle Girl,* and then she
said, 'I heard you're a crack whore but really good in bed,' " he tells a
Gawker ad-sales guy, who snickers.

A Town Car pulls to the curb: It's the most famous young "journalist"
in the city, Julia Allison.

"Don't write about her, don't feed into it," two female bloggers beg me,
stepping out of Allison's way as she approaches.

Allison is what Denton likes to call a "Gawker celebrity": Like all editors of gossip publications, he enjoys thinking of himself as a star-maker
and lays claim to creating the personalities that he promotes, much in the
way that the *New York Post*'s "Page Six" has always said it made Paris
Hilton. But, like Paris, Allison is quite complicit in her star-making
process—although she would never admit it, because that would ruin her
image. She is pretty, though she looks even better on your computer
screen because she chooses her outfits explicitly for the cameras: Her look
is southern deb or, more precisely, an actress playing a southern deb—
a polka-dot Nanette Lepore suit with no blouse underneath, a string of
her grandmother's pearls, thickly applied lavender lipstick, and five-inch
white platform shoes. "I'm just a small yappy dog Nick finds amusing,"
says Allison later, in a deep voice that projects across the room. "He's a
godlike figure at the center of his universe," she says on another occasion.
"The godfather! First he started a company, and now it's a culture."

A recent Georgetown University grad who moved to New York to become Candace Bushnell, Allison had a little-read dating column in *AM
New York*—and a list of paramours that included former Tennessee con-

gressman Harold Ford Jr.—when she decided to change her focus. She grabbed Denton's eye by showing up at one of his Halloween parties in a bustier made entirely of Trojan Magnum XL condom wrappers and developed a sophisticated website ("I dated a computer-science guy!"). She link-whored herself to Gawker on a daily basis, even if it meant sharing videos of herself in a white bikini riding a horse. "Freelancers are like the migrant workers of publishing—when I heard that Tom Wolfe makes $6 a word, I was like, 'Whoa,' " says Allison. "I figure if you make yourself a marquee name, you can't be replaced."

Soon, Allison landed a column in *Time Out,* where she was popular for her ability to get her stories linked on Gawker. Gawker was free advertising, after all: "*Time Out New York* dating columnist Julia Allison tackles the age-old dilemma faced by men around the world: How do you trick a chick into bed? Jules' advice: Be cheesy, surround yourself with hot ass, and buy her greasy food. (Not recommended: Yelling, 'Now suck my cock.')" Next, she was hired by *Star* magazine as an editor-at-large. She doesn't actually write anything, though. Her job is to go on TV and pretend that she works at *Star.*

THE VALUE OF Allison to Denton is not only tits = page views: It's also her popularity with Gawker's commenters, the largely anonymous readers whose responses to Gawker's posts are included on every item page. Commenters are the mob sneering at the tumbrels as they pass by—their comments are sometimes hilarious but always cruel and vicious, an echo chamber of Gawker's meanness. Gawker editors let them know their place by introducing "Commenter Executions," by which they banned a few of the lamest commenters each week (e.g., "Crime: on certain days, comments on every single post—yet says nothing"). But now Denton—impressed by the microblogging capabilities of current Silicon Valley darling Facebook and crushing on its founder, young Harvard dropout Mark Zuckerberg—wants to make more of them. He spent most of the summer working with developers on new software that tailors Gawker's page to the specific commenter who visits it. In fact, he'd love to see a site where half the page is taken up with comments.

"Gawker comments, long an embarrassment, frankly, now represent one of the strongest aspects of the site," he wrote recently (in Gawker's comments!). "They reintroduce an element of anarchy, which was in danger of otherwise being lost, as the site became more professional. I *want* secrets to be exposed, memos leaked, spy photos published, arguments to fly." Noah Robischon, Gawker's new managing editor, adds, "There are no immediate plans to reward commenters, but it is a natural way for us to scout for talent. I wouldn't be surprised if commenters who are promoted regularly end up as paid contributors." But are commenters even close to being in the loop? Last week, Denton tried to get them to step up: "Okay, how about a comment from someone who was actually at the Mediabistro party? Facts, please, people." But no one, of course, could answer such a thing—the best they could do is snipe: "Who would admit to this [being at the party], even under the cloak of i-anonymity?" sneered one.

The success of the comments has even made Denton rethink the compensation he pays his bloggers, the cows he has to pay for milk. Gawker as an automated message board, with commenters generating exponentially greater numbers of page views as they click all over the site to see reactions to their comments, could be the dream. There would then be no editors to pay, even at the rates he has to shell out. Until recently, most Gawker bloggers were paid a flat rate of $12 per post for twelve posts a day, with quarterly bonuses adding to the bottom line; these bonuses could be used to buy equity in the company, which took two years to vest. Now, Denton is moving to a pay-for-performance system. He has always tracked the page views of each individual Gawker Media writer, thinking of them like stocks in a portfolio, with whoever generates the most page views as his favorite. If each writer was only as valuable as the page views he drew, then why shouldn't Denton pay him accordingly?

Balk, the site's primary troublemaker, quickly posted an item on Gawker about this change with the slug "Like Rain on Your Wedding Day, Except for Instead of Rain It's Knives." Denton wasn't amused. "Your item makes the argument for performance pay even stronger," he responded in the post's comments. "This awesomely self-indulgent post—of interest to you, me, and you, and me—will struggle to get 1,000 views. Which, under the new and improved pay system, Balk, will not even buy you a minute on your bourbon drip." (Balk gave notice two weeks later.)

Denton is a visionary tech geek, so it's not surprising that he would be fascinated by such new applications, but his relentless focus on page views may be evidence of restlessness, or even an existential crisis: Now that he's making money, really coining it, he knows he may have reached the top. There is a rush on advertising on the Web now, with TNS Media Intelligence reports showing that online advertising was up 17.7 percent for the first half of 2007, while print and TV were in decline. But in its current form, it's not going to solve the publishing crisis, online or off.

In fact, even Gawker.com has become boring to Denton, because it doesn't get the number of page views of his more popular sites. There were probably only going to be a few big Web companies anyway, as well as Google, and even though he still entertained the notion of holding onto his blogs for posterity, word had started to leak out of his talk about selling them down the road. Eventually, New York media would be like the New York film business—there would still be a lot of work, but except for some small independents, all the platforms would be owned elsewhere, operated out of office parks in San Jose, California. Possibly, Denton is holding onto Gawker.com as a kind of hobby, partly for the fun of having a catalogue of the decline of New York print publishing, an entire history of the fall. His roots are in journalism, and he undoubtedly enjoys the notoriety that Gawker brings—he's running one of the best circuses in the city. But a business model is a business model, and increasingly, in the media business, it's hard to find one. Maybe New York was done as a media town.

ON A CHILLY evening in September, Gould and I went out for sushi. She traipsed down Prince Street in a tight electric-blue shirt, the same color as her fingernail polish, and white knee-high boots she had polished up for the fall season. She had just been at her shrink's, where she says she spends all her time talking about Gawker—"It's just such a weird cross between being an artist and working in a sweatshop," she'd said earlier. She tucked her hair behind her ears and sighed. "Plus I have gotten so much flak over the past year, from everyone from random people who e-mail me that I'm a bitch and a cunt, to my family, to Jimmy Kimmel calling me the devil—to my boyfriend of six years, when we broke up and I was moving my dishes out of his apartment, asking, 'Why did you write that post about that Stevie Nicks song? Now it's obvious to everyone that you were having an affair with your co-worker.' " She shot me a lopsided smile.

I asked her how she felt about the upcoming changes in comments and pay at Gawker. "I can't have feelings about that kind of thing," she said. "It's kind of like you're in jail and you have feelings about the color they paint the walls." Gould published a book last spring, and wasn't sure if she should write another. "At the end of the day, your ideas in a book have less impact than if you had summed them up in two paragraphs on the most widely read blog at the most-read time of the day, so why'd you spend two years on it?" she said, delicately picking up a piece of toro. "But there's other ways to get noticed than the Internet, right?" She laughed bitterly. "There's always TV."

Recently, she'd bonded with Julia Allison—the two went to a psychic in Staten Island together, driving in a Mercedes convertible Allison had borrowed (though the guy who owned it didn't really know she had borrowed it), booming the stereo and singing along to the lyrics of Prince's "Pussy Control." The psychic told Allison that she had to be more "real" and Gould that she was on the road to love—but then she was not, so that was all a waste of time. But at least she decided Allison was cool. "It's not like Julia keeps her enemies close and her friends closer," said Gould. "She doesn't even make a distinction between the two."

In an insult culture, shamelessness is a crucial attribute, was part of the point. Last week at a party, Allison appeared in a particularly revealing top and told me, "I figure if people look at my cleavage they won't listen to my words," then winked. She and Gould were both wearing polka-dots, not on purpose, and they cavorted in their outfits for a photographer, slinging their arms around Allison's boyfriend, even though Gould was sure to overdramatically grimace in some of the pictures.

By Gawker's rules, Allison seemed to be winning the game. Still, the question remained: Could you be successful in New York without becoming a—well, a douchebag? It was something that Gould would have to ponder.

PART TWO

....

THE RISE, THE FALL

★

NAMATH ALL NIGHT LONG

JIMMY BRESLIN

APRIL 7, 1969

There have been many other athletes in New York. But not since Babe Ruth had a sports figure's legend fit so precisely into the city's own story of itself as did that of Joe Namath. The arrogance of his famous guarantee of a Super Bowl victory, and the fact that he delivered on it, summoned to mind Ruth's called shot. And Namath's good-natured, whiskey-fueled womanizing reinforced one of New York's guiding myths—that hard living and huge success are not mutually exclusive. Jimmy Breslin, who was a stalwart of New York *magazine's early years, tracked Namath down and found him completely unabashed about his predilections and living up to his myth. Breslin is the author of many books, most recently* The Good Rat: A True Story *(2008), and won a Pulitzer in 1986. "I should have won ten of them," he says.*

T̲HE BARMAID HAD LONG black hair and she was sitting on top of the bar with her chest coming out of her dress and her skirt useless against the amount of legs she was showing. She had her eyes shut and her hands held out in front of her.

"Excuse me," one of us said.

The barmaid didn't answer.

"Ah, may I ask you something?" I said.

The barmaid frowned. "Shhhhh. I'm driving my Jaguar."

"Oh," I said.

A girl in bell-bottom pants played the juke box and everybody in the place, Bachelors Three on Lexington Avenue in Manhattan, moved their heads with the music. Joe Namath is one of the owners of the place, and also one of its best customers.

"Well, I hate to bother you," I said to the barmaid, "but is Joe around?"

"Not now."

"Expect him?"

"He's at the Palm Bay Club right now. Here, get in. I'll drive you over."

The guy with me, a race track character whose name is Pepe, shook his head. "You know," he said to the barmaid, "I used to be considered a lunatic before kids like you came around."

NAMATH WAS FOUND later at the Palm Bay Club. Later, because the Palm Bay Club is in Miami. In the world of Joe Willie Namath, location and time really don't matter. They are trying to call this immensely likeable twenty-five-year-old by the name of Broadway Joe. But Broadway as a street has been a busted-out whorehouse with orange juice stands for as long as I can recall, and now, as an expression, it is tired and represents nothing to me. And it certainly represents nothing to Joe Willie Namath's people. His people are on First and Second Avenues, where young girls spill out of the buildings and into the bars crowded with guys and the world is made of long hair and tape cartridges and swirling color and military overcoats and the girls go home with guys or the guys go home with girls and nobody is too worried about any of it because life moves, it doesn't stand still and whisper about what happened last night. It is out of these bars and apartment buildings and the life of them that Joe Willie Namath comes. He comes with a Scotch in his hand at night and a football in the daytime and last season he gave New York the only lift the city has had in so many years it is hard to think of a comparison.

When you live in fires and funerals and strikes and rats and crowds and people screaming in the night, sports is the only thing that makes any sense. And there is only one sport anymore that can change the tone of a city and there is only one player who can do it. His name is Joe Willie Namath and when he beat the Baltimore Colts he gave New York the kind of light, meaningless, dippy and lovely few days we had all but forgotten. Once, Babe Ruth used to be able to do it for New York, I guess. Don't try to tell Namath's people on First Avenue about Babe Ruth because they don't even know the name. In fact, with the young, you can forget all of baseball. The sport is gone. But if you ever have seen Ruth, and then you see Namath, you know there is very little difference. I saw Ruth once when he came off the golf course and walked into the bar at the old Bayside course in Queens. He was saying how f'n hot it was and how f'n thirsty he was and he ordered a Tom Collins and the bartender made it in a mixing glass full of chopped ice and then handed the mixing glass to Ruth and the Babe said that was fine, kid, and he opened his mouth and brought up the mixing glass and there went everything. In one shot, he swallowed the mixing glass, ice chunks and everything else. He slapped the mixing glass down and said, give me another one of these f'n things, kid. I still never have seen anybody who could drink like that. After that day, I believed all the stories they told about Ruth.

It is the same thing when you stand at the bar with Joe Namath.

The Palm Bay Club is a private place with suites that can cost you over $2,000 a month, and Namath lives through the winter in one of the biggest, a place with a white leather bar that many people say is the best bar in all of Miami, and a view of sun splashing on blue water. When Joe Namath came to his suite on this day, a guy he knew was taking up the living room floor with a girl. Namath went politely past them into the bedroom. Another guy he knew was there with a girl. Namath shrugged and left to play golf.

He walked around the Diplomat Presidential course in a blue rain jacket and with that round-shouldered, slouchy walk of the campuses and First Avenue. He had sideburns and a mustache and Fu Manchu beard and the thick, shaggy hair at the back of the neck which upsets older people so much, and therefore is a must with the young. I watched the Super Bowl game on television with fourteen-year-old twin boys, and Namath, slouchy and longhaired, came on after the game and said, "All these writers should take their notebooks and pencils and eat them." The two around me burst out of their chairs. "Yeah!" one of them yelled. "Yeah, Joe Willie! Outasight!" the other one yelled. It was Dustin Hoffman in *The*

Graduate all over again. Screw the adults. I knew that Joe Namath was going to mean a lot more than merely the best football player of his time.

AFTER HE FINISHED playing golf, Namath went right for the bar. He had his money up and was ordering whiskey while he kept looking at the people with him to make sure that they didn't get a chance to pay.

"I'm drinking a lot lately," he said.

"Do you drink a lot all the time?" he was asked.

"I might as well. I get the name for it whether I do it or not. In college, this fella Hoot Owl Hicks and I were out one night and we had two cans of beer in the car, that's all we had all night, and we're coming home in one of these four-door, no-door cars. Thing couldn't do over thirty-five miles an hour. But the Tuscaloosa cops stop us. They loved me. Huh. 'Hey, *Penn-syl-vania* kid.' I take the two beer cans and throw them out the car. There's a damn hill there and here come the two sonsofbitches rolling right back to the car. I grab the two cans and throw them back up again. They come rolling down again. The cop says, 'Hey, *Penn-syl-vania* kid, just leave 'em there.' I said to the cop, 'You're a real piece of work. Now I know why mothers like you go on the police. Can't get a job nowhere else.' That did it. I got put in jail for being a common drunk."

"Do you drink during the football season?" he was asked.

"Just about all the time."

"What do you, taper off before the game?"

A grin spread from his mouth. His light green eyes had fun in them. "The night before the Oakland game, I got the whole family in town and there's people all over my apartment and the phone keeps ringing. I wanted to get away from everything. Too crowded and too much noise. So I went to the Bachelors Three and grabbed a girl and a bottle of Johnnie Walker Red and went to the Summit Hotel and stayed in bed all night with the girl and the bottle."

The Oakland game was in late December and it was for the American League championship. On Sunday morning, the Oakland Raiders football team, fresh-eyed from an early bedcheck and a night's sleep, uniform-neat in their team blazers, filed into a private dining room in the Waldorf-Astoria for the pre-game meal. Meanwhile, just across the street in the

Summit Hotel, Joe Willie Namath was patting the broad goodbye, putting an empty whiskey bottle in the wastebasket, dressing up in his mink coat and leaving for the ballgame. It was a cold, windy day and late in the afternoon Namath threw one 50 yards to Don Maynard and the Jets were the league champions. The Oakland team went home in their team blazers.

"Same thing before the Super Bowl," Namath said. "I went out and got a bottle and grabbed this girl and brought her back to the hotel in Fort Lauderdale and we had a good time the whole night."

He reached for his drink. His grin broke into a laugh. "It's good for you," he said. He held his arms out and shook them. "It loosens you up good for the game."

In the Super Bowl game, the Baltimore Colts were supposed to wreck Namath, and they probably were in bed dreaming about this all night. As soon as the game started, the Baltimore linemen and linebackers got together and rushed in at Namath in a maneuver they call blitzing and Namath, who doesn't seem to need time even to set his feet, threw a quick pass down the middle and then came right back and hit Matt Snell out on the side and right away you knew Baltimore was in an awful lot of trouble.

"Some people don't like this image I got myself, bein' a swinger," Namath was saying. "They see me with a girl instead of being home like other athletes. But I'm not institutional. I swing. If it's good or bad, I don't know, but I know it's what I like. It hasn't hurt my friends or my family and it hasn't hurt me. So why hide it? It's the truth. It's what the _____ we are.

"During the season, Hudson and I were drinking a lot and he said to me one day, 'Hey, Joe, we gotta stop all this drinkin'.' And I said, 'Jeez, yes. We'll stop drinking. Let's just drink wine.' Hudson said, no, we had to stop all the way. Well we did. So we don't drink and we go up to Buffalo and we lose, 37–35, and I got five interceptions. I go right into the dressing room and I tell Hudson, 'Jeez, let's not hear any more about not drinking.' Then before the Denver game, I had the flu and I didn't drink. Five interceptions.

"So we're in the sauna before the Oakland game, the first day we were working for the game and I'm saying, 'All right, fellas, this is the big one. Gotta win. Our whole season depends on it. Thinking about not drinking myself.' And Dave Herman yells, 'Jeez, don't do that. Do anything but don't you stop drinking. If you don't drink, I'll grab you and pour it down your throat.' "

Sonny Werblin, who had been on the phone, came back to the bar. He had been taking notes on a small pad. He showed the notes to Namath and spoke to him in a low voice. Sonny Werblin was the head of the Music Corporation of America and he was one of the five or six most important people in show business. He retired from MCA and bought into the New York Jets. In what clearly is the best move made in sports in my time, Werblin decided to base his entire operation on getting Joe Namath and making him a star. Last year, Werblin sold his part of the team. But Joe Namath still calls him "Mr. Werblin" and never "Sonny" and when something comes up in Joe's life, he asks Sonny Werblin about it.

Now, Namath sat and listened to Werblin.

"How much?" Namath asked.

Werblin said something and Namath nodded and they went back to their drinks.

A few minutes later, when everybody else was busy talking about something, Sonny Werblin said, "This thing I was showing him, it's about the movies. You see, I know he's a natural star. I mean, look at him. He's got the face and the eyes. Women'll tell you, bedroom eyes. He's got that animal sex appeal. I knew he was a star the minute I saw him. We'd been going around looking at All-American quarterbacks. They had one at Tulsa. Jerry Rhone. He came into the room, a little, introverted guy. I said, nah, I don't want him. Never mind how good he is, I need to build a franchise with somebody who can do more than play. So we went down to Birmingham and the minute Joe walked into the room, I knew. I said, 'Here we go.' So what I'm doing now. I've got picture offers for him, but I don't want any freaky thing just to cash in on him being a football player. I want to build a broad base for him. I heard about something just now. Paul Newman and Joanne Woodward are doing a film. We'll pay to get into it. We'll *pay* for the chance. I want him in with good actors, where he can look good. I don't want him over his head the first time with something we're doing just for the money. I couldn't care about money. I wouldn't touch a cent of anything I get for him. I just want to do it right for him."

We had to leave the golf club and drive over to a place called the Jockey Club. Before leaving, Namath ordered a round of drinks in plastic cups and everybody got into the car with the drinks. Joe Hirsch, the writer for the *Morning Telegraph*, was driving.

"I'm going up to Pensacola tonight," Namath said.

"Seeing Suzy?" somebody said.

"Yeah, I'll see her," he said.

"She is a lovely, very smart girl," somebody said.

"Is she your girl?" Joe was asked.

"I like her," he said. "She goes to college in Pensacola."

"What school?"

"Jeez, ah, Northern Florida something or other. It's a new college up there."

"Is she a senior?"

"I don't know. What is she, Joe?"

"She gets out this summer," Joe Hirsch said.

"Uh huh," Joe Willie Namath said.

There was a stop at a place with offices and Namath was walking through the hall and the elevator operator came after him and called out, "Mr. Namath, if you don't stop in this office, you'll break the heart of one of your biggest fans."

The operator led Namath to an office where a blonde in a pale yellow dress sat at a typewriter.

"Well, hi," Namath said.

"Hel-lo," the girl beamed.

"How are you?" Namath said.

"Fine," she said. "Do you remember me?"

"Of course I remember you." He repeated her name.

She beamed. "You've got a good memory."

"Still got the same phone number?" She shook her head yes. "That's real good," Joe said. "I'll call you up. We'll have a drink or three."

"That'll be terrific," she said. "Like my hair the new way?"

"Hey, let me see," he said. He looked closely at her pile of blond hair. She sat perfectly still so he could see it better. "It's great," Joe Namath said. She beamed. "See ya," he said.

Walking down the hall, Namath was shaking his head. "Boy, that was a real memory job. You know, I only was with that girl one night? We had a few drinks and we balled and I took her phone number and that's it. Never saw her again. Only one night with the girl. And I come up with the right name. A real memory job."

When the car got to the Jockey Club, Namath, who had been in the back seat, began to get out. Pulling himself by the hands, he got up, turned his body around and came out of the car backwards, hanging on, not moving for long moments while he waited for his two knees to adjust. Now you could see why Sonny Werblin worries about the right chance at the movies for him. All the laughs of Joe Namath are based, as laughs always are, on pain. And this is a kid who has made it to the top on two of the most damaged knees an athlete ever had. His next game could be the last. So today he swings.

In the Jockey Club, he drank Scotch on the rocks. When it was time for him to leave, he asked the bartender to give him a drink in a plastic cup so he could have something in the car. He shook hands and left to get the plane to Pensacola, where his girlfriend goes to a school whose name he doesn't quite know.

COMEDY ISN'T FUNNY

CHRIS SMITH

MARCH 13, 1995

Saturday Night Live, patently, permanently changed comedy after it first aired, in 1975. Twenty years later, when Chris Smith set out to write about SNL, the show was in the doldrums. Its ratings were low, morale lower. The threat to the show was no doubt one reason it took a chance and allowed Smith to wander around for weeks behind the scenes. He went to meetings, to rehearsals, to after-hours parties, and even to an SNL funeral. "It was the kind of journalistic access that's almost nonexistent now," says Smith. Later he ran into a public-relations student who said she'd been assigned his article in class. It was an example, she was taught, of what not to permit clients to do. But the comedy business—like the economy, apparently—is cyclical, and as of this writing the show is doing fine. Smith is a contributing editor at New York.

*I*T'S FRIDAY NIGHT at *Saturday Night Live,* and rehearsal looks like it will drag into Monday. Wedged into one corner of the legendary Studio 8H, where Toscanini made gorgeous music and Dan Aykroyd made cheeseburgers, is the jolly bulk of guest host George Foreman.

Foreman is rehearsing his role as Uncle Joe, a shy wedding guest who is being tormented by Kevin Nealon, playing the wedding reception's smarmy emcee. Nealon goads the reluctant Foreman into making a toast. Nealon wheedles the recalcitrant Foreman into singing a song. Nealon suggests that the annoyed Foreman toss the bouquet. Foreman threatens to slug Nealon. The five-minute sketch isn't particularly complicated—or particularly funny. Yet after an hour of rehearsal, Nealon is still stumbling over his lines. Then Nealon, in his record ninth season at *SNL*, accidentally steps in front of Foreman, blocking the camera and stalling yet another take. There's a metallic clatter as a stagehand knocks lighting poles to the floor. Five actors, fifteen extras, and four musicians sit silently, waiting for the disembodied voice of Dave Wilson, the show's director for most of its two-decade run, to give them instructions. Potbellied technicians jam chocolate-chip cookies into their mouths. A couple of *SNL* writers, waiting for "Uncle Joe" to finish so they can rehearse their own bit, snicker that the sketch should be renamed "Uncle Slow." Adam Sandler tries to cut the boredom, warbling "sing, sing a song . . ." in his trademark idiot-boy voice. At first, there are a few laughs. When Sandler continues into the third verse of the Carpenters song, and then the fourth, people start inspecting their shoelaces.

Standing in the darkness just beyond the set lights is a glum Janeane Garofalo. As *SNL* tried to rebuild from its disastrous 1993–94 season, hiring the smart, sarcastic thirty-year-old comic actress seemed perfect. Besides being funny—she is widely beloved from HBO's *Larry Sanders Show* and became something of a generational mini-icon in the movie *Reality Bites*—Garofalo added two qualities in short supply at *SNL:* She's hip and she's female.

Right now, though, Garofalo looks like a forlorn child trapped at her parents' dinner party. Barely over five feet tall, her lank hair pulled in three directions by pink and yellow baby-doll barrettes, Garofalo droops under the weight of her oversize plaid shirt-jacket, baggy homegirl jeans, and Doc Martens boots. Garofalo watched *SNL* as a kid (she was in fourth grade when it premiered), and after she signed on last summer, she called it a dream come true. Now her mood is as black as her fingernail polish.

For the first three months of the season, Garofalo's largely been stuck in dull, secondary wife and girlfriend roles. In "Uncle Joe," she's a waitress, with a single line near the end of the sketch, and the scene keeps breaking down before reaching her cue.

Finally, it's time for Garofalo to walk up to Foreman, tray of fake cocktails in hand. "Uncle Joe, just sing a song. Okay? Denise's getting upset," Garofalo says perkily. Two or three more takes and she's done. She dashes off to her dressing room.

Upstairs, in the pink-walled cubicle that belonged to Gilda Radner, Garofalo shakes one Marlboro out of a fresh carton and tries to describe how she's been treated on the show. "It's almost like hazing," she says. "Fraternity hazing. It's hard. It takes its toll on you. But I think you come out much better in the end. If nothing else, this experience has just toughened me up."

That's diplomatic—especially since Garofalo has told friends that *Saturday Night* has been "the most miserable experience of my life." What's gotten her through it?

"Cigarettes and Stoli," she says with a tight smile.

SURE *SATURDAY NIGHT LIVE* is bad these days. Everyone from Judge Ito ("hasn't been funny in ten years") to original and recently deceased *SNL* writer Michael O'Donoghue ("It couldn't suck worse if it had rubber lips") says so.

None of the outside critics, however, has pinpointed *why*—why the show that two decades ago revolutionized TV comedy continues to fall on its face. Four weeks spent recently at *SNL* offered up a rare portrait of institutional decay—the gargantuan exertion of sweat, blood, fried food, and bluff self-denial that yields, for example, a mind-bendingly awful sketch about space aliens and rectal probes.

Certainly the loss of Dana Carvey, Jon Lovitz, Jan Hooks, and Phil Hartman, after long runs, has hurt. And even with world-class talent, creating ninety minutes of fresh sketch comedy is a daunting challenge.

But there's more ailing *Saturday Night* than any particular personnel defections: The show that once broke all the rules is now obsessed with maintaining its internal pecking order, from where people sit in meetings to how much airtime new cast members deserve.

What's really killing *SNL* is a deep spiritual funk. There's a lumbering heaviness about every part of the show, from an extravagantly expensive set for a Wizard of Oz sketch to the self-important attitude that squashes bold personalities to the marathon writing sessions that stumble past dawn. "You feel it as soon as you walk into the writers' room," says a young comedian who rejected an offer to join *Saturday Night*. "It's a depressed, kind of lethargic burnout."

The on-camera talent is more spirited; unfortunately, much of that is expressed as petulance. In the middle of a January show, Sandler and David Spade are in an office one floor above the studio, drinking beer and acting cute for a couple of models. "Don't you have a show to do?" someone asks Spade. "Not this week," he sneers. Fifteen minutes later, Spade appears briefly in a sketch, squinting into the middle distance to read his three lines from a cue card.

"They can't even fake forcing themselves to care," says a longtime *SNL* writer who's saddened by the show's decline. "When you watch the show on TV, that comes through—it really seems taken with itself. And when it's as bad as it can be, and people still act like there's nothing wrong, then it's sort of like a fuck-you to the audience—'We don't have to be good, because we're *Saturday Night Live!*' It's like the post office. 'What are you gonna do, deliver the mail yourself?' "

Internal squabbling and raging egos have always been a part of the *Saturday Night* ethos—"It was a combination of summer camp and concentration camp," remembers Anne Beatts, one of the show's original writers; now it's "a cross between *Love Boat* and *Das Boot*," says Mike Myers, the *Wayne's World* star who recently left the show.

But as *SNL* lurches toward its twentieth birthday this October, the turmoil is producing far fewer laughs. For every bright spot—like Norm MacDonald on "Weekend Update"—there are a planeload of bombs, like an interminable October sketch in which Chris Farley and Tim Meadows simply screamed at each other. Last week, Garofalo fled *SNL* to make a movie. Writers phone their agents regularly, begging to escape. With ratings down 19 percent from two years ago, and NBC nervously watching the show's weekly budget climb to an all-time high of $1.5 million, executive producer Lorne Michaels still hasn't figured out how to put the *fun* back in *dysfunctional*.

As arrogant as *Saturday Night* can often be, there's something sad about the slow, woozy fall of a treasured pop-culture institution. For *SNL* fans who grew up on the Coneheads, E. Buzz Miller, Buckwheat, and

Church Lady, watching the current incarnation of the show is like watching late-period Elvis—embarrassing and poignant.

ALL IS TRANQUIL and prosperous in Lorne Michaels's ninth-floor office at 30 Rockefeller Plaza. Postcard-size copies of *SNL*'s colorized host photos form a celebrity quilt behind the executive producer's desk—there's Steve Martin! Sharon Stone! Uh . . . Nancy Kerrigan?

An off-white sectional couch and matching overstuffed chairs look expensive but not ostentatious. Elegant black-and-white photos of the current *SNL* cast line the stark white walls; unfortunately, the group has grown so large that the photo of its newest member, Mark McKinney, is propped against a table leg.

The office décor says taste, money, I'm-all-right-Jack serenity. Two floors down, however, a plastic surgeon is ripping hunks of flesh from the movie-star face of Jeff Daniels.

It's past midnight on a Friday in mid-January. In multiplexes across this great land, Daniels is farting and belching his way through Hollywood's No. 1 box-office hit. But he had to come to *Saturday Night Live* to get really dumb. Tonight, Daniels was being fitted for a prosthetic nose and eyebrows, to help him impersonate Liam Neeson. But the mold used to create the prosthetics has stuck to Daniels's skin. A doctor has been trying to chip the gunk from the star's face, but after two hours of Daniels's screams, he's taking a break.

Michaels's face betrays no sign of the ordeal. "The show is in a transitional period," he says wanly. "I think it's better than last year, and not where it will be by next year."

A cold Amstel Light and a basket of popcorn are on the office table in front of him. Fresh popcorn heralds Michaels's every entrance. Whether he's about to arrive at his seventeenth-floor office at NBC, with its breathtaking view of the Empire State Building; the eighth-floor *Saturday Night* studio; this ninth-floor office overlooking the studio; or his handsome Broadway Video offices a couple of blocks west in the Brill Building, a blond wicker basket of warm kernels precedes him, usually delivered by one of several blonde female assistants in their early twenties. Cast members call these high-strung women the Lornettes. (Nearly four years ago, the fifty-year-old Michaels married one of these assistants, his third wife, a woman eighteen years his junior.)

"Ahhh! Just thinking of [the Lornettes] makes me so happy I quit," says Julia Sweeney, who left the cast last spring. "Because I could not take one fucking more Friday night, trying to get in to see Lorne, outside of Lorne's office on the ninth floor, with this bevy of girls, and their latest outfits and their magazines and their fingernail polish, on the phone, making sure that Steve Martin got the flowers on his anniversary, even though he's broken up with Victoria Tennant, and the hilarious note that Lorne wrote to Steve Martin that *must* go with the flowers, which must be birds-of-paradise! They'd slip in and out of Lorne's office going, 'Shush! Lorne's in a very bad mood today.' "

Though his helpers may be tightly wound, Michaels is unflappable. And he's turned on his "charm beam," as Dana Carvey puts it, for the benefit of a visiting reporter.

"If your angle is going to be that the show is decadent and out of touch," Michaels says wryly, "we have that reduced to a press release to save time."

Michaels's patter is so smooth—his accent, widely imitated by acquaintances, is virtually British, though Michaels grew up in Toronto—that you're almost lulled into believing the peculiar theory he employs to explain the harsh criticism of the show. "I think reviewers hate staying up late," Michaels says. "On every other show, they get a cassette. They view it when they want to. With us, they have to stay up till one o'clock in the morning and then get the story in for Monday. The older ones get cranky."

He doesn't answer questions so much as smother them under a soothing poultice of words. He doesn't get angry. ("Talking to Lorne," says Rosie Shuster, an original *SNL* writer and Michaels's first wife, "is like talking to tundra.") His musings digress so widely that you don't even notice when Michaels slips in the news that he came very close to bringing Carvey back to the cast last summer—a move that would have telegraphed a loss of will for a program traditionally intent on breaking new talent.

Michaels crosses his legs and folds his hands in exactly the way predicted by an intimate of the late William Shawn. Michaels was fascinated by the old *New Yorker* editor, and he gave Shawn an office at Broadway

Video, Michaels's production company, when Shawn was pushed out of the magazine in 1987. "I was amazed at how many of Shawn's mannerisms Lorne had," says the colleague of Shawn's. "And they had similar sensibilities: They're both sort of provincial guys with tremendous romantic ideas of sophistication and the city."

According to a longtime friend of Michaels's, the producer's Shawnophilia went beyond shared tastes: "Lorne had this weird idea that when Shawn retired, he'd be asked to run the magazine. He thinks of himself as the fundamental sophisticated New Yorker. It's one of the weird keys to Lorne's real personality."

One of Michaels's greatest talents is creating an aura of glamour about himself and *SNL*. But as the show sank last year, NBC began to wonder whether Michaels was spending too much time cultivating his urbane image. "You could always tell when the Knicks or the opera were in town," says a recently departed *SNL* star. "That's the only time Lorne made sure the Wednesday-night script read-through started on schedule."

Network executives suggested Michaels increase his "focus" on *SNL* this year, but Michaels stammers when asked what he's doing differently. "Differently? Ahhhhm. Uhhhhmmmm. Just trying to keep people's—ahh, I don't know. Simultaneously sort of pushing people as hard as I can and trying to keep their spirits up."

By all accounts, Michaels is more visible around *SNL* these days—raising the already-therapy-caliber paranoia level. Michaels granted everyone at *SNL* permission to be interviewed for this story, but when I casually say hello to one veteran writer, he lowers his eyes and his voice. "I can't be seen talking to you," he mumbles.

"Lorne wants people to feel insecure," says an ex-cast member. "It's the same techniques cults use—they keep you up for hours, they never let you know that you're okay, and they always make you think that your spot could be taken at any moment by someone else."

Michaels also sends messages through the Brillstein-Grey Company. The powerhouse Hollywood management-and-production team, founded by one of Michaels's closest friends, Bernie Brillstein, handles eight of the fourteen *SNL* cast members as well as its executive producer. The connection makes spinning off movies much easier. "To your face, Lorne always wants to be the hero and Santa Claus. But if you try to do a movie that Lorne's not producing, Brillstein-Grey will let you know he's not happy," says an ex-*SNL* star who's had it happen to him. "Brillstein lets you know you're in the doghouse. Your sketches don't get on, or you get on in the last five minutes of the show.

"Lorne is nonconfrontative," Brillstein confirms. "Sometimes he asks us to talk to people."

VETERANS OF *SNL*'s glorious first five years saw Michaels becoming aloof way back then. "Lorne always wanted to be admired—revered, even. Which is different from being famous. Different from being rich. And different from being sexy," says a man who knows Michaels well from those years. "He wants to be a legend, and he would have LEGENDARY tattooed in his underwear if it were possible." Each week, Michaels poses for dozens of photos with the guest host, adding to his enormous collection.

But there's a sadness, too, when the original crew talks about how Michaels has changed, and it isn't just obligatory nostalgia. "There's a real difference between running a kind of rebel outfit and running an institution," says one famous player. "Castro is not one of my main heroes, but I think I would rather have known him in the hills than in the palace."

Michaels waves off such complaints. He has millions in the bank and has survived more SATURDAY NIGHT DEAD headlines than he can count. His confidence seems genuine, and even when he says the show is "fighting for its life," the words sound more like what he's expected to say than like what he believes.

He takes solace in the fact that *SNL* is still the highest-rated show on late-night TV—*Letterman* included—and that the average rating for this season's first thirteen episodes is just a shade under the numbers for the critically acclaimed shows from the late eighties. As expensive as *SNL* has become to produce, NBC is surely making too big a profit from beer and blue-jeans ads to seriously consider dropping the show—though Fox and CBS, sensing an opening, are planning the first direct challenges to *SNL* in the fall.

"I have a contract for another two years," Michaels says. "The expectation is that I'll be here for another two seasons after this one." Then he's in-

terrupted by a knock on his office door; it's one of the Lornettes. The doctor has returned with more anesthetic for Jeff Daniels's tortured face.
Michaels politely excuses himself and strides off to comfort tomorrow
night's host.

VERY LATE ON a Thursday night, May 1994: A punchy, sleep-deprived
group of *SNL* writers and performers is fooling around in the seventeenth-
floor writers' conference room. Cast member Rob Schneider has an idea
for an imitation. He stretches out on a couch and closes his eyes. "This is
Lorne sleeping," he says. "Okay, somebody wake me up." A writer tugs his
shoulder.

"Uh!" he snorts, snapping to attention. "It wasn't me!"

Laughs all around. "My turn," says a senior writer. He settles onto the
couch as sleeping Lorne and then is startled into consciousness.
"Uhhhh—it was Jim!"

Even Jim Downey laughs. The producer and head writer of *SNL* for
nine years, Downey, forty-two, joined the writing staff in *SNL*'s second
season, in 1976. He left when Michaels quit in 1980, was head writer for
the first year and a half of *Late Night with David Letterman*, then returned to *SNL* in 1984, a year before Michaels came back as executive producer. From "*¿èQuien es mas macho?!*" to a commercial parody for the
"First Citywide Change Bank," Downey has written some of *SNL*'s funniest
and most famous sketches. And in April of last year, weary from holding
together an increasingly ragged show, Downey had learned that NBC
wanted to fire him.

It was one of the few times that Downey, who has day-to-day responsibility for the show, had ever heard from NBC executives. "The network
doesn't know who runs the show!" says a recent cast member. "The only
way they'd know if Jim wasn't doing a good job is if Lorne told them!"

Downey, a moon-faced man with merry Irish eyes, has the distracted
manner of an Ivy League liberal-arts professor (he majored in folklore and
mythology at Harvard); when he's had a rare eight hours of sleep, he could
pass for Dylan Thomas's younger brother. He claims there's a less sinister
corporate explanation: Don Ohlmeyer, the recently installed president of
NBC's entertainment division, simply checked the *SNL* staff list and de-

cided to dispatch the most powerful person beneath Michaels. "We had a rough season; they wanted to make a change. It wasn't personal; it was just business," Downey says. "And Lorne said, 'Absolutely not, I forbid it.' " As he speaks Michaels's name for the first time in the interview, Downey unconsciously puts his right hand to his throat and pulls his shirt collar chokingly tight.

An ex-cast member says Downey was in a very different mood at the party after the final show of last season. "I went up to Jim and said, 'Jim, I want to let you know I think you're a genius. You're the funniest person I've ever known.' And he says, 'Well, I'm quitting.' And I go, 'What?' And of course he didn't quit! *Because Lorne and Jim are like an old married couple! They can't quit!"*

Indeed, Downey flew to Burbank in May to discuss his future with NBC executives. Michaels was there—and, Downey says, had already saved Downey's job. Michaels, however, neglected to mention the reprieve to Downey until *after* the writer's tense meeting with the suits.

"Jim is more sensitive than he is spunky," says a friend of Downey's, "and the more he's beaten up, the more he shrinks away."

AS A JANUARY Thursday night slouches into Friday morning, Downey is where he's been for nearly all of his adult working life. At 2 A.M., the sky is gray, the way it is in paperback detective novels. But no one in the *Saturday Night Live* writers' room could tell you about the weather. They don't glance out the seventeenth-floor windows or step outside the building. Many will sleep tonight on the couches in their tiny offices, if they sleep at all.

Thursday is rewrite night. Each week, the fourteen-man, three-woman writing staff stays up most of Tuesday night, churning out between thirty and forty sketches, supplemented by a half-dozen or so written by cast members. Wednesday evening, about fifty people jam into the writers' room, everyone from Lorne Michaels to the network censor to members of the props department, to listen as the sketches are read aloud. Michaels, Downey, and the week's host then adjourn to Michaels's office and select about a dozen finalists.

The choices are often hard to fathom. Michaels frequently rejects pieces that he thinks are over the heads of *SNL*'s teens and frat-boys demographic. His preference is for the broadest likability, not the sharpest bite—amazingly, he's lately been trying to soften the dark humor of Norm MacDonald on "Weekend Update," one of the few new successes on the show.

Starting at about two on Thursday afternoon, the writers reassemble around the eight-foot-long conference table, where they dissect, line by line, each of the lucky sketches. Friday is for rehearsal and for another bleary-eyed whack at rewriting bits that still aren't working.

This has been, with minor adjustments, the schedule since the show was created in 1975. "Everybody then was on so much coke they didn't notice it was going on until four in the morning," wisecracks new cast member Laura Kightlinger. "We stay up, but we're too lazy to do the drugs."

Suggest that there must be another, less-punishing way to organize the week and you hear self-congratulatory speeches about putting the show on at all. "Look," Downey says, "you get a bunch of Swiss engineers to map out our show, describe to them what's involved, what needs to be written, designed, built, painted, scored, blocked, shot, rehearsed, mounted, and then trimmed, reconfigured, noted, and put back on its feet—they go, 'Okay, you're describing a twelve-day process, maybe ten.' And we go, 'Jeez, that's too bad, 'cause we have to do it in six.' So you just do it, and it involves incredibly long hours for everyone."

The Thursday-night session is a brain-numbing test of endurance, punctuated by moments of giddiness and frequent deliveries of mountains of food. Writers drift in and out, languorously. At the moment, ten writers are perched around the table, but only four speak up regularly: Al Franken, forty-three, a holdover from the early years; Ian Maxtone-Graham, thirty-five, a preppy triathlete in his third season at *SNL;* Fred Wolf, a skeletal stand-up comic and former *Chevy Chase Show* writer in his thirties whose jokes usually involve Satan or spewing bodily fluids; and Downey. Downey commonly works eighty hours a week. Now his eyes are puffy from a catnap on his office couch, and his graying hair is disheveled to the point where it might as well have been attached in random hunks.

During the *SNL* season, the writers don't need to have much interaction with the outside world. As the rewrite session drifts on, they bark out requests for food, and an assistant, Lori Jo Hoekstra, phones them in. At ten o'clock, it's ten Quarter Pounders, eight Big Macs, four bacon double cheeseburgers, and heaps of fries; ninety minutes later, there's an equally hefty delivery of ribs and chicken; at 1 A.M., it's spaghetti, lasagna, and salads.

Meanwhile, they make grudging progress on a sketch written by Norm MacDonald. It's a parody of Andy Rooney—not exactly a fresh target. Rooney, played by MacDonald, is cleaning out his desk and finds a bottle of sedatives, empty except for cotton.

"Should I mention cotton more than once?" MacDonald asks, and it's debated for ten minutes. No—just one cotton reference stays in, but now they can't decide whether the pills are for the treatment of "hallucinations," "mood swings," "dementia," or "NRA dementia."

"That's too much," Downey says. "It's his attitude that's funny, the fact that he's ignoring something that's obviously important."

MacDonald: "So I can say, 'I don't know what the pills are for—what I do know is, the bottle is mostly filled with cotton.' "

Franken: "And, 'I give the pills to Lesley Stahl. Then, when Lesley's passed out, I take her to the closet and rape her.' Or, 'That's why you never see Lesley until February.' Or, 'When she passes out, I put her in various positions and take pictures of her.' "

Downey: " 'Here's a picture of Ed Bradley.' "

MacDonald: "What if Rooney rapes Mike Wallace? And then says, 'I guess that makes me bad.' Is it funnier with a black guy? Or two old white guys?"

Franken: "What about, 'I drag Mike into my office and rape him. Right here! I guess that makes me bad.' "

The discussion sputters for another ten minutes. Then the writers lose interest and drift over to the newly arrived food. "C'mon!" Downey says plaintively. "Let's finish this!"

The sketches eventually get tighter and marginally better. Mostly, all this group writing produces a thin comedy mush. "It's now a much more fey, effete, overthought show," says Rosie Shuster, who did her third tour on the writing staff during the late eighties. "The cud is so well chewed before it goes on the air."

"Talent is essential, and hard work is essential, but there isn't any tight correlation between working your ass off and quality," a frustrated Downey says later. "It's so unfair. You're sitting around, and you just have a great idea—like 'Fred Garvin, Male Prostitute' literally took slightly longer to write than it did to read. It was just easy and fun. And you can stay up all night shitting out some other thing phrase by phrase."

THE MOMENTS OF inspiration have been harder for Downey and everyone else to come by. Lately, the extracurricular action in the writers' room has been more colorful than a lot of the writing.

The show hosted by Sarah Jessica Parker, in November, included a song contrasting love's higher and lower impulses. Michael McKean sang chastely to Parker, plunking an acoustic guitar; then Sandler cranked up his electric guitar to underscore sophomoric lines like "I'm gonna give ya the wood!"

During rewrites of the piece, Kightlinger jokingly suggested to the group that the song be made even more explicit—and found herself the target of a crude barrage. "A couple of them turned on her," says a close friend of Kightlinger's, "with these really vicious, mean sexual things. . . . She's one of the strongest people I know. Very tough to faze. And it made her cry."

Kightlinger, who wrote for *Roseanne* last year, has been reciprocally shocked by the thin skin of her new colleagues. "I've had to pare down my sarcasm big-time," she says, adding that she now feels "really positive" about *SNL*. "In the writers' room at *Roseanne,* you could shit on each other and everybody would laugh. But here, it's like, 'Wait a second—that's a piece I've worked on, dah, dah, dah.' It gets personal in a hurry."

In December, Ian Maxtone-Graham, a self-described anti-smoking zealot, complained about Norm MacDonald's lighting up in the writers' room. MacDonald shrugged it off. So Maxtone-Graham extinguished the cigarette by squirting MacDonald in the face with a water pistol. MacDonald punched Maxtone-Graham in the head, knocking him to the floor.

Tonight, sprawled on a couch a couple of feet from the table, Chris Farley and Adam Sandler alternately listen to the writers debate and cackle at some private joke. Sandler picks up a phone and makes prank calls, talking in a silly elderly woman's voice.

Now it's Farley's turn. Obese, sweating, dressed in a flannel shirt and a white knit skullcap that makes him look like a grunge Muslim, Farley dials. "Excuse me," he says into the phone, "did you hear that? Was it a clap of thunder?" Then he holds the receiver against his butt, unleashes a prodigious fart, and quickly hangs up. The writers laugh louder than they have all night. Except Downey, who's slowly wagging his head.

"Ah, Jim!" Farley exclaims. "That's been a big laugh since sixth grade! Belushi farted, didn't he? Bottom line, farts are funny!"

Downey seems unmoved.

"It'll never happen again," Farley says, but he can't contain a giggle. "It's the goddamn burgers! Lori Jo ordered up about fifty burgers! Jesus!"

"Well, Chris," Downey says, mock solemn. "Look around. All these people are laughing at you. Not *with* you. And they're your friends now, because you're the big clown. But they're gonna all go on . . . and you'll still be there, just farting away."

Farley starts kicking his legs like some demented Rockette, farting after each step.

"Someday, Chris," Downey continues, still in his deadpan mode, "your son will be in a library with a friend, and he'll pull down the *Readers' Guide to Periodical Literature*. 'Oh—January to March 1995. Hey, Dad's in this one!' 'What's it for? The 'Fatty Arbuckle incident'—where he had that incident with the girl, and he was tried?' 'No, this is the one where he farts!' "

The rest of the room is tense, silent, and Farley's face is reddening. Downey's joke, more barbed than anything that makes it on the air at *SNL* these days, refers to a 1994 incident where Farley allegedly groped a female extra. ("He never grabbed her in any sexual area, but he was touching her leg," says a witness who was in the limousine with Farley and the woman. "She was being nice about it, saying, 'Can you just stop now?' But she was annoyed. And we're yelling, 'Will you fucking stop it?' Farley's kind of laughing it off. Then he BA'd [bare-assed] some other limo driver.")

Downey's kidding about the possibility of Farley's being hauled into court (no charges were ever filed, and Farley claims he just told the woman she "looked purty"). But he's serious about shaming Farley into better behavior. And Farley is gasping.

"Daddy was a naughty man," Farley finally says with a shrug. "C'mon—let's all take a break and go down to the Village! Go cattin' around!" He dances crazily, his mammoth belly wobbling. "Me and Adsy [Adam Sandler] are gonna go cattin' around!"

None of the writers move.

Downey clears his throat. "All right. So we were on Andy Rooney . . ."

Farley and Sandler strut out of the room. After a total of about ninety minutes, the Rooney sketch is put aside; there'll be still more tinkering tomorrow. But on Saturday, the sketch gets only weak laughs from the dress-rehearsal audience and is cut from the live show.

Lorne Michaels appears in the *SNL* writers' credits each week, though he hasn't really written a sketch in nineteen years. He has other ways of influencing the writing, however, some of which subtly drive a wedge between the other writers and Downey. "Lorne," says a current writer, "will say, 'You know, there's an enormous desire to make Jim Downey laugh. That's good—Jim Downey's a hard person to make laugh. However, we also need to have pieces that Jim hates on the show—because America likes them.' "

A former key writer, who stays in close touch with the politics at *SNL*, sees all the machinations building to an ugly finish. "I've been in LA, and all I've been hearing is 'Jim Downey's fucking up.' That's the story all these agents and producers are hearing. But Jim's no different [than he ever was]. He's a very funny guy. But Lorne picked that guy for a reason, and he kept him for a reason: Jim is a guy who will internalize everything, will not fight, will just rationalize to himself—and in his heart is just dying. But Lorne doesn't care. Jim's gonna take the fall. It's gonna be in the press"—the writer breaks into Lorne's semi-British murmur—" 'Well, Jim, as wonderful as he is, had allowed himself to get a little out of touch, blah,

blah, blah.' Oh, it's gonna be beautiful!" (Indeed, a tough *New York Times* piece about the show last September depicted Downey as the primary source of *SNL*'s problems.)

Many of the current writers talk tough about quitting if Downey is fired. One of the writers closest to Downey says he'd have quit last year if Downey had been let go—but . . . "That's like saying, 'If I'd been in World War II, I would have been in the French Resistance, man, 'cause that's where all the cool stuff was. As far as collaborating, no way!' And then it comes down to doing it, and it's like, 'Well, you know, I've talked to these Nazis—they have a lot of plans, and this Vichy thing sounds great!' "

FOR SOMEONE SO concerned with nurturing his power, Michaels casts himself as amazingly passive. "When the time is right for people to leave, they generally figure out that that's the time they want to leave," he says, grabbing a handful of popcorn. "I think we'll probably have a smaller group next season. And I think it will become clear by the end of this season the direction that we're going in."

Instead of making difficult decisions and narrowing the cast before the start of this season, Michaels added two recognizable faces—Garofalo and Chris Elliott, famous for his often hilarious, twisted cameos on David Letterman's NBC show—as well as the unknown Kightlinger, and has let the pack battle for scraps of airtime.

On such a rudderless ship, self-interest dominates. Franken, who last summer mounted a relentless and futile campaign to win the "Update" anchorship for himself, continually whines to Downey and Michaels about putting his twelve-step character, Stuart Smalley, on the show.

One Thursday in December, rehearsal is delayed as Sandler uses the studio to videotape a birthday song to Steven Spielberg. Sandler had mentioned Spielberg on the show the week before, in a very funny song; when Spielberg called to praise Sandler on the ditty, Sandler took the opportunity to ingratiate himself further and suggested the birthday greeting. Now several cast members are stewing as they wait for Sandler to clear the stage.

Later, Chris Elliott paces in his smoky dressing room. "You're going to hang around the show for two more weeks?" Elliott asks me. "How can you stand it?"

THE SHOW DOESN'T end when *Saturday Night Live* leaves the air at 1 A.M. There's one more ritual to play out, one more twenty-year-old gesture. Cast and crew trundle off to a publicity-hungry, eager-to-be-cool restaurant—one week it's Planet Hollywood, the next it's Morton's, then Chaz & Wilson's—for a languid party. "They have the show," Chris Elliott cracks, "so they can have the party."

Tonight, after the David Hyde Pierce show, the low-intensity festivities are at Dolce. A fleet of limousines whisks everyone to the restaurant, only three blocks from Rockefeller Center.

The parties began, twenty years ago, with higher spirits and lower regimentation. "Most of us were living at the office in those days," Michaels says. "We naturally just ended up going out somewhere together." They quickly became the coolest, wildest, most important show-business parties in the city, especially when Belushi and Aykroyd bought a seedy joint near Canal Street that they named the Blues Bar—"No relation," Michaels says archly, "to the House of Blues. We would go to the party for the host and cast, and then we would end up at the Blues Bar—sometimes, more often than not, till the sun came up. But that was then and this is now."

Inside Dolce, the mood is strangely stiff for a late-night bash full of comedians. Cast, writers, crew—everyone sticks to his or her table; there's almost no mingling. Kevin Nealon and his wife have brought a clutch of fellow PETA members and are chattering earnestly about "companion animals." Because the Dolce bar is still open to civilians, and the bar crowd is staring at the famous TV faces, the *Saturday Night* group feels like Party Village at a showbiz theme park. Unaffiliated celebrities don't drop in much anymore. Tonight's visitor is Patti Davis, ex-presidential daughter and *Playboy* centerfold.

Seated apart from everyone else is Lorne Michaels. At these events he's always as remote as possible—invariably at the back of the room, preferably in a section of the restaurant raised above the rest of the place. A votive candle flickers light onto Michaels's face as he leans forward from the shadows, making him look mysterious.

Mostly, though, he looks lonely. Young staff members Marci Klein and Erin Maroney sit on either side of Michaels, their blond heads tilted up toward him reverentially.

Across the room, Elliott, Hiscock, Garofalo and a college friend, and Mark McKinney are crammed into a banquette. Jim Downey, jocular, the pressure off for a minute, stops by on his way to the men's room. "Ah," he says with a smile, "the malcontents' table!"

"Jim, you want a drink?" Elliott says.

"I can't keep up with you—you and your *vodka-and-tonics*," Downey says, mocking Elliott in his renowned deadpan. "How many have you had?"

"It's my first!" Elliott says, feigning indignation. "I swear! These are my witnesses."

"One?" Downey says, comically overplaying his disbelief. "'Cause it seems like you've had a fucking million!"

Everyone laughs, then Downey says, "Come over and say hi to my friends from Illinois. They'll say, 'What are you doing slumming with this show?' "

"*Suuuure*," Elliott teases. "I'll come over, so your friends can go back to Illinois and say, 'Oh! I met Chris Elliott!' "

Elliott puts on a big act of giving in. "Awright, awright. Let me finish my drink, and I'll give your friends a little . . ." he says, making wildly insincere, goofily funny smiley faces.

Downey leaves. Garofalo is shaking with laughter. "That's why you say yes to doing this show, 'cause you think this could be the funnest thing—it *should* be the funnest thing in the world." She shrugs. "Doesn't always work out that way."

The next time Garofalo grins so broadly, she's standing at the very front of the *Saturday Night Live* stage. It's the end of the February 25 show, and it's the last one she'll do this season. In interviews, Garofalo says she's open to rejoining the cast in the fall. But as the credits roll, it's plain to see that Janeane Garofalo is waving goodbye as fast as she can.

HARD TO BE RICH

JOHN TAYLOR

JANUARY 11, 1988

The city always seems to be in the throes of a gilded age or coming down from one, and the drama of new wealth and the kinds of things it buys has been at the center of New York experience since Edith Wharton's era. In the past, new wealth had often tried to cleave to old-money traditions, but in the Reagan eighties, the new rich wanted to celebrate themselves. "In order to get socially certified, you didn't have to suck up to old-money people," says John Taylor. "You staked out your social worth by celebrating how rich you were," and also how beautiful and young your wife was. To Taylor, John and Susan Gutfreund were the poster children of this change. John Gutfreund ruled one of Wall Street's preeminent investment firms; Susan reinvented herself, and him, as the Francophilic doyens of ostentation. "They were enacting this fable of Reagan capitalist wealth," Taylor says. He is the author of The Rivalry: Bill Russell, Wilt Chamberlain, and the Golden Age of Basketball.

J OHN GUTFREUND and Malcolm Forbes had been friends for years, so when John married Susan Penn in 1981, Susan and Malcolm naturally became friends. The Gutfreunds went ballooning with Malcolm last June in the south of France. They were among the envied group that spent the Fourth of July on his yacht in New York Harbor. When Malcolm was putting together his guest list for the little lunch he threw in October for

Danielle Mitterrand, wife of the French president, he of course thought of including Susan.

Now, Susan is a woman they all love to snicker at, all those snobs and gossipmongers who lunch at Mortimer's. But they miss the point about the woman. Her excesses (the *four* varieties of caviar) and her frivolities (who can forget the spun-sugar apples?) and even her affectations (*"Bonsoir, Madame,"* she said when introduced to Nancy Reagan) are all just endearing expressions of her—as Susan herself might put it—*joie de vivre.*

Because whatever Susan Gutfreund's flaws may be, she is never dull. And to her credit, she tries to charm and often succeeds. Gianni Agnelli, for example, is absolutely infatuated with her. Also, Susan loves just about anything French. So Malcolm penciled her in for the Mitterrand lunch.

Susan did not disappoint. There they all were—Estée Lauder and the Dillons and the Zilkhas and John Fairchild and Susan Newhouse and Donald Trump—sitting at the table in Malcolm's private office in the *Forbes* magazine building on lower Fifth Avenue. This was a couple of weeks after Black Monday, and Malcolm's guests were all feeling a little shaky. But no one had more reason to be distressed than Susan Gutfreund.

After all, Salomon Brothers, the investment bank that John Gutfreund runs, had suffered heavy trading losses during the crash. Internally, it was still divided by the fact that Gutfreund had sold 12 percent of Salomon's stock to Warren Buffett at a handsome discount to prevent Ronald Perelman from seizing control of the company. Many of the firm's executives were outraged, and rumors ran through Wall Street that a dissident faction at the investment bank was going to force Gutfreund out as chairman and chief executive officer of Salomon, Inc.

Still, everyone at Malcolm's lunch aspired to gaiety, especially Susan. A beautiful blonde with a wide red mouth, she regaled the table with tales of the difficulties of keeping the staffs of two houses running smoothly (she and John divide their time between New York and Paris). At one point, as if in search of just the right insouciant epigram with which to sum up these amusing tribulations, Susan exclaimed, "It's so expensive to be rich!"

Susan Gutfreund didn't come up with this line herself. It was, as a matter of fact, embroidered on a cushion right there in Malcolm's office.

Nonetheless, as Susan observed—and this is what makes her invaluable—it was true! It *is* so expensive to be rich. For the Gutfreunds, anyway. By one estimate, they spent more than $20 million decorating their Fifth Avenue duplex (though that's not much, considering that a single ordinary Impressionist painting can cost a quarter of that sum). Last year, while the French decorator Henri Samuel was doing their mansion in Paris, Susan and her young son, John Peter, and John Peter's nanny stayed for months on end in a lavish suite at the Ritz that cost at least $1,000 a day. "My wife has spent all of my money," John Gutfreund confided to a friend recently, "but it is worth it."

Gutfreund was not really joking. He doesn't seem to care that Susan has been running through his fortune in an incredible sort of beat-the-clock spending frenzy. "She's enriched my life," he told a reporter in 1984. She has, in other words, made him appreciate the finer things, like ormolu and Roederer Cristal. "This guy really thinks he's the frog and she's the princess," says a friend of the couple.

John Gutfreund, fifty-eight, is short and pudgy, with thick lips that give him a vaguely sensual look, and delicate rimmed glasses that add a thoughtful air. Overall, his appearance is rather bland. But people in the securities industry describe Gutfreund as a "brutal trader" and "the king of Salomon" who rules the firm with an iron fist. Those who know him socially, however, say that at the time of his marriage to Susan, now forty-one, Gutfreund saw himself as little more than a bond-trading grind. His life, they say, *was* transformed by the impetuous woman who became his second wife.

This may be more than superficially true. Certainly, Gutfreund's marriage to Susan coincided with his emergence as one of the most powerful—and visible—men on Wall Street. Then, too, the couple's social progress, the ascent of the Gutfreund star, occurred alongside Salomon's rise as the country's preeminent investment bank. The installation of his wife in their Fifth Avenue apartment—arguably one of the most sumptuous homes in the city—proceeded apace with his plans to move Salomon into what would have been a true cathedral of finance, the mammoth skyscraper that Mortimer Zuckerman was to have built at Columbus Circle in partnership with the brokerage.

And today, Susan Gutfreund's setbacks as a figure of consequence in New York society resemble in a most uncanny way John Gutfreund's troubles at Salomon. If in a sense Susan unleashed her husband's ego, if she has enabled him to appreciate more in life than the yield on convertible debentures, she seems also to have instilled in him a dangerous sense of grandeur and diverted a crucial fraction of his attention from the running of his firm.

JOHN GUTFREUND *is* Salomon Brothers, people say. Thus, though the firm has not been hurt as badly as L. F. Rothschild or E. F. Hutton in recent months, its problems, unlike theirs, are in large part attributable to the style of its chairman.

"Gutfreund is getting older," says a top executive at one of the major investment banks. "He's started thinking there's something more to life than all this work. That spells trouble. The ultimate end is that someone who cares only about the bottom line will stab him in the back."

"Say you're a significant partner at Salomon," reasons another investment banker. "All that stuff about Christmas trees and parties and skyscrapers is okay while the firm is making money. But if it starts losing it, assassination teams will begin to surface, saying this guy is out of control."

"It's my theory Susan Gutfreund has had a lot to do with John's problems," says a partner at a large brokerage who knows the couple. "When older guys discover their sexual vitality, they're gone."

Whether he goes or stays, John Gutfreund remains the very embodiment of Wall Street in the eighties, a period in which vast amounts of wealth have been made without—as all those dour economists complain—producing anything tangible. Gutfreund has become rich by presiding over a firm that grew in large part by funding the massive federal deficit. But it is not so much the money Gutfreund has accumulated— a mere trifle compared with the hundreds of millions that Saul Steinberg or Henry Kravis has socked away—as it is the power he wields as the imperial ruler of the country's largest and, until recently, most profitable investment bank, "The King of Wall Street," as *Business Week* called it in a 1985 cover story.

In addition to wealth and power, the eighties have celebrated ruthlessness. And no one has been as ruthless—and as proud of it—as John Gutfreund. At a dinner party in November, he was boasting of how tough-minded he had been the previous month in firing close to eight hundred Salomon employees.

The capacity for political intrigue—a sort of corollary to ruthlessness—has been elevated to a virtue in the eighties. In the past five years, Gutfreund's Machiavellian plotting has made Salomon resemble nothing so much as a Florentine palace during the rule of the Medicis. In his drive for power, he froze out the father figure who made him chairman, pushed aside the man with whom he shared power and who had made him wealthy, and banished the brilliant protégé he had hinted might one day replace him.

The era has also celebrated excess. Many of the merchant princes of the age have left older wives for young honeypots, but none of these women is quite the equal of Susan Gutfreund. She set new standards for ostentatious consumption at the parties she threw at River House, where the Gutfreunds lived in the early eighties. *Le tout* New York attended to swill champagne and feed at troughs of caviar. Grievously, the River House fêtes came to an end when the Gutfreunds left after a dispute with the upstairs neighbors over one of Susan's most outlandish acquisitions, a twenty-two-foot-high Christmas tree (four times as tall as her husband).

THE EIGHTIES, in sum, have been an era defined by Sneering Contempt. One of Gutfreund's characteristic displays is said to have occurred at a party in September. Turning to his dinner companion, a woman from an old New York family of diminished fortune, he said, so the story goes, "Well you've got the name, but you don't have the money."

That sort of remark is vintage Gutfreund. But he's misunderstood, his wife complains. Despite her refining touches, Gutfreund remains a trader. Traders are gruff. They have to be. Have you ever been to the trading floor at Salomon Brothers? It's a barnyard, for God's sake, filled with hundreds of bellowing, shrieking, cursing traders. The only way to be heard above that awful racket is to yell. The only way to get someone's attention is to insult him. You can't take it personally. "He's a trader," Susan said to someone Gutfreund once insulted, as if that excused everything.

John Gutfreund is perhaps the quintessential trader. But, then, he is very much a creature of Salomon Brothers—the only place he has ever worked. And Salomon is perhaps the quintessential trading company.

Gutfreund gets up at around six in the morning. He is chauffeured down to the financial district and arrives by seven at the Salomon offices at One New York Plaza, directly across from South Ferry. He eats breakfast in the elegant partners' dining room and by 7:30 is at his desk, where he is wont to light up a Temple Hall Jamaican cigar and leaf through fresh copies of *The Washington Post, The New York Times, The Wall Street Journal,* the *International Herald Tribune,* and the *Financial Times* that await him.

This desk is not in Gutfreund's formal office. He does have such an office—decorated by Susan with black matte walls and Art Deco fixtures—but he uses it largely for ceremonial occasions. Gutfreund's working desk is at the front of Salomon's gargantuan trading floor. One hundred feet long and two stories high, the floor has double-height windows overlooking New York Harbor, a wraparound visitors' balcony, and a massive electronic quote board that displays the current trading price of about two hundred stocks. The soaring, awesome space is referred to at Salomon simply but reverently as The Room.

From his desk at the front of The Room, Gutfreund presides over a true financial empire. Salomon is the most powerful investment bank on Wall Street. It had a capital base of $3.5 billion before the crash. Salomon uses its vast capital pool—the largest of any American firm until the recent merger of E. F. Hutton and Shearson Lehman—to shoulder aside other firms and buy up massive amounts of stocks and bonds that it resells as quickly as possible for very narrow profit margins. About $20 billion worth of securities change hands every day in The Room, more than are traded on the floor of the New York Stock Exchange.

Salomon has a corporate-finance and a mergers-and-acquisitions department, but the heart of the company is its trading operation. In other major firms, traders are viewed as a lower order—almost, in fact, like bone-through-the-nose savages. But at Salomon, the traders rule. That in turn accounts for the firm's ferocious corporate culture. "You've got to be in shape," Gutfreund reportedly told a group of trainees in the early eighties. "And I don't mean jogging and all that crap. You've got to be ready to bite the ass off a bear every morning."

IN 1953, GUTFREUND was discharged from the army and returned to New York. (He grew up in Scarsdale.) He was thinking of a career teaching literature but needed a job in the meantime. The Gutfreund family belonged to the Century Country Club in Purchase, which at the time was a social center for the German Jewish establishment. Among its members were the Salomon family, of the then very minor Wall Street bond house Salomon Brothers & Hutzler. In fact, William "Billy" Salomon often played golf with Manuel, Gutfreund's father, who arranged an interview. John Gutfreund, then twenty-four, joined the firm as a $45-a-week trainee in the statistical department.

This was nothing to get excited about. "Wall Street in the fifties was not a popular place to work, the way it is today," says Robert Towbin, a longtime friend of Gutfreund's who is now a managing director at Shearson Lehman. "It was just a job, like any other."

After a couple of months, Gutfreund became a clerk in the municipal-bond department (the department he closed down in October). He proved adept at the business and was soon made a trader. He rose swiftly through the ranks and became a partner at thirty-four. "He always had a ferocious drive and ambition," says another old friend.

Gutfreund had also developed the affable salesman's manner that he would turn on and off at will in later life. "John had a good sense of humor," says Towbin. "He could kid around. He didn't take things that seriously. You could go to the Salomon trading floor and ask him what the hell was going on and he would laugh and say, 'I don't know.' "

Through the sixties and seventies, Salomon Brothers (the "& Hutzler" was dropped in 1970) was run by Billy Salomon. He was the son of Percy Salomon, one of the three brothers who helped found the firm in 1910. Under Billy Salomon, it evolved from a house that specialized in making markets in government bonds to a major force in all trading activities.

It also became known for aggressiveness. Though many on Wall Street found this quite disturbing at first, the deregulation of the securities business in the seventies made it ever more rewarding. And no one at Salomon was more aggressive than John Gutfreund. "In the mid-seventies, a client of mine in the Midwest told me Salomon was calling on him," remembers Bob Towbin, who at the time was part of the small firm L. F. Rothschild, Unterberg, Towbin. "I called John, who was a friend. I said, 'It's an old client—it's my account. It's not a big deal for you, so I'd appreciate it if you'd lay off.' He said, 'Nobody has any accounts anymore.' I was shocked. But he was right; the world had changed. The days of the old-boy network were gone. You had to fight in the jungle. He was an old friend, but he taught me that this was business."

William Simon had left Salomon Brothers by that time to join the Nixon administration, and in his absence, Gutfreund was recognized as the inevitable successor to Billy Salomon. "People thought of John Gutfreund as larger than life," says a former partner. "He could see people and size up problems immediately. He had a way of looking at life that was unique." Thus, when Salomon stepped down in 1978, it was to no one's surprise that he appointed Gutfreund managing partner.

Gutfreund's professional success had its cost, however. Just at the time he was beginning to be talked about as the successor to Billy Salomon, his wife, Joyce, left him. "We weren't having fun anymore," a friend recalls Joyce saying at the time.

Gutfreund moved into a bachelor apartment at 900 Park Avenue, at 79th Street. He led a lonely existence, and though he became head of Salomon Brothers, he did not seem happy. "I ran into him at a party in Paris in 1978," says an old friend. "He came up and said, 'Do you remember me? I'm John Gutfreund.' He seemed quite desperate and forlorn."

One of Gutfreund's pals was Huey Lowenstein, an investment banker at Donaldson, Lufkin & Jenrette. In the fall of 1980, Lowenstein's wife, Sandy, told her husband that a friend of hers named Susan Penn had once bumped into Gutfreund, had become intrigued, and was interested in being introduced. Lowenstein arranged for the four of them to have dinner.

SINCE COMING TO New York, Susan Gutfreund has been very secretive about her past. Few people know that she was born in 1946 in Chicago; that her father is Louis Kaposta, a man of Hungarian descent who served for thirty years in the air force; that her mother is of Spanish descent and is named America; and that Susan Kaposta had five brothers.

Because of her father's occupation, the family moved frequently around the U.S. and in Europe. "Susan attended three different high schools her senior year," says America Kaposta. "We had to rely on one another and cling to one another because [my husband] went to different commands." Susan was interested at an early age in society's acclaim. "When we were in Shreveport, Louisiana, when Susan was seventeen, she was chosen mascot of a military organization and was runner-up in a queen contest."

Susan spent some time at LSU, but after Louis Kaposta was assigned to Paris, she studied at the Sorbonne. She was hired in Paris by Pan American as a stewardess. In the late sixties, she met John Roby Penn, the heir to a Texas real-estate fortune. Susan Kaposta and John Roby Penn were married in 1970. They set up house in Fort Worth, where Penn was from, and Susan quickly became known there for her extravagance that would later become her hallmark in New York. "Susan was always sending these lavish flower arrangements," says Cissy Stewart, the former society reporter for the *Fort Worth Star-Telegram*. "People made fun of her for it. But other people said, 'Poor Susan, she's just trying to be friendly.' "

Susan and her husband partied in Fort Worth and Fort Lauderdale, where Penn owned a house, and spent a lot of time sailing in the Bahamas. The marriage lasted only five years. They were divorced in 1976, and Penn has married several times since.

Susan remained in Forth Worth and continued on the social circuit. "Everyone was surprised she stayed around attending all the parties," says Stewart. "But she was out to catch a rich husband." No prospects materialized, however, and Susan Penn (she kept her husband's name) headed north.

John Gutfreund and Susan Penn were so taken with each other during that first evening that when it was time to go, they had to be torn apart. And Susan's parents liked John when they met him. "If he was a plumber, a bus driver, an electrician, it wouldn't matter," says America Kaposta. "He himself is such a wholesome, humble, wonderful son-in-law."

The two became a couple very quickly, and very quickly after that,

Susan moved into Gutfreund's Park Avenue apartment. "Susan had expensive tastes from the beginning," says an acquaintance. "I went to a Christmas party at 900 Park back then, and they had a big silver tree in the living room and under the tree were piles of empty blue Tiffany boxes, nothing but empty blue Tiffany boxes."

AROUND THE TIME John Gutfreund met Susan, some old acquaintances observed that his personality seemed to change. Wall Street noticed, too. If nothing else, the ruthlessness for which he was becoming known reached a new level. When Billy Salomon named Gutfreund to succeed him in 1978, Salomon Brothers was a privately held partnership. Four years later, without even telling Billy Salomon—much less asking his advice—Gutfreund sold the firm for $554 million to Phibro, the giant publicly held commodities-trading company. "Salomon thought he was turning the company he had built over to a man he trusted," says a close observer of the firm, "and the first thing Gutfreund did was sell it."

Gutfreund explained that the firm needed capital to stay competitive and that he knew Billy Salomon would have opposed the sale. Though that may have been true, Salomon (who declined to be interviewed) was upset by the humiliating treatment experienced at the hands of his protégé. What's more, he didn't even get a premium for his limited-partnership interest. Though Salomon had essentially created the firm, he received less than $10 million from the sale. "I would have thought that those of us who had been here forty years deserved to share in the gain," he told a reporter in 1985.

Gutfreund, on the other hand, received cash and securities worth around $32 million for his shares. And if Billy Salomon felt cheated, some people on Wall Street thought he had no one to blame but himself. "It was Billy's fault," says a former partner. "He put on the executive committee a group of tough, hard-nosed, greedy people who weren't going to do anything more than they had to do."

Having frozen out his mentor, Gutfreund turned against David Tendler, the head of Phibro. Under the terms of the merger, Tendler, a commodities broker, was to be chief executive of Phibro-Salomon, and Gutfreund was to run Salomon Brothers as an independent division.

Tendler had believed Phibro would dominate Salomon, but the recession of the early eighties smothered the commodities market, while the stock rally that began in 1982 sent profits soaring at Salomon.

Because his division's earnings were growing, Gutfreund persuaded Phibro-Salomon's board to name him "co-chief executive." Threatened, Tendler secretly began planning to buy back the commodities operation. The deal collapsed when word of it leaked out, and Gutfreund took the opportunity to demand that Tendler be demoted and that he, Gutfreund, be allowed to run Phibro-Salomon singlehandedly.

When the board agreed, Gutfreund set about destroying virtually every trace of the commodities company he had conquered. He sold off a variety of its operations, cut its personnel by two thirds, and then, in 1985, purged all public memory of Phibro by changing the company's name to Salomon, Inc. It was the corporate equivalent of executing the inhabitants and then razing the town.

MEANWHILE, SUSAN GUTFREUND was busy establishing her own reputation. She and Gutfreund had married in 1981, around the time Gutfreund sold Salomon Brothers to Phibro. For a while, they lived in Olympic Tower, but in 1982, the Gutfreunds paid $1.1 million for the duplex on the twenty-fourth and twenty-fifth floors of River House—the same apartment that the building's co-op board had refused to let Gloria Vanderbilt buy.

Susan hired the society decorators Chessy Rayner and Mica Ertegun, who gutted the four-bedroom apartment. By turning more than half—half!—of the second floor into a vast bathroom and dressing room, with closet space Imelda Marcos would envy, they converted the duplex into a one-bedroom apartment. It was dramatic enough to warrant a feature in *House & Garden*. But society decorators aren't hired simply for their taste and skill. They're hired also for the entrée they provide. "Chessy and Mica introduced Susan to all their friends," says a common acquaintance.

Susan by then had adopted a grand style of living. She was, according to another acquaintance, one of the first women to start using a limousine for even the most casual trips, such as those to her exercise lessons. And she began to throw luncheons and dinners that set new standards for lavishness. Her reputation as a society hostess was sealed when she and her husband snared the honor of giving the sixtieth-birthday party for Henry Kissinger, who also lived in River House. Everyone from Stavros Niarchos to the then–Mrs. Johnny Carson attended, but what created the real stir were the green apples of spun sugar that the chef prepared for dessert, using a technique he had learned from the glassblowers of Murano.

SALOMON WAS GOING EVERYWHERE. Proclaiming the "globalization of finance," Salomon opened offices in Zurich, Frankfurt, and Sydney. It also expanded its London office, where the staff was to number six hundred by the end of 1986. To accommodate this staff, Salomon acquired a huge space in Victoria Plaza, right above Victoria Station and just a few blocks from Buckingham Palace, and spent a reported £25 million building a trading floor even more majestic than the one in New York.

But plans were afoot for the New York offices as well. Salomon had expanded so rapidly that people were squeezed in on top of each other. Only top executives had private offices. Extra desks, hundreds of new computer terminals, and miles of cable had been added to The Room, which, for all its size, was severely overcrowded.

So Salomon joined forces with Mort Zuckerman to build a world headquarters at Columbus Circle, where the Coliseum now stands. It was truly a pharaonic project. But Salomon was making so much money—the firm had a net income of $557 million in 1985, the year City Hall decided on the project—that it didn't seem to matter that the firm would pay almost 50 percent above the market rate to lease space in the building. Salomon's name would be linked with one of the most imposing and visible structures ever raised in New York. The planned three-story-high trading room, together with the building's assertive twin towers, would be a fitting projection of the power of Salomon Brothers. Susan Gutfreund was so taken with architect Moshe Safdie's drawings that she rushed out and had the building engraved on a set of Swedish crystal vases.

The firm's attitude toward those who opposed the mammoth project was one of—what else?—Sneering Contempt. During the debate over whether the building could be scaled down to create fewer environmental problems, Salomon president Thomas Strauss declared that he wanted it made "perfectly clear" that if the building were reduced or redesigned for "whatever reason," Salomon would abandon the project.

To many on Wall Street, Gutfreund's sudden preoccupation with grandiose architectural schemes was a harbinger of disaster. "When Salomon announced they were building this monument to themselves, that was clearly the beginning of the end," says a close student of Salomon. "For thirty years, Gutfreund had cared about nothing but the business. Now he was worrying about architecture. It was a clear sign he had taken his eye off the ball."

PEOPLE WILL ALWAYS gossip about the beautiful young wives that rich men marry, particularly if the women have extravagant tastes. What does Susan Gutfreund do? There was some talk that she would start an import company, but nothing seems to have come of it. And while she is on one of the visiting committees at the Met, that is an honorary position without the responsibilities that go with being a trustee. She also attends lots of parties—but not to be seen! "I don't want publicity," she told an acquaintance last year. "You can tell that because whenever you see photographs of me in *W,* I'm not looking at the camera. *My* face is in profile."

What Susan spends so much of her time doing is accumulating possessions. In 1986, the Gutfreunds moved out of the River House—where they were so cramped that their young son was living in a small, glass-walled study—and into the six-bedroom duplex at 834 Fifth Avenue, at 64th Street, that they had bought for $6.5 million. So extensive was the renovation—Susan, of course, had had the apartment gutted—that an elevator was built against the back wall of the building just to ferry detritus and laborers and material up and down. She had originally hired Chessy Rayner and Mica Ertegun to decorate, but before long, she dropped them in favor of the incomparable Henri Samuel.

Samuel has created an opulent eighteenth-century French atmosphere. The capacious double-height entrance hall has stone-paneled walls, one of Monet's water-lily paintings, and a massive central staircase. The library has leather-paneled walls, and there is a plant-filled room with eighteenth-century painted panels and trellises. In other words, a true palace for the very model of the modern prince of finance.

Working with Henri is a thrill, but it leaves little time for anything else. One prominent member of the social circuit asked Susan to work on one of last year's major charity events: "She said she was too busy decorating her apartment."

Oh, yes. Susan also studies French culture under the tutelage of Jayne Wrightsman. When Wrightsman met her husband, the late oil tycoon Charles Wrightsman, who was an ardent collector of eighteenth-century French antiques, she wisely decided to learn everything about the subject herself. Jayne Wrightsman took a shine to Susan and has been passing on her encyclopedic knowledge of things French.

Susan has by now become thoroughly Frenchified. The rooms in the Fifth Avenue apartment are referred to as the boudoir, the salon, and so forth. The butler tells callers on the phone, for example, that "Madame is in the *fumoir*."

The society crowd finds this all pretty rich. "Everything became, '*Oui, oui,*'" says one regular at Mortimer's.

WHEN A COMPANY IS crowned the king of Wall Street, you can be certain that the wheel is about to turn. And it did for Salomon and Gutfreund. While the firm continued to expand madly in 1986, increasing the size of its work force by one thousand in that year alone, the company's stock began to fall. From a high of 59⅝ in April 1986, it fell to 39 by the end of the year. Costs had skyrocketed, while a quiet bond market cut into earnings.

In the spring, Gutfreund began to realize he had seriously overexpanded in London. The firm had positioned itself to take advantage of a trend, but "globalization" had failed to produce the revenues expected. As a result, the huge and vainglorious London trading floor—so close to Buckingham Palace!—had become killingly expensive to run. So, thinking like a trader, Gutfreund moved quickly to cut his losses. Wholesale firings began in London.

The London debacle helped Gutfreund realize that the entire firm was as bloated as a pig's bladder (Salomon Brothers itself had grown from two thousand to six thousand employees in five years). During the first half of 1987, the company's profits continued to plunge. To stem losses, Gutfreund instituted company-wide budgeting for the first time. The move gave Tom Strauss administrative authority over all the firm's independent dukes, including Lewis Ranieri, the rumpled head of mortgage-backed securities, who had run his department with total autonomy.

Given Ranieri's stellar track record, firing him was almost unthinkable. But in the spring, lower interest rates played havoc with the mortgage-securities market. And his weakened position provided Gutfreund and Strauss with an opportunity.

One morning in July, Gutfreund called Ranieri uptown to a meeting in the offices of Martin Lipton, the prominent securities lawyer who frequently represented Salomon. When Ranieri arrived, Gutfreund demanded his resignation. Ranieri was reportedly shocked by the move, all the more so because Gutfreund—his mentor—failed to specify to Ranieri's satisfaction why he wanted him out. One joke circulating on Wall Street is that Gutfreund told Ranieri he wasn't a team player, and Ranieri answered, "What team?"

"There are separatist movements at the firm," Gutfreund told a reporter after the firing. "I guess this restructuring came about because we decided that if we didn't force the firm together, it would grow further and further apart."

Wall Street was as shocked by the decision as Ranieri had been. Gutfreund had fired the firm's hottest star in order to pave the way for the ascension of the somewhat colorless Tom Strauss. "The tragedy of Lewie bespeaks the tragedy of the firm," says a former partner. "Everybody would refer to Lewie as a money-maker. The firm swapped him for an administrator."

AT AROUND THE TIME Ranieri was fired, people began to wonder where Susan Gutfreund was. Not long before this, you couldn't glance at Suzy or Liz Smith or the "Eye Scoop" column in *Women's Wear Daily* without seeing some mention of Susan, often accompanied by a photograph—though rarely one in which she faced the camera. By the summer of 1987, however, she seemed virtually to have dropped from sight.

In fact, Susan was spending much of her time in Paris with her two-year-old son and his nanny. The Gutfreunds had bought a beautiful eighteenth-century mansion on rue de Grenelle. The house was divided by a courtyard. The Gutfreunds lived on one side, the designer Givenchy on the other. Like the Gutfreunds' Fifth Avenue apartment, the Paris mansion was being decorated by the incomparable Henri Samuel.

Susan found Paris so civilized. Then, too, John Gutfreund was sensing that the problems at Salomon were more serious than people generally realized. There were signs that the wonderful party on Wall Street was coming to an end. It was one thing for Susan to flaunt her wealth at balls and auctions when Salomon was at its peak. It was another thing to do so when the company's profits had plunged. "John told Susan to keep a lower profile," says one investment banker.

But Susan still managed to have fun. She was introduced to French society. She took up with the Paris *haute bourgeoisie,* like Victoire and Jacqueline de Ribes, and became particularly tight with the Rothschilds. When she returned to Manhattan, she enthused breathlessly about her new friends. But for the New York society crowd—the people on the Le Cirque circuit—Paris and the Parisians whom Susan had discovered are all pretty familiar and even something of a yawn. Billy Norwich, the *Daily News* columnist, reported that at a gathering in Paris this past fall, one "social arbiter" told Susan to "shut up" and stop talking about these people that "we've known for years."

To spend time with his wife and son, Gutfreund began taking the Concorde to Paris on weekends. Perhaps that experience drained him. Perhaps he was distracted by the political infighting at the firm and the "strategic review" he had undertaken of all its operations. Whatever the case, he neglected another looming crisis. Salomon had an unhappy shareholder.

When Phibro acquired Salomon Brothers, Minorco, an investment company controlled by Harry Oppenheimer, the South African mining magnate, was Phibro's largest shareholder. Minorco had kept that stake during the Phibro-Salomon merger, and though it had sold off some of its holdings since then, it still owned 14 percent of Salomon, Inc.

IN APRIL, Oppenheimer, through his investment banker Felix Rohatyn, of Lazard Frères, indicated to Gutfreund that he wanted to sell his block.

Gutfreund was unwilling to meet the price Oppenheimer asked in April. Nor did he find another friendly buyer. In August, Salomon's stock fell further when it was caught with large inventories of bonds that suddenly declined in value. Oppenheimer's dissatisfaction increased, but Gutfreund still failed to act. "Even I knew, sitting in my office, that the Oppenheimer block was looking for a home," says a senior partner at another investment bank. "Here was his largest shareholder, wanting to get out of the stock, and Gutfreund didn't do anything about it. He just didn't focus on it."

Oppenheimer began looking for buyers elsewhere. That information was conveyed to Ronald Perelman, the chairman of Revlon. Perelman told Gutfreund he wanted to buy the Oppenheimer shares, and he promised to support management if the deal went through.

Gutfreund equivocated, but while Perelman, a devout Jew, was celebrating Yom Kippur, the Salomon chief arranged for Salomon itself to buy the Oppenheimer block for $38 a share, which amounted to a $6 premium over Salomon's stock price at the time. He also arranged to sell what amounted to a 12 percent stake in Salomon to Warren Buffett, the Nebraska investor, for $700 million plus $63 million a year in essentially tax-free dividends.

Gutfreund had refused to accept Perelman's assurance that he would be supportive of management. "Believing Mr. Perelman has no hostile intentions is like believing the tooth fairy exists," he said at the time. In making the deal with his old friend Buffett, Gutfreund was simultaneously getting cash to pay for the Oppenheimer shares, gaining an ally at the firm, and preventing Perelman from acquiring a foothold.

Many of Salomon's insiders were said to be outraged by the deal. They felt it was executed in secrecy and haste, and they feared that the dividend payments to Buffett could affect their yearly bonuses.

Salomon shareholders were furious as well. Nineteen lawsuits were filed by investors against the company's board of directors. Gutfreund had succeeded in retaining control of Salomon, but at some expense to his reputation.

Morale disintegrated further in the aftermath of Black Monday. Salomon lost $75 million in October, largely because of the crash. That set the stage for yet another humiliating setback: Salomon's decision to withdraw from the Coliseum project. All fall, Gutfreund had insisted he was totally committed to the project, regardless of any short-term fluctuations in business. On that assumption, Zuckerman had steel fabricated, stone quarried, and final architectural plans commissioned, spending well over $35 million. Now Zuckerman thinks Gutfreund has reneged on an agreement, and may sue. Salomon, meanwhile, is already paying a reported $55 million for pulling out.

THE PREVAILING EXPLANATION for Salomon's problems is that the firm grew in five years from a bond house to a full-fledged investment bank, while the top executives remained essentially traders in their outlook. Their horizon was short. The trend was their friend, and whether it was globalization or junk bonds or real-estate investments, they muscled in, using the clout of their huge capital base to dominate the game. When the trend turned against them, they had to reverse direction suddenly; in the end, they fared worse than the firms that were following strategies that they had thought through independently.

The sneering contempt with which Gutfreund treated so many people has now returned to haunt him. No one expects a palace coup. Over the summer, Gutfreund craftily eliminated the powerful figures—primarily Ranieri—who might have posed an actual threat. Senior management is now composed of Gutfreund loyalists. But many insiders are said to be unhappy over the Buffett deal, the handling of the layoffs, the subsequent morale problems, and the firm's murky direction. If Gutfreund cannot restore morale and create momentum by next summer, a consensus might develop among the other executives that a younger man should take control. And if it's true that, under his wife's influence, he has developed interests outside of Salomon Brothers, he may be happy to go. If he can afford to. In mid-December, Susan Gutfreund showed up at Marie-Hélène de Rothschild's costume ball in Paris wearing one of those five-figure Lacroix specials and a bizarre feather headdress. It's so expensive to be rich.

HOLLYWOOD'S BRAT PACK

DAVID BLUM

JUNE 10, 1985

*In 1985, David Blum was assigned to profile a young actor, Emilio Es-
tevez, whose father is old-line star Martin Sheen. When the then-twenty-
three-year-old actor invited Blum to hang out with him and his pals at the
Hard Rock Cafe in Hollywood, the writer realized that the article had to be
bigger than Estevez. The actors had a certain swagger, an arrogance that
they would be at the center of new Hollywood. When Blum coined the term
"Brat Pack," he thought of it as an honorific, a way to designate the new
cool kids. Estevez didn't take the compliment. "My friends hate me now,"
he told Blum the day the story appeared. Blum, former editor of* The Village Voice, *is now editor of the* New York Press. *He is the author of*
Tick . . . Tick . . . Tick . . . : The Long Life and Turbulent Times of 60
Minutes.*

*I*T WAS A THURSDAY NIGHT, and like all the Thursday nights in all
the bars in all the cities in all the world where young people live, the Hard
Rock Cafe brimmed over with boys and girls. This was Los Angeles, so the
boys wore T-shirts and sunglasses and shorts, and the girls wore
miniskirts and Madonna hairdos. Over the blare of rock music, the boys
and girls were shouting jokes and stories to one another, talking about
their jobs and their classes and their dreams, eating enormous cheeseburgers and washing them down with swigs from long-necked bottles of

Corona beer. The waitresses were dressed in punk uniforms, and they smiled and laughed as the boys and girls floated from table to table, partying with the endless spirit of those who have no place to return to, no person waiting nervously at home, no responsibility the next day that could possibly be more important than this night, right here, right now.

At one round table in the middle of the room sat a group of boys who seemed to exude a magnetic force. As the boys toasted each other and chugged their beers, the prettiest of the girls would find some excuse to walk by the table, and they would eye the boys as languorously as they possibly could, hoping for an invitation to join them. The boys knew that they had this force, and they stared back with equal vigor—choosing with their eyes the prettiest of the pretty and beckoning them with their smiles. Without fail, the girls would come, and they would stay, bringing with them all the charms they could muster. There were many boys in the bar that Thursday night, many of them as handsome as those at this one round table, but these boys—these young studs, all under twenty-five years old, decked out in Risky Business sunglasses and trendish sport jackets and designer T-shirts—they were the Main Event.

A girl named Alice straightened her long, white T-shirt over her blue skirt, brushed her jet-black bangs away from her eyes, patted her hips with her hands, and walked slowly to the table. She went to the handsomest of the group, the boy with the firmest chin and the darkest sunglasses. She knew that he was Rob Lowe and that he had been in *The Hotel New Hampshire,* and she probably also knew that he was involved with an actress named Melissa Gilbert, but from the open, white-toothed smile he gave her as she walked over, she felt confident.

"Hi," she said. He took her hand and shook it.

"Nice to meet you," he said.

"My name is Alice," she said.

He did not tell her his name. He had already turned his head toward a pretty blonde who had just walked by and turned her head toward him. He flashed the blonde his open, white-toothed smile; she returned it and walked over to the table.

But by the time the blonde girl arrived, Rob Lowe had long since forgotten she was coming. He had turned back to the table, where his friends had once again lifted their bottles in a toast: For no reason, with no prompting, for what must have been the twentieth time of the night, the boys were about to clink bottles and unite in a private pact, a bond that could not be broken by all the pretty young girls in the room, or in the world, or even, perhaps, by the other, less famous young actors who shared the table with them as friends. As the bottles clinked, the boys cried together at the top of their lungs, "*Na zdorovye!*"—Russian for "good health," but really something else, a private signal among the three famous boys that only they understood. After they finished their toast, the three boys turned their attention back to Alice and the other girls who surrounded the table, and smiled. The girls smiled back.

If Rob Lowe seemed to be inviting all too much attention from the girls, Judd Nelson acted as though he wanted nothing to do with it. His fame, too, helped attract them—they recognized his tough-guy looks from his role as the wrong-way kid in *The Breakfast Club* and sought his attention. But as Alice sat down in an empty chair next to him, Judd Nelson announced to anyone within earshot, including Alice, "There is a line. When someone crosses the line, I get angry. And when someone sits down at the table, they have crossed the line. You can let them get close"—he looked around at Alice and the swarm of girls—"but you can't let them sit down."

Only one of the famous young boys seemed to take the attention in stride—perhaps because he grew up the son of a famous actor, Martin Sheen. Just twenty-three years old, Emilio Estevez looks like his famous father and is a star on his own; he played the young punk in *Repo Man* and the jock in *The Breakfast Club*. His sweet smile of innocence drew still more women to the table, and he could not resist them.

"She was a Playmate of the Month," he whispered as an exotic-looking young woman in a purple jumpsuit took the seat next to him and smiled like an old friend. "The last time she was here, we were telling her about a friend who had passed the bar exam, and she said, 'I didn't know you needed to take a test to become a bartender.' " He laughed at her stupidity. But then he turned his attention to her, and before long, the toasts were over. Rob Lowe went back home to his girlfriend, waiting for him in Malibu. And at 1:35 A.M., after leaving the Hard Rock and stopping at a disco and then an underground punk-rock club, Judd Nelson took off by himself in his black jeep. Emilio Estevez and the Playmate went off together into the night.

THIS IS THE HOLLYWOOD "Brat Pack." It is to the 1980s what the Rat Pack was to the 1960s—a roving band of famous young stars on the prowl for parties, women, and a good time. And just like Frank Sinatra, Dean Martin, Peter Lawford, and Sammy Davis Jr., these guys work together, too—they've carried their friendships over from life into the movies. They make major movies with big directors and get fat contracts and limousines. They have top agents and protective PR people. They have legions of fans who write them letters, buy them drinks, follow them home. And, most important, they sell movie tickets. Their films are often major hits, and the bigger the hit, the more money they make, and the more money they make, the more like stars they become.

Everyone in Hollywood differs over who belongs to the Brat Pack. That is because they are basing their decision on such trivial matters as whose movie is the biggest hit, whose star is rising and whose is falling, whose face is on the cover of *Rolling Stone* and whose isn't. And occasionally, some poor, misguided fool bases his judgment on whose talent is the greatest.

The Brat Packers act together whenever possible—and it would be a major achievement for the average American moviegoer not to have seen at least one of their ensemble movies over the past four years. The first Brat Pack movie was *Taps,* the story of kids taking over a military school, a sleeper that took in $20.5 million. Then came *The Outsiders,* adapted from the S. E. Hinton novel and directed by Francis Ford Coppola; *Rumble Fish,* another Coppola-Hinton effort; *The Breakfast Club;* and now the release of the latest matchup of the Brats, *St. Elmo's Fire.*

Emilio Estevez is the unofficial president of the Brat Pack. (He is also the unofficial treasurer; other members seem to forget their wallets when they go out together, and Estevez usually picks up the check.) He may get his best notices yet for his role in *St. Elmo's Fire.*

"I'll bet if you asked everyone in the cast who their best friend is," says Joel Schumacher, who directed and co-wrote *St. Elmo's Fire,* "they'd all say Emilio. He's that kind of guy."

What distinguishes these young actors from generations past is that most of them have skipped the one step toward success that was required of the generation of Marlon Brando and James Dean, and even that of Robert De Niro and Al Pacino: years of acting study. Young actors used to spend years at the knee of such respected teachers as Lee Strasberg and Stella Adler before venturing out onstage, let alone in movies; today, that step isn't considered so necessary.

No one from the Brat Pack has graduated from college—most went straight from high school into acting. Rob Lowe, Sean Penn, and Emilio Estevez all went to Santa Monica High School and acted as much as they could. Estevez made 8mm movies that he acted in and directed; he and Penn wrote and co-starred in one movie about Penn stealing Estevez's dog. Penn later directed a play that Estevez wrote and starred in at Santa Monica High, about Vietnam veterans.

Estevez shares a show-business upbringing with several other Brats; Sean Penn is the son of Leo Penn, a director of such television programs as *Magnum, P.I.* Tim Hutton is the son of the late actor Jim Hutton; and Nicholas Cage's connection to Coppola led to his first film part, in *Rumble Fish*. Tom Cruise grew up in the East, away from the world of Hollywood; still, he found he didn't need much training to succeed.

They all admire the work of those actors who spent years in diligent training, but they do not consider De Niro and Brando, or even Martin Sheen, role models for their careers. There is a spiritual father of the Brat Pack, but it is not an established star, nor is it Frank Sinatra or Sammy Davis Jr. or Peter Lawford. It is a grizzled fifty-eight-year-old character actor named Harry Dean Stanton. He has been a familiar face around Hollywood and a cult hero among film buffs since the 1960s, but has only lately become a real success, as the star of *Repo Man* (with Estevez) and, most recently, *Paris, Texas*. The Brats admire Stanton for his acting gifts—but they have befriended him for his ability to relate to them as kids, sometimes partying with them all night and sleeping till noon.

Stanton lives up in the hills above Hollywood, in a house from which one sees nothing but trees and hawks. As he sits in his living room dressed in an old bathrobe ("This once belonged to Marlon Brando," he remarks), he says of these young stars, "I don't act like their father, I act like their friend." Rubbing sleep from his eyes, he thinks for a minute and then adds,

"Boy, would I have loved to have had everything these guys have when I was twenty-two. That would have been great."

IT WAS A HOT SPRING night in Westwood, perfect weather for movie-going, and the leader of the Brats wanted to see *Ladyhawke,* which stars Matthew Broderick. But it would not behoove one of the Brats to fork over $6 to the industry that made him a star to begin with. So Emilio Estevez stood outside the Mann's Village Theater, five minutes to show time, considering the various ways he might be able to get into the movie free.

"I have a friend who works here who'll get me in free," Estevez said, but as he eyed the man taking the tickets of the paying customers, he muttered, "Guess he's not working tonight." After a moment's thought, he said, "If I could get to a phone, I think I know something I can do."

And so, with three minutes left, Estevez marched down the nearest street in search of a phone. He peered into a pinball parlor and asked, "Do they have a phone in here?" They did not. He walked down to a parking lot and heaved a sigh of relief. "There's a phone," he said, and trotted off to use it. He called the theater and explained that he was Emilio Estevez and that the friend who normally let him in free wasn't working tonight; would there be any way to get Estevez passes for the eight o'clock show? Of course, he was told, and when he arrived, the manager and the ticket taker welcomed him to the theater and told him how much they loved his movies. "Thank you," Estevez said, and with a smile, he dashed off to catch the opening credits.

Estevez, who is only five foot six, stands as a vivid prototype of the Brat Pack he seems to lead. Barely twenty-three years old, he is already accustomed to privilege and appears to revel in the attention heaped upon him almost everywhere he goes. He has a reputation in Hollywood as a super-stud: Dozens of girlfriends, many of them groupies, latch on for brief affairs; his romance with actress Demi Moore (who is also in *St. Elmo's Fire*) is off and on. He is living the life that any American male might dream of—to be young, single, and famous.

IT WAS ALMOST midnight on a boys' night out, and Judd Nelson and Emilio Estevez were still looking for some fun. So Estevez summoned a young writer he'd always wanted to meet, Jay McInerney—the author of a book, *Bright Lights, Big City,* that he'd once wanted to option and turn into a screenplay. It was 1984's trendiest novel, and McInerney was staying at one of Los Angeles's trendiest hotels, the Chateau Marmont, revising the first draft of the screenplay of his book. Coincidentally, the man set to direct the film version of the book is Joel Schumacher—the director of *St. Elmo's Fire.*

McInerney showed up at the Hard Rock at around 11:30 P.M. in a sport jacket and mostly unbuttoned shirt. Estevez was wearing a T-shirt and chic black sport jacket with flecks of color. Nelson was wearing a gray jacket, a dark tie, a gray pullover, and a shirt almost hidden from view. It was 65 degrees, but he did not appear to be sweating. They all shook hands, with McInerney looking slightly mystified that he had been invited. The three of them, along with the Playmate, got into two cars, with McInerney in the backseat of Estevez's Toyota pickup truck, and drove to Carlos 'n Charlie's, a restaurant-discotheque on Sunset Boulevard. The coat-check girls recognized the movie stars and waved the group in without collecting a cover charge.

Estevez wandered around the club, and Nelson went to the dance floor, where the tune of the moment was "ABC," by the Jackson Five. Nobody seemed interested in talking to McInerney. Nelson walked up to one of the loudspeakers and started dancing directly in front of it. But no one was dancing with him, and it was too dark for anyone to notice that there was a movie star dancing with a loudspeaker. So after a few minutes, the anonymity appeared to be too much for him; he sat down with a dejected look and started complaining about what a horrible club it was. Then he suggested they leave.

"There's a punk club open tonight across the street," he said. "Let's go." So Estevez and Nelson and the Playmate and McInerney paid the check and left.

Across the street was the Imperial Gardens Japanese restaurant. Late at night, the Japanese restaurant mysteriously disappears, and a punk club takes its place. A long line snaked through the entranceway and out the door, and two large bouncers stood at the foot of a long staircase to the club, not letting anyone inside.

"Some people have no shame about such things," Estevez said when it was suggested that he approach the bouncers and inform them that two movie stars would like to get in. "I have shame." And so he made no movement. But the rest of the people in line began to notice him and Judd Nelson, and a murmur reached the bouncers.

"The manager would like to speak with you," said one of the bouncers, who left his spot at the staircase to speak to Estevez. And so Estevez put away his shame and headed over. Moments later, he waved his group toward him; the manager stamped their hands, showing proper awe. "I guess we're not as important as they are," muttered a girl standing at the front of the line as Estevez, Nelson, McInerney, and the Playmate made their way inside, pleased with their clout.

Still, each new Brat Packer movie carries with it an increased burden that the young unknowns starring in the hit movie of the moment might come up from behind and replace them. "This word 'hot,' " says Judd Nelson. " 'Hot.' 'Hot!' You can be 'hot' and be a shamelessly poor actor. It's possible, now it's possible to be at the top for half a second and then disappear. It's such a strange thing, to try and build a career on this heat."

ANOTHER NIGHT at the Hard Rock. It was about 11 P.M., and the Brat Pack was in full swing—on their fifth or sixth round of Coronas, and their ninth or tenth round of toasts. The small circle of stars had expanded to include several young actors of their acquaintance, not to mention the dozens of girls who continued to hover near the table.

One of the young actors was Clayton Rohner. He seemed to have most of the credentials necessary to join the Brat Pack: the kind of looks, attitude, and presence that suggested acting talent. He seemed especially ebullient—and the reason, no doubt, was that he was celebrating his first starring role in a movie, something that might bring him closer to the exalted status of his friends. But the film, called *Just One of the Guys,* didn't fit into the same league as *The Breakfast Club*—it was merely another teen exploitation flick, perhaps a little better than average, but still not up to par with those of the Brats.

And so, when a young girl of about sixteen approached him with a pen and slip of paper, asking him for an autograph, Rohner looked immediately at his more famous friends with a skeptical grin. "One of you put her up to this, right?" he asked. They all smiled and denied it. "C'mon," he said, looking at the girl. "One of these guys told you to do this. Which one? I know one of them did." But the girl looked back at Rohner with that special look, the puppy-dog gaze of a groupie who has finally come face-to-face with her fantasy. "Please," she said, thrusting the piece of paper ever closer to him. He took the pen and, with a flourish, signed his name for the girl. As he finished, he looked up again at the members of the Brat Pack. "I know you guys made her do this," he said.

But the Brat Packers just shook their heads and watched, without the trace of a smile, and suddenly it was clear that they were as surprised as he was to see the girl leave the table with his autograph, smiling to herself, not bothering to get theirs too.

THE MEMORY ADDICT

SAM ANDERSON

MAY 5, 2008

As the memoir has become this generation's coming-of-age novel, a confessional of serious events and serious emotions, demands have risen to have something to confess. And therein lies a problem. A series of supposed memoirs with titillating tales of past crime and abuse have turned out to be, in fact, novels. For Sam Anderson, the truth content is just a point of departure in his profile of Augusten Burroughs, the bestselling serial memoirist whose characters seem straight out of a novel. Anderson also explores the pressures on truth and memory that any literary effort produces. "What's interesting in the memoir is the way truth is used," says Anderson. Anderson is the book critic for New York *and winner of the 2007 National Book Critics Circle citation for excellence in reviewing.*

Note: This profile of the allegedly fake memoirist Augusten Burroughs is based on real events. Dialogue has been compressed, and chronology has been changed for dramatic effect.

AUGUSTEN BURROUGHS TRAVELS between Amherst, Massachusetts, where he lives, and New York, where he keeps an apartment, in a hired black Town Car, so he can sit in the back and chew nicotine gum and watch *Trauma: Life in the ER* on his iPod. He has come down, this April afternoon, to walk me around his old neighborhood while I dredge his apparently superhuman memory in an effort to determine whether he is, as millions of readers seem to believe, one of the most honest men on the planet—someone willing to share unvarnished true-life details of his childhood statutory rape and the time he murdered a rat in cold blood in his bathtub—or whether, as others have alleged (some of them in a court of law), he is actually a gigantic liar. I know that his memory is superhuman because he told me so, last week, over lunch. "I can remember being eight months old in my high chair," he said, chewing nicotine gum between bites of a goat-cheese omelette. "I can remember learning to walk. I can remember the exact sound the wooden spoon made on the aluminum pot on the stove. I can remember that the lid of the pot had a little knob, putting it in my mouth like a nipple. I can remember my high chair's tray: The metal was textured, it had peak-valley, peak-valley, peak-valley, a small design element, a striation." Tomorrow he leaves for San Diego to give a speech to someone about something or other. He doesn't remember. "I just show up and talk," he says.

He does, indeed, show up and talk. In person, Burroughs has a focused analytical intelligence that doesn't always come through in his writing, which tends to be emotional and therapeutic and often is written from the perspective of a child. In our first conversation, he gives me speeches about the neglected genius of middlebrow novelist Elizabeth Berg ("If she had a penis, she'd be John Updike"), the origins of southern manners among Belle Époque New York millionaires, and the ecstasy of quantum physics. (He's particularly jazzed about a phenomenon called "entanglement," in which photons at opposite ends of space seem to communicate instantaneously.) He says he can differentiate between the major brands of carbonated water ("Perrier has sharp, broken-glass bubbles; Calistoga's are smaller"), as well as between real homeless people and college kids pretending to be homeless. "There's that look you can't replicate with eye shadow," he says. He is, in person, almost the opposite of his textual persona: tall, athletic, and intense. In an effort not to look "pregnant" for the book tour for his new memoir, he's been working out every day and recently broke his addiction to midnight bags of M&Ms. He is wearing, today, his publicity-tour uniform: jeans, black leather jacket, a blue T-shirt with some kind of Victorian woodcut on it, and a brown mesh trucker hat featuring an artsy cow. The biggest surprise, to me, is that he radiates trustworthiness: He seems open, unrushed, self-deprecating, and willing to discuss any subject with piercingly direct eye contact. He asks questions about my childhood, listens carefully to the answers, and follows up with more questions. He is unfailingly kind to waiters. His voice is dry, higher-pitched than I'd expected, and a little twangy, the product of growing up under highly educated southern parents in western Massachusetts. He puts an especially heavy accent on the word *was:* It comes out sounding like "wahz" or "waaaahz"—as if, even phonetically, the past requires disproportionate emphasis.

I find myself trusting Burroughs far more in person than I ever have in print—and yet I recognize in this trust yet another reason to doubt. Our meeting, after all, is just the first phase of a global marketing campaign whose success depends entirely on the spectacle of his honesty. Trust is the product for sale.

BURROUGHS AND I are sitting looking out the big rectangular plate-glass window of an Equinox fitness center on the corner of Greenwich and 12th. The window is giant and perfectly clean and creates the illusion of containing the entirety of West Village foot traffic like fish in an aquarium. Although Burroughs no longer drinks, he collects lesser compulsions like little girls collect seashells, and he has been drawn to this spot by the lure of two converging addictions, one minor, one major. The minor addiction is Red Bull; they didn't have it, so he settled for a Diet Coke. The major addiction is, as usual, Burroughs's Big One, the master dependency around which all his minor dependencies (M&Ms, the Internet, French bulldogs, nicotine) seem to rotate in twitchy, continuous orbit—the source of pretty much all his wealth and fame and controversy: namely, his allegedly vivid, restless, overstuffed memory. He is giving it a light workout, here at the window, excavating some details mostly for my benefit. This, he says, is an ideal spot for reminiscence, "a very nutrient-dense area." The gym is on the corner of Burroughs's old street, which he hasn't returned to in over ten years. He lived here in the West Village eighteen years ago, when he was twenty-four. "All these little details come back when I'm here," he says. "It's like there's a whole other time layered over this one. And the people that lived here still live here for me, still walk the streets." He says he remembers, for instance, watching a painter—"navy shirt, white pants, brown belt, black boots"—painting a door across from his old apartment. "White drop cloth spread out over the stone steps," he says. "The way the light hit him."

My internal polygraph begins to twitch here, subtly, because what sort of freakishly bloated cortex retains, for eighteen years, the color of a random workman's belt? This is exactly the kind of improbably authenticating detail Burroughs has been accused of inventing in his books—not a big deal on its own, perhaps, but patch enough of them together and your life story is suddenly more imagined than remembered. *"The way the light hit him"*? Seriously?

Burroughs says that, back when he was busy drinking himself to the brink of death in his apartment halfway down the block, this fitness center with its big glass window was an old movie theater called the Art Greenwich. He used to hang out in front of it with a crowd of homeless people, in a kind of informal apprenticeship. "I wasn't doing it to be cool and have homeless friends," he says. "I was doing it to see, How hard can this be? I thought it was inevitable I would become one of them." They got to be such pals they'd do him favors. "They would see me going down to the subway, and all of a sudden there'd be this filthy hand slapping right in front of me, putting a token in." (My polygraph spasms again: a bit Dickensian.) Burroughs fires up his synapses and describes, in detail, the look of the old theater's lobby: its threadbare red carpeting, the off-kilter angle of its back corner, its glass door.

I ask him what movies he saw here.

"Lots," he says, but he can't come up with any names, just something about Robert De Niro as a pedophile on a boat with Juliette Lewis.

Village girls drift past the window in complicated boots. Burroughs points across the street to the diner where he used to have fat-soaked hangover breakfasts to try to absorb some of the alcohol before it reached his swollen liver. He tells me about miserable nights at a now-defunct gay bar called Uncle Charlie's, a place "just exactly as loathsome as the name implies." He remembers, vividly, the embarrassment of trying to sneak Hefty bags full of wine bottles down the stairs of his old building in the middle of the night. But he can't remember which apartment he lived in.

"Something D, maybe?" he says.

At this, my polygraph sketches a quick profile of the Alps. Who can remember the color of a stranger's belt, and the precise angle of the back corner of an old movie theater's lobby, but not the number of his own apartment, or any of the movies he saw? What kind of memory is that?

TO DESCRIBE BURROUGHS'S semi-mythic and exhaustively self-documented life is, at this point, deeply redundant. Over the last six years—as America reached and then passed the red-hot climax of its sado-masochistic affair with memoir—Burroughs has seemed determined to surpass all reasonable human limits of public self-disclosure. In that span, he has published five autobiographical books, and he supplements these with a blog, a MySpace page, and an elaborate promotional website complete with emotive folk songs about his childhood and video of him kissing his dog. We know the names of not only his current pets (Bentley and the Cow) but also his childhood dogs (Cream, Brutus, Grover) and his dead guinea pig (Ernie). Burroughs's new book, *A Wolf at the Table,* is being promoted as "his first memoir in five years"—a gem of self-canceling hype roughly equivalent to "her first wedding since last fall" or "his ninth bar mitzvah since he was thirteen."

And yet somehow here we are. Burroughs was born Chris Robison in 1965, into legendarily unpromising circumstances. His mother was a suicidal bad poet, his father a sadistic, alcoholic philosophy professor. When the marriage flamed out, after years of enthusiastic mutual abuse, Burroughs commenced his world-famous adolescence, as described in his ubiquitous 2002 debut memoir, *Running with Scissors:* His mother abandoned him to her eccentric psychiatrist, a Santa Claus look-alike who searched for hidden messages in his own feces, excused himself during therapy sessions to visit his "masturbatorium," and allowed Burroughs to have a sexual relationship with a thirty-four-year-old man. (According, at least, to *Scissors.*) After escaping this madhouse in his late teens, Burroughs reinvented himself: He went to computer school, changed his name (*Burroughs* after a defunct computer, the Burroughs tabulator; *Augusten* because it "sounded classic—but then, when you looked at it twice, absolutely unfamiliar"), and commenced the second, only mildly less world-famous phase of his life, described in his second memoir, *Dry* (2003): He landed a high-paying job in advertising, moved to New York, blew his money and health on alcohol and drugs, went to rehab, and lost his best friend, Pighead, to AIDS. After all of this tragedy, Burroughs discovered the circular salvation of the memoir. He was rescued from homelessness, alcoholism, crack, and abuse—in short, from everything depicted in his books—by the books themselves.

Today, Burroughs is the last of the big-game memoirists, targeted but still on his feet, still profitably working the cud of his dysfunctional youth, still memoiring, against all odds, under the vengeful glare of Oprah and her increasingly skeptical public. As the culture of memoir has imploded over the last few years—as JT LeRoy dissolved into some kind of conceptual-art project about Truth in Media, as James Frey suffered the most visible public flogging in the long history of global torture, as Margaret "Gangland" Seltzer was outed by her own sister as a pampered suburbanite, as Misha Defonseca admitted that she was neither a Holocaust survivor nor raised by wolves—Burroughs sat at his laptop, undeterred, furiously masticating his chemical gum, and claimed, with a perfectly straight face, to be faithfully transcribing the honest-to-God events of his past.

When Burroughs writes, he tells me, he drifts into a kind of shamanistic memory trance that allows him to travel freely through time. He never stops to look at what he's typing, which he says would only distract him. Instead, his eyes glaze over, and he stares absently at the small aluminum strip between his laptop's keyboard and screen. "When I am writing," he says, "I am there. I'm there. I never, ever, in any of my books, ever, have thought, 'Now, how would I have talked?' That is not how I write. It feels like I just go back and I'm there. It's like a movie. It's extremely vivid. I'm a monkey at a typewriter, writing about the time it got M&Ms, and the time a blue M&M came out instead of a red one." Like Proust, he works in bed, propped up on some pillows. He feels terror, excitement, and sadness; he cries. It's more like a séance than a job.

BURROUGHS'S PUBLICIST has set us up for dinner at an unlikely venue, a tiny West Village cave with tastefully arranged paparazzi outside that also happens to be owned (and frequented) by Graydon Carter, whose magazine, *Vanity Fair,* published a long article about the *Running with Scissors* lawsuit—the biggest dent yet in Burroughs's public credibility. In 2005, the family depicted in *Scissors* sued Burroughs for libel; the case settled last summer, when Burroughs and his publisher agreed to publish the book with a disclaimer recognizing that the family had a different perspective of the events described. (Burroughs called it "a victory for all memoirists.") When I mention the *Vanity Fair* connection, he shrugs. He's still wearing his book-publicity uniform, except this time his hat has a pig on it instead of a cow, and his T-shirt is a lighter shade of blue. When we sit down, he takes off his leather jacket to reveal a pair of tattoos running up each forearm: on his left arm, a mess of winding filigree, on his right, the phrase CICATRIX MANET—Latin for "The scar remains." (He says he also has a spiral tattooed on the back of his shoulder, to remind him not to drink.) He has a way of shrinking already-small New York restaurants. His voice, as it locks into one of his speeches, tends to rise in volume to match the intensity of his thought, and to find its way into distant corners. The dignified elderly couple at the next table leaves not long after we sit down.

Burroughs says he never read the *Vanity Fair* article—in general, he avoids reading his press—but that it doesn't bother him. "It didn't have the impact they thought it would," he says. "No one mentioned it to me. Only reporters. It didn't build. It was like a nothing. There was nothing there." I ask if he'd mind, given that we're at *Vanity Fair*'s unofficial headquarters, responding to the article's main points. He agrees.

I run through the accusations one by one: that Burroughs fudged the book's timeline; that he never saw a six-year-old nicknamed "Poo Bear" poop under the family piano; that there was no masturbatorium; that a shock-therapy machine the kids played with was actually an old vacuum cleaner missing a wheel; that Burroughs and one of the children did not tear down the kitchen ceiling. He responds, vehemently, to every charge.

"Well, no, that's not true at all," he says. "God no, I lived with them far longer. A year and a half, they said that? That's weird. . . . It was not an old vac—I know a shock-therapy machine from an old vacuum cleaner, for God's sake! That's weird, that's just a weird comment. . . . Why would they deny that he has a masturbatorium? How does that harm them? If he were alive, he'd be the first person to tell you where it was. He'd sit right here and say of course it was my masturbatorium. So it's just weird to me. . . . Wow. Wow! I'm flabbergasted. Wow."

His voice begins to fill the little restaurant.

As I watch Burroughs react, my polygraph needle begins to tremble again. Outraged denial is, of course, a reasonable response for an honest writer accused of lying. But is it even remotely possible that, after a well-publicized two-year trial in which his career and reputation hung in the balance, these allegations would come as a surprise to him? Can he possibly be "flabbergasted" by anything I've said?

I ask him if these accusations came up in court. He says he doesn't remember. A minute later he says he thinks they probably did.

Soon he is borderline shouting about how ridiculous it would be for a writer seeking mainstream fame to describe not only a gay sexual relationship between a man and a young boy but *"anal penetration!"*

The new diners at the table next to us, a pair of quiet young gentlemen in nice sweaters, pause momentarily from their conversation about a *Paris Review* party.

I ask Burroughs if all of this makes him angry.

"It doesn't make me angry," he says. "It makes me feel incredulous. It's a very arbitrary list of things. They're reaching, grasping at straws. What it comes down to is they're trying to portray me as a liar and say, 'No, it wasn't sunny that day, it was rainy. He lied. We want our money.'"

Does it ever make him doubt, even for a second, his account of things—or wonder if he might have just misunderstood as a kid?

"Oh, God, no," he says. "How can I explain this? It's not like writing about high school and talking about what yard line the cheerleaders stood at. High school for the most part is unexceptional. These were absolutely extraordinary circumstances. I mean, the terror of my mother going psychotic the way she did, being unable to raise me, and then the wildness of living in this house—it burns into your brain. If you had been on the *Titanic* when it sank, I promise you, I bet you every penny I have, you would know exactly what you were wearing, exactly who was standing next to you, what they were wearing, exactly what people were saying. You would know precisely which side of the lifeboat you climbed into, you would remember if you took your life jacket off or if you left it on, you would remember exactly how that ship sank. You just would. But if you took the *Titanic* and it didn't sink, how much would you really remember? So it doesn't make me second-guess my recollection of it. I don't see how I could be wrong. It isn't. It isn't. I bet my life on it. I bet my life on it."

The maître d' comes over and asks him to lower his voice.

"I did not sit down and cleverly think of a story that I thought would be gripping and make me lots of money and famous," he continues. "I sit down and I go back and I write the stories from my life. It is that simple. All the rest of it I leave to other people to talk about and debate."

We do not order dessert.

THE TENSION BETWEEN "actual" memory and our translation of that memory into words is not, despite the public's perennially fresh outrage, a new problem, nor one that has an easy answer. Every memoir depends on a loose cognitive partnership between notoriously sketchy processes: the subjectivity of memory itself, the spotty and biased power of recall, the translation of images into language. Memory is chaotic, nonsequential, and spotty; marketable narrative is easy, clean, and quick. You might say, in fact, that a certain low-grade lying basically defines the genre, and always has, all the way back to the very first memoirist: Saint Augustine, the fourth-century bishop of Hippo, who confessed, in his *Confessions,* that he was recording "not the events themselves . . . but words conceived from the images of those events." (When I asked Burroughs if he got his first name from the memoiring saint, he said that if he had he "should be taken out back and shot in the fucking head. That would just be so horribly pretentious.")

All of this is, by now, a very familiar can of worms to Augusten Burroughs. "We're a binge culture," he says. "The media will get on one topic and stay on that topic forever. I'm going to be asked about the veracity of my memoirs and the state of memoir when I'm sixty-five. It will never, ever stop." Still, he's happy to make his position clear. He insists that *Running with Scissors* preceded the memoir boom—and that now, after a publishing craze brought on largely by his own success, the genre has spun out of control. "It's just exactly like fucking puppy-mill puppies," he says. "All of a sudden a dog will win Westminster and it will become the 'It' dog and you'll see it in New York everywhere and it'll be in all the pet stores, and what happens is you start off with a really solid, good breed— poodle is a perfect example. Very stable dogs, very good with children, very smart, the smartest breed. Very loyal. And then they get bred, and they get inbred, and they get inbred, and the genetics become weaker and weaker and you get hip dysplasia. Until what you end up with can't even be called a poodle. That's kind of what's happened with memoir."

Burroughs says he rarely reads other memoirs, but when he does he expects the truth. "I find the privileged white girl writing about gangland morally corrupt," he says. "I have a problem with that. I would feel manipulated. JT LeRoy? I would feel really violated. People sort of think now, not 'Do I have a story to tell?' but 'Can I think of a story I could write and call a memoir?' And it's unfortunate because it becomes the focus in the media, and as a result I think there are a lot of incredible stories that may get overlooked because of the big memoir scandals. I mean, how would *Bastard Out of Carolina* do today, you know?"

(*Bastard Out of Carolina*, just for the record, is a novel.)

Burroughs responds to charges of fakery with a denial so bulletproof it almost feels suspicious in itself—it suggests either supreme heroic conviction or a deep, possibly even unconscious, self-deception. He insists, always, that he's telling the absolute truth, even about the details of events that happened thirty years ago. And the bedrock of this defense is always his bionic memory, in which he seems to have total faith.

"I guess it's unusual," he says. "My brother thinks it's because I have a little Asperger's like him, and it's an Aspergian trait. It's an incredible benefit when I'm writing about my past. But it's also a disadvantage in that it's incredibly vivid."

At the center of the skepticism about Burroughs's credibility, even among his admirers, is his work's relentlessly scenic quality. He never recounts dialogue in general terms or describes incidents vaguely. Even the most banal exchanges are quoted verbatim. In the new book, instead of summarizing a thirty-year-old conversation with his mother, Burroughs re-creates it, word by word, gesture by gesture, to a degree that seems humanly impossible.

When I ask him how this works, he is open and adamant.

"Did I get every syllable right?" he says. "No, probably not. But that's the gist of it. That's how she spoke. Those are her inflections. And if it's not exactly word for word, it's certainly nobody else, and it's certainly not my words in her mouth. Was there sun streaming in that day, the actual day that she told me about her marriage? Was the sun at a 47-degree angle? How the fuck would I know? But that's my memory of that period with my mother painting, when the sun was low in the sky like that. I took a sky from one of hundreds of days that were all the same. But that's the painting. I have it downstairs in my house. That's the smell, that turpentine smell. If it wasn't *Tosca* on the stereo it was *La Traviata*.

"The thing with memoir is that it's not court stenography, and it shouldn't be. We have video for that. We have YouTube for that. And I don't understand the criticism. This is not a trial, where I'm recounting a murder and every action must be photographed and documented and measured with a tape measure. It's a life.

"It's a very peculiar fixation. It's like asking the orange: 'Why? Why do you have the pits? Why aren't you smooth like the apple? Why? Why do you have to have the little indentations? No one licks the indentations, no one hides anything in the indentations, it's not like those little indentations are useful. Why do you have them?' "

Burroughs, it should be said, does seem to have an uncanny knack for voices. I notice that, whenever he tells a story about his father, he drops into an impromptu little Dad impression: a slow, low, doltish voice with a southern accent. ("Wul, son, y'know, long time ago. Dudn't matter.") When I ask him if this is really what his father sounded like, instead of answering normally, he breaks eye contact, and his gaze drifts into some kind of wormhole several light-years behind my left ear, and he answers my question by channeling his father himself:

"Uh, uh, a better . . . impression, uh, of my father," he says, in a halting, flat voice. "Wou-would, would, would be—like I say, uh, a better, impression, of my fa—if I were to try, if I were to attempt an impression of my father." He keeps staring blankly at the wall of the restaurant. "What I would do, first, primarily, is, A, I would try to—attempt—the cadence, with which he spoke. And then further if I was, again, engaging in this impression of my father, B, I would try—and though I may fail, like I say, I would try, but I may fail, to imitate: the tone, of his voice."

His eyes click back over to mine. "That's my father," he says.

A WOLF AT THE TABLE is essentially the prequel to *Running with Scissors,* although it's significantly more painful and probably two-thirds less funny. It tells the story of the young Augusten's suffering at the hands of his sadistic father, a dry-lipped, black-toothed, lesion-plagued professor of logic and ethics. (He died three years ago.) The book swings between scenes of pathos and terror. Preadolescent Augusten, desperate for affection, stuffs his father's old clothes with pillows and cuddles with them at night; Dad murders Augusten's guinea pig, magically retrains the family dog to be vicious, and tries to kill his son in a car accident. Burroughs often describes his writing in therapeutic terms, as "venting," or "swatting branches out of the way in a dense forest"; often, his books begin as journal entries (*Dry* was harvested from an 1,800-page computer file called "mess, collected"), and they tend to have the strengths and weaknesses of a diary: They can be artless, repetitive, meandering, and mawkish, but also immediate, heartfelt, connective, and sympathetic.

I talk to Burroughs's older brother, John Elder Robison, about his brother's version of events. Although he and Burroughs grew up largely apart, they are now neighbors in Amherst. Robison tells me, in a voice that sounds a hundred percent identical to Burroughs's impression of it, that he and his brother are opposites. Owing to his Asperger's, he tends to be "flat and logical," while Burroughs is "entirely governed by emotion." (As Burroughs later puts it, "My brother has the emotion of an IBM laptop computer.") Because of this, they often experience the same events in radically different ways. Still, Robison insists that his brother is honest.

"I really feel strongly that people are critical of my brother because he's so emotional. But that absolutely does not mean it's made up. Just because somebody dramatizes the emotional content of something in their mind does not make it false."

Burroughs's mother has said that she, too, remembers some things differently. She's currently working on her own memoir. Robison published his, *Look Me in the Eye*, last year.

After dinner, Burroughs and I walk in continuous disorienting loops around the Village while he extracts more baubles from his memory-hoard. We pass his favorite independent bookstore, which is now a Chase bank. He tells me about the time he met Academy Award winner Linda Hunt while holding a fresh handful of dog feces. ("And I'm thinking, 'Okay, so what are the chances of just an average guy meeting any Academy Award winner in his life? And what are the chances further of meeting that Academy Award winner while holding dog shit? And what are the chances that they would be the only dwarf Academy Award winner?' It just seemed spectacular.") We pass a real-estate agency that used to be a corner store with an oddly distinctive smell—like "sour milk and earth," he says, "but somehow neither." I ask Burroughs what memoir he's going to write next. Growing up with his brother? Nursing his bulldog back from a spinal injury? Overcoming his addiction to M&Ms?

He says he might be done. He wants to go back to fiction, which he says always feels like an adventure. (His first book was the novel *Sellevision*, which he wrote in seven days.) "I'll always write about myself. I just don't know if I'll always publish what I write."

I ask what this novel might be about.

"I should write about the son of a Connecticut senator who writes about a dysfunctional childhood living with a psychiatrist," he says. "It would be very postmodern."

FIVE DAYS AFTER our last meeting, I send Burroughs an e-mail thanking him for his time and warning that I might have some follow-up questions. He responds, quickly, to say that he enjoyed it, then adds, apparently as an afterthought: "what's that little white dot on your front left tooth? a filling?" I'm impressed: The bottom half of that tooth is fake, a mutual gift from my older brother and the concrete edge of our apartment complex's swimming pool when I was eight. One little spot stands out. I haven't noticed or thought about it in years. I write back and tell him so. As I wait for a response, I start to wonder about his motives. Was he actually curious, or was this just some kind of guerrilla-marketing campaign to tout his astounding powers of observation and recall? Again, he writes back quickly, recommending that I see his dentist: "of course, it's not like you have some glaring tooth problem. it's a tiny thing. most people wouldn't even notice. just like most people might notice your glasses? but not that they say Nautica along the temple." I take off my glasses: It's true. This is also impressive, but a little flagrantly calculated for my taste. I begin to doubt his powers altogether. For all I know, he's just memorized a couple of trivial details in order to unleash them on me at exactly this kind of strategic moment.

Now that he's being brazen, I decide to test him: What else does he re-member?

He responds with a detailed 1,200-word recap of our time together: exact phrases we spoke at specific intersections and the cars that passed as we said them; which hand I'd used to straighten my notes at the table; the names of my children; the design of my watch face and wedding ring ("ei-ther white gold or platinum . . . two ridges, or channels—one on top, one on the bottom"). Having been there myself, and having just relived the en-tire experience via five hours of recorded conversation, I find his account (although he gets a word or two wrong) very persuasive.

He even remembers a story I told him about fainting from dehydra-tion in a grocery store in the middle of Queens. He admits that, as I was telling it, he was doubting some of its details, wondering if I'd allowed my-self to embellish the story over the years, eventually even revising my memory to match the more dramatic version. And he was right: I had.

BESS MYERSON IS ONE TOUGH CUSTOMER

SUSAN BERMAN

NOVEMBER 14, 1977

In 1977, Bess Myerson, a former Miss America, and the first Jewish Miss America, lent her considerable glamour to the mayoral campaign of life-long bachelor Ed Koch. She was his constant escort during the campaign, and many credited her with winning him the election. Koch, in return, made her commissioner of cultural affairs. (She'd been head of consumer affairs under Mayor John Lindsay.) As Susan Berman's piece shows, My-erson's New York–size personality and ego were every bit as gargantuan as Koch's own, which is saying something. But the sense, captured beauti-fully by Berman, of a woman careering almost out of control, turned out to be prescient. Eleven years later, after an unsuccessful run for the Sen-ate, Myerson became embroiled in what the tabloids liked to call "the Bess Mess," a bribery scandal involving her boyfriend, Andy Capasso, in which Myerson was charged with obstructing justice. Though she was ac-quitted, her reputation was ruined. Even Koch abandoned her.

Berman played a tragic part in another tabloid case, when she was found murdered in her Hollywood home. The culprit was never found.

I T IS COLUMBUS DAY, and the limousine carrying mayoral candi-date Congressman Ed Koch to the front of the Italian-American parade is stuck. The driver keeps turning down the wrong streets in an attempt to find the proper entrance only to be turned back by officious cops who could care less if the car contained Christopher Columbus himself. Finally, just like in a bad movie, the driver backs up and hits the front bumper of another car.

"Just get out and give him the proper information; I don't want an incident," says an aggravated Koch. All entrances to Fifth Avenue seem forever blocked, and Koch sees his parade appearance being canceled due to the lack of an adequate road map. After five minutes the car starts up again. Everyone in the car offers a different opinion on how to make it to the head of the parade. All suggestions are wrong.

Suddenly, a tightly controlled melodious voice rises from the backseat above the din. An imperious voice. It is a "take charge" voice that speaks in well-defined capital letters. The Voice says, "Ed, Get Out. I'll Take Care of It. Just Make Like the Mouse That Roared." A tall, elegant brunette steps out of the car. She's attired in a classic Jerry Silverman blazer, skirt, and turtleneck sweater, low-heeled black boots, and green sunglasses. She is nearly six feet tall; she looks men in the eye and towers above women. The congressman puts his arm around her so that it appears that he is guiding her, but it is the other way around. Like Marge and Gower Champion, they glide up to a policeman. She gets directions and propels him back to the car. She dispatches orders, mutters "bureaucracy" under her breath, and has him at the start of the parade in ninety seconds flat.

As strains of John Philip Sousa start up, she takes her rightful place beside him in the lead, smiling that God's-gift smile. The music starts: Together they raise their feet high and begin to march. The crowd cheers more loudly and commences to clap. She glances from side to side and realizes the cheers are not for him—they are for her. After all, she has been marching all her life.

THE MARCHING STARTED for Bess Myerson the day she was born, in a lower-middle-class development near Sedgwick Avenue in the Bronx. Her parents, Louis and Bella Myerson, came over from Russia when they were adolescents, and met and married here. They had three daughters: Sylvia; Bess, the beauty in the middle; and Helen.

From the time she was seven, Bess took piano lessons from a Miss LaFollete. There was one thing Bess wanted desperately: a black Steinway grand piano. Someone suggested jokingly she enter the 1945 Miss America contest for the $5,000 prize. And win she did.

An adoring public found her an unusual Miss America. She turned down Broadway offers and modeling jobs. She toured vaudeville for about three minutes before ascertaining that nobody was really interested in her concertos. They were more interested in the bathing suit in which she appeared in the finale. She started losing weight and stopped filling out the bathing suit, so she went home early. She was the first Jewish Miss America, the first New York Miss America, and the first Miss America to go home before the fun began. She took her money and entered Julliard and Columbia for graduate studies in music. In 1946, she played Rachmaninoff's Piano Concerto No. 2 with the New York Philharmonic.

That year, when she was twenty-two, Bess married returning war veteran Allan Wayne. She had known him only six months. In 1947, she bore him a daughter, Barra. The marriage lasted eleven years.

Bess's television career really started in 1951, when she became that Lady in Mink on *The Big Payoff* for CBS. From 1958 until 1967 she was a panelist on *I've Got a Secret*. These and scores of other forgettable shows. And she was a frequent commentator on the Miss America Pageant from 1954 through 1968.

THE TELEPHONE IS an extension of Bess's hand. It was my contact with her. The conversation was ominous. It was also totally one-sided.

"Hello, this is Bess Myerson," the low, resonant, morning voice said. "You're certainly a tenacious reporter. You've left messages everywhere I work and with every friend. I'm sorry but I don't do interviews, I'm much too busy; and now, with the campaign, I have little time at all for myself."

"But, Miss Myerson . . ."

"I'm sorry, that is all I have to say. Now please stop calling people and do understand that I have a meeting I must go to. Good-bye."

After I had pledged that I wanted to do a fair portrait, she agreed to let me attend one parade with her. I was to walk on the other side of Councilman Henry Stern and ask any questions I might have during the march. Later, when I mentioned that I couldn't do the piece without cooperation from her and that perhaps she would rather someone else do it, she said yes, that was a marvelous idea, and, "maybe Shana Alexander could do it."

After repeated exposure, she gave me some time—always with a third person present. But she was always careful, and she had an uncanny mind for detail. If there was anything she thought might be misunderstood, she did not hesitate to call. The Voice in the morning got up around eight and did private things until eleven. When it spoke then, it was going slower than the afternoon or evening voice.

"HELLO, SUSAN? Where were you last night? I was trying to reach you. You know there are certain people who are not going to return your calls about me. Like Mike O'Neill of the *Daily News*. He said he would never return a call from *New York* magazine. He said I was going to get crucified. What is your perspective?"

"HELLO, SUSAN? It's Bess. I'm in Milwaukee. I called one of your boyfriends' numbers and you weren't there. Where were you? Oh, well, I must say he is very polite. I'm glad you're attractive, because I have had such trouble with fat, ugly reporters. They hate me. You said to my niece that you thought I was politically astute and conniving. You know she will tell me everything you said. I'm not conniving—that has a pejorative context. I'm not sitting in back rooms making deals. That's not my style. I relate to people, I understand the issues. I have integrity—when I believe in someone, I will work for them totally like I am for Ed . . .

"You also told her about an instance where I stared someone down on a podium—you said you found it in the clips. I was at a dinner? And someone took my seat when I was speaking? Then told me to sit on his lap? Then I stared him down until he moved? No, I don't remember it. Are you sure it was me? Don't make me into something I'm not in this article."

"HELLO, SUSAN? Bess. I just want to give you some names that you should call. Don't call anyone without talking to me. They won't talk to you. Now call Richard Gelb at Bristol-Myers; William Spencer at Citibank; Henry Stern, he was on my staff in the Consumer Affairs Department; Herb Rickman, I work with him now. What are you going to ask them? . . . All right."

SHE IS IN HER spacious East Side apartment today. It overlooks the Frick and is furnished with understated elegance. There are the *de rigueur* pre-Columbian art objects, the executive couch, the modern prints, the S-shaped contemporary chrome chairs. And there in the entryway is her black Steinway.

Bess is wearing all her hats today, juggling the hours of the day to fulfill her many commitments. Her main incarnation now is as cochairman of the Ed Koch for Mayor campaign. She is also a well-paid, respected consumer consultant to Bristol-Myers and Citibank. She writes a twice-a-week column for the *Daily News* and has a consumer radio program on NBC. She speaks constantly for charities, for Israel, and for other causes in which she believes. She is wearing a red Ultrasuede dress with her ever present low-heeled shoes. She talks with her hands; she touches people; she smiles a wife-bright smile. She straightens ties, jackets, fixing a friend's hair behind her ears. She never looks in the mirror but runs her hands through her brown curly hair constantly. It springs back to place. What does she do to make it spring back like that? "Nothing," she laughs. "I'm just a beauty."

She is eating her usual Spartan lunch: Finn Crisp, tomatoes, and cheese. She complains about her voracious appetite all day long but never eats enough to gain a pound.

She is eating, phoning, ordering, talking, and cleaning. Again and again, she goes to the sink of this fastidious kitchen and sponges things off. "I never like other people to clean for me. I don't want them to invade my own privacy."

The refrigerator is stocked with traditional Jewish food all put away in proper airtight containers. There is sauerkraut, coleslaw, pickles, dairy products; no pastry, no junk food. If coffee is required, Bess makes instant.

The phone, with several different lines, hangs on the wall. When Bess is not at home, the caller hears a taped message which doesn't identify her but asks in the deep resonant voice that is distinctly hers that you leave a message. The campaign headquarters number is tacked up to the wall. The phone is always ringing.

"Hello?" she says in her questioning way.

"Oh, hello, Barra." The tone relaxes; the caller is her daughter, Barra Grant.

"No, darling, you're absolutely right. I wouldn't think of intruding; you wait till the *Post* has finished. I know you're working hard. You call me when you want me, anytime. Good-bye, dear."

"That was Barra, she's in town to film *Slow Dancing in the Big City*, her screenplay. We have a very honest relationship; we don't intrude on each other's space, we respect each other. She was staying with me for a while and I couldn't believe the way she worked. She can sit down at a type-writer for eighteen hours straight, paper and coffee cups all over the place like in a movie. I can't do that, I have to do a little bit at a time."

She is finished cleaning now. She takes out a pocket mirror and outlines her lips in red, then presses them together once. She turns to campaign worker Pam Chanin.

"I'm leaving for Milwaukee tonight, Pam—for two days for Bristol-Myers. I'll leave you a number where I can be reached. But first I want to campaign a little at subway stops, and I'll be back Friday morning. You know, I've been thinking about that Women for Koch breakfast next week at the Americana. I think we should all just say a few words about Ed, then let him announce his platform for women himself so it has the full impact. I don't want to take away from the strength of it," she says, launching into a twenty-minute discussion of Koch's stand on women's rights.

Asked to discuss anything more personal than voting records, she freezes. She turns a half profile and says "Look, I'm a very private person. My private life? My divorce? I was telling Pam yesterday that you're never sorry for anything you do—it's all part of your life's experiences. I don't look upon my divorces as mistakes. Those marriages were right for the Bess that made that decision at that time."

Her childhood? It was demanding.

"Mama never told me, 'Bess, you did good.' She wanted the best for us and she was an incredible administrator. She ran those three kids, that house, the whole bit. But if I looked fine, she'd find something wrong—the color, the hem . . . I used to tell her, 'Mama, don't worry when you're not with me, because you're with me.'

"I guess I am my mother to a certain extent. We all are. But that is another part of me, one of my Besses, and I accepted it and learn from it. . . . I guess my parents are proud of me, I don't know."

When Bess won the Miss America contest, Earl Wilson interviewed her mother, who said, "She's a pretty girl, a nice girl, and she doesn't run around. That's why we're proud of her."

BESS IS SPEAKING at the Women for Koch breakfast at the Americana Hotel. When she takes the podium, a hush falls over the room. She pauses dramatically, then says, "Will the waiters please leave the room? I'm allergic to noise." She applauds the organizers of the breakfast and then introduces the guest of honor, Midge Costanza, assistant to President Jimmy Carter. Costanza takes the podium.

"I'm responsible for Bess's success in politics," Costanza says. "I first met her in 1968 in Monroe County when she was campaigning for Humphrey. I took one look at her and said, 'Bess, clean yourself up, take a shower, get your hair done.' " Bess's expression is pleasant but tense.

Then Costanza says, "I figure Ed Koch needs me, a real woman. He's been with her too long." Bess's laugh is a little less pleasant.

SHE IS TRAVELING in a campaign limousine now.

"Listen, I don't resent the Miss America contest," she said, sitting properly, legs crossed, in the back seat. "Look, I was from the Bronx. There were parts of the television career I enjoyed, but occasionally I felt used for my supposed glamour. I couldn't be the funniest panelist, so I had to play it straight. You know what I did? I did my homework. When I commented on the Rose Bowl Parade, I knew every float by heart. People in New York might say, What difference does it make? But it made a difference to the people in California. They worked hard on those floats. I knew them so well, even if the Teleprompter broke down, I would remember. You can't rely on Teleprompters.

"But all these activities are really a prologue to my life today," Bess says. "You know there's a quote from the Talmud I like: It says we shouldn't weep for the old man who, having lived a useful life, a moral life, dies, but for the baby who is born and doesn't know what awaits him. I think character is destiny, and the one thing that is important to me above all is my character, my reputation."

SHE IS CAMPAIGNING with Koch in Brighton Beach. She moves in crowds of people with *chais* around their necks and among those with crosses. They all kiss her and snap Polaroid pictures. There is one black family on the beach. It seems everyone is avoiding them out of confusion. Bess crosses a pier and bends down and picks up the black baby, telling the mother how beautiful he is. They love her.

She has had a usual campaign day. She has given three speeches, one of them in Brooklyn, where she had a celery tonic. She has worked two hours for Citibank, talking about a new consumer booklet she is writing for them. She has just returned from a trip to Milwaukee for Bristol-Myers.

It is now evening, and she is to have dinner with Ed Koch and Dave Garth, master media strategist, at the Café des Artistes. She is early but doesn't want to wait in the bar, because "I guess I'm traditional, but it makes me nervous." We go upstairs to do the interview in Garth's apartment.

She curls up on a couch, looking guarded. She always looks guarded when she cannot discuss either Koch or consumerism, the two subjects she is completely comfortable with. I ask her about her marriage to wealthy entertainment lawyer Arnold Grant. The marriage lasted from 1962 to 1970, when they divorced. (They had divorced once before, for a year. "I guess the only thing I do impetuously is get married," she had noted earlier.)

"Look, let me explain about my marriage to Arnold. He was a fantastic, brilliant man, okay? He represented some of the most famous clients in the country, and he got them what they wanted. He was tough. But he was very difficult.

"The bars on the windows of our home on Sutton Place began to look like a prison to me; I was so trapped by all the responsibilities of wealth that I had no chance to be me. There was no time to grow.

"I'll tell you a story: One night we had some political people over. It was a terribly stimulating dinner party. After it was over, I said, 'Arnold, I learned so much tonight, it was wonderful.' And he said, 'Yes, but Bess, sit down. I want to discuss something with you. These shrimp forks are too small.' I knew I had to leave then, and I left with just all my clothes in the end."

"I started getting interested in politics when I was married to Arnold, but it was a Pygmalion relationship. In 1969, John Lindsay asked me to be commissioner of consumer affairs. I wasn't his first choice; others had turned it down, saying it would be too difficult. I told him, 'John, give me forty-eight hours to think about it,' and then I took it.

"My Department of Consumer Affairs really fought for the consumer. We passed a consumer-protection act that really protected; we passed unit pricing; we raided supermarkets. With the help of an outstanding staff, we accomplished a great deal. And I campaigned for Hubert Humphrey for president in 1968, and for Senator Henry Jackson in his 1976 presidential bid, and for Senator Patrick Moynihan's race in 1976. I'm a registered Democrat and I would say a moderate centrist, if we use labels. But, above all, I'm issue oriented. . . ." (When asked why she didn't support Bella Abzug, she said: "I don't like Bella. I dislike Bella. She was a fine congresswoman; she would have made an incompetent senator. I don't want her representing me.")

The issue of her own political aspirations brings a stony look. "I came very close to running for mayor in 1973. Nelson Rockefeller invited me up to his estate when the poll showed I could get the Democratic nomination. I thought, 'Sure, I'll go up and talk to him.' I wanted to see the estate anyway. I took a friend, my attorney, Max Kampelman, with me for a steadying hand, but I decided not to run.

"The thing I have felt most strongly is my desire to be as private as possible—to have an opportunity to have as normal an environment as possible so that the public life does not devour me. I hate being in columns; it is not me.

"I want Ed to be mayor. I first met him in 1969, when I was commissioner. He was an unusually responsive congressman, and we agreed on the basic issues. Then we became friends.

"Ed is a fantastic man who will make a fine mayor if he is elected. He isn't a duplicitous man; he's *auf den tisch,* as we say in Yiddish, on the table, on the level. His idea of a good time is to go to subway stops and say, 'Hi, I'm Ed Koch. How'm I doing?' He really cares about New York City."

Garth and Koch have called twice to find out if she wants to go eat. She says no, she is talking. Finally, they finish their meal and come up.

It is late. Koch wants to take her home. She says she wants to walk. He convinces her to let him take her in a cab. They talk about the polls. Koch says, "Bess, you know what I'm going to do for you if this all works out? Someday, I'll invite you to my wedding." They laugh.

"You know, I don't need to get married again," she says later. "I've been married. The only thing I'd marry for is good conversation."

Ed and Bess. Bess and Ed. Ed and Bess hold hands on Rosh Hashanah in temple. Ed and Bess hold hands at a subway stop. Ed and Bess walk arm in arm campaigning. Ed and Bess pose for pictures together. Ed and Bess may run City Hall.

Is it a romance? The official line from both is that "we don't want to discuss our personal lives." But most of their friends and associates agree that it is just a very deep friendship and that there is little chance of Bess Myerson's becoming Bess Myerson Koch.

"Look, I share that part of Ed's life that is politics, and most of his life is politics . . .

"Of course, I will help him in any way I can. But I am outraged by the charge in the campaign that I was Ed's cover-up—there just to dispel rumors that Ed was gay. Ed is not gay. I abhor a campaign of that sort; it makes me furious. Why, Ed said I was 'a very good adviser.' "

"Him? Use me? Nobody uses me. I use me."

UNANSWERED PRAYERS
The Death and Life of Truman Capote

JULIE BAUMGOLD

OCTOBER 29, 1984

When Truman Capote died on August 25, 1984, just shy of his sixtieth birthday, his literary successes were behind him. Even his social renown, which he came to tend even more carefully than his literary oeuvre, had slipped far. In 1966, shortly following the publication of In Cold Blood, *he'd hosted the social event of the decade, the famous Black and White Ball. By the time he died, many of those friends were no longer speaking to him. In his last years, Capote staked his hope for literary, and perhaps social, rehabilitation on his novel-in-progress,* Answered Prayers, *which he often spoke of as his masterwork. Yet when he died, a complete manuscript was nowhere to be found. One month after his death, in a two-part piece running in consecutive issues, Julie Baumgold revealed Capote's intimate world and, for the first time, exposed the truth about his masterwork. The first part is published here. Baumgold is a former contributing editor for* New York, Esquire, *and* Vogue *and is the author of the novels* The Diamond *(Simon & Schuster) and* Creatures of Habit *(Knopf).*

*I*NSIDE MORTIMER'S on the day of Truman Capote's New York memorial service, two small segments of society were in tumult. In the side room, C. Z. Guest was holding a luncheon for twenty-four of Truman's good friends—Katharine Graham (for whom he had given the Black and White Ball), Joanne Carson, Rose and Bill Styron, his producer, Lester

Persky, Judy Green, Joe Fox, Alvin Dewey, the investigator of *In Cold Blood,* his lawyer, Alan U. Schwartz, and some of the Sagaponack friends. Inexplicably, this group was scrunched uncomfortably into the dark area next to the kitchen. The whole center of the room was peculiarly empty, and as far from them as possible, at a long table by the window, Jan Cushing Olympitis, whom Capote once described as "a cat with a cold," was holding her own, smaller, rival Truman Capote lunch with his newer friends. Here were the companions of his night world and members of the Warhol group, among them Kate Harrington, the young woman Capote had loved as a daughter.

"We were the ones he *really* loved," Jan was saying while Mrs. Guest managed to pretend her friends were really quite alone in the room. The two factions, each with its own standing in Capote's life, looked at each other across the gap, few crossing over to lightly sideswipe the cheeks of their chums before scuttling back in loyalty to the rival blonde queen. Meanwhile, in the main room of Mortimer's, one of Capote's last lovers, the father and ex-husband of two women at Jan's table, sat uninvited and unwelcome.

Some of the New York contingent were angry at one of the California contingent, each competing to say who loved him hardest and helped him most. Jack Dunphy, his companion of thirty-six years and heir, had left the service and stayed wisely private. He removed himself, as he always did, from these people he considered "exaggeratedly immature, without much talent," and returned to the beach where he lived, with the ashes of Truman Capote in a hollowed-out book on his mantelpiece.

From both ends of the room, you could hear Truman's friends imitating his voice as they told stories from his good days. There were women who had loved him so much they hadn't wanted to share him, and so there were rivalries and jealousies among these later women as there had been among the earlier ones and among the boyfriends. There were women who had used him for his fame and some he had used. There were those who had courted him, as he had courted the earlier, grander ones, like Babe Paley. And those like Kate and Joanne, one in white, one in black, to whom he had been a mentor, teaching each of them to share his taste in different eras and taking care of them. There was one man in the restaurant who they said had physically abused him, and many who had stayed away and disappeared long ago from his life when he became sloppy in his dress and wobbly on his feet, told their secrets, and brought his careless men into their careful homes. There were those whose talent he encouraged and those who had taken care of him when he collapsed in their houses both grand and simple and those who drove him around, who took him to and from hospitals and drying-out clinics and extricated him from one disaster after another and felt relieved when he would go to the Coast, because then the California people would take over for a while.

The life of an artist had been reduced to this clatter of forks, this last group so fractured and diminished. Except for C. Z. Guest and Katharine Graham, all the stately women were gone. The powerful men were gone, too. In fact, the whole core of the 540 who had rushed to his ball were absent from the day and his life, the result of his social suicide when he published "La Côte Basque 1965" nine years ago. None of *Answered Prayers* had been read at the tribute. But there were readings from *Other Voices, Other Rooms, The Grass Harp, Breakfast at Tiffany's,* and *In Cold Blood,* the beautiful Capote words that were the other truth of this day and this man.

It was not hard to imagine the small figure of Truman Capote in this social landscape, his sensibility always too finely stretched and vibrating, standing in the empty space watching these segments of his life, his felt hat pulled down, his cardigan buttoned, his tongue jammed into the side of his mouth. He would run his finger over his eyebrow as he did in a healthy period when he was enjoying himself, finding it all "hiiiiiiiilarious," perhaps singing one favorite song that the Old Guard had refused to play at the service—"It's my party, and I'll cry if I want to"—his scarf flying out as he twirled from one side to the other on his little feet in pure malicious delight in a ruckus.

Over the afternoon, in the minds of those who knew, hung the last lie, the secret they had begun to suspect, for searches had already been made, that there was no *Answered Prayers*—not a word—except for the four chapters that *Esquire* had published. It was a secret that, if ultimately true, Capote had successfully kept from Gerald Clarke, his biographer for nine years; Joe Fox, his editor since *In Cold Blood;* and his lawyer and literary executor, Alan Schwartz, all of whom had believed the masterwork existed in some form. And so they searched, trying to find a secret drawer in a Chippendale chest, under cabinets, even getting Dunphy to open the trunk of a Buick. For over the last sixteen years, Capote had said he was working. He had given two friends an outline. He had discussed the missing portions in tempting detail, even promising to bring them to various lunches, though he never did. Whenever Fox and Schwartz would meet, they would have this exchange:

"Has he shown it to you?"

"No, has he shown it to *you*?"

"Wouldn't he have shown it to *me*?" says Jack Dunphy. "Truman showed what he did, but *tout de suite*! He had to run down the road with it. Don't you think he would have told me? He was a great conjurer."

Where is *Answered Prayers*? "It's *in* him," says Dunphy.

Well then, what was he doing for the last twelve years when he would go into his house and say he was working?

"He was reading magazines. He was a magazine addict," says Dunphy. But how could *they* know, those capitalists and entrepreneurs who were "minding the store." "They don't see backstage."

As much as he led people on, Capote tried to give clues. Years ago in Palm Springs, Truman had shown Frank Perry a large stack of pages on his typewriter, indicating they were four hundred pages of *Answered Prayers*. When Perry was alone in the room, he went to the pile and found "to my horror," he says, that only the first five pages were typed, the rest blank. At one time, Capote planted a false story in Aileen Mehle's "Suzy" column, saying that all his manuscripts had been lost in a flood at Gloria Vanderbilt's house. He told others that one of his lovers had stolen parts of *Answered Prayers*, but when Alan Schwartz investigated, he decided that the man did not have them. There is always the possibility that they were rewritten out of existence in Capote's obsession with getting his work perfect, though he did not throw away his drafts. Indeed, cartons and stacks of manuscripts had been carried away and sorted.

In the introduction to his last collection, *Music for Chameleons*, Capote wrote about the techniques he would be using for *Answered Prayers*. He did a lot of writing about his writing and his plans to rewrite the book, speeding up the effects, using all his craft. He would practice by writing exercises, combining in a single form all he knew from other genres, setting himself center stage in this "grim gamble." Norman Mailer finds this "a distress call. I made mine early with *Advertisements for Myself.* It was his bad luck it hit him late, when he felt his powers were fading. He loved writing so much and had such pride of offering nothing but his best," says Mailer, "that when he could no longer deliver he lost much of his desire to live." Capote's old antagonist Gore Vidal called his death, at fifty-nine, "a wise career choice." "I'd say," says Mailer, "it was an inevitable career choice. He had more pride than any writer I know. His achievement was to go as far as he went, and it was asking too much of him to be the wise curator of his talent."

Whatever sort of curator he was of his talent, Capote was a poor caretaker of his body. He would cure it to abuse it. He would swim laps, go to gyms; he would go or be carried off to clinics and hospitals, consult doctors; and then he'd sabotage everything. "He had a talent for putting himself in harm's way," Schwartz said at his memorial. "I was involved with him in many heartrending [episodes], but he always got up and threw himself into the fray." At various times, Capote was reported to have throat polyps, prostate problems, a tic douloureux. He did have liver disease, epilepsy, emphysema, and phlebitis, but his hard little body, as stubborn and solid as the bulldogs he collected, kept mending, and his will did the rest. "He could rejuvenate faster than anyone I knew," says a doctor who treated him. "For the last two years, he fought to stay alive. He was kicking his feet to stay above water, not like before, when you felt he was going straight for a nosedive," says Kate Harrington. His death came when he was drinking less, when the turbulent companions were gone, and when he was fighting phlebitis, the disease that frightened him as nothing physical had before. In the last few years, he would have stints when he was spartan, during *Music for Chameleons* and for months last winter and spring, though he had been drinking again over the summer. It was a bad summer. Quite typically, this June he fled his last drying-out place, checking out of Chit-Chat Farms after only five days, paying $600 for a limousine to get him home quick.

"He'd be rueful," says a friend, "but he denied his problem—'It has nothing to do with drinking. It's just bad luck.' He'd take Antabuse and drink right through it."

ALL HIS LIFE, Truman Capote knew how to seduce, the way certain small children (like the child in his story "Miriam") do. He was full of wiles and guile, talking low so you couldn't lean back in your seat with him as he told one of his stories, usually something dreadful about someone impeccable. He loved to shock. The mother of two famous sisters had called her daughters "whores" during one of their screaming fights. The penis of one famous writer was actually "a cross between a dimple and a bellybutton." He had his network of informants and the classic gossip's desire to know it all. In the days when he cared, he was not above asking one editor who on her staff was having affairs. He saw through social poses because, somehow, he knew all worlds, from his underground of pimps, druggies, and whores to the now aging stories from the days of his high life.

Capote was perverse in all things. Though his public mannerisms were effeminate, there was a masculine, almost sexy core to this man who knew himself so well and presented his outrageousness boldly and with calculation. Intensely competitive as he was, and jealous of all his turfs, he was yet a fierce protector of other writers' talent. He was proud of Jack Dunphy's writing all his life. And though he wrote cruelly about a minimally disguised Tennessee Williams in *Answered Prayers,* he dedicated *Music for Chameleons* to him in a low period of Williams's career.

He told women of a certain age to keep to one look, and that way they would never age. He told his women how to dress, what makeup to wear, what to see or read, who to love. He waited at their hairdressers, waited in their libraries. Wear glasses and low heels in reptile, he said to one, happily wasting his writer's eye. He took care of them, moving them into new houses, sending them to Norman Orentreich for their skin, running their lives as he had when he tried to launch Lee Radziwill as an actress in *Laura,* or to set up a house-opening business for his cleaning lady. After he gave a reading to a fashionable audience at the Newhouse Theater, Lester Persky found him in his dressing room cackling away with his cleaning woman and her four friends. When Katharine Graham was nervous about traveling with him without having read all his work, he marked a collection for her of what she should read. He assured her she'd be all right in a more social world than she was used to at the time. Aileen Mehle remembers that when she stayed with him once in Palm Springs "he treated me as though I were a little doll. He tucked me in bed and told me bedtime stories and gave me a bit of *Answered Prayers* to read."

"He was my mentor," says Kate Harrington. "With all his *enfant terrible* behavior, with me he was not that way. He protected me at Studio 54. He taught me what to read, took me on shopping sprees, asking, 'Do you think this is pretty? Isn't this chic?' We went looking at pictures, and he taught me to observe. At the end of parties, he would sit on my bed and say, 'What did you see?' He taught me how to talk. I'd say, 'I'm taking a bath,' and he would say, 'You're not taking a bath, you're *bathing*.' " He made sure she kept out of the sun, having her paged on one California trip whenever she sneaked out to the pool. He had Avedon photograph her for her fourteenth birthday, and gave her pearls from Tiffany for her high-school graduation: "The real thing, for the real thing," he wrote. But as she grew, he changed, and she found herself having to take care of him these last years.

All Capote's friends geared up for him, for he was the best company, not only for the women but for the night people too. Once, he went over to a little gay kid at Studio 54, as thin as a sparrow, and just put his arms around him and held him. The husbands and the big businessmen were comfortable with him, as attracted to the stories and gossip as were their wives. Before the break, William Paley used to call Capote "Tru-boy," and he could be seen sitting parked in front of CBS in Paley's car, waiting for him. Robert O. Anderson, the chairman of Atlantic Richfield, once sent Truman in his private plane to his Mexican house and then took the plane away so Truman would be forced to write. For all of them, Truman always went a bit further: going along 49th Street to find a new shop for his barber, giving a *People* writer copies of his books and driving her all the way to the expressway so she wouldn't get lost, dropping off pies and a quilt at the summer house of Jill Krementz and Kurt Vonnegut, befriending and supporting the family of a lover during and after their affair.

He loved people who were "slightly *manqué*," and he loved pranks and mischief. The first time he met Leo Lerman, he jumped on Lerman's back and said, "Give me a piggyback." He'd call Krementz and imitate a telephone repairman. When Aileen Mehle was going to London, he hurt her by lying about her and a British banker. "I knew you were going there, and I thought it would be fun if we stirred up the pot," he told her later. When he first met one of his later women, she told him she was seeing an analyst he had once gone to. Capote had her go in for her next appointment and say, "Doctor, I'm so happy. I've finally found the man for me. He's warm and stable and everything you told me to look for." A very nervous nurse came in just then to announce that Mrs. X's fiancé was in the waiting room. At that point, Truman burst in, pulling her away, saying, "Darling, you were so quiet when you got out of bed this morning I didn't hear you go." And, laughing, out they ran to lunch at Quo Vadis. "He went from an imp to a gremlin. From something adorable and sweet to hold in your hand to almost a rocklike creature," says a friend.

TRUMAN CAPOTE'S best years ended in the seventies. The mid- to late seventies were very hard times. Then began the desertion of friends, and the feuds with Jacqueline Susann, Gore Vidal, and Lee Radziwill. The collapses, with Capote limp on a stretcher, increased then, too, building to four in two months of 1981. In 1977, he had walked onstage at Towson State University in Maryland announcing he was an alcoholic.

He told a writer about his childhood in Alabama, when he lived with his maiden aunts and an uncle who drank (they were actually his mother's cousins). There was liquor set up in the library. He would talk to his uncle, and when his back was turned, he would drink until he was drunk by the time dinner was called. His aunts would look at him and say, "Truman, we don't understand you. All day you are a monster, and at night, you're so docile and sweet."

"I'd give him a tomato juice," says Judy Green, "and he'd put vodka in it. He'd have one or two openly, but then I'd go out of the room and he'd be up and back at the bar fast." Jan Olympitis would take him home at ten, and call up the UN Plaza concierge, who would tell her Mr. Capote had just gone out. He was known in the bars of 49th Street, where he'd have three doubles at once, drink them in fifteen minutes, and leave. He convinced one friend he was not "a chemical alcoholic but a psychological one." Patrick Shields, the director of Le Club, remembers a dinner with Capote and Tennessee Williams, one of those nights when the language sang, when both were trying so hard not to drink. "Tennessee would look at me and will me with his eyes to pick up the bottle and fill his glass. People like Truman and Tennessee were only alive because of the assertion of their wills. They reach a point where the will does not work anymore, and sort of expire."

There are those who remember Capote's 1978 interview with Stanley Siegel as an example of just how self-destructive he was, to have gone on television drunk and drugged, his upper lip sweating, slurring his half-finished sentences, so that Siegel was obliged to ask him if he wanted to quit before the second question. But what was remarkable about that interview was the bravery and self-understanding that Capote displayed. He performed almost in a trance, too tired and drugged to lie. He had said he was going to show up, and he did, even though he hadn't slept in two days, and he tried very hard to finish the program, answering everything despite the level of some of the questions. He was cut after seventeen minutes.

"My life is so strange—it's not like anybody else's," he tells Siegel.

"You have had this history of alcoholism," says Siegel.

"Oh, my God, alcoholism is the least of it. That's the joker in the cards. My problem was never drinking. [It was] taking different kinds of drugs, but not things that other people would consider drugs."

"But the combination of drugs and alcohol," says Siegel.

"I put them together like some sort of cocktail . . . I think that anybody that starts to do that thing, you know, they get into a kind of pattern of doing. I mean, you start by doing one thing and then you start by doing another thing because you put the two things together."

"You've been doing it lately?" Stanley asks.

"I've been doing it for twenty years."

Siegel asks why.

"I can tell you in exactly one word: anxiety."

About what?

"I don't know. I think certain people have a feeling of anxiety. A lot of analysts call it 'free-floating anxiety.' . . . You know it doesn't mean anything, but it's always there, and I don't know what it is . . . I know people who do fantastic things because of anxiety."

"It began a long time ago?"

"It began because I . . . because my mother. It was all very simple. My mother was a very beautiful girl and only seventeen years old, and she used to lock me in these rooms all the time, and I developed this fantastic anxiety that no analyst has ever been able to . . ."

"Unlock?" says Stanley. "Are you anxious now?"

"I'm pretty anxious about this new book of mine [*Answered Prayers*] . . . really a great sense of anxiety about it," he says and then draws back. "On the other hand, most people who have free-floating anxiety . . . it really has to do with some kind of emotional relationship or something to do with their work. Well, I don't have that at all. I couldn't care less." Siegel asks if he is writing now.

"Yeah, it's almost finished," says Truman. Later, he says, "There's something about me that just got out of it . . . Somebody like me, you really never get through it really to . . . there's just something that's going through your sensibility. It just doesn't work."

"Is it biochemical?"

"It's just something. It's also the reason why you work and create and do something, but it's an awfully high price to pay."

Siegel asks what will happen if Capote can't overcome his problem and says he is sure Capote has thought about it.

"*Well*, you know, I do fret," says Capote, "months and months and months and my writing and everything, but the obvious answer is that eventually I'll kill myself without meaning to."

"Like Marilyn Monroe, for example?" asks Siegel.

"Well, you see . . . it's a really interesting thing, because Monty Clift and Marilyn and I were all great friends. I don't know what it is . . . a particular kind of sensibility."

Siegel wants to know if he could reverse the process.

"Well," says Truman, "I've been in practically every hospital in America you can think of. I don't know. Maybe yes, maybe no. I'm not dishonest about it."

FRIENDS TRIED to help by recommending analysts. Years ago, Jack Dunphy's wife, Joan McCracken, told Dunphy that Truman was "very insecure." "Who isn't insecure?" says Dunphy. "Analysts were a waste of time and money. He'd start to duel with them, and he was always brighter." Friends checked him in and out of Silver Hill, Riggs, Hazelden, Smithers, and various emergency rooms. When he had bad times, "he was forgiven because you always knew that in a month he'd be back in the hospital," says a friend. He was well known to the staff of Southampton Hospital. John Scanlon, there in June of 1982 after a heart attack, remembers Truman being brought in in a straitjacket. The next morning, Scanlon looked out, and there on the misty green lawn was Capote, hiding behind a bush with his sneakers in his hand, pursued by huge female attendants. Later, he saw Capote tied to the bed, a small swollen lump with only his sunglasses showing.

"When he was drinking or on drugs, there was not much you could do," one friend says. "Shake him. Scream at him. I tried, but when one thing stopped, another would start. He could have died a year ago or a year from now."

"I remember sitting on his bed and saying, 'Why are you doing this to yourself?'" says Kate Harrington. "Then he'd 'fall' twice a year. And finally, when I was seventeen, I said, 'Isn't it enough that you have me? I'd be heartbroken if you died.' 'Well, *of course* you would,' he said."

At one dinner in the late seventies at Lester Persky's apartment with two friends, Persky, a kind and true friend of Truman's, decided to talk to him "like a Jewish mother." For forty minutes, he told Capote his forebodings. "The friends' jaws fell slack. Truman took it and was very quiet. He stopped then for a few months."

"His battle was much more difficult because of his cross-addiction to a spectacular panoply of other drugs," wrote a man who lived with him at this time. "When the shakes became untameable through use of alcohol, he moved to downers to stop them and to sleep without the nightmares.

Then, to offset the lethargy . . . he went to uppers. Later, cocaine was added to the already dangerous equation.

"Truman used hospitals quite effectively . . . Indeed, at first, he wanted to get truly well. In the latter stages they merely served as three-day emergency rooms. Which didn't serve cocaine. He could get that only from his 'friends.'

"His addiction was more difficult to treat than most, since he was what is called a 'protected addict.' That is, he had almost unlimited resources to acquire alcohol and other drugs . . . to avoid well-meaning but critical friends, as well as acquire sycophants . . . who abetted his spiral to death."

CAPOTE KNEW ALMOST too much about medicine. He had doctors all over, and since he really was sick and anxious, whenever he walked in, the prescription pads came out. When he died, the coroner found his death complicated by multiple-drug intoxication. He'd taken pills for sleep, anxiety, leg pains, and epileptic seizures. He was always bragging that he knew how much he could take. Once, he said that Sunny von Bulow had sent him a book about recreational drugs: "It describes the maximum dose you can take safely, and it was definitely accurate about every drug I've taken." One day, Gerald Clarke had lunch with him at Bobby Van's when he was waiting for a delivery of sleeping pills. He held up a new violet pill and said, "Aren't these the most beautiful pills you've ever seen? They let me sleep four hours at a time, which I've never been able to do."

It is, of course, presumptuous to go beyond Capote's own words to explain why this happened. Even Jack Dunphy says he does not know. "Fame? Success?" Capote had blamed his childhood, he blamed envy, saying, "People simply cannot endure success over too long a period of time. It has to be destroyed." Certainly, there were external events that hurt him. Some friends, like Phyllis Cerf Wagner, saw his bad times beginning in 1965 with the pain he felt at the execution of the killers of *In Cold Blood*. Ten years later, he was rejected by some of his social friends—in Aileen Mehle's words, "he shot himself in the heart. He went from the pinnacle to the pits." For, as Mailer says, he had tasted a renowned social power. "No one came near it, and he was probably prouder of that. It was harder to do than was the writing for him. His talent was his friend. His achievement was his social life."

It hurt Capote to lose the friendship of the Paleys. He had been at their house every weekend since Babe's daughter Amanda Burden was a girl up until "the dread book," as she calls it. Babe was his "Bobolink." "He'd been her closest confidant for eighteen or twenty years, part of the fabric of her life," says Amanda. "When she saw him later in a restaurant, he was invisible to her. Then he seemed to disappear and begin his serious drug life." Mailer thinks that "La Côte Basque" may have been Capote's deliberate effort to free himself. "Either I grovel at their feet, or I get down to real work," though Judy Green says Capote told her he believed he was giving "immortality" to those he wrote about, and they would, of course, understand. Liz Smith even went so far as to suggest that Capote died of a heart broken by Lee Radziwill's refusal to testify for him in Gore Vidal's lawsuit five years ago, an assumption so embarrassing to Radziwill that she stayed away from his memorial because of it.

Capote's immediate young fame, however desired, was something he always had to deal with. In lulls, the celebrity absorbed his creativity. There was always the dangerous appeal of the verge, sliding into and out of life with the Warhol people, where fame is quick as a photograph and the night rolls on and on. One of the saddest sentences ever written about Capote probably made him the happiest. "In November of 1966, when it all came to a head, the art of the novel was 388 years old and the American system of party-giving was 345," *Esquire* wrote after the Black and White Ball for Kay Graham. "Neither will ever be the same, and all because of one man who managed to become a master at both."

He felt vacant, he needed a family, he had no bourgeois core, he was not hard-thinking, not intellectual enough—he'd lost his looks, his various friends would say. But does anyone really have to go beyond the vision of a writer with a book in his mind that he could not write?

"The pain was always there inside him," says Kate Harrington. "He told me how he saw five things at once and how exhausting it was—a flooding, constantly. Others saw one or two levels, so his writing was his way of getting it out." When he could no longer write as he wanted, he was left with what he called his "dark madness" and the remedies.

"I always felt he brought out something that made you want to hug him, and at the same time, he wanted you to be scathing," says Kate. "Even the first time I met this sweet little man, he had something hurt. When I saw him give a lecture, he came onstage and they laughed and I thought, 'This is what his whole life has been like.' Maybe it's how he became so scathing."

Some blamed his later companions. Just as some men seem to keep marrying the same woman, Capote seemed to be trying to find Jack Dunphy again in the men—sometimes married, usually Irish—with whom he would stay for years. But there was something wrong with them and Truman together. It was said they mistreated him, made him suffer, and brought out his worst. Like Truman, they drank. Once, Capote passed out and fell from a bed he was sharing with one of them. When another man discovered Truman lying on the floor, he said, "Why didn't you help him or call me?" The man said, "What do you want? I'm sick, too." They were toted along now, into worlds Jack had shunned, brought to lunch with Princess Grace. It was hard for them. They "broke things" in every way.

"What is the good of being a famous novelist if you can't have a little vanity," says Mailer. "But he had an outrageously overweening store of it, and that's part of what killed him." Even after he lost the vanity in his appearance that caused him to go to diet doctors and have his face lifted, his hair, eyes, and teeth done, even after he was no longer bothering to get his clothes into eye-pulling combinations or even get fully dressed (he'd wear a seersucker suit with nothing underneath or an overcoat with underwear), he never lost his pride in his work, which may explain why *Answered Prayers* has never been found. It was better to read magazines.

LESTER PERSKY, who is producing the movie of Capote's story "Handcarved Coffins," had several lunches with him in June. With Truman's cooperation, they made some tapes. They decided to return for one lunch to La Côte Basque. On the tape, Truman's voice is thick and very slurred. He says he has taken a new prescription drug: "It has a strange effect—it makes me feel dizzy." He likes the table they have given him right in the front: "I can see every monster as they come in." Eventually, he finds his stride and begins telling stories about Le Pavillon and a wicked tale about the Duchess of Windsor waiting for Jimmy Donahue in the arcade of El Morocco.

He spent a lot of time at the beach last summer with Jack Dunphy. "Jack was always the boy he fell in love with. Truman was so proud of everything he did," says a friend. Kurt Vonnegut thinks Capote was trying to set up a new group of friends. "He would never have bothered with me before," he says, and in fact, Vonnegut had the impression that Capote hadn't read his work or that of Michael Frayn, who was also a guest at the last lunch the Vonneguts had with him, the week before he died. That day, on the way in, Capote lost his balance and seemed faint, and Frayn and Vonnegut supported him. During lunch, he talked all about himself, telling his stories, but then he felt bad again and lay down on a chaise. Vonnegut drove him home, but Capote was insistent about being let off at the end of his driveway, even though it was painful to walk. An arrest for drunken driving the previous summer had changed his life. He was no longer seen barreling along Daniels Lane in his maroon convertible, so small behind the steering wheel that a friend called him the Headless Horseman and those who knew the car would quickly pull over to the side of the road.

Since no one could take care of Truman Capote, who was clearly in a precarious condition and going down, why didn't they take better care of his work? Lester Persky says he has parts of *Answered Prayers* in a black notebook that Truman had asked him to copy, but he can't find it. Fox says a year or six months after the last *Esquire* chapter, Capote gave him another excerpt, "thirty or forty or fifty pages," but he can't remember what was in it, and apparently did not even xerox it, though he had it for "a year or two, maybe three." Capote took it back to make revisions. It was never seen again.

Capote's last conversation with his aunt Marie Rudisill (first reported by Ron Wenzell in the South Carolina newspaper *The State*) took place because she had written him saying she was seventy-three and wanted to make up before she died. Their estrangement, after her book about his boyhood, "preyed on my mind," she said, "He called one night at 12:30. He always called late, never called at a human hour," and told her he knew what she was going through with her book, which had caused her family and friends to stop talking to her. Finally, she wanted to destroy every copy.

"I've been through that," he said. "It caused me more unhappiness. I lost every friend I ever had," he said to her. "Truman cared," she says. "He had that little air that he didn't, but he did."

He told her he was trying to start a new life, he wanted to shake off some people and unshackle himself. I'm bored with most of them, he said, and I think they're getting tired of me.

Towards the end, Capote was deprived of his routines of Bobby Van's and had to swim in the ocean since he could no longer get to pools by himself. In some ways in his later life, he had become like John Cheever's Neddy in "The Swimmer," going from pool to pool wherever he lived, drinking and swimming, not quite realizing what had happened to him. Always, at a pool, he would go to the edge and walk right in without looking. At last he was too sick to swim, and the pool he liked was sold to strangers.

The week before he died, in August, Capote met Kate Harrington for lunch. He was not feeling well. He did not want to go back and stay alone in his apartment. It was soundproof, and even friends felt the silence. This was one of the many lunches Truman would have where he seemed to want it to fill his afternoon, but Kate had to return to work at *Interview*. Later, he spent the night at her place. She had her friends over, and he amused them all with stories, sitting in bed, enchanting a fresh group.

The next week, Kate and Lester Persky had two dinners with Capote. After one, a friend of Kate's took him home, and Truman told him that he could finally let Kate go because he knew she would be all right. During these last dinners, he said he was excited about the movie of "Handcarved Coffins." He talked about Los Angeles, saying, "Who wants to live in a town where the leading social figure is a bald, nearsighted dwarf?" But still, says Persky, he had an "*idée fixe*" about getting to California. He felt comfortable at the Jockey Club and was munching a huge amount of caviar. "I love caviar, but it's no fun unless you order a pound," Truman said. And he talked a bit about his birthday and a party he would give here, maybe a small one, for twenty.

"He would always say, 'I'm coming back in two weeks,' even when he stayed months," says Kate. "This time, he looked at me through his blue-tinted glasses, and I said, 'When will I see you?' and he said, 'I don't know when. But you do what I told you to do. I know about these things. All right, baby doll?' "

"He was anxious to come to California," says Joanne Carson, his friend for twenty years. He'd always arrive with a round-trip ticket, but he told her to make the reservations just one way. "I don't know how long I will stay," he said. He kept calling, wanting to move up the trip, but she told him she was working. "Someone who loves someone like me has to be available at all times," Capote had once said, but now his women worked, like Kate, even C. Z. They weren't those women of fashion who would cancel anything to be with him. It was almost as though there were less room for him in his world.

"Truman was very much in touch with the childlike part of himself," says Joanne Carson. "We both had emotionally deprived childhoods and were looking for playmates . . . He'd call up and say, 'I have a marvelous adventure to take you on.' " Later, he would introduce her to California society, moving the furniture and art from his Palm Springs home into her house. There he always had his rooms. She would cook special food, and she kept the pool heated to 92 degrees.

It was the first time he had come with a suitcase. He brought out new clothes. Friday he was tired, but he wrote under the umbrella. Mrs. Carson had asked him to write something for her that would make him "feel good." He rewrote part of a piece from *Music for Chameleons,* which he called "Remembering Willa Cather." He wrote about lavender roses, and there were lavender roses at the side of his bed, though he was describing a room he remembered from his past. He was still rewriting, even this last story.

All day Friday, he swam and planned his birthday. They had dinner and watched the news, and Capote made a note to call Joe Fox, wanting to get forty copies of *One Christmas* for Christmas presents for his California friends. Joanne Carson says he insisted on writing the notes to go inside the books right then and sat up to do them.

"Usually he fell asleep in my room and then would go to his room and come back. I'd wake to his rustling newspapers. He fell asleep about 2:30 with his notebook and glasses on the table beside him." The next morning, she went in to see if he wanted breakfast. "He was struggling with his little bathing suit, and he let me help. 'Oh, I feel very tired and weak,' he said, and I put a little T-shirt on him and I left and came back to put the tray on his counter and I didn't disturb him. At noon, I went in with the pool towels. The minute I walked in, the room was too still, nothing moved."

Here was the stillness of other rooms, the stillness of his New York apartment, of the rooms he was locked in as a boy. It was the stillness a working writer must live with, a stillness Truman Capote had tried to flee with people and parties and commotions in his blood.

"I usually brush his brow lightly, and I touched his forehead. It was cool . . . There was no pulse. I called the paramedics and waited."

WOODY AND ME

NANCY JO SALES

APRIL 5, 1993

In 1993, Woody Allen was playing the lead in a tabloid drama. In the midst of an acrimonious custody battle with Mia Farrow, his companion of twelve years, he admitted that he was in love with her adopted step-daughter, who was twenty-one. The events caused Nancy Jo Sales, then a twenty-eight-year-old aspiring journalist, to reexamine her own youthful relationship with Allen. It's not what you'd think. As a precocious, bookish, social outcast thirteen-year-old in Coral Gables, Florida, Sales had written to Allen, and the two had become pen pals, corresponding about Kierkegaard and college and other subjects of mutual interest. Sales got back in touch with Allen, who approved her use of the letters. "He's probably responsible for me thinking maybe there's a world outside of Coral Gables, this hot Florida jail," she says. "Woody and Me" was her first serious feature. "Because of this story, I became a journalist for real." Sales is now a contributing editor at Vanity Fair.

*T*HE YEAR I WAS thirteen, my only friend was a famous man who lived far away, and wrote me letters in plain brown envelopes that I told my mother were from "a girl from camp." Hiding behind the stacks in my school library, I had written to him in desperation, skipping math. I didn't like math, or anything else I couldn't understand, which some days seemed like everything.

I was a precocious, too sensitive girl who felt disliked by all, even my family, which was hardly impressed by my knack for delivering lines from Antigone or Barbara Stanwyck movies when asked to do household chores. I escaped into a world of nineteenth-century novels and 1940s movies, after which I styled my clothing: huge thrift-store shoulder pads that stuck out from me like a yoke, and hats—sharp, Mary Astor fedoras that I hid behind. This, according to my high-school yearbook, made me a "Geek/Freak" in sunny Coral Gables, Florida, where girls were supposed to want to be bouncy "Dolphinette" cheerleaders and go to parties where they painted their toenails.

My classmates plucked the hats from my head and threw them across the hallways, amused at my cries of "Halt! Knaves! Infamy!" When I was thirteen, I sat alone every day in a corner of the lunchroom, furtively scribbling my thoughts to my treasured secret sharer on Fifth Avenue. He liked me, I thought, throwing dark looks at whoever had just flung the peas into the brim of my fedora. He understood (I was sure we must be alike, with our red hair and quick-witted eccentricity). And he was better than all of them. He'd even diagnosed me as a "genius."

That year, I floated along on pride and wonder at the thought of this, at the exquisite surprise of my pen pal's identity. His name was Woody Allen.

In 1978, Woody was forty-two. He had made *Annie Hall* and was at a turning point in his career. He was between Diane Keaton and Mia Farrow; he had no children. In the media's indulgent eye, he was both an auteur and a sex symbol, a hybrid that was equal parts Jean-Luc Godard, Jerry Lewis, and Job. For a nation of women beset by newly sensitive men, Woody, with his cringing charisma, had become a generational icon. With the great changes overtaking his life (he was writing *Interiors*, his first serious movie), I don't know how he found the time—and can't say why he had the inclination—to respond to that first letter I wrote him. In it—God knows why—I carried on as if we had always known each other, and told him how unhappy I was, how bored and full of yearning to do something *meaningful*—whatever it might be.

Dear Nancy,

Hard to believe you're 13! When I was 13 I couldn't dress myself, and here you write about one of life's deepest philosophical problems, i.e., existential boredom. I guess it's hard for me to imagine a 13-year-old quoting anything but Batman—but T. Mann!!? [Anyway,] there's too much wrong with the world to ever get too relaxed and happy. The more natural state, and the better one, I think, is one of some anxiety and tension over man's plight in this mysterious universe.

Next time you write, if you ever do, please list some of the books you've enjoyed and movies, and which music you've liked, and also the things you dislike and have no patience with. And tell me what kind of place Coral Gables is. And what school do you go to? What hobbies do you have? How old are your parents and what do they do? Or are you a poor family? Do you speak another language? What are your moods like? Do you brood much? Are you energetic? Are you an early riser? Are you "into clothes"? Does the relentless sun and humidity of Florida have an effect on you? At the moment, I am re-filming some parts of my next film which have not come out so good.

Best—Woody.

I WAS BORN during a hurricane. Water rushed down the halls of the hospital, nurses screamed, and at my rather dramatic thirteen, I took this to be a cosmic warning to the world of my arrival—or perhaps a warning to me of the hostile nature of the world. I'm not sure if I told Woody this in any of the many, many letters I sent. ("Two letters from you in one day!" he once cheerfully exclaimed.) But the young writing student Rain (Juliette Lewis) in *Husbands and Wives* was born during a hurricane too.

Watching Woody's films, as the years go by, I sometimes experience a little jolt of recognition that makes me wonder if I could possibly have had some lasting effect on him, as he so affected me. Since the news of his love affair with Soon-Yi Previn, and the clamor over his breakup with Mia and alleged yen for underage girls, I have listened to all the Woody jokes with discomfort and outrage—because I wonder if they are also, somehow, on me. I prefer to think they aren't. There is a delicate and dangerous line that can be crossed in a relationship between a man and a young girl; but this side of it seems more a cause for celebration than suspicion. At least, that's how I feel about Woody and me.

Dear Nancy,

I am finished with my film [Interiors] *and at work on a new (this time funny) script* [Manhattan]. *I wanted to suggest that you read some books by S. J. Perelman and some essays by Robert Benchley. Both are very funny, and if you enjoyed my books you'll really like theirs. Did you tell me you like jazz music? If so, I'll recommend some records. Don't forget to listen to Mahler's Fourth Symphony (hopefully the Bernstein recording). And of course you're in love with Mozart's 40th Symphony? They are great.*

Sartre is a fine writer. I enjoy many of his fictional pieces even more than his nonfiction. Did you read The Wall *or* The Room? *Kierkegaard is the most romantic of the existentialist thinkers. Camus is the best writer. Also, you might enjoy the films* The Lady From Shanghai, Mr. and Mrs. Smith, Bombshell. *I've been reading too much Carl Jung—a psychoanalyst of dubious merit. I'm blue because the Knicks lost and basketball season is virtually over.*

Keep in touch—Woody A.

The face of Soon-Yi Previn, in the famous photo of her holding hands with Woody Allen courtside at a Knicks game, is full of love and awe and romantic expectation, and, I think, a certain magic cast by secrets, and unexpected attention. Her face is full of discovery—a powerful force, potentially a subversive thing. I believe it's valuable no matter how it's attained. The complex need in girls—and in young women, too—for a guide and teacher is something Woody hasn't explored in his work so much as he has his own delight in playing the teacher.

"I'll give you your lesson for today," he tells the *Annie Hall*–ishly dressed, adorable girl who plays his niece in *Crimes and Misdemeanors.* "Your lesson is this: 'Don't listen to what your schoolteachers tell you' "— a liberating enough message, with the underlying appeal being "Listen to me." He tells this to the niece outside a movie theater where he often takes her to watch his favorite old movies. In *Manhattan*, there is some wonderfully affectionate banter between Woody's character and Mariel Hemingway's Tracy as he explains to her the difference between Veronica Lake and Rita Hayworth; watching late-night TV with her, he smiles blissfully when *Grand Illusion* comes on.

I believe he's trying to convey the irresistible satisfaction of a relationship in which rediscovery of the things one loves best is possible, the joy of being able to give someone the gift of experiencing, for the first time, great things. (At the end of *Manhattan* these things become fused with the loved one they are offered to: "Why is life worth living?" Woody's character, Isaac Davis, asks himself into a tape recorder. "Louis Armstrong. *Sentimental Education* by Flaubert. Those incredible apples and pears by Cézanne. Tracy's face.") Rereading Woody's letters, I am touched by his outpouring of recommendations, his repetition of the word *enjoy*. That he wanted me to enjoy the movies and books he loved fills me with gratitude. I did enjoy them; I still do.

I once asked Woody whom he would like to have dinner with, if he could choose anyone in history. "Perhaps Jelly Roll Morton," he replied, "and Zelda Fitzgerald and maybe Babe Ruth and Chekhov and Sophocles and Charlotte Rampling and Dostoevsky and Tolstoy and Kafka and Proust and Yeats and—oh, I could go on for a long time." We had arguments, one rather heated one about Scarlett O'Hara, whom I idolized all out of proportion and whom he considered unworthy—until I wore him down. "I saw *Gone With the Wind* (at first) four times in four days," he wrote. "I was about 17 or 18. I fell in love with Scarlett. She was my dream. She drove me crazy. Then I saw the film years later (I was 30), and I realized what a bitch she was and how I'd grown up regarding my taste in women. Now I'm not so sure."

Every day I raced home from school hoping to find one of the brown envelopes in our mailbox. When there wasn't one, I was despondent, and when there was, I felt a thrill I have not since experienced—except perhaps when getting an unexpected check. Either way, I would spend the afternoons composing and polishing another letter to my mentor. I realize now it was when I first fell in love with writing. Woody encouraged this in me. I think he saw it happening (he was the inspiration), once telling me that something I wrote "read funny." At the time, I couldn't imagine a greater success than making him laugh.

I MET HIM only once—a day that lives on in the annals of my most misbegotten moments. It was all wrong. I had lost the feather to my fedora. It was raining, a cold, dark, clammy day, and I and my stepmother (who had brought me along on a shopping trip to Manhattan) were trapped in the hospitality of an ultra–Palm Beach female acquaintance who had recently had a nose job and—like something out of a Woody Allen movie—could talk of nothing else.

I had left him a note, and to my delight—and dread—he had called my hotel ten minutes later asking me over. At the last minute I became panic-stricken at the thought of seeing Woody Allen in person, but the stunned and excited women prodded me on. I knew that an epistolary relationship is fragile, like those delicate ferns that crumple when touched. My knees shaking, I tottered into his penthouse on a pair of too tall Katharine Hepburn sandals, with which, because of the cold, I had been forced to wear *socks*.

I remember how pale his skin was behind the trademark glasses, how translucent he looked, like a corpse or an angel. When he opened the door, I don't think he knew which one of us I was. (I was as tall as my two companions, who were both barely thirty.) Couldn't he *tell*? My heart sank. "Sit down!" I remember our Gold Coast acquaintance hissing at me, as she smiled and began to inform Woody of her real-estate-raider husband's financial conquests.

"*We* eat at Elaine's, too," she said.

I fell into Woody's sofa wishing I could silence the woman by feigning vertigo. And he—wearing his very same clothes from *Annie Hall*—sat Indian style in an armchair, much like a thirteen-year-old, nodding politely, trying to catch my eye. I scowled. I have noticed that in Woody's films he often repeats a line about having your worst fears realized. It had been my worst fear, at thirteen, that I would lose this improbable friend. And here it was happening, as if I were watching our letters being shredded by wolves.

What had I imagined? Something, I suppose, very much like the scenario of *Manhattan*—Woody and I taking in art galleries, talking over books and movies. Often discounted in the recent hysteria surrounding adult/child relations are the very real, very romantic fancies entertained by developing girls. Perhaps sometimes girls make too much of them; I think Woody saw that in me the day we met. He had an enormous tray on his coffee table, and I remember a gorgeous array of foods—intensely colored fruits and carefully wrapped candies. It seemed so unlike him, that tray, and yet, in its sumptuous generosity, it seemed to fit. I never got to sample a thing. It was time to go, and I looked into his eyes only at the end of our meeting. "Good-bye," they said sadly.

IT TOOK ME a long time, in my teenage way, to get over him. But when I went away to prep school, on his recommendation, and then on to a college that he had also suggested, I finally met people who were more like me. I made friends. And from time to time, when I felt close enough to one, I would tell him or her about my letters to Woody Allen, and how he wrote back, urging me to read Proust and Kierkegaard, making me feel that I could handle anything. "Your kind of mind and feelings is a prize to have even though you will have to pay a high price for it," he wrote. I never heard from him again.

I RUN TO WIN

JIMMY BRESLIN

MAY 5, 1969

Jimmy Breslin is not usually put in the camp of the New Journalists—his hard-boiled New York voice and longtime tabloid columnizing give him his own genre. But his first-person explorations were just as wild and radical as any of his peers. In fact, he was more than a fellow traveler. In 1969, Breslin ran for City Council president on a ticket with Norman Mailer, who was running for mayor. Their purposes were simultaneously comic, literary, and highly serious. In part, Breslin ran because he despaired of the city's prospects—crime was high, the economy failing. (To deal with these matters, he endorsed the proposal that the city secede and become the fifty-first state.) It was a lark, and great material for a while, but "it got to be a drag," says Breslin. "And you're obliged to go through to the end." In the primary, Breslin won about 75,000 votes— more, he delightedly told one friend, than Mailer received for mayor. Still, the process disappointed Breslin. He finished the primary ahead of just one candidate, Charles B. Rangel, now chairman of the House Ways and Means Committee. "That a Breslin could beat a Rangel, that's a travesty," says Breslin. Also, he says, "I am mortified to have taken part in a process that required bars to be closed."

S OME TIME AGO, I made a basic decision about the way in which I was going to live the little of life available to me. The idea was to place myself in the presence of only those people who give off the warm, friendly vibrations which soothe the coating on my nerves. Life never was long enough to provide time for enemies. Nor is it long enough for people who bore me, or for me to stand around boring and antagonizing others, or for all of us, the others and me, to get into these half-friendly, half-sour fender-bumpings of egos and personalities and ideas, a process which turns a day into a contest when it really should be a series of hours serving your pleasure.

So I gave up jobs which made me uncomfortable. I wrote a book and sold it for a movie without seeing one person involved. I began avoiding any bar or restaurant where there was the slightest chance of people becoming picky and arguing. I reduced conversation, even on the telephone, to the people I like and who like me. One night, my wife had a group of people for dinner and I was not sure of the vibrations around me at the table so I said, "Excuse me, I have to go to bed. I have paresis." It worked wonderfully. I began to do things like this all the time and I wound up doing only what I liked when I liked doing it and always with the people I liked and who liked me.

"Do you want to go out to dinner tonight?" my wife asked me.

"Where?" I said.

"Well, I don't know. We'll go with my sister and her husband."

"Oh, I don't know," I said. "I don't think he had a good time with us last week and he might be a little cold tonight. I'm afraid he might strip my nerves. I'd rather just stay home."

"All right," she said.

So we stayed home. During the night I said hello on the telephone to Jerry Finkelstein, Jack O'Neill, Burton Roberts and Thomas Rand. We all talked nice to each other and I could feel the coating on my nerves being stroked and soothed. On Sunday I went into the office in my house and I spoke to nobody and saw nobody all day. So it was one of the most terrific weekends.

The first phone call on Monday morning was at seven o'clock.

"He's asleep," I heard my wife mumble.

"Wake him up?" she mumbled.

She kicked me and I reached over for the phone.

"Somebody named Joe Ferris," she said. "He needs your correct voting registration for the petitions. What petitions?"

I sat up in bed, with the phone in one hand and my head against the wall and my eyes closed.

"What petitions?" my wife said again.

I knew what petitions Joe Ferris was talking about. I knew about them, but I never thought it would come to the point of an early morning phone call about them. You see, when it started, I was only in this thing for pleasant conversation with nice people.

"Hello," I said to Joe Ferris. I was afraid he would send cold waves through the phone.

"I've got to be at the printer with the petitions this morning," Joe Ferris said. "So what I need is the exact way your name and address appears on the voting rolls. We don't want to have any petitions thrown out on a technicality. Because they're going to be looking for mistakes. Particularly when they see how much support you and Norman are going to get. That's all I've been hearing around town. You and Norman. I think you've got a tremendous chance."

"I'll get the information and call you back," I said to Joe Ferris. He gave me his phone number and I told him I was writing it down, but I wasn't. Maybe if I forgot his number and never called him back, he wouldn't bother to call me anymore.

"What petitions?" my wife said when I hung up.

"Nothing," I said. I put my face in the pillow. Well, to tell you what happened, I really don't know what happened, but I was in a place called the Abbey Tavern on Third Avenue and 26th Street at four o'clock one afternoon, when it was empty and I wouldn't have to talk to anybody I didn't know, and Jack Newfield came in. Jack Newfield is a political writer. He writes for *The Village Voice* and *Life* magazine and he does books and we got to know and like each other during the Bobby Kennedy campaigns last spring. Anyway, I'm having coffee with Jack Newfield and he says, "Did you hear me on the radio the other night? I endorsed you. I endorsed Norman Mailer for mayor and you for president of the City Council in the

Democratic primary." I did two things. I laughed. Then I sipped the coffee. While I did it, I was saying to myself, "Why is Mailer on the top of the ticket?"

And a couple of days later, I had lunch in Limerick's, on Second Avenue and 32nd Street, and here was Newfield and Gloria Steinem, and she likes me and I like her, and Peter Maas, and he is all right with me, too, and we got to talking some more and they kept saying Norman Mailer and I should run in the Democratic primary and finally I said, "Has anybody talked to Norman?"

"No, not recently," Gloria said.

"Give me a dime," I said.

I went to the phone and called Norman. While I was dialing, I began to compromise myself. Norman went to college, I thought. Maybe it's only right that he's the mayor and I'm the president of the City Council. But that's the only reason. He has a Harvard diploma. On ability, I should be mayor.

"Norman?"

"Jimmy, how are you?"

"Norman, let's run."

"I know, they spoke to me. But I have to clean up some business first. I think we could make a great team. Now here's what I'm doing. I'm going to Provincetown for a week to think this over. Maybe we can get together for a night before I go. Then when I come back, we can make up our minds."

"All right," I said.

So two nights later there were about forty people in the top floor of Mailer's house in Brooklyn Heights. They were talking about the terrible condition the city was in, and of the incredible group of candidates the Democrats had in the mayoralty primary, which is on June 17. Norman Mailer began to talk about the right and the left mixing their flames together and forming a great coalition of orange flame with a hot center and I looked out the window at the harbor, down at a brightly lit freighter sitting in the black water under the window, and I was uneasy about Mailer's political theories. I was uncertain of the vibrations. Then I turned around and said something about there being nine candidates for mayor and if

New York tradition was upheld, the one who got in front in the race would be indicted. When I saw Norman Mailer laughing at what I said, I decided that he was very smart at politics. When I saw the others laugh, I felt my nerves purring.

Then he began to talk casually, as if everybody knew it and had been discussing it for weeks, about there being no such thing as integration and that the only way things could improve would be with a black community governing itself. "We need a black mayor," Mailer said. "I'll be the white mayor and they have to elect a black mayor for themselves. Just give them the money and the power and let them run themselves. We have no right to talk to these people any more. We lost that a long time ago. They don't want us. The only thing white people have done for the blacks is betray them."

There hasn't been a person with the ability to say this in my time in this city. I began to think a little harder about the prospects of Mailer and me running the city.

We had another night at Mailer's, with a smaller group, and he brought up the idea of a "Sweet Sunday," one day a month in which everything in the city is brought to a halt so human beings can rest and talk to each other and the air can purify itself. When he got onto the idea of New York taking the steps to become a state, he had me all the way. The business of running this city is done by lobster peddlers from Montauk and old Republicans from Niagara Falls and some Midwesterners-come-to-Washington-with-great-old-Dick such as the preposterous George Romney. I didn't know what would come out of these couple of nights, but I knew we had talked about more things than most of these people running in the Democratic primary had thought of in their lives.

Mailer was leaving for Provincetown the next morning, and we agreed to talk on the phone in a few days.

I stayed around the city and somewhere in here I had a drink with Hugh Carey. He is a congressman from Brooklyn and he is listed as a candidate for mayor. I told Carey I was proud the way he turned down a chance to make a lot of headlines with an investigation into the case of Willie Smith, a poverty worker in New York who had been convicted of great crimes in the newspapers. Carey announced that Willie Smith not only was clear, but also was doing a fine job for the poor. Endorsing the poor is not a very good way of getting votes these days. So I thanked Carey.

"What did you want me to do?" Hugh Carey said.

"Well, I just wanted you to know," I said.

"I wish to God I'd been right on the war when I should have been," he said. He had, from 1965 until only a short time ago, been a Brooklyn Irish Catholic Hawk, of which there are no talons sharper. But now he could look at you over a drink and tell you openly that he had been wrong. "It's the one thing in my life I'm ashamed of," he said. "And I'm going to go in and tell every mother in this city that I was wrong and that we're wasting their sons."

Pretty good, I thought. Let's have another drink.

"How's it look for you?" I asked.

"Well, it's up to The Wag," he said.

"The Wag?" I said.

"The Wag. Bob Wagner."

"What the hell has he got to do with it?"

"Look, if he comes back and runs and I can get on the ticket with him, then in a year he'll run for the Senate against Goodell and I can take over the city and we'll start putting the type of people in . . ."

Well, I told him then what I'm putting down here now. If Robert Wagner, who spent twelve years in City Hall as the representative of everybody in New York except the people who had to live in the city while he let it creak and sag, if this dumpy, narrow man named Robert Wagner, by merely considering stepping back into politics, could have a Hugh Carey thinking about running on the ticket below him, then there was something I didn't like about Hugh Carey. Not as a guy, but as a politician who would run a city which is as wounded and tormented as New York.

You see, the condition of the City of New York at this time reminds me of the middleweight champion fight between the late Marcel Cerdan and Tony Zale. Zale was old and doing it from memory and Cerdan was a bustling, sort of classy alley fighter and Cerdan went to the body in the first round and never brought his punches up. At the start of each round, when you looked at Zale's face, you saw only this proud, fierce man. There were no marks to show what was happening. But Tony Zale was coming apart from the punches that did not leave any marks and at the end of the eleventh round Tony was along the ropes and Cerdan stepped back and Tony crumbled and he was on the floor, looking out into the night air, his face unmarked, his body dead, his career gone. In New York today, the face of the city, Manhattan, is proud and glittering. But Manhattan is not the city. New York really is a sprawl of neighborhoods, which pile into one another. And it is down in the neighborhoods, down in the schools that are in the neighborhoods, where this city is cut and slashed and bleeding from someplace deep inside. The South Bronx is gone. East New York and Brownsville are gone. Jamaica is up for grabs. The largest public education system in the world may be gone already. The air we breathe is so bad that on a warm day the city is a big Donora. In Manhattan, the lights seem brighter and the theatre crowds swirl through the streets and the girls swing in and out of office buildings in packs and it is all splendor and nobody sees the body punches that are going to make the city sag to its knees one day so very soon. The last thing, then, that New York can afford at this time is a politician thinking in normal politicians' terms. The city is beyond that. The City of New York either gets an imagination, or the city dies.

A day or so after seeing Carey, I came into Toots Shor's on the late side of the afternoon, when the place is between-shifts empty. Paul Screvane was finishing lunch. He was sitting with Shor. I tried a cautious drink. The vibrations among the three of us were all right. I settled down to talk with them. For weeks, Screvane had wanted to announce his candidacy for mayor. But he had been waiting until he heard what Wagner was going to do.

"Why wait?" I said.

"Well, because all the financial support I normally would get would go to Wagner," Screvane said.

"Well, what's he going to do?" I asked.

"I've called him for a week. I'm waiting to hear from him right now," Screvane said. "He's next door in the 21 Club. He knows I'm here. I'll just wait."

Screvane waited. He waited while Wagner came out of the 21, walked slowly down the sidewalk to Shor's, stopped and chatted with somebody in front of Shor's, nodded to Shor's doorman, probably looked through the doors and saw Screvane inside, and then ambled off.

"That's a real nice guy," I said to Screvane.

He said nothing. A few minutes later, the headwaiter handed him the phone. Screvane came back muttering, "Wagner just had his secretary call me. 'Where will you be at seven and at nine tonight in case Mr. Wagner wants to get in touch with you?' How do you like that?"

"Why don't you just say the hell with this guy and go ahead and announce you're in it?" I said.

Shor slapped his hand on the table. "Go ahead," he said.

"The hell with it," Screvane said. He got up and went to the phone. He came back smiling. "All right, I called my secretary and told her to start calling the papers and television for a press conference tomorrow morning at eleven o'clock."

"Terrific," I said.

"Are you going to be there?" Screvane said.

"Absolutely," I said.

Well, what happened was, I walked out of the place feeling so good about Paul Screvane standing up and not letting somebody push him around, and this is the way it should be because Screvane is a tough, extremely competent man and nobody should try to take advantage of him. Well, I felt so good about all of this that two hours later I called up Norman Mailer and I said, "Norman, the hell with it. Let's make up our minds right now."

"We're doing it," he said.

The Village Voice promptly came out with pictures of Mailer and myself on the front page. The type underneath the pictures said that we were "thinking" of running for office.

I don't know about the rest of the paper's circulation, but I know of two people who looked at the front page very closely.

One was Paul Screvane.

The other was my wife. "This is a joke, of course," she said.

"Oh, sure," I said.

"Well, if you're that sick for publicity," she said.

There were a couple of calls at the house in the next day or so and my wife handled them, although not too well. "The publicity stunt is tying up our phones," she said. "I don't want these phones tied up. I have real-estate people calling me from the Hamptons. We're going away on a vacation this year. We haven't had one in three years."

"Uh huh," I said. I was looking over the messages she had taken during the day. One was from Gloria Steinem. I knew what that was about. She had a meeting scheduled with some good, young Puerto Rican guys who were interested in politics and wanted to see what Mailer and I looked like. There would be no warm, friendly vibrations from them. These guys would snarl and snap a little, particularly if I said something stupid. So what? I'd learn something from them while I was at it.

So now here we come to this one morning, and this is how I got into what I am into, and I am in bed with my face in the pillows and I am trying very hard to forget Joe Ferris' phone number, and the phone rings again and my wife answers it.

"Yes," she says.

"Oh, I don't know if he's doing that."

"You know that he's doing that? How do you know?"

"Gloria Steinem said what?"

"You're going to write a story? Here, you better talk to him."

She handed me the phone. "This is Sarah Davidson from *The Boston Globe* and she is going to write a nice big story for the first page about you and Mailer running for office. Tell her to make sure she puts in that you're a dirty bastard."

I take the phone and I say hello to Sarah Davidson. A gentle, restrained, cautious politician's hello.

"Sarah, dear, how are you, baby? When are we going to get together for a drink?"

Ten minutes later, the call that makes the whole thing official comes.

"Gabe Pressman," my wife muttered.

"Oh, he's just a friend of mine, you know," I said.

"Hello, Gabe, how are you, baby?" I said.

"Running? Well, we have been talking about it. You know what I mean, Gabe. How many times did we speak about this over a drink? You know how thin the talent is in this city. Look at the names, Scheuer. He says he's going to spend a million dollars for his primary campaign. Well, let me tell you, Gabe. Scheuer has to spend a million-two, just to get known in his own neighborhood. And look at these other guys. Mario Procaccino. How do you like it? How do you like the Democratic party going with Mario Procaccino for mayor in an election? Mario for waiter, yes. For mayor? Good Lord. And the guys they got running in my column, the City Council president, hell, we can't afford to have a thing like this."

"Wagner? Forget Wagner. He's an old man. He won't win a primary."

"Shut up," my wife said.

I held the phone away. "Hey, what are you telling me to shut up for?"

"I said shut up," she said.

I went back to the phone. "Lindsay? Gabe, you know better than I do that Lindsay came into this city like a commuter. He doesn't . . ."

"Shut up," she said again.

"What do you mean, shut up?" I said.

"Because he's going to put down what you say and make you sound like a sour dope."

"What do you mean? Gabe and I are good friends."

"You're not supposed to give long answers to a reporter," she said. "You're going to make yourself look like a jerk and the whole family is going to suffer because of it."

I'm holding the phone against the pillow so Gabe Pressman won't hear.

"Hey, this is a friend of mine calling up. It isn't like an interview. This is personal."

"No it isn't. He'll put down everything you say. He's unethical."

"What do you mean he's unethical? Gabe Pressman is not. He's a friend."

"Hey," she said, "all reporters are unethical. Who knows better than you? You wrote the book."

I made a date to meet Pressman and a camera crew at noon. When I hung up, the phone rang immediately. It was Alice Krakauer, who is handling the scheduling for our college appearances. She told me to write down a date for City College. While I was doing this, my wife got up, got dressed and went out of the bedroom. She called up to me from the front door. "I'm going with my sister to look at houses. We'll be back tomorrow. When I come back, if the phone rings once with this business, I'll have to ask you to leave."

She left. I got up and started for the subway. At the newsstand, the woman said, "Don't I see your picture some place? Are you running for something?"

I stood there and thought for a moment. Thought very deeply. Newsstand Dealer for Mailer and Breslin! My right hand shot out so fast the woman nearly fell over backwards.

"Hi, I'm Jimmy Breslin," I said to her.

PART THREE

CULTURES, SUB- AND OTHERWISE

★

TRIBAL RITES OF THE NEW SATURDAY NIGHT

NIK COHN

JUNE 7, 1976

In 1976, Irishman Nik Cohn made a trip to Bay Ridge, Brooklyn, trawl-ing the disco scene for some new energy in an otherwise boring music era. There he stumbled onto strange synchronized dance routines in clubs like 2001 Odyssey. He immediately recognized this as a scene full of journal-istic potential. Cohn's trouble was, as he later explained, "I couldn't get anyone [at the club] to confide in me." And so, he says, "I faked it." He knit together moments and characters from other encounters. "It was written as a short story in my mind," says Cohn, who revealed the deception, which had been long rumored, two decades later in New York. *Still, Cohn's insights captured truths about working-class kids and music. The story also captured the imagination of Hollywood producer Robert Stig-wood, who turned Cohn's story into* Saturday Night Fever, *starring John Travolta. Cohn is the author of* Awopbopaloobop Alopbamboom: The Golden Age of Rock *and* Triksta: Life and Death and New Orleans Rap, *among other books.*

V —

VINCENT WAS THE VERY best dancer in Bay Ridge—the ultimate Face. He owned fourteen floral shirts, five suits, eight pairs of shoes, three overcoats, and had appeared on *American Bandstand*. Sometimes music people came out from Manhattan to watch him, and one man who owned a club on the East Side had even offered him a contract. A hundred dollars a week. Just to dance.

Everybody knew him. When Saturday night came round and he walked into 2001 Odyssey, all the other Faces automatically fell back before him, cleared a space for him to float in, right at the very center of the dance floor. Gracious as a medieval seigneur accepting tributes, Vincent waved and nodded at random. Then his face grew stern, his body turned to the music. Solemn, he danced, and all the Faces followed.

In this sphere his rule was absolute. Only one thing bothered him, and that was the passing of time. Already he was eighteen, almost eighteen and a half. Soon enough he would be nineteen, twenty. Then this golden age would pass. By natural law someone new would arise to replace him. Then everything would be over.

The knowledge nagged him, poisoned his pleasure. One night in January, right in the middle of the Bus Stop, he suddenly broke off, stalked from the floor without a word, and went outside into the cold darkness, to be alone.

He slouched against a wall. He stuck his hands deep into his overcoat pockets. He sucked on an unlit cigarette. A few minutes passed. Then he was approached by a man in a tweed suit, a journalist from Manhattan.

They stood close together, side by side. The man in the tweed suit looked at Vincent, and Vincent stared at the ground or at the tips of his platform shoes. "What's wrong?" said the man in the suit, at last.

And Vincent said: "I'm old."

BEFORE SATURDAY NIGHT began, to clear his brain of cobwebs and get himself sharp, fired up, he liked to think about killing.

During the week Vincent sold paint in a housewares store. All day, every day he stood behind a counter and grinned. He climbed up and down ladders, he made the coffee, he obeyed. Then came the weekend and he was cut loose.

The ritual never varied. Promptly at five the manager reversed the "Open" sign and Vincent would turn away, take off his grin. When the last of the customers had gone, he went out through the back, down the corridor, directly into the bathroom. He locked the door and took a deep breath. Here he was safe. So he turned toward the mirror and began to study his image.

Black hair and black eyes, olive skin, a slightly crooked mouth, and teeth so white, so dazzling, that they always seemed fake. Third-generation Brooklyn Italian, five-foot-nine in platform shoes. Small purplish birthmark beside the right eye. Thin white scar, about two inches long, underneath the chin, caused by a childhood fall from a bicycle. Otherwise, no distinguishing marks.

That was the flesh; but there was something else, much more important. One night two years before, he had traveled into Queens with some friends and they had ended up in some club, this real cheap scumhole; he couldn't remember the name. But he danced anyhow and did his numbers, all his latest routines, and everyone was just amazed. And then he danced with this girl. He'd never seen her before and he never saw her again. But her name was Petulia, Pet for short, and she was all right, nice hair, a good mover. And she kept staring right into his eyes. Staring and staring, as though she were hypnotized. He asked her why. "Kiss me," said the girl. So he kissed her, and she went limp in his arms. "Oooh," said the girl, sighing, almost swooning, "I just kissed Al Pacino."

In his first surprise, assuming that she must be teasing, Vincent had only laughed and blushed. But later, thinking it over, he knew she had really meant it. Somehow or other she had seen beneath the surface, had cut through to bedrock, to his very soul. That was something incredible. It blew his mind. In fact, if anyone ever asked him and he tried to answer honestly, looking back, he would say that was the happiest, the very best, moment of his life.

Since then, whenever he gazed into the mirror, it was always Pacino who gazed back. A killer, and a star. Heroic in reflection. Then Vincent would take another breath, the deepest he could manage; would make his face, his whole body, go still; would blink three times to free his imagination, and he would start to count.

Silently, as slowly as possible, he would go from one to a hundred. It was now, while he counted, that he thought about death.

It felt just like a movie. For instance, he would see himself at the top of a high flight of stairs, back against a wall, while a swarm of attackers came surging up toward him to knock him down, destroy him. But Vincent stood his ground. Unflinching, he took aim and fired. One by one they went crashing backward, down into the pit.

At one hundred, he let out his breath in a rush. The strain of holding back had turned him purple, and veins were popping all over his neck and arms. For some moments all he could do was gasp. But even as he suffered, his body felt weightless, free, almost as if he were floating. And when he got his breath back, and the roaring in his temples went away, it was true that he felt content.

That was the end; the movie was complete. Turning away from the glass, and away from Pacino, he would flush the toilet, wash his hands. He combed his hair. He checked his watch. Then he went out into the corridor, back into the store. The week behind the counter had been obliterated. No drudgery existed. He was released; Saturday night had begun.

LISA WAS IN love with Billy, and Billy was in love with Lisa. John James was in love with Lorraine. Lorraine loved Gus. Gus loved Donna. And Donna loved Vincent. But Vincent loved only his mother, and the way it felt to dance. When he left the store he went home and prepared for 2001 Odyssey. He bathed, he shaved, he dressed. That took him four hours, and by the time he emerged, shortly after nine, he felt reborn.

He lived on the eleventh floor of a high-rise on Fourth Avenue and 66th Street, close beside the subway tracks, with the remnants of his family. He loved them, was proud that he supported them. But when he tried to describe their existence, he would begin to stammer and stumble, embarrassed, because everything came out so corny: "Just like a soap," he said, "only true."

His father, a thief, was in jail, and his oldest brother had been killed in Vietnam. His second brother was in the hospital, had been there almost a year, recovering from a car crash that had crushed his legs. His third brother had moved away to Manhattan, into the Village, because he said he needed to be free and find himself. So that left only Vincent, his mother, and his two younger sisters, Maria and Bea (short for Beata), who were still in school.

Between them they shared three rooms, high up in a block of buildings like a barracks. His windows looked out on nothing but walls, and there was the strangest, most disturbing smell, which no amount of cleaning could ever quite destroy.

Vincent wanted out. He would have given anything. But there was no chance. How could there be? He could never abandon his mother. "You must understand," he said. "I am the man."

Here he paused. "I am her soul," he said. Then he paused again, pursing his lips, and he cast down his eyes. He looked grave. "Understand," he said, "my mother is me."

It was the guts of winter, bitter cold. But he would not protect himself. Not on Saturday night, not on display at Odyssey. When he kissed his mother good-bye and came down onto Fourth, strutting loose, he wore an open-necked shirt, ablaze with reds and golds, and he moved through the night with shoulders hunched tight, his neck rammed deep between his shoulder blades in the manner of a miniature bull. A bull in Gucci-style loafers, complete with gilded buckle, and high black pants tight as sausage skins. Shuffling, gliding, stepping out. On the corner, outside Najmy Bros. grocery, he passed a Puerto Rican, some dude in a floppy velour hat, and the dude laughed out loud. So Vincent stopped still, and he stared, a gaze like a harpoon, right between the eyes. "Later," he said.

"Later what?" said the dude, lolling slack, sneaking his hand back in his pants pocket, just in case, with a big dumb grin slapped clean across his face. "Later who? Later where? Later how?"

"Hombre," said Vincent, expressionless, "you will die."

It was not quite his own. To be perfectly truthful, he had borrowed the line from Lee Van Cleef, some Italian Western that he'd seen on late-night TV. But he drawled it out just right. A hint of slur, the slightest taste of spit. "Hombre, you will die." Just like that. And moved away. So slick and so sly that the dude never knew what hit him.

Two blocks farther on, Joey was waiting in the car. Joey and Gus in the front, Eugene and John James and now Vincent in the back, trundling through the icy streets in a collapsing '65 Dodge. Nobody talked and nobody smiled. Each scrunched into his own private space; they all held their distance, conserved their strength, like prizefighters before a crucial bout. The Dodge groaned and rattled. The radio played Harold Melvin and the Blue Notes. Everything else was silence, and waiting.

John James and Eugene worked in a record store; Gus was a house painter. As for Joey, no one could be sure. In any case, it didn't matter. Not now. All that counted was the moment. And for the moment, riding out toward 2001 Odyssey, they existed only as Faces.

Faces. According to Vincent himself, they were simply the elite. All over Brooklyn, Queens, and the Bronx, even as far away as New Jersey, spread clear across America, there were millions and millions of kids who were nothing special. Just kids. Zombies. Professional dummies, going through the motions, following like sheep. School, jobs, routines. A vast faceless blob. And then there were the Faces. The Vincents and Eugenes and Joeys. A tiny minority, maybe two in every hundred, who knew how to dress and how to move, how to float, how to fly. Sharpness, grace, a certain distinction in every gesture. And some strange instinct for rightness, beyond words, deep down in their blood: "The way I feel," Vincent said, "it's like we have been chosen."

Odyssey was their home, their haven. It was *the* place, the only disco in all Bay Ridge that truly counted.

It was a true sanctuary. Once inside, the Faces were unreachable.

The basic commandments were simple. To qualify as an Odyssey Face, an aspirant need only be Italian, between the ages of eighteen and twenty-one, with a minimum stock of six floral shirts, four pairs of tight trousers, two pairs of Gucci-style loafers, two pairs of platforms, either a pendant or a ring, and one item in gold. In addition, he must know how to dance, how to drive, how to handle himself in a fight. He must have respect, even reverence, for Facehood, and contempt for everything else. He must also be fluent in obscenity, offhand in sex. Most important of all, he must play tough.

There was no overlapping. Italians were Italian, Latins were grease-balls, Jews were different, and blacks were born to lose. Each group had its own ideal, its own style of Face. But they never touched. If one member erred, ventured beyond his own allotted territory, he was beaten up. That was the law. There was no alternative.

Then there were girls. But they were not Faces, not truly. Sometimes, if a girl got lucky, a Face might choose her from the crowd and raise her to be his steady, whom he might one day even marry. But that was rare. In general, the female function was simply to be available. To decorate the doorways and booths, to fill up the dance floor. Speak when spoken to, put out as required, and then go away. In short, to obey, and not to fuss.

That was why he loved to dance, not talk. In conversation, everything always came out wrong, confused. But out on the floor it all somehow fell into place. There was no muddle, nothing that could not be conveyed. Just so long as your feet made the right moves, kept hitting the right angles, you were foolproof.

Purity. A sacrament. In their own style, the Faces were true ascetics: stern, devoted, incorruptible. "We may be hard. But we're fair," said Vincent. So they gathered in strict formation, each in his appointed place, his slot upon the floor. And they danced.

On the first night when the man in the tweed suit arrived from Manhattan, it was only nine o'clock and Odyssey was still half empty. He had come on the Brooklyn-Queens Expressway and when he descended into Bay Ridge itself, he found himself in a dead land. There were auto shops, locked and barred; transmission specialists, alignment centers. Then the Homestead Bar and Grill, and the Crazy Country Club, advertising "warm beer and lousy food." But there were no people. Only railroads and junkyards, abandoned car seats, hubcaps, tires, scattered by the side of the road. A wasteland.

So he huddled deeper, tighter, into his overcoat, and set off toward a small red light at the farthest end of the street.

This was 2001 Odyssey. On the step outside, Vincent stood waiting, smoking, and did not seem to feel the cold at all. His hair was blow-waved just so, his toe caps gleaming. Brut behind his ears, Brut beneath his armpits. And a crucifix at his throat.

Inside, Odyssey was as vast and still as a Saturday-night cathedral. Music blared from the speakers, colored lights swirled back and forth across the dance floor. But no one answered their call. Perhaps a dozen girls sat waiting, on plastic seats, in scalloped booths. Four Faces in shiny suits stood at the bar, backs turned to the floor. The manager standing by the door scratched himself. That was all.

Gradually, the floor began to fill; the night embarked in earnest. The girls emerged from their booths, formed ranks, and began to do the Bus Stop. A band appeared in blue denim suits embossed with silver studding. Blacks from Crown Heights, who played as loudly and as badly as anyone possibly could, grinning, sweating, stomping, while the dancers paraded beneath them, impassive.

One after another the stock favorites came churning out. "Bad Luck" and "Supernatural Thing," "What a Difference a Day Made," "Track of the Cat," each reduced to the same automaton chugging, interchangeable. Nobody looked and no one ever applauded. Still, the band kept pounding away, kept right on grinning. "These guys. Those shines," said Vincent. "We wind them up like clockwork. We pay, and they perform."

Outside, his companions sat in the car, Joey and Gus in the front, Eugene and John James in the back, drinking whiskey from a bottle in a paper bag. They still made no conversation, did not relax. But as the alcohol hit, they started to mumble.

"Mother," said Eugene.

"Eff," said Gus.

"Mothereffing right," said Joey.

Sometime after ten, feeling ready, they stepped out on the sidewalk and moved toward Odyssey in a line, shoulder to shoulder, like gunslingers. Heads lowered, hands thrust deep in their pockets, they turned into the doorway. They paused for just an instant, right on the brink. Entered.

Vincent was already at work on the floor. By now the Faces had gathered in force, his troops, and he worked them like a quarterback, calling out plays. He set the formations, dictated every move. If a pattern grew ragged and disorder threatened, it was he who set things straight.

Under his command, they unfurled the Odyssey Walk, their own style of massed Hustle, for which they formed strict ranks. Sweeping back and forth across the floor in perfect unity, fifty bodies made one, while Vincent barked out orders, crying One, and Two, and One, and Tap. And Turn, and One, and Tap. And Turn. And Tap. And One.

They were like so many guardsmen on parade; a small battalion, uniformed in floral shirts and tight flared pants. No one smiled or showed the least expression. Above their heads, the black musicians honked and thrashed. But the Faces never wavered. Number after number, hour after hour, they carried out their routines, their drill. Absolute discipline, the most impeccable balance. On this one night, even Vincent, who was notoriously hard to please, could find no cause for complaint.

At last, content in a job well done, he took a break and went up into the bleachers, where he sat on a small terrace littered with empty tables and studied the scene at leisure, like a general reviewing a battlefield.

"How do you feel?" asked the man in the tweed suit.

"I'm thinking about my mother," said Vincent.

"What of her?"

"She's getting old. Sometimes she feels so bad. If I was rich, I could buy her a house, somewhere on the Island, and she could take it easy."

"What kind of house?"

"Big windows. Lots of light," Vincent said, and he spread his hands, describing a shape like a globe. "Space. Chickens in the yard. A grand piano. Grass," he said. "My mother likes grass. And blue sky."

Down below, without his presence to keep control, the order was beginning to fall apart. Around the fringes, some of the dancers had broken away from the mainstream and were dabbling in experiments, the Hustle Cha, the Renaissance Bump, even the Merengue. Vincent looked pained. But he did not intervene. "Chickens," he said. "They lay their own eggs."

A fight broke out. From outside, it was not possible to guess exactly how it started. But suddenly Gus was on his back, bleeding, and a Face in a bright-blue polka-dot shirt was banging his head against the floor. So Joey jumped on the Face's back. Then someone else jumped in, and someone else. After that there was no way to make out anything beyond a mass of bodies, littered halfway across the floor.

Vincent made no move; it was all too far away. Remote in his darkness, he sipped at a Coca-Cola and watched. The band played "You Sexy Thing" and one girl kept screaming, only one.

"Is this the custom?" asked the man in the suit.

"It depends."

"On what?"

"Sometimes people don't feel in the mood. Sometimes they do," said Vincent. "It just depends."

In time, the commotion subsided, the main participants were ushered outside to complete their negotiations in private. Those left behind went back to dancing as if nothing had happened, and the band played "Fly, Robin, Fly."

John James, the Double J, appeared on the terrace, lean and gangling, with a chalky white face and many pimples. There was blood beneath his nose, blood on his purple crepe shirt. "Mother," he said, sitting down at the table. "Eff," said Vincent.

So the night moved on. The Double J talked about basketball, records, dances. Then he talked about other nights, other brawls. The music kept playing and the dancers kept on parading. From time to time a girl would stop and look up at the terrace, hoping to catch Vincent's eye. But he did not respond. He was still thinking about his mother.

Somebody threw a glass which shattered on the floor. But the Faces just went One, and Two, and Tap, and Turn. And Tap, and Turn, and Tap.

"I was in love once. At least I thought I was," said Vincent. "I was going to get engaged."

"What happened?"

"My sister got sick and I had to stay home, waiting for the doctor. So I didn't get to the club until midnight. Bojangles, I think it was. And by then I was too late."

"How come?"

"She danced with someone else."

"Only danced?"

"Of course," said Vincent, "and after that, I could never feel the same. I couldn't even go near her. I didn't hate her, you understand. Maybe I still loved her. But I couldn't stand to touch her. Not when I knew the truth."

Around two, the band stopped playing, the Faces grew weary, and the night broke up. Outside the door, as Vincent made his exit, trailed by his lieutenants, a boy and a girl were embracing, framed in the neon glow. And Vincent stopped; he stared. No more than two yards distant, he stood quite still and studied the kiss in closest detail, dispassionate, as though observing guinea pigs.

The couple did not look up and Vincent made no comment. Down the street, Joey was honking the car horn. "God gave his only son," said John James.

"What for?" said Vincent, absentmindedly.

"Rent," replied the Double J.

It was then that something strange occurred. Across the street, in the darkness beyond a steel-mesh gate, the guard dogs still snarled and waited. Gus and Eugene stood on the curb directly outside the gate, laughing, stomping their feet. They were drunk and it was late. They felt flat, somehow dissatisfied. And suddenly they threw themselves at the steel wires, yelling.

The guard dogs went berserk. Howling, they reared back on their hind legs, and then they hurled themselves at their assailants, smashing full force into the gate. Gus and Eugene sprang backwards, safely out of reach. So the dogs caught only air. And the Faces hooted, hollered. They made barking noises, they whistled, they beckoned the dogs toward them. "Here, boys, here," they said, and the dogs hurled forward again and again, in great surging waves, half maddened with frustration.

Even from across the street, the man in the suit could hear the thud of their bodies, the clash of their teeth on the wires. Gus sat down on the sidewalk, and he laughed so much it hurt. He clasped his sides, he wiped away tears.

When they reached the car, they found Vincent already waiting, combing his hair. "Where were you?" asked Gus.

"Watching," said Vincent, and he climbed into the back, out of sight. Inside 2001 Odyssey, there was no more music or movement, the dance floor was deserted. Saturday night had ended, and Vincent slouched far back in his corner. His eyes were closed, his hands hung limp. He felt complete.

ANOTHER SATURDAY NIGHT. Easing down on Fifth and Ovington, Joey parked the car and went into the pizza parlor, the Elegante. Vincent and Eugene were already waiting. So was Gus. But John James was missing. Two nights before he had been beaten up and knifed, and now he was in the hospital.

It was an old story. When the Double J got home from work on Thursday evening, his mother had sent him out for groceries, down to Marinello's Deli. He had bought pasta and salad, toilet paper, a six-pack of Bud, a package of frozen corn, gum, detergent, tomato sauce, and four TV dinners. Paid up. Combed his hair in the window. Then went out into the street, cradling his purchases in both arms.

As he emerged, three Latins—Puerto Ricans—moved across the sidewalk toward him and one of them walked straight through him. Caught unawares, he lost his balance and his bag was knocked out of his arms, splattering on the curb.

Produce scattered everywhere, rolling in the puddles and filth. The frozen corn spilled into the gutter, straight into some dog mess; and the Latins laughed. "Greaseballs," said John James, not thinking. All that was on his mind was his groceries, the need to rescue what he'd lost. So he bent down and began to pick up the remnants. And the moment he did, of course, the Latins jumped all over him.

In the final count, the damage was three cracked ribs, a splintered cheekbone, black eyes, four teeth lost, and a deep knife cut, right in the meat of his arm, just missing his left bicep.

"Three greaseballs at once," said Gus. "He could have run. But he wouldn't."

"He stuck," said Vincent. "He hung tight."

Judgment passed, the Faces finished their pizzas, wiped their lips, departed. Later on, of course, there would have to be vengeance, the Latins must be punished. For the moment, however, the feeling was of excitement, euphoria. As Eugene hit the street, he let out a whoop, one yelp of absolute glee. Saturday night, and everything was beginning, everything lay ahead of them once more.

But Vincent hung back, looked serious. Once again he had remembered a line, another gem from the screen. "Hung tight," he said, gazing up along the bleak street. "He could have got away clean, no sweat. But he had his pride. And his pride was his law."

DONNA LOVED VINCENT, had loved him for almost four months. Week after week she came to Odyssey just for him, to watch him dance, to wait. She sat in a booth by herself and didn't drink, didn't smile, didn't tap her foot or nod her head to the music. Though Vincent never danced with her, she would not dance with anyone else.

Donna was nineteen, and she worked as a cashier in a supermarket over toward Flatbush. As a child she had been much too fat. For years she was ashamed. But now she felt much better. If she held her breath, she stood five-foot-six and only weighed 140 pounds.

Secure in her love, she lived in the background. Vincent danced, and she took notes. He laughed, and she was glad. Other girls might chase him, touch him, swarm all over him. Still she endured, and she trusted.

And one Saturday, without any warning, Vincent suddenly turned toward her and beckoned her onto the floor, right in the middle of the Odyssey Walk, where she took her place in the line, three rows behind him, one rank to the left.

She was not a natural dancer, never had been. Big-boned, soft-fleshed, her body just wasn't right. She had good breasts, good hips, the most beautiful gray-green eyes. But her feet, her legs, were hopeless. Movement embarrassed her. There was no flow. Even in the dark, when she made love, or some boy used her for pleasure, she always wanted to hide.

Nonetheless, on this one night she went through the motions and nobody laughed. She kept her eyes on the floor; she hummed along with the songs. Three numbers went by without disaster. Then the dancers changed, moved from the Walk to something else, something she didn't know, and Donna went back to her booth.

Obscurity. Safety. She sipped Fresca through a straw and fiddled with her hair. But just as she was feeling stronger, almost calm again, Vincent appeared above her, his shadow fell across her just like in the movies, and he put his hand on her arm.

His shirt was pink and scarlet and yellow; her dress was pastel green. His boots were purple, and so were her painted lips. "I'm leaving," Vincent said, and she followed him outside.

His coat was creased at the back. He didn't know that, but Donna did; she could see it clearly as they walked out. And the thought of it, his secret weakness, made her dizzy with tenderness, the strangest sense of ownership.

"What's your name?" Vincent asked.

"Maria," said Donna. "Maria Elena."

They sat in the back of Joey's car and Vincent pulled down her tights. There was no space, everything hurt. But Donna managed to separate her legs, and Vincent kissed her. "Are you all right?" he asked.

"I love you," said Donna.

"No, not that," said Vincent. "I mean, are you fixed?"

She wasn't, of course. She wasn't on the pill, or the coil, or anything. Somehow or other, she'd never got around to it. So Vincent went away. He simply took his body from hers, climbed out of the car. "Vincent," said Donna. But he was gone.

She didn't feel much, did not react in any way. For the next few minutes, she sat very still and tried not to breathe. Then she went home and she slept until noon the next day, a sleep of absolute immersion, so deep and so silent that, she said later on, it felt like Mass.

Another week went by; another Saturday night arrived. But this time it was different. On Thursday afternoon she had bought her first packet of condoms. Now they nestled in her purse, snug upon her lap. She was prepared.

Everything seemed changed in her, resolved. . . . Even when Vincent danced near her, she hardly seemed to notice. It was as if she were weightless, floating free. But when the man in the tweed suit sat down beside her in her plastic booth, in between dances, and asked her how she felt, she could not speak, could only place her hand above her heart, to keep it from exploding.

Finally, shortly after one o'clock, Vincent decided to leave. He disappeared toward the cloakroom to retrieve his coat, and while his back was turned, Donna slipped by, out onto the street, where she waited.

It was raining hard, had been raining all night. Turning up her collar, tightening the belt on her coat, which had once belonged to her older sister, Donna pressed back into the angle of the wall, right underneath the neon sign. And she began to talk.

At last the door opened and Vincent came out, ducking his head against the downpour. The light fell full on Donna's face; she tried to smile. Her hair was slicked flat against her skull and Vincent looked her over with a look of vague surprise, as if he couldn't quite place her. Her makeup was smudged; the tip of her nose was red. She was fat. Vincent walked straight past her.

He went off down the street, moved out of sight, and Donna remained behind, still standing on the sidewalk. "Oh," she said, and she brought her hand up out of her left coat pocket, loosely holding the packet of unused condoms.

She opened it. Gently, methodically, she took out the sheaths and dangled them, squeezed between her forefinger and thumb. One by one, not looking, she dropped them in the wet by her feet. Then she went home again, back to sleep.

ON WEDNESDAY EVENING, to help time pass, Vincent went to see *The Man Who Would Be King*, and rather to his surprise, he liked it very much. . . . Afterwards, he sat on a low wall outside a basketball court, across the street from the high-rise, and considered. The man in the suit was there again, asking more questions. So Vincent talked about living on the eleventh floor, his windows that looked out on nothing, the smell. And working in a housewares store, selling paint and climbing ladders, grinning for his living. "Stuck," he said. "They've got me by the balls."

"How about the future?" asked the man in the suit.

"What future?" Vincent said, and he looked askance, as though the man must be retarded to ask such a question. This was not the Raj; he was not floating in a film. There were dues to pay, people to support. That took money. And money, in this place, meant imprisonment.

Still the man persisted, asked him to imagine. Just conceive that he was set free, that every obstacle was suddenly removed and he could be whatever he pleased. What would he do then? What would give him the greatest pleasure of all, the ultimate fulfillment?

Vincent took his time. This was another dumb question, he knew that. Yet the vision intrigued him, sucked him in almost despite himself. So he let his mind roam loose. Sitting on the wall, he bent his head, contemplated the cracks in the sidewalk. Pondered. Made up his mind. "I want to be a star," he said.

"Such as?" asked the man in the suit.

"Well," said Vincent, "someone like a hero."

SIX WEEKS PASSED.

Outside the pizza parlor, on another Saturday night, Joey, Vincent, the Double J, and Eugene sat waiting in the Dodge, raring to go. But Gus did not show up.

Twenty minutes passed, then thirty, forty. They were almost ready to go on without him. Then suddenly he came out of the shadows, running, burning. His face was flushed; he was all out of breath. Too wild to make sense, he could only spew out obscenities, kick at the curb, pound his fists, impotent, on the body of the car.

At last he simmered down, choked out his explanations. And the news was indeed enormous. That afternoon, just three hours earlier, his younger sister, Gina, had been violated, debauched, as she crossed a children's playground in the park.

Gus poured out the story. After his sister had finished her lunch, she went to the apartment of her best friend Arlene, who lived about ten blocks away. Both of them were eleven years old and together they spent the afternoon nibbling chocolate candies, trying out different makeups, sighing over photographs of Donny Osmond. Then Gina walked home in the dusk, alone, wrapped in her imitation-leather coat, which was short and showed off her legs. Soon she came to McKinley Park. To make a shortcut, she turned off the street and headed across the park playground.

It was getting dark and the playground was empty, spooky. Gina hastened. Halfway across, however, a man appeared, coming from the opposite direction. He had wispy hair and a wispy beard, and he was talking to himself. When Gina came level with him, he stopped and stared. "Pretty. Pretty. Pretty," he said. Just like that. And he looked at her legs, straight at her kneecaps, with a strange smile, a smile that made her want to run. So she did. She sped out of the playground, into the street, down the block.

Just as she reached the sanctuary of her own hallway, Gus was coming down the stairs. So she bumped straight into him, jumped into his arms. "What's wrong?" he said. But she couldn't say. She just dug her nails into his arms, and she sort of sighed. Then she burst into tears.

When Gus completed his story, he laid his forehead against the roof of the Dodge in order to feel something cold against his skull, which seemed as though it were burning. There he rested for a moment, recovering. Then he straightened up, and he banged his clenched fist into the meat of his left palm, once, twice, three times, just like on TV. "Mother," he said. "I'll kill him."

"Tear his heart out," said Joey. "Eff him in the place he lives."

"Cut off both his legs," said Vincent. "Kill him. Yes."

They all knew who it was. They didn't even have to ask. In Vincent's own building there was a man called Benny, a wimp who had wispy hair and a wispy beard, who shuffled, and he was really weird. He had these crazy staring eyes, this horrible fixed stare. He talked to himself, he mumbled stuff that no one could understand. And often, late at night, blind drunk, he would stand outside people's windows, yell and carry on and keep them from their sleep.

And now this. The final outrage. So the Faces drove back toward the high-rise, piled out of the car, descended on the building in a wedge.

Enforcers. Vigilantes. In silence, they came to Benny's door and Gus rang the bell, banged on the door. A minute passed and there was no answer. Gus banged again. Still no reply. Inside the apartment, everything seemed quiet, absolutely still. Gus banged a third time, a fourth, and then he lost patience. He started raging, kicking the door, barging into it with his shoulder. But nobody moved inside or made a sound, and the door would not give way.

Defeated, the Faces stood around in the hallway, feeling vaguely foolish. At first their instinct was simply to wait it out, keep a vigil till Benny came home. But within a few minutes, hanging about, doing nothing, that plan lost its attraction. The hall was deserted, there was no sign of action. Just standing there grew boring, and they started to fret.

Loitering outside the front doorway, aimless, it was Eugene who came up with the solution. "I don't care. No sweat," he said. "Somebody's going to pay."

"Mothereffing right," said Gus, and he slammed his fist into his palm again; he threw a right cross into space. "Those greaseball bastards."

"Mothers," said the Double J.

"Those mothereffing freaks," said Gus. "We're going to rip them apart." And the man in the tweed suit, who had been watching, was forgotten. The Faces looked past him, hardly seemed to recognize his shape. "We're going," said the Double J.

"Where to? Odyssey?" asked the man.

"Hunting," said Gus.

They moved back to the car, they clambered inside. And the Faces drove away, off into Saturday night. Horsemen. A posse seeking retribution, which was their due, their right.

NIGHT-SHIFTING FOR THE HIP FLEET

MARK JACOBSON

SEPTEMBER 22, 1975

For a generation of postcollegiate kids, driving a New York City taxi was both a rite of passage and a great way of making money—or, at least, the only job they could get. Mark Jacobson, who drove a cab off and on for three years, recalls that once someone stuck a gun through the window of his cab—he managed to speed away. There were also benefits to the job, though. "It was a great way to meet girls," says Jacobson. And also, in Jacobson's case, a good way to advance a writing career. His story about his old cab company landed him a job offer at New York. *"I jumped at it," he says. "Writing is a lot easier than driving a cab." Jacobson's piece became the basis for the television series* Taxi, *starring Judd Hirsch. Jacobson, who has written two novels, recently published a collection of his magazine journalism,* American Gangster and Other Tales of New York City.*

*I*T HAS BEEN a year since I drove a cab, but the old garage still looks the same. The generator is still clanging in the corner. The crashed cars are still in the shop. The weirdos are still sweeping the cigarette butts off the cement floor. The friendly old "YOU ARE RESPONSIBLE for all front-end accidents" is as comforting as ever. Danny the dispatcher still hasn't lost any weight. And all the working stiffs are still standing around, grimy and gummy, sweating and regretting, waiting for a cab at shape-up.

Shape-up time at Dover Taxi Garage #2 still happens every afternoon, rain or shine, winter or summer, from two to six. That's when the night-line drivers stumble into the red-brick garage on Hudson Street in Greenwich Village and wait for the day liners, old-timers with backsides contoured to the crease in the seat of a Checker cab, to bring in the taxis. The day guys are supposed to have the cabs in by four, but if the streets are hopping they cheat a little bit, maybe by two hours. That gives the night liners plenty of time to stand around in the puddles on the floor, inhale the carbon monoxide, and listen to the cab stories.

Cab stories are tales of survived disasters. They are the major source of conversation during shape-up. The flat-tire-with-no-spare-on-Eighth-Avenue-and-135th-Street is a good cab story. The no-brakes-on-the-park-transverse-at-fifty-miles-an-hour is a good cab story. The stopped-for-a-red-light-with-teenagers-crawling-on-the-windshield is not too bad. They're all good cab stories if you live to tell about them. But a year later the cab stories at Dover sound just a little bit more foreboding, not quite so funny. Sometimes they don't even have happy endings. A year later the mood at shape-up is just a little bit more desperate. The gray faces and burnt-out eyes look just a little bit more worried. And the most popular cab story at Dover these days is the what-the-hell-am-I-doing-here? story.

Dover has been called the "hippie garage" ever since the New York freaks who couldn't get it together to split for the Coast decided that barreling through the boogie-woogie on the East River Drive was the closest thing to riding the range. The word got around that the people at Dover weren't as mean or stodgy as at Ann Service, so Dover became "the place" to drive. Now, most of the hippies have either ridden into the sunset or gotten hepatitis, but Dover still attracts a specialized personnel. Hanging around at shape-up today are a college professor, a couple of Ph.D. candidates, a former priest, a calligrapher, a guy who drives to pay his family's land taxes in Vermont, a Rumanian discotheque D.J., plenty of M.A.s, a slew of social workers, trombone players, a guy who makes three-hundred-pound sculptures out of solid rock, the inventor of the electric harp, professional photographers, and the usual gang of starving artists, actors, and writers. It's Hooverville, honey, and there isn't much money around for elephant-sized sculptures, so anyone outside the military-industrial complex is likely to turn up on Dover's night line. Especially those who believed their mother when she said to get a good education so you won't have to shlep around in a taxicab all your life like your Uncle Moe. A college education is not required to drive for Dover—all you have to do is pass a test on which the hardest question is "Where is Yankee Stadium?"—but almost everyone on the night line has at least a B.A.

Shape-up lasts forever. The day liners trickle in, hand over their crumpled dollars, and talk about the great U-turns they made on 57th Street. There are about fifty people waiting to go out. Everyone is hoping for good car karma. It can be a real drag to wait three hours (cabs are first come, first served) and get stuck with #99 or some other dog in the Dover fleet. Over by the generator a guy with long hair who used to be the lead singer in a band called Leon and the Buicks is hollering about the state the city's in. "The National Guard," he says, "that's what's gonna happen. The National Guard is gonna be in the streets, then the screws will come down." No one even looks up. The guy who says his family own half of Vermont is diagnosing the world situation. "Food and oil," he says, "they're the two trump cards in global economics today . . . we have the food, they have the oil, but Iran's money is useless without food; you can't eat money." He is running his finger down the columns of *The Wall Street Journal*, explaining to a couple of chess-playing Method actors what to buy and what to sell. A lot of Dover drivers read *The Wall Street Journal*. The rest read the *Times*. Only the mechanics, who make considerably more money, read the *Daily News*. Leaning up against the pay telephone, a guy wearing a baseball hat and an American-flag pin is talking about the Pelagian Heresies and complaining about St. Thomas Aquinas's bad press. His cronies are laughing as if they know what the Pelagian Heresies are. A skinny guy with glasses who has driven the past fourteen nights in a row is interviewing a chubby day liner for *Think Slim*, a dieters' magazine he tries to publish in his spare time. The Rumanian discotheque D.J. is telling people how he plans to import movies of soccer games and sell them for a thousand dollars apiece. He has already counted a half-million in profits and gotten himself set up in a Swiss villa by the time Danny calls his number and he piles into #99 to hit the streets for twelve hours.

Some of the old favorites are missing. I don't see the guy with the ski tours. He was an actor who couldn't pay his Lee Strasberg bills, and was always trying to sign up the drivers for fun-filled weekends in Stowe. Someone says he hasn't seen the guy for a few months. Maybe he "liberated" himself and finally got to the mountains after all. Maybe he's in a chalet by a brook right now waiting for the first snowfall instead of sweating and regretting at shape-up. Dover won't miss him. Plenty of people have come to take his place.

"I don't look like a cabdriver, do I?" Suzanne Gagne says with a hopeful smile. Not yet. Her eyes still gleam—they aren't fried from too many confrontations with the oncoming brights on the Queensboro Bridge. Suzanne, a tall woman of twenty-nine with patched blue jeans, is a country girl from the rural part of Connecticut. She got presents every time she graduated from something, so she has three different art degrees. When school got tiresome, she came to New York to sell her "assemblages" ("I don't care for the word *collage*") in the SoHo galleries. There weren't many immediate takers and her rent was high, so now Suzanne drives for Dover several nights a week.

A year ago or so, any woman hanging out at shape-up was either waiting to report a driver for stealing her pocketbook, a Dover stiff's girlfriend, or some sort of crazy cabdriver groupie. In those days, the two or three women who were driving were banned from the night line, which is notably unfair because you can make a lot more money with a lot less traffic driving at night. Claire, a long-time Dover driver, challenged the rule and won; now fifteen women drive for Dover, most on the night line. There are a lot of reasons why. "I'm not pushing papers anymore," says Sharon, a calligrapher and former social worker who drove for Dover until recently. "I can't hack advertising." Sharon says many more women will be driving soon because women artists need the same kind of loose schedule that has always attracted their male counterparts to cabdriving. At Dover you can show up whenever you want and work as many days as you can stand. Besides, she says, receptionist and typist positions, the traditional women's subsistence jobs, are drying up along with the rest of the economy. The women at Dover try not to think about the horrors of the New York Night. "You just have to be as tough as everyone else," Sharon says. But since Suzanne started driving, an artwork that she used to do in two or three days is taking weeks. "I'm tired a lot," she says, "but I guess I'm driving a cab because I just can't think of anything else to do."

Neither can Don Goodwin. Until a while ago he was president of the Mattachine Society, one of the oldest and most respected of the gay-liberationist groups. He went around the country making speeches at places like Rikers Island. But now he twirls the ends of his handlebar mustache and says, "There's not too much money for movements, movements are ga-stunk." Don sometimes daydreams in his cab. He thinks about how he used to dress windows for Ohrbach's and how he loved that job. But his salary got too high and now he can't get another window-dresser's job. Don offered to take a cut in pay but "in the window-dressing business they don't like you to get paid less than you got paid before, even if you ask for it. Isn't that odd?" Now Don's driving seven days a week because "after window-dressing and movements, I'm really not skilled to do anything else."

A driver I know named David is worried. David and I used to moan cab stories to each other when I was on the night line. Now he keeps asking me when I'm coming to work. After four years of driving a cab, he can't believe interviewing people is work. David is only a dissertation away from a Ph.D. in philosophy, which makes him intelligent enough to figure out that job openings for philosophers are zilch this year. The only position his prodigious education has been able to land him was a $25-a-night, one-night-a-week gig teaching ethics to rookie cops. David worked his way through college driving a cab. It was a good job for that, easy to arrange around things that were important. Now he has quit school in disgust and he arranges the rest of his life around cab-driving. He has been offered a job in a warehouse for which he'd make $225 a week and never have to pick up another person carrying a crowbar, but he's not going to take it. At least when you're zooming around the city, there's an illusion of mobility. The turnover at the garage (Dover has over five hundred employees for the 105 taxis; it hires between five and ten new people a week) makes it easy to convince yourself this is only temporary. Working in a factory is like surrender, like defeat, like death; drudging nine to five doesn't fit in with a self-conception molded on marches to Washington. Now David's been at Dover for the past two years and he's beginning to think cab freedom is just another myth. "I'll tell you when I started to get scared," David says. "I'm driving down Flatbush and I see a lady hailing, so I did what I normally do, cut across three lanes of traffic and slam on the brakes right in front of her. I wait for her to get in, and she looks at me like I'm crazy. It was only then I realized I was driving my own car, not the cab."

David has the Big Fear. It doesn't take a cabdriver too long to realize that once you leave the joy of shape-up and start uptown on Hudson Street, you're fair game. You're at the mercy of the Fear Variables, which are (not necessarily in order): the traffic, which will be in your way; the other cabdrivers, who want to take your business; the police, who want to give you tickets; the people in your cab, lunatics who will peck you with nudges and dent you with knives; and your car, which is capable of killing you at any time. Throw in your bosses and the hack inspectors and you begin to realize that a good night is not when you make a living wage. That's a great night. A good night is when you survive to tell your stories at tomorrow's shape-up. But all the Fear Variables are garbage compared with the Big Fear. The Big Fear is that times will get so hard that you'll have to drive five or six nights a week instead of three. The Big Fear is that your play, the one that's only one draft away from a possible showcase, will stay in your drawer. The Big Fear is thinking about all the poor stiff civil servants who have been sorting letters at the post office ever since the last depression and all the great plays they could have produced. The Big Fear is that, after twenty years of schooling, they'll put you on the day shift. The Big Fear is you're becoming a cabdriver.

THE TYPICAL Big Fear cabdriver is not to be confused with the archetypal Cabby. The Cabby is a genuine New York City romantic hero. He's what every out-of-towner who's never been to New York but has seen James Cagney movies thinks every Big Apple driver is like. A Cabby "owns his own," which means the car he drives is his, not owned by some garage boss (58 percent of New York's 11,787 taxis are owned by "fleets" like Dover which employ the stiffs and the slobs of the industry; the rest are operated by "owner-drivers"). The Cabby hated Lindsay even before the snowfalls, has dreams about blowing up gypsy cabs, knows where all the hookers are (even in Brooklyn), slurps coffee and downs Danish at the Belmore Cafeteria, tells his life story to everyone who gets into the cab, and makes a ferocious amount of money. But mostly, he loves his work. There aren't too many of them around anymore. The Dover driver just doesn't fit the mold. He probably would have voted for Lindsay twice if he had had the chance. He doesn't care about gypsies; if they want the Bronx, let them have it. He knows only about the hookers on Lexington Avenue. He has been to the Belmore maybe once and had a stomach ache the rest of the night. He speaks as little as possible, and barely makes enough to get by. He also hates his work.

The first fare I ever had was an old bum who threw up in the back seat. I had to drive around for hours in miserable weather with the windows open trying to get the smell out. That started my career of cabbing and crabbing. In the beginning, before I became acquainted with the Big Fear and all its attendant anxieties, the idea was to drive three days a week, write three, and party one. That began to change when I realized I was only clearing about $27 for every ten-hour shift. (A fleet driver makes from 43 percent to 50 percent of his meter "bookings," depending on seniority, plus tips; please tip your cabdriver.)

There were remedies. The nine-hour shift stretches to twelve and fourteen hours. You start ignoring red lights and stop signs to get fares, risking collisions. You jump into cab lines when you think the other cabbies aren't looking, risking a punch in the nose. You're amazed what you'll do for a dollar. But mostly you steal.

If you don't look like H. R. Haldeman and take taxis often, you've probably been asked by a cabdriver if it's "okay to make it for myself." The passenger says yes, the driver sets a fee, doesn't turn on the meter, gets the whole fare for himself, and that's stealing. Stealing ups your Fear Variables immeasurably. You imagine hack inspectors and company-hired "rats" all around you. Every Chevy with black-wall tires becomes terror on wheels. The fine for being caught is $25, but that's nothing—most likely you will be fired from your garage and no one will hire you except those places in Brooklyn with cars that have fenders held on with hangers and brake pedals that flap. But you know that if you can steal, say $12 a night, you'll only have to drive three nights this week instead of four and maybe you'll be able to get some writing done.

All of this is bad for your writer's distance and your actor's instrument, to say nothing of your self-respéct; but nothing is as bad as premonitions. Sometimes a driver would not show up at Dover shape-up for a couple of days and when he came in he'd say, "I didn't drive because I had a premonition." A premonition is knowing the Manhattan Bridge is going to fall in the next time you drive over it and thinking about whether it would be better to hit the river with the windows rolled up or down. On a job where there are so many different ways to die, premonitions are not to be discounted. Of course, a smile would lighten everything, but since the installation of the partition that's supposed to protect you and your money from a nuclear attack, cabdriving has become a morose job. The partition locks you in the front seat with all the Fears. You know the only reason the thing is there is because you have to be suspicious of everyone on the other side of it. It also makes it hard to hear what people are saying to you, so it cuts down on the wisecracking. The partition killed the lippy cabby. Of course, you can always talk to yourself, and most Dover drivers do.

WHEN I FIRST started driving, cabbies who wanted to put a little kink into their evening would line up at a juice bar where they gave Seconals along with the Tropicana. The hope was that some Queens cutie would be just messed up enough to make "the trade." But the girl usually wound up passing out somewhere around Francis Lewis Boulevard, and the driver would have to wake her parents up to get the fare. Right now the hot line is at the Eagle's Nest underneath the West Side Highway. The Nest and other nearby bars like Spike's and the Nine Plus Club are the hub of New York's flourishing leather scene. On a good night, dozens of men dressed from hat to boots in black leather and rivets walk up and down the two-block strip and come tumbling out of the "Tunnels," holes in the highway embankment, with their belts off. Cabdrivers with M.A.s in history will note a resemblance to the Weimar Republic, another well-known depression society.

Dover drivers meet in the Eagle's Nest line after 2 A.M. almost every night. The Nest gives free coffee, and many of the leather boys live on the Upper East Side or in Jersey, both good fares, so why not? After the South Bronx, this stuff seems tame. Besides, it's fun to meet the other stiffs. Who else can you explain the insanity of the past nine hours of your life to? It cuts away some of the layers of alienation that have been accumulating all night. Big Fear cabdrivers try to treat each other tenderly. It's a rare moment of cab compassion when you're deadheading it back from Avenue R and you hear someone from the garage shouting "DO-ver! Do-ver!" as he limps out to Coney Island. It's nice, because you know he's probably just another out-of-work actor-writer stiff like you, lost in the dregs.

SO IT FIGURES that there is a strong feeling of "solidarity forever" in the air at Dover. The Taxi Rank and File Coalition, the "alternative" cab union in town (alternative to Harry Van Arsdale's all-powerful and generally despised Local 3036), has been trying to organize the Dover drivers. Ever since I started cabbing, Rank and Filers have been snickered at by most drivers as Commies, crazy radical hippies, and worse. A lot of this was brought on by the Rank and File people themselves, who used to go around accusing old-timers of being part of the capitalist plot to starve babies in Vietnam. This type of talk does not go over too big at the Belmore. Now Rank and File has toned down its shrill and is talking about more tangible things like the plight of drivers in the face of the coming depression, and members are picking up some scattered support in the industry. Dover, naturally, is their stronghold; Van Arsdale's people have just about given the garage up for lost. Suzanne Gagnes wears a Rank and File button. Suzanne says, "It's not that I'm a left-wing radical or anything. I just think it's good that we stick together in a situation like this."

Last winter a bitter dispute arose over an incident in which a Dover driver returned a lost camera and the garage allegedly pocketed the forthcoming reward money. The Rank and File leaders put pressure on the company to admit thievery. The garage replied by firing the shop chairman, Tom Robbins, and threatening the rest of the committee. Tempers grew very hot; petitions to "Save the Dover 6" were circulated. Robbins appealed to the National Labor Relations Board, but no action was taken. There was much talk of a general strike, but Rank and File, surveying the strength of their hardcore membership, decided against it. Now they have another NLRB suit against Dover and the Van Arsdale union for what they claim is a blacklist against Robbins, who has been turned down in attempts to get a job at twenty different garages in the city.

Gerry Cunningham, who is the boss at Dover, says Rank and File doesn't bother him. "You'd figure there would be a lot of those types here, the way I see it. Big unions represent the median sort of guy, so you'd figure that with the general type of driver we have here, there would be a lot of Rank and File. Look, though, I'm not particularly interested in someone's religion as long as he produces a day's work. If the drivers feel a little togetherness, that's fine with me." Gerry, a well-groomed guy with a big Irish face, is sifting through a pile of accident reports and insurance claims in his trailer-office facing Hudson Street. It seems like all cab offices are in trailers or temporary buildings; it's a transient business. This is the first time, after a year of driving for Dover, that I've ever seen Gerry Cunningham. I used to cash the checks too fast to notice that he signed them. Cunningham smiles when he hears the term "hippie garage." "Oh, I don't mind that," he says. "We have very conscientious drivers here. We have more college graduates here than any other group . . . I assume they're having trouble finding other work." Gerry is used to all the actors and writers pushing around Dover hacks and thinks some of them make good drivers and some don't. "But I'll tell you," he says, "of all the actors we've ever had driving here, I really can't think of one who ever made it."

Gerry Cunningham thinks that's kind of sad, but right now he's got his own problems. "Owning taxis used to be a great business," he says, "but now we're getting devoured. In January of 1973 I was paying 31 cents for gas, now I'm paying 60. I'm barely breaking even here. It costs me $12.50 just to keep a car in the streets for twenty-four hours. Gas is costing almost as much as it costs to pay the drivers."

It's no secret that fleets like Dover are in trouble. They were the ones who pressed for the 17.5 percent fare rise and still say it's not enough to offset spiraling gas costs, car depreciation, and corporate taxes. Some big fleets like Scull's Angels and Ike-Stan, which employ hundreds of drivers, are selling out; many more are expected to follow. There is a lot of pressure for change. *The New York Times* has run editorials advocating a major reshaping of the industry, possibly with all cabs being individually owned.

But Gerry Cunningham, who is the president of the M.T.B.O.T (The Metropolitan Taxicab Board of Trade, which represents the fleets), isn't planning on packing it in. He thinks he can survive if the fleets institute "leasing," a practice the gypsy cab companies have always used. Leasing means, according to Cunningham, "I keep all my cars and lease them out to drivers for about $200 a week. That way only one man drives the car instead of the six or seven who are driving it now, the car lasts much longer, and you cut away a good deal of the maintenance and things like that." Cunningham thinks leasing is the only way the fleets can make it right now. "It's got to be," he says, "because for the first time in my life, it's hard to come to work."

Leasing could really shake up the cabbing and crabbing, although Cunningham claims it won't affect the "parttime actor and writer types" and the guys "who think of cabdriving as a stop along the way." These people, he says, can always "sublet" taxis if they can't come up with the $200.

A COUPLE OF Dover drivers who are really actors and musicians are talking about leasing while waiting in line at the La Guardia lot.

"What a drag leasing would be," says an actor who has only $12 on the meter after four hours out of the garage. "If that happens, I don't know, I'll try to get a waiter's job, I guess."

"Yeah man, that'll be a bitch all right," says the musician. "I hate this goddamn job. Hey, I'd rather be blowing my horn, but right now I'm making a living in this cab. I won't dig it if they take it away from me. Damn, if the city had any jobs I'd be taking the civil-service test."

THE DEATH OF (THE IDEA OF) THE UPPER EAST SIDE

JAY McINERNEY

NOVEMBER 20, 2006

With the publication of his first novel, Bright Lights, Big City, *in 1984, Jay McInerney crystallized and helped create the idea of a new downtown: a cool, youthful, indulgent, nightlife-driven place. Two decades later, McInerney's generation has grown up and gotten rich—and now its members are raising their families in sumptuous lofts where some of them used to go clubbing. And with them, the social center of New York moved out of its longtime East Side precincts downtown. McInerney has lived downtown and uptown (at the Carlyle, in fact). And with his novelist's eye, McInerney is a natural ethnographer—"a double agent" he calls himself—of Manhattan's tribes. McInerney's other novels include* Brightness Falls *and* The Good Life.

—

So I WAS AT a party on Fifth Avenue—one of those grand old apartments that represented the apex of the late-eighties Louis Quinze style. It was way over the top, and yet the vision was so perfectly realized: the quality of the furniture and the art, the proportions of the rooms, and the unity of the vision, such that I couldn't help being blown away. It's not my style, but I have to say it was really awe-inspiring. If the Landmarks commission ever decides to preserve interiors, this one should be at the top of the list. It was like a monument not only to a certain period of French décor but also to a recent period of haute Upper East Side life and Manhattan wealth. The dinner party was being given in honor of the Italian writer Alain Elkann. Along with Robert Hughes, who'd come in from Westchester, I was one of the few people at the gathering who'd traveled more than a few blocks that evening to attend the party.

"Where do you live?" one of the guests asked politely, trying to place me, as if I didn't seem quite local. "The Village," I said. There was a chorus of oohs and aahs and what-hos around the room. Then, you could have knocked me over with a feather duster, John Gutfreund, the former chairman of Salomon Brothers, said, "I want to move to the Village, but my wife won't hear of it."

"Me too," said Jacqui Safra, scion of the Lebanese banking family and longtime consort of producer Jean Doumanian. "I want to move downtown, but Jean won't let me." The topic became general, and debate was joined. All around me, Upper East Siders of long standing—Black Card–carrying members of the tribe that was once called the 400—followed the lead of these two *über*-uptown guys and began to talk about their recent adventures downtown, about friends who'd actually made the move, about lofts with their vast expanses of wall on which to hang paintings, about how . . . fun it was down there. And about how expensive it had become, the last being, in this circle if I read them right, a term of approbation.

In fact, this past spring, *Forbes* announced that Tribeca's 10013 was the most expensive zip code in Manhattan—the twelfth most expensive in the nation, followed by 10007 to the south (No. 19) and Soho's 10012 (No. 31). Venerable 10021, which includes most of the choicest cuts of the Upper East Side, the default zip for generations of cotillion and benefit invitations, received a national rank of No. 255. (No. 1 was Sagaponack, the former stepchild of the Hamptons. Apparently, potatoes are way up.) As recently as 1990, before the dot-com and telecom booms, 10021 was the wealthiest zip code in the country.

LAST YEAR, I started dating an Uptown Girl, and I've been shuttling back and forth between the Village and the Upper East Side ever since, pondering the cultural differences between our respective tribes as well as the question of geographical determinism. Is zip code destiny anymore?

One night, I would accompany her to the black-tie Rita Hayworth Ball; the next night, we'd have dinner at the Spotted Pig and head up to Chelsea for a nightcap and a dance at Marquee. At times, these worlds seemed bizarrely heterogeneous; but then again, Patrick McMullan was snapping pictures at Marquee or at the Waldorf, and Donald Trump was likely to be standing next to you at either venue, so it was possible to see prosperous Bloombergian Manhattan as a melting pot of sorts, for better or worse, rather than the Balkan metropolis of disparate, geographically determined tribes that I'd moved to twenty-five years ago. This summer, after we became engaged, these questions took on a practical urgency as we had to choose between the two realms—if they were two realms—at least in terms of a mailing address.

My fiancée is a post-deb with a venerable surname and a deep, burnished voice that sounds as if it had been passed down through many generations. So 10021-centric is she that after her first twenty-five-minute cab ride to my apartment, she admitted that the Village was fun but complained, "It's so far away from everything." And on our first excursion to Rivington Street, she started to get a little nervous when she saw graffiti on the walls and sidewalks.

Many of her friends live within a few blocks of her apartment on East 72nd, and on any given night she will find some of them at Swifty's or Doubles or La Grenouille. Her children attended Spence and Buckley before they moved on to prep school. The boards on which she serves have their meetings in the neighborhood. The Hampton Jitney stops half a block from her apartment. When we first started looking at real estate downtown, she was shocked to learn that not only wasn't the Village a bargain but it seemed to be more expensive than Park Avenue in the Seventies, which has been the pinnacle of social aspiration for most of the past century. And she couldn't help noticing that all the cool new buildings are going up downtown. There are plenty of crappy Bauhaus-lite towers east of Third, but anything resembling innovative modern architecture doesn't seem too welcome on the Upper East Side—the proposed ovoid glass apartment tower by celebrated architect Lord Norman Foster on upper Madison has been opposed by the local community board; its fate hangs on a decision by the Landmarks commission and the city planning department. The announcement by the board of the Whitney Museum, that after years of struggling to gain approval for its expansion plans it would probably take its toys and move down to Chelsea or the meatpacking district, might be interpreted as a huffy slap at the neighborhood and its preservationists. No one in living memory has suggested that the Upper East Side is, or ought to be, at the cutting edge of the culture, but as the city enters a bold new era of development it risks becoming a museum of Olde New York.

BACK IN THE DAYS when Henry James was in short pants, New York society, such as it was, was huddled around Washington Square Park. Until the 1850s, most of the Upper East Side was common land and pastures. Central Park was completed by 1860, but no one really coveted the land adjacent to this uninhabited wilderness, and upper Fifth Avenue was slow to attract the kind of residents who didn't keep hogs out back. Forty-second Street still qualified as uptown when construction of the Metropolitan Museum began in 1880. In 1888, upper Fourth Avenue was paved over and renamed Park Avenue, although the stretch between 42nd and 57th was still a grimy rail yard. Stanford White finished a house on Madison and 72nd Street for Charles L. Tiffany around 1885, and the cachet of the neighborhood was further bolstered when Caroline Astor had a Richard Morris Hunt château built at 65th and Fifth within the next decade. By the turn of the century, members of the 400 (the supposed number that Mrs. Astor was able to accommodate in her ballroom) like the Schermerhorns and the Rhinelanders had moved up and built townhouses in the area. Clubs like the Metropolitan, the Knickerbocker, the Colony, and the Union, which still define a certain Waspy subset of New York society, rose within a few years of each other. The Vanderbilts and Astors must have been relieved when asphalt was finally laid down on upper Fifth Avenue in 1897. Park Avenue became thoroughly fashionable after the train tracks were moved underground.

Although the Upper West Side developed more rapidly, the blue bloods moved cautiously up the East Side along the artery of Fifth. Montgomery Schuyler, the Lewis Lapham of the Gilded Age, observed that West Side apartment buildings tended toward the gaudy; Fifth Avenue, on the other hand, was the proper address for a gentleman.

Well into the twentieth century, blue bloods and their imitators lived in houses. The concept of apartment living, of different families sharing a common roof, was still wildly outré if not downright scandalous in 1912, when 998 Fifth, a McKim, Mead & White building, arose on Millionaire's Row opposite the Met. Like all the Fifth Avenue apartment buildings that would succeed it, and unlike the towers of Central Park West, it was restrained and understated in its grandeur. Among the new residents at 998 was Levi P. Morton, who served as governor of New York as well as vice-president of the U.S. and who was one of those prominent New Yorkers whose uptown drift was emblematic. "Morton's migrations up Fifth Avenue had always seemed to forge the way for the city's elite," says Elizabeth Hawes in *New York, New York,* her improbably riveting history of the New York apartment building. "From 17th Street to 42nd Street in 1891 (where he provided the setting in which Edith Wharton could come out more discreetly than at Delmonico's); from there to 55th Street in 1894 . . . from 55th Street to 81st Street, where he forsook the genteel traditions of houses altogether." Over the course of the next twenty years, grand apartment buildings on Fifth Avenue and Park redefined the concept of the good life. In a city that was still chaotic and dangerous, the western half of the Upper East Side, with its broad avenues and its doorman-guarded buildings, represented the equivalent of a gated community for the child-bearing wealthy, with Central Park as the ultimate backyard. From that day down to the present, an apartment in one of several dozen buildings built before 1930—the number of "good buildings" is generally agreed to be forty-two—was a necessity for status-conscious New Yorkers, as well as for those who had made their pile in Kalamazoo or Caracas and wanted to plant their flag at the center of the world. At least until recently.

MEMBERS OF THE tribe that inhabits these buildings and whose territory comprises the Upper East Side seldom use the words *society* or *socialite,* although the phrase "social people" is often used to denote its members. It is far more porous today than it was in the days when Mrs.

Astor's Patriarch's Ball defined society; some of its members descend from those old families or newer ones like the Rockefellers and the Vanderbilts who were considered parvenus in the Gilded Age; many of its women, among them some of the fiercest guardians of its ramparts, married up from very humble backgrounds, and some of its fortunes are first-generation. It is most easily defined by the annual circuit-of-charity benefit parties, among which the cocktail preview of the International Fine Art and Antique Dealers Show at the Armory benefiting the Memorial Sloan-Kettering Cancer Center is one of the biggest. "Sloan-Kettering brings out all the Big Girls," says a medium-size girl who is surveying the crowd on a recent October night, looking down the long aisle of antique booths at such Big Girls as Carol Mack, Hilary Geary, Pat Altschul, Somers Farkas, Debbie Bancroft, and Barbara de Portago. It is the wives (and widows and heiresses) who are the keepers of the benefit circuit, although many of the men are here as well: Ambassador Earl Mack, buyout baron Wilbur Ross, sugar heir Pepe Fanjul. It's not a formal event, just a cocktail party, but some of these dresses and gowns could definitely go straight on to major black-tie events; observing the unwritten sumptuary law of their caste, the men are all wearing gray or navy business suits and muted ties. No one would call it a young crowd, with a few exceptions—like flame-haired model-heiress Lydia Hearst-Shaw and professional party boy Fabian Basabe. You can't help wondering where their friends and peers are hanging out tonight and whether, when the time comes, they will bother to dress up and join the boards and carry on the arcane social-philanthropic traditions of their elders.

"This used to be so grand," says my friend, a voluptuous blonde socialite in Carolina Herrera. "It was so great when Nan Kempner and Pat Buckley were chairing. It's really just not the same." This lament sounds frequently up and down Park Avenue. For many people, Nan Kempner's death last year marked the end of a sparkling era of New York social life. The chain-smoking, best-dressing, quick-witted socialite was the embodiment of the tribe, the Platonic ideal of a socialite, the kind of Big Girl who made all the others feel good about being in the tribe, and so far she has no obvious successors. Various candidates have been nominated, privileged and fashionable women in their thirties and forties: Tory Burch,

Gigi Mortimer, Marina Rust Connor, and Lauren Dupont are in the wings, but so far no one has been anointed, and it's not clear that anyone's volunteering. One can only imagine the fierceness of the competition back in the days when Babe Paley and Slim Keith and Capote's other swans roamed the earth.

Donald Trump walks past, poking into a jewelry booth, his hair improbably reddish, and no one seems to notice. Trump is not a member of the tribe, although his territory overlaps theirs; he eats at the same restaurants and attends some of the signature parties. His brother Robert is a member, although somewhat less popular since he left beloved Big Girl Blaine Trump. The feeling on both sides seems to be one of indifference bordering on disdain. The Donald is unclubbable, and he's made it clear he has no use for the genteel rituals of the tribe.

Some of the guests are examining the wares—major furniture and jewelry from the Ming dynasty to mid-twentieth century, and curiosities like an eighteenth-century walnut gentleman's traveling case for $60,000; a carved ivory German crossbow for $220,000—while others complain about last night's Henry Street Settlement benefit party, another major event on the circuit, judged to be overly long and boring this year. A group of women are talking about the funeral earlier today of designer Vera Wang's father, which many of them attended. "Was there a lunch afterward?" asks one of them, sounding slightly aggrieved. "I didn't know there was a lunch."

On this particular chilly Thursday, some of the antiques-show crowd is going on to the '21' club (which wasn't actually named after the zip code where most of its patrons live), where Alex Kuczynski is having a party for her book, *Beauty Junkies*. Not everyone approves of Kuczynski's book, which is something of an exposé of certain tribal rituals. It would be safe to say that most of the women at the Sloan-Kettering party have been the beneficiaries—or victims—of certain cosmetic procedures, and certain surgeons and doctors are the objects of hero worship. "She's just a total bitch for hanging herself and a lot of us out to dry," one of the ladies who lunch griped to Liz Smith. Kuczynski is a member of the tribe by virtue of her marriage to hedge-fund mogul Charles Stevenson, though, as a working journalist, she is something of a maverick.

Still later, you will see many faces from the antiques show at Swifty's, the modest little bistro that has replaced Mortimer's as the canteen of the tribe. At Swifty's, as at '21,' people who fly in front of the plane or in private planes happily dine shoulder to shoulder and cheek by jowl in a space that resembles a subway car at rush hour. Up front, Kathy and Billy Rayner wave to Kimberly Du Ross, while in the tiny back room, Rand and Jessie Araskog are hosting a party for some of the patrons and committee members, and when they eventually head for the front door close to eleven, it's like watching the clowns pour out of a Volkswagen—very expensively dressed, heavily bejeweled, late-middle-aged clowns, many of whom have their own chauffeured cars waiting outside although their apartments are only steps away. "There go the antique people," says a young banker at my table. It takes him a moment to realize he's cracked a joke.

It's 10:45 on the Upper East Side. If you want another drink, then you'd best head downtown.

MY DINNER AT Swifty's reminded me of the Upper East Side period of my own life. Like many Manhattan-dwelling breeders, I just assumed that when I finally spawned, I would—more or less like a salmon—have to move inexorably upstream. Specifically, to the Upper East Side, for the schools. Of course, there were Collegiate and Trinity on the West Side, if you happened to want one of those particular schools, but there weren't any restaurants to speak of back then, and I don't think my then-wife had ever actually set foot on the Upper West Side. She was already living in Turtle Bay when we got married in 1991, more than halfway to the Upper East.

I lived then in the West Village, which I considered by far the most congenial neighborhood in the city. All the amenities of single life were nearby: bars, bookstores, restaurants, and nightclubs. There were a few kids around, most of them belonging to Brian and Keith McNally, as far as I could tell, and I was aware that St. Luke's and Grace Church School and the Little Red Schoolhouse were somewhere nearby . . . but at least half the neighbors were gay men and it was basically a neighborhood where breakfast was taken at eleven and whether you liked it or not the trannies from the adjacent meatpacking district were going to use your stairwell as their place of business and sooner or later you were probably going to get mugged. These minor inconveniences notwithstanding, this was the downtown fantasy that many of us non-native New Yorkers had moved to the city in search of, the New York of the Abstract Expressionists and the Talking Heads, because we'd heard of the Cedar Tavern and CBGB. We didn't want to be Jock Whitney or Carter Burden; we wanted to be Patti Smith or Jim Carroll.

But one day someone got pregnant. Maybe by accident or maybe after a long course of in vitro, in which case you'd probably already thought about moving uptown because that's where most of the fertility clinics were. I convinced myself that saying ciao to the Village was part of growing up, an inevitable rite of passage, like buying a Brooks Brothers suit after graduation. It wasn't just the schools, all the new parents ensconced in the East Seventies would tell you—it was the pediatricians and the park and the nanny network and the whole child-rearing infrastructure from Serendipity to Jacadi. This is where you inevitably ended when you started waking up at 6 A.M.—as everybody assured you you would soon be doing, once the kids came—as opposed to going to bed at 6 A.M.

IF A SINGLE precipitating event can be pinpointed, the beginning of the end for the Upper East Side might be John Kennedy Jr.'s taking up residence in Tribeca. As a young man, John-John had moved first to the Upper West Side, then later downtown, not an unusual trajectory for an Upper East Side scion, even then. But when he became a grown-up and got married and still did not move back—and, in fact, displayed not the slightest inkling that he ought to or ever would—well, that suggested trouble. (It should be noted that John-John apparently did spend the last few weeks of his life, estranged from his wife, at the Stanhope, but that's another story.)

If that defection could be explained away as an act of impetuous youth, there were others that could not, like Diane Von Furstenberg's 1997 move from the Carlyle to a townhouse on far West 12th Street. Von Furstenberg has always crossed social boundaries, and her apartment at the Carlyle was one of New York's great salons, the kind of place where European princesses might find themselves rubbing shoulders with West Chelsea queens; but some of her friends and their drivers must have had to get directions when the salon moved to the West Village. Charlie Rose soon became her neighbor. As the Giuliani era endured and it became clear that the citywide drop in crime was not a momentary blip but an incredible new fact of urban living, fear of those quaint but dark and unfamiliar little streets downtown receded. And then came word that renowned architect Richard Meier, who'd never built in Manhattan, was designing two residential towers along the waterfront in the West Village. While neighborhood activists rallied to fight the development, high-profile, deep-pocketed New Yorkers, the very sort who would never consider living anywhere but on the Upper East Side, started visiting Meier's offices to look at the models and floor plans.

In the midst of my divorce, when I realized that the Upper East Side chapter of my life was over, I trooped down with a Realtor friend who had a very inflated notion of my net worth; I just wanted to see the place even if I couldn't afford it. In the office, I shook Meier's hand and complimented him on the beauty of the shimmering silver-blue architectural model, although I might just as well have complimented him on his own iconic, monumental appearance with that mane of silver-blue hair, since this was probably the first Manhattan building project in decades that was being sold on the basis of the star power of the architect. We then climbed back in the Realtor's Town Car and drove to the site at Perry Street, where we viewed the fourth-floor unit in the northern tower. I was standing in a rough concrete-and-glass box with exposed wiring and, admittedly, a great river view. "Buyers get to finish the interiors themselves," my friend informed me cheerfully. "Calvin's going to take the penthouse. He went up in a helicopter with Richard to inspect the views."

The Meier project put downtown officially on the map for the uptown crowd. Many more fancy downtown buildings have been built or are in the works, bearing names like Calatrava, Gehry, Gwathmey, and Rogers, and creating a new luxury aesthetic that makes ol' Park Avenue seem almost spartan. Despite their sometimes jarring new forms, many of the new buildings already seem to have settled quite comfortably into old neighborhoods—as any good host or D.J. knows, it's all about the mix.

These new downtowners won't have to travel far to visit the Whitney if the museum follows through with its plan to move its new building south. After more than a decade of trying to get approval for plans to expand on Madison Avenue, the Whitney seems to have thrown in the towel. Like some hopeful young suitor bringing one bride after another home to stuffy parents, the Whitney paraded a succession of architects past the neighbors, including Michael Graves, Rem Koolhaas, and Renzo Piano. Now, even as the Piano addition appeared to be on the verge of approval, the board of the Whitney has pulled the equivalent of saying, "To hell with Mom and Dad, we're going to elope with a cocktail waitress." Whatever the details of the decision, the impression seems to be that the old folks want to pull up the drawbridge and keep out anything that doesn't look like it belongs in the 8th Arrondissement. The howls of protest that have greeted the proposal for developer Aby Rosen's twenty-two-story Norman Foster tower atop the Parke-Bernet building reinforce the impression that the Upper East Side wishes to be left out of twenty-first-century Manhattan. The community board slammed the proposal immediately, while the hearing in front of the Landmarks commission drew an overflow crowd of bejeweled and bespoke-suited protesters. William Kahn, a resident of the Carlyle House near the proposed site, compared Lord Foster's proposal to the British occupation of New York during the Revolutionary War.

MY SHRINK, a former student of Hannah Arendt's, lives deep in the Lower East Side, at Houston and Avenue A, in a five-story building that has a stark, army-green, unattended, disinfectant-scented lobby. By the by, she expresses her concern and amazement about the fact that her building has been infiltrated by uptowners—a Wall Street couple and a recent college grad whose Wall Street daddy is setting her up with a nest. She is not entirely convinced that these three are good for the neighborhood that invented the slogans "Eat the rich" and "Die, yuppie scum," which still occasionally appear on brick walls and sidewalks, but obviously they think the neighborhood is good for them. Which raises the question, when everyone and his parents move downtown, in what sense will it still be downtown? Will King Charles spaniels start to replace French bulldogs on Bleecker Street? And speaking of Bleecker, it was one thing for Marc Jacobs to set up shop there, but Ralph Lauren? Now that hedge-fund managers and trust-funders have taken over Tribeca, the former province of painters and sculptors, it may be that Manhattan geography is no longer destiny, that neighborhoods have lost their tribal signification. Or rather, the Upper East Side may be the last neighborhood to preserve its signification and its identity, if only as a kind of prewar retirement community, replete with museums and hospitals, encased in amber.

Designer Robert Couturier, a favorite of the crowd that summers in Southampton and winters in Palm Beach, has noticed a migration even among the rarefied group of his clients. "A number of older people whose children have moved away from home are going downtown. Art dealers—and, of course, the younger generation. As for the really old guard, they are staying entrenched in their Park Avenue and Fifth Avenue buildings. But what is helping kill the Upper East Side is the fact that most of the apartments are occupied by absentee owners; they are in town so seldom that the buildings look depressingly unoccupied. Whether somebody is rich in Lima, Caracas, Paris, London or Rome, Moscow or Shanghai, they all want an apartment in New York that they visit only a couple of months a year. Hence the depressing feeling that the Upper East Side is empty and on any weekend is a desert. The only thing holding many people back is the school factor."

Even that is changing. Last year, Claremont Prep, a K-through-eight private academy, opened its doors on Broad Street in the financial district, providing an alternative for downtown parents who have been sending their kids across the river to Saint Ann's in Brooklyn. The entire neighborhood has been reoriented. "Before, families would look on Fifth, Park, and the Gracie Mansion area and the Upper East Side," says Corcoran broker Maria Pashby. "As recently as five years ago, families with children would tend to come uptown. No more. I just sold 31 N. Moore Street, and everyone who looked was families, families, families. With children. No single people."

Some of those younger kids will go to P.S. 234, on Greenwich Street between Chambers and Warren, where on a typical afternoon you see almost as many dads as moms scooping up kids with Small Paul and SpongeBob backpacks. Whereas you won't see any dads outside Buckley or Allen-Stevenson at this hour, and the mothers will tend to have a certain shade of blonde hair that seems indigenous to the East Seventies. Apparently there's still some truth to geography; certain stereotypes endure for the moment. None of the mothers outside P.S. 234 are wearing Chanel ballet slippers. "It's a great school," shouts one of the fathers, an art dealer in cargo pants and a Black Flag T-shirt who is escorting his fifth-grade son to karate lessons. "The only problem is the construction noise." We can hardly hear ourselves speak over the din emanating from building sites in the area, huge new residential towers at 200 Chambers and 101 Warren. In a year or two, his son will have plenty of new sparring partners.

IN THE MEANTIME, my fiancée sweetly agreed to move downtown, becoming part of what seems more and more like a general migration. We are waiting to close on a prewar apartment in the Village, and we continue to shuttle up and down. Last night, we started at a reading and book signing in the Village, then joined another couple at Le Cirque, where we waved to at least a half-dozen of her friends, admired some major jewelry, winced at some unsuccessful surgery, and talked about acquaintances at nearby tables, people whose names regularly appear in *W* and *Avenue* and *Quest,* none of whom appeared to have any desire to be anywhere else.

ONE BRIEF, SCUZZY MOMENT

GARY INDIANA

DECEMBER 6, 2004

In New York, a person guards his turf, which is not only an actual zip code but a tapestry of memories and associations. In the seventies, when Gary Indiana was in his twenties, his neighborhood was the East Village, a self-reinforcing community of artists and eccentrics (and cheap bars) that thrived outside the mainstream. And then, almost before Indiana's eyes, the scene changed. Some of the locals got famous; many more faded away. And of course, almost everyone became obsessed with real estate. "It's a very uncomfortable place to be now," says Indiana, who still lives in the same rent-stabilized sixth-floor walk-up he occupied thirty years ago. But he does see one bit of encouraging news. "For a while, everybody thought the economy was going to collapse and it would be just like the seventies again. How great!" he says. In this piece, which was written as a preview of a New Museum retrospective of East Village art in the seventies, Indiana revisits the lost comforts of his old neighborhood. Indiana is the author of several books, including the novels Depraved Indifference *and* Do Everything in the Dark, *which is a kind of epilogue to the late seventies.*

I LIVED IN THE East Village when it still had the narcoleptic desuetude of downtown Detroit, and was usually included with today's Loisaida under the less cozy moniker "the Lower East Side." (It had, of course, been called the East Village in the more interesting part of the sixties, but went back to LES in the grim seventies.) So, it's a little thorny for me to flip back a quarter-century to the three years I spent as an art critic at *The Village Voice* in the mid-eighties, or revisit the "East Village Art Scene" they loosely coincided with—a scene that, for one, brief, improbable moment, made the neighborhood the West Chelsea of its day, and forever banished the area's better Detroit-like qualities.

The neighborhood has a jarringly different history for me from the one the New Museum of Contemporary Art chronicles in its new show "East Village USA." I haven't seen it yet, but judging from a checklist of works and curator Dan Cameron's catalogue essay, the show will survey a somewhat parochially defined East Village art world, chronologically speaking. Its true measure of an artist's importance, with a few exceptions, seems to be the amount of publicity he or she got in 1983.

Not that such an approach is historically inaccurate. The Reagan-era scene itself ignored much of the far more interesting East Village art world that had come before it. Until hordes of trust-fund bohemians and storefront art salesmen invaded to give the nabe an entrepreneurial makeover—and lay the groundwork for an explosion in real-estate values that eventually wrecked its wealth of rent-stabilized apartments—the East Village was an ideal refuge for any artist born without a silver spoon. Contrary to its wild and crazy latecomers, they didn't make a rose garden from the Atacama Desert. There was plenty of life in the place before anyone thought to squeeze cash from it.

I was a bit anterior to the Wall-Hanging Art Boom spawned by Morning in America, though I found myself in the whirling center of it before it lapsed into remission. Since 1978, I had been a playwright and stage director who wrote little essays on film and other subjects, and published an occasional bad poem. I never much cared if I had any money. I lived so reclusively that I passed for deceased much of any given year. I was pathologically shy, but I forced myself to become a dervish of sociability whenever I embarked on another play. I believed that actors, like Germans of the thirties, were basically clueless children yearning for a headstrong, visionary father figure, even if he happened to be insufferably overbearing, zonked on speed half the time, and possibly insane.

When I moved into the neighborhood in the late seventies, I immediately assembled a theater troupe with the actor and painter Bill Rice, a sly-boots sage revered in the authentic New York bohemia since Harry Truman. Our theater was a backyard garden—a jumble of bricks, concrete, and cinder blocks with little sprouts of vegetation here and there—behind Bill's floor-through studio at 13 East 3rd. Our company included inspired madcaps like Tina L'Hotsky, Queen of the Mudd Club. And Evan Lurie of the Lounge Lizards (formerly the Eels) composed all the music for our shows. He also appeared in our play *Curse of the Dog People*, as Fludd, an estate archivist hired by a family of werewolves. We never agreed on a name for our company. I favored "Theater of the Obvious," but Bill preferred "Garbage After Dinner." His place was what used to be called "a beautiful mess." Large objects were constantly sliding from shelves. One storm-tossed night when our bal musette had moved indoors, René Ricard recited his electrifyingly caustic poetry from the garden doorway, his back to the audience, while he pissed a full bladder into the pitch-black downpour.

It seems impossible now, but at one time, circa 1979, everyone I saw on Second Avenue, day or night, was either someone I knew or someone I recognized: the vertiginously tall, incomparably fearless photographer Peter Hujar; the sublimely nose-thumbing sculptor Paul Thek; Nico (as in Velvet Underground Nico); Penny Arcade, wacko genius of one-woman stage anarchy; Herbert Huncke, the indomitable drug pusher who inspired much of William Burroughs's *Junky;* Larry Rivers; punk avatars Richard Hell and Tom Verlaine; filmmaker Nick Zedd; actress Black-Eyed Susan; Jean-Michel Basquiat (who went by his graffiti tag SAMO, then); filmmaker Amos Poe; Terri Toye (the most beautiful boy who ever became a girl); and sometimes Debbie Harry. Understand, these familiars didn't graze in packs—there were seldom more than twenty ambulatory individuals scattered between 14th Street and Houston at the same hour.

Before the galleries arrived in the mid-eighties and Avenue A became a beckoning, piquantly semi-dangerous place for kids from Dalton to ferret out a nickel bag of Mary Jane, the "old" East Village already had a full dance card of subterranean amusements. The Bar at Second Avenue and 4th doubled as a pickup joint and giddy living room/salon for a whole community of musicians, writers, actors, and painters, some already famous, like Robert Mapplethorpe and Edward Albee, many others famous later on. John Lurie played pool there in the afternoon. One standout memory is a night when the legendary J. J. Mitchell, Frank O'Hara's lover years before, spilled an entire bottle of poppers up my nose.

A differently eclectic crowd of theater people converged most nights on Phebe's at Bowery and 4th, wired from performing at La MaMa or Theater for the New City. I met Cookie Mueller in Phebe's, and fell in love with her on the spot. Cookie had featured in John Waters's early films. She acted, designed clothes, and also wrote stories and a medical-advice column, "Ask Dr. Mueller."

In a strictly hedonistic way, Eileen's Reno Bar was integral to the East Village community. A narrow pocket of surrealism on Second Avenue between 11th and 12th, its ceiling surfaced in plastic jade plant—brown plastic jade plant—Eileen's had its flaccid nights of dead-room tone. But most evenings brought a steady influx of pre-op transsexuals, clueless walk-ins, bisexual drug dealers, garrulous drunks with a schizophrenic flair, Ricardo Montalban types from Europe lusting after chicks with dicks, and a few black-humored fags like myself, who much preferred the Reno Bar's nightly Halloween party to clocking the aging process in some drippy gay bar. Eileen's had the carnal whoop-de-do of a fetish convention. It was also full of crack whores working the track on 11th Street.

I once took a bar stool beside an enormous black woman I mistook for a drugstore cashier who'd rung up my toothpaste purchase that afternoon, which led to a dyslexic exchange of misunderstandings; I realized my mistake when she leaned close and declared in a tragic whisper: "You know something? My clitoris is as big as a penis. You know what I'm saying? My clitoris is the same size as a penis. I'm talking about a big penis. Can you understand what that makes me feel like?"

One Eileen's habitué named Joel wore a walrusy mustache and the woebegone, sagging face of the chronically defeated. His spot was the last bar stool in back, where a hideous painting, widely assumed to portray the Reno Bar's ancient founder, hovered behind Joel's thinning hair. (There was, and still is, an actual Eileen: I saw her a few weeks ago on the Third Avenue uptown bus. Older, but ever a star.)

My friend Louie Laurita and I felt sad for Joel. Laconic and melancholy as he bolted down five or six G&Ts, Joel would haul himself out to his pickup truck and we'd see it hopelessly circling around at five miles an hour, until Joel returned, slumped and abashed-looking, to drown his abjection in more gin. "Poor Joel," Louie habitually said. "Can't even get laid by a whore."

Around the time when the Barnes & Noble megastore opened on Astor Place, we learned Joel's last name was Rifkin. Over the years, he had strangled seventeen prostitutes in that truck. Here we'd been trying to cheer the guy up, and he'd actually been having the time of his life.

IT MAY SOUND a stretch, but I date the transformation of the East Village from when Jack Henry Abbott, a murderer who'd just been paroled thanks to Norman Mailer's proclaiming him a literary genius, fatally stabbed Richard Adan, a waiter I knew who worked at the Binibon restaurant on Second Avenue, in 1981. It was the beginning of the end for that restaurant.

An obnoxiously trendy, moderately upscale restaurant named 103 opened near the vanished Binibon. It had stupidly angular tables and a snippy, impatient staff. It planted a proprietary yuppie flag in a low-income backwater where eccentricity was normal and having six bucks for a hamburger wasn't. It was only a restaurant, the food was okay. It wasn't Kmart. (We were spared that for another fifteen years.) But more upscale restaurants would soon sprout as the Art Mecca spread its vulpine wings. And already, with 103's arrival, longtime residents understood that one day, gentrification would shove them out of their rent-secure tenements into Hoboken isolation, or possibly a refrigerator crate on the Bowery.

But I'm getting ahead of myself. The globally hyped, short-lived phenomenon known as the East Village Art Scene originated in the basement of the building I live in. One day in 1981, through a doorway under the stoop, I noticed Patti Astor rolling paint over dingy walls, in a space I had long imagined the lair of elderly former concentration-camp guards—the only conceivable background of my landlord's maintenance hires.

Patti was opening a gallery. In Charlie Ahearn's movie *Wild Style*, she played a reporter whose car breaks down in the Bronx, where she befriends a charismatic group of graffiti artists. Patti's character inserts these artists into the downtown art world.

In my experience, life seldom imitates art and certainly never improves on it, but Patti and her partner, Bill Stelling, did smuggle Harlem and the South Bronx into a veritably albino art scene. The Fun Gallery, which later moved farther east, really was fun. Patti served Lava Lamp–colored cocktails. The openings carried the sexy charge of surplus beauty in the room. The place was totally free of pretension. And there were actual black people there. (The endemic racism of the art world speaks volumes about the people who run it.) Patti simply didn't care if she made any money: The point was to zap a little soul into the prevailing rigor mortis.

That was, as the song goes, the start of something big. And the end of something small. Next, monkey see monkey do, more storefront art shops opened, a lot in 1982, and a full invasion by 1985. More, it quickly appeared, than enough worthwhile artists to fill them. I lack the memory cells to proper-name all the galleries whose press releases enhanced the horror of opening my mailbox. But I can recall what distinguishes a period of artistic excellence from a gas leak of mindlessly avid publicity. Consider what the otherwise sensible Dutch laid out for a tulip bulb a few hundred years ago.

The Fun Gallery spawned an embarrassment of epigones, mostly devoted to "Neo-Expressionism." The original Expressionism, of course, had been an effulgence of audaciously painted imagery, aggressively wrought in thick impasto, reflecting the harsh historical upheavals of its time. It dispensed with the delicacies and preciosities of Impressionism in the same way that Dostoyevsky dispensed with the sentimentalized aspects of Turgenev. In these instances, innovation wasn't primarily intended to negate the value of what preceded it, but to keep the recording of consciousness up to date.

But much of the new East Village "movement" amounted to "Self-Expressionism" of the kind that now flowers on television as 24/7 terminal self-revelation. Its crudity effectively captured nothing salient about the movement of history—except, perhaps, as an unconscious reflection of Ronald Reagan's ascendancy and the cultural glorification of greed. These new venues were filled with adolescent energy, prankishness, and their own brand of undifferentiated anger about everything wrong with the world. Unfortunately, few twenty-year-olds even know what world they're living in, much less what's actually wrong with it.

Some who did know, and made very intriguing work from their perception, were Richard Hambleton, a creepy person whose shadow figures painted on all kinds of outdoor surfaces really were disturbing and effective (even more so, strange to say, in broad daylight than at night); Kenny Scharf, who was far more personally engaging than his paintings were for a time, but eventually brought his work up to the same level as his personality; Kiki Smith, a born artist in every sense; and Marilyn Minter, whose paintings of movie-star faces and people wearing excessive makeup hold up much better today than many of the other "Neo-Ex" artists who have been chosen for "East Village USA."

I can easily understand why Rodney Alan Greenblat's playpen defacements of innocent blank canvas would have to be included in a truly comprehensive survey of the period. At the time, he was considered the cynical nadir of Neo-Ex, and a hilarious example of what arriviste orthodontists and jumped-up ambulance chasers in the legal profession were willing to waste money on as "art collectors" before the stock-market crash of 1987. I'm told that one collector couple known then as the "personal hygiene" practitioner and his wife are currently buying a porn channel in Florida. And they were among the better ones.

WHILE MUCH neo-East Village art was tepid, a fair amount of the earlier East Village's more risk-taking chutzpa had started losing steam circa 1982. We should never forget that vast numbers of New York's best people—Peter Hujar, *Flaming Creatures* director Jack Smith, Cookie Mueller, Robert Mapplethorpe, painter Nicolas Moufarrege—died fast in the AIDS epidemic or a few years into it.

Another factor that took the neighborhood's flavor away: Too many esteemed local talents had acquired an insulating crust of uncritical coterie worship. The banal efforts of once-exciting artists received rote adulation from claques less concerned about quality than about sparing a friend's feelings. They no longer cared if what they presented in public sucked, as long as they presented something. You could blame the timidity of artists terrified of wider cultural arenas and their risks, or the small rewards of masochistic, self-induced failure. And, cruel as it sounds, you can also blame living in New York while cowering for decades in the same mousy sliver of it, as if you inhabited an unusually zany alpine village.

There was something necessary and painfully liberating about flushing away preciosity and giving nostalgia a kick in the ass. Even if the flush mechanism itself belonged in a toilet.

David Wojnarowicz, who'd lived in New York forever and had been a teenage hustler in Times Square, straddled the old and new scenes. He and I had a complicated relationship, and I'd like to settle some hash propagated by an art critic named Lucy Lippard in an Aperture publication devoted to David, in which she implied that I'd stalked him.

It happens that for about three months, David and I insistently sought each other's constant company, for differently confused reasons, and mostly in Paris. We said rotten things about each other in public, and in the course of our folie à deux, David wrote many deranged letters to me, and I to him. I disposed of his a year later. He, ever the pack rat, hung on to mine while assuring me he'd burned them. We later made up, but the crux of David's resentment is that I never valued his paintings as highly as his writing. We had basic disagreements about art. David believed that children are natural artists and their spontaneous expression is what an adult artist should approximate as closely as possible. I like children just fine, but that's horseshit. As David was probably the pick of the litter as far as Neo-Ex-slash-graffiti-art went, he also exemplified—not always in his work, but in his attitude—what I found lazy and self-absorbed about most of the artwork produced by the "movement."

After David's death from AIDS in 1992, a curator at the Grey Art Gallery asked my permission to display my deranged letters to David in a vitrine. I refused. I pointed out that I myself wasn't dead yet. I had a great fondness for David. I won't claim that I miss him the way I miss Cookie or my best, best friend, Dieter Schidor, Fassbinder's last producer, who suicided shortly after his HIV diagnosis. Among the dead, we all have our empathetic priorities. I am sorry David's gone.

SOME OF THE gallerists in the new scene were arguably more interesting than the painters. Amid the places where Neo-Expressionism defined the style, Gracie Mansion and her partner, Sur Rodney Sur, stood out. Gracie's instincts and shrewd taste (Peter Hujar, Marilyn Minter, Stephen Lack) deserved, and got, her a lasting career in the biz. I've always respected her as a pioneer, ever since she launched her first "gallery" in her apartment bathroom. I wasn't always crazy about her early choices. At one of her shows, Gracie greeted me as I looked at something very disagreeable on the wall. "What do you think?" she brightly asked. "Oh, Gracie, I can't help it, I think it's a piece of shit." She whooped. "I don't think it's the worst piece of shit," she said. "You should see who I'm showing next, you wanna see shit. The pictures will get better, I hope, or they'll get really bad and he can make a fortune and blow it on heroin."

Pat Hearn also occupied a higher class of startup art dealers. She had panache and daring, beauty and good breeding, but the rarest thing Pat had, in preternatural abundance, was grace. I adored her. I don't think Pat would mind my revealing that our cordial acquaintance ripened into friendship by accident, when we showed up at the same Debtors Anonymous meeting.

Colin de Land, who opened American Fine Arts, was the only matchingly brilliant figure Pat should have married, and she did, and now they're both dead, first her, then him, and nobody who knew them has ever gotten over it. Colin looked like an especially jaded, paling gigolo and card sharp. I'm hardly the only person who ever offered him a blow job in his place of business. I may be the only person who never gave him one at one time or another, though once he married Pat, that was that.

Colin and Richard Prince invented an artist named John Dogg, and put up a well-received show of his work at Lisa Spellman's 303 Gallery. (A lot of people still believe that I was John Dogg. I wasn't. Colin and Richard came up with the ideas, and one or the other "made" the work—Goodyear tires and other store-bought objects. That was one show where presentation was, literally, everything.)

In 1985, *The Village Voice* offered me a job as senior art critic. This made my life easier and lousy at the same time. I now had to actually enter all those galleries instead of peeking in the windows. At times, the only tangible perk was having the chump for a fifth of vodka whenever twenty more phonies had flattered my ass off in the course of a working week.

The East Village was a small quadrant of what I had to "cover," and I was a bit slow to realize that a fresh constellation of galleries there (Nature Morte, Cash/Newhouse, International With Monument) were showing art much more to my liking than the inflatable children's toys of the waning Neo-Expressionist craze. This second wave favored conceptually crisp work by artists fluent in several media: Robert Gober, Gretchen Bender, Ashley Bickerton, Peter Halley, and Jeff Koons.

But year two at the *Voice* brought a distinct slackening of interest in the art world, art, artists, and, frankly, the sound of my own voice. It was also the year when all the galleries began fleeing the East Village. The rents kept soaring, driving some places out of business, while galleries that were making plenty wanted much larger spaces for their money, in one of the two real power centers of the art world, Soho and 57th Street. The East Village had already become a zoo, and NYU would go on to plant some ugly dormitories down and unleash thousands of rich kids whose idea of art was grazing the streets and poking into boutiques while asserting their pathologies by screaming into cell phones. But hey, shit happens.

I still live in the East Village, but now I live in a luxury neighborhood, thanks mostly to an insignificant hiccup in the long burp of art history that created a seismic shift in the history of New York property values. (You knew it was all finished when the methadone clinic moved out.) While this has left the squalor of my apartment building completely intact, an architectural pentimento of former times, being able to get a deli delivery at four in the morning is among many happy improvements that hiccup left in its echoing wake.

I'm not prone to much sentimentality, but you should treasure your own history, however weird it is. William Burroughs once told me, "People like us are lucky because every shitty thing that happens to us is just more material." I want to remember the many people I love who are gone and remind myself how much I love the ones who are still here. And I'll let you in on a little secret: If you live long enough, you even get fond of people you thought you hated.

CRITICS IN THE WORLD OF THE RISING SOUFFLÉ (OR IS IT THE RISING MERINGUE?)

NORA EPHRON

SEPTEMBER 30, 1968

When Nora Ephron entered the gates of New York's food establishment, chefs were not yet stars; few diners even knew their names. No one used the word foodie. *And yet the revolution had begun. In this article, Nora Ephron, who'd worked her way through Julia Child's seminal cookbook, was among the first to observe the food world's monomaniacal passion, a swirl of intense obsessions—there were just a few major figures—that has since been spun into the enormous culinary galaxy in evidence today. "Everything today you can trace to them," the food establishment, she says. The story earned Ephron an invitation to dinner from Julia Child. Ephron, a novelist, journalist, and filmmaker, is currently at work on a film about Julia Child.*

YOU MIGHT HAVE thought they'd have been polite enough not to mention it at all. Or that they'd wait at least until they got through the reception line before starting to discuss it. Or that they'd hold off at least until after they had tasted the food—four tables of it, spread about the four corners of the Four Seasons—and gotten drinks in hand. But people in the Food Establishment are not noted for their manners or their patience, particularly when there is fresh gossip. And none of them had come to the party because of the food.

They had come, most of them, because they were associated with the

Time-Life Cookbooks, a massive, high-budget venture that has managed to involve nearly everyone who is anyone in the food world. Julia Child was a consultant on the first book. And James Beard had signed onto another. And Paula Peck, who bakes. And Nika Hazelton, who reviews cookbooks for *The New York Times Book Review,* and M. F. K. Fisher, usually of *The New Yorker.* And Waverley Root of Paris, France. And Pierre Franey, the former chef of Le Pavillon who is now head chef at Howard Johnson's. And in charge of it all, Michael Field, the birdlike, bespectacled, frenzied gourmet cook and cookbook writer, who stood in the reception line where everyone was beginning to discuss it. Michael was a wreck. A wreck, a wreck, a wreck, as he himself might have put it. Just that morning, the very morning of the party, Craig Claiborne of *The New York Times,* who had told the Time-Life people he would not be a consultant for their cookbooks even if they paid him $100,000, had ripped the first Time-Life Cookbook to shreds and tatters. *Merde alors,* as Craig himself might have put it, how that man did rip that book to shreds and tatters. He said that the recipes, which were supposed to represent the best of French provincial cooking, were not even provincial. He said that everyone connected with the venture ought to be ashamed of himself. He was rumored to be going about town spreading the news that the picture of the soufflé on the front of the cookbook was not even a soufflé—it was a meringue! *Merde alors!* He attacked Julia Child, the hitherto unknockable. He referred to Field, who runs a cooking school and is author of two cookbooks, merely as "a former piano player." Not that Field wasn't a former piano player. But actually identifying him as one—well! "As far as Craig and I are concerned," Field was saying as the reception line went on, "the gauntlet is down." And worst of all—or at least it seemed worst of all that day—Craig had chosen the day of the party for his review. Poor Michael. How simply frightful! How humiliating! How delightful! "Why did he have to do it today?" moaned Field to Claiborne's close friend, chef Pierre Franey. "Why? Why? Why?"

Why indeed?

The theories ranged from Gothic to Byzantine. Those given to the historical perspective said that Craig had never had much respect for Michael, and they traced the beginnings of the rift back to 1965, when

Claiborne had gone to a restaurant Field was running in East Hampton and given it one measly star. Perhaps, said some. But why include Julia in the blast? Craig had done that, came the reply, because he had never liked Michael and wanted to tell Julia to get out of Field's den of thieves. Perhaps, said still others. But mightn't he also have done it because his friend Franey had signed on as a consultant to *The Time-Life Cookbook of Haute Cuisine* just a few weeks before, and Craig wanted to tell him to get out of that den of thieves? Perhaps, said others. But it might be even more complicated. Perhaps Craig had done it because he was furious at Michael Field's terrible review in *The New York Review of Books* of Gloria Bley Miller's *1000 Recipe Chinese Cookbook,* which Craig had praised in the *Times.*

Now while all this was becoming more and more arcane, there were a few who secretly believed that Craig had done the deed because the Time-Life Cookbook was as awful as he thought it was. But most of those people were not in the Food Establishment. Things in the Food Establishment are rarely explained that simply. They are never what they seem. People who seem to be friends are not. People who admire each other call each other Old Lemonface and Cranky Craig behind backs. People who tell you they love Julia Child will add in the next breath that, of course, her husband is a Republican, and her orange Bavarian cream recipe just doesn't work. People who tell you Craig Claiborne is a genius will insist he had little or nothing to do with *The New York Times Cookbook* that bears his name. People will tell you that Michael Field is delightful but that some people do not take success quite as well as they might. People who claim that Dione Lucas is the most brilliant food technician of all time further claim that when she puts everything together, it comes out tasting bland. People who love Paula Peck will go on to tell you—but let one of them tell you. "I love Paula," one of them is saying, "but no one, absolutely no one understands what it is between Paula and monosodium glutamate."

Bitchy? Gossipy? Devious?

"It's a world of self-generating hysteria," says Nika Hazelton. And those who say the food world is no more in-grown than the theatre world and the music world are wrong. The food world is smaller. Much more self-involved. And people in the theatre and in music are part of a culture that has been popularly accepted for centuries; people in the food world are riding the crest of a trend that began less than twenty years ago.

In the beginning, just about the time the Food Establishment began to earn money and fight with each other and review each other's cookbooks and say nasty things about each other's recipes and feel rotten about each other's good fortune, just about that time, there came curry. Some think it was beef stroganoff, but in fact, beef stroganoff had nothing to do with it. It began with curry. Curry with fifteen little condiments and Major Grey's mango chutney. The year of the curry is an elusive one to pinpoint, but this much is clear: it was before the year of quiche lorraine, the year of paella, the year of vitello tonnato, the year of boeuf bourguignon, the year of blanquette de veau, and the year of beef Wellington. It was before Michael stopped playing the piano, before Julia opened L'Ecole des Trois Gourmandes, and before Craig had left his job as a bartender in Nyack, New York. It was the beginning, and in the beginning, there was James Beard and there was curry and that was about all.

Historical explanations of the rise of the Food Establishment do not usually begin with curry. They begin with the standard background on the gourmet explosion—background which includes the traveling fighting men of World War II, the postwar travel boom, and the shortage of domestic help, all of which are said to have combined to drive the housewives of America into the kitchen.

This background is well and good, but it leaves out the curry development. In the fifties, suddenly, no one knew quite why or how, everyone began to serve curry. Dinner parties in fashionable homes featured curried lobster. Dinner parties in middle-income homes featured curried chicken. Dinner parties in frozen food compartments featured curried rice. And with the arrival of curry, the first fashionable international food, food acquired a chic, a gloss of snobbery it had hitherto possessed only in certain upper-income groups. Hostesses were expected to know that iceberg lettuce was déclassé and tuna fish casseroles de trop. Lancers sparkling rosè and Manischewitz were replaced on the table by Bordeaux. Overnight, rumaki had a fling and became a cliché.

The American hostess, content serving frozen spinach for her family, learned to make a spinach soufflé for her guests. Publication of cookbooks tripled, quadrupled, quintupled; the first cookbook-of-the-month club, the Cookbook Guild, flourished. At the same time, American industry realized that certain members of the food world—like James Beard, whose name began to have a certain celebrity—could help make foods popular. The French's Mustard people turned to Beard. The can opener people turned to Poppy Cannon. Pan American Airways turned to Myra Waldo. The Potato Council turned to Helen McCully. The Northwest Pear Association and the Poultry and Egg Board and the Bourbon Institute besieged food editors for more recipes containing their products. Cookbook authors were retained, at sizeable fees, to think of new ways to cook with bananas. Or scallions. Or peanut butter. "You know," one of them would say, looking up from a dinner made during the peanut butter period, "it would never have occurred to me to put peanut butter on lamb, but actually, it's rather nice."

Before long, American men and women were cooking along with Julia Child, subscribing to the Shallot-of-the-Month Club, and learning to mince garlic instead of pushing it through a press. Cheeses, herbs and spices that had formerly been available in Bloomingdale's delicacy department cropped up all around New York, and then, around the country. Food became, for dinner party conversations in the sixties, what abstract expressionism had been in the fifties. And liberated men and women, who used to brag that sex was their greatest pleasure, began to suspect somewhat guiltily that food might be pulling ahead in the ultimate taste test.

Generally speaking, the Food Establishment—which is not to be confused with the restaurant establishment, the chef establishment, the food industry establishment, the gourmet establishment or the wine establishment—consists of those people who write about food or restaurants on a regular basis, either in books, magazines or certain newspapers, and thus have the power to start trends and, in some cases, begin and end careers. Most of them earn additional money through lecture tours, cooking schools, and consultancies for restaurants and industry. A few appear on radio and television.

The typical member of the Food Establishment lives in Greenwich Village, buys his vegetables at Balducci's, his bread at the Zito Bakery, and his cheese at Bloomingdale's. He dines at The Coach House. He is given to telling you, apropos of nothing, how many soufflés he has been known to make in a short period of time. He is driven mad by a refrain he hears several times a week: "I'd love to have you for dinner," it goes, "but I'd be afraid to cook for you." He insists that there is no such thing as an original recipe; the important thing, he says, is point of view. He lists, as one of his favorite cookbooks, the original *Joy of Cooking* by Irma Rombauer, and adds that he wouldn't be caught dead using the revised edition currently on the market. His cookbook library runs to several hundred volumes. He gossips a good deal about his colleagues, about what they are cooking, writing, eating, and whom they are talking to; about everything, in fact, except the one thing everyone else in the universe gossips about—who is sleeping with whom. In any case, he claims that he really does not spend that much time with other members of the Food Establishment, though he does bump into them occasionally at Sunday lunch at Jim Beard's or at one of the publishing parties he is obligated to attend. His publisher, if he is lucky, is Alfred Knopf or Simon and Schuster.

He takes himself and food very very seriously. He has been known to debate for hours such subjects as whether nectarines are peaches or plums, and whether the vegetables that Michael Field, Julia Child and James Beard had one night at La Caravelle and said were canned were in fact canned. He roundly condemns anyone who writes more than one cookbook a year. He squarely condemns anyone who writes a cookbook containing untested recipes. Colleagues who break the rules and succeed are hailed almost as if they had happened on a new galaxy. "Paula Peck," he will say, in hushed tones of awe, "broke the rules in puff paste." If the food establishmentarian makes a breakthrough in cooking methods—no matter how minor and superfluous it may seem—he will celebrate. "I have just made a completely and utterly revolutionary discovery," said Poppy Cannon triumphantly one day. "I have just developed a new way of cooking asparagus."

There are two wings to the Food Establishment, each in mortal combat with the other. On the one side are the revolutionaries—as they like to think of themselves—the home economists and writers and magazine editors who are industry-minded and primarily concerned with the needs of the average housewife. Their virtues are performance, availability of product, and less work for mother; their concern is with improving American food. "There is an awe about Frenchiness in food which is terribly precious and has kept American food from being as good as it could be," says Poppy Cannon, the leader of the revolutionaries. "People think French cooking is gooking it up. All this kowtowing to so-called French cooking has really been a hindrance rather than a help." The revolutionaries pride themselves on discovering shortcuts and developing convenience foods; they justify the compromises they make and the loss of taste that results by insisting that their recipes, while unquestionably not as good as the originals, are probably a good deal better than what the American housewife would prepare if left to her own devices. When revolutionaries get together, they talk about the technical aspects of food: how to ripen a tomato, for example, and whether the extra volume provided by beating eggs with a wire whisk justifies not using the more convenient electric beater.

On the other side are the purists or traditionalists, who see themselves as the last holdouts for haute cuisine. Their virtue is taste; their concern primarily French food. They are almost missionary-like, championing the cause of great food against the rising tide of the TV dinner, clamoring for better palates as they watch the children of America raised on a steady diet of SpaghettiO's. Their contempt for the revolutionaries is eloquent: "These people, these home economists," said Michael Field distastefully, "they skim the iridescent froth off the gourmet department, and it comes out tasting like hell." When purists meet, they discuss each other; very occasionally, they discuss food: whether one ought to put orange peel into boeuf bourguignon, for example, and why lamb tastes better rare.

Although the purists do not reach the massive market available to the revolutionaries, they are virtually celebrities. Their names conjure up a sense of style and taste; their appearance at a benefit can mean thousands of dollars for hospitals, charities, and politicians. The Big Four of the Food Establishment are all purists—James Beard, Julia Child, Michael Field and Craig Claiborne.

Claiborne, a Mississippi-born man who speaks softly, wears half-glasses, and has a cherubic reddish face that resembles a Georgia peach, is probably the most powerful man in the Food Establishment. From his po-

sition as food editor of *The New York Times,* he has been able to bring
down at least one restaurant, crowd customers into others, and play a critical part in developing new food tastes. He has singlehandedly revived
sorrel and cilantro, and if he could have his way, he would singlehandedly
stamp out iceberg lettuce and garlic powder. To his dismay, he played a
large part in bringing about the year of beef Wellington. "I hate the stuff,"
he says.

After thirty-odd unhappy years in public relations and the armed
forces, Claiborne entered the Lausanne Hotel School to study cooking. On
his return—and after a brief stint bartending—he began to write for *Gourmet* magazine and work for Ann Seranne's public relations firm, handling
such products as the Waring Blender and Fluffo the Golden Shortening.
In 1957, he was hired by the *Times,* and he unabashedly admits that his
job has been a dream come true. He loves it, almost as much as he loves
eating, though not nearly as much as he loves cooking.

Claiborne is happiest in his Techbuilt house in Springs, East Hampton, which overlooks an herb garden, an oversized swimming pool, and
Gardiner's Bay. There, he, his next door neighbor Pierre Franey—whom
he calls "my arm and my dear friend"—and a number of other chefs go
fishing, swap recipes, and whip up meals for fifty guests at a time. The
menus are logged into a slender, leather-bound notebook in which Claiborne records every meal he eats throughout the year. On weekdays and
during the winter, he lives in Greenwich Village, where he can be spotted
mornings buying croissants at Sutter's. His other daily meals are taken in
restaurants, and he discusses them as if he were serving penance. "That,"
he says firmly, "is the thing I like least about my job."

Six years ago, Claiborne began visiting New York restaurants incognito
and reviewing them on a star system in the Friday *Times;* since that time,
he has become the most envied, admired, and cursed man in the food
world. Restaurant owners decry his Francophilia and can barely control
their tempers while discussing his prejudice against large management
corporations and in favor of tiny, ethnic restaurants. His nit-picking constantly irritates. Among some of the more famous nits: his censure of a
Pavillon waiter who allowed his pencil to peek out; his disapproval of the
salt and pepper shakers at L'Etoile, and this remark about Lutèce: "One

could wish that the owner, Monsieur Surmain, would dress in a more reserved and elegant style to better match his surroundings."

Surmain, a debonair man who wears stylish striped shirts, sputters when Claiborne's name is mentioned. "He said in a restaurant of this sort I should wear a tuxedo," said Surmain. "What a bitchy thing. He wants me to act like a headwaiter."

The slings and arrows fly at Claiborne—and not only from restaurateurs. Carping about Craig is practically a parlor game in the food world. Everything he writes is pored over for its true significance. It is suggested, for example, that the reason Craig criticized proprietor Stuart Levin's clothes in his recent review of Le Pavillon had to do with the fact that Levin paid too much attention to him during his two visits to the restaurant. It is suggested that the reason Craig praised the clothes of Charles Maisson of La Grenouille in the same review had to do with the fact that Maisson ignores Claiborne entirely too much. It is suggested that Craig is not a nice person; and a story is offered to support the thesis, all about the time he reviewed a new restaurant owned by a friend after the friend had begged him to wait a few weeks. His harsh criticisms, it is said, drove the friend to drink.

But the fact of the matter is that Craig Claiborne does what he does better than anyone else. He is a delight to read. And the very things that make him superb as a food critic—his integrity and his utter incorruptibility—are what make his colleagues envious of him.

"Everyone thinks about Craig too much," says cookbook author and consultant Mimi Sheraton. "The truth is that he is his own man and there is no way to be a friend of his. He is the only writer who is really honest. Whether or not he's reliable, whether or not you like him, he is honest. I know *Cue* isn't—I used to write for them. *Gourmet* isn't. And Michael Field is just writing for Craig Claiborne."

Whenever members of the Food Establishment tire of discussing Craig, they move on to discuss Craig's feuds—though in all fairness, it must be said that Claiborne is usually the less active party to the feuds. The battle currently absorbing the Food Establishment is between Claiborne and Michael Field. Field, who burst into stardom in the Food Establishment after a career as half of the piano team of Appleton and Field, is an energetic, amusing, frenetic man whose recent rise and subsequent candor have won him few friends in the food world. Those who are not his admirers have taken to passing around the shocking tidbit—untrue—that Field had not been to Europe until last year, when he visited Julia Child in Provence.

"Essentially," says Field, "the whole Food Establishment is a mindless one, inarticulate and not very cultivated. These people who attack me are furious because they think I just fell into it. Well, let me tell you, I used to make forty soufflés in one day and throw them out, just to find the right recipe."

Shortly after his first cookbook was published, Field began reviewing cookbooks for *The New York Review of Books,* a plum assignment. One of his early articles, an attack on *The Fannie Farmer Cookbook* which centered on its fondue recipe, set off a fracas that produced a furious series of argumentative letters, in themselves a hilarious inadvertent parody of letters to highbrow magazines. Recently, he attacked *The 1000 Recipe Chinese Cookbook,* a volume that was voted winner of the R. T. French (Mustard) Tastemaker Award (chosen by a hundred newspaper food editors and roughly analogous in meaning to landing on the Best Dressed List). In his attack on Gloria Bley Miller's book, he wrote:

"It would be interesting to know why, for example, Mrs. Miller's recipe for hot mustard requires the cook to bring one cup of water to a boil and then allow it to cool before adding one half cup of dry mustard? Surely Mrs. Miller must be aware that drinking and cooking water in China was boiled because it was often contaminated. . . ."

Mrs. Miller wrote in reply: "I can only suggest to Mr. Field . . . that he immerse his typewriter immediately in boiling water. There are many types of virulence in the world, and 'boiling the water first' is one of the best ways to disinfect anything."

The feud between Field and Claiborne has been simmering for several years, but Claiborne's review of the first Time-Life Cookbook turned it up to full boil. "He has a perfect right to dislike the book," said Field, "but the attack went far beyond that, into personalities." A few months after the review was published, Field counterpunched, with an article in *McCall's* entitled "New York's Ten Most Overrated Restaurants." It is in almost total opposition to Claiborne's "Dining Out in New York"; in fact, reading Field's piece without having Claiborne's book alongside is a little like reading *Finnegans Wake* without the key.

For his part, Claiborne would just as soon not discuss Field—"Don't get me started," he says. And his attitude toward the Time-Life series has mellowed somewhat: he has finally consented to write the text of *The Time-Life Cookbook of Haute Cuisine* along with Franey. But some weeks ago, when asked, he was only too glad to defend his review. "Helen McCully (food editor of *House Beautiful*) said to me, 'How could you be so mean to Michael?' " he recalled. "I don't give a good Goddam about Michael." His face turned deep red, his fists clenched, he stood to pace the room. "The misinformation! The inaccuracies in that book! I made a stack of notes thicker than the book itself on the errors in it. It's shameful."

Claiborne was so angry about the book, as it happened, that he managed to intensify what was, until then, a one-sided feud between James Beard and himself. Beard, a genial, large, round man who receives guests in his Tenth Street house while seated, Buddha-like, on a large pouf, had been carrying on a mild tiff with Claiborne for some time. Just before the first Time-Life Cookbook was published, the two men appeared together on *The David Susskind Show,* and in the course of the program, Beard held up the book and plugged it on the air. Afterward, Claiborne wrote a letter to Susskind with carbon copy to Beard, saying that if he had known he was going to appear on the same show with the Time-Life Cookbook, he never would have consented to go on.

(That Julia Child has managed thus far to remain above the internecine quarrels of the food world probably has more to do with the fact that she lives in Cambridge, Mass., well away from it all, than with her charming personality.)

The success of the Time-Life Cookbook series is guaranteed, Claiborne's review notwithstanding. Offered by mail order to subscribers who care not one whit whether the soufflé on the cover is actually a meringue, the series has already signed up 500,000 takers—for all eighteen books! (*The New York Times Cookbook,* itself a blockbuster, has sold only 200,000 copies.) "The books, whatever their limits, are of enormous quality," says Field. "Every recipe works and is honestly conceived." Yet a few of those intimately connected with the books have complained about the limits Field parenthetically refers to, and most particularly about the technique of group journalism that has produced the books: apparently, the text, recipes and photographs of some of the cookbooks have been done independently of each other.

"It's a joke," says Nika Hazelton, who is writing the text for *The Time-Life German Cookbook*. "First there is the writer, me in this case, but I have nothing to do with the recipes or illustrations. Then there is the photographic staff, which takes recipes from old cookbooks, changes them a little, and photographs them. Then there is the kitchen, under Michael Field's supervision. I think Michael knows about French and Italian food, but he doesn't know quite as much about other cookery. The cook is John Clancy, a former cook in a short-order house who once worked for Jim Beard. I'm the only person connected with the project who knows languages besides French. There is a consultant who hasn't been in Germany for thirty years. My researcher's background is spending three years with the Morgan Bank. It's hilarious. I'm doing it only for the money."

The money that is available to members of the Food Establishment is not quite as much as they would have you think, but it is definitely enough to keep every last one of them in truffles. James Beard—who commands the highest fees and, though a purist, has the most ties with industry—recently turned down a $100,000 offer to endorse Aunt Jemima mixes because he didn't believe in their products. Retainers offered lesser stars are considerably smaller, but there are many jobs, and they suffice. Nevertheless, the impression persists that there are not enough jobs to go around. And because everyone in the food world is freelancing and concerned with putting as many eggs into his basket as possible, it happens that every time someone gets a job, the rest feel that they have lost one.

Which brings us to the case of Myra Waldo. An attractive, chic blonde who lives on Upper Fifth Avenue, Miss Waldo published her first cookbook in 1954, and since then she has been responsible for forty-two others. Forty-two cookbooks! In addition, she does four radio spots a day for WCBS, is roving editor of *Family Circle* magazine, is retained by Pan American Airways, and recently landed the late Clementine Paddleford's job as food editor of *This Week* magazine. Myra Waldo has never been a favorite in the Food Establishment: she is far too successful. Furthermore, although she once made forty-eight soufflés over a July 4th weekend, she is not a truly serious cook. (To a visitor who wanted a recipe for a dinner party, she suggested duck in a sauce made of frozen orange juice, melba sauce, red wine, cognac, lemon juice, and one can of Franco American beef gravy.) For years, it has been rumored that Miss Waldo produces as many cookbooks as she does because she clips recipes and pastes them right onto her manuscript pages, or because she has a gigantic staff—charges she denies. But when she landed the *This Week* job, one that nearly everyone else in the Food Establishment had applied for, the gang decided that too much was too much. Shortly afterward, she went to the Cookbook Guild party, and no one except James Beard even said hello to her.

Says Beard: "You could barely move around at that party for fear someone would bite you in the back."

How much longer life in the Food Establishment—with its back-biting, lip-smacking, and pocket-jingling—will go on is hard to tell. There are some who believe that the gourmet explosion that began it all is here to stay, and that fine cooking is on the increase. "Of course it will last," says Poppy Cannon. "Just in the way sculpture will last. We need it. It is a basic art. We ought to have a National Academy of the Arts to represent the art of cooking."

Others are less sure. They claim that the food of the future will be quite different: pre-cooked, reconstituted and frozen dishes with portion control. "The old cuisine is gone for good and dying out," says Mrs. Hazelton. "Ultimately, cooking will be like an indoor sport, just like making lace and handiwork."

Whatever happens, the Food Establishment at this moment in time has the power to change and influence the way America eats. And, in fact, about all it is doing is showing how to make a better piecrust and fill a bigger breadbox.

"What fascinates me," says Mimi Sheraton, "is that the more interest there is in gourmet food, the more terrible food is for sale in the markets. You can't buy an unwaxed cucumber in this country, the bread thing everyone knows about, we buy overtenderized meat and frozen chicken.

You can't buy a really fresh egg because they've all been washed in hot water so the shells will be clean. And the influence of color photography on food! Oil is brushed on to make it glow. When we make a stew, the meat won't sit on top, so we have to prop it up with oatmeal. Some poor clod makes it at home and it's like buying a dress a model has posed in with the back pinned closed. As a result, food is marketed and grown for the purpose of appearances. We are really the last generation who even has a vague memory of what food is supposed to taste like.

"There have been three revolutionary changes in the food world in past years," Miss Sheraton continued. "The pressure groups have succeeded in changing the labeling of foods, they've succeeded in cutting down the amounts of pesticides used on foods, and they've changed the oversized packages used by the cereal and cracker people. To me, it's interesting that not one of these stories began with a food writer. Where are they, these food writers? They're off wondering about the boeuf en daube and whether the quiche was authentic."

Yes, that's exactly where they are. "Isn't it all a little too precious?" asks Restaurant Associates president Joseph Baum. "It's so elegant and recher-ché, it's like overbreeding a collie." But after all, someone has to wonder about the boeuf en daube and whether the quiche was authentic—right? And there is so much more to do. So many soufflés to test and throw out. So many ways of cooking asparagus to discover. So many pâtés to concoct. And so many things to talk about. Myra's new book. The record Poppy is making. Why Craig finally signed onto the Time-Life Cookbooks. Michael's latest article. So much to do. So many things to talk about . . .

THE BOO TABOO

JOHN SIMON

JUNE 24, 1968

Booing is not good manners in America, not even in New York, one reason that John Simon, whose columns were often the literary equivalent of booing—"You might call it a disposition," he says—seemed so scandalous. Simon, New York's theater critic for thirty-six years, could be effusive in his praise. But he was best known for his vitriolic reviews, which famously included biting, detailed descriptions of an actor's looks: "The vastness of that nose alone as it cleaves the giant screen from east to west," began a description of Barbra Streisand. So shocking was some of Simon's criticism that some producers tried to ban him. For Simon, booing (and criticizing) was not bad manners—he forgave those with vast noses if their acting excelled—but the expression of the critical faculties essential to the production of good art. In "The Boo Taboo," Simon offers a manifesto in defense of booing, and of standards. Simon has published several volumes of his collected criticism.

AND THE VOICE of the booer shall be heard in the land! What our theatres, opera houses and concert halls need is the introduction of the two-party system; as of now, all they have got is a dictatorship. It is the dictatorship of the assenters over the voices of dissent, of the applauders and the cheerers over the booers and hissers, and its effect on our performing arts is to encourage the status quo, however mediocre or lamentable it may be. There is an urgent or, if I may say so, crying need for the voices of protest to be given equal rights and equal time.

In a pioneer essay on the subject, the famous English drama critic, James Agate, wrote: "It seems to me to be unfair to allow the happy fellow to blow off steam by means of applause, and to deny the miserable man that small amount of hissing and booing which presumably are his safety-valve." But although Agate's 1926 essay comes out in defense of booing, it does not pursue its subject beyond a few light-hearted remarks and droll suggestions. Let us examine more closely what makes an American audience in 1968 applaud.

There are, obviously, those who applaud because they genuinely liked the play, opera, concert, recital, or ballet. Their judgment may be questioned, but their motives can not. But what about the others, the fellow-grovelers? There are those who applaud because it is the thing to do. There are those who believe, without any real feelings or opinions about what they have just witnessed, that applause shows discernment, connoisseurship, culture. There are others (and I proceed in an ascending order of sinisterness) who clap to show off: as if the loudness of their palms equaled the weightiness of their opinions. This group excels not only at the manual thunderclap but also at vocal bombardment. They erupt into promiscuous roars of *Bravo,* and even *Bravi* and *Brava,* to display either their knowledge of Italian, or their deftness in distinguishing the number and sex of the performers. At ballets, they applaud every last *entrechat,* drowning out the music and interrupting the flow of the work; at plays, they applaud every witticism, obliterating words and whole lines, and destroying the continuum of a scene. At the opera, they start their din in time to cut off the singer's last notes and the concluding orchestral accompaniment; at concerts, unfamiliar with the music, they applaud at the wrong places, and incite loud shushing. They want to get there with their noise first, loudest, and longest, their motto being, apparently, "I am heard, therefore I exist."

No better, however, are those who applaud because others are doing it, or because they have read favorable reviews, or because they firmly believe that whatever is put on at the Met, Philharmonic, or Carnegie Hall, or at a large Broadway theatre is guaranteed to be good. Things do not change much; back in 1885 Shaw observed: "In every average audience there is a certain proportion of persons who make a point of getting as much as possible for their money—who will *encore*, if possible, until they have had a ballad for every penny in their shilling . . . There is also a proportion—a large one—of silly and unaccustomed persons who, excited by the novelty of being at a concert, and dazzled by the glitter and glory of the Bow-street temple of Art, madly applaud whenever anyone sets the example. Then there are good-natured people who lend a hand to encourage the singer. The honest and sensible members of the audience, even when they are a majority, are powerless against this combination of thoughtless good-nature, folly, and greed."

Needless to say, I am for applause and even for cheering, however magnanimous or misguided the motive. Though I understand the 1609 preface to *Troilus and Cressida,* which recommends the play as one "never clapper-clawed with the palms of the vulgar," I am more in agreement with the imposing rages Paul Henry Lang, then music critic of *The Herald Tribune,* used to fly into every Eastertime when productions of *Parsifal* at the Met were greeted by the audience with reverential silence as though they were attending church services. But audience demonstrations should not interfere with what is happening on stage—does the entrance of a well-known actor have to be heralded by a clash of cymbal-like palms from the fans?—and, above all, they should not be the sole licensed spectator behavior, to the exclusion of counterdemonstrations. The boo and the hiss must be also franchised, as long as they do not obscure the actual sounds of performance.

I have used some actual political terminology deliberately. The American public must be awakened to the dignity and importance of art by education, criticism, and also—yes—by the lowly boo. Art matters fully as much as politics, the public must be told; for it is the politics of the spirit, while the politics proper are the politics of the body. All that good government can give us is material well-being, the political and the economic order and plenty enabling us to cultivate our minds and spirits. This cultivation, however, is the function of several disciplines—science, social science, philosophy, religion, etc.—not the least important, and possibly the most penetrating, of which is art. Thus what happens in the realm of the arts—which help us to see, feel, think and understand—is as significant as what happens in politics. Should then, I repeat, the politics of the mind and spirit be reduced to a one-party system?

The problem with the American audience is that it does not truly apprehend art. It is either in awe of it, or indifferent to it, or regards it as a commodity to be bought from time to time, like chutney or a new doormat. The first attitude stems from the Puritan origins of this country: the stage has taken over from the pulpit—which is quite an irony, considering how the Puritans loathed the theatre. The second attitude derives from general lack of culture: it takes, regrettably, centuries to acquire the kind of culture Europe, India, China, and Japan can boast of (and relatively little time to lose it—but that is another story). The third attitude results from the materialism of this society. But the healthy attitude toward art is a spontaneous give-and-take between stage and auditorium, a frank expression of approval or dispraise.

In a diary entry for April 19, 1897, Gerhart Hauptmann wrote, "The playwright does not write for the stage but for the souls of men. The stage is a mediator between him and these souls." In a 1946 article, Jean Cocteau spoke of "the bouncing back and forth of balls between the audience and the playwright." Whether you think of the relationship as communion or contest, there has to be an easeful exchange between platform and pit. European audiences have not been afraid to boo or hiss (or, according to the local equivalent, whistle) plays, operas, performances, whatever displeased them. The tradition is an ancient one. It is said that Euripides, approaching eighty, was driven from Athens by the jeers of his fellow-citizens. Far from cramping his style, this critical exile elicited from him *The Bacchae*, very possibly his most important play.

In our time, booing or its equivalent flourishes in many European countries. It reaches its acme at the Opera House in Parma, where the din of protesting audiences is sometimes considerably worse than what is being protested. But even this, for all its excess, strikes me as a sounder attitude than supine reverence without discrimination. For one thing, that audience really knows and cares about *bel canto*, and will not accept treasonable facsimiles. The singer may feel hurt, but if he is an artist sure of his ability, he will fight back and live to sing unhampered and applauded another day. As for the author, let me quote again from Agate's little essay: " 'A certain number of fleas is good for a dog,' once said an American humorist, 'it prevents him from brooding upon being a dog.' A certain amount of booing is good for a playwright; at any rate, it prevents him from brooding about being a successful one and thus growing intolerably vain."

Reminiscing about a director whom he admired, Brecht remarked in a 1939 lecture, "On Experimental Theatre," "Piscator's stage was not indifferent to applause but it preferred a discussion." A discussion is all very well, of course, but hard to come by in a theatre or concert hall; the dialogue of applause and booing will, to some extent, take its place. Probably the most famous such contest occurred at the premiere of Victor Hugo's *Hernani,* of which I quote a brief account from *The Oxford Companion to French Literature:* "The first two performances of *Hernani* [at the Comedie Francaise, 25 and 27 Feb. 1830] count among the great battles of the Romantics. News had spread that the piece was in every way—subject, treatment, and versification—a break with the dramatic conventions, and the theatre was packed with partisans. Below, in the expensive seats, were the traditionalists, determined to crush the play and with it the dangerous innovations of the new School. Above were the hordes of Hugo's admirers—young writers, artists, and musicians—led by Theophile Gautier (wearing a cherry-colored satin doublet which became legendary) and Petrus Borel, and all equally determined to win the day. At both performances, they outclapped, outshouted, and generally outdid the occupants of the stalls and boxes, with such effect that the success of the play—and of the Romantic movement—was thenceforth assured." The "Battle of *Hernani*" had actually begun in the street hours before curtain time, while Hugo supporters waited for the doors to open; one of them, Balzac, was hit in the face by a cabbage stalk a jeerer had plucked from the gutter.

But *Hernani* and Hugo prevailed, as Euripides had, as every important author, composer, performer had prevailed against unwarranted booing—and there is hardly an illustrious name in the verbal or musical theatre that escaped without some hisses and catcalls. But catcalls are catnip to genius, and even to talent. On the other hand, I am persuaded that many an unworthy work or artist was hastened to oblivion by well-placed hisses and boos; unfortunately for the documentation of my case, histories of past fakes and no-talents do not get written. As for today's impostors, they are still very much with us—perhaps from a lack of vociferous opposition.

It is not that booing does not occur in New York; but it is usually isolated and ineffectual. One of the rare exceptions took place at Carnegie Hall when the superb Russian cellist, Mstislav Rostropovich, saw fit to compound his error of commissioning a work for cello and orchestra from Lukas Foss by actually performing that work. It was an aleatoric mess, its garishness heightened by having some of the instruments, including the soloist's cello, electronically amplified, and the thing was conducted by the cockily histrionic composer in a manner that was almost more offensive than the piece itself. The battle of jeers and cheers was truly invigorating to experience—I joined in heartily with the former—and the victory, I think, was ours. At any rate, the work (whose pretentious title I have happily forgotten) has not, to my knowledge, shown up in concert since.

As a critic of drama and film I, of course, do not boo plays and movies (it does little good to boo celluloid, in any case); I review them instead. But at other events, where I am a paying customer and not a critic, I feel free to boo. When the Hamburg State Opera brought to New York its production of Gunther Schuller's derivative, pretentious, and vacuous *The Visitation* (an inept transposition of Kafka's *The Trial* into a simplistic American South), there was, I gather, quite some booing at the first performance at the Met. I attended the second, at which, for whatever reason, there were no boos, except for mine at the final curtain. A man came up to me and congratulated me on my good sense and courage. This was typical: the average American theatregoer, even when he realizes that he is being abused, wants someone else to do his protesting for him.

Another good time to protest is when the theatre provides a largely homosexual audience with Instant Camp. I remember, for example, a Poulenc memorial concert in Carnegie Hall, shortly after the composer's death. Among other events, Jennie Tourel performed some Poulenc songs, accompanied by Leonard Bernstein. There was Miss Tourel, the vocal and visual wreck of a once passable singer: splintered voice, wizened and overmade-up face, decrepit figure stuffed into a militantly Shirley

Temple-ish outfit. At the piano, Bernstein was at his ham-actorish best. The two, when they were not loving up the audience, flirted with each other, throwing lateral kisses, curtseys, and lovelorn *oeillades* across the stage. When they did get around to Poulenc, Miss Tourel not only made the songs crack in more directions than her make-up, she even burdened the lovely French words with something like a full-blown Bronx accent. Meanwhile, inverting the usual procedure, the ivories seemed to be tickling Leonard Bernstein, who was carrying on like a cockatoo in orgasm. When this appalling Lenny and Jennie act was over, I naturally booed it. A Frenchwoman, in the intermission, came up to shake my hand; several of my acquaintances in that generally orgiastic audience carefully cut me dead.

The most illuminating occurrence for me was a recent Saturday matinee at the Met. It was Barrault's wretched staging of *Carmen,* with Richard Tucker as Don José. Now Tucker had once been in possession of a good, strong voice; but he had never been a genuine artist with a sense of shading, expressive range, a feeling for the emotional depth of the part or the language in which he was singing. By this time, with even his basic organ gone, Tucker is long overdue for retirement. In this Don José, Tucker's voice was as off as it had been for years, his phrasing as unlovely as it had always been. Visually, he was a geriatric travesty; histrionically, even by the shockingly low standards of operatic acting, a farce. Even his French was, let us say, hyper-Tourelian. After he got through mangling the Flower Song, and after the orchestra was through as well, I added to the general applause three loud phooeys—a phooey cuts through applause better than a boo or hiss.

The reaction was instantaneous. From several boxes around the one I sat in came frantic retaliation—mostly of the "Shut up!" or "How dare you?" or "Go home!" variety, though one middle-aged woman intoned lachrymosely, "He has given you *years* of beauty!" When the lights went on, Rudolf Bing, who was sitting a couple of boxes away, had already dispatched his Pinkerton men after me, right into the box; but I walked out ignoring their reprimands. In the corridor, I was set upon by a mob of some twenty or thirty people berating me and following me almost to the bar with their objurgations and insults. The gist of it was that this sort of thing wasn't tolerated here, and if I was a foreign guest, I should behave or get the hell back wherever I came from. And that if I did not like it, I could not applaud or just leave. I countered that it did not seem to me fair and democratic to allow musical illiterates to clap and bellow their approval to their hearts' content, while someone who recognized the desecration of art was condemned to polite silence. In the following intermission (there had been no further incident during the next act), one of Bing's hugest goons, scowling ferociously, was back in the box once more, this time accompanied by a polite and human-sized person who introduced himself courteously as James Heffernan, house manager.

To summarize the ensuing battle of wits—if that is the term for it—Mr. Heffernan's point was that in Italy, where such a tradition exists, booing was fine, but that in "this house" it just wasn't done. My point was that if there was no such tradition here, it was high time to instigate one for the need was dire. Heffernan put forward that such booing might discourage the singer, to which I replied that that was the general idea. He then said that other people enjoying the performance were disturbed. I indicated that my boos did not come during the performing, which is more than could be said for some of the bravos and applause, and that if the audience had so little confidence in its own enthusiasm that one booer could make them doubt it, maybe doubt was called for. I added that if he wanted to exercise his authority usefully, he might go after the ignorant parvenus who talk through performances when they are not rattling their candy wrappers or jangling their vulgar bracelets. He admitted that this was a nuisance, but that, still and all, if I wished to protest, which he generously granted me the right to do, I should send a letter to Mr. Bing or Mr. Tucker. I told him that I would gladly write both of them my request that they retire, but that I doubted they would get my message. (The eminent poet and librettist, W. H. Auden, has remarked that he will not set foot in the Met while Bing is running it.) So, with a mixture of pleading and threatening looks, Heffernan and his sidekick left. I suspect that had my date and I been less well dressed, and had our seats been less expensive, the treatment accorded us would have been rather less ceremonious.

One understands, without condoning, the management's attitude—

particularly when a boo is heard, thanks to Texaco, across the U.S. and Canada. But the fury of the audience needs analyzing. It is caused, in part, by the middle-class American's confusion of critical indignation with bad manners, his incomprehension that at a theatre or opera house more is at stake than in your or the Jones's parlor. But, more importantly, it is the anger of the insecure *nouveau riche* who has paid a dozen Dollars for his seat, and who, for that much money, wants to be sure he is getting grade-A, U.S.-certified culture. He himself hasn't the foggiest notion what that might be; so if a boo implies that he might be getting damaged goods and, worse yet, be duped by them, his defensive dander is up.

As for the performer's attitude, it is useful to consult the epilogue of William Redfield's *Letters from an Actor* to find out how Richard Burton responded to one solitary booer of his Hamlet: in boundless fury at his wife's refusing to commiserate with him, he kicked in a television screen with his bare foot, damaging his toes as well. And it is even more enlightening to see how Redfield, who acted in that *Hamlet,* interprets the incident: "Now a booer, rare though he be, can be evaluated in a number of ways: (1) He is probably drunk, (2) if he isn't drunk, he is likely a frustrated actor, (3) if he is neither, he is certainly a minority, for booing is not a custom among American audiences, (4) he may very well be wrong." To which I should like to add (5), which hardly occurs to Redfield, that he may very well be right.

It is quite true in this country that the moment someone boos, the majority of the audience, including formerly passive elements, consider it their sacred duty to bravo and applaud for dear life, and prove thereby their dissociation from and superiority to the infamous booer. So booers will not have an easy time of it, either inside the hall or in the corridors outside. Sometimes, as in the case of *Hernani* (a poor play, by the way), history itself will prove them wrong. Yet in a day when the theatre is in sad shape, sinking ever deeper into public apathy, audience participation, sometimes of the most desperate kind, is universally viewed as the salvation. Booing, as long as it does not drown out the actual performance, seems to me a valid form of audience participation, one that would convince the lethargic of how vitally concerned some people are with the theatre. The effect on the authors and performers would be to keep them more in trim. And indignation, unhealthily stifled, would not force many out of the theatres altogether. We must stop being a nation of sheep-like theatregoers who wouldn't say boo to a goose—or turkey.

IF YOU'VE BEEN AFRAID TO GO TO ELAINE'S THESE PAST TWENTY YEARS, HERE'S WHAT YOU'VE MISSED

GEORGE PLIMPTON

MAY 2, 1983

It goes without saying that Elaine's has for decades been the city's indispensable literary saloon. Proprietress Elaine Kaufman was a sometimes stern, always loving mother to all manner of writers (along with machers and cops and many a searcher after the real New York). In trying to describe the restaurant's essence for a series of essays celebrating its twentieth year, George Plimpton considered recounting the evening he was bit on the ankle by an English gossip columnist. He decided instead to focus on the night he introduced an aspiring out-of-town writer to the Large Lady's, as he called Elaine's. Plimpton, the founder of The Paris Review, *died in 2003.*

A COUPLE OF YEARS AGO, Channel 12, the Philadelphia public-television station, had a fund-raising auction with a vast number of items offered, one of which was called "A Night on the Town With George Plimpton." I told the authorities down there that they were welcome to offer such a thing, but I doubted it would fetch very much.

Some weeks later I was telephoned and told that a gentleman named Jerry Spinelli had bid and paid four hundred and some-odd dollars to the television station for the "Evening." He and his wife would be coming up to New York.

I wondered vaguely what to do with them. We have a pool table at home. Perhaps the thing to do was to invite them home for drinks; we'd play some pool, and then leisurely we'd eat at some midtown restaurant— perhaps Gallagher's Steak House—so it would be an easy matter to put the Spinellis on a sensible train back to Philadelphia. I didn't know what else to suggest. I had called Spinelli to see if he and his wife would enjoy the theater . . . was there anything in particular they would like to see?

"Oh, no," he had said in an odd, strangled voice. He seemed very shy.

"How about pool?" I asked. "Would you like to shoot a bit of pool?"

"Pool!"

A couple of weeks later, the Spinellis turned up at the apartment. They arrived at seven o'clock. "How about a spot of pool?" I said to Mr. Spinelli. He was a thin, young man, with a quick, furtive smile.

While Mr. Spinelli and I played a somewhat desultory game, my wife took Mrs. Spinelli, whose name was Eileen, to show her the apartment. It was on their tour that my wife discovered the circumstances of the Spinellis' presence. While the Spinellis were looking at some books in the library, she pulled me out into the hall. She whispered hurriedly, "Jerry Spinelli's a writer."

"Oh, God."

"He's writing a novel." She went on to say that apparently he worked in the dawn, before he went off to his job, and also when he returned home in the evening. The writing had not been going well. That fateful night, Eileen Spinelli had been watching the Channel 12 TV auction—her husband flat out and exhausted in the bedroom—and when the "Plimpton Evening" was offered, she telephoned in her bid on impulse, feeling that the logjam in her husband's literary career might be broken by having a New York literary "connection."

"Oh Lord!"

"To pay for this," my wife said, "Eileen Spinelli told me she took just about *everything* they had out of savings. Four hundred and twenty-five dollars. She left $5 in there to keep the account open."

"What about the husband when he found out?"

"He was shocked."

I glanced into the library. The Spinellis were leafing through a large book on the coffee table.

I wondered aloud if we shouldn't somehow pay the couple's debt to Channel 12 and make ourselves the donors.

"We don't live in Philadelphia," my wife said, practically.

"Then we'll have to turn this into a literary evening."

"Right."

"They won't enjoy Gallagher's Steak House."

"No."

"We'll have to go to Elaine's."

When I told the Spinellis that we were going to Elaine's, Jerry Spinelli brightened visibly. He had heard a lot about it. "Do you think anybody'll be there?"

On the way up by taxi, I murmured a prayer that there *would* be a good literary crowd in Elaine's . . . at the very least the *Saturday Night Live* crowd, who seemed to get twenty of their number around a small table and all talk at the same time; if no luck there, perhaps a couple of *Esquire* editors could be pointed out, even if they were, in fact, stockbrokers. Indeed, I was perfectly willing to stretch a point—anyone with a beard I intended to identify as Donald Barthelme, the *New Yorker* short-story writer.

At Elaine's, the desirable places are what people in the know refer to as "the line"—perhaps ten tables in a row. When we arrived, I took a quick glance at the line: The sudden fancy crossed my mind that Madame Tussaud herself had been working for a week to get it set up for ourselves and the Spinellis. At the first table, just by the front door, Kurt Vonnegut was sitting with Jill Krementz. With them was an older man who looked vaguely like James T. Farrell. "Kurt," I said. I pushed Mr. Spinelli forward. "Kurt, this is Jerry Spinelli, from Philadelphia. Jerry, Kurt Vonnegut." I took a chance. "Jerry, may I present James T. Farrell. This is Jerry Spinelli from Philly."

"Mr. Farrell" looked somewhat bewildered.

I introduced Jill Krementz, and then we moved on to the next table.

Irwin Shaw was sitting there with Willie Morris, the former editor of *Harper's,* and the novelist Winston Groom. I introduced Spinelli to the table; there were pleasant nods and handshakes all around. At the next table, we paused to introduce ourselves to Gay Talese, who had just published *Thy Neighbor's Wife,* and A. E. Hotchner, the author of *Papa Hemingway.* "Mr. Talese, Mr. Hotchner, may I present Jerry Spinelli, the writer from Philadelphia." When he heard me introducing him as "the writer from Philadelphia," Mr. Spinelli beamed. We moved on to Bruce Jay Friedman, sitting with a large crowd. "Bruce, Mr. Spinelli, the writer from Philadelphia." Bruce rose and presented Mr. Spinelli to his friends.

We were approaching—very slowly because of all the bowing and introductions—the most famous table at Elaine's . . . the one just beyond the side door that leads out to the kitchens and the Siberian reaches of the restaurant out back. Often the table is empty, with a plain white RESERVED sign on it; but when the sign is removed, the table is almost invariably occupied by Woody Allen and his entourage. It is an odd table to be the most desired. Not only is it immediately adjacent to the ebb and flow of Elaine's waiters as they rush back and forth from the kitchens, but also it is just off the path of those forlorn people being herded back into the back room— what is officially referred to as the Paul Desmond Room, because the famous musician liked the quiet back there. Not only that, but the Allen table is on the route to the rest rooms; the traffic is considerable, with one of the main reasons being to get to table-hop en route to and from. Thus, the Woody Allen table, on the periphery of all this, is a place where one is jostled constantly, trays of osso buco sail alarmingly overhead like dirigibles, and when Allen is there, people stand in the doorway to the Desmond Room and stare.

At Elaine's, there is one famous house rule. At a place where table-hopping and squeezing in at a table to join even the vaguest of friends ("Mind if I join you?") is very much *de rigueur,* it is not done at Woody Allen's table. Even on the way to the Gents, nothing more than a side glance at the brooding figure of Woody Allen, mournfully glancing down at his chicken francese, which I am told is his favorite dish, is permissible. To interrupt his meal by leaning over and calling out "Hi ya, Woody, how's it going?" would be unheard of.

All of this was very much on my mind as our little band approached the Allen table, where the actor-writer was indeed in residence with a number of his friends. My first inclination was to stick to protocol and pass up his table to move on toward the far corner of the restaurant, where

I spotted Peter Stone, Dan Jenkins, Herb Sargent, Michael Arlen, and others available for introductions.

But I thought of Spinelli's $425, and the long trip up on Amtrak, and the $5 left in the savings account, and the half-finished manuscript in its typewriter-paper cardboard box.

"Woody," I said, "forgive me. This is Jerry Spinelli, the writer from Philadelphia."

Woody looked up slowly. It was done very dramatically, as if he were looking up from under the brim of a large hat.

"Yes," he said evenly. "I *know*."

We stood there transfixed. Allen gazed at us briefly, and then he returned to his contemplation of the chicken francese on his plate.

We moved off to our table. As I recollect, we skipped Peter Stone, Michael Arlen, and the other luminaries in the corner. Jerry Spinelli wanted to talk. He was beside himself. His face shone. He was not quite sure what had happened. "Did you hear *that*?" he asked. "Jesus *Christ!*" He ordered a bottle of Soave wine. He brandished a fork and spoke about Kafka. He asked about agents. He told us a little about his novel, which was about the life of a young boy. He wanted to know if Harper & Row was a good house. In the midst of his euphoria, his wife, Eileen, turned to me. "We've done a terrible thing," she whispered to me. "He's going to be unbearable. We've *spoiled* him!"

Three months ago, I received a letter from Jerry Spinelli. He was writing to tell me that his novel had been published by Little, Brown. It was a cheerful, chatty letter. Though he did not mention it, I knew he would want me to give his best regards to the gang up at Elaine's.

HOW TO DO A *REAL* CROSSWORD PUZZLE
Or What's a Four-letter Word for
"East Indian Betel Nut" and Who Cares?

STEPHEN SONDHEIM

APRIL 8, 1968

Stephen Sondheim, the famed composer and lyricist, had long been an in-veterate puzzle enthusiast, especially of "cryptic" British-style word puz-zles. "Constructing a crossword puzzle is like constructing a lyric," he says. Sondheim composed New York's *puzzles for a year, bicycling down to the office to drop them off himself. "Eventually, I'd go back and do a man's work," he says, and turned to writing the music and lyrics for* Com-pany, *which ran on Broadway for nearly two years. He's won an Academy Award, many Tonys and Grammys, and a Pulitzer Prize. This essay, which was meant to introduce his puzzles, appeared in the very first issue of the magazine.*

T HERE ARE CROSSWORD puzzles and crossword puzzles. The kind familiar to most New Yorkers is a mechanical test of tirelessly esoteric knowledge: "Brazilian potter's wheel," "East Indian betel nut" and the like are typical definitions, sending you either to *Webster's New International* or to sleep. The other kind, prevalent in Great Britain but inexplicably nonexistent in the United States apart from *The Nation* and an occasional Sunday edition of *The New York Times,* is a test of wits. This kind of puz-zle offers cryptic clues instead of bald definitions, and the pleasures in-volved in solving it are the deeply satisfactory ones of following and matching a devious mind (that of the puzzle's author) rather than the transitory ones of an encyclopedic memory.

To call the composer of a crossword an author may seem to be dignifying a gnat, but clues in a "British" crossword have many characteristics of a literary manner: cleverness, humor, even a pseudo-aphoristic grace. In the best puzzles, styles of clue-writing are distinctive, revealing special pockets of interest and small mannerisms, as in any prose style. The clues of the author who calls himself "Ximenes" in the London *Sunday Observer* are, to the eye of a puzzle fan, as different from those in, say, *The Manchester Guardian* as Wilde is from Maugham. But a "Bantu hartebeest" remains a "Bantu hartebeest" whether it's in *The New York Times* or the *Daily News*.

Railway coaches, undergrounds, lunch counters, and offices in England hum with the self-satisfied chuckles of solvers who suddenly get the point of a clue after having stared at it for several baffled minutes. Bafflement, not information, is the keystone of a British puzzle. A good clue can give you all the pleasures of being duped that a mystery story can. It has surface innocence, surprise, the revelation of a concealed meaning, and the catharsis of solution. Solving a British puzzle is far more rewarding than dredging up arcane trivia and is not annoyingly difficult once you've been initiated into the methods of solution. It's a matter of mental exercise, not academic clerk-work, and all it takes is inexhaustible patience, limitless time, and a warped mind.

For crossword fans who, out of fright, have never attempted solving cryptic clues and for those who have, but with limited success, this article will serve as an initiation ceremony, with some ground rules.

In a British puzzle, definitions are called "clues." This is not a pedantic distinction. Each clue, in actuality, is in two parts—a definition (i.e., a synonym) and an elliptical indication of the answer. In a scrupulously written clue these two parts are separate and distinct but blended in such a way as to cause maximum confusion. (The clues in the London *Times*, incidentally, are not always scrupulous.) Theoretically, therefore, this kind of clue is easier than the usual straightforward definition because you get two indications of the answer for the price of one. But a good clue is a deceptive clue and may fool you.

The problem for the solver is that the words in a clue may, if taken literally, mean something quite different from their apparent meaning. Here's a clue, for example: "Stares at torn pages (5)." (Numbers in parentheses following a clue are a conventional notation in British puzzles and indicate the number of letters in the answer, saving you the bother of counting squares in the diagram.) "Stares at torn pages" may suggest at first glance some obscure term in bibliophilia, but what the phrase really means is "A word meaning 'stares at' whose letters are those of 'pages' out of their normal order." In however veiled a way, that is *literally* what it says. "Stares at" is a synonym for GAPES; "torn," in this context, means "separated with violence so that the parts are out of their normal order." So there are two separate and distinct references to GAPES, one a definition and one an elliptical description of the way the word is formed. Your problem is merely to punctuate the clue in an odd way: "Stares at/torn 'pages.' "

Mental repunctuation is the essence of solving cryptic clues. Punctuation in ordinary writing is a guide telling the reader where and how long to pause. But the clue-writer, instead of trying to make the true meaning clear, is trying to hide it.

There are seven basic kinds of clues, according to Ximenes, the current Dean of British puzzles.

1. *Anagrams.* These are indicated by some word or phrase such as "bad," "torn," "confused," "erratically," "naughty," etc., words which imply that a mixture of letters is to take place. The anagram is of the word or words actually printed, not of synonyms. E.g., in "Wed a silly admirer (7)," "silly" is the operative word. A "silly" treatment of the letters in "admirer" would lead to MARRIED, which is defined by "wed." Simple? Yes. Tricky? Yes. Fair? Yes. Try this one: "American confused by wide-screen movie (8)." (Solutions to these examples are at the end of the article.) And don't forget, an anagram can be of more than one word. Like "A snit is the most foolish basis for disagreement (10)."

2. *Multiple meanings.* This form of clue combines two or more definitions (and not always the primary or most obvious defini-

tions) of the answer in a misleading way. E.g., "Fight enclosure in the theater (3)" may look baffling but is simply two meanings of a single word strung together to make a peculiar set of associations. The answer, as you've guessed, is BOX. In this type of clue, watch out for words that look like one part of speech but turn out to be another. "Deliver from bar (4)" leads to SAVE in two senses: "deliver from" and "bar" (as a preposition meaning "except").

3. Reversals. These clues lead to words which, when read backwards, form other words. Indications like "reflex," "looking back," "from East to West" (in the case of Across words), and "upwards," "doing a headstand," "rising" (in the case of Down words), are what you should be on the alert for. E.g., "Emphasized trifles—in a roundabout way (8)." Here there is a small extra deception in that "trifles" doesn't refer to trivia but to desserts, which, when looked at "in a roundabout way" are STRESSED, which means "emphasized." Two or more words may be reversed, too, of course. As in "Push through the District Attorney—otherwise he lies back (8)." Get it? Well, first try to decide which is the definition part of the clue. Still don't get it? Look at the answer at the end of the column.

4. Charades. These lead to words which fall into convenient complete parts. Here's an example from Ximenes: "Remains precisely how he is (5)." You probably wouldn't think of "remains" as a noun in this context, but that's the definition. And the answer is ASHES. "How he is" becomes "As he's"—the whole word is a phrase in itself. Here's another: "One in flames made a landing (4)." "One" = a, "in flames" = lit, "made a landing" = ALIT. Here's one: "Sinister purpose of an auction? (10)." (Question marks and exclamation points at the ends of clues usually indicate some form of pun or outrageous misuse of meaning).

5. Container and Contents. This type of clue resembles the Charades type in having wholes and parts, but the parts are outside and inside instead of side by side. Words in the clue like "in," "around," "holding," and "embraces" are signs of Containers. E.g., "Crooner takes clarinet inside—good manners (8)." What crooner?

Bing, of course. A clarinet is a what? A reed. Let BING take a REED "inside" and you get BREEDING. Good manners.

Both Containers and their Contents often employ symbols and abbreviations, as in fact do all sorts of clues. But only well-known symbols and abbreviations are used and, in the Americanized puzzles on these pages, only those known to the American reader. There are dozens which pop up continually. When you see North, East, West or South or "point" (meaning compass-point) in a clue, think of N, E, W, or S. For "nothing" or "no" or "love" (as in a tennis score), think of O. For "about," keep in mind "re" (meaning "concerning") or "c" (abbreviation for "circa"). "Note" often refers to notes of the scale—"do," "re," "mi," etc. "One" may mean "a," "an," or "I." Other Roman numerals, too: V, X, L, C, D, and M might be indicated by their arabic equivalents. "Steamship" for SS, "saint" or "street" for ST, "glamor" for IT or SA (abbreviation of Sex Appeal), "acceptable" or "high-class" for U (as opposed to non-U), "first-rate" for AI (A1), "soft" or "loud" for P or F (musical dynamics)— these are a few of the devices to watch for. Unusual abbreviations will always be hinted at by "briefly" or "in short." "General, in short" could indicate GEN as part of a word.

Here are some Container clues that use these devices: "When Peg holds a note, it comes out clear (5)." Look for a word meaning "peg" that holds a word meaning "note" that will make a word meaning "clear." How about "High priest seen in the morning in Los Angeles (4)"?

6. *Puns*. Some clues deal with homonyms—words of different meaning which have the same sound. Indications of them usually consist of phrases like "we hear" and "sounds like," as in "We hear the new musical is German (4)." The new musical is *Hair* and we hear it as HERR (German as a noun). Two-word puns are even lower and more frequent, as in "Ethyl alcohol is one way to kill a fish if you listen closely (6)." Ethyl alcohol is SPIRIT (yes, "spirits" can be singular)—listen to it closely.

7. *Hidden*. These clues are both the easiest to solve and the

most deceptive. They involve burying the answer in the letters of the clue—either within a word or as a bridge between words. In point of fact the answer stares you so innocently in the face that you often don't see it. Watch out for indications like "seen in," "within," "containing," "found in," "some of." E.g., "This girl appears in black at every party (4)." Can you see KATE there staring out of "black at every"? Or "Beg for a piece of an apple a day (5)." Which piece? The core—that is, the core of "apple a day," which is PLEAD.

Those are the basic types of cryptic clues in their simplest forms, but you will encounter many which are combinations of two or more types: clues, for example, which contain Anagrams and Reversals within the Container, like "Return to look around the dilapidated tavern for tires (9)." This is a characteristically complex clue. In attacking it, you should first off suspect the word "return" and connect it with "to look." "To look" is to see, so "return" it: EES. "Around" suggests that EES is "around" another word: E. . . . ES. What word? A "dilapidated tavern," of course—and your now-warped mind should tell you that "dilapidated" indicates an anagram. There are six letters missing still in the answer and "tavern" has six letters, so your hunch is confirmed. EntreavES? Check the dictionary to see if it's an obscure word for rubber wheels ("tires"). No—I told you there would be very few obscure words. Ah—EnervatES! "Tires" as a verb, meaning "weakens."

One more complex example should suffice before you plunge in or throw your pencil down in disgust. "*The Last of the Mohicans* is my composition paper (6)." Looks like a needless piece of information instead of a clue, but take it apart. Literally. Suppose that the answer, the word itself, is speaking. Then you could repunctuate the sentence something like this: "The, last of the Mohicans, is—my composition; paper." The first part is what composes "me": i.e., THE, S (last of the Mohicans in the sense of the last letter of "the Mohicans"), IS. THESIS. And what does it mean? Paper (in the sense of a doctorate or term paper). Note two further devices used in this clue: first, that "I" or some other form of the first person may refer to the word itself. "I run," for example, might be the definition part of a clue to MILER or RIVER or even POLITICIAN. Second, part-words are often trickily spliced into a clue. Just as "The Last of the Mohicans" indicated S, so a "tailless bird" might be BIR, "half a sixpence" might be ENCE or SIXP, and a "beheaded King" might be ING. Always look for the possible literal meaning of a clue.

Well, if you've slogged through the undergrowth of all this logodaedaly (a word *worth* going to the dictionary for) and are still unruffled, it should give you a start (pun meaning both "beginning" and "unpleasant surprise"). In the *Listener*-type puzzles which will appear on these pages, the solving of clues is only part of the task. (The *Listener* is a weekly publication of the BBC.) The puzzles have a gimmick of some sort which is fully explained in the Instructions accompanying the diagram. Be prepared for odd shapes, sizes, and problems. Sometimes, for example, the words you enter into the diagram (or "lights," as the British call them) are not the same as the answers to the clues. The light may be a word associated with the answer (e.g., the answer may be ABER-CROMBIE but the light may be FITCH) or it may be the answer in code or the answer with all vowels omitted or whatever the composer of the puzzle has in mind to torture you with. Most often, however, the light and the answer are one and the same, and always there are Instructions if some device is involved, so don't worry. Not this week, anyway.

The puzzle will employ as few East Indian betel nuts as possible and they will hopefully be more challenging and rewarding than those which do. The rewards, by the way, will be material as well as intellectual: each week copies of *Chambers 20th Century Dictionary* (published by Hawthorn Books, Inc. and available at bookstores at $5.50) will be awarded to the senders of the first three correct solutions opened (we will open submissions not in order of receipt but all at once on the day of deadline—some contestants would otherwise suffer from living in outlying postal districts, such as The Bronx). If no solutions are received, the prizes will be held over, accumulating as in a sanitation strike, and the offices of *New York* will eventually open a gift shop.

If you haven't ripped these pages up by now, clip them out and keep them as a guide for future weeks. And as for "Bantu hartebeest," I say it's "lebbek"—and I say the hell with it.

Answers to clues unsolved in the text above:

1. *Anagrams:* CINERAMA (American) ANTITHESIS (A snit is the . . .)
3. *Reversals:* RAILROAD (D.A./or/liar)
4. *Charades:* FORBIDDING
5. *Containers:* PLAIN (p-la-in) LAMA (L.-A.M.-A.)

New York Magazine Puzzle

By Stephen Sondheim

INSTRUCTIONS

The heavy bars in the diagram indicate the beginnings and ends of words, just as black squares do in the usual crossword puzzle. The numbers in parentheses at the end of each clue denote the number of letters in the "light" (the answer to be filled in).

In this puzzle, fifteen of the lights have no written clues: there are five Theme-words, A, B, C, D, and E, which form a familiar group with something in common. Each Theme-word has its own pair of "variations" with a certain relationship to it. The relationship is somewhat different in each case.

E.g., if Theme-word A were SALT, its variations might be SAILOR and TAR; and if Theme-word B were PEPPER, its variations might be VIM and THROUGH (pep = vim, per = through).

Ignore punctuation, which is designed to confuse.

CLUES

ACROSS

1 Theme-word A (8). Variations: 13 (4) and 36 (4)
11 Entertain and wind again? (6)
14 "Foremen Do"—poem in Old English (7)
18 Is it unnecessary to want fewer things? (8)
19 The straight prefix bit—ha! (5)
21 What's gone by sounds like it went by (4)
22 "Tramp, tramp, tramp"—a catchphrase (6)
24 Theme-word B (6). Variations: 28 (5) and 8 Ac. (4)
26 Heavy wig they messed up (7)
27 Uproot the house plant at the station? (5)
29 This Unit is still part of the Resistance (3)
31 Theme-word C (9). Variations: 31 Dn. (5) and 17 (4)
34 State housing South American Men's Club (3)
37 Hydrogen weapon can cause injury . . . (4)
39 . . . or about the opposite (5)
41 Take back the bet—I may explode (4)
42 All ten ruined with anger (6)
43 To carve with hesitation is more dainty (5)
45 Purge from the East—so be it, from the East (5)
46 Theme-word D (8). Variations: 16 (5) and 5 (3)
47 What goes from the center to the edge in the Strad I use (6)
48 Considers an affront almost all the gifts (7)

DOWN

1 Theme-word E (5). Variations: 30 (5) and 12 Ac. (3)
2 Concerning the district income (7)
3 Oh, gosh, the moulding's like an S (4)
4 Water propeller sounds like the alternative (3)
6 Drinks all around might cause song (4)
7 Negative printed in brown-orange (3)
8 One with a lot of gossip (3)
9 Is unable to talk hypocritically (4)
10 Carol is to sing just as Morris is to dance (7)

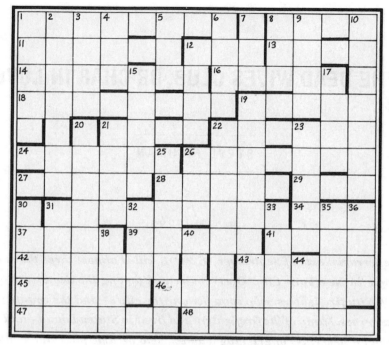

The solution appears on page 571.

12 The last letter is in French relish (4)
15 Lean out of a gas-lantern (5)
19 Members of the ruling class use rash logic, being spoiled (9)
20 Left the role in the middle of the Act (8)
21 Laborer with nothing in prison (4)
22 This is a prison term. This is another. (8)
23 Write for someone else with spirit (5)
25 Ice gliders from Sark, set in motion (7)
26 Half this is an idiot—all this is quite the reverse (3)
32 Dance from "The Spanish Hour" (4)
33 Hesitation in French-born musician's note (5)
35 Concerning part of a permanent wave (5)
38 Does she stick on one note in "La Boheme"? (4)
40 Successor to "The Sound of Music" (4)
44 Heavy French fashion (3)

THE DEAD WIVES CLUB, OR CHAR IN LOVE

STEVE FISHMAN

MAY 31, 2004

The terrorist acts of September 11, 2001, killed almost three thousand people in New York City. Overrepresented among the dead were New York City firefighters, who soon became the city's—and the country's—new heroes. Many of the firefighters had lived in Staten Island—and left behind a new class of grieving widows, who became powerful symbols of the tragedy. Steve Fishman heard that, privately, they had given themselves an irreverent new name, **The Dead Wives Club,** *and he set out to learn more about this exclusive club. His story explores the power and limits of the mourning process. "They were viewed by outsiders as mired in grief, but when you met them they wanted something else entirely," he says. Fishman, a contributing editor, is the author of* A Bomb in the Brain *and* Karaoke Nation; Or, How I Spent a Year in Search of Glamour, Fulfillment, and a Million Dollars, *which began as a* New York *story.*

*C*HARLENE FIORE—everyone calls her Char—was at her regular dinner with ten other Staten Island widows, who had unexpectedly become her closest friends. They'd been meeting weekly at restaurants across the island—Forest Gardens, Brioso, or at R.H. Tugs, where they could peer across the harbor. The widows would occupy one large table and, each time, try a new drink. This particular night, Char was on a tear. The subject was that word, *widow*.

Char is five-eight, with blond hair, a bright smile, light-blue eyes, long legs, on one of which she had tattooed the name Mike. At dinner, she tended to smoke as much as she ate. She had dropped to 112 pounds.

"Widow? Isn't that a horrible word?" she said to her friends. Char's voice sounds a little like a cork popping. "Widow, it's like a bug. It's *yucky*. Who ever came up with it?"

Char was still getting used to being a widow. Or, actually, one of *the* widows. Her husband, Mike, like the husbands of all the women at the table, had been among the 343 firemen who died in the World Trade Center on September 11, 2001. From that day on, Char says, "It was, get the widows into the church, get the widows out of the rain, get the widows to the front of the line."

What else could you do with weepy women? "They had all these emotions," says a fireman who'd known Char's husband. Another reason the widows were escorted to the seat next to the mayor, with whom they would become quite chummy, was that they'd been assigned starring roles in a national tragedy. "Char belongs to the people now," is how another of Char's friends put it. Recently, she'd been invited to a Knicks game—her husband had been a star basketball player for the Fire Department team. At halftime, she and her three teenage kids were ushered to center court, where they blinked into a standing, cheering crowd. *Because my husband died?* thought Char.

But Char knew. She and her friends had become stand-ins for an entire country's tender emotions. "A symbol of America's grief," Char sometimes thought unhappily. In Staten Island, where Char had met her husband on a softball field, the widows were an even more poignant symbol. After all, Staten Island was home to seventy-eight dead firefighters, more per capita than anywhere else. And often it seemed as if the entire borough—blue-collar, Italian, Irish, patriotic, Catholic—had one unyielding goal: to hold fast its dead.

Char sometimes thought she could drive from one end of the island to the other and never leave a street named for a victim of September 11. The dead were memorialized in a corner bar dedicated to a dead fireman—it said so on the sign—as well as a bowling league and a high-school gymnasium and a softball field. A basketball league and a grammar-school playground were named for Char's husband.

Later, Charlene's widow friends would be thought of as the unappeasable widows, the wealthy widows, the lustful widows. But at the start, when they were assuming their new roles, the widows were the perfect virgins of grief, which was how they were supposed to stay. "The public wants you to live up to what they made you," reflects Char. "They don't really want you to move on."

OKAY, CHAR SAID to the dinner table of widows. Wasn't there another way they could refer to themselves? "How about 'the grieving widows'?" Everyone thought of them that way anyhow. After a little discussion, someone shortened it to the GWs, which had a nice ring and was, to Char's mind, funnier. "That was a widow's joke," Char says. "You had to be one to get it."

GWs would become their own best friends, drifting away from many of those Char occasionally thought of as the Alive Wives, meaning their husbands were alive. The widows, Char called the Dead Wives. "You were in one club or the other," Char says. "You wouldn't want to be in the Dead Wives Club, but we found ourselves in it." They really did seem a club. The GWs went to therapy together and to bowling and to the cemetery, though, of course, no one was buried there. They comforted one another and vacationed together.

Also, and this was important, the GWs looked to the future together, a brighter future. A handful of widows (not, for the most part, those who had been married to Staten Island firemen) had turned political. They clung to the past in order to push for investigations. Char's GW friends wanted to let go of the past, at least a little. They shared a secret. Two and a half years after September 11, they didn't really feel like GWs, or not entirely. Lately, when the GWs got together, they didn't talk only about their sadness. They were young, they reminded each other, and they were single and, though they didn't have to say this, wealthy; they had their husbands' salaries and, soon, thanks to the federal government, millions in settlements. The girls—that's how Char refers to them—wanted to date. What a word! It sounded juvenile, embarrassing, guilty, to women who'd almost all met their husbands as teenagers, and, as they well knew, undignified for symbols of a nation's grief. Still, one therapist drew their attention to *Match.com*. Slowly, they took off their wedding rings. "It's difficult to go on a date with a wedding band on," says one. Adds another, "I miss being in love."

WHEN CHAR'S PHONE rang on September 11, 2001, she was already at her friend Jean Fischer's house. Mike had been a fireman for nineteen years, as long as they'd been married. For the past ten, he'd worked at Rescue 5, the elite fire station on Staten Island. Mike hadn't called, but then he never did. Char wasn't the type to think dire thoughts. They joked about the job's dangers. Their son would shout to Mike as he left for work, "Get crispy."

So it was Char's mother—she'd hurried over when she saw the TV— who took the call. The firehouse was on the line. Char distinctly recalls the message her mother relayed: "We don't know where he is, but he's fine."

Char called the station to double-check. They assured her that Mike was fine, though still not located. Later still, she'd get a third reassuring message. *Thank God,* Char thought between cigarettes—Char was usually between cigarettes.

Char turned her attention to Jean, whose husband, a Fire Department lieutenant in Manhattan's Ladder 20, was missing. She hadn't gotten any reassuring messages. Jean's husband and Char's had grown up together in Staten Island. Most summers, the two families vacationed together, a week at Great Adventure. Char left her three kids with her mother and hurried over to Jean's house. It was a six-minute drive in her Tahoe.

Jean refused to put on the TV. She and Char sat on the front stoop and waited for the phone to ring. Jean's neighbor Cheri Sparacio—Jean and Cheri share a driveway—was outside, too. Cheri, three months pregnant, waited for her husband, a currency trader in the World Trade Center, to get off the bus, as he usually did. She joined Jean and Char on the stoop.

Char's kids phoned. "Why hasn't Daddy called?" they asked. "Mommy, come home."

"No, Daddy's fine, but Mrs. Fischer's not fine," Char said. "Daddy's busy. He's working."

Around midnight, Char's mother called. Char had to come home. The kids had been watching TV and were going nuts. At Jean's house, people had started to show up—the Fire Department's efficient support network had kicked in—so Char drove home.

Toward one in the morning, Char was putting out the garbage on the side of her house, thinking the kind of thought she sometimes had: Firemen's wives do everything, since the guys are often gone. Just then, a gray pickup pulled in across the street. In the truck, Char could make out two guys, a fireman from Mike's house, Gerry Koenig, who she figured was driving Mike home. She waited for them to cross the street when she noticed something. All hell had broken loose today, yet Gerry wore a blue uniform shirt and a tie.

Char's reaction was to run. She'd been a fireman's wife long enough. She knew the Fire Department required proper dress of those who deliver unhappy news. Char circled around the truck, away from Gerry. He followed her.

"Why are you here? You shouldn't be here," she shouted over her shoulder. "Mike would never have left you there."

"Char, it doesn't look good," Gerry said.

"Where's Mike? Go get Mike."

Then Char's mother started to call her girlfriends, and the next thing Char knew it was three in the morning, and the house had fifty people in it. (Gerry, meanwhile, drove twenty minutes to Madeline Bergin's house— her husband was in the same firehouse as Char's husband. He had more bad news.)

The next day, people brought over fruit, junk food, flowers, even checks—she got so many flowers she sent some to Cheri, who didn't have the Fire Department's network. (Cheri's news was bad, too, like Jean Fischer's.) And crowds of people, hundreds of them, filled Char's house, which Char thought was irritating and a little funny. Wouldn't Mike, officially just missing, be really impressed when he came home and saw all the friends he had?

A week later, people were still there. Char said, "If I sat on the front steps, there were twelve people on the front steps. I'd go in the backyard, and twenty people were sitting around."

All of a sudden, Char was really wanting to talk to Madeline Bergin. Previously, they'd moved in different circles. Madeline, who'd just turned forty, was a kindergarten teacher. Her husband had recently bought a bar and planned to run it when he retired from the Fire Department. Char, then forty-five, owned a children's-clothing store. Char hunted up Madeline's number, went into her bathroom, locked the door.

"People you haven't seen in twenty years, are they ringing your doorbell?" Char asked Madeline.

"Oh, my God!" said Madeline.

"Me too," said Char. "Do they keep staring at you?"

They did.

"Me too."

Later that night, like at 2 A.M., Char was drinking a glass of wine, and Madeline called.

"Can you sleep?"

"No. Can you?"

"No."

Char was hardly quiet, but Madeline was a real talker. They went on for two hours.

Char's best friend at the firehouse had been another wife, whose husband had survived. She didn't stop by to see Char until three weeks had passed, at which point Char asked, "What are you doing here?" She said something about her kids, but Char knew the real reason: They were in different clubs now. Madeline became Char's new close friend, and not a day went by that they didn't talk two or three times, and often during the night, since they didn't sleep very much. Char and Madeline befriended another widow from the firehouse, Lisa Palazzo, thirty-one at the time.

Char was thrown together with other widows from her husband's firehouse, which had lost eleven guys—almost half its crew—and she remained close to Jean Fischer, though she never saw Jean's neighbor, Cheri. Cheri was a 9/11 widow, too, but she was civilian, and as if that wasn't divide enough, she once publicly bristled that so much attention was paid to fallen firefighters. Was her dead husband's life worth any less? She and the firefighter's wife next door stopped speaking.

The widows became Char's essential friends, especially Mad and Li—Char shortens everyone's name. At the memorial for Lisa's husband, one of the first, Char and Madeline promised to stick by Lisa. Hundreds of people attended, including the mayor, and the firemen ushered the widows up front in their good dresses and manicured nails.

Char, though, was having trouble with all the solemn behavior. She urged Lisa to show the video—Lisa made a tape of the funeral for her young kids—to her husband when he arrived home. "How many people get to witness their own funerals?" Char whispered to Lisa.

Then Char told Mad, "I need a bar." When no one was looking, they grabbed each other and sneaked across the street. Char wasn't much of a drinker, but there she was, trying pink Cosmopolitans, six of them. Eventually, the captain spotted them, and the two tipsy GWs had to return to the funeral home, though before being escorted out, Char managed to grab one last Cosmo in a paper coffee cup.

When they returned, Lisa started shouting, "Where did you two go?" She was nervous about sitting next to the mayor. "I'd never met a mayor before," she said.

"The bar," Char told her. "But don't worry, we brought one for you." Char handed her the coffee cup.

Then Lisa pulled Madeline into the chair of honor—the two of them squeezed into the seat next to the mayor.

"See what it feels like," Lisa said. They put their heads down. Their shoulders, their backs shook. Passersby touched them gently. Later, Madeline said, "They all thought we were crying." Really, though, they couldn't stop their nervous giggling.

Char was stowed behind a row of uniformed firemen, where she sat and pulled the stray threads off their jackets.

At Mike's memorial, a few weeks later, Char was following the A-and-W diet—Altoids and wine. She worked out a system with Joe Sykes, a Staten Island fireman who'd known Mike since they were six years old. Hundreds of people stood on a receiving line. Char hugged so many firemen in polyester uniforms that a red sore spread across the bottom of her chin where it rubbed their shoulders. Civilians in ordinary coats and ties approached, too. Char shook their hands.

When Joe spotted civilians approaching, he'd say, "Char, would you like some water?"

"Thank you, Joe," Char would answer sweetly.

He'd hand her a glass of wine, which she drank as she shook civilian hands. When firemen neared, Joe would hand her the Altoids, and she'd go back to hugging. It was craziness, "accepted craziness," Joe would say later.

At the funeral home, Char finally broke down. Her son had sobbed as the oak coffin came off the fire truck until Char whispered, "He's not in there." (Empty coffins were the original widow's joke.) But how long could she insist Mike was just missing? Char fled to the funeral home's basement.

"The show's waiting for you," Joe said when he found her.

"I don't want to be in the show," Char answered.

"Char, this is the only time the show won't go on if you don't come."

Joe was so great. Char talked to him a couple times every day, the way she'd talked to Mike. He laughed with her—"It's weird, we actually had fun," Joe says—and drove her around, throwing his siren on if traffic backed up. He was by her side at the morgue where Char's kids got their mouths swabbed for DNA identification. Tears ran down her thirteen-year-old's face. The medical examiner, unfazed, just said, "Open."

About a year later, Madeline would fall for the firefighter assigned to help her—it was Gerry Koenig, who'd delivered the bad news to Char—and some didn't like it. He'd been her husband's close friend. Also, he was married, though the marriage was troubled. "In the beginning, nobody was really happy about it" was how one fireman from their station put it. "We were supposed to stay away from that kind of thing." They wondered about Gerry's motives.

By now, everyone knew the widows expected a windfall. Had that affected Gerry's thinking? But Madeline knew Gerry wasn't insincere. "I miss him, too," he'd tell her. "Gerry loved my husband, too," said Madeline, who, nonetheless, sometimes called Char in tears, unsure if she was doing the right thing.

Char knew how sadness could open you up to someone. "It's just total grief and dependency, and you don't realize what's happening. I depended on Joe one hundred percent. I became very attached to this man, as attached as I was to my husband." Joe is happily married and has quadruplets. His relationship with Char wasn't romantic, though she once told him, "I wish you could marry two people. You could stay married to your wife and marry me too."

"That's what she needed to feel at that time," Joe says, "I was grieving, too. She helped me get over a lot of things." Joe counted: He'd worked with more than one hundred of the dead firemen.

"Joe basically stayed around long enough for me to let go of that," Char said. "For me to be able to stand on my own two feet."

STATEN ISLAND IS a boomtown of affordable housing, where every third or fourth block seems to hold a subdevelopment of near-identical homes on tenth-of-an-acre lots. It's the perfect setting for firemen seeking middle-class family life. Firemen tend to be family men, and sometimes live in two-family houses with relatives (who make convenient babysitters), or on the same block with them, or, like some firefighter brothers, back-to-back, so they can share one large backyard. On Sundays, extended families—including, as in Char's case, three generations of men with the same name—convene for dinner or, on a warm day, backyard barbecues, the smell of which carries all the way to the ferry.

After almost twenty years on the job, a fireman can earn a respectable $72,000, though with heavy deductions against future benefits, he takes home just $1,009 every two weeks, one reason so many firemen's wives work. Still, a fireman loves his job. He can schedule an entire workweek in two days, which allows time to work a second job, coach the kids' teams, and still grab an afternoon by the pool he put in with his firehouse buddies. There he'd sit, beer in hand, and wonder, as one fireman phrased it, "What are the poor people doing today?"

Of course, every contented fireman knows one shining irony. As Mike sometimes ribbed Char, "I'm worth more to you dead than alive."

He didn't know the half of it. To start, every fireman's widow received the line-of-duty death benefit—$262,000. And then, the moment the towers collapsed, people across the country wrote checks. The charity totaled $1.4 billion, of which at least $350 million was earmarked for rescue workers. The Twin Towers Fund alone doled out more than $400,000, on average, to each family of a rescue worker. This didn't include donations to firehouses. People had walked checks into Charlene's firehouse, which received, unsolicited, more than $500,000. That money was divided among the families of the eleven victims.

Plus, the government set up the Victim Compensation Fund, which awarded each family an average of $1.7 million.

All told, a fireman's widow would probably receive between $2 million and $3 million, sometimes more, much of it tax-free, plus their husband's salary, also tax-free, for the rest of their lives, as well as any life insurance they'd purchased.

Most widows didn't overhaul their lives, which still revolve around the kids. But some things changed, starting with the anxiety over money. "I don't have to work ever again if I don't want to," Char says. That was just the fact. Madeline, Lisa, and Char don't work these days. Char still has the store, but hardly ever goes in. Staten Island started to seem like a place of fancy new "widow cars," as Char joked. Widows drove Mercedes SUVs and Jaguars and Infiniti SUVs. After her Tahoe fell apart, Char went car shopping with Madeline and Lisa. Madeline had already purchased a minivan, and Lisa an SUV. Char's kids wanted an Escalade, a $50,000 car. Char bought it without even looking at it. She'd buy a spaceship if it put a smile on their faces.

Houses got renovated. Char hardly went crazy. She installed an inground pool to replace her aboveground pool. Another widow redid her house top to bottom. She and her husband had planned to do it together, probably over ten years, doing most of the work themselves. Now she had the money to hire an architect who could finish it in one shot. Some women, single again, spent money on their looks. "I know it's a vain thing, but it makes me feel better," one plastic surgeon recalls being told by a widow. He provided collagen, Botox, and peels to three firemen's widows on Staten Island. One widow went to the plastic surgeon on her wedding anniversary. At the office, she broke down in tears. He didn't charge her. He stopped charging all of them.

Wealth, though, made the widows a more complicated symbol of grief. Could you really be grief-stricken if you never had to work again? Some neighbors and relatives seemed to quiver with resentment. This was blood money; someone died for it. And now the widows were trading up cars, real estate? People inventoried the purchases, the trips, even the Christmas gifts. A relative complained to the Staten Island newspaper about the many expensive Xboxes under one widow's Christmas tree. One dead fireman's sister even went to court to protest how the widow was spending her money. This relative claimed the widow blew through $800,000 that was supposed to benefit the son.

The worst was when the plastic-surgery news got around. "Are those new?" somebody asked one widow, Tina Bilcher, in the supermarket, and pointed at her breasts.

"I feel like Jacqueline Onassis," said one widow, thinking of how people had scrutinized that famous widow.

Recently—how times have changed!—people have approached the widows for help. One friend of Tina's asked her for $10,000—he'd known her husband longer than she had, he didn't fail to mention. Another widow was asked by a co-worker to co-sign a mortgage. It was so awkward that the widow quit her job.

Char hated the backlash, and, what's more, she knew it to be a fraud. Yes, people had been generous. "Now they feel like they have a right to know how we spend it," said Char. "Come on!"

"It's jealousy, it's envy," said another widow of their celebrity and their financial gain. Char, in response, pointed out the limits of her purchasing power. "I can get everything," she said, "but I can't have what I really want," her husband.

THE GWS HAD long been acquainted—firemen's wives in Staten Island run into one another at the kids' school or on the ballfield—but they hadn't been close. Now, though, many felt shut off from non-widows, with whom even small interactions suddenly seemed tense. A casual comment ("I'll check with my husband") sent a chill through a room. "We don't really associate with them," Lisa said, referring to non-widows. Of course, the Alive Wives tried to be sympathetic, but that, too, was uncomfortable. It was, said one widow, " 'Awww,' and then that pitiful look." Then you had to be, as one put it, "a professional widow," in visible distress.

Char sometimes thought that she could only really let loose, be sad or happy or even funny, with other GWs. "We had the same exact feelings," said one widow. Plus, they shared that scandalous widow humor, not at all like the polite jokes of mixed company, which widows couldn't always deal with. "I'm not really laughing," one widow explained. "It doesn't connect anymore." But widow humor, if done right, was funny, at least to them.

Like the time after a group-therapy session when Char and the others, maybe six altogether, climbed into Madeline's minivan. Char, Madeline, and Lisa immediately lit cigarettes. One of the girls who didn't smoke complained, "Are you trying to kill me?"

At which point Lisa whipped around. "And what do you have to live for?" she wanted to know. The GWs laughed so hard Madeline nearly drove the car into a tree.

By now, almost every widow in Staten Island seemed to have three or four widow girlfriends they couldn't get enough of. They talked every day—Char and Mad's first phone call of the day was at 8 A.M. If she couldn't sleep, Lisa called Char in the middle of the night. And Char would get up. For the widows, lots of days were still difficult. "I don't just live my life," a friend of Char's explained. "It's a job." On a day when a widow just couldn't stop crying, an alarm went out. She got calls from half a dozen other widows, trying to put out that fire.

Widows' kids became linked, too, like an auxiliary GW club. One day, Char's sixteen-year-old, Cristen, dark-haired like her dad, long-limbed like her mom, walked home with another widow's kid. They were students at Notre Dame Academy—they wore the same pleated skirt, white shirt, ponytail. They stopped for pizza, then passed the street named for one girl's dad, then the street named for the other's. They talked about the memorials and other stuff, "how we were a lot alike," said Cristen. They were both Pisces, and also, said Cristen, "We're not very emotional."

"People would be like, 'Why aren't you crying?' " Cristen's friend said.

"People don't understand," said Cristen.

The widows started going on vacation together, with their kids, too. Madeline used to host all her family celebrations. Now, to keep the kids from falling apart, she traveled most holidays. That first summer of 2002, just to get a break from being a 9/11 widow—"On vacation, you can be anonymous," Madeline said—Char organized a trip to the Bahamas.

They went for a week to Atlantis, a resort on Paradise Island—seven widows and seventeen kids. The adults lounged by the pool while the kids played on the water slides. It was pricey, but Char loved the place and, on a second trip with Lisa, decided to buy a week every year.

"Mad, we bought a time-share," Char told Madeline excitedly when she returned, then added, "You did, too."

"I did?" Madeline asked, but she was happy to send off a check.

That first Bahamas trip had been a kind of breakthrough—twenty-four of them and no husbands, like a sprawling extended family. One night, four of the widows stayed in Lisa's room, drinking a bottle of wine on the balcony. The air was thick, you could see the water. One widow who'd lost a husband and a cousin said, "Can you still not believe this sometimes?" Then they all cried for a while, though within five minutes they were hysterically laughing about what Lisa—as they knew by now, she had that mouth!—had said to that poor man at the pool.

Every day the seven widows sat by the pool. One day, a gentleman next to them made an observation. Here were all these women and all these kids but no husbands. Where are these lucky guys, he wondered, off golfing?

"No," said Lisa, "they're dead."

Well, the guy lost all his color so fast, and his wife couldn't apologize enough, and Mad and Char had to rush to explain.

IN SOME RESPECTS, firemen were the pivot point around which Staten Island neighborhoods revolved. In eulogies, these men not only ran into burning buildings, they shoveled snow from sidewalks—everyone's on the block. Plus, their homes were meeting places. At Madeline's, where fireman buddies had helped her husband install a backyard pool, a hundred people collected every Fourth of July, without invitations. With firemen gone, family differences gathered centrifugal force. In Staten Island, there were horror stories. "Fractured families," as Char put it. Madeline hardly spoke to her brother-in-law. One mother-in-law had already taken one widow to court, trying to enforce visiting rights to the grandkids. Money fed the differences. A child who was the product of a fireman's one-night stand walked away with $2 million, while the fiancée and his family got nothing (except lawyers' fees).

Perhaps envy was at the root of conflict. But grief was in there, too. And money proved a convenient way to express it. In this regard, parents of the dead suffered especially. Invitations would bypass them, going directly to the widow's house, which was also where their son's firehouse brothers gathered. Who, some parents wanted to know, would recognize their loss, compensate them? "We're the forgotten people. We lost our son. We had him forty-five years. We got nothing," said Chuck Margiotta's father. In some families, old rivalries reasserted themselves. Catherine Buck—Char met her at the nail salon—had been married to fireman Greg Buck for two years. Shortly before September 11, Catherine and Greg had made a down payment on a beat-up house on a pond. In the meantime, they'd lived with Greg's parents.

One morning, Catherine sat in her newly renovated home on the street she'd named for Greg—she lives there with a bunch of cats and a dog—and contemplated why she and her in-laws no longer speak. To Catherine, grief had turned competitive. "It devolved into this total struggle between my mother-in-law and me," said Catherine. She recalled the funeral. "My mother-in-law went up to the casket and would not leave," said Catherine, who then insisted that the funeral director get a chair for her. "Put it next to his body," she told him. "I am his wife, and I will be the last one up there."

One afternoon, the Bucks—Catherine's in-laws—were at home in their hundred-year-old Victorian house twenty minutes from where Catherine now lives. Ernst and Josephine Buck miss Gregory—they call him Gregory—desperately, and constantly relive moments of his life, like a last request to his father: Would he walk the dog? They can't understand why a street named after their Gregory should be near a house he had never lived in. "I couldn't go in *that* house," said his father. "Gregory never went in there." Catherine called her street Greg J. Buck Place. His father purchased his own street sign, Gregory Buck Place, and planted it on the edge of his lawn.

Greg's mother said she always liked Catherine. "I liked her sharing with my son," she said. "She's intelligent, she's pretty, she's got style." But with Gregory gone and no grandkids, is Catherine even family? "To say I miss her, it's like saying I miss the cats," said his father.

Gregory's mother, though, imagines she might eventually pick up the phone and call Catherine. "One day," she said. Meantime, she talks to photos of Gregory she's posted around the house. "I don't really believe I'm hallucinating," she said. But he does respond. She hears his voice. Once, she asked Gregory's photo about Catherine. "Help me," she said to her son. "Help me with this." "Mom," Gregory told her, "Don't worry about it."

CHAR IS A NUT for self-help books. Not long after Mike disappeared, she purchased one about being a widow. Next, she bought every grief book she could find. One day, she drifted toward the relationship shelf and thumbed through a book on dating. *So complicated*, she thought, and put it away.

Char couldn't sort it all out. There was Mike. She was sure she still loved him. She'd been marking the time until the kids grew up, waiting to have him to herself again. But how long should a dead husband's photo patrol the bedroom wall? Tina, now thirty, knew she wanted to be in love again. "I miss being someone's wife. I miss taking something out of the freezer at eight o'clock in the morning and hoping it defrosts in time for dinner."

Char didn't need a husband. Certainly not, as everyone knew, for the financial stuff. "I just want to go to dinner," she explained to a friend one day at lunch. At which point, a good-looking guy named Bobby Nola walked in.

Char looked up at him. "Are you married?" she asked.

"Divorced," he said.

"Well, then I'll go to dinner with you," she said.

At that point—March 2003—she didn't know that Bobby was a Staten Island fireman.

"It's ironic that we all wind up with firemen," Lisa said. Lisa, who recently adopted a son to go with her two girls, had a theory: They fell for similar personalities. "I went to fifteen memorials," she said. "When you listened to people talk about the firemen, it was like you were sitting at the same memorial time and time again."

Lisa met her fireman at a bowling alley. Char, a bowler, had urged Lisa to drop by. "Isn't she beautiful?" Char said to Kevin Tellefsen.

Madeline is still with Gerry Koenig—they live together at Madeline's. They might have been drawn together by grief, Char figured, but romance eventually followed. Even Gerry's firehouse buddies had accepted the relationship as something good to come out of this tragedy.

When Bobby first told Char that he was a fireman, she crossed her fingers like he was a vampire. She said, "I won't marry you as long as you're a fireman." Char later relented, but on the day of the ferry crash, when she couldn't reach him, the old feelings rushed back. (The guys had to call now: Lisa's, who now lives at her place, once phoned from inside a burning building to say he was okay.) Shortly after Bobby moved into Char's house, Bobby decided to retire, and she was thrilled. One Sunday evening, Char and the kids were having dinner at Mike's parents' house. In the kitchen, Char took her mother-in-law aside. "I have something to tell you," she said.

"Good news or bad news?" asked Mike's mother cautiously.

"It depends on how you look at it," Char said.

"It's about Bobby, isn't it?"

In Char's telling, her mother-in-law sounded downhearted. She knew Char was dating. She'd met Bobby.

"Yeah, it is," said Char.

"He wants to marry you, doesn't he?"

"Yeah."

For an instant, Char wasn't sure which way her mother-in-law would go. To Mike's mother, her son was irreplaceable. Plus, in-laws worried, as one put it, "If another man's family comes in, do we get pushed further down?" Finally, Char's mother-in-law spoke. "I think Mike sent Bobby to you." Which, unexpectedly, made Char sad.

Char wondered if being with someone else, if just feeling happy, would always be difficult. It wasn't like a divorce, where you legally cut a person out of your life. "Char struggled for a long time with how could she be so in love with Mike and still be with Bobby and have a good time and laugh?" Lisa said. Sometimes it seemed that Char lived with two men, juggling loyalties. She kept Mike's photo above the fireplace—he was with the kids—not far from a photo of Char leaning over a smiling Bobby. And of course she had the tattoo of Mike's badge on her thigh. "You want to see it?" she'd say, and sometimes show a visitor.

Last September 11, Char and Bobby had been sitting by the pool when the local paper called to ask what she missed most about Mike. She dissolved in tears. "You know I love my husband," she told Bobby, and then, as if husband were an indefinite term, she added, "I love Mike."

Maybe she needed to test Bobby—Madeline knew she was testing Gerry. She'd ask him what to do with a picture of her husband. ("Leave it in the dining room," Gerry said.) By the pool, Char pushed the issue, saying to Bobby, "When I go to heaven, I want to see Mike." Char felt unsure, and gloomy, like the air had come out of her. Suddenly she wasn't certain that she should even get married. "This is never going to end," Char thought.

Bobby stepped in. "I'm not challenged by a ghost," he'd say. He told Char, "Char, if you love me half as much as you love Mike, it's okay."

That was nice. And one night in bed, as Char said good-night to Mike, which she did every night, she mentioned how she loved Bobby, too. September 11 became something they commemorated together. Char bought a plot at Moravian Cemetery, as Madeline had. On an agreed-upon day, Mad and Char and Li went with Windex and flowers, with Bobby and Gerry. Together, they cleaned the headstones and paid their respects. Then they went to Lisa's cemetery, and then to lunch.

Still, as good as things were, "people put things in your head," Char said.

"The first thing people tell you is, 'Oh, he's probably going out with you because you have money,'" said Lisa.

Firemen who'd known Mike warned Char: "Isn't it funny that Bobby wants to marry you now and didn't want to get married for nine years?" which was how long he'd been divorced. If Bobby drove the Escalade, a very nice car on a fireman's salary, someone would say with a wink, "So,

Bobby, you're in an Escalade now?" Char would have to jump in. "The widow car," she'd say and raise her hand. Lisa finally told her boyfriend, "Just tell them you hit the Lotto."

Bobby told Char to stop worrying. "Look, Char, will you cut it out?" he chided her. And Char did. After all, Char knew something else, something she could tell only the other widows.

She loved Mike to death, unconditionally. But also, though Mike was fast at fires and on the basketball court, he was poky everywhere else. "If he could get out of not doing something around the house for as long as possible, he did," says Char, who called him "Mr. P.," for procrastinate.

Bobby, on the other hand, can't sit still. He cooks, not Char. And he doesn't go to bed at night until everything is straightened up. On weekends, he's washing the cars, fixing the pool. Sometimes she has to tell him to lighten up, since we could all be dead tomorrow. But mostly, Char says, "I'm liking it."

As she told one of the widows in what she thought of as a widow joke, the kind that you couldn't say in public, "I sometimes feel like I died and went to heaven."

The wedding is set for the fall in the Bahamas—to coincide with Char, Li, and Mad's time-share. Four widows are coming. Lisa and Madeline will bring their firemen boyfriends. "She's the first from our firehouse to take that step," says Lisa. "It shows that you move on and it's all right." Joe Sykes will attend with his wife. Mike's parents will, too. Mike's father doesn't know how much he'll enjoy himself, but he understands. "Wives usually replace husbands," he says. "That's good." Char, trying to respect her in-laws, told the wedding planner she wanted the evening to be more dinner party than wedding.

Now Char just has to get her dress together. In her mind, it has to be right for Bobby, for Mike's parents, for her kids. That's a lot. Madeline and Lisa went with Char to the fitting, and it was a semi-disaster. "It didn't fit and it wasn't right and the color was off. She was all nuts," says Lisa. In Char's house one afternoon two weeks ago, her sixteen-year-old, Cristen, says that she is happy about her dress, which is pink, brighter than her mom's, which, she says, is beige.

"Off-white," Char corrects.

Two of Char's kids are there, plus a friend. Lisa stopped by with her three kids, one of whom climbs onto Cristen's lap. Char's house is compact, and talk about the dress crosses three connected rooms, until Char, touchy for once, says, "I don't think the dress is that important. Can we talk about something else?"

Outside it's probably 90 degrees. Inside isn't considerably better. "I'm buying you central air," says Lisa. Suddenly Charlene recalls how, when Mike and his firehouse buddies put on the second floor of the house and Mike wrote everybody's name in the concrete, he'd managed to convince her that central air wasn't possible. Oh, well. Char, who is wearing her engagement ring, spots Bobby through the window and fetches him inside. He's hot, and the shamrock tattooed on his arm is covered in dust from the construction site where he now works. Lisa heads out with her kids. Char orders pizza. "Who's staying?" she wants to know. Bobby spots a stray knife, places it in the sink. Char, then, has a thought related to her wedding dress. "Maybe," she says, "we'll all wear bathing suits."

Additional reporting by Lauren DeCarlo.

PART FOUR

....

THE
PERMANENT
REVOLUTION

★

AFTER BLACK POWER, WOMEN'S LIBERATION

GLORIA STEINEM

APRIL 7, 1969

In 1969, Gloria Steinem, at the time a New York *magazine political writer, went to cover a "speakout" at which women told stories about their illegal abortions. "It was a revelation," says Steinem, who'd had an illegal abortion herself. The meeting led to her article "After Black Power, Women's Liberation." It also had the effect of connecting her radical politics to feminism issues. "After I wrote this piece, my friends, other writers, nice guys, essentially said, 'You must not get involved with these crazy women. You've worked so hard to be taken seriously.' They didn't know who I was, and how could they? I hadn't been speaking." After the article, the speaking commenced.* Ms. *magazine, which she co-founded, had its first incarnation as an insert in* New York.

O—NCE UPON A TIME—say, ten or even five years ago—a Liberated Woman was somebody who had sex before marriage and a job afterward. Once upon the same time, a Liberated Zone was any foreign place lucky enough to have an American army in it. Both ideas seem antiquated now, and for pretty much the same reason: Liberation isn't exposure to the American values of Mom-and-apple-pie anymore (not even if Mom is allowed to work in an office and vote once in a while); it's the escape from them.

For instance:

Barnard girls move quietly, unlasciviously into the men's dorms at Columbia; a student sleep-in to protest the absence of "rational communities"—co-ed dorms like those already springing up at other universities.

Wives and mothers march around the Hudson Street alimony jail with posters announcing they don't want alimony.

A coven of thirteen members of WITCH (the Women's International Terrorist Conspiracy from Hell, celebrating witches and gypsies as the first women resistance fighters) demonstrates against that bastion of white male supremacy: Wall Street. The next day, the market falls five points.

More witches and some black-veiled brides invade the Bridal Fair at Madison Square Garden. They carry signs ("Confront the Whore-makers," "Here Comes the Bribe"), sing, shout, release white mice in the audience of would-be brides, and generally scare the living daylights out of exhibitors who are trying to market the conventional delights of bridal gowns, kitchen appliances, package-deal honeymoon trips and heart-shaped swimming pools.

At the end of the Columbia strike, the student-run Liberation School offers a course on women as an oppressed class. Discussions include the parallel myths about women and Negroes (that both have smaller brains than white men, childlike natures, natural "goodness," limited rationality, supportive roles to white men, etc.); the paternalistic family system as prototype for capitalistic society (see Marx and Engels); the conclusion that society can't be restructured until the relationship between the sexes is restructured. Men are kept out of the class, but it is bigger and lasts longer than any other at the school.

Redstockings, an action group in the Women's Liberation Movement, sponsors a one-act play about abortion by the New Feminist Theatre (whose purpose it is to point out how many plays are anti-woman and how tough it is for women playwrights, directors, producers), plus two hours of personal and detailed testimony—in public—by girls who have had abortions and Tell It Like It Is, from humor through sadism. Nobody wants to reform the abortion laws; they want to repeal them. Completely.

What do women want? The above events are in no way connected to the Bloomingdale-centered, ask-not-what-I-can-do-for-myself-ask-what-my-husband-can-do-for-me ladies of Manhattan, who are said by sociologists to be "liberated." Nor do the house-bound matriarchs of Queens and the Bronx get much satisfaction out of reading about feminist escapades. On the contrary, the whole thing alienates them by being a) radical and b) young.

The women behind it, and influenced by it, usually turn out to be white, serious, well-educated girls; the same sort who have labored hard in what is loosely known as the Movement, from the Southern sit-ins of nine years ago to the current attacks on the military-industrial-educational complex. They have been jailed, beaten and Maced side-by-side with their social-activist male counterparts. (It's wonderful to see how quickly police from Selma to Chicago get over a reluctance to hit women.) They have marched on Senate committees, Pentagon hawks, their own college presidents and the Chase Manhattan Bank. But once back in the bosom of SDS, they found themselves typing and making coffee.

"When it comes to decision-making or being taken seriously in meetings," said one revolutionary theorist from Berkeley, "we might as well join the Young Republicans."

Such grumbling noises were being made aloud at Movement meetings as early as five years ago. but women were ridiculed or argued down by men (as well as some "Uncle Tom" women). Eventually, they were assured, "the woman question" would come up on the list of radical priorities—as decided on by radical men. Meanwhile, more backstage work, more mimeographing, more secondary role-playing around the revolutionary cells and apartment-communes. And, to be honest, more reluctance to leave the secondary role and lose male approval.

Finally, women began to "rap" (talk, analyze, in radical-ese) about their essential second-classness, forming women's caucuses inside the Movement in much the same way Black Power groups had done. And once together they made a lot of discoveries: that they shared more problems with women of different classes, for instance, than they did with men of their own; that they liked and respected each other (if women don't want to work with women, as Negroes used to reject other Negroes, it's usually because they believe the myth of their own inferiority), and that, as black militants kept explaining to white liberals, "You don't get radicalized fighting other people's battles."

At the SDS Convention in 1967, women were still saying such integrationist things as "The struggle for the liberation of women must be part of the larger fight for freedom." Many Movement women still are. But members of groups like the Southern Student Organizing Committee and New York Radical Women (a loose coalition of various radical groups whose representatives meet once a month) withdrew to start concentrating on their own problems. They couldn't become black or risk jail by burning their draft cards, but they could change society from the bottom up by radicalizing (engaging with basic truth) the consciousness of women; by going into the streets on such women's issues as abortion, free childcare centers, and a final break with the nineteenth-century definition of females as sex objects whose main function is to service men and their children.

All this happened not so much by organization as contagion. What has come to be known in the last two years or so as the Women's Liberation Movement (WLM) is no more pin-downable than the Black Power Movement; maybe less so, because white groups tend to be less structured, more skittish about leadership than black ones. Nonetheless, when the WLM had its first national conference last fall, women from twenty states and Canada showed up on a month's notice. A newsletter, *Voice of the Women's Liberation Movement,* is published in Chicago. WLM-minded groups are springing up on dozens of campuses where they add special student concerns to their activities: professors who assume women aren't "serious" about careers; advisers who pressure girls toward marriage or traditionally feminine jobs (would-be Negro doctors are told to be veterinarians, would-be women doctors are told to be nurses), and faculties or administrations where few or no women are honored in authority.

In New York, WITCH is probably the most colorful outcropping of the WLM. It got started when women supporters of men being investigated by the House Un-American Activities Committee decided that a witch-hunt should have witches, and dressed up for HUAC hearings accordingly. (In the words of WITCH, "We are WITCH. We are WOMAN. We are LIBERATION. WE are WE. The hidden history of women's liberation began with witches and gypsies . . . the oldest guerrillas and resistance fighters, the first practicing abortionists and distributors of contraceptive herbs. WITCH implies the destruction of passivity, consumerism and commodity fetishism . . . the routine of daily life is the theatre of struggle.") It was the Witch Guerrilla Theatre that hexed Wall Street, and later, as part of a technique called "violating the reality structure," it "freaked out at a Wellesley Alumnae Fund-raising Bridge Party."

Quieter groups seem to be forming everywhere, from the New Women in Manhattan to The Feminists in Oceanside. Redstockings, the most publically active at the moment, has recapitulated the whole WLM in its short history. Women activists rebelled against their subordinate position, but still tried to work within the Movement until a peace-and-liberation protest at Nixon's Inaugural, where girls spoke and were booed by their own fellow radicals. After that moment of truth, they reformed as part of "an independent revolutionary movement, potentially representing half the population. We intend to make our own analysis of the system . . . Although we may cooperate with radical men on matters of common concern . . . our demand for freedom involves not only the overthrow of capitalism, but the destruction of the patriarchal system."

If all this sounds far-out, Utopian, elitist, unnecessary or otherwise unlikely to be the next big thing in revolutions, consider two facts: 1) the WLM is growing so rapidly that even its most cheerful proselytizers are surprised, spreading not only along the infra-structure of the existing co-ed Movement, but into a political territory where anti-Vietnam petitions have rarely been seen; and 2) there are a couple of mass movements, from highly organized through just restless, that the WLM might merge with, becoming sort of a revolutionary vanguard.

The older, middle-class women come first, the ones who tried hard to play subordinate roles in the suburbs according to the post-war-baby-boom-women's-magazine idyll but found Something Missing. Betty Friedan, who explained their plight clearly and compassionately in *The Feminine Mystique,* named that Something: rewarding work. But when these women went out to find jobs, they found a lot of home-truths instead.

For instance, there is hardly a hierarchy in the country—business, union, government, educational, religious, whatever—that doesn't discriminate against women above the secretarial level. Women with some college education earn less than men who get as far as the eighth grade. The median income of white women employed full time is less than that of white men *and* Negro men. The gap between women's pay and men's pay gets greater every year, even though the number of women in the labor force increases (they are now a third of all workers). Forty-three states have "protection legislation" limiting the hours and place a woman can work; legislation that is, as Governor Rockefeller admitted last year, "more often protective of men." The subtler, psychological punishments for stepping out of woman's traditional "service" role are considerable. (Being called "unfeminine," "a bad mother" or "a castrating woman," to name a traditional few.) And, to top it all off, the problem of servants or child care often proves insurmountable after others are solved.

In short, women's opportunities expanded greatly for about fifteen years after they won the vote in 1920 (just as Negroes had more freedom during Reconstruction, before Jim Crow laws took over where slavery had left off), but they have been getting more limited ever since.

The middle-class, educated and disillusioned group gets larger with each college graduation. National Organization for Women (NOW)—founded in 1966 by Betty Friedan, among others, "to bring women into full participation in the mainstream of American society *now*, exercising all the privileges and responsibilities thereof in truly equal partnership with men"—is a very effective voice of this group, concentrating on such reforms as getting irrelevant sex-designations out of Help Wanted ads and implementing Equal Employment Opportunity laws.

If the WLM can feel solidarity with the hated middle class, and vice versa, then an alliance with the second mass movement—poor women of all colors—should be no problem. They are already organized around welfare problems, free daycare centers for mothers who must work, and food prices. For them, equal pay, unequal training and sex discrimination for jobs (not to mention the woman-punishing rules of welfare) exact a daily price: Of all the families living below the poverty level, 40 percent are headed by women.

A lot of middle-class and radical-intellectual women are already working with the poor on common problems, but viewing them as social. If the "consciousness-raising" programs of the WLM work, they'll see them as rallying points for women *qua* women. And that might forge the final revolutionary link. Rumblings are already being heard inside the Democratic party in New York. It's the women who staff and win elections, and they may finally balk at working for only men—not very qualified men at that—in the mayoral primary.

There is plenty of opposition to this kind of thinking, from women as well as men. Having one's traditional role questioned is not a very comfortable experience; perhaps especially for women, who have been able to remain children, and to benefit from work they did not and could not do. Marriage wouldn't go straight down the drain, as traditionalists keep predicting. Women's liberation might just hurry up some sort of companionate marriage that seems to be developing anyway.

But there is bound to be a time of, as social anthropologist Lionel Tiger puts it, "increased personal acrimony," even if the revolution fails and women go right back to darning socks. (Masculinity doesn't depend on the subservience of others, but it will take us a while to find that out.) It might be helpful to men—and good for women's liberation—if they just keep repeating key phrases like, "No more guilt, No more alimony, Fewer boring women, Fewer bitchy women, No more tyrants with all human ambition confined to the home, No more 'Jewish mothers' transferring ambition to children, No more women trying to be masculine because it's a Man's World . . ." (and maybe one more round of "No more alimony") until the acrimony has stopped.

Because the idea is, in the long run, that women's liberation will be men's liberation, too.

RACE: THE ISSUE

JOE KLEIN

MAY 29, 1989

*In 1989, race was New York City's most divisive subject. The event that
roused the city, and prompted Joe Klein's article, was the brutal rape of a
white female jogger in Central Park. Five young men, four black and one
Hispanic, were later convicted of the crime, which became a test of attitudes toward race. For Klein, the discussion was infuriating, framed, as
he saw it, by outdated welfare-state ideologies. Klein argued for a new outlook, one that put a greater emphasis on personal responsibility. Following his article, Klein was labeled a racist and a fascist and later received
a death threat, one sign of the explosiveness of the issue. Certainly, the
liberal-leaning Klein was a heretic, betraying liberal solutions that had
long been orthodoxy. "I never denied white racism," Klein says. "But liberals were in denial." Klein's ideas about race would later gain a kind of currency, but, the five convicted youths were later exonerated after serving
prison terms when a convict with a long criminal history confessed to the
brutal rape. Klein is* Time *magazine's political columnist and the author
of* Primary Colors, *which he wrote under the pseudonym "Anonymous."*

O N A PLEASANT SPRING EVENING, several weeks before the
city was convulsed by the rape of the woman jogger in Central Park,
Richard Ravitch found himself in the heart of Queens—as he often does
these days, pressing his long-shot candidacy for mayor—trying to sell op-

timism to a room full of pessimists. "This city was built by optimists," he insisted. "By people who built the subways two stops beyond where the newest houses were going up. By people who built reservoirs, and roads, and bridges, an infrastructure far more sophisticated and expensive than was needed—because they had faith in the idea of New York, they knew the city would grow and prosper. . . ."

"It was different then," the man next to me muttered. This was an audience of mutterers—the Continental Regular Democratic Club: elderly Jews mostly, the sort of people who sit behind you in matinees and repeat the dialogue.

Ravitch plodded ahead, sensing that his attempt at urban rhapsody wasn't quite cutting it with this crowd, but pushing on anyway—to the immigrant experience, usually a winner with older folks. They loved to hear about the "wave after wave" of immigrants who came to New York "with a dream of building a life for themselves and their families. This city is an incubator," he said. "It provides an atmosphere of opportunity for each newly arrived group, where they can get a job, an education for their children and move into the mainstream. . . ."

"So what happened?" an elderly woman interrupted. "What about the—"

"Shhhh," said the man in front of her.

"No, let me say it," she said, putting a hand on the man's shoulder.

"*Get your hand off me!*" he yelled, and moved away. "Let him talk."

These were wild, inexplicable passions. Ravitch seemed lost, deflated: What was going on here? "Excuse me, Mr. Ravitch," said Arthur Katzman, a leader of the Continental Dems and a longtime member of the City Council. "But I must disagree with you about the immigrants. It was true of the immigrants who came from Europe, and also the Orientals. But these . . . others. The quality is not as good. The ability to contribute used to be greater." There was wild applause, which Katzman took to mean that it was time for a speech—and he careened off on a defense of the mayor and a tour of the homeless crisis, thereby relieving the candidate of the need to respond to that *other* question.

In a perfect world, Ravitch—whose lifelong devotion to the cause of civil rights is unimpeachable—would have gone back and chastised Katzman for the racial implication of his comments. He might have mentioned the thousands of West Indians and Hispanics who have opened stores and worked their way into the mainstream, the tens of thousands of American blacks who—against all odds—have gone to college, become teachers and nurses and public officials. A truly gutsy response would have gone on to acknowledge the social anarchy that has overtaken the black underclass, and the difficulties the city—and the nation—faces in trying to deal with it. But Ravitch should be forgiven his stunned evasion: Each of his fellow candidates would have done the same.

RACE IS AN issue politicians go to great pains to avoid. It has been deemed unfit for open discussion, in all but the most platitudinous manner, for many years. The public is, oddly, complicit in this: People seem to sense that the topic is so raw, and their feelings so intense, that it's just too risky to discuss in mixed company. "It never comes up," says another mayoral hopeful. "Crime does all the time, but it's rarely linked to race. I get questions and comments in public meetings about everything under the sun—but never about race."

In private, though, race seems the *only* thing people are talking about these days—especially since the terrifyingly casual barbarism in Central Park last month. The radio talk shows, the true vox pop of the eighties, are full of it. The subject dominates fancy dinner parties in Manhattan; it comes up on supermarket lines in Queens and around kitchen tables in Brooklyn; it has suddenly become permissible to vent frustrations, to ask questions and say things—often ugly things—that have been forbidden in polite discourse for many years.

And the central question, at least among whites, is a version—more or less refined—of what Arthur Katzman was trying to get across in Queens that night: Why have so many blacks proved so resistant to *incubation*? Why, after twenty-five years of equal rights—indeed, of special remedial treatment under law—do so many remain outside the bounds of middle-class society? Why do even educated blacks seem increasingly remote, hostile, and paranoid? In a society besotted with quick fixes and easy answers to every problem, is this the one that will prove insoluble?

Even though none of the candidates will say it publicly, race is *the* central issue in this year's mayoral campaign. But then, it was the great un-spoken in last year's presidential election as well—remember Willie Hor-ton? It is, and always has been, the most persistent and emotional test of America's ability to exist as a society of equals. In New York, the challenge is immediate and explosive: Race is at the heart of all of the city's most critical problems—crime, drugs, homelessness, the crises in public educa-tion, public health, children's services. All have been exacerbated by racial polarization and antagonism. And also by a conspiracy of silence—by a fear of speaking candidly about the causes and possible solutions to these problems.

The silence may well be about to end. Each new outrage—Howard Beach, Tawana Brawley, the constant drumbeat of crack killings, cops blown away, the jogger raped, the black woman raped and thrown off the Brooklyn rooftop (one of the legion of black victims ignored by white society)—each new barbarity nudges people closer to the moment when the discussion of how black and white Americans can come to terms with each other is reopened.

It is a public debate that was closed down abruptly nearly twenty years ago. The country has been drifting toward disaster ever since. "There is an illness in the community now, a psychosis," says John Lewis, the Georgia congressman and one of the true heroes of the civil-rights movement. "We need to bring all the dirt and all the sickness out into the open. We need to talk again about building what Dr. King called a *beloved community*— a truly integrated society of blacks and whites."

Integration seems an impossibly romantic notion now. Even to pro-pose it as the solution to the racial morass raises derisive hoots in the black community and patronizing shrugs and smiles from whites. Serious talk of integration ended when "black power" began to flourish and *equal rights* was supplanted by *affirmative action* as the rallying cry of the movement. Aggrievement—the notion that blacks deserved special com-pensatory treatment—replaced assimilation at the top of the activists' agenda. Integration withered as a goal; "community control" replaced it. The movement imploded—and white America was only too happy to let it happen. Liberals quickly, romantically—and quite irresponsibly—acceded to the new black demands; conservatives were quietly relieved that blacks no longer wanted in. Only a few brave souls raised the obvious question: How could blacks be included in American society if they insisted on separating themselves from it? For the most part, interracial debate ended.

"White America ceded control of the *definition* of the problem to blacks in the late sixties and early seventies," says Glenn Loury, a black professor of political economy at Harvard's Kennedy School. "But not control of the solution. A situation of mutually reinforcing cowardice has resulted."

Twenty years later, having suffered a generation of black "power" and white indifference, race relations are at a dead end. The usual litany of achievement—the growth of a black middle class, the integration of public life—isn't very convincing. The horrific desperation of the black underclass demands that the racial debate be reopened, and the only logical place for it to begin is where it left off: at the moment when the civil-rights movement resegregated itself. "We made a serious mistake when the movement turned against its first principle: integration," John Lewis laments. "The seeds that were planted twenty years ago have borne very bitter fruit."

THE SHIFT FROM integration to "black power" seems a strange, counterproductive inversion now—and yet it seemed perfectly logical at the time. How did it happen—and happen so quickly? The death of Martin Luther King Jr. is often cited as a turning point—Lewis mentions it—but Stokely Carmichael proclaimed "black power" two years before King's death, and Malcolm X was drawing large crowds well before that. The separatist impulse had always been there, ever since emancipation—and so its revival in the mid-sixties was no great surprise. The surprise was the speed with which it moved from a handful of radicals at the periphery to the heart of the civil-rights movement. The irony was that it occurred at a moment when civil-rights legislation—bills that *mandated* integration— were flying through Congress and the leading integrationist, Martin Luther King, was winning the Nobel Peace Prize. Never had America seemed so open to the idea of inclusion.

And yet the legislation itself—particularly the Voting Rights Act of 1965—contained the seeds of separatism. As Bayard Rustin, a stalwart integrationist until his death in 1987, pointed out early on, "What began as a protest movement is now being challenged to translate itself into a political movement." This meant a shift from nonviolent demonstrations to "the building of community institutions or power bases" to elect black politicians.

There wasn't much percentage in integration for the black mayors and aldermen who soon won election across the black belt in the South and in the urban slums up North. For people like Charles Evers, running for mayor of Fayette, Mississippi, black electoral *power* was a far more immediate concern than the gauzy ideal of "black-and-white together." Their agenda was naturally compensatory: If the streets on the white side of town were paved, equality meant paving them on the black side of town. Like all good politicians, the new black officials pandered to their core constituencies. This was classic ethnic politics, a healthy impulse—but it put the black pols into closer rhetorical proximity with the militant separatists: Both were calling for "black power."

Northern black leaders wanted a piece of the action, too—but they were locked into larger, white-dominated government entities. For them, the naked choice was between power and integration: By separating from the white system—by demanding "community control" of school districts in New York, for example—they could gain a measure of power from the white politicians who ran the town. As Nicholas Lemann observed in *The Atlantic* last December and January, the "community action" component of the federal war on poverty reinforced this tendency by funneling money to a new generation of community leaders, instead of to the established city authorities—even Lyndon Johnson, it seemed, believed in "black power."

There was, less obviously, a certain security in separatism as well. If the schools (and neighborhoods) remained black, there was a good chance blacks would run them. Integration challenged blacks as profoundly as it did whites. It meant competing against *the man* for the top jobs. And a great many blacks were convinced—despite all the new laws and King's Nobel Prize and a president who said, "We shall overcome"—that the competition would be as unfair as it always had been. There were, quite understandably, more than a few who quietly wondered if the racists were right, and secretly feared that they *couldn't* compete. "That impulse was nothing new," said a labor leader deeply involved in the civil-rights movement. "The black teachers in the South were pretty solidly against integration in the 1950s."

So the militants provided the new black class of political leaders with a philosophical rationale for their natural impulses to accumulate power and avoid competition: White society was fundamentally racist, and so integration was pointless. Blacks were victims of a systematic oppression and deserved special treatment—affirmative action, quotas, more programs of every sort—in recompense. This was quite satisfying intellectually. Many fair-minded Americans agreed: Blacks *had* been treated abominably. Their restraint in the face of the most noxious provocation had been remarkable. Even when the great urban riots began in the mid-sixties, these seemed an understandable—if not justifiable—response to white prejudice.

But a line was crossed when blacks demanded—and then got—special treatment. A price was paid, most immediately in heightened antagonism from the white working class, which felt threatened by the new rules. But eventually by the blacks themselves: By defining themselves as victims and separating themselves by race, they had guaranteed their continued isolation from white society. "This . . . is the tragedy of black power in America today," wrote Shelby Steele, the brilliant black essayist, in *Harper's* last year. "It is primarily a victim's power. . . . Whatever gains this power brings in the short run through political action, it undermines in the long run. Social victims may be collectively entitled, but they are all too often individually demoralized."

When aggrievement was proclaimed the central, psychic fact of black life, the most aggrieved and alienated—the most amoral, the criminals— became the definers of "true" blackness in the media and also in the streets. White liberals, guilt-ridden (I write from experience), accepted this spurious definition at face value. Far worse, though: For a brief, truly revolting moment, white radicals celebrated the most antisocial blacks as culture heroes. Criminality was romanticized. Slums were now called "ghettos," which assumed a romantic communalism and immediacy of oppression that simply didn't exist.

The radical looniness reached its apex with the celebration of the Black Panthers and of Eldridge Cleaver's hopelessly perverted *Soul on Ice,* in which black-on-white rape was described as a political act. (As a young reporter in Boston at the time, I interviewed a white rape victim who coolly described her post-violation reaction: "I went to the free clinic to get a tetanus shot, and then went home and reread Eldridge Cleaver, so I could better understand what happened.") There was something incredibly careless—and so ironic as to feed the worst black paranoia—about both the white radicals' celebration and the liberals' acceptance of this pathological behavior. By romanticizing these irresponsible activities— criminality, sexual "freedom," drug use, and general lack of ambition— whites were lending support to a subtle system of oppression that had existed since slavery times.

"One can think of the lower-class Negroes as bribed and drugged by this system," wrote John Dollard in his landmark 1937 study *Caste and Class in a Southern Town.* "The effect of the social set-up seems to be to keep Negroes infantile, to grant them infantile types of freedom from responsibility. . . . The evidence is unmistakable that the moral indolence allowed to Negroes is perceived by them and their white caste masters as a compensating value and gain [for forced labor in a plantation or share-cropping system]."

The words seem rather harsh now, after a quarter-century of euphemisms. But John Dollard wrote as a firm advocate of "Negro" rights; he described a pattern of oppression and prescribed a solution. He made a clear distinction between the determinedly proper black middle class, struggling to assimilate, and the rural underclass, which had not yet shed the behavior patterns imposed by their former slave masters. Then he concluded, "The dominant aim of our society seems to be to middle-classify all of its members. Negroes, including lower-class Negroes, are no exceptions. Eventually they must all enter the competition for higher status which is so basic and compulsive an element in our way of life. This will mean . . . approximating more nearly the ideal of restraint, independence and personal maturity which is implicitly attached to our demands for individual competition and mobility."

This was considered radical race-mixing in the thirties; thirty years later, black activists had come to see any derogation of lower-class black morality as white paternalism. When Daniel Patrick Moynihan wrote a report—in the spirit of Dollard—on the instability of black family structure in 1965, he was pilloried. A sociological ice age ensued. "Liberals became increasingly reluctant to research, write about, or publicly discuss inner-city social dislocations following the virulent attacks against Moynihan," wrote the black sociologist William Julius Wilson in *The Truly Disadvantaged*. Indeed, for nearly twenty years, the only "legitimate" research was conducted by "minority scholars on the strengths, not the weaknesses, of inner-city families and communities."

Meanwhile, the pathology metastasized. When Moynihan wrote his report in 1965, a "staggering" 26 percent of non-white children were born out of wedlock; now the figure is 61 percent. The technology of underclass indolence also has exploded: The Saturday-night knife fights on the black side of the tracks that Dollard says the rednecks found so amusing have become shoot-outs with semi-automatic weapons; "white lightning" has become crack. Sex remains sex—but mixed with hypodermic needles spells AIDS.

A great many blacks and white liberals will argue that these spiraling pathologies are the result of racism, the hopelessness and frustration that are part of growing up desperately poor and "knowing" that the system won't cut you any slack. This is undoubtedly true, as is William Julius Wilson's belief that the departure of the black middle class from the cities to the suburbs removed role models, disciplinarians, and other socializing forces from the slums, hastening the collapse of the social order. "You can't imagine how removed these kids are from life as we know it," says Andrew Cuomo, who runs a program for homeless families. "They have no contact with *anyone* who has succeeded in the system. They don't have an uncle who's a lawyer or an aunt who's a teacher. They see no point to succeeding. The line you hear most often is 'Stay in school so you can go to work in McDonald's.' "

THIS TERRIBLE DEPRIVATION no doubt would have existed if sociologists had been free to ply their trade in the slums, and if the civil-rights movement had kept integration as its goal, but the militant know-nothingism of the black nationalists certainly hasn't helped any. Sadly, when "black power" filters to the streets, it's often little more than a rationale for failure: More than a few scholarly studies, notably one by John U. Ogbu and Signithia Fordham in *The Urban Review,* have shown that there is enormous peer pressure against academic success in black high schools. It is considered "acting white."

The taunts that Ogbu and Fordham describe seem no worse than those endured by generations of Jewish, Irish, and Italian nerds, but the sanctions are cosmic: The black kid who succeeds in school is not only a traitor to the race but a sucker besides. He, or she, is busting his butt for a job at *McDonald's.* There is tremendous pressure on these kids—even those from strict, stable middle-class homes, as some of the children involved in the Central Park rape apparently were—to prove their blackness by misbehaving.

White society offers very few incentives to the black teenagers who resist peer pressure and play "our" game. Indeed, they are treated with the same disdain visited upon the potential hoodlums. In a stunning bit of television several weeks ago, Ted Koppel gave six star black high-school students a camera and sent them out into the white world, asking for change of a dollar. The reactions were depressing. Most whites simply ignored the kids. White women were startled when approached; one seemed to jump back, then hastened to the other side of the street.

Given the levels of criminality now, these reactions are also understandable. They are part of the vicious spiral of racism and reaction that has been allowed to spin out of control during the years of silence. The pattern is clear: The more violent the streets become, the more race-sensitive whites become, and the blacks, in turn, grow more isolated and angry. The rape of the jogger in Central Park seems to have ratcheted the cycle another turn toward anarchy. The white reaction is manifest. Mayoral candidates who never hear questions about race relations in public forums say that *privately* white people seem obsessed by the incident. "Jaws have tightened," says one candidate. "Whites have just *had it* with blacks," says another—that is, they have no tolerance for discussions of racism, oppression, or other excuses for antisocial behavior.

The reaction in the black community is less remarked upon but no less extreme and much more disturbing. "I am just disgusted by how many friends tell me that it was the jogger's fault," says one prominent black leader. "They say she shouldn't have been there."

There is also a new outbreak of the half-crazed paranoia and conspiracy-theorizing that have become quite popular in the black media in recent years. *The City Sun,* considered a "respectable" black weekly, published a truly vomitous account of the incident, including a fantasy description of the victim's body as "the American Ideal . . . a tiny body with round hips and pert buttocks, soft white thighs, slender calves, firm and high breasts."

The author of this trash went on to opine that—if you omit the question of whether the rape actually occurred—the children who committed the Central Park abomination were being subjected to the same sort of treatment as the Scottsboro boys, the blacks falsely convicted of raping a white woman in Alabama fifty years ago. This sort of nonsense is of a piece with the increasing numbers of blacks nationally who, according to one pollster, believe that the drug crisis is a conspiracy on the part of white society to "commit genocide" against blacks. "The really disturbing thing is that the more solid the black middle class becomes," this pollster said, "the more its fundamental views of the issues seems to diverge from middle-class America."

IN THE DAYS since his untimely death, I have been thinking about the asthma that killed Schools Chancellor Richard Green. I had several long conversations with Green during his year or so as chancellor, and the most striking thing about him—in addition to his fierce integrity and caring—was how *constricted* he seemed, physically and figuratively. This was especially true when we were "on the record." He would speak in word clouds, imprecise, clichéd and formal, his inhaler clutched tightly in his hand. When I put the notebook away—and no longer was an official emissary of the white media—he literally seemed to breathe easier. We gossiped freely about politicians and reporters, and how strange the flushed intensity of New York seemed to a fellow from the eminently more rational town of Minneapolis.

The pressure of my "official" station on this proud man—and his relief when the inquisition ended—is haunting. The Richard Greens of the world, *all* the striving, insistently moral black men and women working to overcome four hundred years of stereotyping, are the most poignant victims of the escalating alienation between the races. They are the tightrope walkers, holding their breath as they perform in midair with only a slender strand of support—ever fearful that even the smallest mistake will prove cataclysmic.

I wonder what can be done to make their lives easier, to show appreciation for their efforts. The usual impulse—the *liberal* impulse—is to look to government for a remedy, and there are some things that can be done, but a great deal that can't. The most basic thing, I suspect, is to implement John Dollard's fifty-year-old prescription: make a concerted effort to undo the behavior patterns of the underclass that cause social anarchy, feed the cycle of racism, and undercut the efforts of middle-class blacks to become part of the larger society.

For a quarter-century, this agenda has been avoided. There have been two paradigms for dealing with dilemmas of race, and neither has worked. Conservatives have ignored the problem, left the solution to "market forces" or, worse, to social Darwinism. Liberals seem to have abandoned critical thought entirely, allowing militants to dictate their agenda, scorning most efforts to impose sanctions on antisocial behavior by underclass blacks.

A NEW MODEL is needed, one that returns to the original movement goals of integration and equal rights while addressing the deterioration that has taken place in black family structure and community institutions over the past twenty years. Integration—that is, *assimilation* into the middle-class economy—can be the only possible goal. The society has to "emphasize commonality as a higher value than 'diversity' or 'pluralism,'" wrote Shelby Steele in *Harper's*. Programs that divide by race, even well-intentioned ones like affirmative action, are too costly in *moral* terms. They send the wrong message—of racial division and aggrievement. A more profitable agenda is one that seeks to pull the poorest, regardless of race, into conformity with middle-class standards.

There is no quesiton that the problem of the underclass can't be solved unless an ethic of personal responsibility pervades the entire society, from top to bottom. If black teenagers are going to be made responsible for their sexual conduct, taxpayers will have to be willing to spend the money on education and crime-fighting that will channel the children of the underclass toward inclusion in the middle-class economy. To those few remaining self-destructive militants who say, "You're asking us to become white," the answer is readily apparent in the recent tide of Asian immigrants who practice economic integration while maintaining a fierce cultural pride and even, to an extent, segregating themselves in ethnic enclaves.

"When you are behind in a footrace," Martin Luther King told college students in 1964, "the only way to get ahead is to run faster than the man in front of you. So when your white roommate says he's tired and goes to sleep, you stay up and burn the midnight oil."

There is not much more that government can do than help the runners to the starting line and make sure the lanes are clear for all contestants. There is no way government can guarantee that blacks will succeed, although many seem to believe that to be the case. "It's the greatest difference between blacks and whites in polling—the vast majority of blacks believe government can solve *anything*," says a prominent pollster. "By contrast, the baby-boomers are the ultimate level-playing-field crowd. If you ask them who gets special benefits from the government, they name three groups: big corporations, rich people, and minorities. The good news is that they seem ready to accept anyone who earns what he gets, regardless of race."

Polling data are notoriously sanguine when it comes to problems of race. No doubt, far too many whites *won't* be ready to "accept anyone . . . regardless of race." But what's the alternative? The costs of not competing—of using racism as an excuse for paralysis—have become all too clear these past twenty years. No doubt, the contest will be far more difficult for blacks than it has been for any group that has gone before them. No doubt, a great many won't succeed, and a great many more will be as uncertain and anguished in their pride as Richard Green was. The contest won't be fair.

But consider the possible results of the extra testing, the fearsome struggle that will be required of blacks if they are determined, finally, to compete as equals—even if the race *is* still stacked against them: Their triumphs will be that much sweeter; their success may prove that much more spectacular than the victories won by the less rigorously tried "Europeans" and Asians who have incubated so well—and who have no choice now but to cheer their African brothers and sisters on, since the success of the experiment itself may depend on it.

FEMALE CHAUVINIST PIGS

ARIEL LEVY

JANUARY 22, 2001

Even as the new Times Square was being cleaned up, much of what went on in the old Times Square—porn, strip clubs—was being mainstreamed. But what surprised Ariel Levy was not that the culture was getting raunchier but that her friends—along with many women in the media— were joining right in. Though the sensibility of these "female chauvinist pigs," as she dubbed them, was supposed to be partly comic, Levy, who grew up with an old-school feminist mother, saw that the joke was on them. "My intention was to cut this down. This is not liberation. This is a false bill of goods." Levy's article grew into a book, Female Chauvinist Pigs: Women and the Rise of Raunch Culture. *She is currently a writer at* The New Yorker.

RECENTLY, THE ORGANIZATION New York Women in Film & Television threw a breakfast to honor Sheila Nevins, a twenty-two-year veteran of HBO and its executive vice-president of original programming. The vibe was more *Lifetime Intimate Portrait* than *Sex and the City:* "I was growing up in a society where women were quiet, so I got to listen," Nevins reflected from the podium. "I like to laugh, I like to cry; the rest is paperwork."

All the women wore glazed, reverential expressions as they picked at their melon wedges and admired Nevins's sharp wit, keen intellect, and zebra-printed slides. "Who opened your career doors for you?" one wanted to know. "Me," Nevins replied. A tweedy fellow with a bow tie started his question with "I'm just the token guy . . ." Nevins gave a little snort and said, "You're all tokens," and the gals had a good laugh.

But then a woman in the back brought up *G-String Divas,* the late-night docu-soap that Nevins executive-produces, which treats audiences to extended showings of T&A between interviews with strippers about tricks of the trade and their real-life sexual practices. "Why would a woman—a middle-aged woman with a child—make a show about strippers?" the woman asked. Everyone was stunned.

Nevins whipped around in her chair.

"You're talking fifties talk! Get with the program!" she barked. "I love the sex stuff. What's the big deal?" In fact, there *was* something vaguely Betty Friedan–esque about this woman compared with the rest, in their Eileen Fisher knits and lip liner. She adjusted her glasses, visibly shaken, but persisted: "Why is it still the case that if we're going to have a series about women on television, it has to be about their bodies and their sexuality?"

Nevins shook her head furiously. "Why is it that women will still go after women taking off their clothes and not after all the injustices in the workplace? I don't get it! As if women taking off their clothes is disgusting and degrading. Not being able to feed your kids, that's disgusting and degrading!"

"But—"

"Everyone has to bump and grind for what they want," Nevins interrupted. "Their bodies are their instruments, and if I had that body, I'd play it like a Stradivarius!"

"But—"

"The women are beautiful, and the men are fools! What's the problem?"

"But you're not really answering my question."

Of course not. Because part of the answer is that nobody wants to be the frump at the back of the room anymore, the ghost of women past—it's just not cool. What *is* cool is for women to take a guy's-eye view of pop culture in general and naked ladies in particular. This is an amped-up, horny moment in our culture, and "getting with the program" requires a boys-will-be-boys attitude. Better yet, act like a frat boy in a Wonderbra yourself. Don't worry, everyone's doing it.

There's Madonna gap-toothed in a white cowboy hat in her "Music" video, stuffing a wad of cash into a stripper's G-string. There's the Playboy Mansion in the society pages again, a must-visit Los Angeles stop for female celebrities from Gwyneth Paltrow to Debbie Harry. Last August, California congresswoman Loretta Sanchez scheduled a fund-raiser there. The January issue of *W* magazine features a spread with Balenciaga-clad Playmates, and at Betsey Johnson's spring show, Bunnies went down the runway with neon-orange ears and tufty white tails on their bottoms. The designer gushed to reporters about "empowerment" and "freeing women's sexuality." *Maxim* magazine has a monthly "Letters From Ladies" section to showcase feedback from females (about a quarter of its readership). In November, the film remake of the quintessential jiggle show, *Charlie's Angels,* opened at No. 1 and made $75 million in ten days, reinvigorating the interest of men and women alike in leggy crime fighting. On a flight to Los Angeles a few months ago, I happened to be seated next to Evan Lowenstein of the identical-twin-pretty-boy band Evan & Jaron. He told me he had been partying with some chicks at his hotel room the night before, and "they were trying to convince me to go with them to Scores to meet Howard Stern, but I was too beat."

There was a time when it seemed as if the unintended consequence of the women's movement was the feminized New Age Man. But the newest hybrid of the gender wars is an even more unusual creature: the Female Chauvinist Pig.

I'M TWENTY-SIX, Jewish, raised in Westchester. My mother, a shiatsu masseuse who attended weekly women's consciousness–raising groups for twenty-four years, met my father, a consultant for nonprofits like Amnesty International, NOW, National Abortion Rights Action League, and so on, at the University of Wisconsin, Madison, in the sixties. I went to Wesleyan University, a place where you could pretty much get expelled for saying "girl" instead of "woman." But somewhere along the line, I developed a taste for Howard Stern and started using the word "chick."

You could write it off as an Alex P. Keatonish sort of rebellion in my case, but most people I'm friendly with—both men and chicks, regardless of background—have taken on a similarly loutish posture about what in my Wesleyan days I would have called gender. Partly, it just seems prim to dress up our conversation in the party clothes of political correctness. (Think about it: When was the last time you heard someone you like use the word *objectification*?) But there's also a way in which a certain lewdness, a certain crass, casual humor that has at its core a "me Tarzan, you Jane" mentality, makes us all feel equal. It makes us feel that way because we are all Tarzan, or at least we are all pretending to be.

"Feminism has evolved to the point where women are no longer satisfied being equal to men; they actually have to be men," laments a character on Darren Star's failed series *The Street*.

"What have I been saying?" his friend replies. "They're trying to make us obsolete, dude. You can't turn on the TV without seeing two chicks tonguing each other."

The Female Chauvinist Pig is not a lesbian. But she couldn't have existed before Lesbian Chic magically reconfigured the American conception of lesbian from bull dyke with crew cut to Sharon Stone with ice pick, and made it okay—sexy! racy!—for women to ogle strippers or porn stars or Alyssa Milano on the cover of *Maxim*. The Female Chauvinist Pig doesn't want men to disappear, far from it. She wants to sleep with them and be like them.

By the way, you couldn't have had Female Chauvinist Pigs before the women's movement, either—it's hard to attain that porky swagger when you can't get a job. But whereas the nineties "do me" feminist was a distinctly female, sex-loving, hard-rocking badass, the Female Chauvinist Pig is just mimicking manliness. The she-wolf has had her moment; even Courtney Love has gotten rid of her combat boots and half her nose.

So we've adapted. Women are not about to stand around the sidelines in the frat house of popular culture. If girl rock is going to be about Britney and Christina now, then damn it, we're going to talk about their tushes and learn the words to "Oops! . . . I Did It Again." Because women in America don't want to be excluded from anything—not the board meeting or the cigar that follows it or, lately, even the trip to the strip club that follows that. What we want is to be where it's at, and right now that happens to be a pretty trashy place.

Many of us got tired of being pissed off. Termagant insubordination can be a drag, and no one wants to be a drag. How much easier it is to laugh. How much more appealing to be perceived as funny and with-it. "It's a way of flaunting your femininity—that's what you *think*," says Susan Brownmiller, who's definitely not one of those feminists renowned for their senses of humor. "You think you're being brave, you think you're being sexy, you think you're transcending feminism. But that's bullshit."

This time, however, Brownmiller and the sisterhood aren't going to ruin our fun. Things have changed, we reason. What's the harm? Surely all those Playmates and Angels and strippers are supposed to be ironic. So if you feel stirrings of righteous indignation when you realize that everywhere you look, some demoralizing stereotype is being resurrected in a giggly, bouncy way, just remember: They're *only kidding*. At least that's what they think.

MY FRIEND CHARLOTTE has developed a taste for bimbos. Though she's both an avid heterosexual and a modest dresser, there's something about porn stars and bikini girls in music videos (who more and more frequently *are* porn stars) that grips her the way the Beatles used to bewitch my parents. "The women in these things have these ridiculous bodies with big orb boobs and long legs with fuck-me pumps," she says. "They're plastic—literally plastic—like live Barbie dolls. I grew up playing with Barbie dolls."

Charlotte is from a nice family in Boston, where she attended a top-tier prep school. In college, she worked at the Women's Center, went to Take Back the Night marches, and scared her mother with her hairy armpits. But she feels that this new "guiltiest of pleasures" is just too much to fess up to, so she asked me to refer to her by a pseudonym in this article. "The thing I used to like about this stuff is that at least it was refreshing, it was completely aboveboard," she says. "You felt like Howard was just this one funny, misogynistic guy who said what no one else had the guts to say. But now it's so pervasive: It's like VH1 is covering the porn-rock connection, and it's cool to be a stripper, it's cool to be tarty."

Charlotte has other friends who are unconflicted about their connoisseurship. Getting together with them for the first time, I feel as though I am at a meeting of the Raunch Appreciation Society. Last year, the four of them went to Puerto Rico for a postcollege spring break, and Rachel, a tough, compact girl in platform boots and black pleather pants, has brought Charlotte a memento: a postcard picturing a woman's tumescent breasts against a background of blue sky with the words *breast wishes from puerto rico* scrawled in loopy cursive across the top.

"I was always the girl in the group who showed my tits," Rachel says. "When I first moved to New York, I couldn't get over Robin Byrd. I wouldn't go out till I watched Robin Byrd, and when I did go out, I would talk about Robin Byrd." Rachel is a twenty-five-year-old registered nurse at Beth Israel with a strong southern Massachusetts accent. She pronounces the public-access porn queen's name "Rawbin." "Watching Robin Byrd doesn't turn me on, though," she says. "It's for humor."

"Yeah, it's all comical to me," concurs Sherry, a twenty-five-year-old advertising account executive. Today she started working at a new company, and she's still in her office outfit of cotton blouse and gray stretch-wool skirt. It's Sherry's first big-deal job, and Rachel has brought her a little congratulatory gift: a thick red pencil with a rubber Farrah Fawcett head smiling on one end. "I loved *Charlie's Angels*," Sherry explains.

Lately, Sherry and her roommate, Anyssa, have become "obsessed" with Nevins's show *G-String Divas*. "The other day we were on the subway and I wanted to dance on the pole in the middle," says Anyssa, the daughter of a cop and a florist. "I could never be a stripper myself, but I think it would be so sexually liberating." It isn't her looks that are holding her back; Anyssa is a built, beautiful young woman with icy-pale skin and a broad, lipsticked mouth. Right now she bartends at Bowlmor Lanes, but she wants to be an actress.

"When I'm bartending, I don't dress up because I have to deal with enough assholes as it is," she says. "In college, Sherry and I, by day we would wear these guy outfits, and then at night we'd get dressed up, and people would be like, *Oh, my God!* It's like a card: It's like at first you let them like you for your personality, but then you pull out the hot card and let them look at you like that and it takes it to a whole different level." Anyssa smiles. "And maybe you get to *feel* like a stripper does."

Everyone is quiet for a moment, savoring that possibility.

I suggest that there are reasons one might not want to feel like a stripper; that perhaps spinning greasily around a pole wearing a vapid, sexy facial expression not found in nature is more a parody of female sexual power than an expression of it.

This doesn't go over well. "I can't feel bad for these women," Sherry snaps. "I think they're asking for it."

Sherry considers herself a feminist. "I'm very pro-woman," she says. "I like to see women succeed, whether they're using their minds to do it or using their tits." But she doesn't mind seeing women fail if they aren't using either effectively. She likes the Stern show, for example, because his is a realm in which fairness of a sort pervades. Women who are smart and funny like Sherry, or Robin Quivers, the original Female Chauvinist Pig, get to laugh along with the boys. Women who are pathetic enough to go on national television and strip down to their G-strings in the hopes that Howard will buy them a boob job are punished with humiliation.

"Growing up, I hung out with all guys," says Anyssa. "These are the first girls I ever hung out with who had the same mentality as me and weren't gonna starve themselves and paint their nails every fucking second. I've never been a girly girl, and I've never wanted to compete in that world— I just didn't fit in."

"My boyfriend got mad that I was going out to a strip club!" Rachel offers suddenly. She's drinking an oversize vodka tonic, and it seems to be leading her comments just south of apropos. "We're like the guys in our relationships: We make more money than our boyfriends; we live in better apartments," she explains to me.

"He turned down a chance to work a shoot with Pamela Anderson Lee the other night so he could be with me!" she explodes. "When I found out, I was like, *I would have gone home twelve hours late to see Pamela Anderson Lee!*"

COMEDY CENTRAL AIRS a program called *The Man Show*, which exists solely to celebrate the beer-and-babes lifestyle. I used to watch it once in a while because it's so unbelievably out of hand, and because hey, I can take a joke. When I found out that 38 percent of the viewers are female and that it's co-executive-produced by two women, Jennifer Heftler and Lisa Page, I went out to LA imagining I could confirm what everyone's been saying: that all of this is just a benign goof.

The night I show up for a taping, there isn't enough space for all the guys who've lined up, and a team of heavy-limbed boys in matching green T-shirts from Chico State is pumped to have made it into the audience.

Don, the bald audience fluffer, seems to be looking directly at them when he yells from the stage, "A few weeks ago, we had trouble with guys touching the women here. You can't just grab their asses—you don't do that in real life, do you?" *Beat.* "Welllll . . . so do I!" The frat boys cheer, but not with the alarming gusto of the man in front of them, a scrawny, bespectacled computer technician who resembles one of the *P*'s in Peter, Paul & Mary. "To the women," bellows Don, "today only, you're an honorary man! Grab your dick!"

Snoop is rapping over the loudspeaker:

Guess who back in the motherfuckin house/With a fat dick for your motherfuckin mouth.

Abby, a brunette in tight white jeans, is called up to the stage for her big chance to win a T-shirt. Honorary man status notwithstanding, she is asked to expose her breasts to the crowd. Abby declines, but agrees brightly to kiss another girl instead. A pert redhead in her early twenties races up from the audience to wrap her hands around Abby's back and put her tongue in the stranger's mouth. "Yeah! Yeah! You're making me hard," shrieks Peter/Paul. He is nearly hit in the head by the Chico Statesman behind him, who is pumping his fist in the air in front of his crotch.

Soon after, the stage doors open and out pour the Juggies, nine dancing girls in coordinated pornographic Mother Goose costumes: Little Red Riding Hood in spike-heeled patent-leather thigh-highs, Bo Peep in a push-up bra so aggressive you can almost see her nipples, and, of course, Puss in Boots.

They shimmy their way around the audience, and some of them do tricks on the poles. After the shouting dies down, the show's hosts, Jimmy Kimmel and Adam Carolla, emerge from backstage, fresh as daisies in matching his and his gingham shirts. "Who knows a good joke?" Carolla asks.

"How do you piss your girlfriend off when you're having sex?" a guy in the back volunteers. "Call her up and tell her."

Then they show a pretaped spot about a mock clinic for wife evaluation, where a prospective bride is assessed based on her grasp of football and her aptitude at administering fellatio to Ron Jeremy.

"THERE'S A SIDE of boydom that's fun," declares Jen Heftler, a big woman with frizzy hair and two tattoos, one of a rose and the other of a dragonfly. "They get to fart, they get to be loud—and I think now we're saying we can fart and curse and go to strip clubs and smoke cigars just as easily and just as well."

As for the Juggies, we are supposed to understand that they are kitsch—boobs, yes, but in quotes. "In the sixties, Dean Martin had his Golddiggers, and they were basically Juggies," says Heftler, "but the audience wasn't in on the joke. It was just pretty girls because that's what a guy would have. Then it was, you can never have that, you can't show a woman as a sex object, that's terrible. Now we're back to having it, but it's kind of commenting on that as opposed to just being that. The girls are in on it, and the women watching it are in on it."

But after sitting in that audience, I have to wonder: What exactly are they in on? That women are ditsy and jiggly? That men would like them to be?

Bob Guccione Jr., the publisher and editor of *Gear*, says, "In our pictures, there's a sense of mystery, as if the woman is one step ahead of you. There are women who have a knee-jerk reaction—you know the kind of women I'm talking about—women who just don't like to see guys having fun and are uncomfortable with sex."

The women in front of the camera are *in control*, the argument goes; what's wrong with you that you can't see it? Except that you'd be hard-pressed to argue that the Juggies—who end every episode of *The Man Show* by bouncing around in a section aptly titled "Girls on Trampolines"—are "one step ahead of you."

"Listen, our generation has gone past the point where *The Man Show* is going to cause a guy to walk into a doctor's office and say, *Oh, my God! A woman doctor!*" Heftler counters. "Women have always had to find ways to make men comfortable with where we're at. One of the perks to this job was that we wouldn't have to prove ourselves anymore," she continues. "We could say, 'We worked at *The Man Show*,' and no one would ever think, *Oh, those prissy little women* again."

It's an old strategy. Women who've wanted to be perceived as powerful have long found it more efficient to join forces with men than to try to elevate the entire female sex. Mary McCarthy and Elizabeth Hardwick were famously contemptuous of "women's libbers," for example, and were untroubled about striving to "write like a man." Not everyone cares that this doesn't do much for the sisterhood.

THE NIGHT AFTER the taping, I have dinner with Adam Carolla, Jimmy Kimmel, and *The Man Show*'s co-creator, Daniel Kellison, at the restaurant inside the W Hotel in Westwood, a place that resembles Asia de Cuba in its penchant for hot white lights and giant pieces of fabric draped over everything. I ask why they suppose 38 percent of their viewers are women.

"We did a little research," says Carolla, "and it turns out 38 percent of all women have a sense of humor."

I laugh. I want to be one of those women. The ladies here at the W are like another species: There are lush curves bursting off impossibly thin frames everywhere you look, and miles of hairless, sand-colored skin.

"It's a whole power thing that you take advantage of and career women take advantage of," Kellison offers. "If you read *Maxim* or watch our show or *Howard Stern* or whatever, you have an overview of a cultural phenomenon, you have power. You take responsibility for your life and you don't walk around thinking, *I'm a victim of the press! I'm a victim of pop culture!* So you can laugh at girls on trampolines." He smiles warmly. "There's nothing ominous about this; it's just guys hanging out. You get it."

For a moment, I allow myself to feel vaguely triumphant.

Kimmel sucks an oyster out of its shell and then snickers. "At TCA," the annual Television Critics Association conference in Pasadena, "this woman asked, 'How does having big-breasted women in the Juggy dance squad differ from having black women in the darkie dance squad?' I said, 'First of all, that's the stupidest question I've ever heard.'"

"Then Adam said, 'Let me put your mind at ease: If we ever decide to put together a retarded dance squad, you'll be the first one in it,'" says Kellison, and all three of them laugh.

"What kind of women do you hang out with?" I ask.

Kimmel looks at me as though I'm insane. "For the most part," he says, "*women* don't even want to hang out with their friends."

FOR MY FINAL field trip, I accompany Charlotte and the gang to Ten's on 21st Street. The room—dark, air-conditioned—glints in pink, then green, then orange as dozens of tiny neon stars on the wall flash with color. A bald bouncer in a three-piece suit of sorts leads us to a table near the stage, and we sit down next to two guys in business suits. While one talks on his cell phone, the other is looking up slack-mouthed at the woman twisting in front of him in her underpants. "You're the most beautiful girl in here," he pants. She keeps her face frozen in a slit-eyed half smile until he slips the money in her G-string. Then she walks away, yawning.

Charlotte looks like she may try and make a run for it, but Anyssa decides she's ready for a lap dance. "Oh What a Night" is blaring on the sound system as two strippers approach and peel their dresses off. They don't strictly resemble Barbie dolls, but there is that plastic quality— a body without flaw, skin that looks as if it's been poured from a tube. One stripper slips in between Sherry's legs. Seconds later, a bouncer comes over and grasps her by the arm. "Put your dress on," he says.

"Hey," Sherry yells as the woman is escorted away. "Where'd my girl go?"

Onstage, the blonde who best approximates Pamela Anderson Lee is writhing against a pole. "You should get her on your lap," one of the bouncers tells Sherry, winking.

But her original stripper has returned with a friend, and they settle in next to Sherry and Anyssa. It seems they are getting on swimmingly for a while, but then Anyssa turns to Charlotte, suddenly sullen. "Pass me my wallet," she says. It seems the strippers expect around a hundred dollars for their little chat.

Just then, a tall Russian woman still in her blue polyester dress approaches and rests her hand on my arm. "Are you gay?" she asks. "No? Do you want to be a stripper?"

Because, really—and she was right about this—why else would a woman choose to be here?

SAY EVERYTHING

EMILY NUSSBAUM

FEBRUARY 12, 2007

In the mid-2000s, there was a growing concern among many adults about what young people, the ones who couldn't remember a world without the Internet, were prepared to reveal online. It seemed to some that it was a new form of youthful error, the drinking-and-driving of the digital age. "I was amazed by the hysteria of old people about how young people [on the Internet] are narcissists," says Emily Nussbaum. Her article is both an exploration of a new generation gap, the widest since the sixties, and a defense of the new Web mores. Nussbaum, an editor-at-large at New York, *is a former editor of* Nerve *and a former columnist for* The New York Times.

—

"YEAH, I AM NAKED on the Internet," says Kitty Ostapowicz, laughing. "But I've always said I wouldn't ever put up anything I wouldn't want my mother to see."

She hands me a Bud Lite. Kitty, twenty-six, is a bartender at Kabin in the East Village, and she is frankly adorable, with bright-red hair, a button nose, and pretty features. She knows it, too: Kitty tells me that she used to participate in "ratings communities," like "nonuglies," where people would post photos to be judged by strangers. She has a MySpace page and a Livejournal. And she tells me that the Internet brought her to New York, when a friend she met in a chat room introduced her to his website, which linked to his friends, one of whom was a photographer. Kitty posed for that photographer in Buffalo, where she grew up, then followed him to New York. "Pretty much just wanted a change," she says. "A drastic, drastic change."

Her Livejournal has gotten less personal over time, she tells me. At first it was "just a lot of day-to-day bullshit, quizzes and stuff," but now she tries to "keep it concise to important events." When I ask her how she thinks she'll feel at thirty-five, when her postings are a Google search away, she's okay with that. "I'll be proud!" she says. "It's a documentation of my youth, in a way. Even if it's just me, going back and Googling myself in twenty-five or thirty years. It's my self—what I used to be, what I used to do."

We settle up and I go home to search for Kitty's profile. I'm expecting tame stuff: updates to friends, plus those blurry nudes. But, as it turns out, the photos we talked about (artistic shots of Kitty in bed or, in one picture, in a snowdrift, wearing stilettos) are the least revelatory thing I find. In posts tracing back to college, her story scrolls down my screen in raw and affecting detail: the death of her parents, her breakups, her insecurities, her ambitions. There are photos, but they are candid and unstylized, like a close-up of a tattoo of a butterfly, adjacent (explains the caption) to a bruise she got by bumping into the cash register. A recent entry encourages posters to share stories of sexual assault anonymously.

Some posts read like diary entries: "My period is way late, and I haven't been laid in months, so I don't know what the fuck is up." There are bar anecdotes: "I had a weird guy last night come into work and tell me all about how if I were in the South Bronx, I'd be raped if I were lucky. It was totally unprovoked, and he told me all about my stupid generation and how he fought in Vietnam, and how today's Navy and Marines are a bunch of pussies." But the roughest material comes in her early posts, where she struggles with losing her parents. "I lost her four years ago today. A few hours ago to be precise," she writes. "What may well be the worst day of my life."

Talking to her the night before, I had liked Kitty: She was warm and funny and humble, despite the "nonuglies" business. But reading her Livejournal, I feel thrown off. Some of it makes me wince. Much of it is witty and insightful. Mainly, I feel bizarrely protective of her, someone I've met once—she seems so exposed. And that feeling makes me feel very, very old.

Because the truth is, at twenty-six, Kitty is herself an old lady, in Internet terms. She left her teens several years before the revolution began in earnest: the forest of arms waving cell-phone cameras at concerts, the MySpace pages blinking pink neon revelations, Xanga and Sconex and YouTube and Lastnightsparty.com and Flickr and Facebook and del.icio.us and Wikipedia and especially, the ordinary, endless stream of daily documentation that is built into the life of anyone growing up today. You can see the evidence everywhere, from the rural fifteen-year-old who records videos for thousands of subscribers to the NYU students texting come-ons from beneath the bar. Even nine-year-olds have their own site, Club Penguin, to play games and plan parties. The change has rippled through pretty much every act of growing up. Go through your first big breakup and you may need to change your status on Facebook from "In a relationship" to "Single." Everyone will see it on your "feed," including your ex, and that's part of the point.

IT'S BEEN A LONG time since there was a true generation gap, perhaps fifty years—you have to go back to the early years of rock and roll, when old people still talked about "jungle rhythms." Everything associated with that music and its greasy, shaggy culture felt baffling and divisive, from the crude slang to the dirty thoughts it was rumored to trigger in little girls. That musical divide has all but disappeared. But in the past ten years, a new set of values has sneaked in to take its place, erecting another barrier between young and old. And as it did in the fifties, the older generation has responded with a disgusted, dismissive squawk. It goes something like this:

Kids today. They have no sense of shame. They have no sense of privacy. They are show-offs, fame whores, pornographic little loons who post their diaries, their phone numbers, their stupid poetry—for God's sake, their dirty photos!—online. They have vir-

*tual friends instead of real ones. They talk in illiterate instant
messages. They are interested only in attention—and yet they have
zero attention span, flitting like hummingbirds from one virtual
stage to another.*

"When it is more important to be seen than to be talented, it is hardly surprising that the less gifted among us are willing to fart our way into the spotlight," sneers Lakshmi Chaudhry in the current issue of *The Nation*. "Without any meaningful standard by which to measure our worth, we turn to the public eye for affirmation."

Clay Shirky, a forty-two-year-old professor of new media at NYU's Interactive Telecommunications Program, who has studied these phenomena since 1993, has a theory about that response. "Whenever young people are allowed to indulge in something old people are not allowed to, it makes us bitter. What did we have? The mall and the parking lot of the 7-Eleven? It sucked to grow up when we did! And we're mad about it now." People are always eager to believe that their behavior is a matter of morality, not chronology, Shirky argues. "You didn't behave like that because nobody gave you the option."

None of this is to suggest that older people aren't online, of course; they are, in huge numbers. It's just that it doesn't come naturally to them. "It is a constant surprise to those of us over a certain age, let's say thirty, that large parts of our life can end up online," says Shirky. "But that's not a behavior anyone under thirty has had to unlearn." Despite his expertise, Shirky himself can feel the gulf growing between himself and his students, even in the past five years. "It used to be that we were all in this together. But now my job is not to demystify, but to get the students to see that it's strange or unusual at all. Because they're soaking in it."

One night at Two Boots pizza, I meet some tourists visiting from Kansas City: Kent Gasaway, his daughter Hannah, and two of her friends. The girls are fifteen. They have identical shiny hair and Ugg boots, and they answer my questions in a tangle of upspeak. Everyone has a Facebook, they tell me. Everyone used to have a Xanga ("So seventh grade!"). They got computers in third grade. Yes, they post party pictures. Yes, they

use "away messages." When I ask them why they'd like to appear on a reality show, they explain, "It's the fame and the—well, not the fame, just the
whole, 'Oh, my God, weren't you on TV?' "

After a few minutes of this, I turn to Gasaway and ask if he has a Web
page. He seems baffled by the question. "I don't know why I would," he
says, speaking slowly. "I like my privacy." He's never seen Hannah's Facebook profile. "I haven't gone on it. I don't know how to get into it!" I ask
him if he takes pictures when he attends parties, and he looks at me like I
have three heads. "There are a lot of weirdos out there," he emphasizes.
"There are a lot of strangers out there."

There is plenty of variation among this younger cohort, including a set
of Luddite dissenters: "If I want to contact someone, I'll write them a letter!" grouses Katherine Gillespie, a student at Hunter College. (Although
when I look her up online, I find that she too has a profile.) But these variations blur when you widen your view. One 2006 government study—
framed, as such studies are, around the stranger-danger issue—showed
that 61 percent of thirteen-to-seventeen-year-olds have a profile online,
half with photos. A recent Pew Internet Project study put it at 55 percent
of twelve-to-seventeen-year-olds. These numbers are rising rapidly.

It's hard to pinpoint when the change began. Was it 1992, the first season of *The Real World*? (Or maybe the third season, when cast members
began to play to the cameras? Or the seventh, at which point the seven
strangers were so media-savvy there was little difference between their
being totally self-conscious and utterly unself-conscious?) Or you could
peg the true beginning as that primal national drama of the Paris Hilton
sex tape, those strange weeks in 2004 when what initially struck me as a
genuine and indelible humiliation—the kind of thing that lost former
Miss America Vanessa Williams her crown twenty years earlier—transformed, in a matter of days, from a shocker into no big deal, and then into
just another piece of publicity, and then into a kind of power.

But maybe it's a cheap shot to talk about reality television and Paris
Hilton. Because what we're discussing is something more radical if only
because it is more ordinary: the fact that we are in the sticky center of a
vast psychological experiment, one that's only just begun to show results.
More young people are putting more personal information out in public

than any older person ever would—and yet they seem mysteriously healthy and normal, save for an entirely different definition of privacy. From their perspective, it's the extreme caution of the earlier generation that's the narcissistic thing. Or, as Kitty put it to me, "Why not? What's the worst that's going to happen? Twenty years down the road, someone's gonna find your picture? Just make sure it's a great picture."

And after all, there is another way to look at this shift. Younger people, one could point out, are the only ones for whom it seems to have sunk in that the idea of a truly private life is already an illusion. Every street in New York has a surveillance camera. Each time you swipe your debit card at Duane Reade or use your MetroCard, that transaction is tracked. Your employer owns your e-mails. The NSA owns your phone calls. Your life is being lived in public whether you choose to acknowledge it or not.

So it may be time to consider the possibility that young people who behave as if privacy doesn't exist are actually the sane people, not the insane ones. For someone like me, who grew up sealing my diary with a literal lock, this may be tough to accept. But under current circumstances, a defiant belief in holding things close to your chest might not be highminded. It might be an artifact—quaint and naïve, like a determined faith that virginity keeps ladies pure. Or at least that might be true for someone who has grown up "putting themselves out there" and found that the benefits of being transparent make the risks worth it.

Shirky describes this generational shift in terms of pidgin versus Creole. "Do you know that distinction? Pidgin is what gets spoken when people patch things together from different languages, so it serves well enough to communicate. But Creole is what the children speak, the children of pidgin speakers. They impose rules and structure, which makes the Creole language completely coherent and expressive, on par with any language. What we are witnessing is the Creolization of media."

That's a cool metaphor, I respond. "I actually don't think it's a metaphor," he says. "I think there may actually be real neurological changes involved."

They Think of Themselves as Having an Audience

I'm crouched awkwardly on the floor of Xiyin Tang's Columbia dorm room, peering up at her laptop as she shows me her first blog entries, a thirteen-year-old Xiyin's musings on Good Charlotte and the perfidy of her friends. A Warhol Marilyn print gazes over our shoulders. "I always find myself more motivated to write things," Xiyin, now nineteen, explains, "when I know that somebody, somewhere, might be reading it."

From the age of eight, Xiyin, who grew up in Maryland, kept a private journal on her computer. But in fifth grade, she decided to go public and created two online periodicals: a fashion 'zine and a newsletter for "stories and novellas and whatnot." In sixth grade, she began distributing her journal to two hundred readers. Even so, she still thought of this writing as personal.

"When I first started out with my Livejournal, I was very honest," she remembers. "I basically wrote as if there was no one reading it. And if people wanted to read it, then great." But as more people linked to her, she became correspondingly self-aware. By tenth grade, she was part of a group of about one hundred mostly older kids who knew one another through "this web of MySpacing or Livejournal or music shows." They called themselves "The Family" and centered their attentions around a local band called Spoont. When a Family member commented on Xiyin's entries, it was a compliment; when someone "Friended" her, it was a bigger compliment. "So I would try to write things that would not put them off," she remembers. "Things that were not silly. I tried to make my posts highly stylized and short, about things I would imagine people would want to read or comment on."

Since she's gone to college, she's kept in touch with friends through her journal. Her romances have a strong online component. But lately she's compelled by a new aspect of her public life, what she calls, with a certain hilarious spokeswoman-for-the-cause affect, the "party-photo phenomenon." Xiyin clicks to her Facebook profile, which features eighty-eight photos. Some are snapshots. Some are modeling poses she took for a friend's portfolio. And then there are her MisShapes shots: images from a popular party in Tribeca, where photographers shoot attendees against a backdrop. In these photos, Xiyin wears eighties fashions—a thick belt and an asymmetrical top that give me my own high-school flashback—and strikes a world-weary pose. "To me, or to a lot of people, it's like, why go to a party if you're not going to get your picture taken?"

Among this gallery, one photo stands out: a window-view shot of Xiyin walking down below in the street, as if she'd been snapped by a spy camera. It's part of a series of "stalker photos" a friend has been taking, she informs me: He snaps surreptitious, paparazzi-like photos of his friends and then uploads them and "tags" the images with their names, so they'll come across them later. "Here's one where he caught his friend Hannah talking on the phone."

Xiyin knows there's a scare factor in having such a big online viewership—you could get stalked for real, or your employer could bust you for partying. But her actual experience has been that if someone is watching, it's probably a good thing. If you see a hot guy at a party, you can look up his photo and get in touch. When she worked at American Apparel, management posted encouraging remarks on employee MySpace pages. A friend was offered an internship by a magazine's editor-in-chief after he read her profile. All sorts of opportunities—romantic, professional, creative—seem to Xiyin to be directly linked to her willingness to reveal herself a little.

When I was in high school, you'd have to be a megalomaniac or the most popular kid around to think of yourself as having a fan base. But people twenty-five and under are just being realistic when they think of themselves that way, says media researcher Danah Boyd, who calls the phenomenon "invisible audiences." Since their early adolescence, they've learned to modulate their voice to address a set of listeners that may shrink or expand at any time: talking to one friend via instant message (who could cut-and-paste the transcript), addressing an e-mail distribution list (archived and accessible years later), arguing with someone on a posting board (anonymous, semi-anonymous, then linked to by a snarky blog). It's a form of communication that requires a person to be constantly aware that anything you say can and will be used against you, but somehow not to mind.

This is an entirely new set of negotiations for an adolescent. But it does also have strong psychological similarities to two particular demographics: celebrities and politicians, people who have always had to learn to parse each sentence they form, unsure whether it will be ignored or redound into sudden notoriety (Macaca!). In essence, every young person in

America has become, in the literal sense, a public figure. And so they have adopted the skills that celebrities learn in order not to go crazy: enjoying the attention instead of fighting it—and doing their own publicity before somebody does it for them.

They Have Archived Their Adolescence

I remember very little from junior-high school and high school, and I've always believed that was probably a good thing. Caitlin Oppermann, seventeen, has spent her adolescence making sure this doesn't happen to her. At twelve, she was blogging; at fourteen, she was snapping digital photos; at fifteen, she edited a documentary about her school marching band. But right now the high-school senior is most excited about her first "serious project," caitlinoppermann.com. On it, she lists her e-mail and AIM accounts, complains about the school's Web censors, and links to photos and videos. There's nothing racy, but it's the type of information overload that tends to terrify parents. Oppermann's are supportive: "They know me and they know I'm not careless with the power I have on the Internet."

As we talk, I peer into Oppermann's bedroom. I'm at a café in the West Village, and Oppermann is in Kansas City—just like those Ugg girls, who might, for all I know, be linked to her somehow. And as we talk via iChat, her face floats in the corner of my screen, blonde and deadpan. By swiveling her Webcam, she gives me a tour: her walls, each painted a different color of pink; storage lockers; a subway map from last summer, when she came to Manhattan for a Parsons design fellowship. On one wall, I recognize a peace banner I've seen in one of her videos.

I ask her about that Xanga, the blog she kept when she was twelve. Did she delete it?

"It's still out there!" she says. "Xanga, a Blogger, a Facebook, my Flickr account, my Vimeo account. Basically, what I do is sign up for everything. I kind of weed out what I like." I ask if she has a MySpace page, and she laughs and gives me an amused, pixellated grimace. "Unfortunately I do! I was so against MySpace, but I wanted to look at people's pictures. I just really don't like MySpace. 'Cause I think it's just so . . . I don't know if *su-*

perficial is the right word. But plastic. These profiles of people just parading themselves. I kind of have it in for them."

Oppermann prefers sites like Noah K Everyday, where a sad-eyed, twenty-six-year-old Brooklyn man has posted a single photo of himself each day since he was nineteen, a low-tech piece of art that is oddly moving—capturing the way each day brings some small change. Her favorite site is Vimeo, a kind of hipster YouTube. (She's become friends with the site's creator, Jakob Lodwick, and when she visited New York, they went to the Williamsburg short-film festival.) The videos she's posted there are mostly charming slices of life: a "typical day at a school," hula-hooping in Washington Square Park, conversations set to music. Like Oppermann herself, they seem revelatory without being revealing, operating in a space midway between behavior and performance.

At seventeen, Oppermann is conversant with the conventional wisdom about the online world—that it's a sketchy bus station packed with pedophiles. (In fact, that's pretty much the standard response I've gotten when I've spoken about this piece with anyone over thirty-nine: "But what about the perverts?" For teenagers, who have grown up laughing at porn pop-ups and the occasional instant message from a skeezy stranger, this is about as logical as the question "How can you move to New York? You'll get mugged!") She argues that when it comes to online relationships, "you're getting what you're being." All last summer, as she bopped around downtown Manhattan, Oppermann met dozens of people she already knew, or who knew her, from online. All of which means that her memories of her time in New York are stored both in her memory, where they will decay, and on her site, where they will not, giving her (and me) an unsettlingly crystalline record of her seventeenth summer.

Oppermann is not the only one squirreling away an archive of her adolescence, accidentally or on purpose. "I have a logger program that can show me drafts of a paper I wrote three years ago," explains Melissa Mooneyham, a graduate of Hunter College. "And if someone says something in instant message, then later on, if you have an argument, you can say, 'No, wait: You said *this* on *this* day at *this* time.'"

As for that defunct Xanga, Oppermann read it not long ago. "It was interesting. I just look at my junior-high self, kind of ignorant of what the future holds. And I thought, *You know, I don't think I gave myself enough credit: I'm really witty!*" She pauses and considers. "If I don't delete it, I'm still gonna be there. My generation is going to have all this history; we can document anything so easily. I'm a very sentimental person; I'm sure that has something to do with it."

Their Skin Is Thicker Than Yours

The biggest issue of living in public, of course, is simply that when people see you, they judge you. It's no wonder Paris Hilton has become a peculiarly contemporary role model, blurring as she does the distinction between exposing oneself and being exposed, mortifying details spilling from her at regular intervals like hard candy from a piñata. She may not be likable, but she offers a perverse blueprint for surviving scandal: Just keep walking through those flames until you find a way to take them as a compliment.

This does not mean, as many an apocalyptic op-ed has suggested, that young people have no sense of shame. There's a difference between being able to absorb embarrassment and not feeling it. But we live in a time in which humiliation and fame are not such easily distinguished quantities. And this generation seems to have a high tolerance for what used to be personal information splashed in the public square.

Consider Casey Serin. On Iamfacingforeclosure.com, the twenty-five-year-old émigré from Uzbekistan has blogged a truly disastrous financial saga: He purchased eight houses in eight months, looking to "fix 'n' flip," only to end up in massive debt. The details, which include scans of his financial documents, are raw enough that people have accused him of being a hoax, à la YouTube's Lonelygirl15. ("ForeclosureBoy24," he jokes.) He's real, he insists. Serin simply decided that airing his bad investments could win him helpful feedback—someone might even buy his properties. "A lot of people wonder, 'Aren't you embarrassed?' Maybe it's naïve, but I'm not going to run from responsibility." Flaming commenters don't bug him. And ironically, the impetus for the site came when Serin was denied a loan after a lender discovered an earlier, friends-only site. Rather than delete it, he swung the doors open. "Once you put something online, you really cannot take it back," he points out. "You've got to be careful what you say—but once you say it, you've got to stand by it. And the only way to repair it is to continue to talk, to explain myself, to see it through. If I shut down, I'm at the mercy of what other people say."

Any new technology has its victims, of course: the people who get caught during that ugly interregnum when a technology is new but no one knows how to use it yet. Take "Susie," a girl whose real name I won't use because I don't want to make her any more Googleable. Back in 2000, Susie filmed some videos for her then-boyfriend: she stripped, masturbated, blew kisses at the Webcam—surely just one of many to use her new computer this way. Then someone (it's not clear who, but probably her boyfriend's roommate) uploaded the videos. This was years before YouTube, when Kaazaa and Morpheus ruled. Susie's films became the earliest viral videos and turned her into an accidental online porn star, with her own Wikipedia entry.

When I reached her at work, she politely took my information down and called back from her cell. And she told me that she'd made a choice that she knew set her outside her own generation. "I never do MySpace or Facebook," she told me. "I'm deathly afraid to Google myself." Instead, she's become stoic, walling herself off from the exposure. "I've had to choose not to be upset about it because then I'd be upset all the time. They want a really strong reaction. I don't want to be that person."

She had another option, she knows: She could have embraced her notoriety. "I had everyone calling my mom: Dr. Phil, Jerry Springer, *Playboy*. I could have been like Paris Hilton, but that's not me. That thing is so unlike my personality; it's not the person I am. I guess I didn't think it was real." As these experiences become commonplace, she tells me, "it's not going to be such a big deal for people. Because now it's happened to a million people."

And it's true that in the years since Susie's tapes went public, the leaked sex tape has become a perverse, established social convention; it happens at every high school and to every B-list celebrity. At Hunter College last year, a student named Elvin Chaung allegedly used Facebook accounts to blackmail female students into sending him nude photos. In movies like *Road Trip*, "oops porn" has become a comic convention, and the online stuff regularly includes a moment when the participant turns to the camera and says, "You're not going to put this online, are you?"

But Susie is right: For better or worse, people's responses have already begun to change. Just two years after her tapes were leaked, another girl had a tape released on the Internet. The poster was her ex, whom we'll call Jim Bastard. It was a parody of the MasterCard commercial: listing funds spent on the relationship, then his "priceless" revenge for getting dumped—a clip of the two having sex. (To the casual viewer, the source of the embarrassment is somewhat unclear: The girl is gorgeous and the sex is not all that revealing, while the boy in question is wearing socks.) Then, after the credits, the money shot: her name, her e-mail addresses, and her AIM screen names.

Like Susie, the subject tried, unsuccessfully, to pull the video offline; she filed suit and transferred out of school. For legal reasons, she wouldn't talk to me. But although she's only two years younger than Susie, she hasn't followed in her footsteps. She has a MySpace account. She has a Facebook account. She's planned parties online. And shortly after one such party last October, a new site appeared on MySpace: seemingly a little revenge of her own. The community is titled "The Society to Chemically Castrate Jim Bastard," and it features a picture of her tormentor with the large red letters LOSER written on his forehead—not the most high-minded solution, perhaps, but one alternative to retreating for good.

Like anyone who lives online, Xiyin Tang has been stung a few times by criticism, like the night she was reading BoredatButler.com, an anonymous website posted on by Columbia students, and saw that someone had called her "pathetic and a whore." She stared at her name for a while, she says. "At first, I got incredibly upset, thinking, *Well now, all these people can just go Facebook me and point and form judgments.*" Then she did what she knew she had to do: She brushed it off. "I thought, *Well, I guess you have to be sort of honored that someone takes the time to write about you, good or bad.*"

I tell Xiyin about Susie and her sex tape. She's sympathetic with Susie's emotional response, she says, but she's most shocked by her decision to log off entirely. "My philosophy about putting things online is that I don't have any secrets," says Xiyin. "And whatever you do, you should be able to do it so that you're not ashamed of it. And in that sense, I put myself out there online because I don't care—I'm proud of what I do and I'm not ashamed of any aspect of that. And if someone forms a judgment about me, that's their opinion.

"If that girl's video got published, if she did it in the first place, she should be thick-skinned enough to just brush it off," Xiyin muses. "I understand that it's really humiliating and everything. But if something like that happened to me, I hope I'd just say, well, that was a terrible thing for a guy to do, to put it online. But I did it and that's me. So I am a sexual person and I shouldn't have to hide my sexuality. I did this for my boyfriend just like you probably do this for your boyfriend, just that yours is not published. But to me, it's all the same. It's either documented online for other people to see or it's not, but either way you're still doing it. So my philosophy is, why hide it?"

Future Shock

For anyone over thirty, this may be pretty hard to take. Perhaps you smell brimstone in the air, the sense of a devil's bargain: Is this what happens when we are all, eternally, onstage? It's not as if those fifties squares griping about Elvis were wrong, after all. As Clay Shirky points out, "All that stuff the elders said about rock and roll? They pretty much nailed it. Miscegenation, teenagers running wild, the end of marriage!"

Because the truth is, we're living in frontier country right now. We can take guesses at the future, but it's hard to gauge the effects of a drug while you're still taking it. What happens when a person who has archived her teens grows up? Will she regret her earlier decisions, or will she love the sturdy bridge she's built to her younger self—not to mention the access to the past lives of friends, enemies, romantic partners? On a more pragmatic level, what does this do when you apply for a job or meet the person you're going to marry? Will employers simply accept that everyone has a few videos of themselves trying to read the Bible while stoned? Will your kids watch those stoner Bible videos when they're sixteen? Is there a point in the aging process when a person will want to pull back that curtain—or will the MySpace crowd maintain these flexible, cheerfully thick-skinned personae all the way into the nursing home?

And when you talk to the true believers, it's hard not to be swayed. Jakob Lodwick seems like he shouldn't be that kind of idealist. He's Caitlin Oppermann's friend, the co-founder of Vimeo and a co-creator of the raunchy CollegeHumor.com. Lodwick originated a popular feature in which college girls post topless photos; one of his first online memories was finding Susie's videos and thinking she seemed like the ideal girlfriend. But at twenty-five, Lodwick has become rather sweetly enamored of the uses of video for things other than sex. His first viral breakthrough was a special-effects clip in which he runs into the street and appears to lie down in front of a moving bus—a convincing enough stunt that MSNBC, with classic older-generation cluelessness, used it to illustrate a segment about kids doing dangerous things on the Internet.

But that was just an ordinary film, he says: no different from a TV segment. What he's really compelled by these days is the potential for self-documentation to deepen the intimacy of daily life. Back in college, Lodwick experimented with a website on which he planned to post a profile of every person he knew. Suddenly he had fans, not just of his work, but of him. "There was a clear return on investment when I put myself out there: I get attention in return. And it felt good." He began making "vidblogs," aiming his camera at himself, then turning it around to capture "what I'd see. I'd try to edit as little as possible so I could catch, say, a one-second glimpse of conversation. And that was what resonated with people. It was like they were having a dream that only I could have had, by watching this four or five minutes. Like they were remembering my memories. It didn't tell them what it was like to hang out with me. It showed them what it was like to be me."

This is Jakob's vision: a place where topless photos are no big deal—but also where everyone can be known, simply by making him- or herself a bit vulnerable. Still, even for someone like me who is struggling to embrace the online world, Lodwick's vision can seem so utopian it tilts into the impossible. "I think we're gradually moving away from the age of investing in something negative," he muses about the crueler side of online culture. "For me, a fundamental principle is that if you like something, you should show your love for it; if you don't like it, ignore it, don't waste your time." Before that great transition, some Susies will get crushed in the gears of change. But soon, he predicts, online worlds will become more like real life: Reputation will be the rule of law. People will be ashamed if they act badly, because they'll be doing so in front of all 3,000 of their friends. "If it works in real life, why wouldn't it work online?"

If this seems too good to be true, it's comforting to remember that technology always has aftershocks. Surely, when telephones took off, there was a mourning period for that lost, glorious golden age of eye contact.

Right now the big question for anyone of my generation seems to be, endlessly, "Why would anyone do that?" This is not a meaningful question for a sixteen-year-old. The benefits are obvious: The public life is fun. It's creative. It's where their friends are. It's theater, but it's also community: In this linked, logged world, you have a place to think out loud and be listened to, to meet strangers and go deeper with friends. And, yes, there are all sorts of crappy side effects: the passive-aggressive drama ("you know who you are!"), the shaming outbursts, the chill a person can feel in cyberspace on a particularly bad day. There are lousy side effects of most social changes (see feminism, democracy, the creation of the interstate highway system). But the real question is, as with any revolution, which side are you on?

SWAPPING

JUDITH VIORST

NOVEMBER 2, 1970

From its beginnings, New York *has been a magazine not only for the insider and trendsetter but for the reader observing that trendy city in envy or awe or amusement. Judith Viorst was that reader's in-house ombudsman. "I think I was the voice of the* New York *reader who was not the last word in hip and tuned-in but who was maybe trying to learn how to be that way," she says. Viorst was a carpooling mom with three kids and a husband, a woman who worried that her shoes weren't quite fashionable enough. She used that life as a platform for a weekly column that she wrote in the form of a gentle poem. "I was* New York's *house poet," she says. Before her column, she'd never published a poem. Her columns ran for a dozen years, until she left to study Freudian psychology. She later wrote books about the stages of life, her best known of which is* Necessary Losses. *She is also a children's-book writer. Her* Alexander *series—based on her son's life—has sold four million copies.*

I like to keep up with the new aberrations
And here's what I recently read:
The latest in lust is the swapping of spouses.
The old-fashioned marriage, it's said,
Is just for the frigid, repressed, and neurotic,
Which no modern wife wants to be.
But nobody asks can he swap with my husband.

Is something the matter with me?

It's claimed that the switching of partners produces
A soundness of body and mind
And feelings of intimate group satisfaction
The couples can't manage to find
In cook-outs and bridge clubs and zoning board meetings
And fund drives to build the school gym.
But nobody asks will I swap her my husband.

Is something the matter with him?

Abandoned, insatiable, pulsing with hunger,
It all seems a terrible strain.
Now why did they have to go make things so fancy
When I've been enjoying them plain?
Erotica hasn't appeared at our parties.
We're still talking kids and clogged pipes.
And nobody asks can we swap with each other.

I guess we don't look like the types.

MY BREAST
One Woman's Cancer Story

JOYCE WADLER

APRIL 13 AND APRIL 20, 1992

*When Joyce Wadler wrote about her breast cancer in 1992, the disease was the leading killer of women between thirty-five and fifty-four. Her story helped explode the taboo against talking publicly about such personal matters. Five years later, Wadler, stricken with ovarian cancer, again turned her illness into a journalistic project—*New York *published "Double Exposure" in 1997. Wadler's second cancer led to the discovery that she has a genetic mutation, one found in Ashkenazic Jews like herself. This inheritance proved to be the link between her two cancers and her father's prostate cancer. Though her father did not survive his illness, Wadler says, "My health is excellent." And—because people ask—she adds that her breasts are still intact and, also, excellent. "The girls are still there," she says. Wadler, currently a reporter for* The New York Times, *is the author of two books,* My Breast *and* Liaison.

I HAVE A SCAR on my left breast, four inches long, that runs from the right side of my breast to just above the nipple. Nick, whom I no longer see, once said that if anyone asked, I should say I was attacked by a jealous woman. The true story, which I prefer, is that a surgeon made the cut, following a line I had drawn for him the night before. He had asked me where I wanted the scar, and I had put on a black strapless bra and my favorite party dress and drawn a line in ink just below the top of the bra, a good four inches below the tumor. The surgeon took it out using a local, and when he was done, I asked to see it. It was the size of a robin's egg, with the gray brainlike matter that gives it its name: medullary cancer. It rested in the middle of a larger ball of pink-and-white breast tissue, sliced down the center like a hard-boiled egg, an onionlike layering of whitish-gray tissue about it, and I looked at it hard, trying to figure it out. We did not know it was cancer until twenty minutes later, when they had almost finished stitching me up and the pathology report came back, and then I was especially glad I had looked. Mano a mano, eyeball to eyeball. This is a modern story. Me and my cancer. I won.

Whom do I introduce first, me or my breasts? Formerly, I thought of my body as a unit, indivisible, with my breasts in some small way contributing to my notion of who I am. Now that they have shown the ability to destroy me, I regard them with new respect, thinking perhaps they deserve not only separate but higher billing. As this is a breast-cancer story, maybe they should have it. They are, anyway, good-sized breasts and since I know it would be difficult for me to spot a malignant lump, I have mammograms every year, though I've known of no one with breast cancer in my family.

WHO I AM IS a journalist, forty-four, Jewish, never married, which, as everybody in New York knows, thanks to our one million collective hours of analysis, is a whole other category than single. I was raised in the Catskills, in a boarding house, in a large, noisy, opinionated family headed by my father's mother, who, rather than leaving the Russian *shtetl* of Molov Guburney, brought it to America with her. It enclosed her like a capsule, the Bubble in the Bubble; she never learned to read English and spoke to me in Yiddish, a language I did not entirely understand. I came to New York, to the Village, at seventeen and have lived here since, working for newspapers and magazines. My closest friend is Herb, a comedy writer. We hang out so much that when I am seeing somebody, we joke about how to explain about Herb. Herb's idea is that I throw a sheet over him when he is lying on the couch reading the newspaper, and after each date I pull back the sheet a little bit, and by the time it gets serious, the guy's got the picture. Also, I was in a difficult relationship. His name was

Nick Di Stefano, he was a sportswriter I had known for years, and I had been seeing him, on and off, for eight months. He was Italian, which in my family is considered practically Jewish, except that (1) as children, Italians don't talk back to their parents, and (2) as adults, the men Run Around. Naturally, being so troublesome, we find them very appealing, and anyway, I had always liked Nick. He was smart; he knew all the lyrics to *The Pajama Game;* he dressed like a forties sharpie; he had the requisite newspaper Up-Yours Attitude toward authority.

THE MORNING I DISCOVER the lump, Nick and I are, once again, broken up. It is the first week in March, Monday, a crazy day at *People* magazine, where I am working. I am feeling particularly tense because I'm taking a leave of absence and have one week in which to finish my stories. I am so frantic I have canceled my mammogram at the Guttman, figuring I'll do it when my leave begins.

Then, as I'm showering, I feel it: a large, oval swelling on the upper inner part of my left breast. I have always wondered how women who discover lumps find them, but there is no missing this; it seems to be, as I move my hand around it, the size of an egg, slightly raised, sore to the touch. My breasts, since my mid-thirties, have been sore and swollen before my period, and as I've gotten older the soreness has increased—but I had my period two weeks ago. Another strange thing, this lump seems so big, and I don't remember it being there yesterday. I decide I should get it checked out, but I am not very concerned. What I have heard about breast cancer is that except for a lump, it is asymptomatic; you don't have pain. I figure it's just another one of my fibrocystic lumps, which come and go.

But the Time-Life doctor, provided through *People* magazine, is concerned. And an hour after I see him, I am hailing a cab for the Upper East Side offices of a surgeon we'll call Luke. I am scared. Before I leave his office, the doctor asks if I will have health coverage during my leave, and that has added to my feeling that this is serious. I am now flip-flopping between telling myself I am overreacting and a giddy hysteria.

Standing on Sixth Avenue, I have turned into Zorba the Greek. I want to live. The things I haven't done flash before me, a long list of "But wait, I wanna . . ." But wait, I wanna finish my book; but wait, I wanna get married; but wait, I wanna make some money and take Nick to Paris to meet my friends; but wait, I'm just getting started. . . . I think about Nick and the time we've wasted fighting and make a deal with myself: If everything's okay, I won't worry about monogamy; I won't *hok* him about moving in; I will make the most of every moment. As unwittingly as Newton discovered gravity, I have stumbled upon the key to making me the dream girl of every uncommitting man in Manhattan: breast cancer.

In the doctor's office, there are a dozen women. They seem older than I, and oddly, they all look alike. They look like a truck ran over their faces, I find myself thinking, which I know, as soon as it crosses my mind, is an ugly thought and not correct. Then I realize what I am looking at: fear. I have never seen so much of it sitting together. It's a good thing there's nothing wrong with me, I think. Then, as I have a wait, I go for a walk. I have already called Herb, but now I find I want to talk to Nick too. He tells me it is probably nothing and is very sweet.

"Just tell me what you want me to do, baby," he says.

WHEN I SEE HIM, Luke, the specialist, is reassuring. "Malignancies tend to be hard, almost stony. You can't manipulate them. This you can. I'm 98 percent sure this is not malignant."

What he believes I have, Luke says, is an inflammation of some sort, perhaps a cyst. To find out, he would like to aspirate the lump: take out some liquid with a hypodermic, and send it to be analyzed. It's a painless procedure; all I'll feel is a needle prick. When a cyst is aspirated, a lot of liquid usually comes out, generally clear. It is painless, but it doesn't go as planned.

"Huh, that's odd," Luke says, and he shows me: He has been able to draw out very little liquid. What there is is thick and puslike, though that could be consistent with infection.

I get dressed. Luke tells me he still sees no reason for concern; the signs point to an inflammation, and he's prescribing Dicloxacillin, a form of penicillin. We'll try that for a week or two and see if it reduces the swelling. If not, he will remove the lump. I am concerned: If it's a cyst, I say, how come more liquid didn't come out? And if it's not a cyst, what is it?

"I don't know," says Luke. "That's why we're doing the tests."

I go meet Nick at the Lion's Head, downtown. He's wearing his fedora low on his head and gives me that cocky Bronx grin that has always knocked me out.

"See, I knew it would be nothing," he says, and within hours we are unbroken up.

I AM NOT A HYPOCHONDRIAC, I lean toward the other extreme, associating sickness with weakness and therefore denying being sick. This, I believe, is the legacy of my mother, Milly, who ran off to Florida at seventeen to paint flamingos on glass, in my childhood stole trees from state preserves insisting they were hers because her tax dollars had paid for them, and at sixty-five is still one of the great forces of nature.

"I've never been sick a day in my life," she says. "One hour after I had you, I was eating. The other women in the hospital were screaming their heads off. I made up my mind, 'How it went in, it will go out,' and that was that. This worrying you have about every little thing, *that* you got from your father. He was the worrier. Him and his mother. The Aspirin Addict."

Also, before going off at sixty-two as a volunteer in the Israeli army, "I don't fear death. Death to me is just another adventure. I can think of no greater honor than dying for the state of Israel, the Jewish homeland."

"You're an old dame, Ma," I say. "You think they're gonna put a machine gun in your hand and send you to the front? You're gonna be cleaning toilets."

"Don't even bother to bring back the body," she says.

I do fear death. Even more, I fear a bad death, strapped to machines in a hospital like my father. "Joyce," he had taken to telling me from the mountains, when I called once a week from Paris. "Your father is a very sick man. Your father is dying." I did not entirely believe him. I knew he was sick, very sick. I had been there for the early operations in the city and the last-minute flights to Florida. I knew the cancer was creeping up his spine and down his legs and was eventually going to kill him. But his blood counts were good, he was going to his business every day. It is a rotten thing to admit, but a voice in me, hearing him, was satirizing him: "Joyce, your father is dying"—Hebraic Dramatic Third Person, now replacing that previous family favorite, "You realize, of course, you are killing your father."

I do not, however, dwell on that memory the week of the scare. I trust Dr. Luke, and I know he's good—a friend was a patient; his reputation is excellent. I do mention the lump to my mother, who is in Florida for the winter, but I tell her I don't think it's serious, and I believe it.

The only thing is, I am distracted by this thing in my chest. It's so sore I cannot sleep on my stomach. The penicillin doesn't seem to be doing much after ten days. There is a very bright light in my gym locker room, and I see how vivid and delineated the area around the lump still is.

"I'm starting to feel this thing has a life of its own," I tell Herb one night, as he's stretched out on the couch. "Like it's gonna come flying out of my body any minute, like that thing in *Alien,* and run around the living room and put on a sports channel and tell me to get it a beer."

Eleven days after the discovery of the lump, I go back to see Dr. Luke. He examines my breast and in less than a minute makes a decision.

"This has to come out," he says.

I am not scared now—I am relieved. I don't think it's cancer—I'm too healthy for cancer—I just want this thing out of my body, the sooner the better. I'd be happy if Luke could do it right now in the office. He says that's out of the question.

I spend the night before surgery alone. Nick calls three times, asking when I am leaving for the hospital so he can call and wish me good luck. I remember I have to make my decision about the scar. I put on a bandeau bra that is the skimpiest I own and a skinny little Nicole Miller dress, deep purple, with spaghetti straps, that I wore when Nick took me dancing at the Rainbow Room. I loved that night. I had a thirties evening bag that I had got for forty francs at a flea market in Paris and a Deco rhinestone bracelet from an estate sale in New York, and as I get dressed I wonder about the women who had owned the bag and the bracelet, and where they had worn them, and if they had been as happy as I. Then I take off the dress and turn down the top of the bra a little bit and trace the edge with a ballpoint pen. As I do, I start to cry. I don't have a perfect body by model standards, my breasts are different from what they were in my twenties, but they are my breasts, it is my body, and I like it very much. Now I am making a mark that says, "Cut me."

ROOSEVELT HOSPITAL IS GLOOMY. A group of homeless people has set up housekeeping on the 58th Street side, a sofa and two armchairs arranged in a traditional living-room style. Inside, the hospital needs painting. On the third-floor short-term-stay center, Herb parks himself in a reception area, while I go to a large room, which is partitioned with curtains, and change into baggy hospital clothes. Taking off my bra, I see that the line I have drawn is very low, nearly halfway down my breast. Wonderful, I think. Now the doctor is going to think I'm fast. A few minutes later, the surgical resident who will be assisting Luke drops by.

"Whoa! You can't miss that!" he says when he sees the lump.

Luke comes to get me. He looks very preppy, sockless in clogs, and is very sweet, putting an arm around me as we walk to the operating room. I have a feeling this is politically incorrect behavior and I am not supposed to like it, but I do. The operating team includes a male and a female nurse, as well as the resident and Luke. Seeing the line on my breast, Luke laughs.

"You've sure made this idiotproof," he says.

They paint my breast with a red-brown ointment that smells like iodine and cover the rest of my chest with sterile cloth. I can't see the surgery, because Luke has asked me to turn my face to the right, but he has promised to tell me what I will feel and what he is doing. The anesthetic is Xylocaine. He injects it around my breast, waiting for the area to numb, then makes a cut. I have a feeling of warmth and wetness. Then there are strong sensations of tugging as he pulls back tissue and starts tunneling up to the lump, in the inner upper quadrant of my breast. Sometimes I feel a bit of pain, almost a burning sensation, and he gives me more Xylocaine. The tunneling goes on for twenty minutes, and while it is not as unpleasant as a dentist's drilling, the more tissue that is pulled apart and clamped, the more uncomfortable I become. I am having second thoughts about being so concerned about looking good in a low-cut dress. Luke tells me they've reached the lump, but they're going to go beyond it and take a margin of healthy tissue. I'm getting worried again. I don't know whether the room is cool or I'm feeling a nervous chill, but Luke seems to be cutting a lot of flesh—I know the lump is high, but I feel he is burrowing up toward my collarbone. Then I feel some final tugging and the thing is out, and I see out of the corner of my eye a metal tray and they are cauterizing blood vessels. Luke moves away from the operating table and a few minutes later comes back. It's a tumor all right, he says, sounding serious, but what sort he cannot say. He's sending it to the lab now. I tell him that before he does, I'd like to see it.

"You sure?" he says.

"Yeah," I say. He picks it up. I am astonished at how big it is. The excised flesh is the size of a tangerine and has been sliced down the middle to expose the cross-section of the tumor—that must be what Luke did when he left the table. The tumor, which is the size of a robin's egg, is grayish white, with a layer of whitish-pink tissue. Around that is what appears to be normal breast tissue, pink and white, like very fatty, coarsely ground chopped meat. Luke points out the layering around the tumor, saying it appears to be encapsulated, and that is good. I don't think any of this is good. I can't believe this big gray glob came out of me. I have a bad feeling, a sense of unreality, as if I am in a dream or a place I had no intention to be.

"How soon will we know the results?" I say, as they start stitching me up.

"About twenty minutes," Luke says.

And then, more to myself than to anyone else:

"How am I going to tell my mother?"

I concentrate on being calm. In fifteen minutes, just as they've finished bandaging me, somebody comes into the room.

"Well, it is a tumor, and it is malignant," Luke begins briskly, as if he's giving a lecture to a group of medical students. "It's what's called a medullary carcinoma; it's. . . ."

I am having trouble following. Thoughts are going through my head faster than I was aware thoughts could travel: This can't be real. Is he telling me I'm going to die? Should I ask for a rabbi? No, wait, I'm not a religious Jew, I'm more like an ethnic Jew—that would be hypocritical.

But maybe rabbis in hospitals are more like therapists. Why is he telling me this stuff here, where I'm alone? Wasn't that the point of bringing Herb?

I interrupt him.

"Do you think we could hold off on this until we get upstairs and you can talk to my friend too?" I say.

We find Herb and Luke takes it from the top. It was "a well-circumscribed mass," 2.8 centimeters, with seemingly clean tissue around it—he'll have more detailed results in a few days. It has been caught early; clinically, it's a stage-two cancer. Provided there is no cancer in the lymph nodes under the arm, it is "quite curable."

I'm feeling dreamlike again. I don't get it, I tell Luke. I had mammograms, I had checkups, this thing was enormous; how was it missed? He says medullary is not like other cancers—it may not calcify and can appear on a mammogram as a cyst.

"So how do we know there's not another one of these things somewhere inside me?" I say.

"We don't," he says. "Your breasts are a breast surgeon's nightmare. They're large and dense and full of lumps."

I remember the pictures in the medical book. The real ones are gonna be this dangerous, let them make me a fake.

"Take it off," I say.

I have one more question. I am afraid to ask it, but I have to, anyway.

"What am I looking at here?" I ask. "Statistically?"

He isn't any happier answering than I am asking. He doesn't care much for statistics, he says. You can still have a cancer that has a high cure rate, and if you're in the percentage that is not cured, it doesn't matter. In my case, I have a cancer that has a favorable prognosis and is "more curable than average."

I need something harder.

"When my father was diagnosed with prostate cancer, it was something like a 60 percent survival rate at four years, a 40 percent survival rate at seven years," I say.

"I would say the statistics, in your case, are considerably better than that," he says.

"How much better?" I ask.

"For breast cancer, the overall cure rate is 70 percent. For medullary, it's above that. I would say 80 percent, 90 percent."

I feel better. I like these odds. I don't entirely believe them, but I like them. This leaves me with one immediate problem: how to tell my mother. Herb has the solution: "Lead with the positive." I find my notebook, and we work out the lead and phone it in. The last time I did this, I remember, I was filing a breaking story for *The Washington Post* on a Concerto for Piano and Dog at Carnegie Hall. The dog had stage fright, which was good for me, as it gave me a new top. There is a reason people hate reporters. The phone rings, and I begin the performance.

"Well, Ma, I'm out of surgery, and I'm here at the hospital and everything went great," I say.

"Oh, thank God, I'm so relieved, I don't know what to say, I was so nervous I couldn't sit still, my friends called, I told everybody, 'Get off, get off, I can't talk, my daughter is right now this minute having surgery in New York. . . .' "

I break through the wall of words, power-talking, a skill I developed from forty-three years of training with champions.

"The lump turned out to be malignant, but it's the best kind you can have," I say. "It's called medullary, it tends not to spread, they seem to have got it all. It was in one lump, I saw it, it looks like it was encapsulated, that's a good sign."

Silence. She believes me like I believe the doctors.

"I'm coming north," she says.

Then I call Nick.

"I'm going to tell you something, and I don't want you to get emotional, because it's going to sound worse than it probably is," I say.

I have the feeling, at the other end of the line, of a man who has been slugged in the stomach.

"You just got to give me a minute. I wasn't expecting this," he says.

THEN HERB AND I head downtown. Normally, a glass of wine puts me to sleep. Now we go to the back room of the Lion's Head, where we are known as The Ones Who Only Eat, and I order a margarita. I get a second one. Then I talk tactics. The position I am taking, I say, is not that I have cancer, but that I had a cancer and they cut it out. I am not doing an avoidance number, we will research the hell out of this, but until it is established otherwise, I consider myself healthy.

I go home. I think about Nick, who has said he will get out of work as soon as he can and pick up supper, and wonder what is keeping him. He calls, eventually, from the street near his bar. The bank must have messed up, he says, he can't get any money from the machine, he's got maybe three dollars. I go to meet him at Balducci's, bumping into Sigmund Freud on the way. "You understand the message he is sending you," Freud says. "You vill not depend on him for nossing."

Going public with this is another problem. I am afraid of negativity. Cancer is a scary word; people hear it and think "death," and I don't want that sort of energy around me. I also don't want to hear, however well-meaning, other people's stories.

I also have to figure out how much to tell Ma. They have an interesting way of dealing with illness in my family. They form little whispering cabals, deciding who can "take it." Or, if they must deliver bad news, they hit you in a roundabout way. "You know your uncle Murray, in the hospital in Kingston, he's not doing very well," my aunt Shirley had told me, in a phone conversation years ago. Then she asked to speak to my boyfriend. A few minutes later, he passed back the phone. "Actually," said Shirley, "he's dead."

I never understood this, but now I do: You don't tell the people you love, because you want to protect them. But in doing that, you cut yourself off. I talk to Nick about it. He says mothers are stronger than you think, and anyway, I owe my family the full story. The day after the biopsy, I call her.

"I figured you might be worrying, and I was just wondering if you had any questions," I say.

"Yeah," she says. "What aren't you telling me?"

Trick question. Damn, these mothers are smart. I tell her there is a small possibility "it" may be in the lymph nodes, but if it is, it's not the end of the road. I say because I am concerned another lump might one day be missed, I am leaning toward mastectomy and reconstruction, but that might not be so bad—it would be fun to be able to wear cute little camisoles, and maybe, at forty-three, I could use a perkier pair.

She's scared. I can tell because she hits me with Second-Generation Wadler Cure-All One:

"You know, money is not an issue."

"I know that, Ma," I tell her. "It's okay. I got insurance."

"New underwear, anything cosmetic, that's on me," she says.

"Well, I don't know, Ma," I say. "My bras are very expensive. I don't know if a poor old widow like you can afford them."

"Thirty-four B is a good size," she says. "I'll bring cash. I'll put a thousand in your account." She starts upping the amount, bargaining with some unseen force. "Three. No, five. Six. For the things that aren't covered by insurance. Taxis for back and forth to the hospital. New underwear. A wig." I'm suddenly peeved. What makes her think I'm going to need a wig?

Later, talking to Herb, I realize something.

"You know how we're always saying we miss things," I say. "We weren't around for Paris in the twenties; we weren't reporters in New York in the forties; I had tickets to Woodstock, too much mud, I didn't go. It just hit me: All these stories about breast cancer—for this trend I'm right on time."

I'M HAVING TROUBLE with Nick.

"What's the good news?" he asks whenever I come back from the doctor.

When he hears rough news—the possibility of an ugly reconstruction that could go on for months, the possible problems with chemo—he brushes it off.

"The doctor says you have the best kind," he keeps saying. "You've got nothing to worry about. I wish I could exchange my financial problems for your medical problems."

I think part of this is my fault. After all, the day I was diagnosed, I told him that we had to be positive. I also know this is his way of keeping me from being overcome by terror.

"I could have a very strange look for a few months," I tell Nick one night before bed. "Scars, no nipple . . ."

"So what's a few months?" he says. "When it's over, you have a great new pair. Maybe better."

"I thought you liked these," I say.

"I *love* them," he says. "But you know what they say—variety is the spice of life."

Meanwhile, his demand that I lead with "good news" is making me feel that he just doesn't want to hear the bad. One day, I blow up.

"There is no good news," I say to him. "This is cancer. I could lose a breast; I could die; I could be spending the summer with a hole in my chest. If you want good news, get yourself a twenty-four-year-old California girl. With no health problems."

"What's to be scared?" says Nick. "You die on the table, you never know what hit you. I keep telling you, it's the best way to go."

"You're just saying that because you're a guy and you don't like to admit to fear of dying," I say.

"My mother isn't a guy; she wouldn't be scared," Nick says.

"Your mother is seventy," I tell him.

"Eighty," says Nick. "But she wouldn't be scared if she was forty. If she was twenty, she still wouldn't be scared."

"What is it with Italian guys and their mothers?" Herb says. "Jewish guys insult their mothers and make jokes about them. Say anything to an Italian guy about his mother and he's ready to get in a fight."

"Why would anyone say anything about my mother?" says Nick. "She's an incredible woman."

I move back to medical concerns. I have a bone scan and liver ultrasound to show the presence of cancer cells. They come back negative. I go to a lawyer and make a will. I sign a health-care proxy, sent to me by Sloan-Kettering, giving Herb the right to make medical decisions on my behalf in case I am incapacitated during surgery to remove lymph nodes, and write an outline of the last chapters of my book, assigning rights again to Herb. I have been going to the gym a lot, to strengthen my heart and lungs for surgery; now I focus on a psychic attack for my hospital stay.

Most of the patients I see in hospitals, except new mothers, shuffle around like depressed shlubs. Analyzing it, I think I know why: bathrobes. Only Rex Harrison could look good in a bathrobe. Hospital pajamas aren't that great, either, though the floppy drawstring pants, matched with the oversize shirts, have possibilities. Casual clothing, I decide, is what is called for. I pull out a bunch of Hawaiian shirts and bright, oversize beach tops, and flowered tights and pink sandals. I have a pre-surgical session with the shrink, tell her that even if cancer is in the nodes, I will try to beat this disease, and if not, or something goes wrong on the table, I have an interesting life behind me. I have friends who love me, I got to have two grandmothers, I've been in love in Paris, I drank champagne with a spy at ten in the morning, I wrote a few things I liked, I had Herb. I had really wanted to stand with someone under a wedding canopy, but maybe it is silly to think you can have everything.

"You have a good life ahead of you," the shrink says. "It isn't finished."

THE MOOD ON THE eighteenth floor of Sloan-Kettering, which is known as the breast-cancer floor, is surprisingly up. Women come and go, sharing stories. The first day after surgery, I have very little pain. I can't raise my left arm straight up over my head or touch the middle of my back, but Sloan has stretching classes to get the arm back to normal as quickly as possible, an estimated four to six weeks. My roommate, a research biochemist in her mid-fifties who had multiple lesions in her breast, has had a mastectomy but seems unconcerned: Maybe she'll have a reconstruction, maybe she won't, she says. There is no guy in her life, but if one comes along, she figures if he's a good man, he'll love her for who she is; if not, the hell with him.

The most helpful is a former breast-cancer patient exactly my age, who has also had a lumpectomy—somewhere, somebody is doing some careful matching. She's a strikingly pretty woman, in a flowered, V-neck dress, and she asks if I understand the next step of my treatment, radiation therapy. When it comes to cancer treatment, I consider myself the smartest kid in the class:

"Takes about fifteen minutes a session; you have five treatments a week for six weeks. Some people get tired; your breast can get a little swollen and pink, like you're sunburned. They mark where they're going to radiate you with ink."

"Wrong," she says. "In most places they mark you with ink. At Sloan-Kettering, they give you tattoos."

I stare at her. A tattoo? What's it gonna be? A picture of a single-breasted mermaid and SEMPER CARCINOMA on my breast?

"They're very small," she continues. "They give you four or five of them; it's better than ink, which comes off on your clothes. You can have them removed after the treatment, but I know only one person who's bothered. Can you see mine?"

I look closely at her chest. She has a sprinkling of freckles, like me, and after a minute, I can see one tattoo, above her cleavage. It's the size of an ink dot.

Monday morning, Nick switches on Lucy. We fight. I wait till I'm in the street to call Nick.

"It may seem to you like this cancer thing is over, but it's not," I tell him. "My breast hurts, my side hurts; every week I see another doctor. I just sometimes need to be held."

"Then get yourself another guy," Nick says. "We don't have that kind of relationship."

THE DOCTORS TOOK OUT twelve lymph nodes. They were all clean. Radiation therapy goes off without a hitch. I have some tiredness, but I attribute that mostly to psychological factors and feel well enough to take myself off medical leave and return to my book. By the end of June, my cancer treatment is over. The medical bills come to $32,300, but almost all of it is covered by insurance. Life returns to normal. Herb and I watch TV and complain about editors. My mother re-ups in the Israeli army, as her way of giving thanks for my health.

In early March, I begin a course of chemotherapy called CMF—a combination of the anti-cancer drugs Cytoxan, Methotrexate, and 5-Fluorouracil, as well as an anti-nausea sedative called Ativan. I take my Walkman with me for my chemo treatments and listen to *Beauty and the Beast* and *La Cage aux Folles* and, because Ativan has a mild narcotic effect, get pleasantly high. In my five weeks of treatment to date, I have increased my weights at the gym to prove that I am not a sick guy. I have not had hair loss or any other physical problems. My breasts are the same size. While the doctors have said the drugs will probably put me into early menopause, I am for once going against statistics and taking the position that is unlikely to happen to me.

And even if it does, I consider myself a lucky guy. Not just because in the time of the great breast-cancer uprising, mine was so benign, but for the terror of the ride. Nothing is real until you are close to it, and for a few weeks, I was given something few people have: a dress rehearsal of my mortality. And though cancer has not made me a model of mental health, though I remain tempted by the drama and danger of gangsters and ladies' men and continue to worry about every little thing, my experience with serious illness has changed me. Death, I now see, may not come when I am eighty-five and weary, or after I have solved all my problems or met all my deadlines. It will come whenever it damn well pleases; all I can control is the time between. So when I see something I want, I grab it. If the tulips are particularly yellow, I buy them. If I hear Pavarotti is in town, I make a run to the Met and work the crowd for a scalper. I make time for my friends the way I used to make time for work. If someone treats me disrespectfully, I leave.

As for the mark on my left breast, I am happy to have it. It is the battle scar over my heart, and if no one but my doctor and the girls at the gym have seen it lately, I am certain, believing as I do in musical comedies, that somebody will soon.

"So how'd ya get that?" he'll ask, our first lazy morning, and I'll say, delighted that he has found me, listening for the bells to ring, "Glad you asked, 'cause it's a wonderful story. . . ."

THE "ME" DECADE

TOM WOLFE

AUGUST 23, 1976

One of Tom Wolfe's advantages as a journalist was that he never drank the Kool-Aid. "People assumed that because I wrote in what they took be a psychedelic style I was half a hippie myself," he says. "Nothing could be further from my natural tendencies. I'm a good southern boy." And so while some journalists approached the seventies fetish for self-fulfillment as a phenomenon to be understood and even experienced, Wolfe, an instinctive satirist, never sympathized. "I realized I wasn't going to fit into any of these worlds, and so I didn't try," he says. When a friend told him over a restaurant meal about the consciousness-raising group that forms the story's opening anecdote, he knew he'd found one of his great subjects. Wolfe is the author of many books, including Bonfire of the Vanities *and* The Electric Kool-Aid Acid Test.

I. Me and My Hemorrhoids

The trainer said, "Take your finger off the repress button." Everybody was supposed to let go, let all the vile stuff come up and *gush out*! They even provided vomit bags, like the ones on a 747, in case you literally let it gush out! Then the trainer told everybody to think of "the one thing you would most like to eliminate from your life." And so what does our girl blurt over the microphone?

"*Hemorrhoids!*"

Just so!

That was how she ended up in her present state . . . stretched out on the wall-to-wall carpet of the banquet hall of the Ambassador Hotel in Los Angeles with her eyes closed and her face pressed into the stubble of the carpet, which is a thick commercial weave and feels like clothes-brush bristles against her face and smells a bit *high* from cleaning solvent. That was how she ended up lying here concentrating on her hemorrhoids.

Eyes shut! deep in her own space! her hemorrhoids! the grisly peanut—

Many others are stretched out on the carpet all around her; some 249 other souls, in fact. They're all strewn across the floor of the banquet hall with their eyes closed, just as she is. But Christ, the others are concentrating on things that sound serious and deep when you talk about them. And how they had talked about them! They had all marched right up to the microphone and "shared," as the trainer called it. What did they want to eliminate from their lives? Why, they took their fingers right off the old repress button and told the whole room. My husband! my wife! my homosexuality! my inability to communicate, my self-hatred, self-destructiveness, craven fears, puling weaknesses, primordial horrors, premature ejaculation, impotence, frigidity, rigidity, subservience, laziness, alcoholism, major vices, minor vices, grim habits, twisted psyches, tortured souls—and then it had been her turn, and she had said, "Hemorrhoids."

You can imagine what that sounded like. That broke the place up. The trainer looked like a cocky little bastard up there on the podium with his deep tan, white tennis shirt, and peach-colored sweater, a dynamite color combination, all very casual and spontaneous—after about two hours of trying on different outfits in front of a mirror, *that* kind of casual and spontaneous, if her guess was right. And yet she found him attractive. *Commanding* was the word. In any event, *hemorrhoids* was what had bubbled up into her brain.

Then the trainer had told them to stack their folding chairs in the back of the banquet hall and lie down on the floor and close their eyes and get deep into their own spaces and concentrate on that one item they wanted to get rid of the most—and really feel it and let the feeling gush out.

So now she's lying here concentrating on her hemorrhoids. The strange thing is . . . it's no joke after all! She begins to feel her hemorrhoids in all their morbid presence. She can actually *feel* them. The sieges always began with her having the sensation that a peanut was caught in her anal sphincter. That meant a section of swollen varicose vein had pushed its way out of her intestines and was actually coming out of her bottom. It was as hard as a peanut and felt bigger and grislier than a peanut. Well—for God's sake!—in her daily life, even at work, *especially* at work, and she works for a movie distributor, her whole picture of herself was of her . . . *seductive physical presence.* She was not the most successful businesswoman in Los Angeles, but she was certainly successful enough, and quite in addition to that, she was . . . *the main sexual presence in the office.* She could feel her sexual presence go through the place like an invisible chemical, like a hormone, a scent, a universal solvent.

The most beautiful moments came when she would be in her office or in a conference room or at Mr. Chow's taking a meeting—nobody "had" meetings anymore, they "took" them—with two or three men, men she had never met before or barely knew. The overt subject was, inevitably, eternally, "the deal." She always said there should be only one credit line up on the screen for any movie: "Deal by . . ." But the meeting would also have a subplot. The overt plot would be "The Deal." The subplot would be "The Men Get Turned On by Me." Pretty soon, even though the conversation had not strayed overtly from "The Deal," the men would be swaying in unison like dune grass at the beach. And she was the wind, of course. And then one of the men would say something and smile and at the same time reach over and touch her . . . on top of the hand or on the side of the arm . . . as if it meant nothing . . . as if it were just a gesture for emphasis . . . *but in fact a man is usually deathly afraid of reaching out and touching a woman he doesn't know* . . . and she knew it meant she had hypnotized him sexually. . . .

Well—for God's sake!—at just that sublime moment, likely as not, the goddam peanut would be popping out of her tail! As she smiled sublimely at her conquest, she also had to sit in her chair lopsided, with one cheek of her buttocks higher than the other, as if she were about to crepitate, because it hurt to sit squarely on the peanut. If for any reason she had to stand up at that point and walk, she would have to walk as if her hip joints were rusted out, as if she were sixty-five years old, because a normal stride pressed the peanut, and the pain would start up, and the bleeding, too, very likely. Or if she couldn't get up and had to sit there for a while and keep her smile and her hot hormonal squinted eyes pinned on the men before her, the peanut would start itching or burning, and she would start double-tracking, as if her mind were a tape deck with two channels going at once. In one she's the sexual princess, the Circe, taking a meeting and clouding men's minds . . . and in the other she's a poor bitch who wants nothing more in this world than to go down the corridor to the ladies' room and get some Kleenex and some Vaseline and push the peanut back up into her intestines with her finger.

The Sexual Princess! On the outside she has on her fireproof grin and her Fiorio scarf as if to say she lives in a world of Sevilles and 450SLs and dinner last night at Dominick's, a movie-business restaurant on Beverly Boulevard that's so exclusive, Dominick keeps his neon sign (DOMINICK'S) turned off to make the wimps think it's closed, but *she* (Hi, Dominick!) can get a table—but inside her it's all the battle between the bolus and the peanut—

—and is it too late to leave the office and go get some mineral oil and let some of that vile glop roll down her gullet or get a refill on the softener tablets or eat some prunes or drink some coffee or do something else to avoid one of those horrible hard-clay boluses that will come grinding out of her, crushing the peanut and starting not only the bleeding but . . . *the pain!* . . . a horrible humiliating pain that feels like she's getting a paper cut in her anus, like the pain you feel when the edge of a piece of bond paper slices your finger, plus a horrible hellish purple bloody varicose pressure, but lasting not for an instant, like a paper cut, but for an eternity, prolonged until the tears are rolling down her face as she sits in the cubicle, and she wants to cry out, to scream until it's over, to make the screams of fear, fury, and humiliation obliterate the pain. But someone would hear! No doubt they'd come bursting right into the ladies' room to save her! and feed their morbid curiosities! And what could she possibly say? And so she had simply held that feeling in all these years, with her eyes on fire and her entire pelvic saddle a great purple tub of pain. She had repressed the whole squalid horror of it—*the searing peanut*—

—until now. The trainer had said, "Take your finger off the repress button!" Let it gush up and pour out!

And now, as she lies here on the floor of the banquet hall of the Ambassador Hotel with 249 other souls, she knows exactly what he meant. She can feel it all, all of the pain, and on top of the pain all the humiliation, and for the first time in her life she has permission from the Management, from herself, and from everyone around her to let the feeling gush forth. So she starts moaning.

"Oooooooooooooooohhhhhhhhhhhh!"

And when she starts moaning, the most incredible and exhilarating thing begins to happen. A wave of moans spreads through the people lying around her, as if her energy were radiating out like a radar pulse.

"Oooooooooooooooohhhhhhhhhhhh!"

So she lets her moan rise into a keening sound.

"Oooooooooooooohhhhhhhhhhhhhhhhheeeeeeeeeeeeeeeee!"

And when she begins to keen, the souls near her begin keening, even while the moans are still spreading to the prostrate folks farther from her, on the edges of the room.

"Eeeeeeeeeooooooohhhhhhhhheeeeeooooooooooh!"

So she lets her keening sound rise up into a real scream.

"Eeeeeeeeeeeeeeeeeaiaiaiaiaiaiaiaiaiai!"

And this rolls out in a wave, too, first through those near her, and then toward the far edges.

"Aiaiaiaiaiaiaiaiaiaiaiaiaieeeeeeeeeeeeeeeohhhhhhhhhhheeeeeeaiaiai!"

And so she turns it all the way up, into a scream such as she has never allowed herself in her entire life.

"AiaiaiaiaiaiaiaiaiaiaaaaAAAAAAAAAARRRRRRGGGGGGHHHHHH!"

. . . until at last the entire room is consumed in her scream, as if there are no longer 250 separate souls but one noosphere of souls united in some incorporeal way by her scream . . .

"AAAAAAAAAAARGGGGGGGGHHHHHH!"

Which is not simply *her* scream any longer . . . but the world's! Each soul is concentrated on its own burning item . . . my husband! my wife! my homosexuality! my inability to communicate, my self-hatred, self-destruction, craven fears, puling weaknesses, primordial horrors, premature ejaculation, impotence, frigidity, rigidity, subservience, laziness, alcoholism, major vices, minor vices, grim habits, twisted psyches, tortured souls—and yet each unique item has been raised to a cosmic level and united with every other until there is but one piercing moment of release and liberation at last—a whole world of anguish set free by . . .

My hemorrhoids.

"Me and My Hemorrhoids Star at the Ambassador" . . . during a three-day Erhard Seminars Training (est) course in the hotel banquet hall. The truly odd part, however, is yet to come. In her experience lies the explanation of certain grand puzzles of the 1970s, a period that will come to be known as the Me Decade.

II. *The Holy Roll*

In 1972 a farsighted caricaturist did a drawing of Teddy Kennedy captioned "President Kennedy campaigning for re-election in 1980 . . . courting the so-called Awakened vote."

The picture shows Kennedy ostentatiously wearing not only a crucifix but also (if one looks just above the cross) a pendant of the Bleeding Heart of Jesus. The crucifix is the symbol of Christianity in general, but the Bleeding Heart is the symbol of some of Christianity's most ecstatic, nonrational, holy-rolling cults. I should point out that the artist's prediction lacked certain refinements. For one thing, the odd spectacle of politicians using ecstatic, nonrational, holy-rolling religion in presidential campaigning was to appear first not in 1980 but in 1976.

The two most popular new figures in the 1976 campaign, Jimmy Carter and Jerry Brown, are men who rose up from state politics . . . absolutely aglow with mystical religious streaks. Carter turned out to be an evangelical Baptist who had recently been "born again" and "saved," who had "accepted Jesus Christ as my personal Savior"—i.e., he was of the Missionary lectern-pounding amen ten-finger C-major-chord Sister-Martha-at-the-Yamaha-keyboard loblolly piny-woods Baptist faith in which the members of the congregation stand up and "give witness" and "share it,

Brother" and "share it, Sister" and "Praise God!" during the service. Jerry Brown turned out to be the Zen Jesuit, a former Jesuit seminarian who went about like a hair-shirt Catholic monk, but one who happened to believe also in the Gautama Buddha, and who got off koans in an offhand but confident manner, even on political issues, as to how it is not the right answer that matters but the right question, and so forth.

Newspaper columnists and newsmagazine writers continually referred to the two men's "enigmatic appeal." Which is to say, they couldn't explain it. Nevertheless, they tried. They theorized that the war in Vietnam, Watergate, the FBI and CIA scandals, had left the electorate shell-shocked and disillusioned and that in their despair the citizens were groping no longer for specific remedies but for sheer faith, something, anything (even holy rolling), to believe in. This was in keeping with the current fashion of interpreting all new political phenomena in terms of recent disasters, frustration, protest, the decline of civilization . . . the Grim Slide. But when *The New York Times* and CBS employed a polling organization to try to find out just what great gusher of "frustration" and "protest" Carter had hit, the results were baffling. A Harvard political scientist, William Schneider, concluded for the *L.A. Times* that "the Carter protest" was a new kind of protest, "a protest of good feelings." That was a new kind, sure enough—a protest that wasn't a protest.

In fact, both Carter and Brown had stumbled upon a fabulous terrain for which there are no words in current political language. A couple of politicians had finally wandered into the Me Decade.

III. Him?—The New Man?

The saga of the Me Decade begins with one of those facts that is so big and so obvious (like the Big Dipper), no one ever comments on it anymore. Namely: the thirty-year boom. Wartime spending in the United States in the 1940s touched off a boom that has continued for more than thirty years. It has pumped money into every class level of the population on a scale without parallel in any country in history. True, nothing has solved the plight of those at the very bottom, the chronically unemployed of the slums. Nevertheless, in Compton, California, today it is possible for a family at the very lowest class level, which is known in America today as "on welfare," to draw an income of $8,000 a year entirely from public sources. This is more than most British newspaper columnists and Italian factory foremen make, even allowing for differences in living costs. In America truck drivers, mechanics, factory workers, policemen, firemen, and garbagemen make so much money—$15,000 to $20,000 (or more) per year is not uncommon—that the word *proletarian* can no longer be used in this country with a straight face. So one now says *lower middle class*. One can't even call workingmen *blue collar* any longer. They all have on collars like Joe Namath's or Johnny Bench's or Walt Frazier's. They all have on $35 Superstar Qiana sport shirts with elephant collars and 1940s Airbrush Wallpaper Flowers Buncha Grapes and Seashell designs all over them.

He didn't look right, and he wouldn't . . . *do right*! I can remember what brave plans visionary architects at Yale and Harvard still had for *the common man* in the early 1950s. (They actually used the term "common man.") They had brought the utopian socialist dream forward into the twentieth century. They had things figured out for the workingman down to truly minute details such as lamp switches. The new liberated workingman would live as the Cultivated Ascetic. He would be modeled on the B.A.-degree Greenwich Village bohemian of the late 1940s—dark wool Hudson Bay shirts, tweed jackets, flannel trousers, briarwood pipes, good books, sandals and simplicity—except that he would live in a Worker Housing project. Worker Housing would be liberated from all wallpaper, "drapes," Wilton rugs with flowers on them, lamps with fringed shades and bases that looked like vases or Greek columns. It would be cleansed of all doilies, knickknacks, mantelpieces, headboards, and radiator covers. Radiator coils would be left bare as honest, abstract sculptural objects.

But somehow the workers, incurable slobs that they were, avoided Worker Housing, better known as "the projects," as if it had a smell. They were heading out instead to the suburbs—the *suburbs!*—to places like Islip, Long Island, and the San Fernando Valley of Los Angeles—and buying houses with clapboard siding and a high-pitched roof and shingles and gaslight-style front-porch lamps and mailboxes set up on top of lengths of stiffened chain that seemed to defy gravity and all sorts of other unbelievably cute or antiquey touches, and they loaded these houses up with "drapes" such as baffled all description and wall-to-wall carpet you could lose a shoe in, and they parked twenty-five-foot-long cars out front and Evinrude cruisers up on tow trailers in the carport just beyond the breezeway.

By the 1960s the common man was also getting quite interested in this business of "realizing his potential as a human being." But once again he crossed everybody up! Once more he took his money and ran— determined to do-it-himself!

IV. Lemon Sessions

In 1971 I made a lecture tour of Italy, talking (at the request of my Italian hosts) about "contemporary American life." Everywhere I went, from Turin to Palermo, Italian students were interested in just one question: Was it really true that young people in America, no older than themselves, actually left home, and lived communally according to their own rules and created their own dress styles and vocabulary and had free sex and took dope? They were talking, of course, about the hippie or psychedelic movement that had begun flowering about 1965. What fascinated them the most, however, was the first item on the list: that the hippies *actually left home and lived communally according to their own rules.*

To Italian students this seemed positively amazing. Several of the students I met lived wild enough lives during daylight hours. They were in radical organizations and had fought pitched battles with police, *on the barricades,* as it were. But by 8:30 P.M. they were back home, obediently washing their hands before dinner with Mom&Dad&Buddy&Sis&the MaidenAunt.

That people so young could go off on their own, without taking jobs, and live a life completely of their own design—to Europeans it was astounding. That ordinary factory workers could go off to the suburbs and buy homes and create their own dream houses—this, too, was astounding. And yet the new life of *old* people in America in the 1960s was still more astounding. Throughout European history and in the United States up to the Second World War, old age was a time when you had to cling to your children or other kinfolk, and to their sufferance and mercy, if any.

In the 1960s, old people in America began doing something that was more extraordinary than it ever seemed at the time. They cut through the whole dreary humiliation of old age by heading off to "retirement villages" and "leisure developments"—which quickly became Old Folks communes. Some of the old parties managed to take this to a somewhat psychedelic extreme, joining trailer caravans . . . and rolling . . . creating some of the most amazing sights of the modern American landscape . . . such as thirty, forty, fifty Airstream trailers, the ones that are silver and have rounded corners and ends and look like silver bullets . . . thirty, forty, fifty of these silver bullets in a line, in a caravan, hauling down the highway in the late afternoon with the sun at a low angle and exploding off the silver surfaces of the Airstreams until the whole convoy looks like some gigantic and improbable string of jewelry, each jewel ablaze with a highlight, rolling over the face of the earth—the million-volt billion-horsepower *bijoux* of America! The Trailer Sailors!

It was remarkable enough that ordinary folks now had enough money to take it and run off and alter the circumstances of their lives and create new roles for themselves, such as Trailer Sailor or Gerontoid Cowboy. But, simultaneously, still others decided to go . . . *all* the way. They plunged straight toward what has become the alchemical dream of the Me Decade.

The old alchemical dream was changing base metals into gold. The new alchemical dream is: changing one's personality—remaking, remodeling, elevating, and polishing one's very *self* . . . and observing, studying, and doting on it. (Me!) This had always been an aristocratic luxury, confined throughout most of history to the life of the courts, since only the very wealthiest classes had the free time and the surplus income to dwell upon this sweetest and vainest of pastimes. It smacked so much of vanity, in fact, that the noble folk involved in it always took care to call it quite something else.

Much of the satisfaction well-born people got from what is known historically as the "chivalric tradition" was precisely that: dwelling upon Me and every delicious nuance of *my* conduct and personality. At Versailles, Louis XIV founded a school for the daughters of impoverished noblemen, called L'Ecole Saint-Cyr. At the time most schools for girls were in convents. Louis had quite something else in mind, a secular school that would develop womenfolk suitable for the superior *race guerrière* that he believed himself to be creating in France. Saint-Cyr was the forerunner of what was known up until a few years ago as *the finishing school*. And what was *the finishing school*? Why, a school in which the personality was to be shaped and buffed like a piece of high-class psychological cabinetry. For centuries most of upper-class college education in France and England has been fashioned in the same manner: with an eye toward sculpting the personality as carefully as the intellectual faculties.

At Yale the students on the outside wondered for eighty years what went on inside the fabled secret senior societies, such as Skull and Bones. On Thursday nights one would see the secret-society members walking silently and single file, in black flannel suits, white shirts, and black knit ties with gold pins on them, toward their great Greek Revival temples on the campus, buildings whose mystery was doubled by the fact that they had no windows. What in the name of God or Mammon went on in those thirty-odd Thursday nights during the senior years of these happy few? What went on was . . . lemon sessions!—a regularly scheduled series of *lemon sessions*, just like the ones that occurred informally in girls' finishing schools.

In the girls' schools these lemon sessions tended to take place at random on nights when a dozen or so girls might end up in someone's dormitory room. One girl would become "it," and the others would light into her personality, pulling it to pieces to analyze every defect . . . her spitefulness, her awkwardness, her bad breath, embarrassing clothes, ridiculous laugh, her suck-up fawning, latent lesbianism, or whatever. The poor creature might be reduced to tears. She might blurt out the most terrible confessions, hatreds, and primordial fears. But, it was presumed, she would be the stronger for it afterward. She would be on her way toward a new personality. Likewise, in the secret societies: They held lemon sessions for boys. Is masturbation your problem? Out with the truth, you ridiculous weenie! And Thursday night after Thursday night the awful truths would out, as he who was It stood up before them and answered the most horrible questions. Yes! I do it! I whack whack whack it! I'm *afraid* of women! I'm afraid of *you*! And I get my shirts at Rosenberg's instead of Press! (Oh, you dreary turkey, you wet smack, you little shit!) . . . But out of the fire and the heap of ashes would come a better man, a brother, of good blood and good bone, for the American *race guerrière*. And what was more . . . they loved it. No matter how dreary the soap opera, the star was *Me*.

By the mid-1960s this service, this luxury, had become available for one and all, i.e., the middle classes. Lemon Session Central was the Esalen Institute, a lodge perched on a cliff overlooking the Pacific in Big Sur, California. Esalen's specialty was lube jobs for the personality. Businessmen, businesswomen, housewives—anyone who could afford it, and by now many could—paid $220 a week to come to Esalen to learn about themselves and loosen themselves up and wiggle their fannies a bit, in keeping with methods developed by William C. Schutz and Frederick Perls. Fritz Perls, as he was known, was a remarkable figure, a psychologist who had a gray beard and went about in a blue terry-cloth jump suit and looked like a great blue grizzled father bear. His lemon sessions sprang not out of the manly virtues and cold showers Protestant-prep-school tradition of Yale but out of psychoanalysis. His sessions were a variety of the "marathon encounter." He put the various candidates for personality change in groups, and they met in close quarters day after day. They were encouraged to bare their own souls and to strip away one another's defensive facades. Everyone was to face his own emotions squarely for the first time.

Encounter sessions, particularly of the Schutz variety, were often wild events. Such aggression! such sobs! tears! moans, hysteria, vile recriminations, shocking revelations, such explosions of hostility between husbands and wives, such mud balls of profanity from previously mousy mommies and workadaddies, such red-mad attacks! Only physical assault was prohibited. The encounter session became a standard approach in many other movements, such as Scientology, Arica, the Mel Lyman movement, Synanon, Daytop Village, and Primal Scream. Synanon had started out as a drug rehabilitation program, but by the late 1960s the organization was recruiting "lay members," a lay member being someone who had never been addicted to heroin . . . but was ready for the lemon-session life.

Outsiders, hearing of these sessions, wondered what on earth their appeal was. Yet the appeal was simple enough. It is summed up in the notion: "Let's talk about Me." No matter whether you managed to renovate your personality through encounter sessions or not, you had finally focused your attention and your energies on the most fascinating subject on earth: *Me*. Not only that, you also put *Me* up on stage before a live audience. The popular "est" movement has managed to do that with great refinement. Just imagine . . . *Me and My Hemorrhoids* . . . moving an entire hall to the most profound outpouring of emotion! Just imagine . . . *my life* becoming a drama with universal significance . . . analyzed, like Hamlet's, for what it signifies for the rest of mankind. . . .

The encounter session—although it was not called that—was also a staple practice in psychedelic communes and, for that matter, in New Left communes. In fact, the analysis of the self, and of one another, was unceasing. But in these groups and at Esalen and in movements such as Arica there were two common assumptions that distinguished them from the aristocratic lemon sessions and personality *finishings* of yore. The first was: I, with the help of my brothers and sisters, must strip away all the shams and excess baggage of society and my upbringing in order to find the Real Me. Scientology uses the word "clear" to identify the state that one must strive for. But just what is that state? And what will the Real Me be like? It is at this point that the new movements tend to take on a religious or spiritual atmosphere. In one form or another they arrive at an axiom first propounded by the Gnostic Christians some 1,800 years ago: namely, that at the apex of every human soul there exists a spark of the light of God. In most mortals that spark is "asleep" (the Gnostics' word), all but smothered by the façades and general falseness of society. But those souls who are clear can find that spark within themselves and unite their souls with God's. And with that conviction comes the second assumption: There is another order that actually reigns supreme in the world. Like the light of God itself, this other order is invisible to most mortals. But he who has dug himself out from under the junk heap of civilization can discover it.

. . .

VI. Only One Life

In 1961 a copywriter named Shirley Polykoff was working for the Foote, Cone & Belding advertising agency on the Clairol hair-dye account when she came up with the line: "If I've only one life, let me live it as a blonde!" In a single slogan she had summed up what might be described as the secular side of the Me Decade. "If I've only one life, let me live it as a ——!" (You have only to fill in the blank.)

This formula accounts for much of the popularity of the women's-liberation or feminist movement. "What does a woman want?" said Freud. Perhaps there are women who want to humble men or reduce their power or achieve equality or even superiority for themselves and their sisters. But for every one such woman, there are nine who simply want to *fill in the blank* as they see fit. "If I've only one life, let me live it as . . . a free spirit!" (Instead of . . . a house slave: a cleaning woman, a cook, a nursemaid, a station-wagon hacker, and an occasional household sex aid.) But even that may be overstating it, because often the unconscious desire is nothing more than: *Let's talk about Me.* The great unexpected dividend of the feminist movement has been to elevate an ordinary status—woman, housewife—to the level of drama. One's very existence as *a woman*—as *Me*—becomes something all the world analyzes, agonizes over, draws cosmic conclusions from, or, in any event, takes seriously. Every woman becomes Emma Bovary, Cousin Bette, or Nora . . . or Erica Jong or Consuelo Saah Baehr.

Among men the formula becomes: "If I've only one life, let me live it as a . . . Casanova or a Henry VIII" . . . instead of a humdrum workadaddy, eternally faithful, except perhaps for a mean little skulking episode here and there, to a woman who now looks old enough to be your aunt and has atrophied calves, and is an embarrassment to be seen with when you take her on trips. The right to shuck overripe wives and take on fresh ones was once seen as the prerogative of kings only, and even then it was scandalous. In the 1950s and 1960s it began to be seen as the prerogative of the rich, the powerful, and the celebrated (Nelson Rockefeller, Henry Ford, and show-business figures), although it retained the odor of scandal. Wife-shucking damaged Adlai Stevenson's chances of becoming president in 1952 and Rockefeller's chances of becoming the Republican presidential nominee in 1964 and 1968. Until the 1970s, wife-shucking made it impossible for an astronaut to be chosen to go into space. Today, in the Me Decade, it becomes normal behavior, one of the factors that have pushed the divorce rate above 50 percent.

Much of what is now known as "the sexual revolution" has consisted of both women and men filling in the blank this way: "If I've only one life, let me live it as . . . a Swinger!" (Instead of a frustrated, bored monogamist.) In "swinging," a husband and wife give each other license to copulate with other people. There are no statistics on the subject that mean anything, but I do know that it pops up in conversation today in the most unexpected corners of the country. It is an odd experience to be in De Kalb, Illinois, in the very corncrib of America, and have some conventional-looking housewife (not *housewife,* damn it!) come up to you and ask: "Is there much tripling going on in New York?"

"Tripling?"

Tripling turns out to be a practice, in De Kalb, anyway, in which a husband and wife invite a third party—male or female, but more often female—over for an evening of whatever, including polymorphous perversity, even the practices written of in the one-hand magazines, all the things involving tubes and hoses and tourniquets and cups and double-jointed sailors.

One of the satisfactions of this sort of life, quite in addition to the groin spasms, is talk: *Let's talk about Me.* Sexual adventurers are given to the most relentless and deadly serious talk . . . about Me. They quickly succeed in placing themselves onstage in the sexual drama whose outlines were sketched by Freud and then elaborated upon by Wilhelm Reich. Men and women of all sorts, not merely swingers, are given just now to the most earnest sort of talk about the Sexual Me.

A key drama of our own day is Ingmar Bergman's movie *Scenes from a Marriage.* In it we see a husband and wife who have good jobs and a well-furnished home but who are unable to "communicate"—to cite one of the signature words of the Me Decade. Then they begin to communicate, and there upon their marriage breaks up and they start divorce proceedings. For the rest of the picture they communicate endlessly, with great candor, but the "relationship"—another signature word—remains doomed. Ironically, the lesson that people seem to draw from this movie has to do with . . . "the need to communicate." *Scenes from a Marriage* is one of those rare works of art, like *The Sun Also Rises,* that not only succeed in capturing a certain mental atmosphere in fictional form . . . but also turn around and help radiate it throughout real life. I personally know of two instances in which couples, after years of marriage, went to see *Scenes from a Marriage* and came home convinced of the "need to communicate." The discussions began with one of the two saying, Let's try to be completely candid for once. You tell me exactly what you don't like about me, and I'll do the same for you. At this, the starting point, the whole notion is exciting. We're going to talk about *Me*! (And I can take it.) I'm going to find out what he (or she) really thinks about me! (Of course, I have my faults, but they're minor, or else exciting.)

She says, "Go ahead. What don't you like about me?"

They're both under the Bergman spell. Nevertheless, a certain sixth sense tells him that they're on dangerous ground. So he decides to pick something that doesn't seem too terrible.

"Well," he says, "one thing that bothers me is that when we meet people for the first time, you never know what to say. Or else you get nervous and start babbling away, and it's all so banal, it makes me look bad."

Consciously she's still telling herself, "I can take it." But what he has just said begins to seep through her brain like scalding water. What's he talking about? . . . makes *him* look bad? *He's saying I'm unsophisticated, a social liability, and an embarrassment. All those times we've gone out, he's been ashamed of me!* (And what makes it worse—it's the sort of disease for which there's no cure!) She always knew she was awkward. His crime is: He *noticed*! He's known it, too, all along. He's had *contempt* for me.

Out loud she says, "Well, I'm afraid there's nothing I can do about that."

He detects the petulant note. "Look," he says, "you're the one who said to be candid."

She says, "I know. I *want* you to be."

He says, "Well, it's your turn."

"Well," she says, "I'll tell *you* something about when we meet people and when we go places. You never clean yourself properly—you don't know how to wipe yourself. Sometimes we're standing there talking to people, and there's . . . a smell. And I'll tell you something else. People can tell it's you."

And he's still telling *himself,* "I can take it"—but what inna namea Christ is *this?*

He says, "But you've never said anything—about anything like that."

She says, "But I *tried* to. How many times have I told you about your dirty drawers when you were taking them off at night?"

Somehow this really makes him angry. . . . All those times . . . and his mind immediately fastens on Harley Thatcher and his wife, whom he has always wanted to impress. . . . From underneath my $250 suits— I smelled of shit! What infuriates him is that this is a humiliation from which there's no recovery. *How often have they sniggered about it later?— or not invited me places?* Is it something people say every time my name comes up? And all at once he is intensely annoyed with his wife, not because she never told him all these years—but simply because she knows about his disgrace—and she was the one who *brought him the bad news!*

From that moment on they're ready to get the skewers in. It's only a few minutes before they've begun trying to sting each other with confessions about their little affairs, their little slipping around, their little coitus on the sly—"Remember that time I told you my flight from Buffalo was canceled?"—and at that juncture the ranks of those who can take it become very thin, indeed. So they communicate with great candor! and break up! and keep on communicating! and then find the relationship hopelessly doomed.

Well, my dear Mature Moderns . . . Ingmar never promised you a rose garden!

VII. How You Do It, My Boys!

In September of 1969, in London, on the King's Road, in a restaurant called Alexander's, I happened to have dinner with a group of people that included a young American named Jim Haynes and an Australian woman named Germaine Greer. Neither name meant anything to me at the time, although I never forgot Germaine Greer. She was a thin, hard-looking woman with a tremendous curly electric hairdo and the most outrageous Naugahyde mouth I had ever heard on a woman. (I was shocked.) After a while she got bored and set fire to her hair with a match. Two waiters ran over and began beating the flames out with napkins. This made a noise like pigeons taking off in the park. Germaine Greer sat there with a sublime smile on her face, as if to say: "How you do it, my boys!"

Jim Haynes and Germaine Greer had just published the first issue of a newspaper that All London was talking about. It was called *Suck*. It was founded shortly after *Screw* in New York, and was one of the progenitors of the sex newspapers that today are so numerous that in Los Angeles it is not uncommon to see fifteen coin-operated newspaper racks in a row on the sidewalk. One will be for the *Los Angeles Times*, a second for the *Herald-Examiner*, and the other thirteen for the sex papers. *Suck* was full of pictures of gaping thighs, moist lips, stiffened giblets, glistening nodules, dirty stories, dirty poems, essays on sexual freedom, and a gossip column detailing the sexual habits of people whose names I assumed were fictitious. Then I came to an item that said, "Anyone who wants group sex in New York and likes fat girls, contact L—— R——," except that it gave her full name. She was a friend of mine.

Even while Germaine Greer's hair blazed away, the young American, Jim Haynes, went on with a discourse about the aims of *Suck*. To put it in a few words, the aim was sexual liberation and, through sexual liberation, the liberation of the spirit of man. If you were listening to this speech and had read *Suck*, or even if you hadn't, you were likely to be watching Jim Haynes's face for the beginnings of a campy grin, a smirk, a wink, a roll of the eyeballs—something to indicate that he was just having his little joke. But it soon became clear that he was one of those people who exist on a plane quite . . . Beyond Irony. Whatever it had been for him once, sex had now become a religion, and he had developed a theology in which the orgasm had become a form of spiritual ecstasy.

The same curious journey—from sexology to theology—has become a feature of *swinging* in the United States. At the Sandstone sex farm in the Santa Monica Mountains, people of all class levels gather for weekends in the nude, and copulate in the living room, on the lawn, out by the pool, on the tennis courts, with the same open, free, liberated spirit as dogs in the park or baboons in a tree. In conversation, however, the atmosphere is quite different. The air becomes humid with solemnity. Close your eyes and you think you're at a nineteenth-century Wesleyan summer encampment and tent-meeting lecture series. It's the soul that gets a workout here, brethren. And yet this is not a hypocritical cover-up. It is merely an example of how people in even the most secular manifestation of the Me Decade—free-lance spread-'em, ziggy-zag rutting—are likely to go through the usual stages. . . . Let's talk about Me. . . . Let's find the Real Me. . . . Let's get rid of all the hypocrisies and impedimenta and false modesties that obscure the Real Me. . . . Ah! At the apex of my soul is a spark of the Divine . . . which I perceive in the pure moment of ecstasy (which your textbooks call "the orgasm," but which I know to be Heaven). . . .

Every major religious wave that has developed in America has started out the same way: with a flood of *ecstatic experiences*. The First Great Awakening, as it is known to historians, came in the 1740s and was led by preachers of "the New Light" such as Jonathan Edwards, Gilbert Tennent, and George Whitefield. They and their followers were known as "enthusiasts" and "come-outers," terms of derision that referred to the frenzied, holy-rolling, pentecostal shout tempo of their services and to their visions, trances, shrieks, and agonies, which are preserved in great Rabelaisian detail in the writings of their detractors.

The Second Great Awakening came in the period from 1825 to 1850 and took the form of a still wilder hoe-down camp-meeting revivalism, of ceremonies in which people barked, bayed, fell down in fits and swoons, rolled on the ground, talked in tongues, and even added a touch of orgy.

We are now—in the Me Decade—seeing the upward roll (and not yet the crest, by any means) of the third great religious wave in American history, one that historians will very likely term the Third Great Awakening. Like the others it has begun in a flood of *ecstasy*, achieved through LSD and other psychedelics, orgy, dancing (the New Sufi and the Hare Krishna), meditation, and psychic frenzy (the marathon encounter). This third wave has built up from more diverse and exotic sources than the first two, from therapeutic movements as well as overtly religious movements, from hippies and students of "psi phenomena" and Flying Saucerites as well as charismatic Christians. But other than that, what will historians say about it?

The historian Perry Miller credited the First Great Awakening with helping to pave the way for the American Revolution through its assault on the colonies' religious establishment and, thereby, on British colonial authority generally. The sociologist Thomas O'Dea credited the Second Great Awakening with creating the atmosphere of Christian asceticism (known as "bleak" on the East Coast) that swept through the Midwest and the West during the nineteenth century and helped make it possible to build communities in the face of great hardship. And the Third Great Awakening? Journalists (historians have not yet tackled the subject) have shown a morbid tendency to regard the various movements in this wave as "fascist." The hippie movement was often attacked as "fascist" in the late 1960s. Over the past several years a barrage of articles has attacked Scientology, the est movement, and "the Moonies" (followers of the Reverend Sun Myung Moon) along the same lines.

Frankly, this tells us nothing except that journalists bring the same conventional Grim Slide concepts to every subject. The word *fascism* derives from the old Roman symbol of power and authority, the *fasces*, a bundle of sticks bound together by thongs (with an ax head protruding from one end). One by one the sticks would be easy to break. Bound together they are invincible. Fascist ideology called for binding all classes, all levels, all elements of an entire nation together into a single organization with a single will.

The various movements of the current religious wave attempt very nearly the opposite. They begin with . . . "Let's talk about Me." They begin with the most delicious look inward; with considerable narcissism, in short. When the believers bind together into religions, it is always with a sense of splitting off from the rest of society. We, the enlightened (lit by the sparks at the apexes of our souls), hereby separate ourselves from the lost souls around us. Like all religions before them, they proselytize—but always on promising the opposite of nationalism: a City of Light that is above it all. There is no ecumenical spirit within this Third Great Awakening. If anything, there is a spirit of schism. The contempt the various seers have for one another is breathtaking. One has only to ask, say, Oscar Ichazo of Arica about Carlos Castaneda or Werner Erhard of est to learn that Castaneda is a fake and Erhard is a shallow sloganeer. It's exhilarating!—to watch the faithful split off from one another to seek ever more perfect and refined crucibles in which to fan the Divine spark . . . and to *talk about Me.*

Whatever the Third Great Awakening amounts to, for better or for worse, will have to do with this unprecedented post-World War II American development: the luxury, enjoyed by so many millions of middling folk, of dwelling upon the self. At first glance, Shirley Polykoff's slogan—"If I've only one life, let me live it as a blonde!"—seems like merely another example of a superficial and irritating rhetorical trope (*antanaclasis*) that now happens to be fashionable among advertising copywriters. But in fact the notion of "If I've only one life" challenges one of those assumptions of society that are so deep-rooted and ancient, they have no name—they are simply lived by. In this case: man's age-old belief in serial immortality.

The husband and wife who sacrifice their own ambitions and their material assets in order to provide "a better future" for their children . . . the soldier who risks his life, or perhaps consciously sacrifices it, in battle . . . the man who devotes his life to some struggle for "his people" that cannot possibly be won in his lifetime . . . people (or most of them) who buy life insurance or leave wills . . . and, for that matter, most women upon becoming pregnant for the first time . . . are people who conceive of themselves, however unconsciously, as part of a great biological stream. Just as something of their ancestors lives on in them, so will something of them live on in their children . . . or in their people, their race, their community—for childless people, too, conduct their lives and try to arrange their postmortem affairs with concern for how the great stream is going to flow on. Most people, historically, have not lived their lives as if thinking, "I have only one life to live." Instead they have lived as if they are living their ancestors' lives and their offspring's lives and perhaps their neighbors' lives as well. They have seen themselves as inseparable from the great tide of chromosomes of which they are created and which they pass on. The mere fact that you were only going to be here a short time and would be dead soon enough did not give you the license to try to climb out of the stream and change the natural order of things. The Chinese, in ancestor worship, have literally worshiped the great tide itself, and not any god or gods. For anyone to renounce the notion of serial immortality, in the West or the East, has been to defy what seems like a law of Nature.

Hence the wicked feeling—the excitement!—of "If I've only one life, let me live it as a ——!" Fill in the blank, if you dare.

But once the dreary little bastards started getting money in the 1940s, they did an astonishing thing—they took their money and ran. They did something only aristocrats (and intellectuals and artists) were supposed to do—they discovered and started doting on Me! They've created the greatest age of individualism in American history! All rules are broken! The prophets are out of business! Where the Third Great Awakening will lead—who can presume to say? One only knows that the great religious waves have a momentum all their own. Neither arguments nor policies nor acts of the legislature have been any match for them in the past. And this one has the mightiest, holiest roll of all, the beat that goes . . . *Me . . . Me . . . Me . . . Me. . . .*

PART FIVE

....

CRIMINAL ACTS

★

THE CRACK IN THE SHIELD

MICHAEL DALY

DECEMBER 8, 1986

By the early 1980s, crime was indisputably the central story in New York City. Citizens were frightened, cops disheartened. "We're just shoveling shit," was the attitude police voiced to Michael Daly for this article. "There's no way to win." In this demoralized landscape, the 77th Precinct in Brooklyn held a place of distinction. It was a dumping ground for problem cops, and in a largely unsupervised environment, many of them went wild, robbing drug dealers and peddling drugs and guns themselves. Eventually, after tapes and testimony were provided by a bad cop turned informant, Henry Winter, who had been the worst of the offenders, thirteen members of Precinct 77 were charged with corruption. Daly's account, based on a series of interviews on the eve of their sentencing, tells the story of a good man, Brian O'Regan, who became a bad cop. Shortly after the interviews were conducted, O'Regan shot himself. "Hopefully O'Regan haunted Winter for the rest of his life," says Daly. Perhaps he did. In 1995, Winter, too, committed suicide. Daly is now a columnist for the Daily News.

*E*ARLY ON THE MORNING he was to be arrested, police officer Brian O'Regan of the 77th Precinct arrived at his mother's house with a cardboard box. He filled the box with a three-page will, a pair of spit-polished police shoes, an identification card from when he was a deputy sheriff in Florida, a thank-you letter from a citizen he had helped after a burglary, and a Christmas card from more than a decade ago that still held a $10 bill his grandmother had enclosed. He then neatly sealed the top with tape.

Shortly before dawn, Brian's mother came out of her room in a flannel nightgown. She saw that her forty-one-year-old second son's soft blue eyes were reddened and that his face was stubbled with a five-day beard. She asked if he wanted to talk.

"He said he didn't have time," Dorothy O'Regan remembers. "He said, 'I can't, I have to appear.' "

In the basement, Brian found his dead father's razor. He shaved and told his mother he had to leave. She followed him as far as the back door of the small brick house. She called to him as he hurried into the dark and misty morning.

"I said, 'Brian, you're very upset. Drive very carefully,' " Dorothy re-members.

The mother closed the door against the chill. Brian drove his gray Su-baru down the treelined lane where he had been raised. He rolled through the hushed suburban town of Valley Stream, and he came to the turn that would have taken him toward Brooklyn. He pulled the steering wheel the other way and headed east.

At 6:20 A.M., Brian checked into the Pines Motor Lodge on Route 109 in Lindenhurst. He registered as Danny Durke and paid $35. The desk clerk gave him the key to Room 1.

On a fluorescent-light fixture across from the bed, Brian propped a laminated Honor Legion plaque he had received for facing down a gun-man armed with a .45-caliber automatic. He sat alone in this room thirty-two miles from Brooklyn as the twelve other indicted cops of the "Seven-Seven" surrendered on charges ranging from peddling crack to selling stolen guns. He opened a small notepad and wrote of watching a television report of his friends being arrested.

"Good morning, I missed my appointment," Brian wrote.

Around noon, a Suffolk County police officer cruised the parking lot in search of a trio who had been robbing cash machines. Brian apparently panicked at the sight of the squad car, and he checked out. Desk clerk John Drake later discovered that he had left behind the Honor Legion plaque sitting on the light fixture.

"We figured he'd be back," Drake says. "A cop would want to keep it. It would be important to a cop."

By 12:30 P.M., Brian was again in the Subaru. He traveled farther east, and the housing developments gave way to bleak pine barrens. He kept driving into the gray afternoon and turned down Route 27 into Southampton.

At 3:30 P.M., Brian checked into the Southampton Motel. He registered as Daniel Grant and paid $37.65 for a night. He went into Room 2 with a green garbage bag containing his frayed uniform. He also had a pint of Seagram's 7 Crown and a plastic bottle of 7UP.

As he sipped a 7 and 7 from a paper cup, Brian again opened the notepad and began writing about his years as an officer in the 77th Precinct in Crown Heights–Bedford Stuyvesant. He had joined the Police Department in 1973 with the aim of being a good cop. He had soon discovered that this was not a simple ambition in a ghetto precinct that had become a dumping ground for the department's misfits, malcontents, and rebels.

"*I can't swim in a cesspool, can you?*" Brian now wrote.

Day after day, Brian had commuted to a combat zone where each year saw as many as eighty people murdered, an additional one hundred raped, some four hundred shot, and more than three thousand robbed. He had made an arrest for drugs or gun possession again and again, only to see the "skel" back on the street the next day. The written law had seemed to leave him powerless. An unwritten law had kept him silent when he first saw an officer steal.

"*I will not turn. No. Never. I won't turn on another cop.*"

By 1982, twin desires to be "one of the boys" and to get back somehow at the skels had led Brian to start shaking down drug dealers. He and several other cops were eventually seized by a frenzy of stealing. One of them would put a coded call over the radio, and they would assemble to hit narcotics spots with sledgehammers and ladders and sometimes axes borrowed from a firehouse. They had gleefully kicked in doors and swung on ropes through windows.

"I thought if you hooked up with them, I would be a big shot."

At first, they had just taken cash. They had later begun selling narcotics and firearms. They had twice hit a location and then sold drugs to the customers who continued to arrive. Whatever pangs of guilt they had felt had apparently been numbed by a few hours of racing from shooting to robbery to rape to beating.

"No right. No wrong."

In 1984, Brian had apparently begun to find his double life as a cop and criminal unbearable. He had begun to sink deeper and deeper into depression. He had eventually resolved to get out of the Police Department, and he had conspired to get a disability pension by having a fellow officer shoot him in the hand.

"I want to be normal. I want a life, I want a child."

Finally, this same fellow officer and another cop had been caught shaking down a drug dealer. The two had agreed to cooperate with the special prosecutor, and Brian had been among those they had ensnared. The Brian Francis O'Regan who was known to his friends and family as good and kind and honest had been indicted on eighty-two counts in the biggest police scandal since the Knapp Commission investigation of the early seventies.

"I am guilty, but not guilty as you understand. I need help."

At 5:40 A.M. on Friday, Brian woke in the motel. He went out twice for coffee and newspapers. He opened a second small notebook and wrote.

At 9:20 A.M., Brian was still writing. He wrote that he had turned on the television and that the only clear channel was showing *Donahue*. He wrote that he loved his girlfriend, Cathy, and that he was afraid a SWAT team was going to burst through the door at any moment and that he did not own the proper clothes to wear to court. He noted that the motel's noon checkout time was nearing.

"Only have about $4. What a choice. Death or jail. Got no place to go. Do you think God wants me? Does it hurt to die?"

Then Brian set down his pen. He left the two notebooks on the dresser and set his birth certificate and PBA membership card on the nightstand. He stretched out on the bed in a pair of denims and a light-blue sweatshirt bearing the legend 77TH PRECINCT—THE ALAMO—UNDER SIEGE. With his right hand, Brian raised a .25 Titan automatic pistol he had most likely acquired while raiding a narcotics spot. He pressed the chrome muzzle to his right temple. He fired.

"The precinct is hell," Brian had said some thirty hours before. "I know when I die I'm going to heaven."

BRIAN O'REGAN came to the New York Police Department from Valley Stream Central High School and the Marine Corps. His mother was the daughter of a Flushing truck farmer. His father was an oil-burner mechanic locally renowned for having built a Ford with two front ends and for riding a motorcycle down Merrick Road while standing on the seat. The father also had a practical streak that led him to approve of twenty-eight-year-old Brian's career choice.

"My father used to say, 'One thing about the Police Department, they never lay anybody off,' " the oldest son, Greg, remembers.

For his part, Brian seemed to come out of the academy with a dreamy vision of heroic comrades and daring deeds. He was assigned by chance to the 77th Precinct, and he arrived at the Utica Avenue stationhouse on October 29, 1973, raring to do battle with crime. He had only to be told what to do.

"Pride and glory," Brian later said. "That's what I liked."

With a rookie's blind enthusiasm, Brian was always ready to race to do a job or scramble up a fire escape or leap to an adjoining roof. He often returned to the suburbs with cuts and scrapes. His father suggested calling a family friend who was an inspector and arranging for a transfer to a less busy precinct.

"Brian said, 'No, I'm new, I need some time there,' " Greg remembers.

On July 30, 1975, the fiscal crisis caused the city to lay off 2,864 cops. Brian was forced to turn in his gun and shield and search for another job. He heard that the Broward County sheriff was hiring, and he went down to Fort Lauderdale to sign on as a deputy.

When his nieces visited Brian in Florida, they found him driving a police cruiser that gleamed right down to the steam-cleaned engine. He wore a fitted white shirt and a shiny brass badge and a Smokey the Bear hat. He had begun collecting thank-you letters from citizens he had assisted, and supervisors spoke of promoting him to detective.

"He always had a smile on his face," says his niece Kathleen. "He'd say, 'How do I look? How do I look in my uniform?' "

In 1980, Brian's father died of a heart attack. Brian flew north and attended the wake at the Moore Funeral Home in Valley Stream. The New York Police Department was hiring again, and he announced that he was moving home. The family urged him to stay in Broward County.

"I said, 'You should go back to Florida where you're happy,' " remembers his sister-in-law, Carole. "He said, 'No, I have to take care of my mother.' "

ON JANUARY 13, 1981, Brian returned to the 77th Precinct stationhouse, on Utica Avenue. He climbed into a grimy squad car with coffee stains on the seats, and he drove onto the Atlantic Avenue viaduct. As far as he could see were abandoned buildings and housing projects.

"I said to myself, 'What the hell am I doing here?' " Brian later remembered.

As he began patrolling these battered streets, Brian learned that black Brooklyn was the department's dumping ground and that his fellow officers included a large number of drunks, shirkers, boss fighters, rule benders, rebels, and crooks who were not quite crooked enough to fire. An officer would misbehave in some choice command and Brian would see another new face in the Seven-Seven.

"You would ask the guys, 'What did you do wrong to get here?' " Brian later said. "They might not tell you, but you knew something."

On one of his first radio runs, Brian pulled up to a dress shop on Nostrand Avenue that had been burglarized. The plate-glass front window had been smashed, and Brian followed several other officers inside. He watched one of the cops punch open the cash register and grab a stack of bills.

"I could not believe what I saw," Brian later remembered. "He said,

'What do you want?' and I said, 'I don't do that. I do not do that. I don't want anything.' "

During another tour, Brian responded with lights and siren to a radio report of three men with guns. Other cars screamed up to the scene, and several cops crashed through the Plexiglas front of a smoke shop in apparent pursuit of the perpetrators.

"Somebody said, 'Did you drop a dime?' " Brian later remembered. "I didn't understand. I just looked at him."

On an evening tour, Brian shone his flashlight from an upper-floor tenement window and saw a tiny dark form down below he could not immediately recognize. He then realized that the woman in the apartment had thrown her newborn child down the air shaft. Brian later said, "I stood there and stared at it and I kept thinking, It's so little, it's so little."

At the stationhouse, police officer Peter Heron warned Brian that the routine of mayhem and misery could change a person. Heron was later fired for shooting heroin. Brian went on patrolling the streets of the Seven-Seven. He delivered eight babies. He made nine gun arrests in a single month.

On Lincoln Place, Brian grabbed a dope dealer named Mitch twice for guns and once for drugs. None of the arrests seemed to interrupt Mitch's business for more than a few days, and the man flashed a big smile each time Brian's squad car pulled onto the block.

"You put somebody in jail and the next day he's out waving to you," Brian later said. "So what did you accomplish?"

Other officers experienced similar frustrations and sometimes administered summary punishment to dope dealers by flushing the drugs down a toilet, tossing the money to neighborhood kids, or otherwise "busting chops." These cops included police officer Henry "Hank" Winter, a fellow Valley Stream Central High School alumnus who lived across the street from Brian's uncle and who was known to have once left a pusher naked on Jones Beach in December. He now became something of a precinct legend by burning a dope dealer's bankroll on a table in the roll-call room.

"Henry Winter has personality," Brian later said.

At some point, Winter began slipping confiscated cash into his pocket.

He kicked in doors and rappelled through windows to rob pushers of their "nut." He then went back to the stationhouse joking and laughing. Brian had an adjoining locker and sometimes saw Winter count a wad of cash.

"He'd say, 'Not a bad night,' " Brian later said.

IN MARCH 1983, another cop was suspended for suspicion of robbing a smoke shop on Dean Street. Brian's younger brother, Kevin, heard of the incident and called to ask what had happened. Kevin remembers, "Brian said, 'I don't know, but sometimes you just work too long in a precinct and things can happen.' "

Around this time, police officer William Gallagher asked Brian to be his regular partner on the steady midnight shift. Gallagher was the precinct union delegate. He called himself a "hero cop."

"He was cement," Brian later said. "He wanted me because I'm easy, because I'm a follower."

As they began riding together, Gallagher sometimes did not deign to speak even when Brian asked him a direct question. Brian accepted the insult and seemed to become devoted to his new partner. A friend named Patricia Cuti says, "It made him feel very macho just being in a car with Gallagher."

Early one morning, Gallagher pulled the squad car over and led Brian into a smoke shop. Brian later remembered, "He said, 'I want to *do* this place.' I didn't know what he meant."

Behind the counter, Gallagher found a bin filled with cash. Brian later said that Gallagher grabbed the money and returned to the squad car. There, Gallagher held out $150. Brian hesitated. Gallagher kept his hand out. Brian took the money.

"I felt like I was one of the boys," Brian later said.

At roll call, Brian began standing off to the side with Gallagher and the other "Raiders" of the late tour. He then joined the nightly prowl for drug locations. Brian proved to have a real talent for spotting lookouts and other signs that meant a dope dealer was operating nearby.

"I would have done great in narcotics," Brian later said.

When the cops wanted help hitting a spot, they got on the radio and said, "Buddy Bob, meet at 234." The code phrase summoned all interested officers to gather at St. Johns Recreation Park, near Engine Company 234's firehouse. They then set out together to make a raid.

Since many of the spots were fortified, one cop took to borrowing sledgehammers, axes, ladders, and ropes from Engine Company 234. Gallagher and Brian began keeping a sledgehammer in the trunk of the squad car. They would splinter the door with a great blow of the hammer and rush screaming into the room. They would see fear and anger in the face of a once smug dope peddler.

"It was glory," Brian later said. "It was *not* money. It was you finally getting back at all the slaps you took. It was getting back at the skels, back at people you couldn't hit."

One night, Gallagher and Brian went with Winter to a construction site. They then rode through the precinct with a stolen ladder atop the squad car. They stopped in front of an apartment building on Eastern Parkway and propped the ladder on the car's roof. Gallagher scrambled up and began kicking in the windows of a narcotics spot.

"I wanted adventure, some kind of excitement," Brian later said.

During one tour, several officers of the Seven-Seven came upon a van filled with cigarettes. They correctly guessed that this was bait set out by the Internal Affairs Division. They then had great fun banging the sides of a second van where the IAD men were hiding.

"They must think we're stupid," Gallagher was later heard to say.

Even as rumors began circulating that a number of officers were about to be arrested for shakedowns, Brian and the others continued hitting narcotics spots. They gave each other nicknames, and Brian became "Space Man." Gallagher was "Junior," and his swaggering presence seemed to keep Brian fearless. Brian later said, "He was infallible. He could get out of anything."

After work, the cops became family men and good citizens. Brian did not smoke and seldom drank, and his idea of a good time was going to a flea market.

IN LATE 1983, Brian met a rookie policewoman at the stationhouse. She later remembered, "He said, 'Get out of here as soon as you can. Just leave this place. Get out before it changes you.'"

"Sometimes, I used to get a feeling, a deep, deep feeling of guilt," Brian later said. "But then it would go away. I would go back on patrol and it would go away."

As the days passed, Brian began to take less and less care with his appearance. He let himself get out of shape, and he began to get a paunch. He turned out in a uniform that was stained and frayed.

"I had no pride," Brian later said. "Nobody becomes a cop to steal."

At a family gathering, relatives noticed that Brian seemed troubled and agitated. He had begun to suffer a sort of numbness, and he later said, "Anything could happen, and I just wouldn't care. . . . I said, 'I'm dead and I don't know it.'"

The gloom deepened, and Brian spoke to Henry Winter about somehow leaving the Police Department with a disability pension. Brian later remembered, "He said, 'We'll get you shot,' and I said, 'That sounds good.'"

As they discussed the matter, Winter offered to help Brian stage a fake gun battle. Brian suggested that Winter shoot him in the leg, and he later remembered, "He said, 'No, too many arteries.' He said, 'The hand's better.'"

One evening, the two cops went into an abandoned building on Porter Avenue, and Winter gave Brian a .22-caliber pistol. Brian took the weapon with one hand and held out the other. He aimed and curled his finger on the trigger and then lost his nerve at the last instant. He returned the gun to Winter and asked him to do the job. Winter refused, and they handed the gun back and forth, saying, "You do it." "No, you do it." "I'm not doing it, you do it."

As they continued to steal, Winter appeared to share none of Brian's anguish. He was forever laughing and joking. On a dare, he did a striptease on top of the front desk.

In early 1985, Winter and his partner, Tony Magno, were sharing $50 a week in protection money from a pusher who also ran a dice game. A pair of anti-crime cops demanded a cut and raided the game when Winter and Magno refused. The pusher resolved the matter by paying the four cops a total of $800 a week.

That October, Gallagher got word that a pusher had complained to IAD of shakedowns and that detectives were putting together a case against Winter and Magno. Gallagher passed on a warning, and Winter and Magno grew cautious. The others went right on raiding spots.

"You just couldn't stop from happening what was happening," Brian later said.

ON FEBRUARY 17, 1986, an unmarked car pulled Winter's car over on the Belt Parkway as he returned from a fishing trip. Winter was whisked in handcuffs to the IAD building on Poplar Street. There, he and Magno were sat down before a television set and a VCR.

A lawyer from the Special Prosecutor's Office played a videotape showing Winter and Magno taking protection money from a drug dealer outside a St. Johns Place building. The lawyer then said that they had two alternatives. They could go to jail or they could cooperate.

"You just show them what you have," says Special Prosecutor Charles J. Hynes. "It's very dispassionate. You just say, 'Here's your choice.'"

Winter and Magno now settled for being what Hynes calls "unarrested."

In May, the two arrived at the stationhouse wearing micro-recorders. They joined in raids on narcotics spots and recorded cops talking about other scores. They put out the word that they were willing to "fence" stolen property, and cops brought them drugs and guns.

At the end of each tour, Winter and Magno met secretly with IAD and handed over their ninety-minute micro-cassettes. One cop was recorded boasting of pilfering $8,000 in cash and $3,900 in food stamps from a burglarized supermarket on Franklin Avenue. Another chatted about stealing cars while on duty. Another gossiped about a cop who had killed a man and woman for $1,500.

On June 17, Gallagher put a "Buddy Bob, meet at 234" call on the radio. Winter met Gallagher and Brian at the park across from the firehouse, and they all went off to hit a spot at 143 Albany Avenue. They first searched a second-floor apartment, without success.

When Brian shone his flashlight down an air shaft, he spotted a paper bag. Winter lowered himself down and discovered that the bag contained crack vials. Brian then found a .357 Magnum and a potato-chip sack filled with more of the drug.

Back in the park, Brian helped count the total score and discovered they had more than a half-ounce. Brian "fenced" the .357 Magnum through Winter for $200. The drugs were sold to a West Indian drug peddler. Winter turned over his $1,000 share to IAD.

On June 18, Brian and Gallagher spotted a couple buying drugs in the doorway of an apartment at 261 Buffalo Avenue. Winter helped hit the spot, and he discovered a trapdoor in a third-floor apartment. He pulled out a bag containing marijuana and $107 in cash.

Brian pocketed the money, and Winter offered to sell the marijuana. Winter then took the pot to IAD, and an investigator gave him $400. Three days later, Winter passed the bills to Gallagher.

That same day, Brian told Winter that he had spotted a new narcotics spot, on Classon Avenue. He telephoned Winter the next day and said that he and Gallagher had raided the place and come away with $70 and fifty-eight vials of crack. He asked Winter to handle the sale.

On July 1, Brian and Gallagher got into a car with Winter. Brian placed a package containing crack in the glove compartment. Gallagher spoke about an upcoming sergeant's test and other PBA business and then handed Winter a slip of paper with the notations "52/10" and "19/5." The figures apparently corresponded to the number of $10 and $5 vials.

"Fifty-two and nineteen," Brian was recorded as saying.

On July 4, Winter met with Gallagher and said he had sold the drugs. Winter then gave $400 to Gallagher, who returned $100 as an apparent commission. Winter spoke to Brian later that day and told him of his transaction.

"You work, you stick your neck out, you get paid," Brian was recorded as saying.

On July 30, Brian joined Gallagher and Winter in a foray to the Soul Food shop on Franklin Avenue. Brian rummaged through a hallway trash bin and found a .25-caliber automatic pistol that he later "fenced" through Winter for $100. The other cops stuffed the spot's drugs and cash in a bag.

Apparently, everybody thought someone else had the bag, and the cops managed to leave behind the booty when they departed. Winter's micro-recorder picked up one of the officers saying, "What are we, a bunch of f——ing Keystone Cops?"

At one point, Brian sat with Winter in a car and spoke once again of somehow getting a disability pension. Brian later remembered, "I said, 'I wish I could care about something. I wish I could give a f— if somebody jumps out a window.'"

RUMORS WERE BY THEN circulating that Winter and Magno were wired. An officer named Rathbun, who'd been with Winter on a narcotics shakedown, patted Winter down, without discovering the micro-recorder. Brian arrived for work and saw that somebody had scrawled the word "rat" on Winter's locker.

"I didn't believe it," Brian later said. "Not Hank."

By then, Brian had begun speaking of marrying a young woman named Cathy. He looked at a modest house in Rockville Centre and started negotiating with the owner. He later said, "All I want is a house. Just a house and a wife and a child."

Still, Brian would leave Cathy's apartment each work night and find himself in another raid on a narcotics spot. He and Gallagher allegedly agreed to assist the pusher Herbie by eliminating a competing location at 233 Utica Avenue. They hit the place again and again.

On the night of September 17, the dealer named Roy approached Winter in the precinct and said that the proprietors of the Utica Avenue location had decided to shoot the next cop who came through the door. Winter immediately relayed the information to IAD.

The same evening, an officer named Crystal Spivey, who'd allegedly taken five hundred dollars to help Winter escort a narcotics shipment a couple of weeks before, went up to Winter at the stationhouse. She asked to speak to him in private, and they went outside to his car. She announced she had been tipped by a sergeant from another precinct that he was wearing a wire. She frisked him and failed to find the recorder taped to his crotch. Her suspicions were apparently allayed.

"*You* wouldn't dog me like this," Spivey was recorded saying.

In the morning, the Special Prosecutor's Office instructed Winter to take Spivey on a second narcotics run. She is alleged to have immediately agreed, and she was recorded as saying, "I want to buy a condo."

On Winthrop Avenue, detectives stopped the car and took Winter and Spivey to the IAD building. The Special Prosecutor's Office offered Spivey a reduced sentence if she would help determine how word of the investigation had leaked. She agreed and headed out with a micro-recorder of her own.

At the same time, Hynes said that the leak left Winter in too much jeopardy to continue. Hynes canceled plans to send Winter and his micro-recorder to a beach party with a new group of suspected cops.

That night, Brian reported for duty and heard that an IAD investigator had returned Winter's portable radio to the stationhouse. Brian immediately checked the stationhouse log and saw a notation by the names Winter and Magno.

"It said, 'Transferred to IAD,' " Brian later remembered.

In the back, Brian checked Winter's locker. The IAD investigators had cut off the lock. They had carried away everything except for a single brass collar device bearing the numerals "77."

ON SATURDAY, September 20, Brian drove to Winter's white frame house in Valley Stream. He saw a woman he recognized from pictures as Winter's wife. He later recalled, "She looked like she had been through a war. I said, 'I'm Brian.' She said, 'He's not here and I gotta go.' "

As Brian began to pull away, he saw Winter drive up with some relatives. Brian later remembered, "I said, 'Hank, how are you doing?' He said, 'Hey, buddy boy.' He has a big smile on his face and he says, 'I'll see you later.' "

Brian returned to his apartment in Rockaway. The owner of the house in Rockville Centre called to accept Brian's latest offer. Gallagher also telephoned and warned Brian to stay away from Winter. Brian went to Gallagher's house in Marine Park and found his partner sitting in the dining room.

"I said, 'What's the problem? What's going on?' " Brian later recalled. "He said, 'I told my wife everything.' I said, '*Everything*?' He said, 'Yeah. We could be in big trouble.' "

THAT MONDAY, Crystal Spivey appeared at the Special Prosecutor's Office and said she would continue to wear a wire only if Hynes guaranteed her probation. Hynes said she would have to do at least a one- to three-year term. She balked, and Hynes canceled the deal.

On Tuesday morning, Chief John Guido of IAD decided he could not risk having a noncooperating Spivey tip off other officers. He reached for a folder on his desk that contained the names of thirteen targeted cops.

"Take them! Take them!" Guido was reported to have said.

Rathbun was processing a prisoner at Central Booking when he called his wife and learned that he had been suspended. Another cop was waiting with his fiancée to be seated at a restaurant when the news came over the television in the bar. Brian first understood that something had happened when his friend Patricia Cuti telephoned.

"Pat said, 'What's the matter, what's going on at the precinct?' " Brian later recalled. "She said, 'Turn to Channel 4.' "

When he flicked on the television, Brian heard himself named as one of the thirteen cops who had been suspended. The others included a sergeant who was often the sole supervisor of Brian's shift in the field. Brian called the sergeant to break the news.

"I had to tell him five times. He wouldn't believe it," Brian later remembered.

Later that day, Brian drove to the stationhouse and went through a side door to avoid the crowd of reporters out front. An IAD investigator instructed him to surrender his guns, identification card, and gas card. The investigator followed him to his locker.

"I guess they're afraid you're going to blow your brains out," Brian later said.

The next day, Brian and some of the other suspended cops went to the PBA to seek legal assistance. Gallagher cried six times, and Brian later remembered, "I said, 'Holy shit, I can't believe this here. He was always *cement.*' "

Afterward, Brian sat with Rathbun in a car. Rathbun was also crying, and Brian later recalled, "I said, 'Maybe it's not so bad.' He took out his wallet and showed me a picture of his son and said, 'See this? How could you ever tell him?' "

When he reached Cathy's house, in Brooklyn, Brian still had not broken down. She was red-eyed when she met him at the door, and he later remembered, "I said, 'Are you crying?' She said, 'No.' I went upstairs and I burst out crying."

Winter began testifying before a grand jury. He and Magno helped the Special Prosecutor's Office secure indictments against thirteen cops and prepare cases on about a dozen more. Brian was charged with some eighty crimes.

"It's funny how you can be good for your whole life, for so long, and then. . . ." Brian later said.

On November 4, Brian called Cuti and said that he had been notified to surrender the following Thursday. He said he planned to show up in dark glasses, a hooded sweatshirt, and a hat.

"He was scared to death," Cuti says.

The following day, Brian stopped by Cathy's house and gave her white carnations for her twenty-fifth birthday. He also drove to a notary public in Queens with a will he had typed himself. He later made an appointment with Mike McAlary, the New York *Newsday* reporter who had broken much of the story behind the investigation.

At 10 P.M., Brian met with McAlary and this writer at the Ram's Horn diner in Rockaway. Brian spoke for four hours and then went home. Cathy called him, and he told her that he planned to surrender with the others and that he might shave for the arraignment. He then drove through the rainy pre-dawn darkness to his mother's house.

Five hours later, all the indicted cops except Brian arrived at the IAD building. They came out an hour later in handcuffs and rode to Central Booking. They had all taken prisoners there in the past, and they did not have to be told the procedure for photographing and fingerprinting.

At 11 A.M., a clerk on the fifth floor of Brooklyn Supreme Court announced that the first item on the calendar was Indictment SPOK 224. Gallagher shuffled in wearing a black jacket. His shoulders were slumped. His head was bowed.

"Step up, please, Mr. Gallagher," the clerk said.

After entering a plea of not guilty, Gallagher's lawyer noted that his client had received thirty-five medals and commendations during his seventeen years as a cop. Hynes responded that Gallagher was accused of eighty-seven felonies and misdemeanors. The charges included the sale of crack and of loaded handguns.

His bail set at $50,000, Gallagher shuffled back out. Rathbun then appeared and pleaded not guilty to thirty-seven counts that included selling drugs. He was followed by Spivey and nine other cops who pleaded not guilty to charges ranging from the sale of cocaine to burglary to the theft of two garbage cans from the stationhouse. Spivey's face was blank as she listened to a prosecutor say she was charged with an A-I felony. The prosecutor added that this carries a maximum penalty of life in prison.

By that time, the police had put out an APB for Brian's gray Subaru. Winter and Magno are said to have kept searching for him for the next two days. Brian's brother Greg began to fear the worst when the mail brought a brown envelope containing a one-page typewritten letter.

"I've always considered myself to be an honest, upstanding person."

"I was firmly convinced that nobody cared in the ghetto, from the people who lived there to the police and the city."

"I'm sorry it had to happen this way, but it did."

"Try your best to take care of mom."

On the afternoon of Friday, November 7, a neighbor told Greg that the radio was reporting that Brian had been found dead in a Southampton motel. Greg and Kevin went to the Suffolk County medical examiner's office and identified the body. Two other relatives then took the Subaru to Greg's house.

That Sunday night, Brian was laid out in the room at the Moore Funeral Parlor where his father's wake had been, six years before. The family gathered for a private viewing, and afterward Greg went to his mother's house. The phone rang, and Greg spoke for a moment to Gallagher's wife. Gallagher himself then got on the line.

"All he kept saying was 'I'm sorry, I'm sorry,'" Greg remembers.

Wednesday morning, a police color guard escorted the hearse to the Holy Name of Mary Church in Valley Stream. The officers of the 77th Precinct stood at attention in white shirts and white gloves. They saluted as Brian's flag-draped coffin was carried up the steps.

During the Sign of Peace, Greg went down the right side of the aisle and shook hands with one cop after another. Rathbun was hunched off to the left with his wife, sobbing. Gallagher sat in the back, gripping the pew before him with both hands, his eyes welling with tears.

Just before noon, the coffin was carried back into the sunlight. The officers again saluted, and many of them went off to start another tour at a stationhouse that is expected to see as many as twelve more indictments.

With a squad of leather-jacketed officers on motorcycles clearing traffic, the O'Regan family followed the hearse to a cemetery in Westbury. There, they each laid a red carnation by the grave of the man who had left Valley Stream to be an officer in the Police Department of the City of New York.

"You tell me why I did this," Brian O'Regan had said one week before.

THE HEADMISTRESS AND
THE DIET DOCTOR

ANTHONY HADEN-GUEST

MARCH 31, 1980

In the history of New York scandals, Jean Harris's murder of her lover, Herman Tarnower, occupies a place d'estime. For one thing, it played as film noir: a spurned lover, a prominent victim, a gun, and a lethal encounter in a bedroom. And then it was staged in a kind of Masterpiece Theater setting in Westchester, the sort of place where such things weren't supposed to happen. "The upper-middle class were restrained and controlled," says Anthony Haden-Guest. Harris, who served twelve years in prison, was granted clemency by Governor Mario Cuomo. Haden-Guest is the author of, among other books, The Last Party: Studio 54, Disco, and the Culture of the Night *and* Bad Dreams, *which grew out of another* New York *magazine cover story.*

I T WAS THE LAST Friday of the term, and tinged with discontent. This marijuana business, the expulsion of a handful of seniors for flirting with the weed, had some of the girls nervous, mutinous. But Jean Struven Harris, headmistress of the Madeira School, did not flinch. Her vision of Madeira was, as always, pure, crystalline, hostile to error. She spoke of Duty, and of Caliber, and, above all, of Integrity.

But—some of the girls noticed—Jean Harris seemed unusually ill at ease. Run-down. That Friday, she dropped in at the infirmary, where a nurse gave her some shots for anemia. She proceeded with the day's business calmly enough—she had announced that she intended to stay on campus for the three-week break—but, showing some distress, she unexpectedly canceled a 3:30 appointment.

The girls left Madeira that Saturday morning, except for some forty-odd juniors who had holiday internships on Capitol Hill. One of the juniors went to see Jean Harris on Sunday. Jean Harris lived in a two-story red-brick house called "The Hill," and she had said that it was "always open."

It was seldom open quite so literally, however. The door was open wide, the girl says, and the usually meticulous place was the biggest mess you can imagine. "Clothes were thrown all over the floor," she recalls, "and the kitchen looked as if she hadn't been in there for a week." Jean Harris herself was nowhere to be seen, and the girl departed, puzzled, her problem unresolved.

Jean Struven Harris spent much of Monday writing. She wrote a letter, extraordinarily long and rambling, and then she put the sheets together in no particular order and stuffed them into a manila envelope. She addressed the letter to Dr. Herman Tarnower and dropped it off at the small post office on the Madeira campus.

Just to make completely sure, she sent it by registered mail, which requires a signature. No prevarications, no excuses. Herman Tarnower, best known as the millionaire creator of the "Scarsdale Diet," had been her lover for fourteen years. But, since her coming to Madeira, perhaps even since his newly found celebrity, he had been slip-sliding away. There was Another Woman. Her shining world—*Duty, Caliber, Integrity*, those safe and shining abstractions—lay about her in ugly shreds and splinters.

That night Jean Harris was expected for dinner with John and Kiku Hanes. It was a typical "intelligent" Washington dinner, a sit-down for fourteen, nothing to do with Madeira, no alums, no parents, just well-informed people, like Jean Harris.

"I had spoken to her the day before," Kiku Hanes says. "She was looking forward to it. There was an empty place, but I wasn't worried at all. I know what being a headmistress is like."

In fact, Jean Harris did dress as if for dinner: a trim ensemble of black jacket, white shirt, black skirt. It seems she changed her mind. She wrote some further notes, these detailing her inner ferment, and she scattered them around the small and comfortable house that (she wrote) she had no intention of ever seeing again.

Jean Struven Harris fetched her gun, a Harrington & Richardson .32-caliber revolver, which she had acquired a couple of years back at Irving's Sport Shops in Tysons Corner. It was still in its box. She dumped it in her car, an unshowy blue-and-white 1973 Chrysler, and took off on the five-hour drive.

The weather, so unseasonably mild, broke while she was still on the road. An inconsiderate thunderstorm lashed the rich suburbs, and she arrived to find Dr. Tarnower's house, that half-million-dollars' worth of neo-japonaiserie where she had spent so much pleasant time, muffled with black and steaming blankets of rain.

The burglary call came through to the Harrison police at 10:59 P.M. When he arrived, patrolman Brian McKenna found the angular body of Herman Tarnower, sixty-nine, sprawled crooked and awkward in an upstairs bedroom, dying in beige pajamas. Tarnower tried to speak, but managed only random sounds. Jean Harris stood there, distraught, her natty outfit rain sodden. The headmistress of Madeira School, whose roster of pupils, past and present, reads like a *Fortune*-hunters' 500, was booked for Murder Two.

THE HEADMISTRESS AND THE MILLIONAIRE DOCTOR, the headlines ran.

Certainly, it has a better sound to it than the sleazy mayhem that usually occupies the tabloids and the TV news. There's a ring of that comfortably titillating British detective-story world, those clubs and country houses where the upper middle classes plot one another's baroque demises. No wonder that cigar box of a courtroom in Harrison allured such media luminaries as Shana Alexander (who wore black mink), sitting behind the defendant, just as she had done through the seven months of the equally classy Patty Hearst trial: the Shana Alexander position.

And add to Agatha Christie pinches of Cheever and John O'Hara. Consider the venues: Shaker Heights, Cleveland; Grosse Point, Michigan; Chestnut Hill, Philadelphia; a smart girls' school in Virginia; and Westchester County. Was ever a crime of passion more fashionably suburban than this?

But there is much more to this odd affair than class. Kennett Rawson, who published the Scarsdale diet book in hardback, finds himself bewildered. "Tarnower was not a man who anybody ever got anything out of," he says. "That's what makes it so incongruous that he was involved with these torrid love affairs."

A prominent Madeira alumna is equally puzzled. "Mrs. Harris is most genteel," she told me. "She's so very proper. The whole thing sounds so *incongruous*."

The echo proves to be eerily appropriate. Yes, this case does turn out to be a most incongruous affair.

THE ROMANTIC LIAISON of Jean Struven Harris and Dr. Herman Tarnower had begun, friends say, fairly soon after her 1966 divorce. There was a certain symmetry to it. Jean Harris was a director at the Springside School, a girls' academy in Philadelphia. She and her two sons lived in a house in one of the city's fancier neighborhoods, Chestnut Hill. She dressed with conservative chic and took care to keep abreast of the times. A divorcee in her early forties, with her high forehead, fair hair, and pale blue eyes, she cut a fine figure. One observer saw a resemblance to middle-period Bette Davis.

Herman—"Hi"—Tarnower was in his mid-fifties. He appeared to most an austere and private figure with no capacity for small talk. He came across as a warmer man to his patients at the Scarsdale Medical Group, which he had founded with Dr. John Cannon, and which kept him comfortably rich. "He always had very attractive women friends," says Mrs. Arthur Schulte, who had known him for years. "He was always very generous with time and money. But he never married. I don't know why."

It was a deeper symmetry than this. Tarnower and Harris were, in certain respects, similar. Both had achieved their positions with huge expenditures of effort, and both masked their formidable competitive streaks with a manner of cool self-containment. Quite fittingly, their relationship was, it seems, both decorous and intense.

Herman Tarnower came from a solid middle-class Jewish family in

New York. And he was a driven man from the beginning. Ignoring his father's prosperous hat-manufacturing business, he studied medicine at Syracuse, graduating in 1933. A residency in Bellevue was followed by the first of his travels, a 1936–37 postgraduate fellowship: six months studying cardiology in London, and six months in Amsterdam.

In 1939, Tarnower was back home, an attending cardiologist at White Plains Hospital. War came. The end of the war found him a lieutenant colonel stationed in Japan. He was a member of the Casualty Survey Commission, the casualties in question coming from Hiroshima and Nagasaki. The experience, understandably, marked him. He would talk of it frequently.

In due course, Herman Tarnower returned to White Plains Hospital. He moved to Scarsdale. In quiet, exemplary fashion, his career progressed, carrying him toward his meeting with Jean Struven Harris.

Jean Witte Struven was born in 1924 and grew up in the fashionable Cleveland suburb of Shaker Heights. She was educated at a private school, the Laurel School, and spent the war reading history and economics at Smith. Contemporaries say that she was ambitious, organized, and personable, but showed scant interest in the pleasant dillydallying of college days. She graduated magna cum laude. Shortly thereafter, she married the good-looking son of a Detroit industrialist, James Harris. They settled, of course (seeing that low-rent neighborhoods do not figure widely in this story), in Grosse Pointe, Michigan.

The Harris family was every bit as socially registered in Detroit as the Struvens were in Cleveland, but James Harris was a second son, and well-bred does not invariably mean well-heeled, nor does the whole of Grosse Pointe look custom-built for the Ford family. As Jane Schermerhorn, editor of the Detroit *Social Secretary*, put it, the residents mostly "aspire to the life-style they can't afford."

The Harrises moved into a two-story "colonial" house on Hillcrest, a narrow road lined with trees and closely spaced houses, which runs into the back lot of a Sears shopping center. In 1946, four months after her marriage, Jean entered the world of private education, teaching history and current events at Grosse Pointe Country Day School.

This was in keeping with her ambitions. "It's always been a fashionable school," Jane Schermerhorn says. "If you couldn't send your children to Dobbs Ferry or Andover, you sent them there. Edsel Ford worked very hard for the school and all his boys went there."

She took some time off to raise her sons, David, born in 1950, and James, born twenty-four months later, but remained at the school for the next several years. Bertram Shover, then the lower-level director, remarks that "she was definitely ambitious and wanted to become more than a first-grade teacher."

James Harris, meantime, had also taken a job, though not necessarily at a level guaranteed to make an ambitious Grosse Pointer swell with pride: He became a supervisor at the Holly Carburetor Company. It seems he simply wasn't that ambitious. "James Harris wasn't as forceful as she was," Bertram Shover says, "but a lot more fun to be with. I liked him a lot." A neighbor spoke directly to the point. "All I'm saying is that everyone loved him," the neighbor said. "She was very pretty and very brilliant, but everyone loved *him*. He was a nice, quiet man."

Jean Struven Harris, however, was forging ahead. She was a good teacher, impressing parents with her creativity and administrators with her competence and drive. Although teachers made less in the private sector than at the public schools, there were other, very tangible advantages. The Harris boys were enrolled free, for instance, and, as Shover puts it, there was "social prestige with the job; an entry into social circles." She became increasingly active in such pleasant milieus, and increasingly independent. Shover remembers that in 1958 she went to Russia, quite alone, and gave a well-attended lecture about her experiences on her return. Jean Harris was very good at giving lectures.

In 1964, however, Mrs. Harris had to deal with certain obstacles. She was one of three recommended as Bertram Shover's assistant, but lost by a nose. Also that October, she filed for divorce, complaining of "extreme and repeated cruelty." It was stated that the weekly salary of James Harris was $203.80 gross, $165.30 net, and that he had a net worth of $27,000, including a $900 Renault. Jean Harris—who listed her own salary as $132.90 per week—asked for custody of the two boys and possession of the house, upon which she requested that James Harris continue to pay the mortgage. James Harris agreed to the cruelty complaint but said that his wife was guilty of the same. The court found against him, and ordered that he make weekly payments of $54. The divorce was granted February 23, 1965. In June, Jean Harris decided to leave Grosse Pointe. In the years ahead she was often to allude, with justifiable pride, to the way she brought up her boys. Of James Harris, who died in 1977, she seldom, if ever, spoke.

Jean Harris moved to Chestnut Hill, Philadelphia, in September 1966, and took up a post as director of the middle school at the Springside School for girls. She is remembered as rather a formidable person there, a keen administrator and a tough disciplinarian. "It was a reign of terror. We were glad when she left," one of her pupils told a Philadelphia reporter. Her views regarding cigarettes, let alone beer or pot, were inflexible, and her eye vis-à-vis dress lengths was as beady as *Women's Wear Daily*'s. More ominously, one pupil reports that she was "very, very high-strung."

Socially, she was active, of course. Philadelphians recall frequent visits from one escort in particular: Dr. Herman Tarnower. To the few permitted any insight into the relationship of these two very private people, it seemed a fitting arrangement. True, Tarnower was a decade and a half older and showed every sign of being a committed bachelor, but he had a shrewd eye for a handsome woman.

Impelled perhaps by memories of Japan, he had recently taken one such lady friend to the Far East. They had made the then unusual trip to mainland China, and Tarnower would sometimes discourse on his dinner with Zhou Enlai. It was this woman friend who was now being phased out in favor of another woman: Jean Struven Harris.

It was true that those who didn't know the vulpine and thin-featured Tarnower often found him forbidding, what with his formal manners, his probing stare, his correct English clothing. "I don't think anybody knew him very well," says Kennett Rawson. "He was very self-contained, very opinionated. Nobody talked to him. He lectured you. He reminded me of the Hollywood idea of a Prussian major general." Said an acquaintance, "He hated chitchat, gossip, small talk." But what of that? There wasn't too much of the chitchatter about Jean Struven Harris.

Also, the eminent cardiologist's intimates had a different view. What else are intimates for? "He was a very outgoing guy. A very humorous guy," says architect Robert Jacobs, a close friend of Tarnower's. Jacobs attended many of the doctor's excellent dinner parties, where the wines would be chosen with expertise, and the food—prepared by Dr. Tarnower's French-born cook-housekeeper, Suzanne van der Vreken—was likewise. The parties were also where the ascetic gourmet's guests—"usually six to eight, all interesting people"—would eschew froth, hewing to the issues of the day. Mrs. Schulte also notes an absence of frivolity, saying that Tarnower "didn't like fiction. He liked reading biography, history, books about people who had achieved something, made a difference in the world" but agrees that the doctor always liked a laugh. "He had a very quick sense of humor," she says. "My husband had been his closest friend for twenty-five years. They used to throw semihumorous insults at each other."

Here are hints of the singularity that put off so many, but drew some—including, one must presume, Jean Harris—so close. Those superlative medical skills, which showed the kindlier side of Tarnower's nature—"He was one of the last old-style doctors," says a patient, "he really cared"—ran alongside a sort of competitiveness, a controlled aggression.

To a certain extent, this showed itself in traditional upper-middle-class pursuits. Tarnower drew most of his friends from either his patients' register or his country club, the Century, which is to say, the same list. He was a seventeen-handicap golfer. "He was excellent at gin rummy," says Robert Jacobs. "He was excellent at backgammon. He was excellent at everything he did."

And some of the things he did were more exotic. He loved to travel. The travels yielded objets d'art. Tarnower brought back numerous Buddhas from the East, for instance. One such holy figure, covered with a crackle of gold paint, sits on an islet in a pool on Tarnower's cultivated six-acre estate. The doctor would sometimes row across and contemplate. Agatha Christie herself would have gloried in the touch.

Hi Tarnower's other pursuit was in a contrary direction. He liked to *hunt*. He fished for marlin in the Bahamas, bonefish off Mexico, shot birds in North America, and went on six African safaris with Arthur Schulte alone. There are few varieties of legal game that the imperious hat manufacturer's son did not, at one time or another, add to his bag, the choicer items being brought back so that they might adorn his Purchase house, alongside the stone and golden Buddhas and the large collection of guns.

Jean Harris, understandably, was fascinated. The relationship grew deeper. When she left Springside in 1972 to become head of the Thomas School in Rowayton, Connecticut, Philadelphia acquaintances speculated that it was to be closer to Tarnower. She bought a house in Mahopac, just a forty-five-minute drive from both the doctor and the school.

Thomas was a private girls' school and was in a sorry state. It was a bad time for private schools generally, with enrollments declining, and the posh boys' schools—Exeter, Saint Paul's, Choate—going co-ed. Jean Harris was supposed to turn it around. The reputation she earned was familiar—efficient, though inflexible—but there was a disturbing new ingredient. She could be temperamental, sources say. Moody. A former staffer said that she would "scream at students."

In 1975, at any rate, the Thomas School closed. Jean Harris, whose sons were now both in their twenties, left private education and took a $32,500-per-year job with the Allied Maintenance Corporation. Allied does such necessary, but unglamorous, tasks as supplying janitors to Madison Square Garden. Jean Struven Harris of Shaker Heights, Grosse Pointe, and Chestnut Hill, was a supervisor of sales. The money was good, but, after eighteen months, when she heard that there was an opening at the head of the Madeira School, one of the glittering prizes of the profession, she did not hesitate before applying.

THE MADEIRA SCHOOL was started by Miss Lucy Madeira in a Washington, DC, townhouse in 1906. Considering what was to come, it is a pleasant touch that Lucy Madeira was a determined young woman with a strong inclination to the theories of Fabian socialism. Portraits of Madeira show a pleasant Late Victorian face with a smile of steely shyness and the round, thin-rimmed specs so popular later with that girls' school problem, the Woodstock Generation. Her will is still much a factor in the school. "She had these sayings," an alumna tells me, "like 'Function in Disaster' and 'Finish in Style.' Just mention them to any Madeira girl—she heard those phrases over and over and over again."

The first disaster was the Depression. Lucy Madeira wished to move, expand. Funds were not forthcoming. Help came. Eugene Meyer, owner of *The Washington Post,* presented several hundred acres of unused woodland alongside the Potomac, which is where Madeira School is today.

In many respects, the Fabians might be pleasantly surprised by the New Woman as she has emerged from Madeira. Alumnae include Eugene Meyer's daughter, Kay Graham; Ann Swift, now a diplomatic hostage in Tehran; and Diane Oughton, a member of the Weatherman collective, who died so brusquely in an exploding Greenwich Village townhouse and who, friends say, cherished fond memories of the school to her rigorously Marxist end. Students today include the daughters of ABC reporter Sam Donaldson, commentator Eric Sevareid, Republican senator from Wyoming Malcolm Wallop, and a granddaughter of Nelson Rockefeller.

That great Fabian George Bernard Shaw might have found himself more ambivalent about other aspects of the school. It is, of course, true that the first visible sign on the campus reads, STOP: HORSE CROSSING, just as it is true that the most splendid new building is a $3.5 million indoor riding ring, but Madeira alumnae are sensitive to the merest hint that it's a fairly fancy setup.

"We are not a finishing school," alums told me over and over. Madeira has a 100 percent college-entrance rate. Madeira is practically a *natural resource* where the Ivy League is concerned. Madeira integrated during the last decades, the administration told me, and now has twelve black pupils. Indeed, they are actively looking for more, but there is a sort of problem, given the fees—"$6,100 a year for boarders, after taxes"—and the shortage of scholarship endowments. As to the other all-girl schools, Madeira tends to be a bit sniffy. "Foxcroft?" said one. "That's a glorified riding academy." I repeated this remark to another alum who had, till then, been talking of Madeira rather as if it were the Académie Française. She struck like a terrier embedding its teeth in my calf. "We *always* beat Foxcroft," she said.

But, for all its equable progress, some felt that the years since Lucy Madeira departed had represented a decline. Many of the problems had been classic. One senior official, it was found, had a drinking problem. The late sixties and early seventies brought contemporary travails. "We could get expelled for smoking a cigarette," one ex-pupil remarks. "But there was no shortage of druggies."

The headmistress then was Barbara Keyser. Barbara Keyser was a girls' school headmistress in the indomitable British mold—unmarried, wholly engrossed in her role. Many swore by her, but some were intimidated. "She was really quite a threatening figure," one pupil says. "She looked and acted like a drill sergeant."

Many say that girls' schools in those turbulent years needed a hand. It was, after all, at this time that a dead baby in a plastic bag was discovered at that genteel Connecticut school, Miss Porter's. Anyway, when the problem did come to Madeira, it was less natural, more horrible. A man had taken to roaming the grounds. It seemed to go on and on. A malaise overhung Madeira until the deranged male was caught, and locked up.

What happened next is not crystal clear. At any rate, the man was at large and the school wasn't told. Hitherto harmless, he struck. One of the pupils was assaulted and tied to a tree. She died of exposure. It seemed that the sickening event preyed on Barbara Keyser's mind. She did everything that could be done, but the memory didn't leave her. It hung about the school like memories of a bad dream.

Barbara Keyser retired three years later, in 1977. The board of alumnae in charge of choosing a successor thought long and hard. They decided they knew exactly what they were looking for. A woman was needed with managerial skills appropriate to the modern business of education. Also, one of them says, "we wanted somebody *womanly*."

There were a hundred applicants. "The committee investigated *in depth*," an alumna says. And Jean Struven Harris seemed perfect. The business background at Allied Maintenance. The marriage, the family. Nobody, it seems, got an adverse reading from the former schools. The Thomas School, anyway, was closed. Jean Harris was appointed headmistress of Madeira, taking a salary cut of some $10,000 a year. Things seemed rosy.

Things were less rosy between Jean Harris and Herman Tarnower. They were still close. Tarnower had accompanied Harris to the 1974 graduation ceremonies at the Thomas School, for instance, and she frequently left Madeira for weekends in Purchase. But two things were happening.

Herman Tarnower's affections were quite perceptibly cooling. Also, Herman Tarnower had become a celebrity.

The celebrity business first. There was nothing new about the Scarsdale Diet, of course. Tarnower had been circulating it as a single mimeographed sheet for years, though his expertise was not the belly but the heart. Yet the diet got good word of mouth. In early 1978, the *Times* featured it in a piece, mentioning especially its exemplary effects on a vice-president of Bloomingdale's.

This article was read by Samm Sinclair Baker. Baker says he has written twenty-seven books. A couple of mysteries first, then five books on Creative Thinking, and so into medicine by way of "a book on skin problems written with a couple of dermatologists." The Scarsdale Diet was a natural.

"We met in May '78 and we liked each other immensely," Baker says. "He was a total gentleman. Very straight arrow." He discovered that Tarnower had discussed the idea of a diet book with his neighbor, Alfred Knopf. "But Knopf was discouraging," Samm Sinclair Baker says. He discussed things with Tarnower, mainly the strictly formal problem of how to turn a mimeographed sheet into a full-length book—"I said what we will do is answer all your readers' questions as though they were your patients"—and, writing night and day over four months, they delivered the book on October 1. "We were both workaholics," Baker concludes with satisfaction. The book, which carried a prominent acknowledgment to Jean Harris, sold 750,000 copies in hardback, two million in paperback, and made Herman Tarnower very celebrated and even richer.

Herman Tarnower himself, a meager performer on talk shows and poor at public appearances, tended to play the thing down. Indeed, he probably felt ambivalent about the unexpected stardust. A friend, hearing that he was to deliver a speech in Washington, once asked what branch of cardiology he would be discussing.

"Heck no," Tarnower said. "Nobody wants to hear me on the subject of *cardiology*."

Dr. Tarnower's new celebrity made another change that much more conspicuous. Over the last couple of years, Hi Tarnower had begun to date another woman. She was Lynne Tryforos, thirty-seven, a comely blond employee of his Scarsdale Medical Group. She was two decades younger than the woman Tarnower had refused to marry for a dozen years.

The new affair seemed cruelly public to Jean Harris. Tarnower would take Lynne Tryforos to dinner parties like the one given by Bernard "Bunny" Lasker, former chairman of the New York Stock Exchange—the sort of upper-echelon Westchester and New York functions to which he had taken Jean Struven Harris.

Jean Harris compressed her private griefs. "Integrity" was as stressed as ever in her Monday-morning talks to the girls. If anything, she was re-trenching. Last fall she was applauded by parents for announcing that she was putting that insidious district, Georgetown, off limits. She seemed to be ever more vigilant that the girls not succumb to weaknesses of the flesh.

Not everyone was favorably impressed. Some parents—like a father whose daughter was suspended for quaffing a glass of beer—were irritated by her inflexibility. The girls, by and large, decided that she was a cold fish. A few sensed something else. "She was really always a nervous wreck," an-nounces a pupil. "Pulling at her hair, walking bowed over. She could never joke around. I've never seen a woman so ill-assured. One time a kid asked some critical question, a ridiculous question. She cried onstage in front of the whole school."

Last December, Hi Tarnower shot quail at the South Carolina ranch of Christian Herter Jr., then calmly took Jean Harris to spend Christmas and the New Year with the Schultes in Palm Beach. They read, talked, fished. Tarnower worked avidly through the Manchester book on General MacArthur.

Toward the end of January, Hi Tarnower took another trip. He went to Montego Bay, Jamaica. His companion was Lynne Tryforos. Some sort of decision was approaching. This last Tuesday, March 18, was to have been Tarnower's seventieth birthday. A dinner party was planned. His guest was to have been Lynne Tryforos.

Lynne Tryforos was also among Tarnower's dinner guests—they had all left a couple of hours earlier—the night Jean Harris arrived in the raging rain. When the police came, Jean Harris spoke in broken and contradictory fashion. "I shot him—I did it," she said at one point. But she also said that she had asked him to kill *her*.

If Joel Aurnou, Harris's lawyer, can prove that such was indeed her intention, the charge of murder automatically gets lowered to one of manslaughter. Jean Harris sits and waits, her pale blue eyes unreflecting as china. She laughs aloud when something funny is said, but kindness makes her weep. Mostly, though, even in the courtroom, even in the sanitarium, she has a forlornly elegant dignity. It is as though those Late Victorian Madeira maxims shield her still. *Function in Disaster. Finish in Style.*

Perhaps all she wanted to do, as schoolchildren say, was teach Hi Tarnower a lesson. Certainly she cut Tarnower off just as an apotheosis of sorts was approaching this ambitious man. On April 19, Dr. Charles Bertrand, president of the Westchester County Medical Society, was to have presented Tarnower with an award at a very grand dinner. A cardiac center was to be named after him. The cardiac center, like the jail in which Jean Harris was held, was in a place called Valhalla.

Dr. Bertrand sighs. The Thursday before the murder, he had been chatting with Tarnower, who said he was about to start another book.

"What's the title?" asked Bertrand.

"*How to Live Longer and Enjoy Life More*," said Hi Tarnower.

Lucy Madeira's sayings have a more durable ring.

THE $2,000-AN-HOUR WOMAN

MARK JACOBSON

JULY 10, 2005

When Mark Jacobson happened upon him, Jason Itzler was the self-described "King of All Pimps," a kind of P. T. Barnum of the prostitution world, who didn't seem to worry about getting arrested. At first, Jacobson found most of the prostitutes he met uninteresting. "All they did was sleep, fuck, or snort cocaine," he says. But Natalia, Itzler's girlfriend and favored prostitute, was different: an actress—she'd done Shakespeare—she was now playing a different kind of role, as the city's most expensive prostitute. Itzler's hucksterism cost him—he went to prison, though he claims to have recently made several hundred thousand dollars selling photos of Ashley Dupré, one of his former prostitutes who serviced New York's former governor Eliot Spitzer. Natalia now works at a spa in Canada—"It really is a spa," says Jacobson. Her book on her experience will appear soon.

J ASON ITZLER, the self-anointed world's greatest escort-agency owner, prepared to get down on his knees. When a man was about to ask for the hand of a woman in holy matrimony, especially the hand of the fabulous Natalia, America's No. 1 escort, he should get down on his knees.

This was how Jason, who has always considered himself nothing if not "ultraromantic," saw it. However, as he slid from his grade-school-style red plastic seat in preparation to kneel, the harsh voice of a female Corrections officer broke the mood, ringing throughout the dank visitor's room.

"Sit back down," said the large uniformed woman. "You know the rules."

Such are the obstacles to true love when one is incarcerated at Rikers Island, where Jason Itzler, thirty-eight and still boyishly handsome in his gray Department of Corrections jumpsuit, has resided since the cops shut down his megaposh NY Confidential agency in January.

There was also the matter of the ring. During the glorious summer and fall of 2004, when NY Confidential was grossing an average of $25,000 a night at its 5,000-square-foot loft at 79 Worth Street, spitting distance from the municipal courts and Bloomberg's priggish City Hall, Jason would have purchased a diamond with enough carats to blow the eye loupe off a 47th Street Hasid.

That was when Itzler filled his days with errands like stopping by Soho Gem on West Broadway to drop $6,500 on little trinkets for Natalia and his other top escorts. This might be followed by a visit to Manolo Blahnik to buy a dozen pairs of $500 footwear. By evening, Itzler could be found at Cipriani, washing down plates of crushed lobster with yet another bottle of Johnnie Walker Blue label and making sure everyone got one of his signature titanium business cards engraved with NY Confidential's singular motto: ROCKET FUEL FOR WINNERS.

But now Jason was charged with various counts of criminal possession of a controlled substance, money laundering, and promoting prostitution. His arrest was part of a large effort by the NYPD and the D.A.'s office against New York's burgeoning Internet-based escort agencies. In three months, police had shut down American Beauties, Julie's, and the far-flung New York Elites, a concern the cops said was flying porn stars all over the country for dates. Reeling, pros were declaring the business "holocausted" as girls took down their websites and worried johns stayed home.

Many blamed Itzler for the heat. In a business where discretion is supposed to be key, Jason was more than a loose cannon. Loose A-bomb was more like it. He took out giant NY Confidential ads in mainstream magazines (the one you're holding included). In restaurants, he'd get loud and identify himself, Howard Stern style, as "the King of All Pimps." Probably most fatally, Itzler was quoted in the *Post* as bragging that he didn't worry about the police because "I have cops on my side." After that, one vice guy said, "it was like he was daring us."

Only days before, Itzler, attired in a $5,700 full-length fox coat from Jeffrey, bought himself a Mercedes S600. Now the car, along with much of the furniture at Jason's lair, including the $50,000 sound system on which he blared, 24/7, the music of his Rat Pack idol, Frank Sinatra, had been confiscated by the cops. His assets frozen, unable to make his $250,000 bail, Jason couldn't even buy a phone card, much less get Natalia a ring.

"Where am I going to get a ring in here?" Jason said to Natalia on the phone the other night. He suggested perhaps Natalia might get the ring herself and then slip it to him when she came to visit.

"That's good, Jason," returned Natalia. "I buy the ring, give it to you, you kiss it, give it back to me, and I pretend to be surprised."

"Something like that," Jason replied, sheepishly. "You know I love you."

That much seemed true. As Jason doesn't mind telling you, he has known many women since he lost his virginity not too long after his bar mitzvah at the Fort Lee Community Jewish Center, doing the deed with the captain of the Tenafly High School cheerleader squad. Since then, Jason, slight and five foot nine, says he's slept with "over seven hundred women," a figure he admits pales before the twenty thousand women basketball star Wilt "The Stilt" Chamberlain claimed to have bedded. But, as Jason says, "you could say I am a little pickier than him."

Of these seven hundred women, Jason has been engaged to nine, two of whom he married. "It was really only one and a half," Itzler reports, saying that while living in Miami's South Beach he married "this hot Greek girl. She was gorgeous. The first thing I did was buy her this great boob job, which immediately transformed her from a tremendous A/B look to an out-of-sight C/D look. But her parents totally freaked out. So I got the marriage annulled."

This aside, not counting his sainted late mother, Jason says Natalia, twenty-five, about five foot three and perhaps a hundred pounds soaking wet, reigns as the love of his life.

Without Natalia, she of the smoldering brown eyes that have excited who knows how many hedge-fund managers, billionaire trust-fund babies, and NFL quarterbacks, Jason would never have been able to build NY Confidential into the sub rosa superhotness it became. It was Natalia who got top dollar, as much as $2,000 an hour, with a two-hour minimum. In the history of Internet escorting, no one ever matched Natalia's ratings on TheEroticReview.com, the Zagat's of the escort-for-hire industry. On TER, "hobbyists," as those with the "hobby" of frequenting escorts are called—men with screen names like Clint Dickwood, Smelly Smegma, and William Jefferson Clinton—can write reviews of the "providers" they see, rating them on a scale of 1 to 10 for both "appearance" and "performance."

In 2004, Natalia recorded an unprecedented seventeen straight 10/10s. On the TER ratings scale, a 10 was defined as "one in a lifetime." Natalia was the Perfect 10, the queen of the escort world.

"Yo! *Pimp Juice!* . . . that her?"

It was Psycho, a large tattooed Dominican (PSYCHO was stenciled on his neck in Gothic lettering) who was referring to Jason by his jailhouse nickname. Itzler nodded. There was no need to gloat. Moments before, Jason scanned the grim visiting room. "Just making sure I've got the hottest chick in the room." Like it was any contest, Natalia sitting there, in her little calfskin jacket and leather miniskirt, thick auburn hair flowing over her narrow shoulders.

Besides, half of Rikers already knew about Jason and NY Confidential. They'd read, or heard about, the articles Itzler had piped to his pulp enablers at "Page Six," including how he could get "$250,000 an hour for Paris Hilton with a four-hour minimum."

But you couldn't believe everything you read in the *New York Post*, even at Rikers. Natalia's presence was proof. Proof that Jason, a little Jewish guy who still sported a nasty black eye from being beaten silly in his sleep by some skell inmate, wasn't full of shit when he told the homeys that he was the biggest pimp in the city, that he got all the best girls. How many other Rikers fools could get the Perfect 10 to visit them, at nine o'clock in the morning, too?

"Psycho . . . Natalia," Jason said. "Natalia . . . Psycho."

"Hey," Natalia said with an easy smile. She was, after all, a girl you could take anywhere. One minute she could be the slinkiest cat on the hot tin roof, wrapping her dancer's body (she was the tap-dance champion of Canada in 1996) around a client's body in a hotel elevator. Then, when the door slid open, she'd look classic, like a wife even, on the arm of a Wall Street CEO or Asian electronics magnate. She was an actress, had played Shakespeare and Off Broadway both. Ever the ingénue, she'd been Juliet half a dozen times. Playing opposite Jason's however-out-of-luck Romeo was no sweat, even here, in jail.

Not that Natalia had exactly been looking forward to coming to Rikers this raw late-spring morning. Riding in the bus over the bridge from East Elmhurst, freezing in her lace stockings as she sat beside a stocky black man in a Jerome Bettis jersey, she looked out the window at the looming prison and said, "Wal-Mart must have had a two-for-one on barbed wire."

It wasn't that she didn't miss Jason, or the heyday of when they lived together at 79 Worth Street, the harem stylings of which came to Jason while getting his hair cut at the Casbah-themed Warren Tricomi Salon on 57th Street. It was just that this marriage thing was flipping her out, especially after Jason called the tabs to announce the ceremony would be held inside Rikers.

"Every little girl's dream, to get married at Rikers Island," Natalia said to Jason. "What are they going to get us, adjoining cells?"

But now, holding hands in the visiting room, surrounded by low-level convicts, just the sort of people who rarely appeared in either of their well-to-do childhoods or in the fantasy life of 79 Worth Street—neither of them, pimp or escort, could keep from crying.

"Are those happy tears or sad tears?" Jason asked.

"Just tears," answered Natalia.

"Crying because your boy is in jail?"

"That and . . . everything else."

It was a tender moment. Except then, as he always does, Jason began talking.

"Don't worry about this Rikers marriage," he said, back in schemer–boy genius mode. "This isn't the real marriage . . . When I'm out we'll have the princess marriage . . . the white dress, everything. Your mom will be there. My dad . . . This is just the publicity marriage. You know: getting married at Rikers—it's so . . . rock star!"

Natalia looked up at Jason, makeup streaming from her face.

"It's great, isn't it?" Jason enthused. "A brilliant idea."

"Yeah," Natalia said wearily. "Great, *in theory*." Almost everything Jason Itzler said was great, in theory.

NOT YET FORTY, Jason Itzler has a story that is already a mini-epic of Jewish-American class longing, a psycho-socio-sexual drama crammed with equal parts genius (occasionally vicious) boychick hustle, heartfelt neo-hippie idealism, and dead-set will to self-destruction. Born Jason Sylk, only son of the short-lived marriage between his revered mother, Ronnie Lubell, and his "sperm dad," Leonard Sylk, heir to the Sun Ray drugstore fortune built up by Harry Sylk, who once owned a piece of the Philadelphia Eagles, Jason spent his early years as one of very few Jewish kids on Philly's Waspy Main Line. If he'd stayed a Sylk, says Jason, "I would have been the greatest Richie Rich, because Lenny Sylk is the biggest thing in the Jewish community. He's got a trust that gives money to stuff like the ballet, a house with an eighteen-car garage, and a helicopter landing pad. Golda Meir used to stay with us when she was in town."

After his parents' divorce, Itzler moved to New York with his mother, whom Jason describes as "the hottest mom in the world. She had this Mafia princess–Holly Golightly thing about her. Her vanity license plate was TIFF. My mother being beautiful made me into who I am today, because when you grow up around a beautiful woman, you always want to be surrounded by beautiful women."

Also a big influence was his mom's father, the semi-legendary Nathan Lubell, "the biggest bookmaker in the garment industry, a gangster wizard," says Jason. "He owned a lot of hat stores, a bunch of the amusement park in Coney Island, and was hooked up with Meyer Lansky in Las Vegas hotels. I used to love it when he took me to the Friars Club, where he was a king. Even as a kid, I could feel the action."

With his mom remarried, to Ron Itzler, then a lawyer in the firm of Fischbein, Badillo (as in Herman), Wagner, and Itzler, the family lived in the Jersey suburbs. Displaying his compulsive intelligence by setting the all-time record on the early-generation video game Scramble, Jason, "pretty much obsessed with sex from the start," wrote letters to *Mad* magazine suggesting it put out a flexi-record of "teenage girls having orgasms." Summers were spent in the Catskills, where as a cabana boy at the Concord Hotel he befriended people like Jason Binn, now the playboy publisher of the *Hamptons* and *Los Angeles Confidential* magazines, a name Itzler paid homage to with his NY Confidential.

Itzler remembers, "At the Concord, when Jason Binn said he was the son of a billionaire, and my stepfather told me, yeah, he was, I got light-headed."

In the late eighties, after getting through George Washington University, even though he was "mostly running wet-T-shirt contests," Itzler entered Nova Southeastern University, a bottom-tier law school in Fort Lauderdale, Florida, where he embarked on what he calls "my first great chapter" as "the twenty-two-year-old phone-sex king of South Beach." Advertising a "Free Live Call" (after which a $4.98-a-minute charge set in), Itzler's company was doing $600,000 a month, hitting a million and a half within a year.

"I had so much money," Jason recalls. "I bought an Aston Martin Virage, three hundred feet of oceanfront property. Like a moron, I spent half a million decorating a one-bedroom apartment."

Alas, it would all soon come tumbling down, owing to what Jason now calls a "kind of oversight," which left him owing $4.5 million at 36 percent interest. Forced to declare bankruptcy in 1997, he lost everything, including his visionary acquisition of one of the fledgling Internet's most valuable URLs: pussy.com.

The demise of Itzler's phone-sex company set a pattern that would be repeated in 2000 with his next big act, the SoHo Models fiasco. With typical overreach, Jason rented an 8,000-square-foot space at the corner of Canal and Broadway and declared himself the new Johnny Casablancas. Unfortunately for the young models hoping to find their faces on the cover of *Vogue*, the true business of SoHo Models was to supply Webcam porn. For a fee, the voyeur would type in "take off blouse . . . insert dildo."

Squabbling among gray-market partners soon ensued. Within months, Jason found himself dangling over the side of the Canal Street building, held by the ankles by a guy named Mikey P.

Jason says he would have gotten through these setbacks more easily if his mother were still alive, but Ronnie Itzler died of cancer in 1994, "after which I went kind of a little nuts." Following the collapse of the phone-sex firm, he twice attempted suicide, once running himself through with a steak knife and on another occasion drinking "a milk shake" he claims contained "seventy-five Valium, seventy-five Klonopin, and a couple bottles of Scotch." Much to his surprise, he survived both times.

Desperate for money after the SoHo Models disaster, Itzler decided his best option was to go to Amsterdam to buy four thousand tabs of Ecstasy. "In retrospect, it was a totally retarded idea," says Jason, who would leave Newark airport in handcuffs. He was sentenced to five years in the Jersey pen. The fact that his grandfather, whom he'd idolized as a gangster, stopped talking to him when he got locked up "was hard to take."

"Jail is terrible, really boring," says Jason. "But it does give you plenty of time to plan your next move."

ON PAROLE AFTER SERVING seventeen months of his smuggling sentence, living in a funky third-floor walk-up in Hoboken per the terms of his release, Jason started NY Confidential (he would remain on parole his entire pimp career) in late 2003. Business was spotty at first but picked up dramatically in early 2004, when Natalia walked into the company's place at 54th Street and Sixth Avenue, an office previously occupied by the magician David Blaine.

"It was my birthday," Natalia remembers. "I'd just been cast as Ingrid Superstar in this play, *Andy & Edie.* I wanted to be Edie, but Misha Sedgwick, Edie's niece, also wanted it, so forget that. I was eating in a restaurant with Peter Beard, the photographer. I was a kind of party girl for a while. I met Peter one night, and we hit it off. He said I should meet this guy Jason."

Beard, a nocturnal bon vivant known for his "discovery" of exotic models like Iman, and who had been associated with Jason during the SoHo Models episode, warned Natalia off Itzler's new venture. Eventually, however, Natalia decided to give Jason a call. "Being an escort never crossed my mind. It wasn't something girls like me did. I was an actress. From a very nice home. But I was involved in an abusive relationship, with this Wall Street guy," she says. "In the beginning, all I wanted was enough money to move out."

Jason says, "When Natalia came over with Peter, I said, *Wow, she's so hot. She has one of the all-time great tushes.* But there was this other girl there, too. Samantha. When she took off her shirt, she had these amazing breasts. So it was Natalia's butt against Samantha's boobies. I went with the tits. But when Natalia came back from making a movie, she moved in with us. Samantha could tell I was kind of more into Natalia. So we became boyfriend and girlfriend."

At the time, Jason's top girl was Cheryl, a striking blonde ballroom dancer from Seattle who says she got into the business to buy her own horse. "I did NY Confidential's first date," Cheryl recalls. "I had on my little black dress and was shaking like a leaf. Jason was nervous, too. He said, 'Just go up there and take your clothes off.' I told him, 'No, you've got to make it romantic. Special.' "

It was Cheryl who came up with the mantra Jason would later instruct all the NY Confidential girls to repeat, "three times," before entering a hotel room to see a client: *"This is my boyfriend of six months, the man I love, I haven't seen him for three weeks . . . This is my boyfriend of six months, the man I love . . ."*

"That's the essence of the true GFE, the Girlfriend Experience," says Jason. As opposed to the traditional "no kissing on the mouth" style, the GFE offers a warmer, fuzzier time. For Jason, who says he never hired anyone who'd worked as an escort before, the GFE concept was an epiphany. "Men see escorts because they want to feel happier. Yet most walk away feeling worse than they did before. They feel dirty, full of self-hatred. Buyer's remorse big-time. GFE is about true passion, something genuine. A facsimile of love. I told guys this was a quick vacation, an investment in the future. When they got back to their desks, they'd tear the market a new asshole, make back the money they spent at NY Confidential in an hour.

"What we're selling is rocket fuel, rocket fuel for winners."

Jason decided Natalia would become his great creation, the Ultimate GFE. It mattered little that Natalia, for all her French-Scottish sultriness, might strike some as a tad on the skinny side. Brown-eyed, dark-haired, olive-skinned, not to mention lactose-intolerant, she didn't fit the usual description of a big ticket in an industry filled with PSE (Porn-Star Experience) babes with store-bought bazangas out to here. Jason took this as a challenge. If he was into Natalia, he'd make sure everyone else was, too. It was a simple matter of harnessing the available technology.

The main vehicle was the aforementioned TheEroticReview.com, "the Consumer Reports of the escort industry," according to the site's founder and owner, the L.A.-based Dave Elms, a.k.a. Dave@TER. "The most important thing was to break Natalia out big," Jason says. "To get the ball rolling with a number of fabulous reviews, I sent her to some friends, to sort of grease the wheel. I knew those 10/10s would keep coming, because no man wants to admit he got less. They're brainwashed that way."

If any hobbyist had the temerity to hand out a paltry 8/8, or even a 9/10, he would be contacted. "Don't break my girl's streak, this is history in the making," Jason cajoled, offering to throw in a couple hours of free time to get the customer to do a little recalculating. If that didn't work, good reviews could be ensured by the $5,000 everyone working at NY Confidential (except Jason) swears was FedExed to Dave@TER on the 15th of every month.

Jason's hyping sometimes was faintly embarrassing. "Jason would be saying, 'Natalia is the greatest escort in the history of the world, as good as Cleopatra or Joan of Arc,'" says Natalia, "and I'd be like, 'Jason! Joan of Arc was not an escort, she was a religious martyr.' Then he'd be saying I was the greatest escort since Mary Magdalene."

But all the hype in the world (an Asian toy manufacturer wanted to mass-produce Barbie-style Natalia dolls, complete with tiny lingerie) wouldn't have helped if Natalia, who never imagined she'd wind up staying in "every expensive hotel in New York," hadn't turned out to be a natural.

"I'm a little moneymaking machine, that's what I am," she says as she takes a languorous drag of her Marlboro while stretching out on her apartment couch in a shiny pink satin corset, Marlene Dietrich style.

Then she cracks up, because "you know, the whole thing is so ridiculous sometimes."

People wonder what it is about Natalia that made her the Perfect 10. "From the start, you know this is going to be fun," says one client. "It is like having sex in a tree house." Says another, "Nat isn't this all-knowing geisha thing. But in a way, it's deeper, because she gets to a place inside where you used to be free." And another: "With her, there's none of that shit like this is costing enough for a first-class ticket to London and the girl's in the bathroom for, like, half an hour. Natalia's this one, total this-is-all-about-you."

Suffice it to say, it's in the pheromones. According to Natalia, she's always gotten along with men. "Jason understood who I was," she says. "Yes, he sold the shit out of me, but he sold me as myself, someone anyone can be comfortable with, someone who really likes sex. Because the truth is, I do. I loved my job, totally."

It is another old story, along with the heart of gold, that many "providers" actually like what they do. But even if she professes to be "horrified" by stories about sexual trafficking and "sickened" by nightmarish exploitation of the street prostitute, Natalia says, "At the level NY Confidential was at, the guys I was meeting, I would have gone out with 80 percent of them anyway. People have so many misconceptions, preconceptions, about my life. Last year, I got a call to play an escort in a Broadway play. But the part was so dark, so icky. I said no. It didn't fit my experience at all."

You never knew who might be behind the hotel door. Once, she was summoned to a guy's room, told only that he was a famous, championship athlete. "I'm not a big sports fan, but I recognized him, the quarterback. He turned out to be very laid-back. He mostly wanted to make me happy. In the middle, he looks up and says, 'Well, you know me, I'm more of a giver than a receiver.' "

Some weeks were particularly frenetic. From July 29 to August 1, she had a four-day date in the Florida Keys for which Itzler charged $29,000. The very next day was a four-hour appointment. August 3 was filled with a ten-hour appointment and another two-hour job. August 4, three hours. August 5, a three-hour followed by another four-hour. August 6, two hours. August 7, one four-hour job and a two-hour. August 8, she was off. But the 9th was another ten-hour day, followed by a pair of two-hour jobs on August 10. "It was like a dream," Natalia says. "I never got tired."

Asked if the work affected her relationship with Itzler, Natalia says, "Sometimes he'd say, 'Everyone gets a chance to spend time with you except me.' I'd say, 'You're the one booking me.' " As for Jason, he says, "If she ever did it with anyone for free, it would have broken my heart."

Moving from 54th Street following a nasty fallout with partner Bruce Glasser (each party claimed the other had taken out a contract on his life), Itzler ran NY Confidential out of his parolee apartment in Hoboken. One visitor describes the scene: "The place was full of naked women and underwear. It was a rain forest of underwear. In the middle on the couch is Jason with all these telephones, one in either ear, the other one ringing on the coffee table."

For Jason, the loft was an opportunity to make real his most cherished theories of existence. "To me, the higher percentage of your life you are happy, the more successful you are," says Jason, who came upon his philosophy while reading Ayn Rand. "I was really into the 'Who is John Galt?' *Atlas Shrugged* thing. I thought I could save the world if I could bring together the truly elite people, the most beautiful women with the most perfect bodies, best faces, and intelligence, and the elite men, the captains of industry, lawyers, and senators. This would bring about the most happiness, to the best people, who most deserved to be happy."

Years before, Jason wrote out the precepts of what he called "The Happiness Movement." Assuming his findings to be big news, Itzler packed up the manifesto, a copy of his half-finished autobiography, and a naked centerfold picture of Elisa Bridges, his girlfriend at the time, and mailed it to Bob Woodward. "I stuck it in this $3,000 Bottega Veneta briefcase so he'd notice it. He said I was a nut job and to leave him alone. I was so bummed I told him to keep the stupid briefcase."

Seventy-nine Worth Street became a well-oiled machine, with various calendars posted on the wall to keep track of appointments. The current day's schedule was denoted on a separate chart called "the action board." But what mattered most to Jason was "the vibe . . . the vibe of the NY Confidential brand" (there was franchising talk about a Philadelphia Confidential and a Vegas Confidential). To describe what he was going for, Jason quotes from a favorite book, *The Art of Seduction,* a creepily fascinating tome of social Machiavellianism, by Robert Greene.

Discussing "seductive place and time," Greene notes that "certain kinds of visual stimuli signal that you are not in the real world. Avoid images that have depth, which might provoke thought, or guilt . . . The more artificial, the better . . . Luxury—the sense that money has been spent or even wasted—adds to the feeling that the real world of duty and morality has been banished. Call it the brothel effect."

Accentuated by the fog machine at 79 Worth Street, people seemed to come out of the shadows, float by, be gone again. "It was full of these familiar faces . . . like a soap-opera star, a politician you might have seen on NY1, a guy whose photo's in the *Times* financial pages," says one regular. In addition to Sinatra, music was supplied by the building's super, a concert pianist in his native Russia, who appeared in a tuxedo to play on a rented Baldwin grand piano.

"It was like having my own clubhouse," says Jason now, relishing the evenings he presided as esteemed host and pleasure master. He remembers discussing what he called a "crisis in Judaism" with a top official of a leading Jewish-American lobby group. Jewish women were often thought of as dowdy, Jason said. If the American Jew was ever going to rise above the prejudice of the goyishe mainstream, creativity would be needed. A start would be to get Madonna, the Kabbalist, to become the head of Hadassah. The official said he'd look into it.

Seventy-nine Worth Street was supposed to be Jason and Natalia's home, where they would live happily ever after. They had their own bedroom, off-limits to everyone else. Natalia wrote her mom that she'd moved into a beautiful new place with a highly successful businessman. Her mom, a sweet cookie-baking lady leery of her daughter's life in New York, wrote back that she'd like to come down to visit. Looking around the loft at the naked women, Natalia asked, "How am I going to have my mom come here?" Jason said he would close the place, and take the loss, for the time Natalia's mom was in town. Family was the most important thing, he said.

"Well," Natalia says, "Jason never closed the loft. My mom and I stayed in a little apartment uptown. Jason was supposed to come by to meet her, but it started getting late. Then the doorbell rings at 2 A.M. It's Jason, in his knee-length coat with these two nineteen-year-old girls. I'm totally flipping out: *Like, what the fuck are you doing?* He looked like the pimp from *Superfly*. My mom is saying, '*This is him?*' But then Jason sits down and starts telling my mom I'm a great young actress and my career is going to take off, how living in New York is so terrific for me. He charmed her, completely. She left saying, 'Well, your boyfriend is kind of weird. But he's very, very nice.'

"It was always like that."

FEW EXPECTED 79 Worth Street to last very long. The parole situation led to certain traumas. Court-mandated drug tests caused Jason to alter his intake. Always "on the Cheech-and-Chong side of things," Itzler couldn't smoke pot, which turned up on piss tests. Instead, Jason, who never touched coke and often launched into Jimmy Swaggart–like speeches about the evils of the drug, dipped into his personal stash of ketamine, or Special K, the slightly unpredictable anesthetic developed for use by veterinarians. "They didn't test for it," Jason says by way of explanation. He was also drinking a $200 bottle of Johnnie Walker Blue a day. Natalia's drug use cut into her Perfect 10 appearance. One night, she cracked her head into the six-foot-tall statue of an Indian fertility goddess Jason had purchased for their room. Knocked cold, she had to go to the emergency room.

Still, the business charged on. It takes a singular pimp to think it is a good idea to stage a reality-TV show at his place of business, but Jason Itzler is that kind of guy. "It was incredible," says independent producer Ron Sperling, who shot the film *Inside New York Confidential*. "Big-shot lawyers and Wall Street bankers flipped when they saw the cameras. Jason told them the movie was no problem. That it was a good thing. If they didn't want to be in it, they should just walk behind the camera. That's Jason. If he was a billionaire and no one knew about it, it wouldn't be anything to him."

Jason's manic spending increased. One afternoon, splashing on Creed Gold Bottle cologne ($175 per bottle) as "kind of a nervous tic," he bought twenty-six antique crystal chandeliers at $3,000 apiece. "We had so much furniture, there was nowhere to walk. I used to jump over the stuff for exercise," says Natalia. Jason's Utopian house of happiness turned into a stage for an ongoing paranoid soap opera. Feeling his grip slipping, Itzler begged his former fiancée Mona to help with the day-to-day running of the place. With Jason's parole problems increasingly keeping him in Hoboken, Mona soon filled the power vacuum at 79 Worth Street. Her key ally would be Clark Krimer, a.k.a. Clark Kent or Superman, a muscle-bound young banker hired by Itzler to manage credit-card accounts. This way, those wanting to disguise their use of NY Confidential services would appear to be spending their $1,200 or so at venues like the fictitious Gotham Steak. Clark and Mona soon became an item, consolidating their power.

The Clark-and-Mona regime upset "the vibe" of 79 Worth Street, turning it into, in the words of one working girl, "just another whorehouse." First to feel the fallout was Natalia. As queen of the castle, Natalia always dismissed the jealousies of the other escorts as "stupid girl stuff." This was different. She says, "Mona was a psycho-bitch. She hated me, and now she was running the place." When clients called, instead of Jason's rapturous invocations of Natalia's charms, Mona said, "I've got this girl, she's six-one, a rower on an Ivy League college scull team. She's cheaper than Natalia and way better." Natalia's bookings fell off.

One November afternoon, Natalia arrived at the loft to find Mona standing in front of the door to her room—*her room!*—demanding she turn over her keys to the loft. "This is where I live. My home," Natalia screamed. Eventually, however, Natalia decided to move out.

Through this, people began telling Jason he'd better cool things out, not keep bringing parties of vacationing second-grade schoolteachers by the loft for fun. With guys in Con Edison vans watching the place from across the street, the least he could do was make sure the front door stayed locked.

"What do I have to hide?" Jason scoffed. "I'm not doing anything illegal."

Much of this self-deluding assessment was based on the contract Jason, utilizing his best Nova U. legalese, worked up between himself and the NY Confidential escorts. The document, signed by all the girls, stated they were "specifically forbidden" to have sex with the clients. "I'm bulletproof. Rich people don't go to jail," Jason proclaimed. He was certain that if anything came up, his lawyers, Mel Sachs and Paul Bergrin, a former Army major, could handle it. "Mel's my personal Winston Churchill, and Paul's the tough Marine general," Jason rhapsodized, either unaware or not caring that Bergrin is currently under federal investigation for his alleged part in the death of a police informer slated to testify against one of his drug-dealer clients.

AMID THIS GATHERING train wreck, one incident in November 2004 stands out as the beginning of the end. That evening, accompanied by a mutual friend, two mobsters, members of the Genovese family, according to Jason, stopped by the loft.

"I never did any business with them. I just thought it might open a new line of high-priced clients," says Jason, who bought a $3,500 Dior suit for the occasion, with a matching one for his bodyguard, a former Secret Service agent. The meeting had barely begun when a girl named Genevieve burst through the door. A tall blonde, she was returning from her first NY Confidential date, reputedly stoned out of her mind, and was demanding to be paid immediately. Told to wait, Genevieve started yelling, threatening to call the police to adjudicate the matter.

"What's wrong with that girl?" one of the mobsters asked. Itzler asked the bodyguard to quiet Genevieve down. But as the bodyguard approached, Genevieve pulled a can of pepper spray from her handbag and blinded him. With the bodyguard writhing on the floor, Genevieve locked herself in a room and called 911. A dozen cops and an engine company of firemen arrived.

There was some debate about whether to open the door, but the mobsters said, "It's the cops, you got to let them in."

"I'm looking at the security-camera monitors," remembers one witness. "In one is the cops, another the gangsters, the third the screaming girl, the fourth the Secret Service guy rubbing his eyes. That's when I thought I'd take a vacation from this place."

The encounter would end relatively harmlessly. "It looked like one of the cops recognized one of the gangsters," says the witness. "They started talking, everyone exchanged business cards and left."

After that, the cops started coming to the loft almost every day. "They'd knock on the door, come in, look around, and leave," remembers Hulbert Waldroup, one of the workers. Almost always, they took a stack of Jason's distinctive metal ROCKET FUEL FOR WINNERS business cards. The card had become something of a collector's item at headquarters, one cop says. "Everyone wanted one." Rumor has it that one ended up on Mayor Bloomberg's desk, to the mayor's amusement.

When the big bust inevitably came down on January 7, the loft was nearly empty. Krimer and Waldroup were at an art gallery when someone's cell phone rang. The caller said no one was picking up at NY Confidential. That was a bad sign, Waldroup said.

Frantically, Krimer and Waldroup attempted to connect to the Webcam security system Itzler had installed so he could watch the activities at 79 Worth Street from his Hoboken apartment. The cam was available from any wired-up computer. But no one could remember the password. "Fuck!" screamed Krimer. Eventually the connection was made.

"The place is being raided, and we're watching it on the Internet," says Waldroup. "The cops were like ants, over everything, taking all the files, ledgers, computers. On the couch were these people I'd worked with for months, in handcuffs. It was very weird."

Jason wouldn't find out about the bust until sometime later. "I was shopping for rugs with Ed Feldman, who is kind of a legend in the fashion business," Jason says. It was Feldman who, years before, had given the young Jason Itzler a copy of Budd Schulberg's all-time delineation of the Hebrew hustler, *What Makes Sammy Run?*

"Read it," Feldman said. "It's you."

Jason says, "I immediately checked into the Gansevoort Hotel and began partying. Had a couple of girls come over because I figured I wouldn't be doing that for a while. When the cops came, I thought, 'Well, at least I'm wearing my $2,800 rabbit-fur-lined sweater from Jeffrey's, because who wants to look like a guy in a sweatshirt?'"

DOWN DEEP, he always knew that when all was said and done, after everyone had had their fun, he'd be the one to pay for it. As a "predicate" felon from his ill-considered Ecstasy importation, Itzler's facing a four-

and-a-half-to-nine-year sentence. Even if he beats that, there is the matter of his busted parole in New Jersey. Sitting in Rikers, playing poker for commissary food, once again Jason has a lot of time on his hands. "I'm staying optimistic," Jason says, free of bitterness. "It is like I told the girls, if you smile a fake smile, keep smiling it because a fake smile can become a real smile."

"The problem with NY Confidential was it didn't go far enough," Jason says now. "If you really want to put together the elite people, the best-looking women and the coolest guys, you can't stop with a couple of hours. It has to be a lifetime commitment." Jason has consulted his prison rabbi, who presided over the recent Passover ceremony during which Itzler got to sit with recently arrested madam Julie Moya (of Julie's) during the asking of the Four Questions. The rabbi told Jason that as a Jewish pimp who sold women to Jewish men, he was liable for the crime of *kedesha*. The rabbi did not, however, think this transgression necessarily prevented Jason from becoming a *shadchan*, or a traditional matchmaker.

"I'm thinking about the future, the next generations," Jason says from his un-air-conditioned prison dorm. "I think I have a chance to do something good before I die. Who knows, the answer to the question 'Who is John Galt?' could be 'Jason.' "

As for Natalia, she is "keeping a low profile." Last week, she went to see Jason again. Thankfully he didn't talk too much about getting married inside the prison. Mostly they talked about the strange times they'd been through and how, even if it turned out the way it did, somehow it was worth it.

"I was a young actress who came to New York like a lot of young actresses, and I wound up with the role of a lifetime. I was the Perfect 10. I totally was. It wasn't the rabbit hole I expected to tumble down, but Jason and I . . . we were happy . . . for a time, really happy."

Since she received hardly any of her booking money and is pretty broke these days, people ask Natalia if she's planning on coming back to "work." The other night, a well-known provider, who said she used to hate Natalia when she was getting those 10/10s, offered to "pimp her out."

"That would be a feather in my cap," said the escort. "To be the one who brought back the famous Natalia."

"No, thanks," said Natalia, which is what she tells her old clients who call from time to time. "I say I'm retired, in repose. They say, 'Come on, let me buy you a drink. I'll be good.' I tell them, 'Look, we had fun and I love you. But that is over.' Mostly, they understand. Some are willing to stay friends, some can't wait to get off the phone. They've got other numbers in their book."

That doesn't mean a girl has to stay home at night. New York, after all, is a big place, full of opportunity. In a way, things have gone back to the way they were before she met Jason. "Wiser, but not necessarily sadder," Natalia says. Tonight she's going downtown. It is always good to look good, so Natalia goes through what was a familiar ritual back in the days when she was the Perfect 10—getting her nails done at the Koreans' on 29th Street, combing out her wavy hair. For old times' sake, she's got on what she used to call her "money dress," a short satin pink number with gray jersey inserts, with the shoes to match. About ten, she's ready. She goes out into the street, lifts her arm, gets into a cab, and disappears into the night.

WISEGUY

NICHOLAS PILEGGI

JANUARY 20 AND 27, 1986

Nick Pileggi had covered the Mafia for New York *magazine for years when he was introduced to Henry Hill. The writer was a regular at a mob restaurant and knew most of Hill's former colleagues, and Hill at first believed Pileggi was a wiseguy himself. When Hill was in hiding, a new member of the federal witness-protection program, he slipped Pileggi his phone number at a court appearance. Soon the two began taking long car rides together. Pileggi drove, his tape recorder on, while Hill reminisced. "Once in a while you meet a great storyteller who has a great story," says Pileggi. "I could have sat around on peyote buds for a year and couldn't have made up that stuff." Pileggi's research became the bestselling book* Wiseguy *and then the Martin Scorsese movie* GoodFellas. *Hill's testimony helped convict some fifty of his former colleagues.*

O<small>N TUESDAY</small>, May 22, 1980, a man named Henry Hill did what seemed to him the only sensible thing to do: He decided to cease to exist. He was in a Nassau County jail, facing a life sentence for his part in a huge narcotics conspiracy. The federal prosecutors were asking him about his role in the $6 million Lufthansa German Airlines robbery, the largest successful cash robbery in American history. The New York City police were in line behind the Feds to ask him about ten murders. The Justice Department wanted to talk to him about his connection with a murder that also involved Michele Sindona, the convicted Italian financier. The Organized Crime Strike Force wanted to know about the Boston College basketball players he had bribed in a point-shaving scheme. Treasury agents were looking for the crates of automatic weapons and Claymore mines he had stolen from a Connecticut armory. The Brooklyn district attorney's office wanted information about a body, found in a refrigeration truck, that was frozen so stiff it needed two days to thaw before the medical examiner could perform an autopsy.

When Henry Hill had been arrested, only three weeks earlier, it hadn't been big news. There were no front-page stories in the newspapers and no segments on the evening news. His arrest was just another of the dozens of slightly exaggerated multi-million-dollar drug busts that police make annually in their search for paragraphs of praise. But it was a prize beyond measure. Henry had grown up in the mob. He was only a mechanic, but he knew everything. He knew how the mob worked. He knew who oiled the machinery. He knew, literally, where the bodies were buried. If he talked, the police knew that Henry could give them the key to dozens of indictments and convictions. And even if he didn't talk, Henry knew that his own friends would kill him, just as they had killed nearly everyone else who had been involved in the Lufthansa robbery as a way to guarantee their silence. In jail, Henry heard the news: His protector, Paul Vario, the seventy-year-old mob chief in whose house Henry had been reared from childhood, was through with him; James "Jimmy the Gent" Burke, Henry's closest friend, the man he had been scheming and hustling with since he was thirteen years old, was planning to murder him.

Under the circumstances, Henry made his decision: He became part of the Federal Witness Security Program. His wife, Karen, and their children, Judy, fifteen, and Ruth, twelve, ceased to exist along with him. They were given new identities. It should be said that it was slightly easier for Henry Hill to cease to exist than it might have been for an average citizen, since the actual evidence of Henry's existence was extraordinarily slim. His home was apparently owned by his mother-in-law. His car was registered in his wife's name. His Social Security cards and driver's licenses—he had several of each—were forged and made out to fictitious names. He had never voted and he had never paid taxes. He had never even flown on an airplane using a ticket made out in his own name. In fact, one of the only pieces of documentary evidence that proved without doubt that Henry Hill had lived—besides his birth certificate—was his yellow sheet, the police record of arrests he had begun as a teenage apprentice to the mob.

HENRY HILL WAS introduced to life in the mob almost by accident. In 1955, when he was eleven years old, he wandered into a drab, paint-flecked cabstand at 386 Pine Street, near Pitkin Avenue, in the Brownsville–East New York section of Brooklyn, looking for a part-time job. The storefront cabstand and dispatch office was across the street from the house where he lived with his mother, father, five sisters, and two brothers, and Henry had been intrigued by the place almost as far back as he could remember. Henry had seen the long black Cadillacs and Lincolns glide into the block. He had watched the expressionless faces of the cabstand visitors, and he always remembered their huge, wide coats. Some of the visitors were so large that when they hauled themselves out of their cars, the vehicles rose by inches. He saw glittering rings and jewel-studded belt buckles and thick gold wristbands holding wafer-thin platinum watches.

The men at the cabstand were not like anyone else in the neighborhood. They wore silk suits in the morning and would drape the fenders of their cars with handkerchiefs before leaning back for a talk. He had watched them double-park their cars and never get tickets, even when they parked smack in front of a fire hydrant. In the winter, he had seen the city's sanitation trucks plow the snow from the cabstand's parking lot before getting around to cleaning the school yard and hospital grounds. In the summer, he could hear the noisy, all-night card games, and he knew that no one—not even Mr. Mancuso, who lived down the block and groused about everything—would dare complain.

At first, Henry's parents were delighted that their energetic young son had found a job just across the street. Henry's father, Henry Hill Sr., a hardworking construction-company electrician, always felt youngsters should work and learn the value of the money they were forever demanding. Since he was twelve years old, when he had come to the United States from Ireland shortly after his own father died, Henry Hill Sr. had had to support his mother and three younger brothers.

Henry's mother, Carmela Costa Hill, was pleased—almost ecstatic, really—when she learned that the Varios, the family who owned the cabstand, came from the part of Sicily where she had been born.

It wasn't too long, however, before Henry's parents began to change their minds. After the first couple of months, they found that what had started out as a part-time job for their son had become a full-time compulsion.

In 1955, the Euclid Taxicab and Limousine service was more than a dispatch center for neighborhood cabs. It was a gathering place for horseplayers, lawyers, bookies, handicappers, ex-jockeys, parole violators, construction workers, union officials, local politicians, truck drivers, policy runners, bail bondsmen, out-of-work waiters, loan sharks, off-duty cops, and even a couple of retired hit men from the old Murder Incorporated days. It was also the unofficial headquarters for Paul Vario, a rising star in one of the city's five organized-crime families and the man who ran most of the rackets in the area.

Paul Vario was a large man, six feet tall and over 240 pounds, and he appeared even larger than he was. He had the thick arms and chest of a sumo wrestler and moved in the lumbering manner of a big man who knew that people and events would wait for him. At the age of twelve, Henry began running Paul Vario's errands. Soon he was getting Vario his Lucky Strikes and coffee—black, one sugar—and delivering his messages. Henry got in and out of Vario's black Impala two dozen times a day when they made their rounds of meetings throughout the city. While Vario waited behind the wheel, Henry would bring supplicants and peers to the car for conversations.

"AT THE AGE OF TWELVE, my ambition was to be a gangster. To be a wiseguy," says Henry. "To me, being a wiseguy was better than being president of the United States. It meant power among people who had no power. It meant perks in a working-class neighborhood that had no privileges. To be a wiseguy was to own the world. I dreamed about being a wiseguy the way other kids dreamed about being doctors or movie stars or firemen or ballplayers.

"After I got my first few bucks and the nerve to go shopping without my mother, I went to Benny Field's on Pitkin Avenue. That's where the wiseguys bought their clothes. I came out wearing a dark-blue pin-striped double-breasted suit with lapels so sharp you could get arrested just for flashing them. I was a kid. I was so proud. When I got home, my mother took one look at me and screamed, 'You look just like a gangster!' I felt even better.

"It was a glorious time. Wiseguys were all over the place. It was when I met the world. It was when I first met Jimmy Burke. He used to come to the card games. He couldn't have been more than twenty-four or twenty-five at the time, but he was already a legend. He'd walk in the door and everybody who worked in the joint would go wild. He'd give the doorman a hundred just for opening the door. He shoved hundreds in the pockets of the guys who ran the games. The bartender got a hundred just for keeping the ice cubes cold.

"Jimmy was the kind of guy who cheered for the crooks in movies. He named his two sons Frank James Burke and Jesse James Burke. He was a big guy, and he knew how to handle himself. He'd whack you. There was no question—Jimmy could plant you just as fast as shake your hand. It didn't matter to him. At dinner he could be the nicest guy in the world, but then he could blow you away for dessert.

"For most of the guys, the killings were just accepted," says Henry. "It didn't take anything for these guys to kill you. They liked it. They would sit around drinking booze and talk about their favorite hits. They enjoyed talking about them. They liked to relive the moment while repeating how miserable the guy was. He was always the worst son of a bitch they knew. He was always a rat bastard, and most of the time it wasn't even business. Guys would get into arguments with each other, and before you knew it, one of them was dead.

"One night, we were having a party in a bar for Billy Batts. Billy had just gotten out of prison after six years. We usually gave a guy a party when he got out. Food. Booze. Hookers. Billy was a made guy. He was with

Johnny Gotti from near Fulton Street, and he was hooked up with the Gambinos. We're all bombed. Billy turned around and he saw Tommy DeSimone, who he knew from before he went away. Tommy was only about twenty at the time, so the last time Billy saw him, Tommy was just a kid. Billy started to kid around. He asked Tommy if he still shined shoes. It was just a side remark, but you couldn't kid around with Tommy. He was wired very tight. One of Tommy's brothers had ratted people out years ago, and he was always living that down. He always had to show he was tougher than anyone around. He always had to be special. He was the only guy in the crew that used to drink Crown Royal. It was a Canadian whiskey that wasn't imported back when he was a kid. Tommy had it smuggled in. He was the kind of guy who was being so tough he managed to find a bootleg hooch to drink, thirty years after Prohibition.

"I looked over at Tommy, and I could see he was fuming at the way Billy was talking. Tommy was going nuts, but he couldn't do or say anything. Billy was a made man. If Tommy so much as took a slap at Billy, Tommy was dead. Still, I knew he was pissed. We kept drinking and laughing, and just when I thought maybe it was all forgotten, Tommy leaned over to Jimmy and me and said, 'I'm gonna kill that f——.' I joked back with him, but I saw he was serious.

"A couple of weeks later, Billy was drinking at the Suite [a Queens Boulevard nightclub Henry owned]. It was late. I was praying he'd go home, when Tommy walked in. It didn't take long. Tommy immediately sent his girlfriend home, and he gave me and Jimmy a look. Right away, Jimmy started getting real cozy with Billy Batts. He started buying Billy drinks. I could see he was setting Billy up for Tommy.

" 'Keep him here, I'm going for a bag,' Tommy whispered to me, and I knew he was going to kill Billy right in my own joint. He was going for a body bag—a plastic mattress cover—so Billy wouldn't bleed all over the place. Tommy was back with the body bag and a .38 in twenty minutes. I was getting sick.

"By now, Jimmy has Billy Batts in the corner of the bar near the wall. They were drinking, and Jimmy was telling him stories. Billy was having a great time. As it got late, almost everybody went home. The bartender left. Jimmy had his arm hanging real loose around Billy's shoulder when Tommy came over. Billy didn't even look up. Why should he? He was with friends. Fellow wiseguys. He had no idea Tommy was going to kill him.

"I was on the side of the bar when Tommy took the .38 out of his pocket. The second Billy saw what was happening, Jimmy tightened his arm around Billy's neck. 'Shine these f——in' shoes,' Tommy yells, and smashes the gun right into the side of Billy's head. Billy's eyes opened wide. Tommy smashed him again. Jimmy kept his grip. The blood began to come out of Billy's head. It looked black. I locked the front door, and when I turned back, I saw that Billy's body was spread out on the floor. His head was a bloody mess. Tommy had opened the mattress cover. Jimmy told me to bring the car around back.

"We had a problem. Billy Batts was untouchable. There has to be an okay before a made man can be killed. If the Gambino people ever found out that Tommy killed Billy, we were all dead. There was no place we could go. They could even have demanded that Paulie Vario whack us himself. Tommy had done the worst possible thing he could have done, and we all knew it. Billy's body had to disappear. We couldn't leave it on the street. There would have been a war. With no body around, the Gotti crew would never know for sure.

"Jimmy said we had to bury the body where it couldn't be found. He had a friend upstate with a dog kennel, where nobody would ever look. We put Billy in the trunk of the car, and we drove by Tommy's house to pick up a shovel. His mother was already up and made us come in for coffee. We have to have breakfast—with a body parked outside.

"Finally, we left Tommy's and got on the Taconic. We'd been driving about half an hour when I heard a funny noise. I'm in the back, half asleep, with the shovel. Tommy was driving. Jimmy was asleep. I heard the noise again. It was like a thump. Jimmy woke up. The banging began again. It dawned on all of us at once. Billy Batts was alive. He was banging on the trunk. We were on our way to bury him and he wasn't even dead.

"Now Tommy really got mad. He slammed on the brakes. He leaned over the seat and grabbed the shovel. Nobody said a word. We got out of the car and waited until there were no more headlights coming up behind us. Then Tommy opened the trunk. The second it sprang open, Tommy smashed the sack with the shovel. Jimmy grabbed a tire iron, and he started banging away at the sack. It took only a few seconds, and we got back in the car. When we got to the spot where we were going to bury Billy, the ground was so frozen we had to dig for an hour to get him down deep enough. Then we covered him with lime and drove back to New York.

"But even then, Billy was like a curse. About three months after we planted the guy, Jimmy came up to me at the Suite and said Tommy and I would have to dig up the body and bury it somewhere else. The guy who owned the kennel had just sold his property to a housing developer. He had been bragging to Jimmy about how much money he was going to make, but all Jimmy knew was that workmen might find the body. That night, Tommy and I took my brand-new yellow Pontiac Catalina convertible and we dug Billy up. It was awful. We had put lime on the body to help it decompose, but it was only half gone. The smell was so bad I started to throw up. All the time Tommy and I worked, I was throwing up. We put the body in the trunk and took it to a junkyard we used in Jersey. Enough time had passed so nobody was going to think it was Billy.

"I stayed sick for a week. I couldn't get away from the smell. Everything smelled like the body. I couldn't stop smelling it. I threw away the clothes, even the shoes I wore that night, thinking they were the problem. I couldn't get the smell out of the trunk of my car. I ripped out all the upholstery and threw it away. I gave the car a real scrubbing. I tossed a bottle of Karen's perfume inside and closed the lid. But I couldn't get rid of the smell. I finally had to junk the car. Jimmy and Tommy thought I was nuts. Tommy said if he could have smelled it, he would have kept the car, just to remind him about how he took care of that miserable bastard Billy Batts."

Soon, Henry heard the good news that Tommy DeSimone was to become a full-fledged wiseguy.

"Tommy was going to be made. He was finally getting his button," says Henry. "For Tommy, it was a dream come true. If you wanted to be a wiseguy, you had to be made. It was like being baptized.

"We had heard that Bruno Facciolo and Petey Vario were going to vouch for him. They were supposed to pick him up and drive him to where they were having the little ceremony, but when Jimmy called, Tommy's mother said it was snowing so much it had been called off. The next day, Jimmy called again. I saw him in the phone booth. He listened, and then I saw him raise his hand and jam the phone down on the hook with all his strength. The whole booth shook. I never saw him like that. I never saw such anger. I was scared.

"He came out of the booth, and I saw he had tears in his eyes. I don't know what's going on, and he says that they just whacked Tommy. The Gotti crew. They whacked Tommy. It was over Tommy's having killed Billy Batts and a guy named Foxy. They were made guys with the Gambinos, and Tommy had killed them without an okay. Nobody knew Tommy had done it, but the Gambino people had somehow gotten the proof. They had a sit-down with Paulie, and they got Paulie's okay to kill Tommy.

"The way they did it was to have Tommy think he was going to get made. He thought he was going to his christening. He got all slicked up. He wanted to look good. Two of his crew came to pick him up. He was smiling. Nobody ever saw him again. Even Jimmy couldn't revenge Tommy. It was between the Italians, and on that level Jimmy didn't belong, any more than I did, because my father was Irish."

"ON THE DAY I finally got arrested, my friends and family were driving me crazy," Henry recalls. "I was working such long hours that I was snorting about a gram of coke a day just to keep all the insanity together. I was under so much pressure that the day I got pinched almost came as a relief. I left the house about seven in the morning. I was going to pick up my brother Michael at the New York Hospital. He was being treated for spina bifida. On the way to the hospital, I planned to drop by Jimmy's house. Jimmy had ordered some guns from a guy I had been doing business with in a Connecticut armory. The guy had dropped off Jimmy's guns at my house the night before. Jimmy had some .32-caliber silencers, and he wanted guns to go along with his silencers. Here's Jimmy, heat all over him from Lufthansa, on parole, just like me, and he's looking to buy guns.

"I figured I'd stop off at Jimmy's, drop off the guns, then drive into the city, pick up my brother, and drive him back to my house. I threw the guns in the trunk of the car, and I heard this helicopter. I looked up and saw it. It was hovering right over my head, and it was red. You notice a red helicopter over your house at seven o'clock Sunday morning. I got in the car and drove toward Jimmy's house in Howard Beach. For a while, I noticed that the copter seemed to be following me, but by the time I got near his house, it was gone.

"Jimmy was already awake. He was waiting in the doorway like a kid at Christmas. He came out, and he started to look at the guns before we got into his foyer. I reminded him about the heat. I told him about the helicopter. He looked at me like I was nuts. He wanted to see the guns. When we got into the foyer, he ripped open the paper bag, took one look, and screamed, 'F——! These are no good! My silencers won't fit these things. I don't want these things.' I'd bought the damn things for him. He had wanted them, not me. And now I was stuck. I didn't say anything.

"By 8:30, we had all finished eating. Judy [Wicks, one of his drug couriers] had an eleven o'clock flight. At 9:30, she said she had to go home to Rockaway to get her hat. I'd been carrying a pound of heroin around in my jacket all day, and I wanted Judy to start taping it to her leg. No, she said, it's her lucky hat. She needs it. She's afraid to fly without it. It was a blue-and-pink thing that sat on top of her head. It was the most midwestern, rube thing you ever saw. The point is, if she insisted, I had to drive her home for her damn hat.

"When I got into the car, I suddenly realized that I was still carrying half a kilo of heroin in my pocket. I remember saying to myself, 'What do I have to drive around with this stuff for?' So while the engine was still idling, I got out of the car and went back inside the house and stuck the packages in a recessed light near the entry steps. I then got back in the car and started to drive Judy home. I wasn't fifty feet out of the driveway when my car was blocked. There were cars all over the place. I thought maybe there'd been an accident in front of my house. Then I thought, 'It's my turn to get whacked for Lufthansa.' I saw this guy in a Windbreaker who popped up alongside the car and jammed a gun against the side of my head. For a second, I thought it was over. Then he screamed, 'Make one move, motherf——er, and I'll blow you away!' That's when I began to relax. I knew they were cops. Only cops talk that way. If it had been wiseguys, I wouldn't have heard a thing."

"I KNEW THAT ARREST on the drug charge made me vulnerable," says Henry. "Maybe too vulnerable to live. There wouldn't have been any hard feelings. I was just facing too much time. The fact that I had never made a deal before, the fact that I had always been stand-up, the fact that I had done two years in Nassau and four years in Lewisburg and never gave up a mouse, counted for nothing. It's what you're doing today and could do tomorrow that counts. From where my friends stood, I was a liability. I was no longer safe. I didn't need pictures.

"In fact, I knew even before the Feds played me the tape of [Angelo] Sepe and [Anthony] Stabile [two of Hill's Mafia associates] talking about getting rid of me. Sepe sounded anxious to get it over with. He said that I was no good, that I was a junkie. But Jimmy was calm. He told them not to worry about it. And that was all I heard.

"If you're a part of a crew, nobody ever tells you that they're going to kill you. It doesn't happen that way. There aren't any great arguments or finger-biting curses like in Mafia movies. Your murderers come with smiles. They come as friends, people who have cared deeply about you all your life, and they always come at a time when you are at your weakest and most in need of their help and support."

"THE HARDEST THING for me was leaving the life I was running away from. Even at the end, with all the threats, I still loved the life. We walked in a room and the place stopped. Everyone knew who we were, and we were treated like movie stars with muscle. We had it all, and it was all free. Truckloads of swag. Fur coats, televisions, clothes—all for the asking. We ran everything. We paid the lawyers. We paid the cops. We walked out laughing. We had the best of everything. In Vegas and Atlantic City, somebody always knew someone. People would come over and offer us shows, dinners, suites.

"And now all that is over, and that's the hardest part. Today, everything is very different. No more action. I'm an average nobody. I get to live the rest of my life like a schnook."

Today, Henry Hill has a successful business and lives in a $150,000 neo-Colonial house in an area with such a low crime rate that garden-shed burglaries get headlines in the weekly press. His children go to private schools. He and Karen have their own cars, and she has a small business. He has a Keogh plan. One of his few complaints is that he cannot get good Italian food in the area where he has been assigned to live.

SID VICIOUS AND NAUSEATING NANCY
A Love Story

RON ROSENBAUM

OCTOBER 30, 1978

In 1978, when Sid Vicious was accused of stabbing his girlfriend Nancy Spungen, in the Chelsea Hotel, his notorious band the Sex Pistols had already broken up. Vicious had come to New York with Nancy searching for a second act, as a solo performer and also perhaps as part of a married couple. Vicious claimed he was innocent of the violence, and Ron Rosenbaum found some evidence for believing him. Despite his name, given him by the band's manager, Malcolm McLaren, he wasn't particularly vicious. "He was a gentle junkie," says Ron Rosenbaum. Vicious never went to trial. He died of a heroin overdose while out on bail. Rosenbaum is the author of several books, including Explaining Hitler *and* The Shakespeare Wars.

T HERE'S A STORY about the time Sid Vicious tried to inject heroin into his forearm with a ball-point pen. Sid chose the pen for its utilitarian rather than its metaphoric value (he couldn't find a proper needle and was apparently too desperate for the drug to take the time to look), but it's peculiarly appropriate that Sex Pistol Sid should use a pen, the primal fountain of hype, as a hypodermic for his heroin habit.

There is something in that image that illuminates the linkage of addictions—to fame, love, and heroin—in a chain of circumstances that concluded with Sid's longtime love, "Nauseating Nancy," bleeding to death from a stab wound in a room at the Chelsea Hotel.

The ball-point-pen fix reportedly took place last January during the frenzy of the heavily hyped but almost deliberately hidden concert tour of the United States by the Sex Pistols, the Bizarro Beatles of British punk rock. It was a tour which many had predicted would establish the Sex Pistols as the biggest rock-'n'-roll phenomenon in the world, a demonic second coming of the Beatles.

Bass-guitar man Sid had prepared for the tour with the best intentions. He'd begun actually learning how to play his guitar and he'd finally kicked his habit.

Well, almost. He'd kept himself clean until pre-tour farewell night with Nancy Spungen, his American-born girl friend. According to Sid, it is said, Nancy, a longtime junk user who may have hooked Sid on heroin in the first place, suggested the two of them shoot up just once for old times' sake, a romantic gesture before parting.

By the time Sid arrived in Atlanta for the first Sex Pistols concert, he apparently was heavy into his habit again.

In one instance, lacking a needle, Sid reportedly took apart a ball-point pen, frantically flushing the ink out of the inner tube, filing down the point with a knife, cooking up some junk to fill the tube, tying off his arm, and making a stab at a forearm vein.

No luck. The ball-point was too blunt. It could tear the skin but lacked the precision to puncture and deliver the heroin without spilling it out uselessly in the bloody laceration.

But Sid, the story goes, had an inspiration. He used a safety pin. Safety pins had, after all, been Sid's trademark. It was Sid who started the London punk fashion of piercing the lips, cheek, and nose with safety pins, symbolic self-mutilation, a prime element in the imagemaking the Sex Pistols used to hype themselves.

Sid himself never really pierced his cheeks with safety pins; he just made it look that way. But in this extremity, Sid was ready to go beyond symbolism. He took one of his safety pins, made a neat little pinhole in that forearm vein, and then sought to stick the smack-filled, filed-down ball-point pen into the opening. The trouble was that Sid's hands were shaking so badly by this time that he couldn't get the ball-point pen to hit that safety-pin hole. He kept jabbing and missing with the pen point, ultimately tearing a bloody four-inch trench in his arm.

Sudden and massive self-injections—whether they be of heroin or hype—are not uncommon in the rock-'n'-roll life. Nor are the scars on the skin and the psyche that accompany them. Rock-'n'-roll history is littered with the bodies of rock stars who have died through an overdose of one or the other or both—Brian Jones, Jimi Hendrix, Janis Joplin, most recently Keith Moon.

The lesson of history is that rock stars tend to kill themselves, not other people. In fact, until October 12, it was impossible to find a single instance of a rock star charged with murder. On the afternoon of that day, detectives from the Third Homicide Zone took Sid Vicious into custody and charged him with stabbing his girl friend to death with a five-inch hunting knife. Sid has pleaded not guilty. According to his manager, "He's gonna come out like a matador and fight this and win it."

What did happen in Room 100 that morning? What kind of addictive relationship between these punk lovers led them to this end?

In a peculiar, sordid way the story of Nancy Spungen and Sid Vicious is an old-fashioned love story. There's an element of those doomed romances of late-fifties, early-sixties rock: "Teen Angel," "Leader of the Pack," and the like. Sid Vicious was a big fan of such early heroes of fifties rock as Eddie Cochran and Elvis. And in the late-seventies whirl of groupies and group gropes, Sid and Nancy clung fiercely to each other with the single-minded fervor of an old-fashioned fifties rock-'n'-roll romance, defiantly resisting—just like in the old songs—the many people who wanted to break them apart. However strained the comparison may seem, more than one intimate described Sid and Nancy as the Romeo and Juliet of punk rock.

WHEN SHE FIRST HEARD of the Sex Pistols, Nancy had been on the New York rock scene long enough to make the transition from groupie to super-groupie. As one rock-club figure explained the distinction, "A groupie is someone who will fuck a rock star and disappear the next morning. A super-groupie is someone who picks out an up-and-coming rocker before he's a star, becomes his girl friend, supports him until he makes it, then enjoys the rewards. Sort of like an A&R man scouting talent for record companies."

Back in 1975 when Nancy dropped out of college and came to New York, she picked up a job as a topless go-go dancer to support herself and began hanging out with the crowd around the New York Dolls and the Heartbreakers, key transition groups between glitter and punk. She was said to be aggressive and energetic and early on scored some big coups— nights with David Bowie and Iggy Pop. She began to get a reputation for being too aggressive with other girls' boyfriends. Nasty graffiti about her began to appear in the rest rooms of Max's and CBGB's. But she was riding high. She'd come back to Max's from a night at her go-go bar flushed with the thrill of being the center of attention, a star herself, dancing to rock music. She'd buy everyone champagne with the bills men had stuffed into her bikini bottom.

But the rock-club scene in New York was still in transition. She was looking for something more. She was eighteen years old when she began reading about the Sex Pistols and the furor they were stirring in England. She decided she had to get to London and into the excitement of that scene.

Do you remember back in 1963 when the first reports about the Beatles began to appear over here? How wild and shaggy and strange and, yes, offensive they seemed? How the sensibilities of the English public were outraged? Of course the Beatles seem tame now, and perhaps the Sex Pistols in their brief moment of media glory were no more threatening, but to many English and American observers the Sex Pistols had the intensity and sound that portended an equally momentous future.

Nancy sacrificed a lot to make the trip to London. Three times, she said, she'd tried to kick her heroin habit to save enough money for plane fare. Finally she gave up trying to kick and raised the money by other means. The heroin habit she brought over was one she said she'd picked up very early, back when she was thirteen or fourteen and rebelling against what she called the boring, pampered life her parents had given her.

Nancy arrived in London on a March morning in 1977, and by that night she was in bed with Sid Vicious. By the next morning he was under her spell. Actually she wasn't really after Sid at first. Her first choice was Johnny Rotten, the lead singer and songwriter for the Pistols, whose snarling demeanor and decaying teeth had made him a defiant cult figure among hordes of working-class teenagers.

As soon as she got off the plane, Nancy went right to the King's Road boutique operated by Malcolm McLaren, the Sex Pistols' manager and chief media manipulator. She and McLaren had mutual friends from the days when he lived in New York and designed costumes for the New York Dolls. Nancy told McLaren she wanted to meet Johnny Rotten.

She found him that night in a Soho punk club called Louise's. Sid was there drinking with Rotten, but Nancy didn't pay him much attention at first. He was a new addition to the Sex Pistols; he barely knew how to play his bass guitar and hadn't developed the fame or fanatical following of his childhood friend Rotten.

Nancy tried to make it with Rotten that night but it didn't work out.

It did with Sid. "Sid was almost a virgin then," recalled one intimate. "He spent all his time fighting and hanging around the streets and all he'd talk about was fighting. He once said he hated sex, described it as two minutes and fifty seconds of squelching sounds and then you forget it. But after he hooked up with Nancy, all he could talk about was sex."

But there was more to it than that. People in the punk world don't hesitate to use the words "love" and "fifties romance" to describe the relationship between Sid and Nancy. "You have to forget about his name, which was a joke anyway, and think of Sid as a romantic," said one. "The first time Sid was asked to join the Sex Pistols he didn't because he was trying to form his own group, which he was going to call the Flowers of Romance. See what I mean? He'd wanted to be a flower of romance more than a sex pistol."

"Sid was an incredible romantic," manager McLaren says. "He dived into everything totally and it was like that when he fell in love with Nancy."

Unfortunately it was also like that when he fell in love with heroin. Some who knew them claimed that it was Nancy who got Sid hooked the first time. His friend overheard them bickering about who got strung out first, with Sid indignantly claiming he'd been a junkie long before he'd met Nancy.

"But that could be Sid indulging in that junkie romanticism, you know, of the fifties. They were both into that romantic glamour of being junkies," said the friend.

Certainly they both got deeper into junk together than Sid had ever been before Nancy. They began to keep themselves withdrawn from the company of the rest of the band. Friends, manager, and some band members began to try to keep them apart. Manager McLaren confessed to going as far as executing a kidnap attempt to spirit Nancy away from Sid. A friend lured Nancy into a car, handed her a one-way ticket to the United States, and began speeding toward Heathrow Airport. Nancy aborted the plot by screaming her lungs out as the car passed through a quiet neighborhood, forcing her would-be abductor to stop.

These same forces prevented Nancy from accompanying Sid on what was to be the Sex Pistols' frenzied and bizarre tour of the United States, a triumphal return she had hoped to share with Sid. She did, however, according to several sources, manage to get Sid hooked on heroin again after he had gone clean just before the tour departed.

With him strung out again, the tour became a nightmare and a triumph for Sid. Onstage he acted like a true believer in the Sex Pistols' anarchic mystique, taking a smash to the face with a bottle from a fan in the Longhorn Ballroom in Dallas, smearing himself with his own blood, stalking around the stage mesmerizing the audience with his manic presence. Offstage, Sid found himself under constant surveillance from record-company security men who kept him virtual prisoner on the tour bus for the hours and hours of driving they did through the South.

Once he slipped his guard and stalked the corridors of a Memphis Holiday Inn motel searching for smack, only to be captured shortly thereafter. They began punching him. Sid whipped off his metal-studded belt and whomped them across the face until they were as bloody as he was.

There's a dramatic two-hour interview with Sid and Nancy in London about this time made by filmmaker Leck Kowalski. Sid, in a red swastika-printed T-shirt, and Nancy, in a black rubber two-piece suit, are lying in bed, both downed-out on something heavy. Sid can barely croak out a single word. Nancy keeps harping on him to "wake up . . . don't be a fuck-up . . . answer the question," while she interprets his grunts and rattles on about the conspiracy of the rest of the world to badmouth her, put down Sid, rip them off, and beat them up. Sid occasionally responds to her nagging by trying desultorily to burn her with a lighted cigarette; occasionally he drifts away entirely to play with a knife. Nancy offers to do a porn film for £100.

Nonetheless, Nancy is still romantic about their relationship. "Sid and Nancy," she says, sighing like a fifties teenager over her dream date. "I've been with Sid ever since the first day we met," she says. "We were partners in crime, we helped each other out. Sid would have died fifteen deaths if I hadn't been around."

SID AND NANCY were getting restless in London. The ferment was now in New York. They wanted to be part of it. They talked about getting married. They made plans to visit her parents in Philadelphia. Nancy would become Sid's manager and take charge of his great future. They arrived in New York in late August and rented a room at the Chelsea Hotel.

They were not exactly treated like the new John and Yoko. Many on the American punk scene were resentful of the whole Sex Pistols hype. "The Sex Pistols killed punk in New York," one declared. "Just for instance, a week after the Sex Pistols arrived, the Dead Boys got haircuts to look like them. People who had been playing good music went into theatrics; the thing became a freak circus."

And Sid had to compete with the aura his adopted name and career as a Sex Pistol had given him. People came to his first gig in New York (at Max's in September) expecting to see a savage animal raving and drooling. When they saw a downed-out twenty-one-year-old kid doing "My Way," there was a lot of negative overreaction.

Nor was Nancy making much progress building his career.

Sid had problems booking any future tours because he couldn't go more than a day's travel from his methadone clinic without going into severe withdrawal. Increasingly, their life together centered on the problem of getting up in time to make it to the methadone center before it closed.

When they missed they'd spend the day scoring Tuinals on 14th Street or scouring the Chelsea neighborhood for smack.

Still they clung to each other. Nancy went around calling herself Mrs. Sid Vicious. They spent almost a week with her parents in the Main Line (yes) of Philadelphia and came back talking of marriage.

But they also talked about death and the horror of growing old. She was quoted as saying she wanted to "die before I get a single wrinkle." People noticed a change in her. "When she first arrived on the scene, she was all party, party. This time when they came back from London she was very down, talked about being depressed, falling down, passing out during Sid's gig."

Sid's behavior was getting more and more erratic during their last days together. He'd get into fights at methadone centers, getting himself beaten up and robbed by gangs. His plans for a new backup band fell through when his first choice for lead guitarist turned him down. He kept saying he wanted to kick smack and methadone, but there weren't many hopeful signs of that happening.

How did it end? Defenders of Sid tend to support the suicide-pact theory: The two planned to kill themselves, but Sid nodded out before he could get around to stabbing himself, waking up horrified at what he'd allowed Nancy to do to herself. In support of this, they cite a late-night visit Sid and Nancy paid to "Neon Leon," a fellow musician down the hall in the Chelsea. They presented him with Sid's prized leather jacket and a collection of Sex Pistols clippings, a gesture some have interpreted as a kind of final bequest. In a *Soho News* interview, Neon Leon, who has since disappeared, said they had also displayed to him a five-inch knife Nancy had bought Sid that day. The chief medical examiner's autopsy reported that the stab wound in Nancy's belly had been made with a five-inch knife.

Other defenders of Sid promote a shadowy third-party involvement in Nancy's death. One cites their chief intermediary to smack dealers, with whom Nancy had a loud public argument in Max's not long before her death. Others suggest the possibility of an intruder's trying to rip off the bags of money Nancy was seen carrying or the drugs they might have been expected to possess. Who was the outside caller who told the hotel switchboard about somebody hurt in Room 100? Still others suggest the possibility of an accident—Sid and Nancy playing at violence as they were wont to do. (The doctor who did the autopsy reported "old and fresh bruises all over her body.") Could the stabbing have been some stupid accident with Sid and Nancy nodding off without knowing only one of them would wake up? Why was there blood on the bed and in the bathroom where the body was found propped beneath the lip of the sink?

Homicide detectives will say very little about what convinced them to charge Sid with murder. When they arrived at Room 100 in the Chelsea, they found Sid standing in the hall outside. He reportedly told them he woke up to find Nancy dead and assumed she had committed suicide while he was asleep. After five hours' investigation, Detective Thomas and Sergeant Kilroy of the Third Homicide decided not to believe that story and charged Sid with second-degree murder. Sid's ex-manager, Malcolm McLaren, flew into town, charged the police with a railroad job, and offered TV stations clips of Sid from his soon-to-be released movie. Sid went into seizures of methadone withdrawal in his detention cell, was hospitalized and put on a methadone phase-out dose. McLaren helped raise $50,000 bail to get Sid released and disappeared with him "into seclusion."

According to McLaren, when Sid emerged from Rikers Island he had two specific requests:

"First, he said, 'Where's my fucking leather jacket?' " reports McLaren. Then, in the car on the way to seclusion, Sid asked if he could call Nancy's parents and tell them how bad he felt.

PART SIX

. . . .

THE
NATIONAL
INTEREST

★

*P*RESIDENTIAL POLITICS, with all its noise and ego and argument and huge amounts of money spent on media, is a New York sort of activity, even when the action takes place beyond the city's borders. The White House and its aspirants have been an integral part of the magazine's portfolio since the earliest days. The writers collected in this political medley—Gloria Steinem, David Halberstam, Richard Reeves, Garry Wills, Joe Klein, Kurt Andersen, John Heilemann, and Jennifer Senior—are among many who have written on national affairs for the magazine. For all these writers, from Steinem's psycho-political portrait of Richard Nixon to Senior's visit with Barack Obama as he was testing the presidential waters, personality is the crucial lens.

IN YOUR HEART, YOU KNOW HE'S NIXON

GLORIA STEINEM   OCTOBER 28, 1968

Beaten by John F. Kennedy in 1960, then by Pat Brown for governor of California in 1962, Richard Nixon was a moldering political relic. Then, in 1968, came the so-called New Nixon, with gestures and speech patterns retooled for a different moment. Gloria Steinem, who wrote regularly about politics in the magazine's early years, is a "congenital liberal," as she explains. But when she went out to interview him on the eve of his victory, she was looking for hopeful signs. She'd lost all confidence in Nixon's opponent, Hubert Humphrey, and wondered if the pragmatic Nixon might be the one to end the Vietnam War. She looked for signals in "Nixon's behavior and the atmosphere of the men around him, and anecdotes revelatory of character." The signs weren't promising.

—

THE NEW GESTURES of the New Nixon are very evident—since '60, he has given up the keep-your-elbows-in stance recommended by his high-school debating coach—but what doesn't show up on these short takes is in the difference between form and content. For the phrase "We must reach up . . . ," he may stretch both arms downward; for "the whole world," he may gesture close to his chest, or tick off the first of two points on the third finger; for the one-arm thrust that marks important statements, he may find himself with his arm raised too soon, and pause visibly to get co-ordinated. This is a man who has, to an extraordinary degree, created himself; who has worked hard, who never stops working, to fulfill his idea of what a public man should be.

Colleagues say he has one of the highest IQs in Washington. The State Department officials who briefed him for his many trips as Vice President were invariably impressed that he had "done his homework." In recent years of law practice, fellow attorneys have commented on his ability to grasp all the essentials of a problem quickly, and to analyze afterward what did or did not go wrong. If it can be learned, Nixon will learn it.

But if it has to be understood, Nixon—and possibly the country—may be in deep trouble. He has worked so long and so consciously to better himself that instinct and spontaneity have somehow got buried. ("He has a better grasp of Africa's overall economic problems than any other American politician," said a visiting official, "but he doesn't understand Africans.")

Over the years, aides have tried to humanize his image with everything from hobbies (in '60, one of them said he was too neat and should take up something messy like chicken-raising) to posed photographs in sport clothes. Yesterday on the suburban tour, an announcement was made to all three buses that Nixon had lost a cufflink to the crowd. ("Next thing you know, someone will snatch the paper-clips from Wallace's cuffs," said one reporter.) But the emphasis now is on being statesmanlike instead of, as Nixon puts it, "a buddy-buddy boy," so the candidate seems much more at ease.

But there is a philosophical tree-in-the-forest question that will never be answered, one that he raises in our minds by being so relentlessly conscious, politically and personally, of the way he appears to others. When Nixon is alone in a room, is there anyone there?

WALLACE AGONISTES

GARRY WILLS JULY 10, 1972

The attempted assassination of Alabama governor George Wallace in 1972 was an event of remarkably complex symbolism. It made Wallace a kind of martyr, like Robert Kennedy and Martin Luther King Jr., men whose beliefs were the diametrical opposite of Wallace's own. It also, as Garry Wills wrote in this 1972 story, "somehow shrove and decontaminated him." Among the Democrats making pilgrimages to his hospital room was Georgia governor Jimmy Carter, who appears in Wills's telling as a cold-eyed pragmatist with the kind of talent that could hold the Democratic Party together.

—

THE LIGHTNING that hit Wallace somehow shrove and decontaminated him. Getting shot is, by now, a way of joining the club—as the sad visiting of various Kennedys proved. Ted, Joan, and Ethel came, reminding one reporter, who called Wallace just after Bobby had been shot, of the eerie conversation: "Well, if I had been shot first, he would have said something nice about me, I guess." Wallace anticipated, even then, joining the club whose tone has been set by the Kennedys (though others, like the Everses or Mrs. King, have also joined). And now George, of all people, had paid his dues.

So they all came on pilgrimage to this rather dingy mecca. A ten-foot pole should have been kept at the door for those who, earlier, would not touch him with one. But it was safe to court him now, when praising had become a way of upstaging him, angling for his votes, hoping to pick up some of his appeal.

GOVERNOR JIMMY CARTER of Georgia put it this way: "The Wallace voters are now somewhat detachable from Wallace himself, and they must be kept in the Democratic Party." I was flying, in the governor's frail leaf of a private plane, to Albany, Georgia, where he would speak to a sheriff's convention near his own peanut fields and warehouses. But what intrigued me was the journey he would take the next day, the eve of Wallace's second operation, to Red Level, Alabama. Huge pits were at that moment being dug, hundreds of hogs being butchered, to raise Miami money for the continuing miracle of Wallace's nickel-and-dime operation. Why was Carter, a New South hope, hailed as a dawn of reason after the dark night of Lester Maddox, going to address rednecks for George?

"I'm not endorsing Wallace," said Carter. "I've never voted for him. But it is important to keep him in the party, and even more important to keep the people he represents—who are not only Southerners, by any means. He has appeal all over the country, more than his own staff ever expected.

I want to keep Wallace in the race, just as I want to keep all the other candidates in—in fact, I've done something to accomplish that. We worked on Harold Hughes in Houston [at the Democratic Governors' conference] to keep Muskie from dropping out, just when he was about to. We might lose Shirley Chisholm, but the others seem to be holding. I'm not trying to stop McGovern, as they said in Houston. I just want an open convention. If McGovern comes to Miami with it all sewed up, there'll be no reason for him to listen to others.

"That is why I am willing to speak for George Wallace's candidacy tomorrow. He is stricken down, and his delegates are under heavy challenge."

Carter can be very plausible when he says, "I do not agree with George Wallace's program," though Carter has hit busing very hard. He is the last remnant of the dream that a Kennedy South could be forged for the Democratic Party. He even looks like JFK—the same filmy dip of hair over his forehead; the same features somehow quashed or jumbled inward; the slight frame and wry diffident air (at once casual and cautious); the same rinsed outdoor eyes (color of blue jeans often washed) set in almost liquid pouches of flesh. He even has a mother who was in the Peace Corps. Some governors pestered McGovern on his abortion stand, but Jimmy Carter cannot be shocked by it after his mother spent two years in India giving out contraceptives.

But Carter never plans to out-lib his constituents. The South gets only so new each time.

Often, in Southern politics, political roots ramify out into family tangles. Carter's only brother, Billy, who runs his peanut warehouses, is married to Wallace's cousin—he goes to all the Wallace family affairs. Lots of people here in South Georgia come from Clayton (Wallace's Alabama hometown). But Jimmy, unlike Billy, has gravitated toward the Wallaces with class. His wife is one of George Wallace's wife Cornelia's best friends: both Carters rode, unknown to the Alabama press, with Cornelia in the pace car at the Talladega races. "In Houston, Cornelia came to see us," he said, "and told us all about George's condition. He has his own kind of inside track."

Carter does not think as highly of George as of Cornelia. He admits, "His genius is the ability to talk with a gas-station attendant on his own level." Another state official, along in the plane, leans over and touches Carter's knee, using an acolyte's tones even over the engine's roar: "That's your strength, too, Governor." Carter admits, "I can talk to the people as one of them—to these sheriffs, for instance. But George cannot talk to anyone above the gas-station man's level. He has an inferiority complex when he comes to our governors' conventions." That is not Jimmy's problem.

WE COME BACK, always, to the bullet. Dr. Joseph Schanno had called it a "dirty bullet" that left postoperative infections in Governor Wallace. But it was a cleansing bullet too, and a sterilizing one. It made Wallace just clean enough for many people to touch him in passing, to "appreciate" and pay tribute to "his people." It made Wallace*ism* marginally respectable. But what of Wallace himself? Cleansed, he is nothing. He always depended on himself alone, and on a gritty appeal closely linked with his body. Disembodied, he is safe for others, because lost to himself. He had carried with him the Southern haze of suspended earth in air; the sultriness, direct yet insinuating, of his birthplace; the vulgar realism with an overlay of sorghumy rhetoric. Above all, the muggy atmosphere of mixed sex and violence, continual, subliminal, like a never-ending cicada screech. Wallace without the use of his lower body is like Elvis told to sing without his pelvis.

What this year's response to Wallace signified was a spread of diluted redneckism over the country. Sexual frankness, earthy language, the fad for various "populisms," TV shows like *All in the Family*—all these are indications, along with the Wallace vote. The dogmatists of a New South always waited for that region to catch up with the rest of the country. But the South, with its dazzling underdog's optimism, always claimed that America would have to catch up with it.

Not that Wallace himself could have entered the promised land, no matter how close he brought others to it. Away from home, he felt inferior even when he said he was not. The South must be mediated outward through voices with a wider range than his—like Cornelia's. Or Jimmy Carter's. George just provides them with a wheelchair they can ride, at least part way.

THE LUCK OF SPIRO AGNEW

DAVID HALBERSTAM OCTOBER 30, 1972

Spiro T. Agnew's resignation from the vice presidency in disgrace after a federal bribery investigation was a farce on the way to the tragedy of Watergate. It's easy to forget that at the time David Halberstam profiled him for New York, *he'd enjoyed one of the swiftest rises in American political history, having traveled from Baltimore County executive to vice president in six years. Part of Agnew's success was that he embodied what Nixon had taken to calling "the silent majority." But, as Halberstam found, that came at a price. Halberstam was a Pulitzer Prize–winning journalist and the author of many books including* The Best *and the* Brightest, *about the Kennedy and Johnson administrations and the Vietnam War.*

—

T
HE PLANE ARRIVES; Agnew strides down the ramp steps, eyes forward, not looking at the steps, bearing self-consciously erect. He looks like a Vice President, a man you can turn to in a time of hippies and smut peddlers. The clothes are well tailored; he is, in fact, a bit of a dude, though given to civic-club gray. The suits are well pressed—Agnew always careful in his young manhood to lean forward in a chair and not wrinkle his jacket, careful not to cross his legs and wrinkle his pants. (Was this your immigrant's son sensitive about being Greek, sensitive about his father's accent, not wanting to go to Greek schools, wanting to be more American? Were the well-pressed suits a sign of upward mobility, a sign of his Americanization?) In a time of turbulence, when people are looking for some-

one to draw the line, there is Agnew: Wallace simply was not respectable enough, Nixon was too clearly the politician (one might vote for him, but taking moral guidance from him was another thing), but Spiro was stern, unbending, a strong man drafted from the outside to stop the abuses.

Here in Indiana, and later in the week, he seems to welcome the hecklers; they allow him to depart from the rather narrow and boring confines of being the good Agnew. The orders from above, of course, are that he must not become an issue in this year's campaign. In this he was lucky, as he has been in every part of his political career. The Democrats had hoped to make the case against him with the excellence of their own Vice Presidential candidate, Tom Eagleton; they ended up with the Eagleton affair. This killed the issue of the Vice Presidency, and more, the entire balance of the campaign seemed to change. McGovern lost his balance, went on the defensive; the press, which in the past had praised his organizational sense, now began to look for mistakes (thus recalling the words of Gene McCarthy in 1968: "Reporters are like blackbirds on a telephone wire. One flies off, they all fly off; one flies back, they all fly back"). Suddenly bad staff work was blamed on McGovern when, in fact, he had nothing to do with it. But thus died the issue of the Republican Vice President, and thus began a reversal of momentum which allowed the Republicans to campaign from Olympian heights, and forced the Democrats to raise their voices. Such is Agnew's luck.

WHO COULD BE BETTER prepared to touch the new alienation of old Democratic workers than this serious, ambitious, self-conscious young man, sensitive about his own immigrant origins, the outsider as a young man, working his way through a night law school with the shoddy third-rate jobs that followed (the legal jobs paying so badly that he was forced for a time to leave the law and work as an assistant in a Baltimore supermarket) when the richer kids were going through the better law schools and getting the better jobs with their better connections. Those were hard years with thin jobs and a thin margin of security; Agnew was classically the American ethnic coming into middle class in the post-war years. Someone with a background like that who finally made it—nouveau Establishment—was not likely to look upon a future change of mores with great sympathy. Had he worked all that hard to become respectable, only to find that respectable was no longer respectable? Now, of course, the society was opening up and among those who wanted to open it more were the upper-class Wasps who, not threatened by the immediacy of the new upward thrust, were willing to see some change in the society. But not Agnew and many like him whose victories were hard-won, whose hold on their newfound status was precarious. If he had encountered certain hardships and overcome them, then others could do the same, and never mind a different consciousness and a greater complexity of problem. Nor were these sham views; they were very real. In 1968 Agnew's staff worked very hard on his speeches to make them seem balanced on social issues, yet somehow when he gave them they came out hard—it was simply his manner, his emphasis. For he, at a time when values were changing, knew what was good and what was bad and he would draw the line. Even as governor of Maryland he had represented the changing definition of liberality; he had run as a semi-liberal, but as civil rights demands had escalated under the new consciousness, he had changed. Faced with black student demands, he would not be moved. This, he said in effect, was how far it went; he would set the limits. More important, he would not succumb to direct pressure from them: do not demand of us, we will tell you. He would set the limits of speech, action, aspiration.

SO HE GRADUALLY in all those years became the spokesman for those who felt most threatened by sweeping social change, and similarly and inevitably the spokesman for entrenched power, for the world as it was, for existing status and traditional virtue. It was in fact a reflex action, more a part of him than he knew. Indeed, there was a revealing moment recently during a press conference in Omaha. Ralph Nader had just released his report on the Congress, saying that the Congress was too aligned with the executive branch and the big interests. Now Nader in an odd way fits into Agnew's definition of America as the greatest country in the world—the most open, the most responsive to citizen pressure—if those views are genuinely held. So this could have been an easy question to handle. He could praise Nader in theory, praise the vitality and openness of a society which produces a Nader, or if nothing else, simply slip off the question and say that he simply had not read the report—which was the basic truth of the occasion. But no, the reflex was simply too strong: Who, he asked, was Ralph Nader to criticize the Congress? What were his credentials, anyway? Who are the outs to criticize the ins, the weak to judge the strong, the poor to object to the weak? Particularly in a country as open and re-markable as this, where anything could happen, a country so wondrous, in fact, that Spiro Agnew could become Vice President. Did we need further proof of America's greatness?

JERRY FORD AND HIS FLYING CIRCUS: A PRESIDENTIAL DIARY

RICHARD REEVES NOVEMBER 26, 1974

In politics, with its baby-kissing, corn-dog-eating necessities, can often be found comedy. But Gerald Ford, who became president after Nixon re-signed in 1974, took this to a new level, as Richard Reeves found when he accompanied him on a barnstorming trip in Ford's first year. Reeves's, who wrote the magazine's "National Interest" column for several years, found in Ford a good-natured, guileless, politically challenged everyman. He was an antidote to Nixon—but the cure had its own side effects. Reeves's story carried the cover line "Ladies and Gentlemen, the Presi-dent of the United States." Bozo the Clown appeared behind the podium.

—

WILLIAM WALTER and David Hopkins, the Huntley-Brinkley of Grand Junction, Colorado, looked into the perfect blue sky above the Con-tinental Divide as a dot of black expanded into a silver jet roaring over mountains, mesas, and, finally, silhouetted horsemen.

"There it is! There's Air Force One!" they told the listeners of KREX, the Voice of the Intermountain West. "Here it comes, landing full flaps . . ." "It's touched down . . ." "It's only, maybe, I would guess three hundred yards from us, Dave . . ." "It's turning toward us . . ." "They're rolling up two ramps, one to the front and one to the back. We're walking toward the plane. We're walking toward the plane now. Which ramp will the president use? . . ." "Probably the back, Bill . . ." "The president of the United States will be out any moment now . . ."

Unfortunately for KREX fans, the president was already out. He had come down the front ramp, as always, and Walter and Hopkins had just walked right by Gerald R. Ford. Actually, Walter and Hopkins were not supposed to be out there on the tarmac, but then Gerald R. Ford was not supposed to be the president.

It was something like the joke the president tried to tell in Indianapolis. He began a speech there by saying that he was traveling around the country because his advisers said he needed more visibility. Then he was supposed to say he passed a lady in the hall who said, "You look familiar," and he helpfully answered, "Jerry Ford?" Then she said, "No, but you're close."

Unfortunately, what Ford told the Indianapolis crowd was that he answered, "I am Jerry Ford," and the lady answered, "No, but you're closer."

Oh, well. On to Grand Junction and the crowning of the Mesa College homecoming queen. "A college homecoming is a happy time and I wish Meesa College . . ."

Students and friends let out an embarrassed little gasp at the mispronunciation, but Ford recovered quickly, "Messa College." Oh! "Mesa?" the president said. "Well, we have some community names out in Michigan all of you could not pronounce, either. I love you, anyhow."

So it went as President Ford traveled 16,685 miles campaigning for Republican candidates in the month before Election Day, 1974. It was a big story—Nightly News, Page One!—with airport announcers parodying The China Trip at every stop. But journalism has its limits. Journalism is covering something, even when there is nothing. There is no accepted technique that deals adequately with the president's travels. Do you write:

GRAND JUNCTION, Colorado, Nov. 2—President Ford had nothing to say and said it badly to a friendly and respectful but slightly stunned crowd of 5,000.

It is not a question of saying the emperor has no clothes—there is a question of whether there is an emperor.

This, then, is one report of the last 9,545 miles of the travels of the president of the United States, from October 24 to November 2:

DES MOINES, IOWA. OCT. 24.

The basic Ford message is delivered from the steps of the Iowa State House and at a Republican fund-raising lunch in the Val Air Ballroom, across the street from the national headquarters of Roto-Rooter:

"I know there are some so-called experts who say the president ought to sit in the Oval Office and listen to bureaucrats telling him what to do, yes or no, or sitting in the Oval Office reading documents that are prepared by people in Washington. I reject that advice. It is more important that I come to Des Moines . . .

"I remind you a government big enough to give us everything we want is a government big enough to take from us everything we have . . . What we need is not a veto-proof Congress. What we need is an inflation-proof Congress."

On the flight to Des Moines, the president's press secretary, Ron Nessen, tells reporters that Ford has no plans to visit Richard Nixon next week when he campaigns in California.

SIOUX CITY, IOWA. OCT. 31.

On the flight from Washington to Sioux City, Nessen says the president has no plans to visit Nixon tomorrow in California. The press secretary also emphasizes that there has been no change in United States policy toward Palestinian refugees, even though the president, at a news conference the day before, had seemed to back off the U.S. position that all negotiations on Israeli-occupied territories on the west bank of the Jordan River must include only Israel and Jordan, by saying: "We, of course, feel there must be a movement toward settlement of the problem between Israel and Egypt on the one hand, between Israel and Jordan or the PLO on the other."

Whatever the president meant by that—he seemed to be equating the legitimacy of Jordan and the Palestine Liberation Organization—the White House press corps doesn't take the thing particularly seriously. The unstated assumption is that Henry Kissinger handles American foreign policy. One senior correspondent says: "What the hell, it was just Jerry talking about things he doesn't understand."

LOS ANGELES, CALIFORNIA. OCT. 31.

At 7:16 P.M., Nessen announces that the president has just telephoned Mrs. Richard Nixon in Long Beach and said: "I don't want to push, but would it help if I came down there?" Nessen said Ford was checking to see if his schedule allowed him time—in fact, there has always been a suspiciously blank spot on the schedule for the morning of November 1.

After meetings with Governor Ronald Reagan and a couple of cocktail parties, the president goes to a $250- and $500-a-plate Republican dinner at the Century Plaza Hotel. It's a rather classy affair and as I walk into the hotel, a man in a Cadillac asks, "Do you park the cars around here?"

The president sits on the dais for an hour and thirty-eight minutes listening to a succession of local Republicans, Bob Hope, and the music of Manny Harmon, who says Ford asked him to play the songs from *Oklahoma!*

Hope is very funny, perhaps closer to the truth than he knows: "The president and Henry Kissinger are both early risers. Whoever gets to the airport first gets the plane." The press, at least, are absolutely convinced that Ford is traveling to avoid being president. Nessen, battered by questions about who's running the country, says, "Look, he enjoys this. He's having a good time." Ford himself adds that he enjoys the food at political dinners.

LOS ANGELES, CALIFORNIA. NOV. 1.

At 8:15 A.M., Nessen announces that Ford will leave at 9:35 to visit Nixon. In talking later about the visit, Ford always refers to Nixon as "the president."

PORTLAND, OREGON. NOV. 1.

The president's staff is furious when *Air Force One* lands in Portland—Ford has been taken by someone named Diarmuid O'Scannlain.

O'Scannlain is the Republican candidate for Congress in Oregon's First District and he appeared in Fresno to hitch a ride north on Air Force One. He then wanted to talk to Ford, and did, for a couple of minutes—then he ran back to the press section of *Air Force One* and said he had just told the president of the United States that he was wrong to pardon Nixon and wrong to propose a 5 percent income-tax surcharge.

On the flight, Ford also looks over a cable from Kissinger outlining the secretary of state's speech next week to the World Food Conference in Rome. The president does not review all Kissinger speeches, Nessen says, but he does see "major" ones, and the press secretary says the incident is proof that the president is the president no matter where he travels.

At the Benson Hotel, the president meets with six representatives of the Oregon Cattlemen's Association and receives a $10 beef gift certificate, which someone says he can use to buy bacon.

"I love beef," the president says. "I'm a great advocate of it. But I don't know about breakfast."

"There is such a thing as beef bacon," a cattleman says.

"Really?" Ford answers. "Is it a special part of the cattle?"

After the usual round of Republican receptions, Ford heads for the annual auction of the Oregon Museum of Science and Industry, a black-tie fund-raising affair in the Portland Coliseum. Boats and even airplanes are being auctioned off to a handsome, champagne-drinking crowd that seems pretty recession-proof. The president is there twenty-five minutes—he autographs two footballs that bring $2,700 each; one pair of his cuff links goes for $11,000 to a lumber dealer, and another goes for $10,000 to a food distributor.

It is a high good time. Ford is bouncing around like a kid, and when the bidding on the first football reaches $500, he grabs the microphone and says: "Double it and I'll center it to you." Which is exactly what the center of the 1934 Michigan team does—after moving around when he suddenly realizes three dozen camera lenses are focused on what his quarterback used to see. Finally, an auto-parts dealer pays $1,100 for the chair Ford had sat in for a moment.

SALT LAKE CITY, UTAH. NOV. 2.

Radio and television are waiting, of course, when Ford arrives at Salt Lake City International Airport at 10:35 A.M. Howard Cook of KSXX Radio sees it this way:

"The president of the United States is not just President Ford, a Republican. He is an institution. He is the most powerful man in the world. You say what about the Russians? They have the same power we have, but there it takes more than one man to pull the trigger. Here we're set up so that one man can do the job. He would never dream of doing it, of course, but it's within his power."

The man with the power is introduced to 8,000 people at the University of Utah by Jake Garn, the mayor of Salt Lake City and Republican candidate for the U.S. Senate, who tells a charming and revealing story of a meeting between fourteen mayors and Ford just five days after he succeeded Nixon:

"We were just standing around talking and somehow the president slipped into the room and came up behind me and said, 'Hi, Jake, how are things in Salt Lake City?' Then he walked around the room, shaking hands and saying, 'Hi, I'm Jerry Ford.' . . . When the meeting was over, someone asked, 'Is there anything we can do for you, Mr. President?' He said: 'Go home and pray for me. This is a very big job.' "

Air Force One lands at Andrews Air Force Base early on Sunday, November 3, and the president of the United States is back at the White House at 1:15 A.M.

The press back-up plane—six "pool" reporters travel on Air Force One—touched down at Andrews about an hour later and thirty reporters headed for home, hearth, and wife. Like a lot of young newspapermen, I was once told by a city editor that the lead of a story is what you tell your wife when she asks you what went on that day. I am willing to bet that on that particular late night what reporters were telling their wives was a hell of a lot different from what they had been writing.

What would I say at home? I would choose my words carefully and say, "The president of the United States is a very ordinary man." He is, in a phrase coined by Saul Friedman of the Knight Newspapers, our "Commoner-in-Chief." It is not hard to walk by him without noticing, as Bill Walter and Dave Hopkins did in Grand Junction.

President Ford stayed in Washington for fourteen days before taking off on his first foreign trip—the first of many, according to some of the men close to him. Our last president was a recluse; this one cannot stand being alone. Much of his Oval Office time was spent in post-mortems of the last trip and briefings for the next.

Welcome home and sayonara, Mr. President! There are times, and this is one of them, when Herblock is deeper than *The New York Times*. We have always cherished the promise that any one of us could be president. Any one of us now is.

BILL CLINTON: WHO IS THIS GUY?

JOE KLEIN JANUARY 20, 1992

When Joe Klein wrote his profile on Bill Clinton in 1992, the Arkansas governor was hardly an unknown. But the idea that he had what it took to get all the way to the White House was held by a fairly small circle. Joe Klein, New York's political columnist for many years, was an an early believer, and in this piece, he helped bring the future president, in all his fascinating complexities, to a wider audience. Klein, who would later write the novel Primary Colors *about Clinton, was among the first journalists to explore the psychological implications of the future president's troubled upbringing, including his violent, alcoholic stepfather. Bill Clinton's thirteen appearances on the magazine's cover would eventually be joined by his wife's nine (and the four on which they appeared together). In 2008, Chelsea made a cover appearance as well.*

—

WHEN CLINTON WAS SEVEN, the family moved to Hot Springs, where Roger Clinton became service manager in his brother's Buick dealership. Hot Springs was a wild town in those days—a spa for rich northerners, a debauch of illegal gambling, fancy nightclubs, and the Oaklawn racetrack. The Clintons were known for living a "fast" life, hanging out at casinos and clubs like the Vapors. Bill's mother developed a passion for the horses and remains a devoted $2 bettor to this day. The drinking and violence continued at home, but quietly so—Clinton's childhood friends say they were never aware of it.

There are many possible ways to respond to an alcoholic parent. Bill Clinton's was to become the perfect child: "He was always so thoughtful," his mother says. "From the very start. And later, when he was a teenager, if he was out on a date and knew his stepfather had been drinking, he'd always call in a couple of times to see that I was all right. . . . The only bad mark he ever had in school was in conduct one time, when the teacher decided to send him a message to stop trying to answer every question"— a tendency Clinton has brought to the presidential campaign.

"I was forty years old by the time I was sixteen," he admitted. "I think my desire to accommodate is probably due in part to the sense that I had from my childhood, that I was the person who had to hold things together in my home, to keep peace. And on balance, those skills are very good— I mean, basically we're living in a world where cooperation is better than conflict."

The need to smooth things over, the eagerness to please, had a desperate quality at times. When Clinton moved to officially change his name at the age of fifteen, the family was in a state of collapse. His mother says that Clinton made the move because his half-brother, Roger Jr., was entering school, "and Bill didn't want people confused by them having different names." But he'd been known as "Billy Clinton" ever since the family had arrived in Hot Springs and now admits that the change was "an expression of family solidarity."

Ultimately, though, there was no way to massage the situation. "When he would get drunk, he was so consumed with self-destructive impulses," Clinton recalled. "And one of the most difficult things for me was being fourteen years old and putting an end to the violence."

"How did you do that?" I asked.

Clinton sighed. "I just broke down the door of their room one night when they were having an encounter and told him that I was bigger than him now, and there would never be any more of this while I was there."

OH, THE HUMILITY

KURT ANDERSEN NOVEMBER 13, 2006

By the president's words shall ye know him. In 2004, Kurt Andersen, who writes a column for the magazine called "The Imperial City," traced the concept of humility through several of George W. Bush's utterances and his administration's actions, analyzing how it has served him at some points and was abandoned at others. Andersen, a former editor of the magazine who is also a novelist and radio host, locates the sense of entitlement in the solipsism implicit in Bush's personal relationship with God.

—

S EVEN YEARS AGO, at a debate in Iowa among the Republican candidates for president, each man was asked to name the political philosopher with whom he most identified.

"Christ," George Bush answered, famously, "because he changed my heart."

The follow-up exchange isn't well known, but it's at least as telling. When the questioner asked Bush to elaborate on the heart-changing part, he demurred. "Well, if they don't know, it's going to be hard to explain."

It was a year later, in a one-on-one debate with Al Gore, that Bush was asked about his foreign-policy vision—how he would "project us around the world."

"If we're an arrogant nation, they'll resent us. If we're a humble nation, but strong, they'll welcome us. . . . Our nation stands alone right now . . . in terms of power. And that's why we've got to be humble. . . . One way for us to end up being viewed as the Ugly American is for us to go around the world saying, 'We do it this way, so should you.' "

It was a perfect answer—and, in retrospect, of course, perfectly ironic. Bush's rise and fall are so stark and clockworkish it's like a play, a tragedy and farce in three acts.

Act One, 1999–2001: the nice Christ-y talk of humility plus the blithe arrogance (we get it, you don't) of true believers—and then, with 9/11, the opportunity to be born again, geopolitically, and divide the whole world in two, "either with us or against us."

Act Two, 2001–2005: the moment push came to shove, all humility abandoned in favor of highfalutin Wilsonian hubris about our place in the world and lazy, stupid, Ugly American hubris concerning the particulars of Iraq.

Act Three, 2006: nudged by Karl Rove or reminded of Jesus' promise in Luke ("He who humbles himself will be exalted"), an eleventh-hour show of humility (press-conference regrets over "Bring 'em on" and Abu Ghraib)—but his own chief Middle East spinmeister carries the new candor a truth too far, confessing in Arabic on Al-Jazeera two weeks ago that we are "witnessing failure in Iraq" and that "undoubtedly, there was arrogance and there was stupidity from the United States in Iraq."

And let the final line of this play be the other half of Jesus' injunction in Luke 14:11: "Everyone who exalts himself will be humbled." Amen. The end. Curtain.

The war is lost. The question now is just how hideous the outcome will be, and the timing—whether the last U.S. convoy (or, if the Vietnam analogy becomes foursquare, helicopter) leaves Baghdad's Green Zone in 2007 or 2008. America has been humbled—and we'll see this week if Bush and the Republicans will be humbled politically in turn, having so monstrously exalted themselves these last several years.

Even some Republicans want Bush and the GOP punished. Christopher Buckley is one of seven conservatives who wrote an extraordinary *Washington Monthly* cover package last month called "Time for Us to Go." He said that "one has no sense . . . that the president or the Republican Congress is in the least bit chastened by their debacles."

I discovered the essay posted on a website called Republicans for Humility. Which got me thinking that the GOP used to be the party of humility, for better or worse: skepticism about big government and deficits, buzzkill pragmatism and competence over utopian wishfulness, a strict obedience to the authority of the Constitution—nothing like Bushism.

Of course, this country has always had an iffy relationship with humility. John Quincy Adams was a founding imperialist ("North America [is] destined by Divine Providence to be peopled by one nation"), but also warned against overreach ("America does not go abroad in search of monsters to destroy"). We're the country of Jimmy Stewart and Warren Buffett and a reflexive disapproval (as I heard incessantly as a child in the Midwest) of "getting too big for your britches." But we're also the nation of Orson Welles, Donald Trump, and "America, Fuck Yeah!"

And now we are faced with a paradoxical, almost oxymoronic national challenge: to operate as a superpower with humility and magnanimity—as Bush suggested in 2000. The right choice is neither a bullying America-rules moralism nor a weenie-ish blame-America moralism. Rather, it's to temper our long-standing sense of righteous superiority with our equally hardwired pragmatism—to maintain a clear-eyed view of what's practical and sensible, to avoid believing our own bullshit. The salient, illuminating presidential comparison is not George W. Bush versus Jimmy Carter, as the Republicans would now like us to think, but Bush 43 versus Bush 41. As Chris Buckley wrote, the senior Bush, for whom he worked, is "the most . . . humble and cautious man on the planet."

George H. W. Bush's weakness as a politician boiled down to several connected problems: He seemed like a Wasp wimp, someone with neither fierce convictions nor any knack for rhetorical grandeur—too plainly humble. In 1988, his offhand derision of "the vision thing" fixed his image as ludicrously passionless, flat-footed. During the same election, when he needed to sell the idea that he wasn't a wimp, he refashioned himself as a Clint Eastwood: "Read my lips," Peggy Noonan had him snarl. "No new taxes."

AFTER HE WAS ELECTED and worked out a deal with a Democratic Congress (sensibly, humbly) to raise taxes, he was a goner. And while the "vision thing" remark will dog him forever, in retrospect its mistrust of fancy rhetoric looks like a healthy instinct, born of a truly conservative humility about what's reasonable to expect of government. He was the President Bush, remember, who during the Gulf War in 1991, having removed the Iraqis from Kuwait—mission actually accomplished—decided against sending U.S. forces on to Baghdad to remove Saddam. Humility in action.

When his son was running in 2000 and needed to sell the idea that he wasn't a cowboy, he stuck to his humble-foreign-policy talking point—but then did a 180 as soon as he acquired a big, simple, stark vision of America vengefully, mightily, miraculously remaking the Middle East. Unlike his humble old man, who plainly never subscribed to the fiscal or religious or geopolitical certainties of his party's newfangled base, George W. Bush after 9/11 was vulnerable, like a callow, feckless kid seduced by a cult at a moment of personal crisis—this is a man, after all, who suddenly swung from boozy, irreligious party boy to Evangelical teetotaler at age forty.

Two cults: After Bush signed on at age fifty-five to both the Ayn Randian certitude of his neocon *Übermenschen* and the credulous biblical certitude of the religious right, his regime has embodied an awful hybrid of the worst of both—PowerPoint know-it-alls stoked with messianic zeal and a crusading Christianity shorn of real humility. On a personal level, I'm sure he still considers himself a steadfast exemplar of Christian humility—that he's an unworthy sinner in obeisance to Jesus Christ—notwithstanding the Iraqi debacle into which his arrogance has dragged us all.

Perhaps his solipsism—his absolute trust of his "gut" and his ability to detect someone's "good heart"—was part of his personality before his Christian rebirth. But you can't help notice that a proud solipsism is what distinguishes the ascendant, wingnuttier types of Protestants from the theologically humbler mainliners. For Evangelicals, it's all me me me, from the born-again experience to the personal relationship with the savior to speaking in tongues, interpreting the fancies and feelings that happen to flicker through their central nervous system as messages from God.

"God wants me to do it," Bush reportedly told people when he first ran for president. After 9/11, he said he didn't consult his father for advice but "a higher Father." So in other words, he relies on his own instincts concerning politics and policy, but recasts them as divine instructions. Humble? The absolutely freakish opposite, it seems to me.

THE MEME PRISONER

JOHN HEILEMANN FEBRUARY 25, 2008

With her formidable operation and her former-president husband and her steely focus, Senator Hillary Clinton was widely thought to be a shoo-in for the Democratic presidential nomination in 2008. Then, suddenly, shockingly, Hillary went from lock to long shot. John Heilemann, New York's *national-politics correspondent, found that the reasons didn't have only to do with the intrinsic strength or weakness of the candidates but with interplay of media story lines. Heilemann is the author of* Pride Before the Fall: The Trials of Bill Gates and the End of the Microsoft Era.

—

The day after the notably down-and-dirty Nevada caucuses, I asked Hillary Clinton if, on occasion, her campaign had been wont to play the game a tad too rough. Now and then, Clinton allowed—then quickly pivoted and trained her fire on Barack Obama's operation. She argued that his campaign had incited racial animus by playing up her remarks about Lyndon Johnson and Martin Luther King. That it had made "what I thought was a breathtaking charge that I was in some way responsible for Benazir Bhutto's assassination." That it had "basically condoned a really mean-spirited" Spanish-language ad in Nevada that asserted Hillary "does not respect our people." Without pausing to catch her breath, Clinton concluded, "There's no outcry. There's no drumbeat. And so I accept that I will always be under a higher level of scrutiny; it goes with the territory."

The scrutiny Clinton was talking about was media scrutiny, of course. So I asked if she agreed with her husband's loudly voiced view that there was a double standard inherent in the coverage of her and Obama. "I don't go there," she replied, waving one hand in the air. "Certainly, a lot of my supporters express their feelings about it. But I just don't think about that because it's not a useful thing for me to think about."

Whether Clinton is actually so Zen-like about this topic—and, really, who would be?—her adjutants are adamantly not. Instead, for the better part of a year, they have complained to any reporter who would listen about what they regard as a manifest pro-Obama, anti-Hillary tilt in the press corps. With the contretemps over David Shuster's "pimped out" comments about Chelsea Clinton, this line of argument has become more heated, to be sure, especially as it pertains to NBC and MSNBC. ("A horror show" is how one Clinton adviser describes her nightly treatment by Chris Matthews, Tim Russert, and even Brian Williams.) But it's connected to a long-simmering sense of grievance that's deeper and more subtle.

That the campaign exaggerates its degree of outrage, and Hillary her victimhood, in order to gain a tactical advantage is obvious. But that doesn't mean their critique is meritless—quite the contrary. The more interesting question, however, is what role each campaign has had in fostering a media dynamic that has clearly favored Obama and plainly damaged Clinton. And also whether that dynamic will come back to bite Obama if he's the Democratic nominee.

Divergence in tone is one thing, double standards are another. And it's the latter that most galls the former advisers to the other, now-departed, Democratic candidates. "Obama has been able to get away with a stunning amount of hypocrisy that would get called on her," says one such operative. "They've run the nastiest, most deceptive pieces of paid media: the mailer they did lying about her health-care plan, with the Harry and Louise look-alikes. The idea that it took Hillary growling Tony

Rezko's name in a debate to get any national coverage. How he complained in Iowa about 527s and then had them supporting him like crazy
in Nevada and California. And nobody says a peep about it. It's fucking
comical!"

Campaigns are, at bottom, a competition between memes: infectious
ideas that gather force through sheer repetition. The most powerful of
these memes are what Marion Just, a political scientist at Wellesley,
refers to as meta-narratives, the backdrops against which everything
plays out in the media. "Clinton's meta-narrative," she says, "is that she'll
do anything to win; she can't be trusted, she's ethically challenged; she's
manipulative, calculating, and programmed." Obama's meta-narrative is
decidedly otherwise. "It's the same, in a way, as John McCain's," says
Just, who has made a systematic study of the race. "He's authentic, honest, free of taint. Then you add in new, charismatic, and an agent of
change."

For any candidate and his or her team, the formation and management of the meta-narrative are paramount strategic challenges. And
these challenges were especially daunting for Clinton because she started
out with much of hers already baked in. Even so, early on, her campaign
had ample opportunity to alter the vestigial perceptions of her. They had
done so effectively, after all, when she first ran for the Senate in New
York. But instead, the affect she presented to reporters was in perfect
keeping with all the stereotypes about her: She was guarded and relentlessly, robotically on-message on the rare occasions when she sat for interviews, displaying little of her charm or humor. She adopted an
arch-Establishmentarian posture rather than an inspiring, transforma-
tional one—an alterna-stance that wouldn't have been such a stretch for
someone who stood a reasonable chance of becoming our first female
president.

And, in fact, it was worse than that. By arguing that one of Clinton's
key virtues was her ability to go toe-to-toe with the GOP attack machine,
her campaign exacerbated instead of ameliorated her reputation for ruthlessness. "By bragging about how tough they were," says John Edwards's
former chief strategist, Joe Trippi, "they reinforced the sense of the media

that everything they did had a negative cast to it." At the same time, Trippi argues, "it made it really hard for them to call Obama on his shit. How can you complain about Obama being negative when you're bragging about your willingness to do the same thing against the Republicans?"

Obama, by contrast, was in the enviable position of being able to author his own meta-narrative. With his two autobiographies, he was able at once to accentuate his positive qualities and, in pointing out the potentially damaging aspects of his past (his teenage drug use preeminent among them), to inoculate himself against attacks. The grassrootsy, bottom-up, decentralized campaign structure that he and his team built, funded by small donors via the Internet, enhanced the impression of him as a man committed to a different kind of politics. And his strategists were wise enough to understand that when it was time to go negative, they should never do so with TV ads but stick instead to more sub-rosa media, from radio and direct mail to robo-calls. "In my experience in politics," Trippi says, "nobody ever really gets called out on that crap."

The implications of Obama's and Clinton's respective meta-narratives for their press coverage have been profound. For Clinton, the inability to change the story line meant that any vaguely negative maneuver was interpreted in the darkest possible light, for it reinforced a preexisting supposition. For Obama, however, any criticism could be fended off as a manifestation of grubby old politics. And any act he committed that could be perceived as nefarious created cognitive dissonance. As Just points out, a prime example is the case of Tony Rezko, the now-indicted Chicago fixer and slumlord to whom Obama has been linked for many years. "There was no way for the press to believe it wasn't true—because, you know, it looks like people are going to jail," she says. "So instead the press dismisses the story as an aberration."

The trouble for Obama is that the Republicans aren't terribly likely to let that dismissal stand—nor the polite avoidance of discussing his controversial minister, his wayward youth, or, indeed, his blackness itself. Again and again, as Clinton often points out, the GOP has proved painfully adept at taking compelling, carefully honed meta-narratives and blowing them to pieces. In ways too numerous to mention, Obama has been toughened up by the primary process. But no matter what his handlers say, the notion that he's been subjected to the most withering press scrutiny imaginable is—how to put this?—a fairy tale. His success has turned in no small part on his skill at avoiding such flyspecking, and on his rival's inability to muster the same kind of dexterity. If Obama winds up facing John McCain, a man whose meta-narrative is spun from pure gold, he is unlikely to be so fortunate again.

IS JOHN McCAIN BOB DOLE?

JOHN HEILEMANN APRIL 21, 2008

As Hillary Clinton and Barack Obama battled for the nomination, John McCain was having an easier time. Columnist John Heilemann wondered why was this so, and in exploring the question, he uncovered deep similarities between McCain's attitudes and postures and those of the media, ones that existed below any simple left-right schism. McCain, he argued, was a kind of meta-candidate who always saw the sport in it. Like the media, he was in on the joke—a kind of political David Letterman whose closest previous analog had been Bob Dole.

—

B Y THE TIME John McCain trundles into the ballroom of the Fairmont hotel in Dallas, he has already had what for most men his age would have been a very full day. He has met the press at a Mexican restaurant in San Antonio. He has held a town-hall meeting at a barbecue joint in Houston. He has fielded yet another question about the "North American Union," the latest conspiracy theory from the nutters who brought us the New World Order. He has uttered the salutation "my friends" at least forty times. And, oh yes, he has won the Republican primaries in Texas, Ohio, Rhode Island, and Vermont, dispatched that holy-rolling goober Mike

Huckabee back whence he came, and secured his party's nomination for president of the United States.

So McCain is feeling pretty chuffed when he mounts the stage with his canary-yellow-suited, Barbie-blond gal, Cindy. The crowd before him is measly by Barack Obama standards, just a few hundred people, but it's plenty loud and lusty. The confetti cannons are loaded and cocked, the balloons pinned to the ceiling.

Out in the audience, Mark Salter and Steve Schmidt look twitchy. The goateed Salter is McCain's chief wordsmith; the shaven-headed Schmidt his mouthpiece. Through experience, the two men have learned that prepared addresses are not McCain's best friends—and teleprompters his mortal enemies. On a good day, McCain merely looks shifty when he's reading off a prompter, as his eyes track the flowing text; on a bad day, he stutters, stammers, yammers, making him seem . . . well, let's not go there.

As McCain begins to speak, Salter and Schmidt position themselves so they can see both their boss and the giant flat-panel on the camera riser directly in front of him. The speech is short. It's going smoothly. McCain is nearly done. "Their patience," he is saying of the American people, "is at an end for politicians who value ambition over principle, and for partisanship that is less a contest of ideas than an uncivil brawl over the spoils of power."

And then . . . Oh, shit!

The screen goes blank!

McCain is flying blind!

Up onstage, McCain wears a mask of misery. He shuffles some papers, blinks, smiles tightly, checks the prompter repeatedly. Schmidt and Salter, eyes bugging, heads swiveling, are in full panic mode. Ten seconds pass. Then twenty, then thirty, then forty without a word from McCain. The crowd cheers and chants, filling up the dead air that threatens to throttle him on national TV—until suddenly, voilà, the text reappears and McCain picks up where he left off. Salter shakes his head. Schmidt shrugs and mops his brow. Soon they're tapping away at their BlackBerrys as if nothing momentous had occurred, let alone a near-death experience.

By the standards of the McCain campaign, of course, nothing momentous had occurred. Less than a year ago, the Arizona senator really was kaput—or so some of us geniuses thought. His operation was broke, his poll numbers anemic, his team in tatters, his image muddied and muddled. But today McCain stands as good a chance as any of the remaining runners of being the next resident of 1600 Pennsylvania Avenue. His approval rating, according to Gallup, is 67 percent, as high as it's ever been. In head-to-head matchups, he runs roughly even with Hillary Clinton and Barack Obama, and his prospects seem to brighten each day that the rancorous contest between his potential rivals rumbles on. "The Democrats are destroying themselves," says GOP strategist Alex Castellanos, who recently signed on with McCain. "They're engaged in killing Obama. It's like killing Santa Claus on Christmas morning—the kids won't forget or forgive."

That McCain's political resurrection owed as much to the weakness of the Republican field—not to mention blind shithouse luck—as to his talent and grit makes it no less remarkable. Yet for all the hosannas being sung to him these days, and for all the waves of fear and trembling rippling through the Democratic masses, the truth is that McCain is a candidate of pronounced and glaring weaknesses. A candidate whose capacity to raise enough money to beat back the tidal wave of Democratic moola is seriously in doubt. A candidate unwilling or unable to animate the GOP base. A candidate whose operation has never recovered from the turmoil of last summer, still skeletal and ragtag and technologically antediluvian. ("Fund-raising on the Web? You don't say. You can raise money through those tubes?") Whose cadre of confidantes contains so many lobbyists that the Straight Talk Express often has the vibe of a rolling K Street clubhouse. Whose awkward positioning issues-wise was captured brilliantly by Pat Buchanan: "The jobs are never coming back, the illegals are never going home, but we're going to have a lot more wars." A candidate one senior moment—or one balky teleprompter—away from being transformed from a grizzled warrior into Grandpa Simpson. A candidate, that is, who poses an existential question for Democrats: If you can't beat a guy like this in a year like this, with a vastly unpopular Republican war still ongoing and a Republican recession looming, what precisely is the point of you?

DREAMING OF OBAMA

JENNIFER SENIOR OCTOBER 2, 2006

Jennifer Senior found her way to Senator Barack Obama at a privileged moment: on the eve of the publication of his second book, his candidacy not yet declared, shortly before he went from being a hopeful to a full-blown phenomenon. Senior's article explores Obama's generational appeal and provides a kind of road map for the campaign that was to follow. Senior has written about politics and other topics at New York *for many years.*

—

THE FIRST TIME I have a chance alone with Obama, I ask why he thinks the world has gone gaga over him. "It's interesting," he says, smiling. "It is interesting." We're in his aide's car, driving from a town called Palestine to another called Paris. He thinks for a moment, then suggests that perhaps the answer lies in the unique circumstances of his 2004 Senate campaign. "I sort of got a free pass, because I wasn't subjected to a bunch of negative ads," he says. "And nobody thought I was going to win. So I basically got into the habit of pretty much saying what I thought. And it worked for me. So I figured I might as well keep on doing it."

AT SOME LEVEL, possibly the most basic one, the mania surrounding Barack Obama is a simple function of his age—or, as John F. Kennedy would have said, his vigor. At forty-five, he's fifteen years younger than the average senator in the 109th Congress, and he's thirteen years younger than Hillary Clinton, the presumptive Democratic nominee in 2008. (Al Gore is also fifty-eight. And John Kerry is sixty-three.) As Simon Rosenberg, head of the New Democratic Network, says, "Obama has already established himself as the paramount leader of the next generation. There's no one even close." There's something to be said for a politician who didn't come of age wearing sideburns and listening to Simon and Garfunkel. Obama suggests there might be another way to think about politics, to speak about politics, to write about politics. It's certainly what Crown Publishing was counting on when it awarded him with a $1.7 million, two-book contract twenty-one months ago. The first book, *The Audacity of Hope*, will be hitting bookstores in mid-October.

"To some degree—and I say this fairly explicitly in my book—we have seen the psychodrama of the baby-boom generation play out over the last forty years," says Obama as we're driving through ravishing acres of corn and soy. "When you watch Clinton versus Gingrich or Gore versus Bush or Kerry versus Bush, you feel like these are fights that were taking place back in dorm rooms in the sixties. Vietnam, civil rights, the sexual revolution, the role of government—all that stuff has just been playing itself out, and I think people sort of feel like, Okay, let's not re-litigate the sixties forty years later." He rattles off some of the familiar dichotomies—isolationism versus intervention, big government versus small. "These either/or formulations are wearisome," he says. "They're not useful. The reality outstrips the mental categories we're operating in."

Perhaps the most captivating component of Obama's appeal, though, is that he is only the third black candidate to be elected to the U.S. Senate since Reconstruction. And if you're only the third black senator in 130 years, you are bound to be the vessel for many people's hopes. To white progressives, Obama represents the fantasy of racial reconciliation, the black RFK. To affirmative-action skeptics, he's Horatio Alger, proof that this country affords equal opportunities to anyone who works hard enough. (Obama's mother was a middle-class woman from Kansas; Obama's father started out as a goatherd in Kenya.) Whatever the case, Obama's Senate campaign certainly understood the power of white guilt. Its slogan was *Yes we can*—an energetic rallying cry, certainly, but also a subtle appeal to black pride and white self-respect. It dared the voters of Illinois to change the face of a lily-white institution. Which they did.

And to a younger generation of black politicians, Obama is the embodiment of progress, advancement, hope. Before July of 2004, no one had even heard of Barack Obama. He was a promising but modest figure in Illinois politics, a seven-year veteran of the state senate who'd already made one disastrous attempt for a congressional seat in 2000. But in 2004, he made a longshot bid to run for an open Senate seat. In small towns where the typical response to a person of color was to roll up the car windows, people came pouring out to hear Obama speak. He was immensely popular in both the suburbs of Chicago and the city's whitest wards. "Twenty years ago, if I'd said there would be lawn signs with pictures of an African-American—with an African surname—all over my district on the northwest side of Chicago, people would have had me tested for drugs," says Rahm Emanuel, head of the Democratic Congressional Campaign Committee. "Yet there they were."

"BARACK, I THINK, represents a point of transition," says Artur Davis, a thirty-eight-year-old African-American congressman from Alabama and former law-school classmate of Obama's. "This is the first generation of African-American politicians who essentially have the same aspirations as their white compatriots. A twenty-five-year-old black kid today who's talented, who's well educated, and who's interested in politics wants to be president—and doesn't view that as some bizarre goal. That's what I think Barack will represent: the leading edge of the generation of African-American politicians for whom there are no glass ceilings."

There are still plenty of black politicians who'd disagree with this, of course. At the very least, they'd point out that there's no such thing as transcending race. It's not an accident that black politicians who appeal broadly to whites are called "crossover" candidates—the problem's buried right in the word. "Crossing over" suggests deserting your own kind, or being insufficiently, inauthentically black somehow (whatever on earth being sufficiently, authentically black even is). In a famous *New Yorker* essay, Henry Louis Gates took a long, hard look at this burdensome problem when writing about Colin Powell. He asked the general about how he'd come to be seen "as a paragon of something like racial erasure." It was a devastating moment, I thought. I ask Obama about it during our car ride, wondering whether that perception, too, will be his lot. Clinton was who he was, I say. Kennedy was who he was. Bush is who he—

"And I feel like I'm very much who I am," he says, cutting me off. "Do you ever get a sense that I'm not?" He looks at me pointedly, eyes over his shades, waiting for an answer.

No, I say. I don't.

"I mean, the fact that I conjugate my verbs and, you know, speak in a typical midwestern-newscaster voice—there's no doubt this helps ease communication between myself and white audiences," he says. "And there's no doubt that when I'm with a black audience, I slip into a slightly different dialect." He turns and stretches his legs for a moment. He's been facing me this entire car ride, though he's in the passenger seat and I'm in the back. He turns back around and looks at me again. "But the point is," he says, "I don't feel the need to talk in a certain way before a white audience. And I don't feel the need to speak a certain way in front of a black audience. There's a level of self-consciousness about these issues the previous generation had to negotiate that I don't feel I have to."

AT A QUICK STOP outside Palestine, a woman grabs Obama by both arms. "We need you to run for president. You must. You must. Are you running?"

Obama demurs. "I can't make news."

"Obama for president," her husband repeats. "That's the answer."

He thanks them both, moves on—and then another couple tells him the same thing about six seconds later.

So much hope and so much fuss. All over a man whose father was from Kenya and whose mother might have been a distant relation of Jefferson Davis. Whose meals in Indonesia were served, for a time, by a male servant who sometimes liked to wear a dress. Whose first and last names inconveniently rhyme with "Iraq Osama." And whose middle name, taken from his Muslim grandfather, is, of all things, Hussein.

Where else but here, though, right?

ACKNOWLEDGMENTS

★

A book spanning forty years of magazine history gives us much to acknowledge. To begin: This anthology could not have been contemplated if *New York* did not have such a rich magazine history; for four decades, outstanding editors have shaped that history, and they have our deep gratitude. First and foremost among them is the magazine's founding editor, Clay Felker. Much was said about Felker in the remarks that open this book. Right here, we'll only say the obvious. This is an anthology of stories that appeared in *New York*. *New York* would not exist without Felker; probably much of contemporary journalism wouldn't either. The vision Felker, who died in July 2008, had for the magazine continues to inspire editors at *New York,* and elsewhere. Succeeding editors of *New York* built on Felker's work, shaping the magazine to their tastes and ideas as well as to their sense of a changing city. We thank the magazine's chief editors, in order of their tenure: after Felker, James Brady, Joe Armstrong, John Berendt, Ed Kosner, Kurt Andersen, and Caroline Miller. Other gifted editors went out of their way to aid the selection process, including Peter Herbst and Byron Dobell. We're indebted to Tom Wolfe for his exquisite and exquisitely Wolfean foreword; even his handwritten faxes with their calligraphic markings were a delight.

And of course we're indebted to Wolfe for his pieces we have anthologized here, and to all of the magazine's four decades of writers; they are the true stars of this anthology. Reading through literally thousands of articles was an exhilarating exercise. It was impossible not to be impressed by the stylish writing, the prodigious reporting, the smart thinking, and the journalistic enterprise that have shaped the magazine for generations, often under weekly deadlines. One unexpected pleasure has been to reconnect with many of the magazine's past writers and to learn from them about their city, and their *New York*. But the culling process was also painful, and much excellent work was inevitably left out. To those writers whose work is included in the anthology, we are grateful for the work itself but also for their generosity. They accepted a modest honorarium, much less than they are worth but as much as we could afford. To a one, they could not have been more gracious.

We owe a special debt of gratitude to Serena Torrey, whose efforts on this book's behalf were at times heroic. Without her charm, firmness, and talents, the project would not have gotten off the ground and certainly would have stalled. Jennifer Coughlin, Lauren Starke, and Jill Weiskopf did great service as well. We also thank the incomparable Ann Clarke, who in her politic way keeps us on track.

This book would not have seen the light of day without the intrepid, forceful persistence of Mary Burke, who secured the many permissions necessary to publish these stories.

We could not have completed the contract or permissions process without the help of our diligent lawyer Eric Bergner, whose legal expertise is rivaled only by his ability to translate our non-lawyer-speak into binding written language and back again.

This book could not have been put together with the swiftness required without the research and organizing talents of Jocelyn Guest. *New York* magazine does not yet have a digitized archive for poring through back issues, and so collecting far-flung stories fell to her. Interns Ben Kawaller, Kathleen Reeves, Alexa Battista, and Scott Ward helped with a variety of tasks. Emma Pearse made the complex process of assembling all the elements of this book simple and painless.

Carl Rosen and Tricia Brick sped each story's introduction and the introduction to this book through a rigorous fact- and copy-checking process while simultaneously doing the same for the weekly magazine.

New York's book agent, David McCormick of McCormick and Williams, was an early champion of this project and one without whom it would not have seen print. He was aided in this effort by the capable Gillian Linden.

Thanks especially to Bruce Tracy, executive editor at Random House, whose enthusiasm for this anthology was immediate and sustaining. This book was put out on a schedule closer to a magazine's than a book's; Bruce—and his enormously capable assistant Ryan Doherty—allowed their patience to be tried (but not broken). Also at Random House, Dana Maxson, Kristina Miller, Evan Camfield, Sandra Sjursen, and so many others were instrumental in hastening this book through channels.

New York magazine's design director, Chris Dixon, created the very handsome cover of this anthology. His elegant touch is so unerring it would be easy to take it for granted. We don't.

And finally, a special note of gratitude to Bruce Wasserstein, *New York*'s owner. In believing in the original mission of the magazine, he ensured that *New York* would have a fortieth anniversary worth celebrating.

SOLUTION TO THE *NEW YORK* MAGAZINE PUZZLE

. . . .

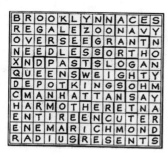

Theme-words: Five boroughs of New York
Variations: Brooklyn Navy Yard; Queens,
kings, aces; Manhattan, manna, that (anagrams); Richmond, Lee, Grant (Civil War);
Bronx, cheer, zoo (associated phrases)

ACROSS

11 re-gale
14 O.(verse)E.
18 need less
19 ort-ho
21 passed
22 slog-an
26 wig they (anag.)
27 de-pot (pun)
34 S.A.-Y(MCA)
37 H.-arm
39 o(the)r
41 ante (rev.)
42 ten(anag.)-ire
43 cut-er
45 E.-amen (rev.)
47 hidden
48 (p)resents

DOWN

2 re-venue
3 O,gee
4 or
6 song (anag.)
7 hidden
8 an-a
9 pun
12 Z-est
15 hidden
19 rash logic (anag.)
20 de(part)ed
21 pe(O)n
23 two meanings
25 Sark set (anag.)
32 pun
33 ne(um)e
35 hidden
38 mi,mi
40 air
44 two meanings

ABOUT THE EDITORS

STEVE FISHMAN is a contributing writer who has written several of *New York* magazine's most notable stories.

JOHN HOMANS has served as executive editor of *New York* magazine for the past twelve years.

ADAM MOSS has been *New York* magazine's editor-in-chief since 2004.